ASIA SMALL AND MEDIUM-SIZED ENTERPRISE MONITOR 2022

VOLUME I—COUNTRY AND REGIONAL REVIEWS

NOVEMBER 2022

ASIAN DEVELOPMENT BANK

ADB

6 ADB Avenue, Mandaluyong City, 1550 Metro Manila, Philippines
Tel +63 2 8632 4444; Fax +63 2 8636 2444
www.adb.org

ISBN 978-92-9269-872-0 (print); 978-92-9269-873-7 (electronic); 978-92-9269-874-4 (ebook)
Publication Stock No. SGP220540-2
DOI: http://dx.doi.org/10.22617/SGP220540-2

Notes:
In this publication, "$" refers to United States dollars, "€" and "EUR" refer to euro, "AMD" refers Armenia dram, "AZN" refers to Azerbaijan manat, "GEL" refers to Georgian lari, "KGS" refers to Kyrgyz Republic som, "KZT" refers to Kazakhstan tenge, "SUM" refers to Uzbekistan sum, and "TJS" refers to Tajikistan somoni.

ADB recognizes "China" as the People's Republic of China, "Korea" as the Republic of Korea, "Kyrgyzstan" as the Kyrgyz Republic, "Turkey" as Türkiye, "Vietnam" as Viet Nam, "Russia" as the Russian Federation, "Hanoi" as Ha Noi, and "Bombay" as Mumbai.

Cover design by Claudette Rodrigo.

Contents

Tables, Figures, and Boxes

Tables

Regional Review

Armenia

Azerbaijan

Figures

Boxes

Foreword

Central and West Asian economies saw a relatively fast V-shaped recovery from the economic slowdown brought on by the coronavirus disease (COVID-19) pandemic. But the 2022 Russian invasion of Ukraine has slowed their growth momentum once again—from 5.7% growth in 2021 to 3.9% forecast for 2022. With the Russian Federation the region's major trade partner, the invasion and associated sanctions have affected all Central and West Asian economies. Most private sector businesses have suffered, though to differing degrees by country. A third of micro, small, and medium-sized enterprises (MSMEs) in the region rely on exports, and they have been heavily affected.

Policymakers across the region prioritize MSME development and financial inclusion as part of their growth strategies as they strive for resilient, diversified, and sustainable economies. Finance, especially access to growth capital, is critical for MSMEs. National financial inclusion strategies—including financial education programs for MSMEs—are also important. However, increased global economic uncertainty makes it more difficult for the region's governments to design feasible and effective MSME policies. To provide the right policy support for MSME development, they need timely access to comprehensive, comparative databases and information on the evolving business environment and other factors.

To help satisfy this growing demand, the Economic Research and Regional Cooperation Department at the Asian Development Bank annually publishes the Asia Small and Medium-Sized Enterprise Monitor (ASM)—a multicountry analytical report on MSMEs and regional best practices. The ASM provides in-depth analysis on MSME development, access to finance, and government policies, covering a different Asian region each year. Since 2020, it has covered Southeast Asia and South Asia. In 2022, it turns its focus to Central and West Asia. This new edition comprises two volumes: one containing country and regional reviews (Volume I) and a theme chapter assessing the impact of the ongoing Russian invasion of Ukraine on the region's MSMEs (Volume II). I hope this first volume will continue to help governments use evidence-based policy design in crafting their MSME development strategies and will promote more regional and global dialogue on how to adapt MSME policies to increased global uncertainty.

Albert Park
Chief Economist and Director General
Economic Research and Regional Cooperation Department
Asian Development Bank

Acknowledgments

The *Asia Small and Medium-Sized Enterprise Monitor (ASM)* 2022 was prepared by Shigehiro Shinozaki, senior economist, Economic Research and Regional Cooperation Department (ERCD) of the Asian Development Bank (ADB). The work was supervised by Albert Park, chief economist and director general of ERCD, and supported by Yevgeniy Zhukov, director general of ADB's Central and West Asia Department (CWRD); Paolo Spantigati, country director of the Armenia Resident Mission; Candice McDeigan, country director of the Azerbaijan Resident Mission; Shane Rosenthal, country director of the Georgia Resident Mission; Nariman Mannapbekov, country director of the Kazakhstan Resident Mission; Kanokpan Lao-Araya, country director of the Kyrgyz Republic Resident Mission; Shanny Campbell, country director of the Tajikistan Resident Mission (TJRM); Cynthia Malvicini, senior advisor of CWRD and former country director of the Uzbekistan Resident Mission; and Satoru Yamadera, advisor of the ERCD's financial cooperation and integration team. The ASM team included Shigehiro Shinozaki, team leader; Muhammadi Boboev, senior economics officer of the TJRM; Sergey Tantushyan, ADB consultant for Armenia; Rashad Huseynov, ADB consultant for Azerbaijan; Phaikidze Grigoli, ADB consultant for Georgia; Berik Tankimov, ADB consultant for Kazakhstan; Malik-Aidar Abakirov, ADB consultant for the Kyrgyz Republic; Iskandar Davlatov, ADB consultant for Tajikistan; Timur Nuratdinov, ADB consultant for Uzbekistan; ADB consultant Josephine Penaflor Ferre; and ADB consultant Romeo Arahan. Administrative support was provided by Richard Supangan and Maria Frederika Bautista.

Shigehiro Shinozaki wrote the Highlights, Regional Review, and Rationale and Methodology. He provided substantive comments/inputs and initially edited the Country Chapters. Sergey Tantushyan wrote the Armenia Chapter, Rashad Huseynov the Azerbaijan Chapter, Phaikidze Grigoli the Georgia Chapter, Berik Tankimov the Kazakhstan Chapter, Malik-Aidar Abakirov the Kyrgyz Republic Chapter, Iskandar Davlatov the Tajikistan Chapter, and Timur Nuratdinov authored the Uzbekistan Chapter. Shinozaki and Arahan led the estimates of the Small and Medium-Sized Enterprise Development Index. The report was peer reviewed by Giacomo Giannetto, principal financial sector specialist of CWRD. Ferre and Arahan prepared the ASM 2022 database, guided by Shinozaki.

We thank all data contributors listed in this report for preparing the Country Chapters and thank all CWRD Resident Mission staff for their administrative support, including virtual mission arrangements.

Data Contributors in Participating ADB Developing Member Countries

Central and West Asia

Country	Data Contributors
Armenia	Armenia Securities Exchange, Ameria Group Inc., Central Bank of Armenia, CIVITTA (former EV Consulting), Datamotus LLC, Ministry of Economy, Ministry of Finance, Statistical Committee of the Republic of Armenia
Azerbaijan	Agrarian Credit and Development Agency under the Ministry of Agriculture, Azerbaijan Credit Bureau LLC, Baku Stock Exchange Closed Joint-Stock Company, Central Bank of the Republic of Azerbaijan, National Depository Center of the Republic of Azerbaijan, Ministry of Energy of the Republic of Azerbaijan, Mortgage and Credit Guarantee Fund of the Republic of Azerbaijan, Republic of Azerbaijan Chamber of Commerce and Industry, Small and Medium Business Development Agency under the Ministry of Economy of the Republic of Azerbaijan, State Statistical Committee of the Republic of Azerbaijan
Georgia	Enterprise Georgia, Georgian Stock Exchange, Ministry of Economy and Sustainable Development, Ministry of Environmental Protection and Agriculture, Ministry of Finance of Georgia, National Bank of Georgia, National Statistics Office of Georgia, Revenue Service of Georgia
Kazakhstan	Agency for Regulation and Development of the Financial Market, Association of Credit Unions, Bureau of National Statistics under Agency on Strategic Planning and Reforms of the Republic of Kazakhstan, "Damu" Entrepreneurship Development Fund, Kazakhstan Stock Exchange, Ministry of National Economy, National Bank of Kazakhstan, National Chamber of Entrepreneurs
Kyrgyz Republic	Development and Investment Agency, Kyrgyz Stock Exchange, Ministry of Economy and Commerce; Ministry of Finance, Ministry of Foreign Affairs, National Bank of the Kyrgyz Republic, National Statistic Committee of the Kyrgyz Republic, State Service for Regulation and Supervision of the Financial Market under the Ministry of Economy and Commerce

Tajikistan	Agency for the Development of Securities and Specialized Registration under the Ministry of Finance, Agency on Statistics under President of the Republic of Tajikistan, Association of Microfinance Organizations of Tajikistan, Central Asian Stock Exchange, Chamber of Commerce and Industry of the Republic of Tajikistan, Credit Guarantee Fund Tajikistan, Entrepreneurship Support Fund of Tajikistan/SUE Sanoatsodirotbank, Ministry of Economic Development and Trade of the Republic of Tajikistan, Ministry of Finance of the Republic of Tajikistan, National Bank of Tajikistan, State Committee on Investment and State Property Management of Tajikistan, The National Association of Small and Medium Businesses of the Republic of Tajikistan, The State Enterprise Business—Incubator Tajikistan
Uzbekistan	Agrobank of Uzbekistan; Central Bank of Uzbekistan; Chamber of Commerce, CRIFKAX; Export Promotion Agency; Microcredit Bank of Uzbekistan; Ministry for the Development of Information Technologies and Communications; Ministry of Agriculture; Ministry of Economic Development and Poverty Reduction; Ministry of Innovative Development; Ministry of Investments and Foreign Trade; Ministry of Finance; Ministry of Justice; Ministry of Labor; Republican Stock Exchange (Toshkent); State Committee on Statistics of Uzbekistan

South Asia (Updates)

Country	Data Contributors
Bangladesh	Bangladesh Bank, Bangladesh Securities and Exchange Commission, Chittagong Stock Exchange,Dhaka Stock Exchange
India	Bombay Stock Exchange; National Stock Exchange; Reserve Bank of India; Small Industries Development Bank of India; Department of Commerce, Ministry of Statistics and Program Implementation; Securities and Exchange Board of India
Nepal	Central Bureau of Statistics; Credit and Information Bureau, Deposit and Credit Guarantee Fund; Ministry of Finance; Ministry of Industries Commerce and Supplies; Nepal Planning Commission; Nepal Rastra Bank; Nepal Stock Exchange; Securities Board of Nepal
Pakistan	Federal Board of Revenue; Karandaaz; Ministry of Industries and Production; National Incubation Center, Pakistan Bureau of Statistics; Pakistan Stock Exchange; Securities and Exchange Commission of Pakistan; Small and Medium Enterprise Development Authority; State Bank of Pakistan
Sri Lanka	Central Bank of Sri Lanka, Colombo Stock Exchange, Department of Census and Statistics, Ministry of Finance, Ministry of Industries and Commerce, National Enterprise Development Authority, Securities and Exchange Commission of Sri Lanka

Southeast Asia (Updates)

Country	Data Contributors
Brunei Darussalam	Bank Usahawan; Brunei Darussalam Central Bank; Department of Economic Planning and Statistics; Darussalam Enterprise; Ministry of Energy, Manpower, and Industry; Ministry of Finance and Economy
Cambodia	Cambodia Securities Exchange, Ministry of Economy and Finance, National Bank of Cambodia, National Institute of Statistics, Securities and Exchange Regulator of Cambodia
Indonesia	Bank Indonesia, Bandan Pusat Statistik, Coordinating Ministry for Economic Affairs, Indonesia Stock Exchange, Ministry of Cooperatives and SMEs, Otoritas Jasa Keuangan
Lao People's Democratic Republic (Lao PDR)	Bank of the Lao PDR, Lao Securities Commission Office, Lao Securities Exchange, Lao Statistics Bureau, Ministry of Industry and Commerce—Department of SME Promotions, Department of Industry and Handicraft
Malaysia	Bank Negara Malaysia, Bursa Malaysia, Credit Guarantee Corporation, Department of Statistics Malaysia, Malaysia Digital Economy Corporation, Ministry of Entrepreneur Development and Cooperatives, Securities Commission Malaysia, SME Corporation Malaysia
Philippines	Bangko Sentral ng Pilipinas, Bureau of Small and Medium Enterprise Development—Department of Trade and Industry, Cooperative Development Authority, Philippine Guarantee Corporation, Philippine Statistics Authority, Philippine Stock Exchange Inc., Securities and Exchange Commission, Small Business Corporation—Department of Trade and Industry
Singapore	Enterprise Singapore, Singapore Department of Statistics, Ministry of Trade and Industry, Monetary Authority of Singapore, Singapore Exchange
Thailand	Office of Small and Medium Enterprises Promotion, National Statistical Office, Bank of Thailand, Securities and Exchange Commission, The Stock Exchange of Thailand, Thai Credit Guarantee Corporation, The Fiscal Policy Office—Ministry of Finance
Viet Nam	Agency for Business Registration—Ministry of Planning and Investment, Agency for Enterprise Development—Ministry of Planning and Investment, General Statistics Office of Vietnam, Hanoi Stock Exchange, Ho Chi Minh Stock Exchange, Ministry of Finance, Ministry of Science and Technology, State Bank of Vietnam, State Securities Commission of Viet Nam

Abbreviations

ARDFM	–	Agency for Regulation and Development of Financial Markets (Kazakhstan)
AKIA	–	Agrarian Credit and Development Agency (Azerbaijan)
ArCa	–	Armenian Card CJSC
ACB	–	Azerbaijan Credit Bureau LLC
ACRA	–	Armenian Credit Reporting Agency
AMX	–	Armenian Securities Exchange
ADB	–	Asian Development Bank
AIFC	–	Astana International Financial Centre (Kazakhstan)
ATM	–	automated teller machine
AZPROMO	–	Azerbaijan Export and Investment Promotion Foundation
BCC	–	Bank Center Credit (Kazakhstan)
BANA	–	Business Angels Network of Armenia
B2B	–	business-to-business
CPC	–	Caspian Pipeline Consortium
CASE	–	Central Asian Stock Exchange (Tajikistan)
CBA	–	Central Bank of Armenia
CJSC	–	Close Joint Stock Company
C4D	–	Clusters4Development (Georgia)
CIS	–	Commonwealth of Independent States
CAGR	–	compound annual growth rate
C2C	–	consumer-to-consumer
CIBT	–	Deep and Comprehensive Free Trade Area
DCFTA	–	deep and comprehensive free trade area
DICA	–	Development and Investment Corporation of Armenia
DBK	–	Development Bank of Kazakhstan
EDF	–	Entrepreneurship Development Fund (Azerbaijan)
EEC	–	Eurasian Economic Commission
EAEU	–	Eurasian Economic Union
EU	–	European Union
FCI	–	Financial Capability Index
FCB	–	First Credit Bureau LLP (Kazakhstan)
FDI	–	foreign direct investment
GAAP	–	Generally Accepted Accounting Principles
GITA	–	Georgia Innovation and Technology Agency
GCCI	–	Georgian Chamber of Commerce and Industry
GAF	–	German-Armenian Fund
G2B	–	government-to-business
GDP	–	gross domestic product
GVA	–	gross value added
IRIS	–	Increased Resilience of Syrian Armenians and Host Population (Armenia)
ICT	–	information and communication technology

IT	–	information technology
IPO	–	initial public offering
IFI	–	international finance institution
IFRS	–	International Financial Reporting Standard
ISO	–	International Organization for Standardization
KASE	–	Kazakhstan Stock Exchange
KSE	–	Kyrgyz Stock Exchange
MFI	–	microfinance institution
MCI	–	Monthly Calculation Index
MSE	–	micro and small enterprise (Uzbekistan)
MSME	–	micro, small, and medium-sized enterprise
NBK	–	National Bank of Kazakhstan
NBT	–	National Bank of Tajikistan
NBKR	–	National Bank of the Kyrgyz Republic
NCE	–	National Chamber of Entrepreneurs (Kazakhstan)
NDP	–	National Development Plan (Kazakhstan)
NPED	–	National Project on Entrepreneurship Development (Kazakhstan)
NSFE	–	National Strategy for Financial Education (Georgia)
NBFI	–	nonbank finance institution
NGO	–	nongovernment organization
NPL	–	nonperforming loan
OJSC	–	open joint stock company
OECD	–	Organisation for Economic Co-operation and Development
PFI	–	partner financial institution
P2P	–	peer-to-peer
PRC	–	People's Republic of China
POS	–	point of sale
QR	–	quick response
ABAD	–	Simplified Support to Family Businesses (Azerbaijan)
SMBDA	–	Small and Medium Business Development Agency (Azerbaijan)
SME	–	small and medium-sized enterprise
SMECA	–	Small and Medium Enterprise Cooperation Association (Armenia)
SMEDA	–	Small and Medium Enterprise Development Association (Georgia)
SME DNC	–	Small and Medium Entrepreneurship Development National Center (Armenia)
SCB	–	State Credit Bureau (Kazakhstan)
UCO	–	Union of Credit Organizations
UNDP	–	United Nations Development Programme
US	–	United States
VAT	–	value-added tax
VTB	–	VneshTorgBank
WTO	–	World Trade Organization

Highlights

Central and West Asian economies recovered quickly from the COVID-19 pandemic. But the ongoing Russian invasion of Ukraine is stunting growth momentum once more, with MSMEs having to deal with multiple, differing impacts by country.

Central and West Asian economies recovered relatively quickly from the contraction brought on by the coronavirus disease (COVID-19) pandemic. While a V-shaped recovery led to 5.7% economic growth in 2021, the 2022 Russian invasion of Ukraine has interrupted renewed growth momentum. The region's economies are now forecast to expand by 3.9% in 2022. With the Russian Federation the dominant trade partner for most countries in the region, the invasion of Ukraine and associated sanctions have seriously affected businesses—including micro, small, and medium-sized enterprises (MSMEs). The impact of the invasion differs by country, but in general Armenia, Azerbaijan, and Georgia have been less affected than Kazakhstan, the Kyrgyz Republic, Tajikistan, and Uzbekistan. Those countries experiencing limited impact do not for now need comprehensive anti-crisis plans, while those more affected have created action plans, including MSME support, to minimize adverse effects.

National export strategies should be reassessed and refined to support changes in MSME foreign trade, while developing domestic commodity markets can replace imported goods with those produced domestically.

As in other Asian regions, MSMEs dominate the private sector in Central and West Asia. Based on available data through 2021, they accounted for on average 98.9% of all enterprises, 46.1% of the workforce, and 40.7% of a country's economic output—whether in gross domestic product (GDP) or gross value added (GVA). Globalized MSME exporters and importers tend to contribute most to national output. The data show MSME exports accounted for an average of 32.4% of total export value—more than in other Asian regions (19.2% for Southeast Asia). MSME exports were hit hard by the 2014–2016 Russian financial crisis and the COVID-19 pandemic. In turn, the impact of the ongoing Russian invasion of Ukraine and related sanctions are upending MSME export operations, given their high reliance on the Russian Federation as a trading partner. Thus, governments in the region should reassess and refine their national export strategies to support MSME foreign trade and domestic commodity market development—to replace imported goods with those produced domestically.

MSMEs mainly trade in domestic markets, with their entrepreneurial base yet to be established. Making them more growth-oriented will help unlock new productivity.

Most MSMEs are in services (mainly wholesale and retail trade), followed by manufacturing. Agriculture's share of MSMEs is relatively high (8.1% in 2021), especially among those in Kazakhstan, Tajikistan, and Uzbekistan, which exclusively focus on domestic markets. The entrepreneurial base—essential for inclusive growth—has yet to take hold across Central and West Asia. Expanding this growth-oriented base will help unlock new productivity. Internationalizing MSMEs, business clustering, and innovation will accelerate economic recovery and inclusive, resilient growth. MSME participation in domestic and global supply chains must deepen. And entrepreneurial development should continue to target youth, women, agribusiness, and tech startups.

New mechanisms—like entrepreneurship development—will create more quality MSME jobs nationally.

Despite the large number of MSMEs operating in each economy, they account for less of the labor force than in other Asian regions—67.3% in Southeast Asia and 76.6% in South Asia—though the average differs by country. Job creation remains a critical issue for MSME development. In manufacturing and services, MSMEs tend to concentrate in capital cities. Promoting innovative rural businesses would create more new jobs. Youth and women entrepreneurs hold much potential to improve the region's labor markets and accelerate inclusive growth.

The shocks of the pandemic and the Russian invasion of Ukraine—along with increased global economic uncertainty in general—have accelerated MSME digitalization of both operations and administration; increased financial and technical assistance must support this process.

E-commerce and other forms of digitalization are spreading rapidly across Central and West Asia, supported by national payment systems and government assistance. However, the proportion of digital business transactions remains small. Developing adequate infrastructure and strengthening MSME digital literacy are key to developing the digital economy.

Finance is essential for MSMEs, especially access to growth capital. Diversified financing options—particularly market-based financing and digital finance platforms—will benefit both the growth and depth of MSME operations.

Finance is the foundation for business growth, but the MSME credit market remains small in Central and West Asia. Based on available data through 2021, bank lending to MSMEs averaged 9.0% of GDP and 31.4% of total bank lending. Nonperforming loans (NPLs) remain high, averaging 19.2% of MSME bank loans during 2015–2021. But the MSME NPL ratio has been dropping rapidly (a 13.7% compound annual decrease).

The nonbank finance industry, primarily microfinance institutions, remains in its infancy and cannot meet demand. During 2015–2021, financing by nonbank finance institutions (NBFIs) accounted for an average 2.3% of a country's GDP and 8.9% of total bank lending. High lending rates and nonperforming financing remain problems. The share of nonperforming financing to total NBFI financing averaged 10.1% over the period. Mobile and internet banking increased in several countries but needs to expand with wider product options covering credit, savings, insurance, and remittances.

Capital markets remain small. Based on operating equity markets in the region, market capitalization averaged 7.5% of a country's GDP during 2015–2021. Dedicated equity markets for small firms were created only recently in Kazakhstan and Tajikistan, offering simplified listing requirements. MSMEs can issue corporate bonds, but there are few. It is critical to strengthen capital market literacy programs and training to attract MSME issuers and potential investors.

The small lending markets in the region have led governments to offer financial assistance to MSMEs—such as refinancing facilities, special funds, soft-loan programs with interest rate subsidies, and credit guarantees. These tools have provided emergency assistance to MSMEs hit by financial crises and shocks like the COVID-19 pandemic. Demand for public financing schemes have surged since the start of the pandemic and the Russian invasion of Ukraine, creating a risk of bloated national budgets. There has been long debate on using subsidized loans as they can distort markets. Shifting from high reliance on subsidy-backed to more market-based finance should be one focus during policy discussions.

ADB's Small and Medium-Sized Enterprise Development Index (SME-DI) shows that limited lending to MSMEs with low-quality loan assets slows MSME development in the region. By contrast, increased lending to MSMEs with better loan assets, enhanced job creation, expanded foreign trade, and increased productivity all contribute to MSME development. This suggests that developing quality financial markets, a functioning labor market, expanding foreign trade, and enhancing productivity help MSMEs recover from crises more rapidly.

Complete and functioning MSME data infrastructure is the foundation of workable MSME policy design. Strengthening granular firm-level data nationally will promote more evidence-based policy support and financial inclusion.

Developing better credit data is crucial to improve MSME access to finance and contributes to more efficient MSME development, inclusive growth, and economic resilience. There are standard credit bureau systems across countries in Central and West Asia, with most having a collateral registry—or plan to introduce one—to improve credit reporting systems. However, company data and lists of pledged assets lack even basic company profiles, with many not tracking credit information over time. A credit risk database that comprehensively covers both positive and negative granular firm-level data over time should be considered to help build more sophisticated MSME data infrastructure.

Central and West Asia

Regional Review

Summary

Central and West Asian economies recovered relatively quickly from the contraction brought on by the coronavirus disease (COVID-19) pandemic. While they could revel in a V-shape recovery to 5.7% growth in 2021, the 2022 Russian invasion of Ukraine slowed growth momentum, with the region's economies now forecast to expand by 3.9% in 2022. With the Russian Federation a dominant trade partner, the invasion and associated sanctions also seriously affected the region's business operations—including micro, small, and medium-sized enterprises (MSMEs).

Like other Asian regions, MSMEs dominate private sector business. Based on available data through 2021, they accounted for an average 98.9% of all enterprises, 46.1% of the workforce, and 40.7% of a country's economic output—whether in gross domestic product (GDP) or gross value added (GVA).

Most MSMEs deal in services (mainly wholesale and retail trade), followed by manufacturing. But agriculture's share of MSMEs is relatively high (8.1% in 2021), especially Kazakhstan, Tajikistan, and Uzbekistan. The geographical distribution of MSMEs differs by country. Around half or more are concentrated in the capital cities of Armenia, Azerbaijan, Georgia, and the Kyrgyz Republic, with rural MSMEs spread across Kazakhstan, Tajikistan, and Uzbekistan.

Despite the large number of MSMEs operating nationally, they account for less of the labor force than in other Asian regions—67.3% in Southeast Asia and 76.6% in South Asia—although the average differs by country. Job creation remains a critical issue for MSME development in Central and West Asia. In manufacturing and services, MSMEs tend to concentrate in capital cities. Promoting innovative rural businesses would create more new jobs.

MSME contributions to a country's output is relatively large in Central and West Asia—nearly equal Southeast Asia's (40.8%). Contributing sectors differ by country. Services are the largest component to MSMEs' contribution to GDP or GVA, except in Uzbekistan, where agriculture contributed 47.3% in 2021. Globalized MSME exporters and importers tend to contribute most.

One-third of MSMEs in the region are export-oriented. Based on available data through 2021, MSME exports accounted for an average 32.4% of total export values—more than other Asian regions (19.2% for Southeast Asia). In the past, MSME exports were hardest hit by the 2014–2016 Russian financial crisis and the 2020 COVID-19 pandemic. The ongoing Russian invasion of Ukraine and related sanctions are hitting MSME exporters hard, given their high reliance on the Russian Federation as a trading partner.

Like the rest of Asia, e-commerce and other forms of digitalization are spreading rapidly, supported by national payment systems and the government assistance. However, it remains a small fraction of total business transactions. Developing digital infrastructure and strengthening MSME digital literacy are key to developing the digital economy across the region.

Private sector organizations—such as chambers of commerce and MSME associations—play a critical role in promoting MSME development. This was particularly true during the COVID-19 pandemic. As peer support, they provide training, business networking, and advisory services. They also actively lobby with governments in designing and implementing national MSME policies.

Finance is essential for business growth, but the MSME credit market is small in Central and West Asia. Based on available data through 2021, bank lending to MSMEs averaged 9.0% of GDP and 31.4% of total bank lending—compared with a 14.2% GDP share and 15.6% bank lending share in Southeast Asia. Nearly half (42.0% in 2021) of MSME loans went to services, followed by agriculture (18.0%). Nonperforming loans (NPLs) remain high, averaging 19.2% of MSME bank loans during 2015–2021. But the MSME NPL ratio has been dropping sharply (a 13.7% compound annual decrease).

Given the small lending market, governments offer financial assistance to MSMEs—such as refinancing facilities, special funds, soft-loan programs with interest rate subsidies, and credit guarantees. These tools provided emergency assistance to MSMEs hit by financial crises and shocks like the COVID-19 pandemic. Among them, subsidized loans and credit guarantees are the most popular.

Public financial assistance has increased as national budgets expand—though not to the point of dominating lending markets across the region. Demand for public financing schemes surged due to the pandemic and the ongoing Russian invasion of Ukraine, creating the risk of bloated national budgets. There has also been a long debate on using subsidized loans as they can distort markets. Shifting from a high reliance on subsidy-backed to more market-based finance needs to be reconsidered in policy discussions.

The nonbank finance industry remains in its infancy and does not meet demand. Nonbank finance institutions (NBFIs) include microfinance institutions (MFIs), credit unions, leasing, and pawnshops. During 2015–2021, NBFI financing in the region accounted for an average 2.3% of a country's GDP (2.0% compound annual growth rate [CAGR]) and 8.9% of total bank lending (2.9% CAGR). High lending rates and nonperforming financing remain problems. The share of nonperforming financing to total NBFI financing averaged 10.1% over the period, much higher than other Asian regions—an average 1.2% in Southeast Asia and 6.6% in South Asia.

Digital financial infrastructure—such as interoperable payment systems—has developed rapidly with government policy support. Mobile and internet banking increased in several countries, but needs to expand with wider product options covering credit, savings, insurance, and remittances.

Capital markets remain small in Central and West Asia. Based on operating equity markets in the region, market capitalization averaged 7.5% of a country's GDP during 2015–2021. Dedicated equity markets for small firms were created only recently in Kazakhstan and Tajikistan. The Kazakhstan Stock Exchange opened an Alternative Board catering to MSMEs in 2017, offering simplified listing requirements to encourage them to use the stock market for financing. MSMEs are not taxed on income from securities listed and traded. MSMEs can also issue corporate bonds on the Alternative Board. Under certain conditions, bond guarantees are available for up to 5 years. Since opening, the Alternative Board has steadily expanded, except in 2020 due to the pandemic.

In Southeast Asia and South Asia, qualified MSMEs can raise working capital from banks—supported by government assistance—while firms that benefited from the pandemic's mobility restrictions, like those in information and communication technology (ICT), could still raise growth capital from equity markets. In Central and West Asia, those firms tended to issue corporate bonds rather than tap equity markets for growth capital. Developing better corporate governance standards, increasing transparency and public awareness, and further developing financial intermediation could help securities markets in the region become more attractive. It is also critical to strengthen capital market literacy programs and training to attract MSME issuers and investors.

Developing better credit data is also crucial to improve MSME access to finance. All Central and West Asian countries covered here have standard credit bureau systems, with most having a collateral registry—or plan to introduce one—and improving credit reporting systems. However, company data and lists of pledged assets lack even basic company profiles with many not tracking credit information over time. A credit risk database that comprehensively covers both positive and negative granular firm-level data over time would be worth considering.

This report estimates a Small and Medium-Sized Enterprise Development Index (SME-DI) for Central and West Asia, using the Asia SME Monitor 2022 database. It identifies the critical factors affecting MSME development by using a probabilistic principal component analysis. ADB began designing this benchmark index in 2020.

The SME-DI shows that limited lending to MSMEs with low-quality loan assets slows MSME development in the region. By contrast, increased lending to MSMEs with better loan assets, enhanced job creation, expanded foreign trade of MSMEs, and increased MSME productivity—all these factors contribute to MSME development. Thus, developing quality financial markets, a functioning labor market, expanding foreign trade, and enhancing productivity all help MSMEs recover following crises.

The region's policymakers prioritize MSME development and financial inclusion as part of their national growth strategies. The Central and West Asian countries covered here all have long-term MSME development policies that include financial and nonfinancial assistance. They aim to strengthen MSME competitiveness by promoting international trade; adopting available technology; developing entrepreneurship; upgrading skills; diversifying financing options; and targeting assistance toward youth and women entrepreneurs, startups, agribusiness, and exporters.

In general, countries frequently use government subsidies and grants to implement policies. Preferential taxation and subsidies directly support MSMEs, although they risk bloating national budgets unless there is an appropriate exit strategy. For example, public-private partnerships should be considered in helping policy implementation, especially in providing technical support for businesses and funding assistance programs.

There are comprehensive national financial inclusion strategies in the Kyrgyz Republic, Tajikistan, and Uzbekistan, while Azerbaijan, Georgia, and Kazakhstan focus on a national financial education strategy. Armenia does not have a financial inclusion strategy. The common goals of financial inclusion strategies include (i) diversifying financial products (digital finance), (ii) financial literacy, (iii) consumer protection, (iv) financial assistance for targeted groups (youth and women), and (v) financial regulatory reforms. Central banks generally coordinate and implement financial inclusion strategies.

The pandemic stunted growth momentum. Lockdowns or mobility restrictions hampered domestic and foreign trade and significantly reduced economic activities. Remittances from migrant workers dropped sharply. MSMEs were hardest hit. Retail service outlets, hotels and restaurants, tourism, and education were severely affected. Several business surveys show that MSMEs faced immediate supply chain disruptions, a sharp drop in sales and revenue, reduced availability of raw materials (at higher prices), and delayed customer payments. Many public and private institutions switched to remote operations. Private businesses cut costs by laying off workers or reducing wages. Governments in the region used timely economic stimulus packages to limit economic damage and allow for a quick recovery.

The impact of the Russian invasion of Ukraine differs by country, but can be split into two groups: (i) countries with a relatively limited impact—Armenia, Azerbaijan, and Georgia, and (ii) those hit hard by the invasion and sanctions—Kazakhstan, the Kyrgyz Republic, Tajikistan, and Uzbekistan. Those with limited impact do not have comprehensive anti-crisis plans, while those more affected have action plans to minimize the adverse effects. Given continuing global economic uncertainty, governments should reassess and refine their national export strategies to support MSME foreign trade and domestic commodity market development to replace imported goods with those produced domestically.

Overall, MSMEs are mainly trade on domestic markets, with their entrepreneurial base—essential for inclusive growth—yet to be established. Making MSMEs more growth-oriented will help unlock new productivity. There is also a need to develop mechanisms to create quality MSME jobs.

Over the long term, Central and West Asian economies should increase their resilience to shocks by making MSME more robust as they grow. Internationalizing MSMEs, business clustering, and fostering innovation will accelerate economic recovery and inclusive growth. It is critical to promote MSME participation in domestic and global supply chains and encourage entrepreneurial development targeting the youth, women, agribusiness, and tech startups. Digitalizing MSME operations and administration should be another policy priority. A recent COVID-19 study suggests that digitalization may encourage businesses to register as it saves costs and provides support for more business transparency.

Finance, especially access to growth capital, is critical for MSMEs to survive and grow. Diversified financing options are needed, with attention paid to market-based financing (capital market development) and digital finance platforms.

Finally, developing data infrastructure promotes evidence-based assistance for MSMEs. ADB's Asia SME Monitor supports its development. More advanced discussion on this is to support creating an effective credit risk database, allowing MSMEs to access more diversified financing options.

1. Overview of the Regional Economy

Most economies in Central and West Asia were hit hard by the COVID-19 pandemic. GDP fell sharply across the region, leading to a 2.0% contraction in 2020. The recovery came quickly, however, with GDP growing by 5.7% in 2021, in part due to large government assistance packages (Figure 1.1A). However, the 2022 Russian invasion of Ukraine sapped growth momentum and increased inflationary pressures. The region is forecast to grow by 3.9% in 2022 with inflation rising from 8.9% in 2021 to 11.5% in 2022 (Figure 1.1B).

Based on Russian Federation trade data, goods exports to Central and West Asia—the region's imports from the Russian Federation—was $32.7 billion in 2021 (Figure 1.1C). The Russian Federation's imports from the region (Central Asia's goods exports to the Russian Federation) amounted to $11.7 billion. All Central and West Asian economies, especially Kazakhstan, rely on international trade with the Russian Federation. Thus, the Russian invasion of Ukraine and associated global sanctions against the Russian Federation seriously affected the region and its business operations, including those of MSMEs (one-third export their products).

Figure 1.1: Economic Overview in Central and West Asia

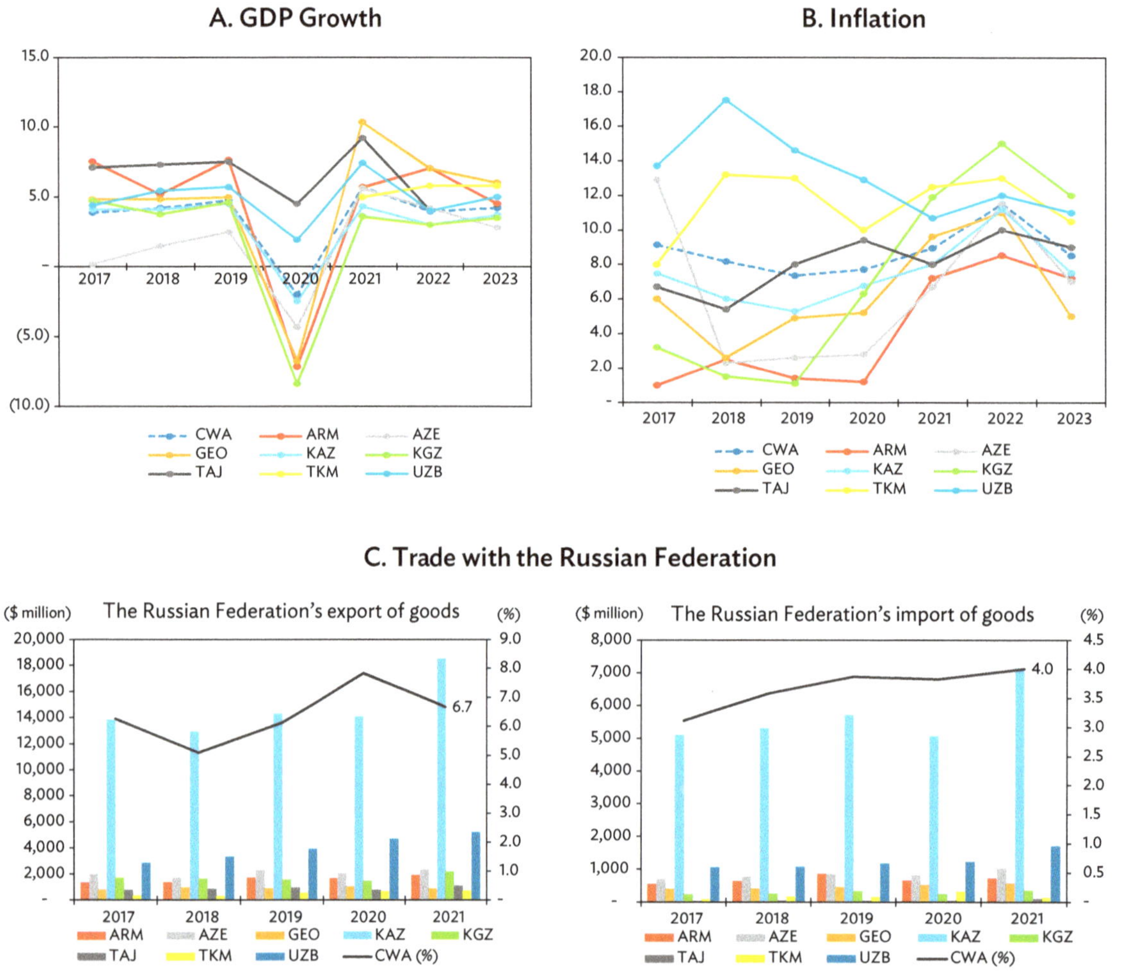

ARM = Armenia, AZE = Azerbaijan, CWA = Central and West Asia, GEO = Georgia, GDP = gross domestic product, KAZ = Kazakhstan, KGZ = Kyrgyz Republic, TAJ = Tajikistan, TUR = Turkmenistan, UZB = Uzbekistan.

Source: For GDP growth and inflation, ADB Asian Development Outlook 2022 and Update September 2022; for trade with the Russian Federation, calculations based on its trade in goods, UN Comtrade.

2. MSME Development

MSMEs in Central and West Asia, 2010–2021

	Percentage share	*Compound annual growth*
• **Number of MSMEs to total enterprises**	***98.9%***	***+0.1%***
• **MSME employees to total employees**	***46.1%***	***+0.7%,***
• **MSME contribution to national GDP***	***40.7%***	***+2.0%,***
• **MSME exports to total export value****	***32.4%***	***-3.1%***

GDP = gross domestic product; MSME = micro, small, and medium-sized enterprise.
* Based on GDP for the Kyrgyz Republic, Tajikistan, and Uzbekistan; gross value added for Armenia, Azerbaijan, Georgia, and Kazakhstan.
** Data for 2015–2021.
Reporting countries only. Data based on latest available data until 2021.

Scale of MSMEs

MSMEs are defined in the region either by law or policy, using criteria on the number of employees, asset values, and annual revenue (Table 1.1). Categories vary by country; (i) micro, small, and medium-sized enterprises in Armenia, Azerbaijan, Kazakhstan, and the Kyrgyz Republic; (ii) small and medium-sized enterprises in Georgia and Tajikistan; and (iii) micro and small enterprises for Uzbekistan. For the Kyrgyz Republic and Uzbekistan, the definition also differs by business sector, while other countries use a single definition regardless of sector. This report uses country-specific MSME definitions for comparative analysis as they are the benchmarks for national MSME policies. Although the definition differs by country, the region's MSMEs make a homogeneous group by employment (firms with fewer than 200 or 250 employees are roughly categorized as MSMEs across the region). For convenience, this chapter uses "MSME" throughout unless otherwise stated.

Table 1.1: MSME Definitions in Central and West Asia

		Definition						
Country	Category	Employee	Asset	Revenue	Capital	By Sector	Legal Basis	Remarks
Armenia	Micro, small, and medium-sized firm	√	√	√			√	Law No.121 of 2000 on State Support for Small and Medium Entrepreneurship.
Azerbaijan	Micro, small, and medium-sized firm	√		√			√	Decree of the Cabinet of Ministers No.556 of 2018 on the approval of the "criteria for the division of micro, small, medium, and large business entities."
Georgia	Small and medium-sized firm	√		√				Defined by the SME Development Strategy of Georgia for 2021-2025.
Kazakhstan	Micro, small, and medium-sized firm	√		√			√	Entrepreneurial Code No.375-V of 2015.
Kyrgyz Republic	Micro, small, and medium-sized firm	√		√		√	√	Government Resolution No.78 of 1998.
Tajikistan	Small and medium-sized firm	√		√			√	Law No.1107 of 2014 on Government Protection and Support of EntrepreneurshipState Support for Small and Medium Entrepreneurship; amended in 2020.
Uzbekistan	Micro and small firm	√				√	√	Resolution of the Cabinet of Ministers No.275 of 2016.

MSME = micro, small, and medium-sized enterprise, SME = small and medium-sized enterprise.

Source: Compiled from Country Reviews of Asia SME Monitor 2022.

MSMEs dominate private sector businesses. Latest available data through 2021 show they accounted for an average 98.9% of all enterprises—higher than the Southeast Asian average (97.7%).[1] The share remained stable over the decade with a CAGR of 0.1% during 2010–2021. But the number of MSMEs increased in every country during the period (2010–2020 for Armenia, Azerbaijan, and Georgia), particularly in Georgia (11.8% CAGR), Kazakhstan (7.3%), and Uzbekistan (9.9%) (Figure 1.2A).

Most MSMEs are in services—in wholesale and retail trade (an average 33.9%), transportation and communication (8.1%), and other services such as accommodation and food services (28.0%). Services was followed by manufacturing (10.3%) and construction (6.7%) (Figure 1.2B). Compared with other regions, agriculture's MSME share (8.1%) was higher in Central and West Asia than Southeast Asia (1.6%), but similar to South Asia (8.7%). The share of agricultural MSMEs was relatively higher in Kazakhstan (18.2%), Tajikistan (15.2%), and Uzbekistan (9.9%).

1 Data refer to 2020 for Armenia, Azerbaijan, and Georgia, and 2021 for Kazakhstan, the Kyrgyz Republic, Tajikistan, and Uzbekistan. Southeast Asia data are based on the Asia SME Monitor 2022 database for Association of Southeast Asian Nations (ASEAN) members.

For geographical distribution, the majority of MSMEs operate outside the capital or rural areas, but the share of those in capital cities was relatively high in Central and West Asia as compared to other Asian regions. While an average 62.8% of MSMEs operated in provinces, 37.2% were based in capital cities, whose share was higher than in Southeast Asia (17.1% in capitals) and South Asia (21.1%) (Figure 1.2C).[2] At the country level, however, the share varied. Around half or more concentrated on the capital for Armenia, Azerbaijan, Georgia, and the Kyrgyz Republic, while MSMEs spread in rural areas for agriculture-oriented countries like Kazakhstan, Tajikistan, and Uzbekistan.

Figure 1.2: Number of MSMEs

A. Number of MSMEs, 2021

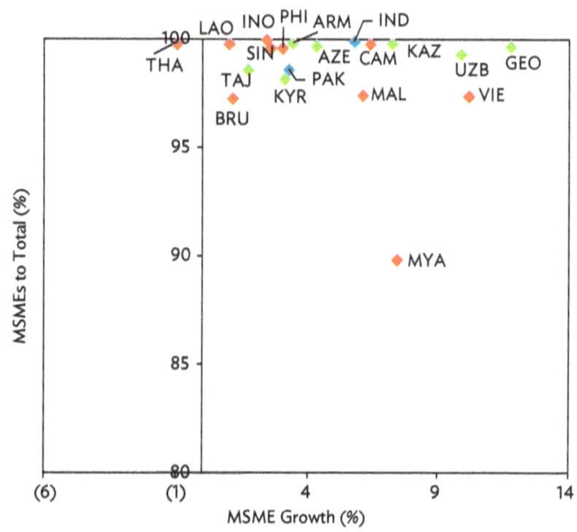

B. MSMEs by Sector, 2021

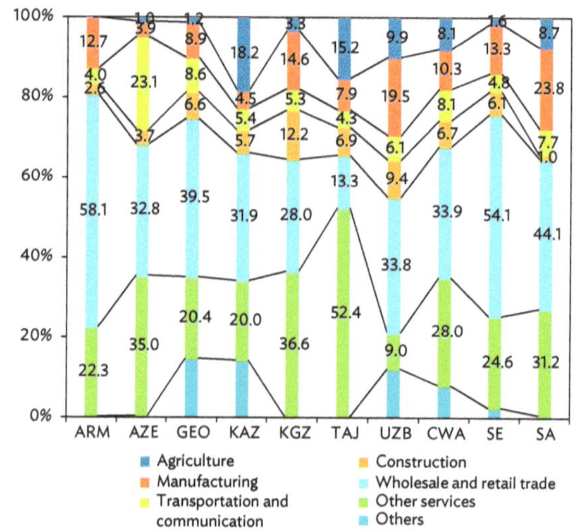

C. MSMEs by Region, 2021

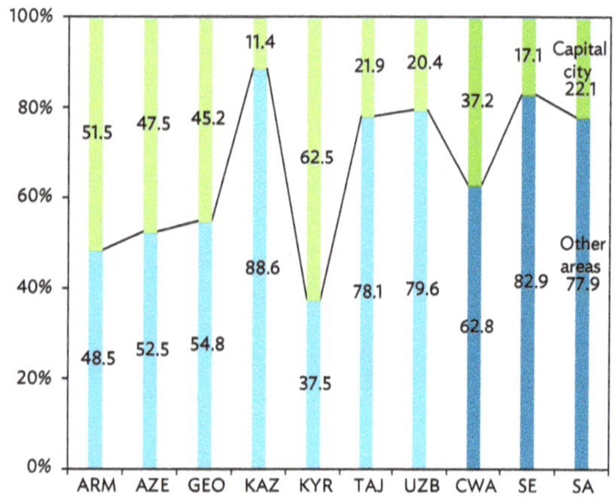

ARM = Armenia; AZE = Azerbaijan; BRU = Brunei Darussalam; CAM = Cambodia; CWA = Central and West Asia; GEO = Georgia; IND = India; INO = Indonesia; KAZ = Kazakhstan; KGZ = Kyrgyz Republic; LAO = Lao People's Democratic Republic; MAL = Malaysia; MSME = micro, small, and medium-sized enterprise; MYA = Myanmar; PAK = Pakistan; PHI = Philippines; SA = South Asia; SE = Southeast Asia; SIN = Singapore; TAJ = Tajikistan; THA = Thailand; UZB = Uzbekistan; VIE = Viet Nam.

Notes: For Figure 1.2A, the share of MSMEs to the total (%) refers to the latest available end-of-year. MSME growth (%) refers to compound annual growth during 2010–2020 for ARM, AZE, and GEO; 2010–2021 for KAZ, KGZ, TAJ, and UZB. For Figures 1.2B and 1.2C, CWA, SA, and SE refer to the average of reporting countries.

Source: ADB Asia SME Monitor 2022 database.

[2] Capitals include Yerevan in Armenia, Baku in Azerbaijan, Tbilisi in Georgia, Astana in Kazakhstan, Bishkek in the Kyrgyz Republic, Dushanbe in Tajikistan, and Tashkent in Uzbekistan.

Employment

Although MSMEs in Central and West Asia grew in number over the past decade, they absorbed relatively less new workers. Job creation is a critical issue for MSME development in the region. Based on available data through 2021, MSMEs employed an average 46.1% of the workforce (a 0.7% CAGR during 2010–2021), less than the Southeast Asian average (67.3%) and South Asian average (76.6%, based on data through 2020). By country, however, employment varied from a 2021 high of 74.4% for Uzbekistan to a low of 20.4% for Tajikistan. The growth in number of MSME employees also differed by country, from high growth in Tajikistan (26.0% CAGR) and Azerbaijan (14.1%) to a contraction in Armenia (1.0%) and slow growth in the Kyrgyz Republic (0.4%) (Figure 1.3A).

More than half of MSME employees work in services—an average 20.6% in wholesale and retail trade, 5.8% in transportation and communication, and 31.9% in other services—followed by manufacturing (15.9%), agriculture (12.0%), and construction (10.8%) (Figure 1.3B). The average share of agricultural workers—most in Uzbekistan (34.3%), Tajikistan (13.6%), and Kazakhstan (13.0%)—was higher than in Southeast Asia (3.6%).

Figure 1.3: Employment by MSMEs

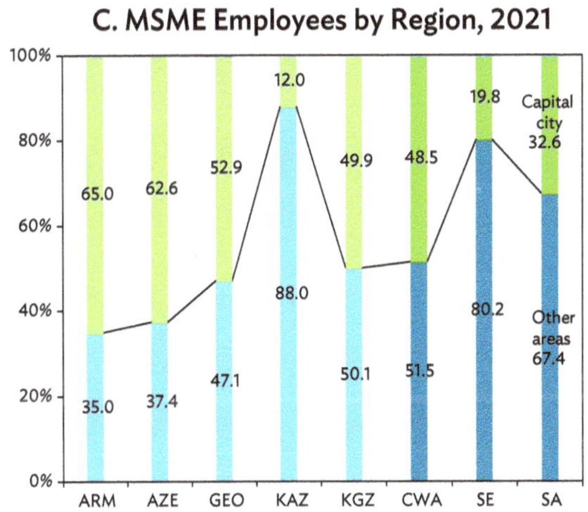

ARM = Armenia; AZE = Azerbaijan; BRU = Brunei Darussalam; CAM = Cambodia; CWA = Central and West Asia; GEO = Georgia; INO = Indonesia; KAZ = Kazakhstan; KGZ = Kyrgyz Republic; LAO = Lao People's Democratic Republic; MAL = Malaysia; MSME = micro, small, and medium-sized enterprise; NEP = Nepal; PAK = Pakistan; PHI = Philippines; SA = South Asia; SE = Southeast Asia; SIN = Singapore; TAJ = Tajikistan; THA = Thailand; UZB = Uzbekistan; VIE = Viet Nam.

Notes: For Figure 1.3A, the share of MSME employees to total (%) refers to the latest available year (end-of-year). The growth of MSME employees (%) refers to compound annual growth during 2010–2020 for ARM, AZE, and GEO; 2010–2021 for KAZ, KGZ, TAJ, and UZB. For Figures 1.3B and 1.3C, CWA, SA, and SE refer to average of reporting countries. Data on agriculture is unavailable for ARM.

Source: ADB Asia SME Monitor 2022 database.

Around half (an average 51.5%) of those employed by MSMEs work in provinces, while the remaining half (48.5%) work in capital cities. The share of MSME workers in capitals was higher than the average in Southeast Asia (19.8%) and South Asia (32.6%) (Figure 1.3C). MSME workers were concentrated in the capital cities of Armenia (65.0%), Azerbaijan (62.6%), and Georgia (52.9%) as of end-2020; while provincial MSME workers were highest in Kazakhstan (88.0% in 2021).

As workers tend to concentrate in industrial capital cities, promoting more innovative rural MSMEs would result in more new jobs.

Business Productivity

Data on MSME contributions to GDP are available for the Kyrgyz Republic, Tajikistan, and Uzbekistan. Where data on MSME GDP are unavailable, gross value added (GVA) is used to measure productivity in Armenia, Azerbaijan, Georgia, and Kazakhstan. Although it is difficult to compare MSME productivity given the different definitions, overall, MSME contributions to country output in Central and West Asia was largely the same as in Southeast Asia. Based on available data until 2021, the MSME output share averaged 40.7% in Central and West Asia (2.0% CAGR during 2010–2021), while Southeast Asia averaged 40.8% during the same period.

Contributions to GVA or GDP varied significantly, with MSMEs in Georgia contributed 60.8% to GVA in 2020, followed by Kazakhstan (33.5% in 2021), Armenia (26.3% in 2020), and Azerbaijan (16.7% in 2020). Those in Tajikistan contributed 59.4% of GDP, followed by Uzbekistan (54.9%) and the Kyrgyz Republic (42.8%) as of end-2021 (Figure 1.4A). MSME GVA or GDP growth (based on local currency values) also differed by country—Armenia (0.9% CAGR), Azerbaijan (25.6%), Georgia (14.9%), Kazakhstan (18.1%), the Kyrgyz Republic (11.8%), Tajikistan (15.6%), and Uzbekistan (21.9%) in 2010–2021 (2010–2020 for Armenia, Azerbaijan, and Georgia).

Some countries expanded their MSME share of GVA—Azerbaijan (19.6% CAGR in 2010–2020) and Kazakhstan (4.5% in 2010–2021)—while some shares contracted (Armenia –4.8% in 2010–2020 and Uzbekistan –0.9% in 2010–2021) (Figure 1.4B).

In United States (US) dollar terms, MSME output was highest in Kazakhstan ($65.1 billion in 2021), followed by Uzbekistan ($34.5 billion in 2021), Azerbaijan ($6.4 billion in 2020), Tajikistan ($5.2 billion in 2021), Georgia ($4.1 billion in 2020), the Kyrgyz Republic ($3.7 billion in 2021), and Armenia ($3.1 billion in 2020) (Figure 1.4C).[3] These are small compared with Southeast Asia ($689 billion in Indonesia, $179 billion in Thailand, $141 billion in Singapore, and $128 billion in Malaysia) and India ($594 billion).

Services (combining wholesale and retail trade, transportation and communication, and other services) contributed most to MSME GVA or GDP across the region, except in Uzbekistan—Armenia (62.3% in 2020), Azerbaijan (68.3% in 2020), Georgia (61.5% in 2020), the Kyrgyz Republic (47.2% in 2021), and Uzbekistan (32.0% in 2021) (Figure 1.4D). In Uzbekistan, agriculture's share of GDP was 47.3% in 2021. The main contributors to GVA or GDP were globalized MSMEs (exporters and importers).

[3] Exchange rates of local currency to US dollar refer to end-of-year rates from the International Monetary Fund's International Financial Statistics in designated years.

Figure 1.4: MSME Contribution to GDP

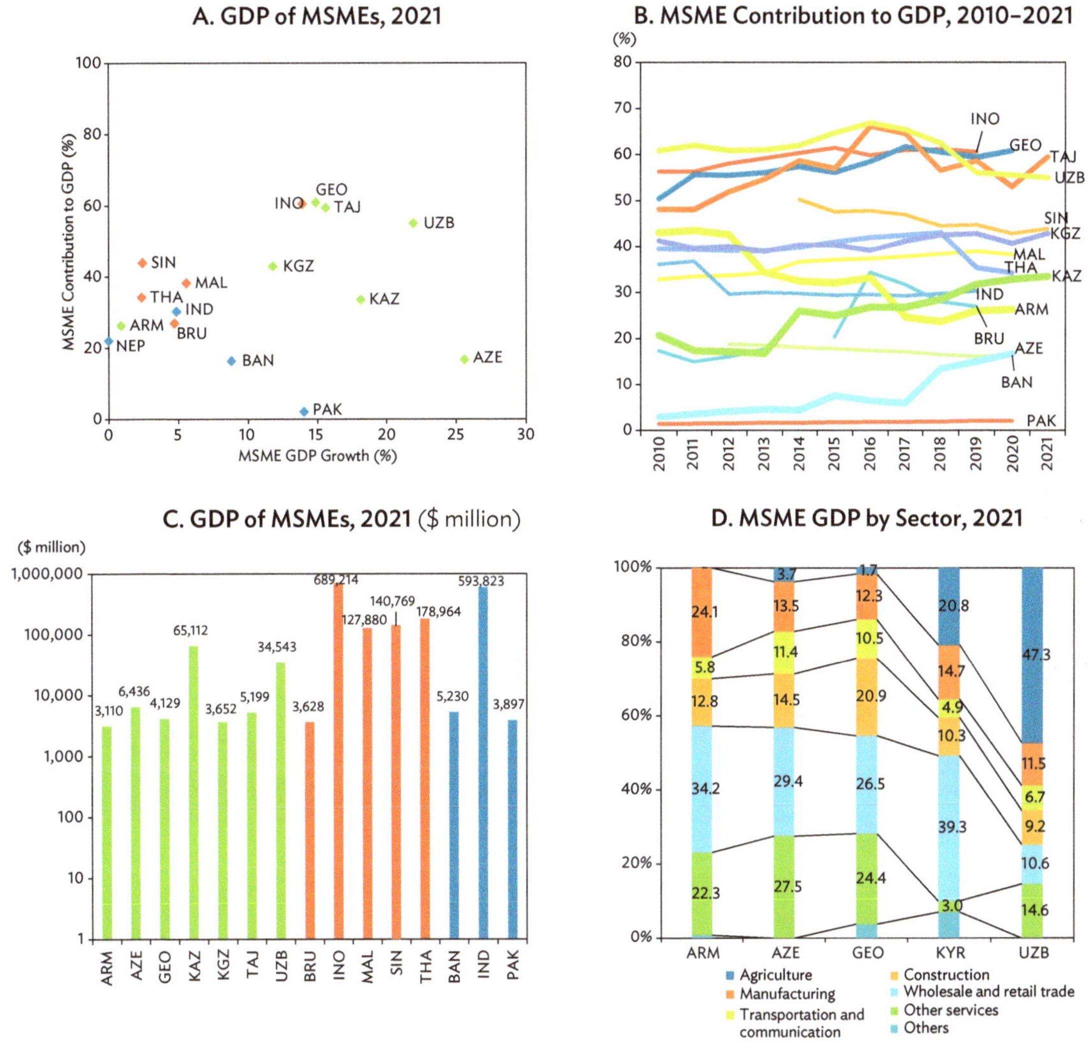

ARM = Armenia; AZE = Azerbaijan; BAN = Bangladesh; BRU = Brunei Darussalam; GDP = gross domestic product; GEO = Georgia; IND = India; INO = Indonesia; KAZ = Kazakhstan; KGZ = Kyrgyz Republic; MAL = Malaysia; MSME = micro, small, and medium-sized enterprise; PAK = Pakistan; SIN = Singapore; TAJ = Tajikistan; THA = Thailand; UZB = Uzbekistan.

Notes: For Figure 1.4A, MSME contribution to GDP (%) refers to the latest available year (end-of-year). MSME GDP growth (%) refers to compound annual growth during 2010–2020 for ARM, AZE, and GEO; 2010–2021 for KAZ, KGZ, TAJ, and UZB. Data refer to GDP for KGZ, TAJ, and UZB; gross value added for ARN, AZE, GEO, and KAZ. For Figure 1.4C, data refer to 2020 for ARM, AZE, and GEO; and 2021 for KAZ, KGZ, TAJ, and UZB. Exchange rates of local currency to US dollar refer to end-of-year currency rates from the International Monetary Fund's International Financial Statistics in designated years.

Source: ADB Asia SME Monitor 2022 database.

Market Access

While many Central and West Asian MSMEs are in distributive trade, one-third are export-oriented. Based on available data through 2021, MSME exports accounted for an average 32.4% of total export value (falling –3.1% CAGR during 2015–2021). Although the share contracted, it remained well above the Southeast Asia average (19.2% in 2010–2020). MSME shares in exports was again quite varied across countries. Georgia's MSME export share of total export value in 2021 was 55.9%, while Uzbekistan had the strongest growth in MSME export local currency value—25.7% CAGR in 2010–2021 (Figure 1.5A).

MSME exports were hard hit by both the 2014–2016 Russian financial crisis and the 2020 COVID-19 pandemic. During 2015–2021, the MSME export share to total exports contracted in Georgia (–1.6% CAGR), the Kyrgyz Republic (–4.7%), and in Uzbekistan (–4.9%) (Figure 1.5B). Although data are not yet available for 2022, the impact of the Russian invasion of Ukraine certainly forced MSME exporters to adjust their operations.

In US dollar terms, MSME export value was highest in Uzbekistan ($3.3 billion in 2021), followed by Georgia ($766 million in 2021), the Kyrgyz Republic ($752 million in 2020), and Armenia ($121 million in 2009) (Figure 1.5C).[4] Compared with Southeast Asia and South Asia, MSME export values in Central and West Asia remain relatively small. Given continuing global economic uncertainty, the region's governments need to realign their national export strategies to both support internationalized MSMEs as they adjust and domestic commodity markets to continue replacing imported goods with domestic inputs for production.

Figure 1.5: MSME Exports

A. MSME Exports, 2021

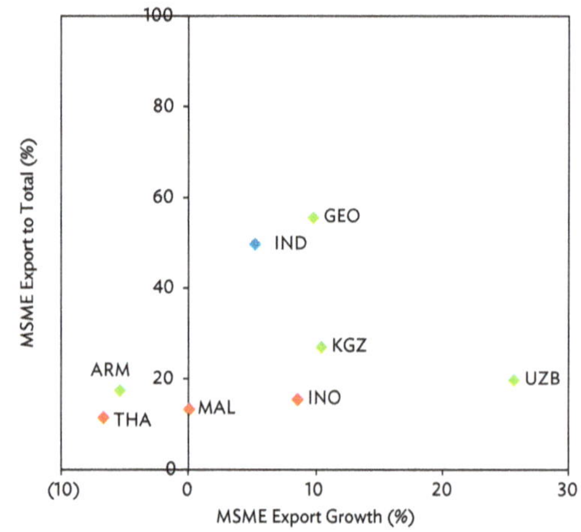

B. MSME Exports to Total, 2004–2021

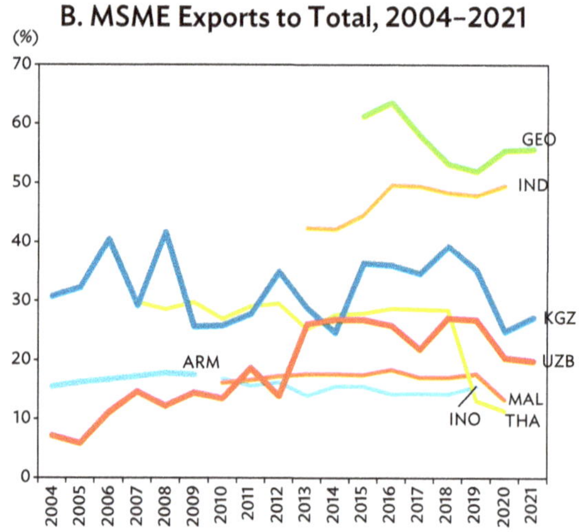

C. MSME Exports, 2021 ($ million)

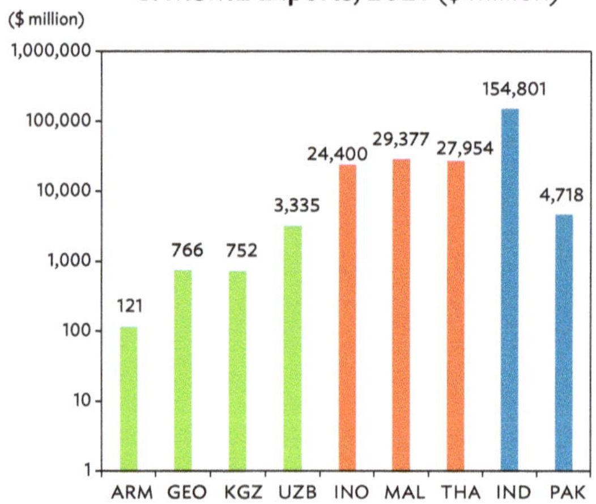

ARM = Armenia; GEO = Georgia; IND = India; INO = Indonesia; KGZ = Kyrgyz Republic; MAL = Malaysia; MSME = micro, small, and medium-sized enterprise; THA = Thailand; UZB = Uzbekistan.

Notes: For Figure 1.5A, MSME export to total (%) refers to the latest available year (end-of-year): 2009 for ARM; 2019 for INO; 2020 for IND, MAL, and THA; and 2021 for GEO, KGZ, and UZB. MSME export growth (%) refers to compound annual growth during past and latest available data. Data covers: 2010–2019 for INO, 2010–2020 for MAL and THA, 2013–2020 for IND, 2004–2009 for ARM, 2015–2021 for GEO, and 2010–2021 for KGZ and UZB. For Figure 1.5C, exchange rates of local currency to US dollar refer to end-of-year currency rates from the International Monetary Fund's International Financial Statistics in designated years.

Source: ADB Asia SME Monitor 2022 database.

[4] Exchange rates of local currency to US dollar refer to end-of-year rates from the International Monetary Fund's International Financial Statistics in designated years.

Technology and Innovation

As in many regions, mobile phones and internet use is increasing across Central and West Asia. In 2020, mobile cellular subscriptions exceeded the population in nearly all countries—Armenia (118 subscriptions per 100 people), Azerbaijan (102), Georgia (128), Kazakhstan (129), the Kyrgyz Republic (130), Tajikistan (121), and Uzbekistan (100). Individual internet use remains limited but has been growing—Armenia (77% of the population in 2020), Azerbaijan (85%), Georgia (73%), Kazakhstan (86%), the Kyrgyz Republic (51% in 2019), Tajikistan (22% in 2017), and Uzbekistan (71% in 2020) (Figure 1.6).

With interoperable payment systems developing, e-commerce has grown rapidly, though at varying rates across countries. In Armenia, international online shopping sites like Amazon and eBay are supplemented by domestic online shopping platforms—mostly MSMEs. The government is considering new e-commerce legislation that would include collecting value-added tax (VAT) on international online transactions.

In Azerbaijan, COVID-19 lockdowns accelerated e-commerce growth as several domestic online platforms opened (including MSMEs); e-commerce transaction value in 2020 was more than 20 times the amount in 2015. Azerbaijan's Digital Trade Hub, a government startup built through a public-private partnership, offers several technical and advisory services to develop the national e-commerce industry.

Georgia's SMEs had high internet penetration before the pandemic outbreak in 2020. But online business is limited by the lack of appropriate infrastructure for transacting and paying online. In 2021, 96% of SMEs had no sales online, while less than 4% conduct e-commerce. A lack of innovation and technology use remains a major challenge for SME development. The government has supported startups and innovative small businesses by providing grants or training.

The pandemic accelerated Kazakhstan's adoption of digital business technologies, including MSMEs. As most MSMEs are in low-tech industries, the government offers several assistance programs (training and advisory services) to startups centered on digitalization. The government also promotes MSME participation in e-commerce through international trade platforms like Alibaba.

The Kyrgyz Republic has a High-Tech Park that supports businesses, including low-tech MSMEs, in adopting technology for commercial use. As in many countries, e-commerce and digitalization have expanded rapidly. The Association of E-commerce supports technology-based business growth, targeting local and small businesses. The government has also helped develop tech-based agribusiness.

In Tajikistan, upgrading digital infrastructure is critical, given the current high cost of mobile subscriptions and low internet speeds. With most bandwidth sourced from the Russian Federation, the Russian invasion of Ukraine disrupted the limited internet connectivity, partially explaining the country's small e-commerce footprint. Most SMEs have yet to digitalize nor use e-commerce.

E-commerce in Uzbekistan has developed slowly due to poor digital infrastructure and a lack of digital skills. Still, micro and small firms have been gradually digitalizing using international trade platforms to export products to neighboring Commonwealth of Independent States members, the Middle East, Europe, and the United States (US). The government supports information technology (IT) firms with tax exemptions and advisory services through an IT park. The development of online payment systems is also gaining momentum.

Overall, business digitalization—by developing e-commerce—is gaining momentum with government support. Digital infrastructure and digital literacy must be prioritized, especially for MSMEs. The Russian invasion of Ukraine exacerbated the problems facing the digital development in the region, given the high reliance on Russian Federation providers for IT infrastructure and digitally operated firms exporting to the Russian Federation.

Figure 1.6: Mobile and Internet Penetration, 2020

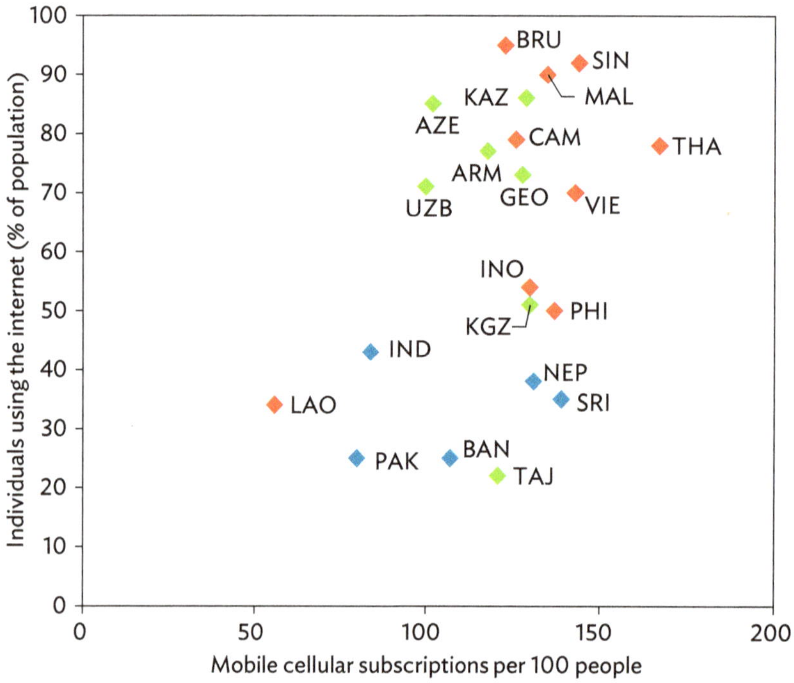

ARM = Armenia, AZE = Azerbaijan, BAN = Bangladesh, BRU = Brunei Darussalam, CAM = Cambodia, GEO = Georgia, IND = India, INO = Indonesia, KAZ = Kazakhstan, KGZ = the Kyrgyz Republic, LAO = Lao People's Democratic Republic, MAL = Malaysia, NEP = Nepal, PAK = Pakistan, PHI = Philippines, SIN = Singapore, SRI = Sri Lanka, TAJ = Tajikistan, THA = Thailand, UZB = Uzbekistan, VIE = Viet Nam.

Source: World Bank. World Development Indicators. https://data.worldbank.org/indicator/

Networking and Support

Many private organizations and associations, as well as government agencies, help MSMEs develop their business through training, business networking, and advisory services. They also actively lobby with governments on designing and implementing national MSME policies.

Armenia's SME Cooperation Association, National Center for Innovation and Entrepreneurship, and Chamber of Commerce and Industry play a key role in supporting MSME business through various services, including incubation and startup programs.

Several government authorities in Azerbaijan provide networking, capacity building, government-to-business (G2B), and business-to-business (B2B) services to MSMEs and startups, along with incubation and acceleration opportunities. The Small and Medium Business Development Agency offers one-stop advisory services through the SME House, SME Development Centers, and "SME Friends" project. The Chamber of Commerce and Industry also supports local business.

Government authorities like Enterprise Georgia and the Georgia Innovation and Technology Agency with the private sector's Chamber of Commerce and Industry and SME Development Association support industrializing SMEs. They are helping develop business clusters and additional infrastructure through advisory and training services, grants, and other funding.

Kazakhstan's international technopark, Astana Hub, promotes startups and provides a wide range of business and educational programs. The National Chamber of Entrepreneurs supports MSMEs and local entrepreneurs through its small and medium business development committee.

In the Kyrgyz Republic, MSME associations and the Chamber of Commerce and Industry (about 100 active business associations) support MSME development and industrialization through consulting and training services, as well as business clusters and infrastructure development.

Tajikistan has adopted several initiatives to develop businesses—especially SMEs and entrepreneurships—led by government and private sector groups such as the Chamber of Commerce and Industry. A state enterprise—Business Incubator of Tajikistan—promotes individual entrepreneurs, SMEs, and startups through regular consultations, incubation programs, training, and other educational activities. The Chamber of Commerce and Industry offers customized advice and support to individual SMEs through its "Hot Line," which helped them make it through the pandemic.

Uzbekistan has several business associations and various groups actively supporting small businesses—such as the Chamber of Commerce and Industry, and the Business Women's Association. The government also supports micro and small enterprise development and entrepreneurships through its special State Fund for Entrepreneurial Development Support.

In sum, private sector groups use their tight business networks to support MSME development across the region, especially during unexpected shocks like the COVID-19 pandemic and the Russian invasion of Ukraine. They closely communicate with government authorities responsible for MSME policies to supplement government MSME initiatives. They focus targeted group assistance by providing training and advisory services for agribusinesses, exporters, tech-based startups, and women entrepreneurs.

3. Access to Finance

MSMEs in Central and West Asia, 2015–2021

Bank credit	*Percentage share*	*Compound annual growth*
• **MSME loans to national GDP**	*9.0%*	*+2.7%*
• **MSME loans to total bank loans**	*31.4%*	*-2.2%*
• **MSME NPLs to total MSME loans**	*19.2%*	*-13.7%*
Nonbank and market-based finance		
• **NBFI financing to national GDP**	*2.3%*	*+2.0%*
• **NBFI financing to total bank loans**	*8.9%*	*+2.9%*
• **NBFI NPF to total financing**	*10.1%*	*+7.2%*
• **MSME market capitalization to GDP***	*7.5%*	*-1.3%*

GDP = gross domestic product; MSME = micro, small, and medium-sized enterprise; NBFI = nonbank finance institution; NPF = nonperforming financing; NPL = nonperforming loan.

* Data include primary market data if MSME market data is unavailable (average percentage of available markets). Reporting countries only.

Bank Credit

During 2015–2021, bank lending to MSMEs in Central and West Asia averaged 9.0% of GDP (2.7% CAGR) and 31.4% of total bank lending (–2.2%). The MSME credit market in the region is smaller than in Southeast Asia's (14.2% share of GDP and 15.6% of total bank lending during 2010–2021), but relatively larger than in South Asia's (6.2% share of GDP and 15.2% of total bank lending during 2015–2021).

As of end-2021, bank lending to MSMEs stood at 19.3% of GDP in the Kyrgyz Republic—the highest among countries covered—followed by Armenia (16.8%), Georgia (14.1%), Uzbekistan (8.1%), Azerbaijan (4.8%), Kazakhstan (4.6%), and Tajikistan (2.5%) (Figure 1.7A). The share of MSME bank loans to total bank lending in 2021 was also highest in the Kyrgyz Republic at 76.8%, followed by Armenia (31.6%), Azerbaijan (26.7%), Kazakhstan (20.0%), Georgia (19.8%), Uzbekistan (18.2%), and Tajikistan (16.0%). In US dollar terms, in 2021, MSME lending was highest in Kazakhstan ($8.7 billion), followed by Uzbekistan ($5.5 billion), Georgia ($2.7 billion), Azerbaijan ($2.6 billion), Armenia ($2.4 billion), the Kyrgyz Republic ($1.6 billion), and Tajikistan ($134 million) (Figure 1.7B).[5]

While still relatively small, bank loans to MSMEs are expanding gradually across the region. MSME loans (based on local currency) grew most rapidly in Uzbekistan (29.8% CAGR in 2015–2021), followed by the Kyrgyz Republic (18.5% in 2010–2021), Azerbaijan (15.7% in 2018–2021), Georgia (15.4% in 2015–2021), Kazakhstan (9.5% in 2010–2021), Tajikistan (3.9% in 2011–2021), and Armenia (–0.9% in 2020–2021). As can be seen here, available time series data can vary significantly by country.

While MSME credit by value has expanded, the share of MSME loans to GDP and total bank loans have fluctuated, reacting to shocks like the 2014–2016 Russian financial crisis and the 2020 COVID-19 pandemic (Figures 1.7C and 1.7D). During 2015–2021, the share of MSME loans to GDP fell in Tajikistan (–6.8% CAGR) and Kazakhstan (–1.6%), while it grew in Uzbekistan (6.3%), Georgia (4.8%), and the Kyrgyz Republic (1.5%). During the same period, the share of MSME loans to total bank loans contracted in Uzbekistan (–8.6% CAGR), Tajikistan (–3.4%), Georgia (–2.2%), and the Kyrgyz Republic (–0.8%), while it increased in Kazakhstan (3.8%).

An average 42.0% of MSME loans went to firms in services—wholesale and retail trade (24.1%), transportation and communication (3.9%), and for other services (14.0%)—followed by agriculture (18.0%), construction (8.8%), and manufacturing (8.3%) (Figure 1.7E). The average share of MSME loans in agriculture was higher than in Southeast Asia (4.4%) and South Asia (6.2%), with Kazakhstan (24.1%), the Kyrgyz Republic (23.8%), and Tajikistan (31.1%) the main borrowers. Meanwhile, the share in services was lower than in Southeast Asia (69.0%) and South Asia (62.9%).

NPLs remained high, averaging 19.2% of total MSME bank loans during 2015–2021, although the MSME NPL ratio decreased sharply (–13.7% CAGR). The NPL ratio in Central and West Asia was higher than the Southeast Asian average of 4.4% (–0.9% CAGR in 2010–2021) and the South Asian average of 13.5% (–6.0% CAGR in 2015–2021).

MSME NPL ratios in 2021 are available for Armenia (2.1%), Azerbaijan (6.8%), Georgia (6.5%), and Tajikistan (4.6%); decreasing sharply during 2015–2021 (Figure 1.7F). The MSME credit market responds quickly to shocks, crises, and neighbors' economies. For instance, the rise of NPLs in Tajikistan in 2016 was caused by the impact of sanctions imposed on the Russian Federation during the 2014–2015 Russian financial crisis, which weakened remittances to Tajikistan, sharply reduced aggregate demand, and increased NPLs in the SME credit market. Two commercial banks were liquidated, with the government recapitalizing the two-remaining large banks at a cost equal to 5% of GDP. Across the region, several governments had to assist banks as a result of these shocks, which helped reduce NPLs.

[5] Exchange rates of local currency to US dollar refer to end-of-year rates from the International Monetary Fund's International Financial Statistics in designated years.

Figure 1.7: Bank Credit

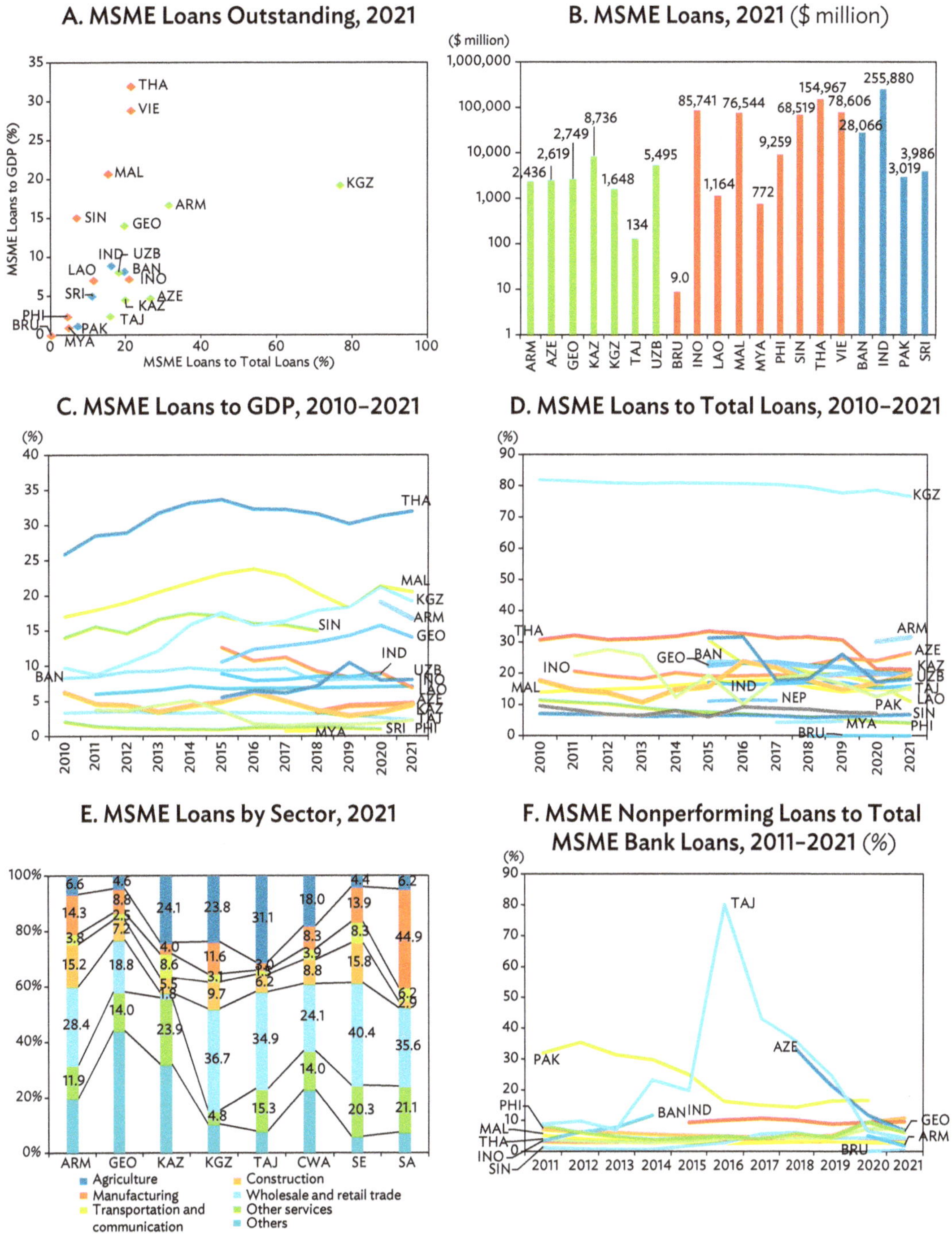

ARM = Armenia; AZE = Azerbaijan; BAN = Bangladesh; BRU = Brunei Darussalam; CWA = Central and West Asia; GEO = Georgia; IND = India; INO = Indonesia; KAZ = Kazakhstan; KGZ = Kyrgyz Republic; LAO = Lao People's Democratic Republic; MAL = Malaysia; MSME = micro, small, and medium-sized enterprise; PAK = Pakistan; PHI = Philippines; SA = South Asia; SE = Southeast Asia; SIN = Singapore; SRI = Sri Lanka; TAJ = Tajikistan; THA = Thailand; UZB = Uzbekistan; VIE = Viet Nam.

Notes: For Figure 1.7A, MSME loans to GDP (%) refers to the latest available year (end-of-year). 2021 data for ARM, AZE, GEO, KAZ, KGZ, TAJ, and UZB. For Figure 1.7B, exchange rates of local currency to US dollar refer to end-of-year currency rates from the International Monetary Fund International Financial Statistics in designated years. Figure 1.7E, CWA refers to average of ARM, GEO, KAZ, KGZ, and TAJ. SE refers to average of eight Association of Southeast Asian Nations (ASEAN) countries except CAM and PHI. SA refers to average of BAN, PAK, and SRI.

Source: ADB Asia SME Monitor 2022 database.

Public Financing and Guarantees

With credits markets relatively small, governments and central banks in Central and West Asia use several MSME financial assistance packages to supplement financing—refinancing facilities, special funds, soft-loan programs with interest rate subsidies, and credit guarantees. These tools were actively used as emergency assistance to MSMEs hurt by financial crises and shocks like the COVID-19 pandemic. They expanded existing programs or created new ones, providing debt relief, concessional lending, liquidity support for financial institutions, and reduced regulatory requirements. These emergency measures helped MSMEs survive during the pandemic (Table 1.2).

There are focal public agencies for these government MSME support measures including, for example, Enterprise Armenia, Enterprise Georgia, and the Damu Entrepreneurship Development Fund (DAMU) in Kazakhstan.

Interest subsidies through special government funds or refinancing facilities and public credit guarantee schemes are the most frequently used government instruments for MSMEs. Currently, they comprise a small fraction of total MSME lending at the national level. However, subsidized loans and public credit guarantees are increasing as national budgets expand. Governments generally provide assistance to MSMEs, targeting farmers and agribusinesses, tech industries and startups, youth and women entrepreneurs, among others.

The COVID-19 pandemic and the continuing Russian invasion of Ukraine caused a surge in demand for public finance at the risk of bloating national budgets. There has also been a long debate on using subsidized lending at the risk of market distortions—whether to shift from a high reliance on subsidy-backed finance to market-based finance.

a. Subsidized loans

Launched in 2018, Azerbaijan's Entrepreneurship Development Fund (EDF) provides subsidized loans to MSMEs and entrepreneurs. The number of MSMEs receiving subsidized loans more than doubled in 2021 (1,895) from 2020 (903), primarily due to a reduction in average loan size. There remains huge unmet MSME demand for subsidized lending. Only 0.3% of MSMEs accessed EDF loans in 2020. The Agrarian Credit and Development Agency also offers subsidized loans for farmers and small agricultural firms.

Subsidized loans were frequently used in Georgia for SMEs, agribusinesses, and farmers suffering from the COVID-19 pandemic. New subsidized loans increased sharply in 2021 (439 loans from 141 in 2020). The share of subsidized loans to total SME loans increased from 3.8% in 2015 to 17.4% in 2021.

In Kazakhstan, DAMU provides public funds to MSMEs through subsidies, guarantees, and soft loans. Subsidized loans to MSMEs increased sharply (158.2% in 2020 and 83.6% in 2021) due to emergency financial support amid the pandemic. These loans helped 7,269 MSMEs in 2021, nearly double (98.5%) the number in 2020 (3,662 firms), though they reached just 0.5% of operating MSMEs.

The Kyrgyz Republic's "Financing of Agriculture" program, launched in 2013, provides subsidized agricultural loans for crops, livestock, agricultural processing, and related businesses, including MSMEs, mainly through two state-owned banks. There were 10,407 MSME newly approved borrowers in 2021, a 13.1% drop from 2020. To use government funds more effectively, the Cabinet of Ministers plans to gradually transfer all subsidized loans to state banks by increasing their capitalization.

In Tajikistan, subsidized loans to SMEs fell during the 2020 pandemic, but increased sharply in 2021. They remain a small fraction of all SME loans.

The Uzbekistan government launched a large-scale concessional lending program for small businesses in April 2022, providing commercial banks a $300 million credit line from its Fund for Reconstruction and Development. There are several public funds supporting small businesses, such as the State Fund for Entrepreneurship Support, which offers financial support in local or foreign currency through commercial banks. The fund offers credit guarantees and partial compensation for interest expenses.

b. Credit guarantees

All Central and West Asian economies have special credit guarantee programs for MSMEs. They are provided by special credit guarantee corporations or public agencies.

As part of its national MSME policy, Enterprise Armenia provides partial credit guarantees covering 70% of credit to small startups with a maximum loan maturity of 5 years, up to 6 months grace period, and no collateral requirements.

Enterprise Georgia offers portfolio guarantees for SMEs by commercial banks and microfinance institutions (MFIs). It offers credit guarantees covering up to 80% of the loan principal and not more than 35% of the loan portfolio allowed for each financial institution.

In Kazakhstan, guaranteed loans to MSMEs have increased sharply since 2017, especially during the COVID-19 pandemic (a 168% increase in 2020 and 32.6% increase in 2021). A rapid approval process—10 days maximum for approvals and sector limits lifted—drove the sharp growth. Still, MSME credit guarantees remained just 1.2% of guarantees approved in 2021.

The Open Joint Stock Company (OJSC) Guarantee Fund corporation in the Kyrgyz Republic provides individual guarantees, portfolio guarantees, guarantees based on Islamic principles, and mixed guarantees. The maximum guaranteed amount is up to 50% of the loan and 10% of capitalization, or KGS660 million ($7.8 million). The scheme was limited to 2.5% of total MSME lending in 2021.

The Credit Guarantee Fund Tajikistan provides guaranteed loans to SMEs through seven partner financial institutions. SME access to credit guarantees was limited to 1.5% of all SME loans in 2021.

Credit guarantee markets remain extremely small in Central and West Asia compared with other Asian regions. In US dollar terms, in 2021 (2020 for Armenia), guaranteed MSME loans amounted to $846 million (disbursed) in Kazakhstan, $67.9 million (outstanding) in the Kyrgyz Republic, $66.0 million (outstanding) in Georgia, $15.6 million (outstanding) in Tajikistan, and $0.2 million in Armenia (disbursed). These were far smaller than in India, Indonesia, Malaysia, and Thailand (Figure 1.8).[6] In Central and West Asia, the main reasons behind lower usage of credit guarantees for MSMEs are attributed to fundamental issues from both demand side (insufficient MSME documentation such as financial statements) and supply side (a lack of incentives for banks to work with MSMEs due to the nature of their credit risks).

6 Exchange rates of local currency to US dollar refer to end-of-year rates from the International Monetary Fund's International Financial Statistics in designated years.

Figure 1.8: Credit Guarantees, 2021 ($ million)

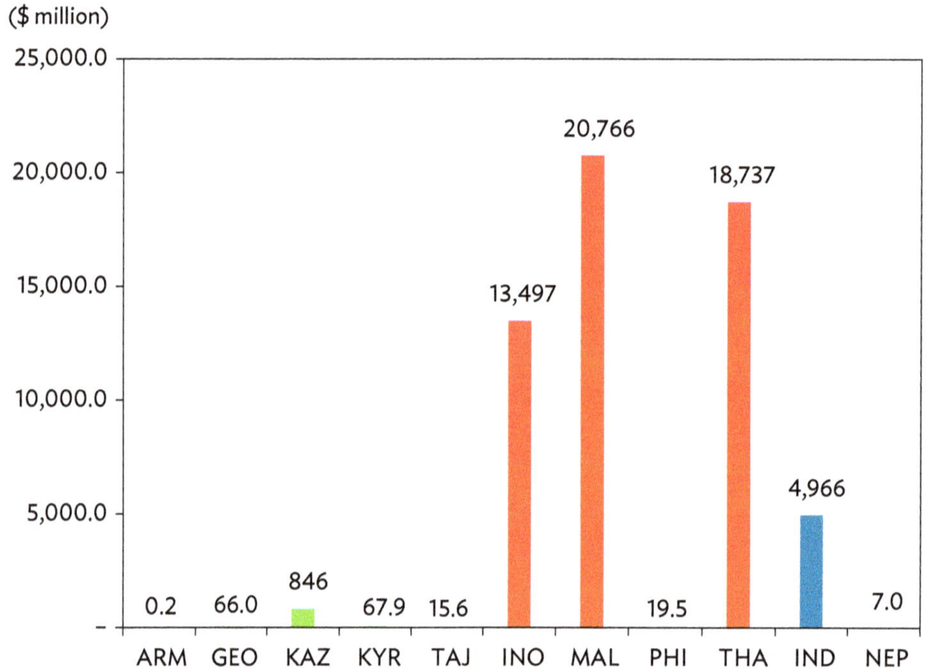

ARM = Armenia, GEO = Georgia, IND = India, INO = Indonesia, KAZ = Kazakhstan, KGZ = Kyrgyz Republic, MAL = Malaysia, NEP = Nepal, PHI = Philippines, TAJ = Tajikistan, THA = Thailand.

Notes: Data refer to 2021, except ARM (2020) and NEP (2018). Exchange rates of local currency to US dollar refer to end-of-year currency rates from the International Monetary Fund's International Financial Statistics in designated years.

Source: ADB Asia SME Monitor 2022 database.

Table 1.2: Assistance and Infrastructure for MSME Access to Finance

Item		Bank Credit						Public Finance			Nonbank Finance			Digital Finance			
		Refinancing facilities to banks	Credit guarantees/ credit risk sharing	Mandatory lending to MSMEs	Interest rate subsidy	Credit bureaus/ credit information system	Secured transaction legal system/ collateral registry	Specialized bank/state agency with MSME finance programs	Direct lending/ special funds/ soft loans	Focused groups financing	MFI development support	NBFI industry development (except MFIs)	Consumer/ client protection policies	Branchless/ agent banking strategy	Peer-to-peer (P2P) lending regulations	Equity crowdfunding (ECF) regulations	National payment system and digital infrastructure
Lower-middle-income economies	KGZ		√		√	√	√		√	√ (agriculture)	√ (NBKR)		√ (NBKR)				√ (Elcard; digital wallets)
	TAJ	√	√		√	√			√	√ (NDS priorities, tech-industry, youth, women)							√ (e-wallets)
	UZB	√	√		√	√	√		√	√ (agriculture, industry, services)							√ (Humo; digital banks)
Upper-middle-income economies	ARM	√	√		√	√		√ (Enterprise Armenia)	√	√ (startups)							√ (ArCa; Idram)
	AZE	√	√		√	√	√		√	√ (non-oil sectors, agribusiness, farmers)				√ (Azerpost)			√ (IPS)
	GEO		√		√	√		√ (Enterprise Georgia)	√	√ (agriculture)	√ (micro bank reform)				(discussed under CMDS)	(discussed under CMDS)	
	KAZ	√	√		√	√	√	√ (DAMU)	√	√ (DAMU priority sectors)						√ (AIFC)	√ (IPS; digital tenge planned)

Item		Capital Markets: Equity/bond markets that MSMEs can tap	Capital Markets: Venture capital and private equity investments	Capital Markets: Tax incentive for MSME issuers/ investors	Financial education programs and training	Dedicated financial inclusion strategy	Emergency Assistance (Response to COVID-19): Liquidity support for financial institutions/ capital injection	Emergency Assistance (Response to COVID-19): Debt restructuring/ deferral of debt payments	Emergency Assistance (Response to COVID-19): Relaxed lending conditions/ interest rate reduction	Emergency Assistance (Response to COVID-19): New lending to MSMEs/ emergency refinaning facility	Emergency Assistance (Response to COVID-19): Special credit guarantees	Emergency Assistance (Response to COVID-19): Regulatory forbearance
Lower-middle-income economies	KGZ	(some MSMEs issued bonds/KSE)			√ (GPFL)	√ (SIFI)	√	√	√	√	√	√
	TAJ	√ (SME Board/ CASE)			√	√ (NSFI)	√	√	√	√	√	√
	UZB	(some MSEs issued bonds)			√	√ (NSIFI)		√	√	√	√	
Upper-middle-income economies	ARM	(no dedicated market but C Platform available for MSMEs)			√				√	√		
	AZE		√ (venture capital fund)		√				√	√	√	√
	GEO	(considered easing listing requirements, CMDS)			√ (NSFE)		√		√	√	√	
	KAZ	√ (Alternative Board/KASE)	√		√ (CIFL)			√	√	√	√	

AIFC = Astana International Financial Centre (Kazakhstan); ARM = Armenia; AZE = Azerbaijan; CASE = Central Asian Stock Exchange (Tajikistan); CIFL = Concept of Improving Financial Literacy for 2020-2024; CMDS = Capital Market Development Strategy (Georgia); GEO = Georgia; GPFL = Government Program on Financial Literacy 2016-2020 (Kyrgyz Republic); IPS = instant payment system (Azerbaijan and Kazakhstan); KASE = Kazakhstan Stock Exchange; KAZ = Kazakhstan; KSE = Kyrgyz Stock Exchange; KYR = Kyrgyz Republic; MSE = micro and small enterprise (Uzbekistan); MSME = micro, small, and medium-sized enterprise; NBKR = National Bank of the Kyrgyz Republic; NDS = National Development Strategy for 2030 (Tajikistan); NSFE = National Strategy of Financial Education 2016 (Georgia); NSIFI = National Strategy for Increasing Financial Inclusion for 2021-2023 (Uzbekistan); NSFI = National Strategy for Financial Inclusion for 2022-2026 (Tajikistan); SIFI = Strategy for Improving Financial Inclusion for 2022-2026 (Kyrgyz Republic); SME = small and medium-sized enterprise; TAJ = Tajikistan; UZB = Uzbekistan.

Note: World Bank country classification by income in 2021.

Source: ADB Asia SME Monitor 2022 database.

Nonbank Financing

The nonbank finance industry remains in its infancy and cannot yet meet demand. Microfinance institutions (MFIs), credit unions, leasing, and pawnshops are the nonbank financing options for businesses in Central and West Asia. Although they do not specifically target MSMEs, they play a critical role of supplying MSME working capital, especially MFIs. High lending rates and nonperforming financing remain critical issues.

Financing from nonbank finance institutions (NBFIs) in the region during 2015–2021 remained small, accounting for an average 2.3% of GDP (2.0% CAGR) and 8.9% of total bank lending (2.9%). The share of GDP was lower than the Southeast Asian average (4.2% of GDP during 2010–2021) and South Asian average (3.5% of GDP during 2015–2021). The Central and West Asian share to total bank lending was slightly higher than other Asian regions (8.8% for Southeast Asia and 6.4% for South Asia over the same period).

NBFI financing in 2021 was equivalent to 4.4% of GDP in Armenia, followed by Georgia (3.8%), Kazakhstan (3.6%), Tajikistan (3.0%), the Kyrgyz Republic (2.8%), Azerbaijan (0.4%), and Uzbekistan (0.2%) (Figure 1.9A).[7] By comparison, NBFI financing in 2021 was 26.4% of total bank lending in Tajikistan, followed by Kazakhstan (13.6%), the Kyrgyz Republic (11.3%), Armenia (8.4%), Georgia (5.4%), Azerbaijan (2.1%), and Uzbekistan (0.4%). The growth in nonbank financing in value (based on local currency) differed by country, with high CAGRs during 2015–2021 in Kazakhstan (64.4%), Uzbekistan (50.7%), Georgia (11.4%), Armenia (8.8%), the Kyrgyz Republic (7.1%), and Tajikistan (3.8%)—Azerbaijan contracted by –8.1%.

7 NBFI data differ by country: Armenia (microfinance institutions and pawnshops); Azerbaijan (microfinance institutions and credit unions/cooperatives); Georgia (microfinance institutions, credit unions/cooperatives, and pawnshops); Kazakhstan (microfinance institutions, credit unions/cooperatives, finance companies, and pawnshops); the Kyrgyz Republic (microfinance institutions, credit unions/cooperatives, finance companies, pawnshops, and leasing companies); Tajikistan (microfinance institutions and nonbank credit institutions); and Uzbekistan (microfinance institutions and pawnshops).

In US dollar terms, nonbank finance in Kazakhstan reached $5.8 billion in 2021, followed by Georgia ($745 million), Armenia ($645 million), the Kyrgyz Republic ($242 million), Tajikistan ($221 million), Azerbaijan ($204 million), and Uzbekistan ($123 million) (Figure 1.9B).[8] Compared with Southeast Asia and South Asia, the nonbank finance industry in Central and West Asia remained relatively small.

Figure 1.9: Nonbank Finance

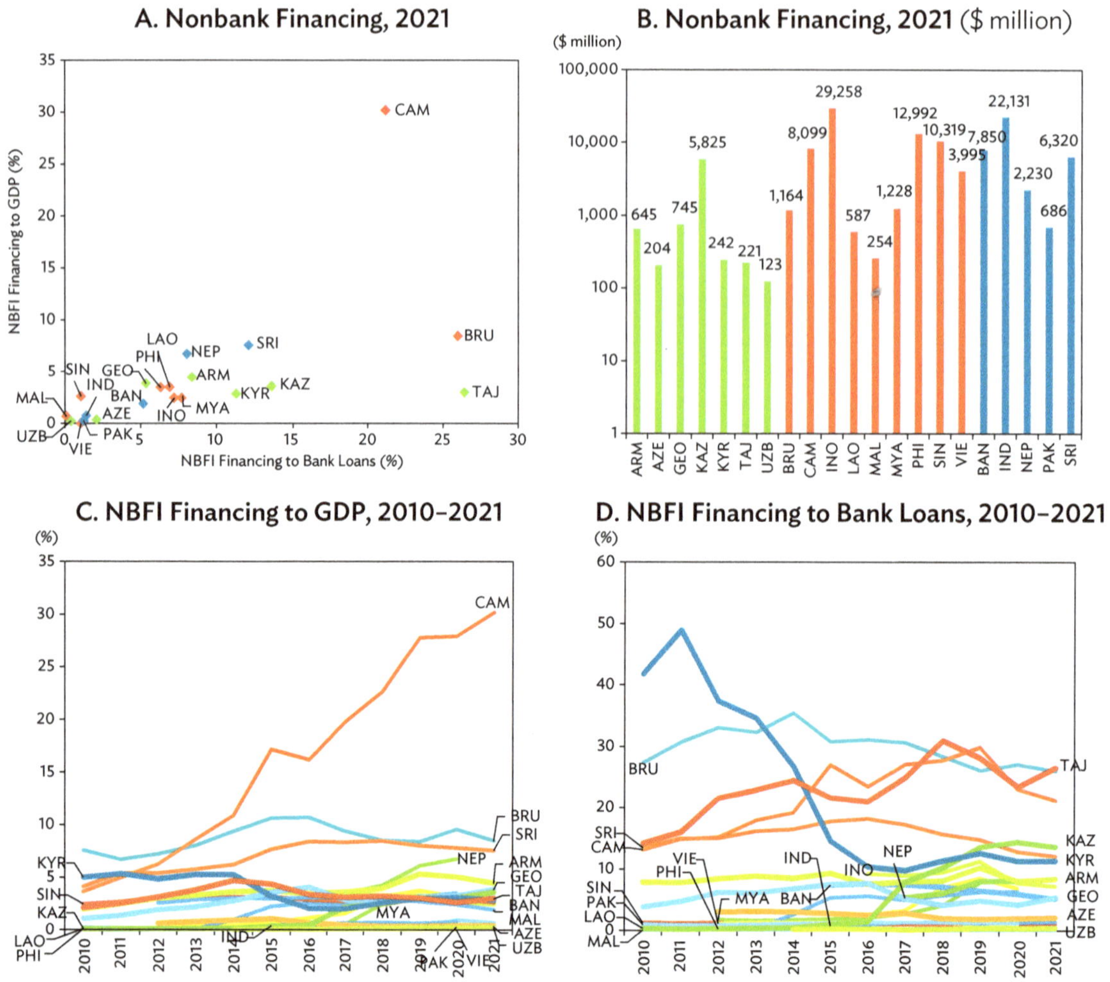

ARM = Armenia, AZE = Azerbaijan, BAN = Bangladesh, BRU = Brunei Darussalam, CAM = Cambodia, GDP = gross domestic product, GEO = Georgia, IND = India, INO = Indonesia, KAZ = Kazakhstan, KGZ = Kyrgyz Republic, LAO = Lao People's Democratic Republic, MAL = Malaysia, MYA = Myanmar, NBFI = nonbank finance institution, NEP = Nepal, PAK = Pakistan, PHI = Philippines, SIN = Singapore, SRI = Sri Lanka, TAJ = Tajikistan, UZB = Uzbekistan, VIE = Viet Nam.

Notes: NBFI data varies by country: Armenia (microfinance institutions and pawnshops); Azerbaijan (microfinance institutions and credit unions/cooperatives); Bangladesh (NBFIs regulated by Bangladesh Bank); Brunei Darussalam (finance companies and pawnbrokers); Cambodia (microfinance institutions and leasing companies); Georgia (microfinance institutions, credit unions/cooperatives, and pawnshops); India (NBFIs regulated by Reserve Bank of India; MSME financing only); Indonesia (finance companies, microfinance institutions, and government pawnshops); Kazakhstan (microfinance institutions, credit unions/cooperatives, finance companies, and pawnshops); the Kyrgyz Republic (microfinance institutions, credit unions/cooperatives, finance companies, pawnshops, and leasing companies); the Lao PDR (microfinance institutions, pawnshops, and leasing companies); Malaysia (private equity, venture capital, factoring, and leasing companies); Myanmar (microfinance institutions); Nepal (microfinance institutions); Pakistan (microfinance institutions and leasing companies); the Philippines (credit unions and cooperatives [2015–2018], pawnshops [2009–2018], and nonstock savings and loans associations [NSSLAs; 2014–2020]); Singapore (finance companies); Sri Lanka: (NBFIs regulated by Central Bank of Sri Lanka); Tajikistan (microfinance institutions and nonbank credit institutions); Uzbekistan (microfinance institutions and pawnshops); and Viet Nam (People's Credit Funds and microfinance institutions). For Figure 1.9A, NBFI financing to GDP (%) refers to the latest available year: 2021 data for ARM, AZE, GEO, KAZ, KGZ, TAJ, and UZB. For Figure 1.9B, exchange rates of local currency to US dollar refer to end-of-year currency rates from the International Monetary Fund's International Financial Statistics in designated years.

Source: ADB Asia SME Monitor 2022 database.

8 Exchange rates of local currency to US dollar refer to end-of-year rates from the International Monetary Fund's International Financial Statistics in designated years.

The share of NBFI financing to GDP fluctuated by country over the decade. It increased in Kazakhstan (36.9% CAGR in 2010–2021), Uzbekistan (25.3% in 2014–2021), Georgia (11.9% in 2010–2021), Armenia (7.5% in 2010–2021), and Tajikistan (3.1% in 2010–2021). It decreased in Azerbaijan (–5.6% CAGR in 2012–2021) and the Kyrgyz Republic (–5.0% in 2010–2021)(Figure 1.9C). The share of NBFI financing to bank credit also fluctuated by country. It fell in the Kyrgyz Republic (–11.2% CAGR in 2010–2021) and Azerbaijan (–4.1% in 2012–2021), while it increased in Kazakhstan (43.7% CAGR in 2010–2021), Uzbekistan (9.4% in 2014–2021), Tajikistan (5.9% in 2010–2021), Georgia (3.1% in 2010–2021), and Armenia (0.6% in 2010–2021) (Figure 1.9D).

The share of nonperforming financing to total NBFI financing averaged 10.1% over the period with a 7.2% CAGR in 2015–2021. It was much higher than the 1.2% Southeast Asia average (7.3% CAGR in 2010–2021) and the 6.6% South Asia average (15.0% CAGR in 2015–2021). The NBFI nonperforming financing ratio is gradually decreasing, yet remained high in Azerbaijan (42.1% in 2018 to 21.0% in 2021) and Uzbekistan (19.8% in 2020) (Figure 1.10). The ratio also decreased in Georgia (8.3% in 2019 to 5.9% in 2021 [MFIs only]), Kazakhstan (8.3% in 2017 to 5.4% in 2021), and Tajikistan (3.4% in 2011 to 3.2% in 2021 [MFIs only]).

Figure 1.10: NBFI Nonperforming Financing to Total Financing, 2011–2021 (%)

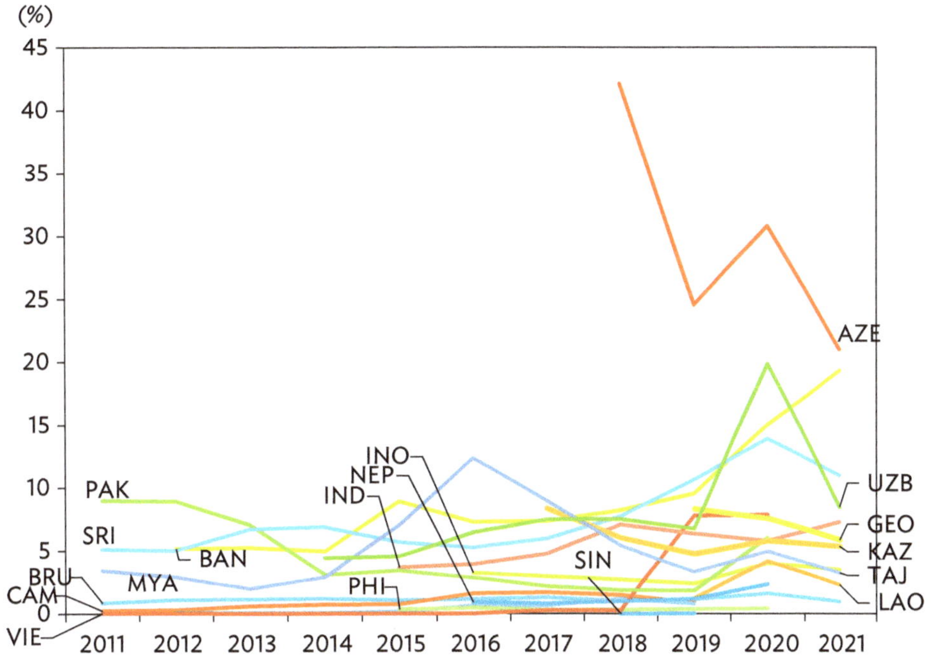

ARM = Armenia, AZE = Azerbaijan, BAN = Bangladesh, BRU = Brunei Darussalam, CAM = Cambodia, GEO = Georgia, IND = India, INO = Indonesia, KAZ = Kazakhstan, KGZ = Kyrgyz Republic, LAO = Lao People's Democratic Republic, MAL = Malaysia, NBFI = nonbank finance institution, NEP = Nepal, PAK = Pakistan, PHI = Philippines, SIN = Singapore, SRI = Sri Lanka, TAJ = Tajikistan, UZB = Uzbekistan, VIE = Viet Nam.

Source: ADB Asia SME Monitor 2022 database.

Digital Financial Services

There is no available data on digital financial services in Central and West Asia. But with the relatively high penetration of digital devices, mobile phones, and the internet (see *Technology and Innovation*, p.15), there is much potential in developing digital finance across the region. Most countries have an interoperable national payment system, central to e-commerce. And there is some progress in boosting digital finance infrastructure.

The Armenian Card CJSC (ArCa) unified card payment system expanded and accelerated the use of card transactions. Idram is the interoperable payment system used by registered firms or individual entrepreneurs using e-commerce. There are more than 9,000 point-of-sale (POS) terminals that use *Idram* quick response (QR) codes, with around 7,000 partners. Tellcell is a licensed financial operator that, since 2007, has offered MSMEs a full range of financial services and products. In July 2022, the Law on Cashless Payments became effective, under which payments exceeding AMD300,000 (around $600) should be cashless—via wire transfer, payment cards, or payment systems.

Recent digital banking reforms in Azerbaijan include establishing an instant payment system, use of QR codes, and a blockchain-based digital identification system. The instant payment system uses QR codes for MSMEs to accept noncash payments. The central bank's Digital Payment Strategy allows businesses to access more affordable financial services by expanding use of digital payments.

In Kazakhstan, the central bank launched an upgraded platform in June 2022 for its instant payment system between customers of various banks. It allows transfers via mobile phone and payments using a QR code between clients of different banks. The central bank is also exploring the viability of creating a "digital tenge," with a decision likely by the end of 2022.

The Kyrgyz Republic uses a national payment system *Elcard* for bank card transactions. In 2021, more than 53% of payments by value came via the *Elcard*, with transactions consistently rising. By end-2021, more than 20 organizations were licensed to operate payment systems. In 2021, the number of electronic wallets totaled more than 4.4 million, 40.8% more than in 2020.

Since 2018, Tajikistan's credit financial institutions (payment service providers) have started offering their customers the option of noncash payments. As of June 2022, 17 credit financial institutions provided electronic wallet services. There were 4.9 million electronic wallets by then, a 39.1% increase over 2021.

Uzbekistan is developing *Uzcard* and *Humo* retail payment systems to service bank cards, as well as services provided within payment systems. As of July 2021, there were 23.7 million bank cards in circulation. In 2020, the central bank launched a QR-online instant payment information system that allows customers to make payments for goods and services using bank card funds without directly using the card or payment terminal.

Government policy support for developing digital finance infrastructure in Central and West Asia varies. While mobile and/or internet banking has increased in some countries, others have yet to establish digital financial services involving credit, savings, insurance, and remittances, as they lack an appropriate regulatory framework.

Mobile and digital banking in Azerbaijan is part of most credit organization operations. Software using artificial intelligence and chatbots running customer services are also given to customers by some banks. Nevertheless, the current legislative framework is insufficient to regulate e-money and payment companies. Peer-to-peer (P2P) lending and crowdfunding for financing startups and MSMEs are rare. There is no legal definition of "crowdfunding."

In Georgia, P2P lending and equity crowdfunding have not developed and there is no regulatory legislation. The government is working on a Capital Market Development Strategy to address these issues.

Internet and mobile banking in Kazakhstan accounted for 66.0% of transactions and 84.1% of the value of noncash payments and money transfers, with POS-terminals covering 33.9% by number and 15.7% by value. The pandemic accelerated digital finance for individuals and MSMEs. Local banks offer digital services for financing, purchasing goods, and some public services.

As of January 2022, there were more than 20 million users of remote banking services in Uzbekistan, of which more than 900,000 were businesses or individual enterprises. Many banks have developed their own mobile applications, which people use to carry out real-time P2P transfers from card to card, make budgetary and utility payments, receive and repay microloans, make online deposits, open remote deposit and loan accounts, access international bank card accounts, and perform online conversion operations. Three registered digital banks banks—Anorbank, TBC Bank, and Apelsin Bank—offer a full range of digital services through mobile applications or personal computers.

There are several challenges to developing digital financial services for MSMEs. These include insufficient digital infrastructure (high costs and low internet speeds, especially in remote regions), a lack of legal frameworks on digital financial services, and the low level of digital finance literacy in general. It is critical for any financial inclusion agenda to strengthen financial education, upgrade nationwide digital infrastructure, and create and improve digital finance legislation that promotes alternative financing options for individual entrepreneurs and MSMEs.

Capital Markets

Specialized SME equity markets operate in several developing Asian countries.[9] They include Indonesia's Acceleration Board (launched in 2019); the Access, Certainty, Efficiency (ACE, 2009) and Leading Entrepreneur Accelerator Platform (LEAP, 2017) markets in Malaysia; the market for alternative investment (*mai*, 1998) in Thailand; Catalist in Singapore (2007); SME Board in the Philippines (2001); and Bombay Stock Exchange (BSE) SME Exchange and the National Stock Exchange (NSE) Emerge in India (2012 for both), along with SME platforms in Bangladesh (2019). These markets help SMEs raise growth capital and target qualified, accredited investors. They apply either concessional listing requirements or require a sponsor.

In Central and West Asia, most countries have yet to establish an SME board. Only Kazakhstan and Tajikistan recently created a dedicated SME market.

In June 2017, the Kazakhstan Stock Exchange (KASE) opened an Alternative Board catering to MSMEs. It offers simplified listing requirements to encourage them to use the stock market for financing. MSMEs are not taxed on income (dividends and coupon interest) from securities listed or income from the increase in stock values through open trading. If issuers on the Alternative Board have rating of at least "BB-" by Standard&Poor's and/or an equivalent rating from Fitch and/or Moody's Investors Service, the listed company will be transferred to the Main Board. Aside from equity, MSMEs can issue corporate bonds on the Alternative Board to support and attract financing for MSME investment projects. Most corporate bonds carry a 1- to 5-year maturity and are increasingly popular among MSMEs (particularly medium-sized firms). Government incentives for MSMEs to raise funds through KASE include the corporate bond option. The coupon rate on bonds issued by medium-sized firms can be subsidized under the National Project on Entrepreneurship Development for 2021–2025 (NPED), with DAMU providing bond guarantees up to 5 years and KZT2.5 billion.

There are two registered stock exchanges in Tajikistan—the Central Asian Stock Exchange (CASE, established in 2015) and the Asian Stock Exchange (ASE, 2018)—which in part target SMEs. ASE never began operating due to the pandemic and lack of highly qualified specialists (as of end-August 2022). CASE has a main board, intended for large issuers, and a specialized board created for SMEs, with simplified listing requirements to encourage them to list.

9 In this section, SME is used instead of MSME following capital market terminology, unless otherwise stated.

Specialized equity markets available to SMEs across developing Asia in 2021 had very small market capitalizations—0.0002% of GDP in Indonesia, 2.2% in Malaysia, 0.002% in the Philippines, 2.2% in Singapore, 2.9% in Thailand, 0.14% in India (2020), and 0.6% in Kazakhstan (Figure 1.11A).

Market capitalization (based on local currency) of specialized SME equity markets have grown rapidly though remain small—Indonesia's Acceleration Board grew 201.4% in 2021 over 2020; Malaysia's ACE 17.4% CAGR in 2012–2021; Malaysia's LEAP 116.6% in 2017–2021; the Philippines' SME Board 54.8% in 2012–2021; Singapore's Catalist 6.3% in 2012–2021; Thailand's *mai* 15.1% in 2012–2021; India's BSE SME Exchange 76.4% in 2012–2021; India's NSE Emerge 58.8% in 2012–2021; and Kazakhstan's Alternative Board –2.2% in 2017–2021.

In US dollar terms, Thailand's *mai* had the highest market capitalization ($14.1 billion), followed by Malaysia's ACE ($7.0 billion), India's BSE SME Exchange ($6.4 billion), India's NSE Emerge ($1.3 billion), Kazakhstan's Alternative Board ($1.2 billion), the SME Board in the Philippines ($590 million), and Indonesia's Acceleration Board ($226 million) (Figure 1.11B).[10]

During the 2020 COVID-19 pandemic, SME markets expanded market capitalization, except for the Philippines and Kazakhstan (Figure 1.11C). Across developing Asia, SMEs could raise working capital from banks, supported by government financial assistance programs, while those that benefited from mobility restrictions, such as those in ICT, likely raised growth capital from equity markets during the pandemic.

The number of listed companies on specialized SME equity markets increased somewhat—15 firms on Indonesia's Acceleration Board, 141 on ACE in Malaysia, 44 on LEAP in Malaysia, 7 on SME Board in the Philippines, 217 on Catalist in Singapore, 183 on *mai* in Thailand, 358 on BSE SME Exchange in India, 236 on NSE Emerge in India, and 89 on the Alternative Board in Kazakhstan (Figure 1.11D).

In Central and West Asia, small firms tend to issue corporate bonds rather than tap equity markets to raise growth capital. In the Kyrgyz Republic, MSMEs are not listed on the stock exchange, but some issue bonds to raise funds. Three MSMEs have issued corporate bonds (for manufacturing, agri-processing, and sewing and trade). In Tajikistan, three issued bonds on the CASE Board as of end-2021. In Uzbekistan, some SMEs also raised funds by issuing bonds.

Armenia has no specialized SME market, but the government plans to start a dedicated SME board, though it is not clear when. Also, the Armenian Securities Exchange has three types of listing venues: A and B for normal listing, with C less regulated but riskier (considered a logical place for SMEs to list).

Georgia does not find creating a dedicated SME market feasible, given the relatively high listing fees and requirements for issuers along with its difficulty in attracting investors. SMEs can list, but they tend to seek bank credit or alternative finance instead. The government is considering easing certain listing requirements for SMEs in its capital market development strategy.

Capital market regulators cite several barriers and challenges to developing SME capital markets in the region: (i) the fear of diluting the value of SME owners' shares; (ii) poor institutional structures and inadequate SME corporate governance; (iii) poor accounting (SME financial statements not complying with International Financial Reporting Standards [IFRS] or Generally Accepted Accounting Principles [GAAP]); (iv) weak capital market literacy; (v) high cost of compliance with legal requirements (such as the cost of financial advisory services, auditing,

10 Exchange rates of local currency to US dollar refer to end-of-year rates from the International Monetary Fund's International Financial Statistics in designated years.

listing, and annual fees); (vi) lack of diverse investor base (including institutional investors); (vii) the large share of state joint-stock companies; and (viii) limited availability of tools to protect shareholder interests.

Developing better corporate governance standards, increasing transparency and public awareness, and further developing financial intermediation could help securities markets become more attractive in the region. It is also crucial to strengthen capital market literacy programs and training to attract SME issuers (including youth, green, women entrepreneurs, and startups) and investors (including venture capital firms and business angels). This should be stated clearly in national financial inclusion strategies or capital market development roadmaps.

Figure 1.11: Equity Markets for MSMEs

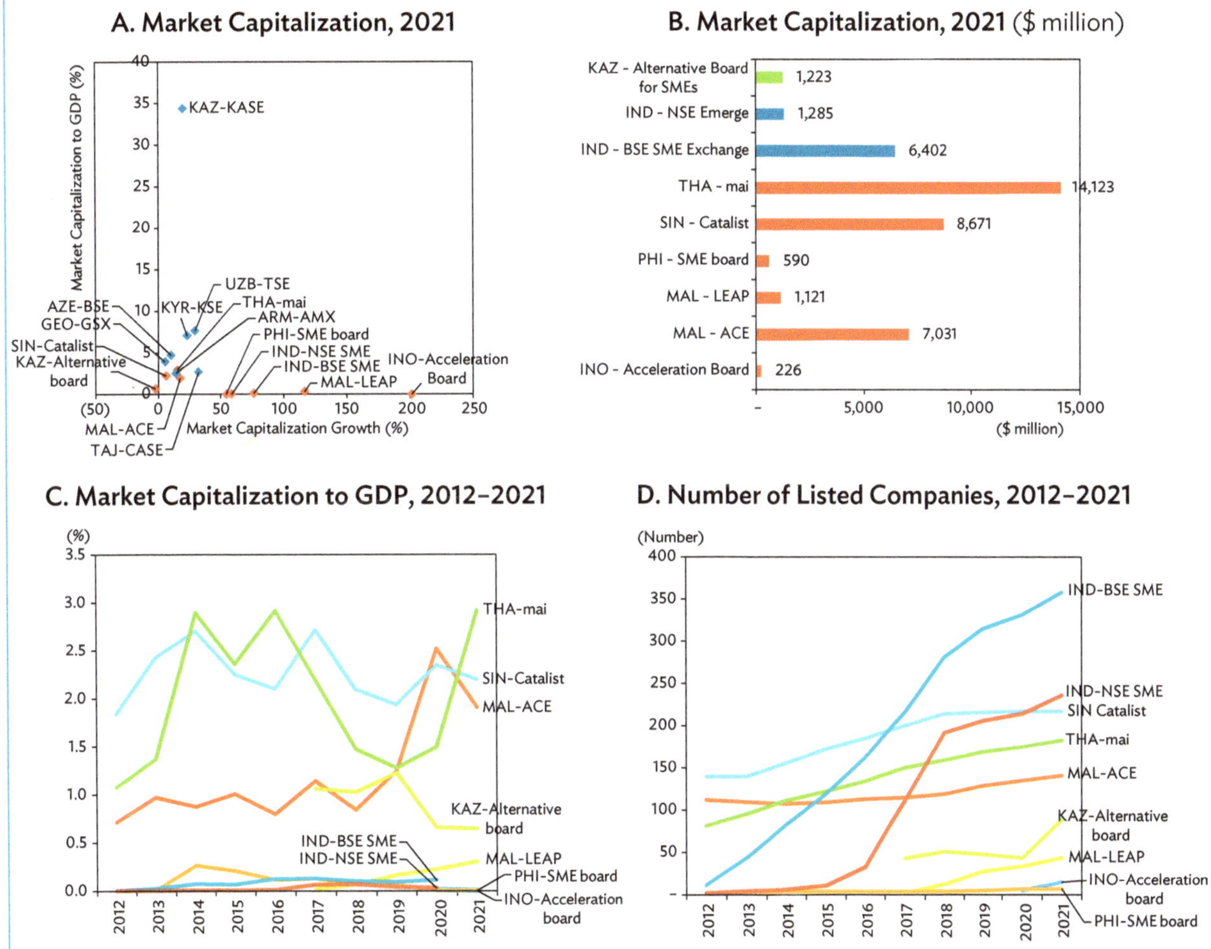

AMX = Armenian Securities Exchange, ARM = Armenia, AZE = Azerbaijan, BSE = Baku Stock Exchange/Bombay Stock Exchange;,CASE = Central Asian Stock Exchange, GEO = Georgia, GSX = Georgian Stock Exchange, INO = Indonesia, KAZ = Kazakhstan, KASA = Kazakhstan Stock Exchange, KGZ = Kyrgyz Republic, KSE = Kyrgyz Stock Exchange, MAL = Malaysia, NSE = National Stock Exchange, PHI = Philippines, SIN = Singapore, SME = small and medium-sized enterprise, TAJ = Tajikistan, THA = Thailand, TSE = Republic Stock Exchange "Toshkent", UZB = Uzbekistan.

Notes: End-of-year data. Exchange rates of local currency to US dollar refer to end-of-year currency rates from the International Monetary Fund's International Financial Statistics in designated years.

Source: ADB Asia SME Monitor 2022 database.

Financial Infrastructure

Easily accessible and complete credit data infrastructure is crucial for improving MSME access to finance. All countries covered here have a standard credit bureau system, and most countries have a collateral registry or plan to introduce one. Good credit reporting systems that hedge credit risks of financial institutions and promote access to finance for individuals and businesses are key to MSME development. In general, however, company data and pledged assets remain incomplete, relatively shallow with limited data—many lacking even basic company profiles. Many do not track credit information over time. A credit risk database that comprehensively covers both positive and negative granular company data over time is an essential part of financial infrastructure. Central and West Asian countries should ensure they are complete and function efficiently.

In Armenia, the Armenian Credit Reporting Agency (ACRA) is a private credit bureau, founded in January 2004, working with banks and MFIs. Its primary purpose is to gather data from banks and NBFIs, processing and updating information while providing security and confidentiality. ACRA also offers new, innovative risk assessment services and offers other solutions to clients in banking, finance, insurance, and business in general.

The Azerbaijan Credit Bureau (private credit bureau) and the State Register of Encumbrances of Movable Property were established in 2018 as part of reform measures outlined in the Strategic Roadmap for the Development of Financial Services. The state register allows borrowers to obtain loans by mortgaging real estate and movable assets. Registering allows financial institutions to receive information on business collateral, including those from MSMEs.

CreditInfo Georgia offers credit information reports (existing and closed loans) and credit scoring (Creditinfo Predictor). The central bank began collecting credit registry data as a pilot test in 2021. The Credit Registry is a database that collects comprehensive credit risk information. The central bank requires data to be submitted monthly, including credit details, refinancing loans, investments, and rejected credit applications.

There are two credit bureaus operating in Kazakhstan—the public JSC State Credit Bureau (SCB) and the private First Credit Bureau LLP (FCB). In 2017, FCB launched "The Strongest" to assess the creditworthiness, reliability, and payment histories of MSMEs. There is also an active collateral registry. The nonprofit JSC state corporation "Government for Citizens" registers collateral for both individuals and legal entities as a "one-stop shop" for registering movable and immovable collateral. It is integrated with a database covering all public agencies and generates online public services through the Egov portal.

There are two private credit bureaus in the Kyrgyz Republic—*Ishenim,* established in 2003, and CRIF KG in 2018—and a centralized collateral registry. These credit bureaus partner with of more than 240 financial-credit institutions. The government also uses a state credit registry to improve MSME access to credit. In February 2019, credit registry functions were transferred to the Pledge Registration Department of the Ministry of Justice.

Tajikistan also has two active credit bureaus: (i) the Credit Information Bureau (CIB) and (ii) the Bureau of Credit Histories Somoniyon. The CIB has a database of 3-4 million borrowers, including SME loans with banks and NBFIs. There are plans to open a credit registry.

Uzbekistan's two credit bureaus are the Credit Information Analytical Center (KIAC) and CRIF Kredit-Axborot Xizmatlari (CRIF KAX). The information database holds consumer and corporate records, and acts as a collateral registry for loans. It remains weak, however, and needs to collect more information. There is also a pledge registry, an information database containing records of the rights of creditors to debtor collateral and their disposal. In 2021, a scoring system with banks was set up through Wings Partners—one of Asia's largest scoring companies.

As a regional effort to develop credit data infrastructure, the Association of Credit Information Providers of Eurasia was formed in 2018 to ensure information from credit reporting systems follow international best practices. Credit registries and bureaus representing Azerbaijan, Belarus, Georgia, Kazakhstan, the Kyrgyz Republic, Tajikistan, Ukraine, and Uzbekistan are members.

4. Factors Affecting MSME Development

Here we discuss the factors affecting MSME development in Central and West Asia by using an SME Development Index (SME-DI). ADB began designing this benchmark index in 2020 to measure the level of MSME development by using a multivariate analytical approach based on real data collected through the Asia SME Monitor project. Because available data on MSMEs are limited across countries, the SME-DI uses probabilistic principal component analysis (P-PCA) to compensate for missing data, which are estimated by an expectation maximization (EM) algorism.[11] The data set comes from the Asia SME Monitor 2022 database covering the seven Central and West Asian countries discussed here. It stores various MSME-related variables measured for each country and year (2007–2021).

To estimate the regional SME-DI for Central and West Asia, the P-PCA was applied to country-level panel data to obtain three factors—principal components (PC)1 to PC3 (Figure 1.12 and Table 1.3). The three factors formed three different time-series dynamics. PC1 remains low over the first half of the sample period (2007–2014), which includes the 2008–2009 global financial crisis (GFC), and rises afterward. PC2 remains low until 2010, goes up and peaks in 2014, declining afterward, including the 2014–2016 Russian financial crisis (still positive) and the 2020 COVID-19 pandemic (negative). PC3 rises after the GFC with its first peak in 2011, bottoms out in 2015 (Russian financial crisis), and rises again with a second peak in 2019, just before the 2020 COVID-19 pandemic.

Figure 1.12: Time-Series Plots of Estimated Principal Components— Central and West Asia

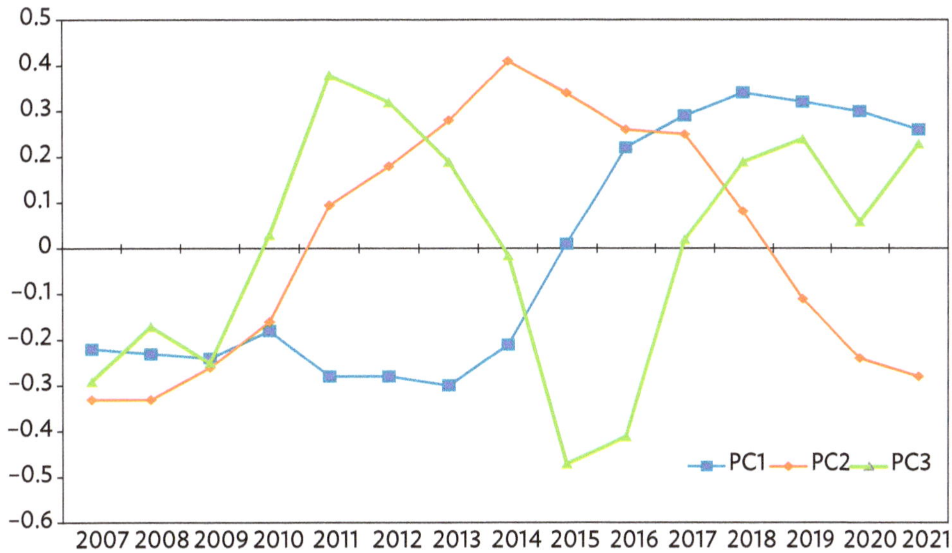

PC = principal component.

Source: Calculated based on Asia SME Monitor 2022 database.

11 The detailed methodology refers to *Asia SME Monitor 2021 Volume IV—Pilot SME Development Index: Applying Probabilistic Principal Component Analysis*. https://www.adb.org/publications/asia-sme-monitor-2021-volume-4.

Table 1.3: Time-Series of Estimated Principal Components— Central and West Asia

Year	2007	2008	2009	2010	2011	2012	2013	2014	2015	2016	2017	2018	2019	2020	2021
PC1	−0.22	−0.23	−0.24	−0.18	−0.28	−0.28	−0.30	−0.21	0.01	0.22	0.29	0.34	0.32	0.30	0.26
PC2	−0.33	−0.33	−0.26	−0.16	0.10	0.18	0.28	0.41	0.34	0.26	0.25	0.08	−0.11	−0.24	−0.28
PC3	−0.29	−0.17	−0.25	0.03	0.38	0.32	0.19	−0.02	−0.47	−0.41	0.02	0.19	0.24	0.06	0.23

PC = principal component.
Source: Calculated based on Asia SME Monitor 2022 database.

PC1 makes the largest contribution to the variation in country-level panel data (63%), followed by PC2 (16%) and PC3 (10%), explaining 88% (Table 1.4).

Table 1.4: Contribution of Each Estimated Principal Component

Principal Component	PC1	PC2	PC3
Contribution ratio	0.63	0.16	0.10
Cumulative contribution rate	0.63	0.78	0.88

PC = principal component.
Source: Calculated based on Asia SME Monitor 2022 database.

Factor loadings are sorted in descending order (Table 1.5). A darker red color indicates a positive and large impact to the trend in the principal component, while a darker blue means a negative and small impact. Each factor is orthogonal to each other and related to each variable with specific factor loadings. Key factors that form each PC can thus be extracted.

In PC1, negative and small factor loadings were found for variables such as bank loans (-0.97) and NPLs (-0.88) in Kazakhstan; microfinance (-0.95), NBFI financing (-0.83), and bank loans (-0.83) in Azerbaijan; and microfinance (-0.79) and NBFI financing (-0.78) in the Kyrgyz Republic. This suggests that poor bank lending and increasing MSME NPLs in Kazakhstan and stagnant nonbank financing in Azerbaijan and the Kyrgyz Republic contributed to the region's slow MSME recovery from the GFC until 2015.

PC1 also found positive and large factor loadings for variables such as bank loans and the number of MSMEs in the Kyrgyz Republic (0.94 and 0.93) and Georgia (both 0.92); the number of MSMEs (0.89) and MSME employees (0.9) in Kazakhstan; bank loans (0.91), microfinance (0.87), market capitalization (0.86), and NBFI financing (0.85) in Armenia; and the number of MSME employees (0.87) in Azerbaijan. This indicates that the region's MSME business recovery after 2016 came from improved MSME loan assets in banking and nonbank financing (Armenia, Georgia, and the Kyrgyz Republic), as well as job creation and the expanded number of MSMEs (Kazakhstan).

PC2 shows a faster recovery of MSME business than PC1, and after a 2014 peak, their performance slows, dropping further during the pandemic. PC2 had positive and large factor loadings for variables such as microfinance (0.88), GDP of MSMEs (0.76),[12] and nonperforming NBFI loans (0.51) in Tajikistan; microfinance (0.79), GDP of MSMEs (0.64), MSME imports (0.6), and number of MSME employees (0.54) in Georgia; number of MSME employees (0.72) and MSME exports (0.51) in Uzbekistan; and nonperforming bank loans (0.87) in Azerbaijan. This suggests that increased productivity/outputs of MSMEs (Tajikistan and Georgia), expanded MSME exports (Uzbekistan)

[12] "GDP of MSMEs" is a variable name. Data refer to GDP for the Kyrgyz Republic, Tajikistan, and Uzbekistan; and GVA for Armenia, Azerbaijan, Georgia, and Kazakhstan.

and imports (Georgia), improved MSME employment (Uzbekistan and Georgia), and increasing microfinance (Tajikistan and Georgia) contributed to region's MSME business recovery from the GFC.

PC2 also had negative and small factor loadings for variables like microfinance (–0.96), bank loans (–0.96), NBFI financing (–0.95), nonperforming NBFI loans (–0.87), market capitalization (–0.87), and NPLs (–0.76) in Uzbekistan. This indicates that deteriorated MSME loan assets and capital market in Uzbekistan were likely to push down the region's MSME development during the GFC and COVID-19 pandemic.

PC3 showed a complicated pattern of the region's MSME development but linked more clearly to the impacts of the GFC, Russian financial crisis, and COVID-19 pandemic. It had negative and small factor loadings for variables like NPLs (–0.82), nonperforming NBFI loans (–0.67), bank loans (–0.63), and NBFI financing (–0.57) in Tajikistan; and GDP of MSMEs (–0.81) in Uzbekistan. This indicates that deteriorated SME loan assets in Tajikistan and decreased MSME output in Uzbekistan likely pushed down the region's MSME development during the GFC and Russian financial crisis.

PC3 also found positive and large factor loadings for variables like MSME exports (0.81) and MSME imports (0.68) in Georgia; GDP of MSMEs (0.58), MSME imports (0.57), NBFI financing (0.55), microfinance (0.54), and MSME exports (0.43) in the Kyrgyz Republic; and GDP of MSMEs (0.56) in Azerbaijan. This suggests that increased MSME exports and imports (Georgia and the Kyrgyz Republic) and MSME outputs (the Kyrgyz Republic and Azerbaijan) were likely to fuel a quick recovery from the GFC, the Russian financial crisis, and the pandemic.

The SME-DI shows that limited lending activities to MSMEs with low-quality loan assets will slow the region's MSME development. In contrast, increased lending to MSMEs with improved loan assets, enhanced MSME job creation, expanded MSME foreign trade, and increased MSME productivity will help drive the region's MSME development. Thus, developing quality financial markets, functioning labor markets, international business expansion, and enhanced productivity are all major factors behind the ability of the region's MSMEs to grow following the GFC, Russian financial crisis, and COVID-19 pandemic. Developing sophisticated MSME finance markets and boosting MSME productivity through internationalization play a critical role in promoting a smooth economic recovery from crises and shocks in the region.

Table 1.5: Factor Loadings Based on Probabilistic PCA—Central and West Asia

Country	Indicator	PC1	Country	Indicator	PC2	Country	Indicator	PC3
Kyrgyz Republic	Bank loans outstanding	0.94	Tajikistan	Microfinance loans	0.88	Georgia	MSME exports	0.81
Kyrgyz Republic	Number of MSMEs	0.93	Azerbaijan	Nonperforming bank loans	0.87	Georgia	MSME imports	0.68
Georgia	Bank loans outstanding	0.92	Georgia	Microfinance loans	0.79	Kyrgyz Republic	GDP of MSMEs	0.58
Georgia	Number of MSMEs	0.92	Tajikistan	GDP of MSMEs	0.76	Kyrgyz Republic	MSME imports	0.57
Armenia	Bank loans outstanding	0.91	Uzbekistan	Number of MSME Employees	0.72	Azerbaijan	GDP of MSMEs	0.56
Kazakhstan	Number of MSME Employees	0.9	Georgia	GDP of MSMEs	0.64	Kyrgyz Republic	NBFI outstanding	0.55
Kazakhstan	Number of MSMEs	0.89	Georgia	MSME imports	0.6	Kyrgyz Republic	Microfinance loans	0.54
Armenia	Microfinance loans	0.87	Georgia	Number of MSME Employees	0.54	Kazakhstan	GDP of MSMEs	0.49
Azerbaijan	Number of MSME Employees	0.87	Uzbekistan	MSME exports	0.51	Kyrgyz Republic	MSME exports	0.43
Armenia	Market capitalization	0.86	Tajikistan	Nonperforming NBFI loans	0.51	Georgia	GDP of MSMEs	0.39
Armenia	NBFI outstanding	0.85	Azerbaijan	NBFI outstanding	0.48	Armenia	Bank loans outstanding	0.34
Armenia	Nonperforming bank loans	0.76	Georgia	NBFI outstanding	0.47	Uzbekistan	MSME imports	0.33
Uzbekistan	MSME imports	0.76	Azerbaijan	Bank loans outstanding	0.44	Armenia	NBFI outstanding	0.32
Georgia	Number of MSME Employees	0.73	Kyrgyz Republic	MSME imports	0.43	Georgia	Market capitalization	0.31
Kyrgyz Republic	Market capitalization	0.7	Tajikistan	Nonperforming bank loans	0.42	Kazakhstan	Nonperforming bank loans	0.3
Kazakhstan	NBFI outstanding	0.69	Kazakhstan	GDP of MSMEs	0.36	Kyrgyz Republic	Market capitalization	0.29
Georgia	NBFI outstanding	0.67	Georgia	Market capitalization	0.29	Kazakhstan	Microfinance loans	0.29
Uzbekistan	Number of MSMEs	0.66	Azerbaijan	Microfinance loans	0.25	Kazakhstan	NBFI outstanding	0.25
Kyrgyz Republic	GDP of MSMEs	0.64	Tajikistan	Bank loans outstanding	0.21	Armenia	Microfinance loans	0.24
Uzbekistan	Number of MSME Employees	0.63	Armenia	Nonperforming bank loans	0.18	Uzbekistan	Number of MSMEs	0.24
Kyrgyz Republic	Nonperforming bank loans	0.58	Kyrgyz Republic	NBFI outstanding	0.17	Georgia	Bank loans outstanding	0.18
Georgia	GDP of MSMEs	0.53	Kyrgyz Republic	Microfinance loans	0.17	Kyrgyz Republic	Nonperforming bank loans	0.17
Tajikistan	GDP of MSMEs	0.47	Kazakhstan	Nonperforming bank loans	0.16	Uzbekistan	MSME exports	0.12
Azerbaijan	Number of MSMEs	0.42	Kazakhstan	Number of MSME Employees	0.1	Kazakhstan	Bank loans outstanding	0.12
Uzbekistan	MSME exports	0.36	Kazakhstan	Number of MSMEs	0.1	Azerbaijan	Nonperforming bank loans	0.11
Kazakhstan	GDP of MSMEs	0.35	Kyrgyz Republic	GDP of MSMEs	0.079	Georgia	Number of MSME Employees	0.072
Tajikistan	Nonperforming NBFI loans	0.29	Georgia	Number of MSMEs	0.07	Kyrgyz Republic	Bank loans outstanding	0.036
Georgia	Nonperforming bank loans	0.26	Georgia	MSME exports	0.047	Azerbaijan	Bank loans outstanding	0.032
Tajikistan	Nonperforming bank loans	0.23	Uzbekistan	GDP of MSMEs	-0.0088	Armenia	GDP of MSMEs	0.028
Kyrgyz Republic	Number of MSME Employees	0.13	Armenia	Bank loans outstanding	-0.016	Azerbaijan	NBFI outstanding	0.0025
Tajikistan	Market capitalization	0.00025	Kazakhstan	Bank loans outstanding	-0.03	Georgia	Number of MSMEs	0.002
Kyrgyz Republic	MSME exports	-0.024	Kyrgyz Republic	Bank loans outstanding	-0.048	Kyrgyz Republic	Number of MSMEs	-0.01
Tajikistan	Microfinance loans	-0.064	Armenia	NBFI outstanding	-0.068	Uzbekistan	Nonperforming bank loans	-0.018
Kyrgyz Republic	MSME imports	-0.15	Azerbaijan	Number of MSME Employees	-0.076	Uzbekistan	Microfinance loans	-0.023
Uzbekistan	Market capitalization	-0.16	Kyrgyz Republic	MSME exports	-0.096	Uzbekistan	Bank loans outstanding	-0.027
Uzbekistan	Bank loans outstanding	-0.19	Armenia	Microfinance loans	-0.11	Georgia	Nonperforming bank loans	-0.031
Uzbekistan	Nonperforming NBFI loans	-0.23	Georgia	Bank loans outstanding	-0.17	Tajikistan	GDP of MSMEs	-0.035
Uzbekistan	NBFI outstanding	-0.24	Armenia	Market capitalization	-0.17	Uzbekistan	Market capitalization	-0.048
Uzbekistan	Microfinance loans	-0.26	Kyrgyz Republic	Number of MSMEs	-0.18	Azerbaijan	Microfinance loans	-0.059
Azerbaijan	Nonperforming bank loans	-0.27	Georgia	Nonperforming bank loans	-0.22	Kyrgyz Republic	Number of MSME Employees	-0.087
Georgia	MSME imports	-0.29	Tajikistan	Market capitalization	-0.25	Tajikistan	Microfinance loans	-0.14
Georgia	Microfinance loans	-0.44	Uzbekistan	MSME imports	-0.29	Uzbekistan	Number of MSME Employees	-0.15
Uzbekistan	Nonperforming bank loans	-0.44	Azerbaijan	GDP of MSMEs	-0.29	Uzbekistan	NBFI outstanding	-0.15
Georgia	MSME exports	-0.47	Tajikistan	Number of MSMEs	-0.32	Kazakhstan	Number of MSMEs	-0.16
Kazakhstan	Microfinance loans	-0.5	Armenia	Number of MSME Employees	-0.33	Georgia	NBFI outstanding	-0.18
Uzbekistan	GDP of MSMEs	-0.5	Armenia	GDP of MSMEs	-0.38	Armenia	Market capitalization	-0.18
Armenia	Number of MSMEs	-0.51	Tajikistan	NBFI outstanding	-0.4	Kazakhstan	Number of MSME Employees	-0.24
Georgia	Market capitalization	-0.53	Kyrgyz Republic	Market capitalization	-0.41	Uzbekistan	Nonperforming NBFI loans	-0.24
Tajikistan	NBFI outstanding	-0.53	Kyrgyz Republic	Nonperforming bank loans	-0.52	Georgia	Microfinance loans	-0.32
Azerbaijan	GDP of MSMEs	-0.58	Uzbekistan	Number of MSMEs	-0.57	Armenia	Nonperforming bank loans	-0.32
Tajikistan	Bank loans outstanding	-0.66	Armenia	Number of MSMEs	-0.58	Azerbaijan	Number of MSME Employees	-0.39
Tajikistan	Number of MSMEs	-0.67	Kazakhstan	NBFI outstanding	-0.6	Armenia	Number of MSMEs	-0.39
Armenia	Number of MSME Employees	-0.77	Kyrgyz Republic	Number of MSME Employees	-0.74	Tajikistan	Market capitalization	-0.41
Armenia	GDP of MSMEs	-0.78	Kazakhstan	Microfinance loans	-0.75	Azerbaijan	Number of MSMEs	-0.42
Kyrgyz Republic	NBFI outstanding	-0.78	Azerbaijan	Number of MSMEs	-0.76	Armenia	Number of MSME Employees	-0.47
Kyrgyz Republic	Microfinance loans	-0.79	Uzbekistan	Nonperforming bank loans	-0.76	Tajikistan	NBFI outstanding	-0.57
Azerbaijan	Bank loans outstanding	-0.83	Uzbekistan	Market capitalization	-0.87	Tajikistan	Bank loans outstanding	-0.63
Azerbaijan	NBFI outstanding	-0.83	Uzbekistan	Nonperforming NBFI loans	-0.87	Tajikistan	Number of MSMEs	-0.64
Kazakhstan	Nonperforming bank loans	-0.88	Uzbekistan	NBFI outstanding	-0.95	Tajikistan	Nonperforming NBFI loans	-0.67
Azerbaijan	Microfinance loans	-0.95	Uzbekistan	Bank loans outstanding	-0.96	Uzbekistan	GDP of MSMEs	-0.81
Kazakhstan	Bank loans outstanding	-0.97	Uzbekistan	Microfinance loans	-0.96	Tajikistan	Nonperforming bank loans	-0.82

GDP = gross domestic product; MSME = micro, small, and medium-sized enterprise; NBFI = nonbank finance institution; PCA = principal component analysis.

Source: Calculated based on Asia SME Monitor 2022 database.

5. Policies and Regulations

Central and West Asian policymakers consider MSME development and financial inclusion priority components of national growth strategies for a resilient, diversified, and sustainable economy. All countries in the region have a long-term MSME development policy framework that comprehensively covers financial and nonfinancial assistance for MSMEs—in line with their national development strategies (Table 1.6). Here we summarize the region's MSME policies.

MSME Development

Countries across the region have a set of MSME development targets under their national strategies. They commonly aim to strengthen MSME competitiveness by promoting their participation in global business; technology adoption and commercialization; entrepreneurship development; worker skills development; diversified financing options; and focused group assistance for youth and women entrepreneurs, startups, agribusiness, and internationalized MSMEs. Each country has a guiding strategy:

- Small and Medium Entrepreneurship Development Strategy 2020–2024, Armenia;
- SME Roadmap for 2017–2020, Azerbaijan;
- SME Development Strategy 2021–2025, Georgia;
- Development Concept of SMEs for 2030, Kazakhstan;
- National Development Strategy for 2018–2040, the Kyrgyz Republic;
- National Development Strategy for 2030, Tajikistan; and
- Strategy for Five Priority Areas of Development for 2017–2021, Uzbekistan.

Each government in Central and West Asia conducts policy coordination, implementation, and monitoring through a focal government agency—Enterprise Armenia, the Small and Medium Business Development Agency in Azerbaijan, Enterprise Georgia, DAMU in Kazakhstan, the Ministry of Economy and Commerce in the Kyrgyz Republic, and the State Committee on Investment and Property Management in Tajikistan—or a central government body like Uzbekistan's Cabinet of Ministers. They support MSMEs as classified under their different yet single national definitions to help government authorities and the central bank design and implement MSME policies and assistance measures (see Table 1.1 for country MSME definitions).[13]

Although MSME policy aims are homogeneous across countries in the region, there are some different approaches to providing assistance. In Armenia, there is preferential tax treatment for MSMEs called the "turnover tax," which replaces income and value-added taxes, thus reducing the MSME tax burden. Azerbaijan focuses on entrepreneurship and startup development, strengthening their international business, knowledge base, and investments in research and development (R&D). The government also provides income tax exemptions and grants for innovative startups. Georgia sets annual SME growth targets—SME output (average annual 10% growth), job creation (by 15%), labor productivity (by 7%), and for adopting technology. Policy priorities include skills development, SME exports, and innovation and R&D.

Kazakhstan's strategic MSME priorities address legal issues that simplify business procedures, reforms in agriculture, transport, and tourism, digitalization, and venture capital MSME financing. The Kyrgyz Republic targets priority sectors for MSME development—agriculture, manufacturing, energy, and tourism. Its thematic assistance

[13] By contrast, in South Asia, even within the country, several MSME definitions are used by different government agencies and central banks. Using a single national definition is critical for effectively implementing government MSME assistance nationally.

prioritizes women-led MSMEs, high-tech firms, exporters, and business cluster development. Tajikistan also has strategic goals, including job creation in high-tech industries, empowering youth and women, and improving the business and investment climate ("core infrastructure development"). Other priority policy measures include legal reforms that promote entrepreneurship development, modernizing production, attracting investments to domestic businesses, widening access to finance, and providing government subsidies and guarantees to SMEs. In Uzbekistan, policy priorities include legal reforms that reduce the administrative burden for businesses, improving the investment climate for exporters (free-trade zone development), and creating more women entrepreneurs.

MSME policies in Central and West Asia tend to rely on government subsidies and grants to implement planned policy measures. Preferential taxation and subsidies are powerful tools that directly support MSMEs, even with the risk of overtaxing national budgets. There is a need to provide exit strategies from purely public assistance. It would be worth considering how best to use public-private partnerships to help implement MSME policies, especially in supplying technical support for businesses and funding for assistance programs.

Financial Inclusion

A comprehensive national financial inclusion strategy exists in the Kyrgyz Republic, Tajikistan, and Uzbekistan, while Azerbaijan, Georgia, and Kazakhstan focus on financial education strategies. Armenia does not have a specific national financial inclusion strategy. Strategic goals include (i) diversifying financial products (including digital financial services), (ii) enhancing financial literacy, (iii) consumer protection, (iv) providing financial assistance for targeted groups like youth and women, and (iv) reforming financial regulations. Central banks coordinate and implement financial inclusion strategies across the region with guiding strategies:

National financial inclusion strategies

- Strategy for Improving Financial Inclusion for 2022–2026, Kyrgyz Republic
- National Strategy for Financial Inclusion for 2022–2026, Tajikistan
- National Strategy for Increasing Financial Inclusion for 2021–2023, Uzbekistan

National financial education strategies

- Strategic Roadmap for Development of Financial Services for 2017–2020 (includes financial literacy), Azerbaijan
- National Strategy of Financial Education 2016, Georgia
- Concept of Improving Financial Literacy for 2020–2024, Kazakhstan

The financial inclusion strategy in the Kyrgyz Republic sets targets such as increasing the number of payment terminals, bank cards, and digital payment transactions. Diversifying financial products covers green finance, specific products for women, agriculture finance, savings and remittances, and Islamic finance. Tajikistan's financial inclusion strategy encourages the use of digital financial services for youth, women, and SMEs, with some numeric targets such as POS terminals available to 95% of adults and digital payment services covering at least 60%, among others. Uzbekistan's financial inclusion strategy promotes alternative financing for small businesses, agent banking, and digital financial services with digital identification and modern payment systems. The action plan for 2023 focuses on gender inclusiveness. All countries are developing digital financial infrastructure and embracing new products.

Response to COVID-19

Several waves of COVID-19 infections hit Central and West Asian countries beginning in March 2020. Governments quickly imposed strict quarantines and lockdowns, including travel bans, border closures, school and business closures, mobility restrictions, and social distancing. Economic growth in the region was stunted by the pandemic. Lockdowns hampered domestic and foreign trade and significantly reduced business operations. Remittances from migrant workers dropped sharply. MSMEs were hardest hit by the pandemic and mobility restrictions, especially local firms and microenterprises. Retail service outlets, hotels and restaurants, tourism, and education were particularly affected. Several business surveys conducted across countries showed that firms, including MSMEs, faced immediate supply chain disruptions, a sharp drop in sales and revenue, reduced availability of raw materials (and at higher prices), and delayed customer payments. Many public and private institutions switched to remote operations. Private businesses took several cost-cutting measures—reducing wages and increasing layoffs to keep their businesses operating during the pandemic.

Along with quarantine measures and lockdowns, each government introduced timely economic stimulus packages, which allowed the region to quickly recover from the pandemic (Table 1.7).

Armenia took over 25 initiatives to support MSMEs hit by the pandemic. Most important were measure "one" (temporary access to finance for individual businesses through cofinancing and refinancing facilities, along with interest subsidies); "three" (maximum 36-month loans for MSMEs); and "nineteen" (maximum 60-month loans at 7%-10% interest rates for innovative, competitive businesses).

In Azerbaijan, a COVID-19 action plan included three broad pillars: (i) support for economic growth and entrepreneurs (temporary tax relief, credit guarantees, interest subsidies, exemption from rents on state property and government-owned land, and custom duty exemptions for essential goods and medical products); (ii) support for employment and social welfare (cash handouts to the unemployed, financial assistance on tuition fees, and electricity discounts); and (iii) macroeconomic and financial stability (such as regulatory holidays for credit institutions).

Georgia offered several assistance packages to SMEs, including nonfinancial support (such as online marketing showrooms organized and training for SME exporters, tax exemptions for tourism businesses, and subsidies for farmers) and financial support (a new credit line for SMEs and credit guarantees).

The Kyrgyz Republic adopted an Anti-Crisis Response Plan, which included financial assistance packages for MSMEs (interest-free loans and portfolio guarantees), debt restructuring (deferral of debt repayments), and simplified documentation requirements for loans, among others.

Kazakhstan also offered several assistance programs for MSMEs, such as compensation for income losses, tax and fee exemptions for worker salaries in affected sectors, subsidies for the agro-industrial complex, loan payment deferrals, concessional loans at 6% interest, and guaranteed loans.

Similarly, Tajikistan provided debt restructuring for affected businesses, loan payment deferrals, temporary waiving of supervisory sanctions for banks, concessional loans for food and medical supply companies, among others. SMEs also received subsidies. Grain, seeds, and fuel were provided to farmers to improve food security.

Uzbekistan's Anti-Crisis Fund increased the State Fund for Entrepreneurship Support. Stimulus included reduced social tax, suspension of tourist (hotel) fees, and eased business requirements for exporters. The state fund covered 8% of an entrepreneur's loan expenses with interest rates not exceeding 24% and provided credit guarantees of up to 75% of the loan amount. Tax payments on turnover, land, property, social and water resources were deferred for small businesses that saw their revenue drop by 50% or more.

Response to the Russian Invasion of Ukraine

The impact of the Russian invasion of Ukraine differed by country. They can be split into two groups: (i) countries with relatively limited impact—Armenia, Azerbaijan, and Georgia, and (ii) those hit hardest by the invasion and sanctions—Kazakhstan, the Kyrgyz Republic, Tajikistan, and Uzbekistan. Countries in the first group have no comprehensive anti-crisis plan, while those in the latter group prepared a set of action plans to mitigate the harmful effects of the invasion and associated sanctions (Table 1.7).

Armenia has no specific policy measures as the invasion and sanctions increased business opportunities. Armenian banks were not affected by the sanctions (such as the Russian Federation's disconnection from SWIFT). Rather, the Russian Federation-based firms and individuals are moving to Armenia and opening bank accounts. Travel restrictions from the Russian Federation to Europe drove many tourists to Armenia. Also, major trading partners with the Russian Federation have shifted to Armenia, benefiting its export industry.

Azerbaijan also did not take any anti-crisis measures as the economic damage is limited. Revenues from the oil industry increased due to high prices has at least temporarily compensated for the negative impact from the invasion like decreased inward remittances and high inflation.

Georgia has no general anti-crisis plan as well. But given the long-term effects of shrinking foreign trade, Enterprise Georgia implemented an export assistance program for SMEs, offering (i) product licenses and certificates based on international standards, (ii) support for product branding, and (iii) support for marketing globally.

Kazakhstan was hit by sanctions—as 42% of its imports come from the Russian Federation. Sanctions caused a sharp drop in trade with the Russian Federation and disrupted supplies of food and essential commodities. US sanctions on three Russian Federation banks (Sberbank, Alfa Bank, and VneshTorgBank) in April 2022 damaged livelihoods and business operations as many people had accounts with their Kazakhstan branches. Also, the Russian Federation- and Belarus-based firms have been moving their business base to Kazakhstan, risking the country to secondary sanctions. In response, the government established an anti-crisis command center in March 2022 which has discussed several countermeasures focusing on food security, such as expanding the state subsidy for insurance premiums to support agricultural producers, increasing preferential leasing of agricultural machinery for domestic production, and forwarding purchases of agricultural products from state stabilization funds to prevent food shortages and food price inflation (as of August 2022).

The economy of the Kyrgyz Republic also relies on the the Russian Federation economy. In 2021, 24% of exports went to the Russian Federation, with 34% of imports emanating from the Russian Federation. The potential trade losses high. In March 2022, the government launched an anti-crisis plan with three components: (i) food security and price stability, (ii) social protection and price stability, and (iii) MSME employment. The plan provides seeds and fertilizer to farmers, while the government is seeking alternative trading partners to import crops and fuel for food security. The government is also helping returning migrant workers find jobs, promoting entrepreneurship development, providing refinancing facilities for agricultural producers and agriculture value chain development, and offering currency risk-sharing with MSME exporters.

Tajikistan is also highly dependent on the Russian Federation for exports, trade routes and logistics, its labor market and remittances, and several infrastructure development projects. Sanctions immediately hurt the Tajikistan economy. In response, the government launched an anti-crisis program in March 2022. Like the Kyrgyz Republic, the program offers (i) social protection for the poor and vulnerable (via cash transfers); (ii) food security (seeds and fertilizer to farmers; with food stocks secured); and (iii) support for SMEs hit hardest (vocational training for returning migrant workers and concessional loans to SMEs in agriculture, trade, and services).

Uzbekistan was also hit hard by the invasion and related sanctions, as the Russian Federation is a major trading partner and main destination for Uzbekistan migrant workers. The sanctions brought supply chain disruptions, high inflation, and reduced inward remittances. In response, the government imposed countercyclical measures addressing (i) food security and price stability (exemptions of VAT and customs duties on essential food products), (ii) social protection (cash transfers to the vulnerable), and (iii) support for businesses and employees (financial assistance for entrepreneurs and job opportunities for the unemployed and returning migrants). Like Armenia, many foreign IT experts have moved to Uzbekistan along with many tourists from the Russian Federation and Belarus, in effect benefiting tourism and IT development.

Table 1.6: Policies and Regulations—Central and West Asia

Country	Item	Regulators and Policymakers	Regulations	Policies
Armenia	Small and medium-sized enterprise (SME) Promotion	Small and Medium Enterprise Development Council	Prime Minister Decision No.638 of 2011 on Establishing a Small and Medium Enterprise Development Council of the Republic of Armenia	1) Strategic Development Plan of Armenia for 2014-2025 (Governmnet Decision No.442 of 2014)
		Ministry of Economy	Law No.121 of 2000 on State Support for Small and Medium Entrepreneurship	2) Small and Medium Entrepreneurship Development Strategy 2016-2018 (Government Decision No.44 of 2015)
			Law No.232 of 2001 on Joint Stock Companies	3) Small and Medium Entrepreneurship Development Strategy 2020-2024 (Government Decision No.1443 of 2020)
			Law No.252 of 2001 on Companies with Limited Liability	
		Ministry of Finance	Tax Code No.165 of 2016 of the Republic of Armenia	
		State Revenue Committee		
		Enterprise Armenia (fromer Small and Medium Enterpreneurship Development National Center)	(implementing agency of SME policies)	
	Banking Sector	Central Bank of Armenia (CBA)	Law No.68 of 1996 on Banks and Banking	(There is no national financial inclusion strategy.)
	Nonbank Sector			
	Digital Finance			
	Capital Markets		Law No.195 of 2007 on Securities Market	
Azerbaijan	SME Promotion	Ministry of Economy Small and Medium Business Development Agency Export and Investment Promotion Agency Entrepreneurship Development Fund	Law No.673-IQ of 1999 on State Support to Small Business	1) Azerbaijan 2030: National Priorities for Socio-Economic Development
			Tax Code of the Republic of Azerbaijan No.905-IQ of 2000	2) Strategic Road Map for the Production of Consumer Goods at the Level of SMEs (SME Roadmap) for 2017-2020
			Law No.878-IQ of 2000 on Privatization of State Property in Azerbaijan	3) State Programme on Socio-Economic Development of Regions of the Republic of Azerbaijan for 2019-2023
			Law No.245-IIQ of 2001 on Public Procurement	4) Socio-Economic Development Strategy of the Republic of Azerbaijan for 2022–2026
			Law No.560-IIQ of 2003 on State Registration and the State Register of Legal Entities	
			Customs Code of the Republic of Azerbaijan No.164-IVQ of 2011	
			Law No.1410-IVQ of 2015 on Suspension of Inspections of Entrepreneurial Activities	
			Presidential Decree No.1771 of 2017 on further improvement of management of small and medium enterprises	

continued on next page

Table 1.6 *continued*

Country	Item	Regulators and Policymakers	Regulations	Policies
			Presidential Decree No.148 of 2018 on ensuring the activities of the Small and Medium Business Development Agency of the Republic of Azerbaijan	
			Decree of the Cabinet of Ministers No.556 of 2018 on the approval of the "criteria for the division of micro, small, medium and large business entities"	
			Presidential Decree No.713 of 2019 on the approval of the "guidelines on providing state support for internal market research for the purpose of stimulating the competitive production of micro, small and medium-sized enterprises"	
			Decision of the Cabinet of Ministers No.364 of 2020 on approval of the "regulation on the financing of education, science, research and support projects related to the development of micro, small and medium entrepreneurship"	
			Decision of the Cabinet of Ministers No.20 of 2021 on the approval of the "criteria for determining the startup"	
			Presidential Decree No.1415 of 2021 on the approval of the "regulations on the e-KOB evi (e-SME house) portal"	
			Presidential Decree No.1482 of 2021 on the approval of the "rule of support for the expansion of the sale of products produced by micro and small business entities using the trade networks"	
		State Agency for Public Service and Social Innovations	Presidential Decree No.685 of 2012 (for establishment of the agency)	
		Agrarian Credit and Development Agency, Ministry of Agriculture	Presidential Order No.467 of 2004 on Measures to Improve Management in the Agrarian Division (for establishment of the agency)	5) State Program on the Development Production of Cotton between 2017–2022 6) State Program on the Development Production of Tobacco between 2017–2022 7) State Program on the Development Production of Citrus between 2018–2025 8) State Program on the Development Production of Winemaking between 2018-2025 9) State Program on the Development Production of Cocoon and Silk between 2018-2025 10) State Program on the Development Production of Rice between 2018-2025
	Banking Sector	Central Bank of the Republic of Azerbaijan	Law No.590-IIQ of 2004 on Banks	11) Strategic Road Map for Development of Financial Services for 2017-2020
	Nonbank Sector		Law No.933-IIIQ of 2009 on Non-Bank Credit Institutions	
			Law No.876-IQ of 2000 on Credit Unions	
	Digital Finance			12) State Program on Expansion of Digital Payments for 2018-2020
	Capital Markets		Law No.1284-IVQ of 2015 on Securities Market	
			Law No.551-VIQ of 2022 on Investment Activity	

continued on next page

Table 1.6 *continued*

Country	Item	Regulators and Policymakers	Regulations	Policies
Georgia	SME Promotion	Ministry of Economy and and Sustainable Development		1) SME Development Strategy of Georgia 2016-2020
		Enterprise Georgia	Government Resolution No.365 of 2014 on establishment of Enterprise Georgia	2) SME Development Strategy of Georgia 2021-2025
		Ministry of Environmental Protection and Agriculture		3) Agriculture and Rural Development Strategy for 2021-2027; Action Plan for 2021-2023
		Rural Development Agency (RDA)		
		Ministry of Finance	Minister of Finance Order No.996 of 2010 on Administration of Taxes (with subsequent amendments)	
		Department of Tax and Customs Policy	Tax code of Georgia No.3591 of 2011 (with subsequent amendments)	
		Revenue Service of Georgia (GRS)		
		Service for Accounting, Reporting and Auditing Supervision (SARAS)	Law No.5386 of 2016 on Accounting, Reporting, and Auditing	
		Agency for Innovations and Technologies of Georgia	Resolution No.1-1/66 of 2014 on the approval of the regulations of the Agency for Innovations and Technologies of Georgia	
			Law No.1388 of 2005 on Public Procurement	
	Banking Sector	National Bank of Georgia (NBG)	Law No.121-11s of 1996 on Activities of Commercial Banks	4) National Strategy of Financial Education (2016)
			Decree No.51/04 of 2014 of the Governor of NBG on the approval of the "Regulation on Assets Classification and the Creation and Use of Reserves for Losses by Commercial Banks"	
			Decree No.44/04 of 2020 of the Governor of NBG on the approval of the "Regulation on Lending to the Individuals"	
	Nonbank Sector		Law No.3482 of 2006 on Microfinance Organizations	
			Government Resolution No.163 of 2019 on Credit Guarantee Scheme	
	Digital Finance		NBG Digital Bank Licensing Principles	5) National Bank's supervisory strategy for 2020-2022 (including digital bank licencing)
	Capital Markets		Law No.1745 of 1998 on Securities Market	6) Capital Market Development Strategy (drfat as of end-August 2022)
			Law No.6805 of 2020 on Investment Funds	
			Stock Exchange Licensing, Financial Reporting, and Minimum Capital Requirement Rule, 169/01 of 2010	
			Rule of Financial Instruments Trading System Recognization as Organized Market, 33/04 of 2018	
Kazakhstan	SME Promotion	Ministry of National Economy	Entrepreneurial Code No.375-V of 2015	1) Development concept of small and medium-sized enterprises until 2030 2) National project on entrepreneurship development for 2021-2025 (instead of state program "Business Road Map-2025")
			Civil Code No.268-XIII of 1994	3) "Business Road Map-2025" state program

continued on next page

Table 1.6 *continued*

Country	Item	Regulators and Policymakers	Regulations	Policies
		Ministry of Labor and Social Protection	Labor Code No.414-V of 2015	4) "Enbek" State Program for the Development of Productive Employment and Mass Entrepreneurship for 2017–2021 (closed)
		Ministry of Agriculture	Law No.372-V of 2015 on Agricultural Cooperatives	5) National project for the development of the agro-industrial complex for 2021–2025
			Law No.66-III of 2005 on State Regulation of the Development of the Agro-industrial Complex and Rural Areas	
		State Revenue Committee, Ministry of Finance	Tax Code No.120-VI of 2017	
			Law No.434-V of 2015 on State Procurement	
		Ministry of Trade and Integration		
		Ministry of Industry and Infrastructure Development		
		Ministry of Digital Development, Innovations and Aerospace industry		
	Banking Sector	National Bank of Kazakhstan		6) "Economy of Simple Things" (financing for manufacturing and agro-products)
	Digital Finance			
	Nonbank Sector	Agency for Regulation and Development of Financial Markets	Law No.56-V of 2012 on Microfinance Activities	
		"Baiterek" National Managing Holding JSC (parent company of "DAMU")		7) Development Strategy of the Damu Fund for 2014–2023
		"DAMU" JSC Entrepreneurship Development Fund		
	Capital Markets	Agency for Regulation and Development of Financial Markets	Law No.6-I of 1996 on Copyright and Related Rights	
			Law No.220-1 of 1998 on Limited and Additional Liability Partnerships	
			Law No.78-II of 2000 on Financial Leasing	
			Law No.330-II of 2002 on Complex Entrepreneurial License (franchising)	
			Law No.461-II of 2003 on the Securities Market	
			Law No.415-II of 2003 on Joint Stock Companie	
			Law No.576-II of 2004 on Investment and Venture Funds	
			Law No.234-III of 2007 on Accounting and Financial Reporting	
Kyrgyz Republic	SME Promotion	Ministry of Economy and Commerce (MEC)	Government Resolution No.78 of 1998	1) National Strategy on the Development of the Kyrgyz Republic for 2018–2040 (2018)
			Law on State Support for Small Business, 2007	2) Strategy for Sustainable Development of Industry for 2019–2024
			Law on Public-Private Partnership, 2007	3) Program to support and develop women's entrepreneurship for 2022–2026
			Presidential Decree on State Support for Small Businesses, 2021	
			Presidential Decree on Protecting Property and Supporting Entrepreneurs and Investors, 2021	

continued on next page

Table 1.6 *continued*

Country	Item	Regulators and Policymakers	Regulations	Policies
		Ministry of Foreign Affairs		4) Export Development Program for 2019–2022
		Development and Investment Agency		
	Banking Sector	National Bank of the Kyrgyz Republic (NBKR)	NBKR Instructions on Limitations of Credit, 2004	5) Strategy for Improving Financial Inclusion for 2022–2026
			Law on Pledge, 2005	6) Government Program on Financial Literacy 2016–2020 (2016)
			NBKR Regulation on the minimum requirements for credit risk management in commercial banks and other financial institutions, 2010	7) Financing of Agriculture Program (2022)
			Law on Banks and Banking Activities, 2016	
			NBKR requirements to Banks and Other Financial and Credit Institutions when Granting Loans to Individual Clients, 2017	
	Nonbank Sector		Law on Credit Unions, 1999	
			Law on Microfinance Organizations, 2002	
			Law on Exchange of Credit Information, 2014	
			Law on Guarantee Funds, 2019	
	Digital Finance			
	Capital Markets	Service for Regulation and Supervision of the Financial Market, MEC	Law on Joint Stock Companies, 2003	
			Law on Securities Market, 2009	
			Code of Corporate Governance, 2020	
Tajikistan	SME Promotion	State Committee on Investment and State Property Management	Law No.1107 of 2014 on the Government Protection and Support of Entrepreneurship	1) Program for Government support of entrepreneurship in Tajikistan up to 2020 (2012)
		Entrepreneurship Support Fund		2) Creation of the Entrepreneurship Support Fund of Tajikistan (2013); Transformation of Entrepreneurship Support Fund of Tajikistan to State Unitary Enterprise Industrial and Export Bank of Tajikistan "Sanoatsodirotbonk"
		Ministry of Economic Development and Trade		3) National Development Strategy of the Republic of Tajikistan for 2030 (2016)
		Ministry of Finance (MOF)	Tax Code No.549 of 2021	
		Ministry of Industrial and New Technologies		
	Banking Sector	National Bank of Tajikistan	Law No.524 on Banking Activities (2009)	4) National Strategy for Financial Inclusion for 2022-2026 (Governmnet Decision No.314 of 2022)
	Nonbank Sector		Law No.816 on Microfinance Organisations (2012)	
	Digital Finance			
	Capital Markets	Agency for the Development of Securities and Specialized Registration, MOF	Law No.745 of 2011 on Securities Market	

continued on next page

Table 1.6 *continued*

Country	Item	Regulators and Policymakers	Regulations	Policies
Uzbekistan	SME Promotion	Cabinet of Ministers	Presidential Decree N UP-101 of 2022 on the next reforms to create conditions for stable economic growth by improving the business environment and developing the private sector	1) Development Strategy of New Uzbekistan for 2022-2026
			Presidential Decree N PP-3777 of 2018 on the implementation of the program "Every family is an entrepreneur"	2) Program "Every family is an entrepreneur"
			Presidential Decree N PP-4720 of 2020 on additional measures to finance the program "Every family is an entrepreneur"	
		Ministry of Finance	Presidential Decree N PP-4525 of 2019 on measures to further improve the business environment and improve the business support system in the country	3) "Roadmap" to improve the position of the Republic of Uzbekistan in the annual report of the World Bank and the International Finance Corporation "Doing Business"
			Presidential Decree N PP-5214 of 2021 on additional measures to further support entrepreneurship and develop cooperation between business entities and the population in mahallas	
			Presidential Decree N PP-5228 of 2021 on additional measures to create a favorable investment climate, encourage small businesses and family entrepreneurship in the Surkhandarya region	
			Presidential Decree N PP-5084 of 2021 on measures to further support entrepreneurship and develop engineering and communication networks in the Namangan region	
			Presidential Decree N PP-5087 of 2021 on additional measures to improve the business support system, further improve the business climate	
		State Tax Committee	Presidential Decree N UP-6314 of 2021 on measures to further reduce the administrative and tax burden for business entities, improve the system for protecting the legitimate interests of business	
		Ministry of Labor	Resolution of the Cabinet of Ministers No.313 of 2020 on measures to establish youth technology parks in the country	4) Action strategy for five priority areas of development of the Republic of Uzbekistan in 2017-2021 in the "Year of Youth Support and Public Health Promotion"
			Decree of the Cabinet of Ministers No.222 of 2021 on measures to support talented young people in scientific and innovative activities	
			Presidential Decree N UP-6208 of 2021 on additional measures to support entrepreneurial activity, promote employment, social protection and meaningful organization of free time for young people	
			Presidential Decree N PP-4742 of 2020 on measures to simplify state regulation of entrepreneurial activity and self-employment	

Table 1.6 *continued*

Country	Item	Regulators and Policymakers	Regulations	Policies
		Ministry of Justice	Resolution of the Cabinet of Ministers N 584 of 2019 on measures for the effective organization of the activities of the Commissioner under the President of the Republic of Uzbekistan to protect the rights and legitimate interests of business entities	5) "Roadmap" to facilitate doing business and improve the system for protecting the legitimate interests of business
		Ministry of Economic Development and Poverty Reduction	Presidential Decree N UP-5690 of 2019 on measures to radically improve the system for protecting business activities and optimizing the activities of the prosecutor's office	6) "Roadmap" for attracting grants and concessional long-term financing for measures to counter the negative consequences of the global coronavirus pandemic
			Presidential Decree N UP-5718 of 2019 on measures to radically improve the system of support and protection of entrepreneurial activity	
		Ministry of Innovative Development	Resolution of the Cabinet of Ministers No.468 of 2017 on measures to organize the activities of the innovation technology park in Yashnabad district of Tashkent	
			Presidential Decree No. UP-5544 of 2018 on "Innovative Development Strategy of the Republic of Uzbekistan for 2019-2021"	7) Innovative Development Strategy for 2019-2021
			Presidential Resolution No.PP-3855 of 2018 on additional measures to increase the effectiveness of commercialization of scientific developments and scientific-technical activities	
			Decree of the Cabinet of Ministers N 643 of 2019 on measures to support the development of entrepreneurship and the expansion of industrial production in the Jizzakh region	
			Resolution of the Cabinet of Ministers No.133 of 2020 on measures to further improve the normative and legal basis for the development of research and innovative activity	
		Ministry of Investments and Foreign Trade	Presidential Decree No.UP-6091 of 2020 on measures to further expand financial support for export activities	
		Ministry of Agriculture	Presidential Decree No.UP-53 of 2022 on measures to stimulate deep processing, production and export of finished products with high added value by textile and sewing and knitting enterprises	
	Banking Sector	Central Bank of Uzbekistan (CBU)	Presidential Decree No.UP-5992 of 2020 on the strategy for reforming the banking system of the Republic of Uzbekistan for 2020-2025	8) Banking Reform Strategy for 2020-2025
	Nonbank Sector			9) National Strategy for Increasing Financial Inclusion for 2021-2023
	Digital Finance			
	Capital Markets	Ministry of Finance (MOF)	Presidential Decree No.PP-5073 of 2021 on measures to further improve the capital market regulation system	

Source: Compiled from country reviews of Asia Small and Medium-Sized Enterprise Monitor 2022.

Table 1.7: COVID-19 Lockdowns, Economic Stimulus Packages, and Emergency Measures in Response to the Russian Invasion of Ukraine

Item	Country	2020 (Mar–Dec)	2021 (Jan–Dec)	2022 (Jan–Jun)
1. COVID-19 pandemic	ARM	1st wave pandemic; 2nd wave pandemic (the peak)	3rd wave pandemic	
	AZE	1st wave pandemic; 2nd wave pandemic	3rd wave pandemic; 4th wave pandemic; 5th wave pandemic	6th wave pandemic
	GEO	1st wave pandemic; 2nd wave pandemic	3rd wave pandemic; 4th wave pandemic; 5th wave pandemic	6th wave pandemic
	KAZ	1st wave pandemic	2nd wave pandemic[1]	
	KGZ	1st wave pandemic	2nd wave pandemic	
	TAJ	1st wave pandemic	2nd wave pandemic	
	UZB	1st wave pandemic; 2nd wave pandemic	3rd wave pandemic	
2. COVID-19 quarantine measures and lockdowns	ARM	1st large-scale social restriction; 2nd large-scale social restriction (requirement for certification on non-infected)	Vaccination required	
	AZE[2]	Special Quarantine Regime[3]		
	GEO	1st lockdown and social/economic restrictions; Social, economic, and mobility restrictions	Social, economic, and mobility restrictions (2nd year)	Social, economic, and mobility restrictions (3rd year)
	KAZ	1st State of Emergency with strict containment measures; 2nd strict containment measures[4]		All quarantine restrictions were lifted.
	KGZ	1st social restriction	2nd social restriction	
	TAJ[5]	1st social restriction[6]	2nd social restriction[7]	Partial mobility restriction[8]
	UZB	1st social restriction; 2nd social restriction	3rd social restriction	
3. Economic stimulus packages responding to the COVID-19	ARM	More than 10 economic stimulus packages	New subsidized business loans (1st package) Continuation of the 2–3 year subsidized loans that were given in 2020 (3rd package) MSME subsidized loans (19th package) Agricultural subsidized loans	
	AZE	Fund to Support for Fight Against Coronavirus; Presidential Decree on the allocation of funds to improve the provision of microcredits to producers of agricultural products in the conditions of the coronavirus pandemic and in the subsequent period.		
	GEO	Anti-Crisis Economic Plan	Anti-Crisis Economic Plan (2nd year)	Anti-Crisis Economic Plan (3rd year)
	KAZ	Comprehensive plan on recovery of economic growth (CPoREG)	CPoREG (2nd year)	
		Program of concessional lending to business entities	Program of concessional lending to business entities (2nd year)	
		Funding for expansion of the state programs		
		Funding of "Employment Road Map" program	Funding of "Employment Road Map" program (2nd year)	
		Funding of tax exemption for business entities		
		Expansion of funding under the "Economy of simple things" (EST) program	EST (2nd year)	EST (3rd year) until December 2022
		Financing working capital of MSMEs	Financing working capital of MSMEs (2nd year)	
	KGZ	Anti-Crisis Plan	Anti-Crisis Plan (2nd year)	MSMEs support program
	TAJ	Country Preparedness Plan and Response Plan (PPRP)[9]	PPRP (2nd year)	PPRP (3rd year)
	UZB	Anti-crisis measures to support business (Resolution and Decrees)	Anti-crisis measures to support business (2nd year)	
4. Emergency measures on MSMEs in response to the Russian invasion of Ukraine	ARM			
	AZE[10]			
	GEO			Export Assistance Program
	KAZ			Allocating the necessary preferential volume of fuel and lubricants to farmers for ensuring the sowing campaign
				Anticrisis Command Center established
	KGZ			NBKR anti-crisis program
	TAJ			Government anti-crisis program[11]
	UZB			

ARM = Armenia, AZE = Azerbaijan, COVID-19 = coronavirus disease, GEO = Georgia, KAZ = Kazakhstan, KGZ = Kyrgyz Republic, TAJ = Tajikistan, UZB = Uzbekistan.

1 The time range for the 2nd wave came from the speech of former vice-minister and chief sanitary doctor of the Ministry of Healthcare, January 2021 (https://24.kz/ru/news/social/item/448688-v-kazakhstane-nachalas-vtoraya-volna-covid-19-minzdrav).
2 Operational Headquarter (Task Force) was established under the Cabinet of Ministers of the Republic of Azerbaijan in February 2020.
3 Special Quarantine Regime includes various social restriction measures that were relaxed and then reinstated throughout March 2020–August 2022.
4 After the 2nd strict containment measures there were less stringent quarantine measures but with mandatory wearing of masks, PCR testing, and vaccination requirements.
5 More than 12,500 people quarantined, including foreign arrivals as of 5 May 2020 (World Health Organizations Statistics).
6 Border with the People's Republic of China (PRC) closed in January 2020, with citizens of five high-risk countries prohibited from entering Tajikistan from February 2020. All flights suspended and the airport closed from 20 March 2020.
7 Travelers entering Tajikistan were confined to state facilities for 14 days upon arrival.
8 Quarantine requirement at government-designated site. Travelers arriving in Tajikistan may be screened and may be required to have a PCR test on arrival. Travelers entering Tajikistan are not subject to quarantine if tested negative (as of August 2022). If tested positive, travelers will be required to self-isolate.
9 The government approved the Tajikistan COVID-19 Country Preparedness Plan and Response Plan on 19 March 2020.
10 There are no emergency measures (action plans, programs, or other documents) adopted by the government (as of August 2022).
11 The Government of Tajikistan adopted an anti-crisis program in March 2022. On 16 March 2022, the President signed a decree imposing a moratorium on checking activities of entrepreneurs from April 2022 until January 2023.

Southeast Asia Update

1. MSME Development

MSMEs in Southeast Asia, 2010–2021

	Percentage share	*Compound annual growth*
• **Number of MSMEs to total enterprises**	***97.7%***	***+0.1%***
• **MSME employees to total employees**	***67.3%***	***+0.6%***
• **MSME contribution to national GDP**	***40.8%***	***+1.7%***
• **MSME exports to total export value***	***19.2%***	***-4.6%***

GDP = gross domestic product; MSME = micro, small, and medium-sized enterprise.
* 2010–2020. Reporting countries only.
Source: ADB Asia SME Monitor 2022 database.

2. Access to Finance

MSMEs in Southeast Asia, 2010–2021

Bank credit	*Percentage share*	*Compound annual growth*
• **MSME loans to national GDP**	***14.2%***	***-3.3%***
• **MSME loans to total bank loans**	***15.6%***	***-0.6%***
• **MSME NPLs to total MSME loans**	***4.4%***	***-0.9%***
Nonbank and market-based finance		
• **NBFI financing to national GDP**	***4.2%***	***+13.4%***
• **NBFI financing to total bank loans**	***8.8%***	***+2.5%***
• **NBFI NPF to total financing**	***1.2%***	***+7.3%***
• **MSME market capitalization to GDP***	***7.8%***	***+0.6%***

GDP = gross domestic product; MSME = micro, small, and medium-sized enterprise; NBFI = nonbank finance institution; NPF = nonperforming financing; NPL = nonperforming loan.
* 2012–2021. Data include primary market data if MSME market data is unavailable; average percentage of available markets. Reporting countries only.
Source: ADB Asia SME Monitor 2022 database.

South Asia Update

1. MSME Development

MSMEs in South Asia, 2020

	Percentage share	*Compound annual growth*
• **Number of MSMEs to total enterprises**	***99.6%***	***n/a,***
• **MSME employees to total employees**	***76.6%***	***n/a,***
• **MSME contribution to national GDP***	***16.3%***	***-6.9%***
• **MSME exports to total export value****	***47.0%***	***+2.2%***

FY = fiscal year; GDP = gross domestic product; MSME = micro, small, and medium-sized enterprise.

* For Bangladesh, contribution of cottage and small enterprises to manufacturing gross value added. For Pakistan, only small manufacturing contribution to GDP.

** Only India for FY2013–FY2020.

Reporting countries only. Data based on latest available data until 2020.

Source: ADB Asia SME Monitor 2022 database.

2. Access to Finance

MSMEs in South Asia, 2015–2021

Bank credit	*Percentage share*	*Compound annual growth*
• **MSME loans to national GDP***	***6.2%***	***-2.3%***
• **MSME loans to total bank loans**	***15.2%***	***+3.6%***
• **MSME NPLs to total MSME loans**	***13.5%***	***-6.0%***
Nonbank and market-based finance		
• **NBFI financing to national GDP**	***3.5%***	***+9.0%***
• **NBFI financing to total bank loans**	***6.4%***	***-1.5%***
• **NBFI NPF to total financing**	***6.6%***	***+15.0%***
• **MSME market capitalization to GDP***	***18.2%***	***-4.2%***

GDP = gross domestic product; MSME = micro, small, and medium-sized enterprise; NBFI = nonbank finance institution; NPF = nonperforming financing; NPL = nonperforming loan.

* 2015–2020. For the share of market capitalization to GDP, data include primary market data if MSME market data is unavailable; average percentage of available markets. Reporting countries only.

Source: ADB Asia SME Monitor 2022 database.

References: Data for SME Development Index—Central and West Asia

A. MSME Related Variables—Central and West Asia, 2007–2021

Country	Variables	Unit	Obs	Mean	Median	S.D.	Min	Max
Armenia	Number of MSMEs		14	80,930	75,817	22,562	59,267	132,923
	Number of employees		13	311,647	280,927	101,816	168,185	471,394
	Nonbank loans outstanding	$ million	15	371	367	182	126	725
	Microfinance loans	$ million	15	351	341	183	118	708
	Market capitalization	$ million	15	211	176	82	105	362
	GDP of MSMEs	$ million	14	3,685	3,547	585	2,833	4,851
	Bank loans default	$ million	15	144	154	100	15	360
	Bank loans outstanding	$ million	15	4,377	4,206	2,048	1,344	7,702
Azerbaijan	Number of MSMEs		14	201,733	194,334	48,713	135,353	316,370
	Number of employees		14	187,419	112,006	105,928	90,182	348,723
	Nonbank loans outstanding	$ million	15	326	239	180	174	775
	Microfinance loans	$ million	10	278	192	163	134	596
	GDP of MSMEs	$ million	14	2,854	2,287	1,986	562	6,513
	Bank loans default	$ million	15	707	792	318	125	1,220
	Bank loans outstanding	$ million	15	10,981	9,799	4,516	5,694	22,346
Georgia	Number of MSMEs		14	77,426	64,626	37,780	32,961	129,268
	Number of employees		14	376,016	389,050	94,526	226,064	491,668
	Nonbank loans outstanding	$ million	15	354	409	210	35	744
	Microfinance loans	$ million	15	314	365	170	34	555
	Market capitalization	$ million	10	859	745	257	552	1,280
	MSME imports	$ million	7	1,745	1,830	193	1,426	1,980
	GDP of MSMEs	$ million	14	3,301	3,708	1,219	1,378	4,760
	MSME exports	$ million	7	626	616	85	520	765
	Bank loans default	$ million	15	509	500	185	76	971
	Bank loans outstanding	$ million	15	6,904	6,672	3,451	2,816	13,898
Kazakhstan	Number of MSMEs		15	1,000,171	926,844	279,139	643,376	1,431,647
	Number of employees		15	2,842,480	2,810,962	500,462	2,121,198	3,472,606
	Nonbank loans outstanding	$ million	15	1,634	276	2,147	121	5,825
	Microfinance loans	$ million	7	733	590	522	190	1,721
	GDP of MSMEs	$ million	15	37,308	37,756	13,482	11,393	57,578
	Bank loans default	$ million	14	8,660	3,384	7,699	1,414	22,862
	Bank loans outstanding	$ million	15	50,111	51,468	13,558	34,075	73,274

Country	Variables	Unit	Obs	Mean	Median	S.D.	Min	Max
Kyrgyz Republic	Number of MSMEs		15	13,720	13,505	2,171	9,852	17,050
	Number of employees		15	91,773	89,400	5,928	86,000	107,800
	Nonbank loans outstanding	$ million	15	237	223	78	139	379
	Microfinance loans	$ million	15	201	193	71	110	328
	Market capitalization	$ million	15	233	165	149	72	602
	MSME imports	$ million	15	2,645	2,837	634	1,139	3,398
	GDP of MSMEs	$ million	15	2,692	2,697	641	1,702	3,814
	MSME exports	$ million	15	585	578	123	386	773
	Bank loans default	$ million	14	65	56	36	18	147
	Bank loans outstanding	$ million	15	1,235	1,238	583	560	2,144
Tajikistan	Number of MSMEs		13	35,374	31,144	10,356	25,451	55,750
	Nonbank loans outstanding		15	288	219	164	99	647
	Nonbank loans default	$ million	15	9	7	7	1	27
	Microfinance loans	$ million	15	186	195	88	44	357
	Market capitalization	$ million	14	542	449	474	64	1,647
	GDP of MSMEs	$ million	14	4,087	4,492	1,051	2,227	5,344
	Bank loans default	$ million	12	244	236	152	52	556
	Bank loans outstanding	$ million	15	986	908	247	702	1,465
Uzbekistan	Number of MSMEs		15	229,432	196,014	99,178	129,211	462,834
	Number of employees		15	9,471,127	9,865,700	909,244	7,743,100	10,541,500
	Nonbank loans outstanding	$ million	8	60	46	34	24	123
	Nonbank loans default	$ million	8	6	3	6	1	18
	Microfinance loans	$ million	8	47	33	33	16	107
	Market capitalization	$ million	12	3,345	2,896	1,227	1,825	5,512
	MSME imports	$ million	15	6,740	5,677	3,707	2,155	14,972
	GDP of MSMEs	$ million	9	35,457	34,543	8,922	22,724	48,167
	MSME exports	$ million	15	2,843	3,101	1,006	1,334	4,715
	Bank loans default	$ million	8	435	268	476	121	1,566
	Bank loans outstanding	$ million	8	19,523	18,176	6,338	13,276	30,116

GDP = gross domestic product; MSME = micro, small, and medium-sized enterprise.

Source: Calculated based on the Asia SME Monitor 2022 database.

B. Missing Data—Central and West Asia

Country	Variables	2007	2008	2009	2010	2011	2012	2013	2014	2015	2016	2017	2018	2019	2020	2021
Armenia	Number of MSMEs															NA
	Number of employees							NA								NA
	Nonbank loans outstanding															
	Microfinance loans															
	Market capitalization															
	GDP of MSMEs															NA
	Bank loans default															
	Bank loans outstanding															
Azerbaijan	Number of MSMEs															NA
	Number of employees															NA
	Nonbank loans outstanding															
	Microfinance loans	NA	NA	NA	NA	NA										
	GDP of MSMEs															NA
	Bank loans default															
	Bank loans outstanding															
Georgia	Number of MSMEs															NA
	Number of employees															NA
	Nonbank loans outstanding															
	Microfinance loans															
	Market capitalization	NA	NA	NA	NA	NA										
	MSME imports	NA	NA	NA	NA	NA	NA	NA	NA							
	GDP of MSMEs															NA
	MSME exports	NA	NA	NA	NA	NA	NA	NA	NA							
	Bank loans default															
	Bank loans outstanding															
Kazakhstan	Number of MSMEs															
	Number of employees															
	Nonbank loans outstanding															
	Microfinance loans	NA	NA	NA	NA	NA	NA	NA	NA							
	GDP of MSMEs															
	Bank loans default	NA														
	Bank loans outstanding															
Kyrgyz Republic	Number of MSMEs															
	Number of employees															
	Nonbank loans outstanding															
	Microfinance loans															
	Market capitalization															
	MSME imports															
	GDP of MSMEs															
	MSME exports															
	Bank loans default	NA														
	Bank loans outstanding															

Country	Variables	2007	2008	2009	2010	2011	2012	2013	2014	2015	2016	2017	2018	2019	2020	2021
Tajikistan	Number of MSMEs	NA			NA											
	Nonbank loans outstanding															
	Nonbank loans default															
	Microfinance loans															
	Market capitalization	NA														
	GDP of MSMEs	NA														
	Bank loans default	NA	NA	NA												
	Bank loans outstanding															
Uzbekistan	Number of MSMEs															
	Number of employees															
	Nonbank loans outstanding	NA	NA	NA	NA	NA	NA	NA								
	Nonbank loans default	NA	NA	NA	NA	NA	NA	NA								
	Microfinance loans	NA	NA	NA	NA	NA	NA	NA								
	Market capitalization	NA	NA	NA												
	MSME imports															
	GDP of MSMEs	NA	NA	NA	NA	NA	NA									
	MSME exports															
	Bank loans default	NA	NA	NA	NA	NA	NA	NA								
	Bank loans outstanding	NA	NA	NA	NA	NA	NA	NA								

GDP = gross domestic product; MSME = micro, small, and medium-sized enterprise; NA = not applicable.

Source: Calculated based on the Asia SME Monitor 2022 database.

Country Review
Armenia

Overview

After contracting by 7.2% in 2020, the economy started to recover in 2021 as gross domestic product (GDP) grew by 5.7% to $13.9 billion (per capita GDP of $4,670). It was driven by private and public consumption with smaller contributions from investment and net exports. On the production side, services rebounded from a sharp drop in 2020, with industry and construction contributing moderately to growth. Agriculture contracted for the sixth straight year, reflecting unreformed land markets, uneven access to irrigation, and low resilience to changing weather patterns.

Following a period of relatively low inflation, prices picked up in late 2020 and remained elevated in 2021. Inflation peaked at 9.6% in November before moderating to 6.5% in February 2022. Food inflation peaked at 17% in November 2021, driving two-thirds of overall inflation. In response, the Central Bank of Armenia increased the policy rate nine times by a cumulative 500 basis points between December 2020 and March 2022.

The poverty rate, defined as the population living on less than $5.5 a day, was 44.7%, according to 2019 data, with life expectancy at birth 75.1 years, according to 2018 data.[14] The population was 3 million in 2021.[15] Armenia stands out for its inexpensive but highly skilled labor force, solid yet rather liberal banking regulations, favorable investment laws, and its free economic zones.[16] The labor force participation rate was around 52% in 2021.[17]

Prudent macroeconomic policies, including more-effective inflation targeting, robust fiscal control, sound financial sector oversight, and pro-competition reforms, helped Armenia weather the twin crises in 2020 with a lower-than-expected increase in poverty. Domestic political uncertainty has subsided since the snap mid-2021 elections. Yet, Armenia still faces significant structural constraints, such as weak connectivity, closed borders, and no economic relations with two of its four neighbors (Azerbaijan and Türkiye). There are challenges related to high unemployment, skill mismatches, and firm competitiveness.

Micro, small, and medium-sized enterprises (MSMEs) represented 99.8% of all enterprises in 2020, with its share growing since 2017. MSMEs employed 232,955 workers or 68.7% of the workforce in 2020, with 65% of MSME employees concentrated in the capital city Yerevan. MSME contributed over 26.3% to gross value added (GVA) in 2020. By sector, one-third of MSMEs were in wholesale and retail trade, one-fifth were engaged in services, with almost a quarter in manufacturing.

14 WDI, Macro Poverty Outlook, and official data. a/ Most recent value (2020), 2011 PPPs; b/ WDI for School enrollment (2020); Life expectancy (2019).

15 Armenia Overview: Development news, research, data, World Bank.

16 World Bank. Doing Business 2020 - Armenia Economy Profile. https://www.doingbusiness.org/content/dam/doingBusiness/country/a/armenia/ARM.pdf.

17 The percentage of the population aged 15 and up (modeled ILO estimate), according to World Bank Development Indicators, compiled from officially recognized sources.

Market access is generally favorable domestically but limited internationally. According to the World Bank's Ease of Doing Business report in 2020, Armenia was ranked 47th among 190 countries, with business registration being the highest-ranked component (10th out of 190), due to the introduction of a one-stop-shop agency for registering businesses and simplified legislation. The government is proactive on legislative initiatives that provide better access to international markets. Still, of the country's four borders, two—Azerbaijan and Türkiye—remain closed, limiting international trade and market access. Technology is being adopted rapidly by Armenian firms, but mostly in the capital.

The financial sector is dominated by the banking sector, with 17 commercial banks regulated by the central bank. The percentage of nonperforming loans (NPLs) in 2020 rose to 4.5% from 3.4% in 2019, but fell to 1.9% in 2021 as the recovery took hold. MSME loans amounted to AMD1,170 billion (31.6% of total bank credit) in 2021. MSME NPLs decreased from 5.3% in 2020 to 2.1% in 2021.

There are 134 nonbank finance institutions (NBFIs) operating as of end-2021, of which over one-third are microfinance institutions (MFIs). They are mostly universal credit organizations helping MSMEs finance their working capital. Capital markets, as well as venture capital and angel networks, have yet to be well used for financing MSMEs. There is no dedicated MSME market, but is currently under consideration. Digital financial services are developing rapidly under a new law that promotes noncash payments and limits the volume of cash transactions. Financial education initiatives are led by the central bank in corporation with bilateral and multilateral donors.

In 2000, the government established a legal framework to support MSMEs using preferential tax measures for businesses, including MSMEs (turnover tax). There is no comprehensive national financial inclusion strategy, but several financial assistance programs have been implemented in cooperation with international organizations. To mitigate the damage caused by the coronavirus disease (COVID-19) pandemic, the government undertook over 25 measures, with two (third and 19th)—worth around AMD10 billion—specifically targeting MSMEs.

1. Impact of the Global Economy on MSMEs

COVID-19 Impact

As in most countries, Armenia's economy suffered from the pandemic. In January–August 2020, the initial COVID-19 outbreak cut 5.3% off of GDP (average, year on year).[18] The government responded with more than 25 special measures and support mechanisms for MSMEs with costing AMD113 billion ($225 million). The measures—called "Packages of Measures to Alleviate the Consequences of COVID-19 Outbreak"—covered business, health, social issues, and education, among others. Much more is needed to ensure that recovery moves quickly to return the economy to its pre-COVID-19 level, while building resilience against future external shocks.

The number of registered employees decreased during the pandemic across many sectors. Beginning in March 2020, employment began to fall countrywide (Figure 2.1). By the end of the second quarter, government measures began to take effect and new jobs were added. In the third quarter, employment fell due to global economic stagnation, offsetting some of the benefits due to government support. By the fourth quarter, however, stricter lockdowns, restrictions led to another wave of business suspensions or closings and thus more job losses, particularly those in hospitality, tourism, and entertainment.

[18] Statistical Committee of the Republic of Armenia. https://armstat.am/file/article/sv_03_21a_112.pdf.

Figure 2.1: Employment in Armenia, 2020

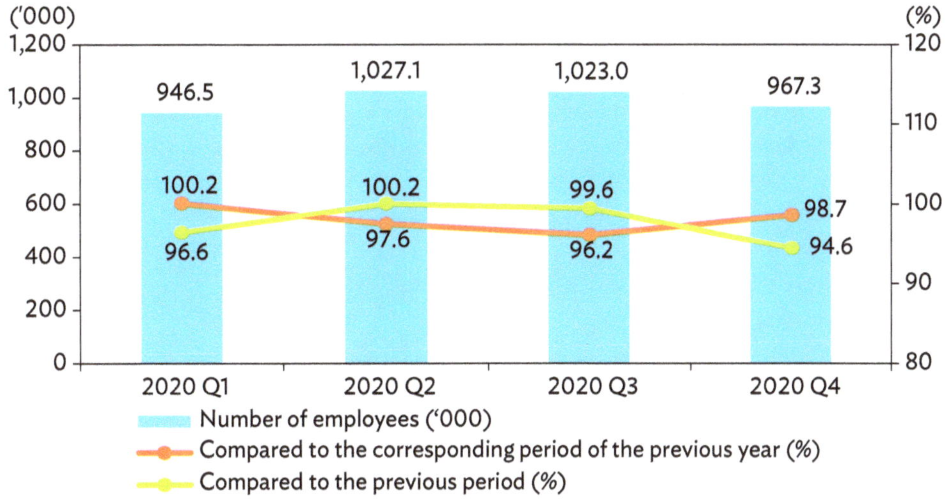

Source: Statistical Committee of the Republic of Armenia. https://www.armstat.am/am/?nid=12&id=17003.

The pandemic hurt trade as well. In January 2020, monthly exports were more than 20% above the January 2019 level, the result of economic growth.[19] By March-April, however, the state of emergency and lockdowns resulted in a drop in exports. As restrictions loosened, export volumes began to return to their 2019 levels.[20] Imports fell 8%–12% in January–May 2020, compared to 2019 (footnote 20).

While many types of assistance measures were approved, their effect was not always as planned. Several measures to ensure access to finance appeared insufficient to maintain normal economic development during the pandemic. And aside from the impact of COVID-19, the border area conflict had a serious impact on the economy. The twin crises show that, despite the desire to concentrate on long-term measures that have positive development impact, less-effective short-term solutions were dictated by events, delaying longer-term economic objectives.

According to the United Nations Economic Commission for Europe (UNECE) to COVID-19 Report, "the Government of Armenia limited trade restrictions to the minimum; implemented expansionary monetary and fiscal policies, and launched sweeping relief measures, such as credit schemes and tax deferrals, to curb unemployment and support the hardest-hit sectors."[21] Yet, capacity shortfalls aggravated the impact of lockdowns, compounded by Armenia's limited access to international transport routes and its underdeveloped transport system. This disrupted supply chains, slowing the recovery and development prospects. MSMEs also suffered as a consequence.

Impact of the Russian Invasion of Ukraine

The Russian invasion of Ukraine and international sanctions imposed on the Russian Federation have affected economies worldwide. In particular, developing countries in Europe and Central Asia are feeling the brunt—for example, together the Russian Federation and Ukraine account for more than 75% of wheat imports in Central Asia and the South Caucasus. The invasion led to a sharp increase in global oil prices, and limited natural gas exports to Europe threaten just as temperatures begin to drop. The region's economy is forecast to contract by 4.1% in 2022,

19 https://bit.ly/39Po2Mk
20 Statistical Committee of the Republic of Armenia. https://armstat.am/am/?nid=12&id=10003.
21 The Impact of COVID-19 on trade and structural transformation in Armenia. Evidence from UNECE's survey of MSMEs. The assessment was carried out over the period May-August 2020 among over 370 enterprises from across the country.

compared with the pre-invasion forecast of 3% growth, as the economic shock from the invasion compounds the ongoing impact of the pandemic. This would be the second contraction in as many years, and twice as large as the pandemic-induced contraction in 2020 (World Bank 2022).[22]

The Russian Federation is Armenia's the largest trading partner. In 2021, exports to the Russian Federation made up 28% of Armenian exports, while imports from the Russian Federation were 33% of total imports (Figure 2.2).[23] Almost 50% of individual remittances to Armenia come from the Russian Federation, given the latter's large Armenian community and the flow of seasonal migrant workers to the Russian Federation. Also, about 40% of foreign direct investment (FDI) comes from Russia—recently, there has been a shift from the power sector to telecommunications and metal extraction. Five of the 10 largest tax-paying companies in Armenia operate with Russian capital—they have created thousands of jobs and pay billions of drams to the state budget.[24] The services sector was also affected, as 40% of the revenues generated from tourism in 2021 derived from Russian tourists.

The initial impact of the invasion on the Armenian financial system was felt on the foreign exchange market. In February 2022, the *dram* began to depreciate against the US dollar, reaching AMD518.28 to USD1 on 11 March, about 7.5% down from 25 February.[25] Tides have changed since—from 1 January to 20 June 2022, the dram appreciated against the dollar by 11.4%.[26]

Figure 2.2: Armenia's Financial Inflows from the Russian Federation—Selected Sectors
(% share of Armenian total)

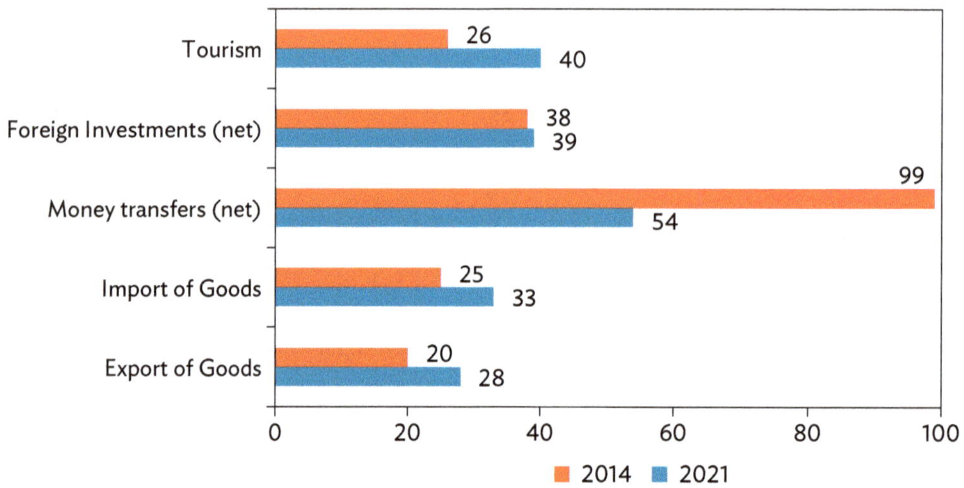

Source: Statistical Committee of the Republic of Armenia. https://armstat.am/am/.

[22] World Bank. 2022. Russian Invasion to Shrink Ukraine Economy by 45 Percent this Year. Press Release. 10 April. https://www.worldbank.org/en/news/press-release/2022/04/10/russian-invasion-to-shrink-ukraine-economy-by-45-percent-this-year.

[23] Imports include energy, metals, construction materials, sugar, wheat, dairy products, chicken meat, oil, and consumer goods—with Armenia's food self-sufficiency at 56%, the uninterrupted supply of essential goods imported from the Russian Federation (wheat, oil, buckwheat, among others) is of strategic importance.

[24] EVN Report. https://evnreport.com/arm/economy-arm/economic-implications-of-the-russian-ukrainian-war/.

[25] https://bit.ly/3NDyJzg

[26] https://www.msn.com/en-xl

In addition, the *dram's* dependence on the Russian *ruble* is increasing dramatically. For example, during the first half of May–June 2022, the equivalent of AMD135 billion in *US dollars* and *euros* were transferred out of the Armenian market—or 13.5% of Armenia's foreign currency reserves in just 1.5 months.

The vast majority of inward remittances were sourced from the Russian Federation until 2019. But beginning in 2020, remittances from other countries—particularly the US—began to rapidly increase, reaching 46% in July 2022.[27] This was due to a decrease in income from the Russian Federation during the pandemic and restrictions on Armenian seasonal migrant workers, along with an increase in remittances from Armenian residents in the US.

Russian Federation banks disconnected from SWIFT will not be able to serve their clients when making international transfers. Thus, Armenian banks established with Russian capital may fall under these restrictions. But there are commercial banks in Armenia that can freely perform their transactions with non-sanctioned Russian commercial banks. Several Russian companies and individuals have opened accounts in banks operating in Armenia, benefiting the banking system.

The structure of tourists arriving in Armenia have also changed in recent years, with the proportion Russian tourists doubling (41.5% in 2021 compared to 26.2% in 2014). Restrictions on Russian travel to Europe has also helped Armenian tourism.

Ukraine is also important to the Armenian economy, especially in trade, investments, remittances, and tourism. In 2021, it accounted for 2.7% ($143.1 million) of Armenia's imports and 0.9% ($25.6 million) of exports.[28]

There is no specific assessment of the impact of the Russian invasion of Ukraine on MSMEs as of end-August 2022. Still, the impact is expected to be significant, particularly in a prolonged invasion.

2. MSME Development

- In 2011, the MSME definition was harmonized with the European Union's—MSMEs are firms with fewer than 250 employees. In 2020, there were 83,032 MSMEs, or 99.8% of all Armenian enterprises (94.6% were microenterprises).
- In 2020, MSMEs employed 232,955 people, or 68.7% of the labor force. Wholesale and retail trade held the largest share (31.6%). Most worked in the capital, Yerevan (65%).
- MSMEs contributed 26.3% to gross value added in 2020, with the largest share (34.2%) in wholesale and retail trade.
- International market access for MSMEs is difficult as two Armenian borders remain closed—Azerbaijan and Türkiye. In 2018, 6.1% of MSMEs exported their products, while 25.5% imported goods and services.
- E-commerce continues to develop rapidly due to growing internet availability and credit card use. Consumers use a variety of platforms—all local and international MSMEs—for making online purchases.
- There are many private organizations and associations helping MSMEs advocate and lobby their positions with government and help them access finance.

[27] Statistical Committee of the Republic of Armenia. https://armstat.am/am/.
[28] UN Comtrade Database. https://comtrade.un.org/data/ (accessed 31 August 2022).

Scale of MSMEs

In 2011, Armenia's definition of MSMEs was harmonized with that by the European Union (EU), which classifies MSMEs for administrative purposes according to the Law on State Support for Small and Medium Entrepreneurship of 2000 (5 December) (Table 2.1). It defines microenterprises as firms with 0-9 employees and annual revenues and assets (book value) not exceeding AMD100 million ($200,000). Small enterprises have 10–49 employees and revenues/assets less than AMD500 million ($1 million). Medium-sized enterprises are firms employing 50–249 people with revenues less than AMD1.5 billion ($3 million) and assets not exceeding AMD1 billion ($2 million).

Most MSMEs are labor-intensive. In 2020, they employed 68.7% of the labor force (232,955 workers). They concentrate primarily on small markets, where economies of scale do not offer major benefits, or where there are no larger corporations, in particular, sectors considered "other services"—such as real estate; professional, scientific, and technical work; administrative and support services; computer repair; and personal and household goods.[29] They include manufacturing (C as classified under the Nomenclature of Economic Activities); construction (F); wholesale and retail trade, repair of motor vehicles and motorcycles (G); transportation and storage (H); accommodation and food service activities (I); and other professional services. The national statistical report analyzes these areas, but excludes small-scale agriculture as the National Statistics Bureau considers it "household" work with no legal (firm) status.

Historically, MSMEs dominate in terms of number of enterprises. They continue to grow. Since 2017, an official statistical bulletin—Small and Medium Enterprises in the Republic of Armenia—has been published. Although there are data available starting from 2004 (collected by international organizations and the Small and Medium Entrepreneurship Development National Center [SME DNC], among others), the data sets are not comparable due to methodological differences. The analysis here uses the data set from 2017 onward.

There were 83,032 MSMEs in 2020, up from 59,467 MSMEs in 2017—a compound annual growth rate (CAGR) of 8.7% (Figure 2.3A and Table 2.2). They grew moderately since 2018 (up 1.2% over 2017), dropping slightly in 2019 (-1.1%), with pandemic-affected 2020 increasing (1.1%) due to the government's State Support Program for Small and Medium Entrepreneurship.

The vast majority of MSMEs are microenterprises, with many simply self-employed individuals. The government has been working to formalize unregistered MSMEs by attacking corruption among tax authorities, promoting equal enforcement of existing regulations, and simplifying MSME taxes.[30]

In 2020, the majority of MSMEs were in wholesale and retail trade (58.1%), followed by other services (16.2%), manufacturing (12.7%), accommodation and food services (6.1%), transportation and storage (4.0%), and construction (2.6%) (Figure 2.3B).

Because of its large consumer market, MSMEs are concentrated in Yerevan, with about half located there (42,889 or 51.5%) (Figure 2.3C). The next largest is the Kotayk region (adjacent to the capital) with 7,127 MSMEs and Ararat (5,267 firms). The government hopes more will spread to other regions as it pursues more inclusive development.

29 Small and Medium Entrepreneurship in the Republic of Armenia, Statistical Bulletin as of January 2021. Structure of turnover follows Nomenclature of Economic Activities sections and sales, 2020.

30 Orbitax. Amendments to Armenia's Tax Code Signed into Law — Orbitax Tax News & Alerts. https://www.orbitax.com/news/archive.php/Amendments-to-Armenia-Tax-Co-38713.

Figure 2.3: Number of MSMEs

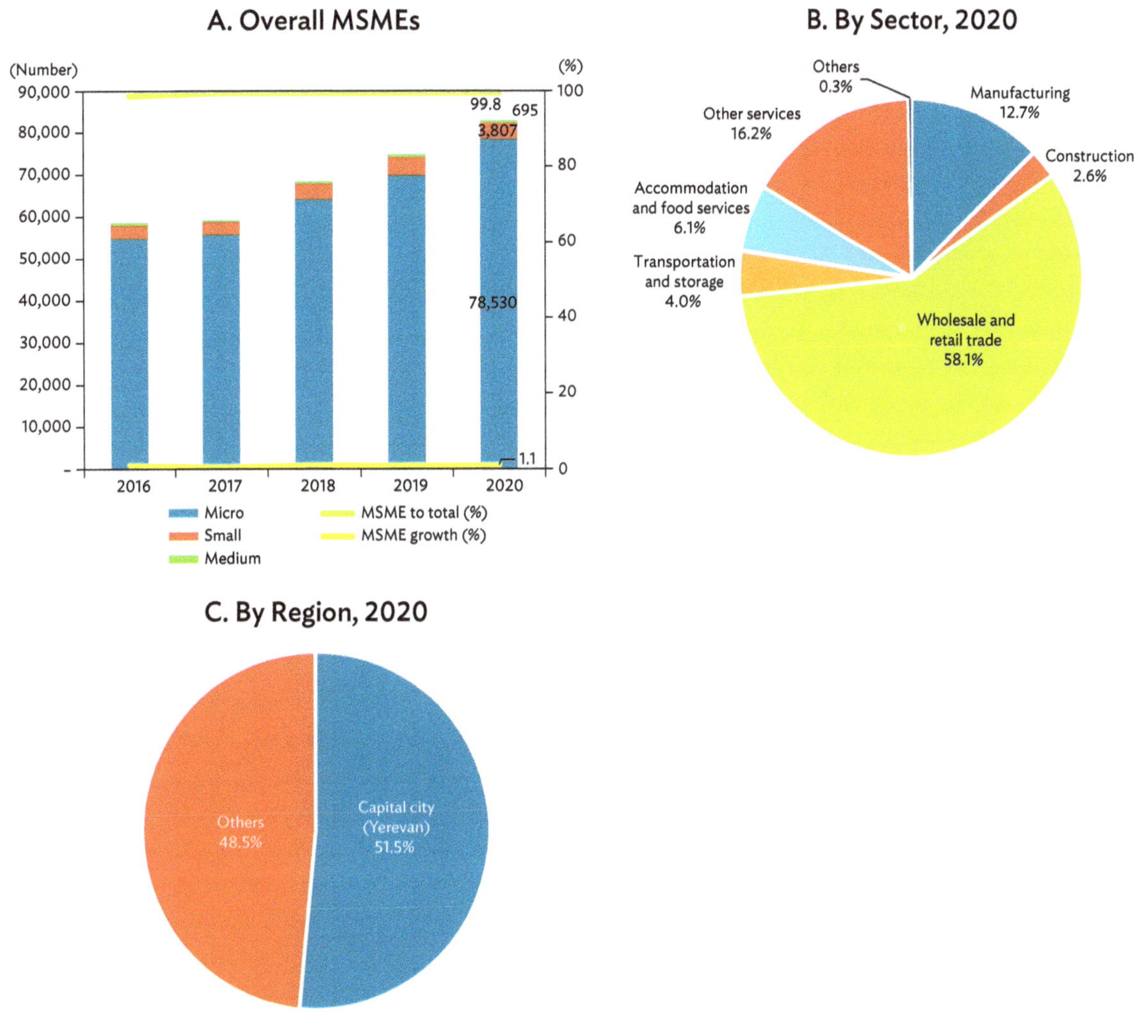

MSME = micro, small, and medium-sized enterprise.

Source: ADB Asia SME Monitor 2022 database. Data from the Statistical Committee of the Republic of Armenia.

Employment

In 2020, there were 232,955 MSME employees, or 68.7% of the country's labor force (338,998)—an 8.5% CAGR from 2017 (168,185 or 66.2%) (Figure 2.4A and Table 2.2). Due to the pandemic, however, the number of MSME workers decreased by 6.0% in 2020 from 2019.

Also, due to some changes in legislation, many informal entrepreneurs registered their business to become legal entities. The reforms now allow microentrepreneurs to enter the pension system by paying a modest AMD1,000 monthly fee—around $2. The vast majority of microenterprises are individual entrepreneurs (no salaried employees).

Wholesale and retail trade employs the largest number of MSME workers (31.6% in 2020), followed by other services (22.4%), manufacturing (22.2%), accommodation and food services (9.9%), construction (8.9%), and transportation and storage (3.9%) (Figure 2.4B). After the late 1991 collapse of the Soviet Union, Armenia went through a period of deindustrialization. During the Soviet era, many small towns were built around factories or clusters of factories. These dissipated after the collapse. Retail trade and services have the fewest barriers of entry and require little capital investment. Thus, many MSMEs turned to these sectors.

Agriculture is a primary employer given limited job opportunities elsewhere; and thus signals underemployment. Widening disparities in wealth and income have led to a socioeconomic gap between urban and rural areas. Poverty remains a serious problem—estimates show 33% of the rural population live at or below the national poverty line (2019), up from 30% in 2015. Social hardships and insufficient employment opportunities, particularly in the regions, have led to out-migration.[31]

Figure 2.4: Employment by MSMEs

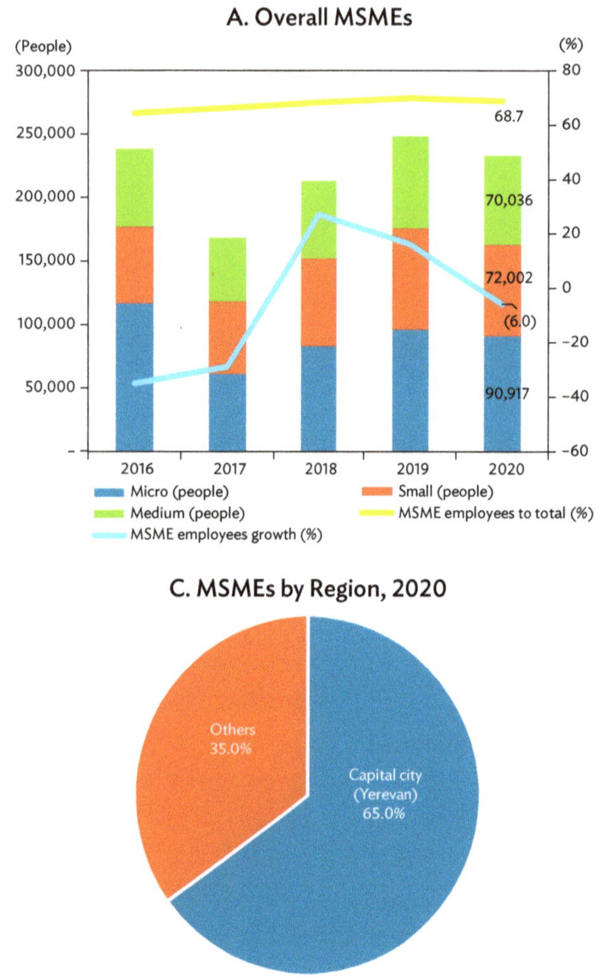

MSME = micro, small, and medium-sized enterprise.

Source: ADB Asia SME Monitor 2022 database. Data from the Statistical Committee of the Republic of Armenia.

31 From a technical needs assessment of entrepreneurial households and micro/smallholder farmers, prepared by Civitta Armenia, March 2022.

In terms of rural economic development, farm and rural nonfarm incomes are low and labor underutilized. While over 22% of the labor force works in agriculture, its share of GDP remains at 11.2% due to low productivity (2020).[32]

In 2020, around 65% of MSME employees were concentrated in Yerevan (Figure 2.4C).

Business Productivity

The official statistical bulletin provides data on MSME contributions to gross value added (GVA). In 2020, MSMEs added AMD1.6 trillion, a 4.3% increase (CAGR) from 2017 (AMD1.4 trillion)—it fell 4.9% in 2020 as the pandemic struck) (Figure 2.5A and Table 2.2). Still, the share of MSMEs to total GVA was 26.3% in 2020.[33] However, labor productivity of MSMEs has been declining—it fell from AMD8.2 million in 2017 to AMD7.0 million in 2020.

MSMEs in wholesale and retail trade held the highest MSME GVA share in 2020 (34.2%), followed by manufacturing (24.1%), other services (19.6%), construction (12.8%), transportation and storage (5.8%), and accommodation and food services (2.7%) (Figure 2.5B).

Figure 2.5: MSME Contribution to Gross Value Added

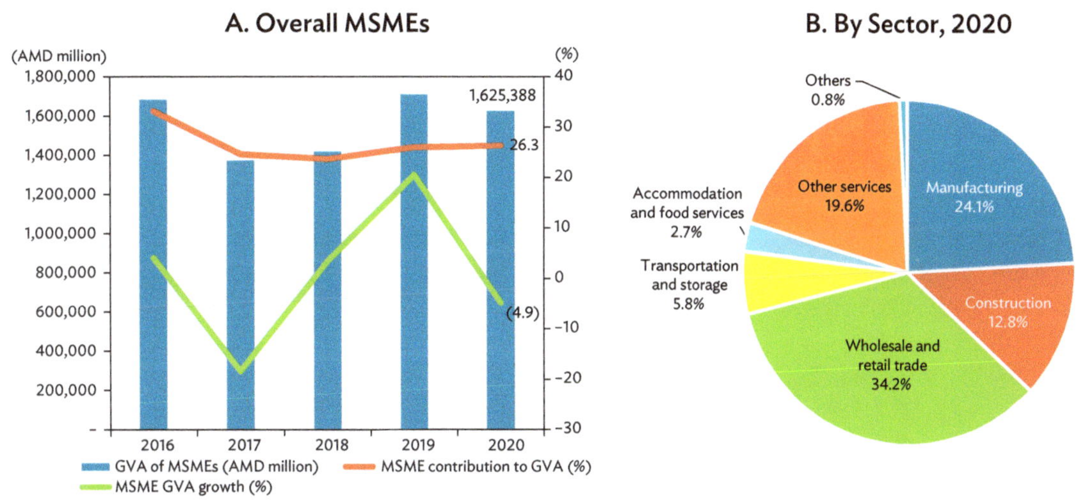

GVA = gross value added; MSME = micro, small, and medium-sized enterprise.

Source: ADB Asia SME Monitor 2022 database. Data from the Statistical Committee of the Republic of Armenia.

Market Access

Armenia was ranked 47th among the 190 economies surveyed in the World Bank's Ease of Doing Business Index 2020 (down from 41st in 2019).[34] Its highest ranking (10 out of 190) was received in "Starting Business," which measures the number of procedures, time, cost, and paid-in minimum capital requirement for a small- to medium-sized limited liability company to start up and formally operate in thew economy's largest business city.[35] It takes

32 Statistical Committee of the Republic of Armenia. Link: https://www.armstat.am/en/

33 Official statistics do not provide data on GDP by business size, or the share of MSME output to overall GDP.

34 World Bank, Ease of doing business index for Armenia [ICBUSEASEXQARM], retrieved from FRED, Federal Reserve Bank of St. Louis; https://fred.stlouisfed.org/series/ICBUSEASEXQARM, May 25, 2022.

35 World Bank. Doing Business 2020 - Armenia Economy Profile. https://www.doingbusiness.org/content/dam/doingBusiness/country/a/armenia/ARM.pdf.

up to 2 days to register a business at the one-stop shop agency (launched in 2011) within the State Register of the Legal Entities of the Ministry of Justice of the Republic of Armenia. There are two documents required for registration (company's charter and the decision of owners to open a new limited liability company). Companies and individual entrepreneurs can obtain the name reservation, business registration, and tax identification number (TIN) at a single location and at the same time. An application for a taxpayer identification number is filed at the one-stop shop with the TIN issued by the State Registrar.[36]

Since January 2019, value-added tax (VAT) registration can be done a year after a business meets the AMD58.4 million revenue threshold. Starting January 2018, entrepreneurs could opt for voluntary VAT registration when applying for company registration. The legal time limit is 2 working days, but the application can be approved in 1 day if the firm uses the templates provided by the Ministry of Justice. Electronic registration is available at www.e-register.am/am, but is not frequently used due to an e-signature requirement which adds cost and time.[37]

According to a 2019 Armenian Business Coalition survey, MSMEs find the Armenian market too small for operating efficiently.[38] Some 22% of those surveyed said that the market is too small to run any business, while 20% think the market is not large enough. About 25% said the market is sufficiently large to run a business, with 23% saying it is not a concern. One in 10 MSMEs found it difficult to answer. As for foreign markets, 43% of those surveyed said their business was purely domestic, 14% said foreign markets held some potential, while 28% said their business was ready to enter foreign markets (15% found it difficult to answer the question). Of MSMEs surveyed, 32% said they would need support to enter foreign markets, while 11% said that they urgently needed support.

In 2020, Armenia ranked 132nd worldwide in GDP, 128th in exports, 136th in imports, 112th in GDP per capita, and 77th in complexity, according to the Economic Complexity Index. Armenia trades primarily with Europe, the Middle East, and the Commonwealth of Independent States (CIS). With only two open trade borders—with Iran and Georgia—most of its gas, oil, and other supplies must transit these two countries. Top exports include (i) copper ore ($739 million), (ii) gold ($464 million), (iii) rolled tobacco ($241 million), (iv) hard liquor ($202 million), and (v) ferroalloys ($149 million).

Exports go mostly to Russia ($671 million), Switzerland ($594 million), the People's Republic of China (PRC) ($323 million), Iraq ($164 million), and Bulgaria ($151 million). The fastest-growing export markets in 2019–2020 were the United Arab Emirates ($38.4 million, up 65.7%), the PRC ($103 million, 46.8%), and India ($144 million, 3.4%). The fastest-growing import markets were Belarus ($11.9 million, 22.3%), Germany ($12 million, 5.5%), and the Russian Federation ($32.4 million, 2.2%).

Armenia has diplomatic relations with more than 180 countries. It is a member of the Eurasian Economic Union (EEU), the Council of Europe, and the Collective Security Treaty Organization. Armenia has joined more than 40 international organizations—including the United Nations, the Council of Europe, the Asian Development Bank (ADB), the CIS, the World Trade Organization (WTO), World Customs Organization, the Organization of the Black Sea Economic Cooperation, and La Francophonie. It is a member of the Collective Security Treaty Organization military alliance, and participates in NATO's Partnership for Peace Programme.[39]

---

36 World Bank Group, Doing Business 2020, Armenia: ARM.pdf (doingbusiness.org)

37 World Bank Group, Doing Business 2020, Armenia: ARM.pdf (doingbusiness.org)

38 ՓՄՁ ՈԼՈՐՏԻ ԳՆԱՀԱՏՄԱՆ ՀԵՏԱԶՈՏՈՒԹՅՈՒՆ ՀԱՅԱՍՏԱՆՈՒՄ (armla.am) Armenian SME Sector Assessment Research, The Armenian Business Association.

39 OECD. 2019. *Roadmap for a National Strategy for Financial Education in Armenia*. https://www.oecd.org/financial/education/Armenia-Roadmap-National-Strategy-for-Financial-Education-EN.pdf.

In general, there are six categories of MSMEs working internationally: (i) direct exporting; (ii) direct importing; (iii) investing abroad; (iv) subcontracting to foreign firms; (v) having foreign subcontractors; and (vi) cooperating with foreign enterprises under joint ventures, non-equity alliances, licensing, and franchising.[40] Armenia's foreign trade policy aims to attract FDI and liberalize trade regimes. As a WTO member since 2003, Armenia has worked to reduce the customs burden and reform the existing customs system. Examples include an online customs declaration system (e-declaration), a traffic light system for inspection of goods entering the country, and reducing the number of import documents required from nine to three.

Armenia offers a liberal trade and investment regime, with its average applied tariff—2.7%—one of the lowest among WTO members. It benefits from Most Favored Nation treatment with all WTO members. In turn, it grants Most Favored Nation status and National Treatment to foreign investors. Its customs policy is administered by the State Revenue Committee, with procedures defined by the Customs Code of the Republic of Armenia, among other legal documents, which comply with rules defined by WTO agreements and other international treaties. Armenia is a member of the World Customs Organization and uses a harmonized tariff classification system under the 1984 International Convention on Harmonized Commodity Description and Coding System. Only two tariff rates apply on imports —0% or 10%. The 0% tariff applies to imports of capital goods, with the 10% tariff on imports of consumer products. All imports pay 20% VAT, and alcoholic beverages, tobacco products, and fuels also pay an excise tax. There are no tariff quotas, licensing requirements, or quantitative restrictions on imports. Nor does Armenia maintain a system of minimum import prices. It does not tax exports and does not have any export licensing requirements. There are neither export duties nor VAT obligations or limitations.[41]

Entering the EEU market has become easier: paperwork has been reduced, procedures have been simplified, and electronic reporting has been introduced. Procedures are easy for non-animal and plant-based products. For those of animal or vegetable origin, a permit is issued by the Food Safety Inspection Body. The main obstacle to MSME exports remains product quality. Proper quality assurance for entering international markets requires export insurance—in case of nonpayment. With insurance premiums high and nonpayment rates low, many exporters avoid buying insurance.

Official statistics of MSME exports and imports is available until 2009. As of end-2009, MSME export amounted to AMD45.7 billion or 17.7% of total export value, while MSME import was AMD316.7 billion or 26.2% of total import value; international trade of MSMEs remained limited with decreasing trend (Figure 2.6 and Table 2.2). According to research by Ameria Management Advisors, in 2018, more than one-quarter of MSMEs (25.5%) were importers, over four times more than those exporting (6.1%).[42]

[40] B. Z. Yuhua. 2015. SME Internationalization and Measurement. *APEC Policy Support Unit Policy Brief No. 12.*

[41] Import and Export Regime (investinarmenia.am)

[42] Ameria Management Advisory. Small and Medium Business in Armenia. http://ameriaadvisory.am/wp-content/uploads/2020/08/SME-conference-presentation-ENG-1.pdf.

Figure 2.6: MSME Exports and Imports

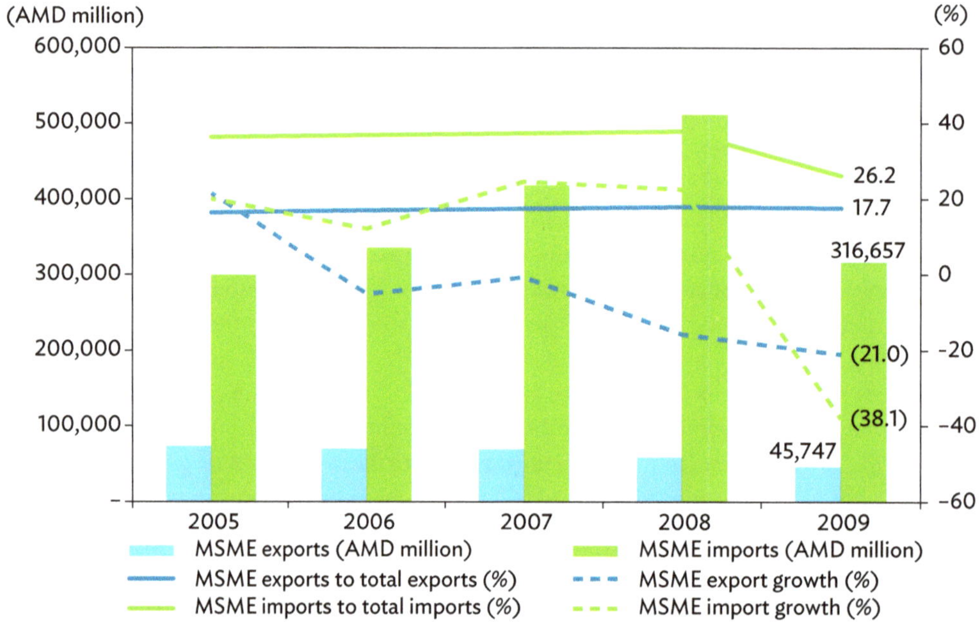

MSME = micro, small, and medium-sized enterprise.

Source: ADB Asia SME Monitor 2022 database. Data from the Statistical Committee of the Republic of Armenia.

Box 2.1: Overcoming the COVID-19 Impact—Arcolad Chocolate Company

Arcolad Chocolate Company was founded in October 2004 by Emil Harutyunyan and three family members and friends—with an initial investment of about $180,000. A year later it produced its first chocolate. Initially the company sold several kilos of chocolate a day and had a staff of just six people. As of May 2022, the company has over 30 employees helping produce around 300 kilograms of chocolate a day. It is a successful case of how to produce high quality chocolate (over 50% of cocoa content), and exports to more than 20 countries.

The company deviated from the old Soviet model by using value chains to their fullest—importing cocoa, producing chocolate, and marketing abroad. It imports industrial chocolate—semi-finished cocoa-based raw-material, also known as couvertures—from Poland, Belgium, and Switzerland. This is refined into the final product and packaged in-house.

Arcolad found its success through trial and error, losing money for the first 5 years. The company began strengthening its domestic market during 2006–2011. In 2007, a new partner joined to help the company regain market presence. In 2009, Arcolad showed a profit for the first time (only 5% of production was exported). The rise of tourism helped a lot, with the majority of sales (around 60%) in duty-free shops and other tourism-related sales outlets (gift shops and hotel shops, among others). The Armenian diaspora and tourists are the primary target market, along with local corporate customers who use Arcolad products as signature Armenian gifts to their international partners.

continued on next page

Box 2.1 *continued*

During 2010–2018, the company saw rapid growth. It built a factory (opened in 2018) using a government-supported low-interest loan, grant financing (AMD23 million), and company resources. The company began exporting to several countries on a one-time-basis, while stable export markets were established with Belarus, the Russian Federation, France, Kazakhstan, and Lithuania.

The impact of the coronavirus disease (COVID-19) was devastating. Due to the pandemic, the major sales partner of the company—the duty-free shop—stopped operations for several months, restarting on a very limited scale, resulting in 55% drop in sales. For a long time corporate sales completely stopped, as did sales through the Ararat Cognac Factory Museum shop, another important outlet. According to Harutyunyan's estimates, another 25% decrease in sales was due to the 44-day war between Armenia and Azerbaijan in 2020.

Losses were mitigated thanks to the 3rd Government Emergency Programs—the company received a AMD45 million loan (around $100,000)—which allowed Arcolad to keep most of its staff (only three people were laid off, with 36 working currently). The company also received a program loan from the World Bank to further expand its operations. The company expects rapid growth during the recovery as tourism picks up. Arcolad is currently working to expand its operations further, establishing dedicated trade partnerships in the Russian Federation and the United States.

Source: Interview with co-founder of Arcolad, Emil Harutyunyan, May 2022.

Technology and Innovation

The pattern is similar across much of the developing world. While Armenia has roughly 14 fixed lines per 100 people, it boasts 118 mobile phones per 100 population (Figure 2.7). Both fixed line and mobile cellular services are reliable across the capital, Yerevan, and in major cities and towns. Cellular coverage is also available in most rural areas.[43] Internet penetration was 68.2% in January 2021, with the number of internet users up by 5.6% between January 2020 and 2021. Over 60% of the population are actively using social media (20% more than in January 2020). There are one-quarter more mobile subscriptions (127.4%) than there are people in Armenia.[44]

According to the World Economic Forum Global Competitiveness Index (Pillar 3, ICT Adoption, Rank), Armenia ranked 59th out of 139 countries (2019).[45] The Global Innovation Index 2020 ranked the country 61st of the 131 economies surveyed, ahead of neighbor Georgia (63rd) and EEU partner Belarus (64th).[46]

E-commerce continues to develop rapidly, given growing internet use, use of credit cards, and rising household incomes. Consumers shop online for a variety of goods—household appliances, consumer electronics, apparel, cosmetics, toys, meals, and groceries. More business-to-business (B2B) transactions are driving e-commerce growth, particularly as more sectors digitize operations.

Local consumers use a variety of platforms—many of them MSMEs—both domestic and international. While giants Amazon and eBay are widely used by local consumers—with the help of shipping consolidators—many homegrown platforms serve local consumers, using e-payment systems for grocery delivery, ride hailing, and for a wide range of consumer goods.

43 CIA World Fact Book: Armenia - The World Factbook (cia.gov)

44 DIGITAL 2021: Armenia by DataReportal.com.

45 World Bank. GovData360. https://govdata360.worldbank.org/indicators/h432dbf3b?country=ARM&indicator=41526&viz=line_chart&years=2017,2019&compareBy=region (accessed 31 August 2022).

46 Cornell University, INSEAD, and WIPO. 2020. Global Innovation Index 2020: Who Will Finance Innovation? Geneva: World Intellectual Property Organization.

Figure 2.7: Fixed Broadband Subscriptions in Armenia, 2015–2020 (per 100 population)

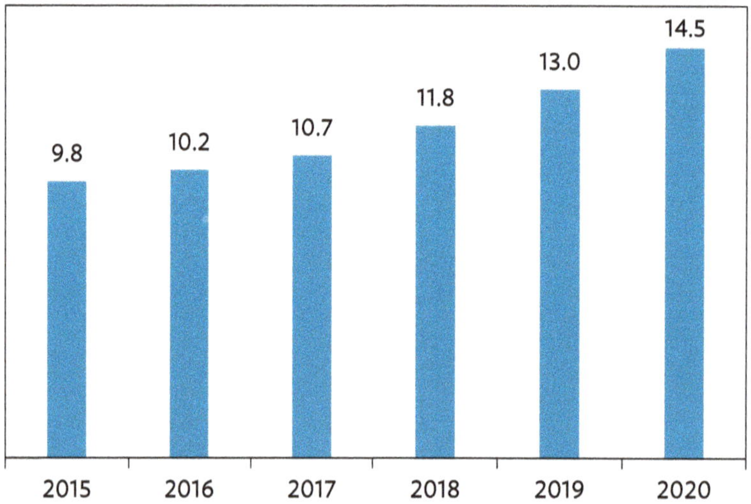

Source: International Telecommunication Union (ITU) World Telecommunication/ICT Indicators Database.

There are two main competitors for delivering retail purchases from the US, the PRC, the Russian Federation, France, Belarus, Germany, and the United Kingdom—Globbing and Onex. There are other smaller international delivery companies as well. Aside from remote online and terminal-based payment systems, innovative contactless locker boxes are available across the country, as well as 24/7 customer service when problems arise. This drove "HayPost" CJSC—the official national postal operator—to modernize operations and introduce its own international and local delivery service "BerBer."

According to the central bank, Visa and Mastercard are the most commonly used cards for international transactions. Yet, despite the growth in the use of payment cards, cash upon delivery remains the dominant method of paying for domestic e-commerce transactions.

Several laws regulate key aspects of Armenian e-commerce—including the Civil Code, Law on Trade and Services, Law on Consumer Rights Protection, and Law on Implementation of Cashier Machines. The government is formulating new legislation focused specifically on e-commerce. It is also working on legislation for collecting VAT on international online transactions—in line with discussions under the Organisation for Economic Co-operation and Development (OECD). The country's tax authority wants an environment conducive for e-service providers under other jurisdictions to self-declare and pay VAT on services provided. It has not indicated whether it is considering levying a digital services tax.

While email for business communication is becoming increasingly common, the telephone remains the primary method of business communication—though that is changing as most companies have their own website. Online banking is becoming increasingly popular. The increased use of electronic payment systems, whether through traditional cards, mobile money, or digital platforms, is helping boost the effectiveness of e-commerce, and thus drive its growth.[47]

[47] International Trade Administration. Armenia - Country Commercial Guide. https://www.trade.gov/country-commercial-guides/armenia-ecommerce.

Box 2.2: Creating Digital Infrastructure in Armenia—Mer Soft LLC

Mer Soft LLC is an Armenian software development company, founded in 2008 by a team of enthusiastic information technology (IT) specialists. It aims to equip businesses with software that simplifies complex, time-consuming tasks, to lower customer costs and motivate entrepreneurs to use IT management solutions, customized to their specific needs.

Mer Soft works with customers to automate business processes in fields such as human resource management, customer relationship management, warehouse and trade (distribution and production), navigation, healthcare, pharmacies, dental clinics, restaurants, and hotels. The company develops and implements solutions to automate business processes, regardless of their complexity or uniqueness.

Initially the staff had just five employees. As of April 2022, it had 25 software engineers and project managers working on enterprise resource planning, specialists on quality assurance, and a technical support team of eight specialists. As a medium-sized enterprise with 73 employees, Mer Soft works together with customers to create, install, and support business management and automation. Over 1,000 Armenian businesses in various fields are using Mer Soft solutions.

In 2018, Mer Soft launched a new project—bonee digital solution (https://en.bonee.net). It is a platform for creating digital menus and catalogs, and organizing online orders using innovative technologies. Bonee uses a research and development team of 15 specialists and a marketing and sales support team of five specialists. As of April 2022, bonee had more than 500 clients worldwide, mostly from the United States (US), the Middle East, and the Commonwealth of Independent States. There were 3 million average monthly page views with an average 100,000-150,000 monthly users. Bonee recently launched a multivendor online food ordering platform Ofoodo (https://ofoodo.com) with Georgia.

Mer Soft also works on custom software development and outsource projects with a team of 20 developers, project managers, and quality assurance specialists. One of the projects involves developing a document flow system for six US counties in collaboration with Granicus, a US-based software development company.

As one Mer Soft co-founder says, “There are many IT companies that write code, however, those who do that with passion and love are quite few. We believe in the integrity of a programmer—when the customer has a fully functional product for many years”.

Source: Interview with Mer Soft chief executive officer Tigran Manukyan, April 2022.

Networking and Support

There are several nongovernment organizations (NGOs) and associations working with MSMEs to advocate and lobby with associations and the government for their interests. They also offer training and consulting, business incubation, improve MSME access to finance, and help establish and develop business promotion activities. They also work on business incubators and link crowdfunding organizations to MSMEs, both domestically and internationally.

SME Cooperation Association (SMECA). With almost 30 members (as of April 2022), SMECA—an NGO—offers three main services, it (i) lobbies to protect MSME rights in government relations; (ii) networks SMECA members to boost cooperation; and (iii) provides consulting, training, and incubation through the Increased Resilience of Syrian Armenians and Host Population (IRIS) business incubator foundation—co-founded by SMECA and the "Armenian Caritas" benevolent NGO. It is a member of various MSME development councils working in partnership with public authorities (government and parliament).

IRIS. The business incubator was founded in 2020 in response to the Syrian crisis and is funded by the EU Regional Trust Fund, the Austrian Development Cooperation, and the Austrian Red Cross. The IRIS business incubator emphasizes project diversity: (i) more than 50% of business incubator resident-entrepreneurs are from Armenia regions; (ii) 63% of IRIS business incubator residents are women; (iii) it has extensive experience working with target groups in need of economic integration, including repatriates, migrants, refugees, other displaced persons, and persons with disabilities (32% of IRIS residents are from these target groups); (iv) supports tourism and hospitality services, creative industries, agriculture, food processing and production, among others; and (v) provides business incubation, mentorship programs, and office space.

National Center for Innovation and Entrepreneurship. Its special program for MSMEs (i) raises awareness of investors about business opportunities, (ii) creates favorable conditions for setting up a business, (iii) provides ways the state can support business, (iv) creates working mechanisms business and government to interact, and (v) introduces Armenian businesses to new markets.

The Chamber of Commerce and Industry. The chamber aims to improve the business climate, promote exports and investments, and support MSMEs to promote economic growth. It promotes competitive manufacturing to enhance export potential, assists cooperation between business organizations, acts as a bridge between business organization and the government, and offers business development and incubation services to startups, among others.

Business Angels Network of Armenia (BANA). The NGO has 45 members including Armenia's diaspora, foreigners, and local investors. It is financed through annual membership fees paid by business angel members. It also receives a percentage of the syndicated investments it arranges. As of April 2022, BANA helped establish 22 deals, predominantly IT businesses, with typical investments of $100,000–$500,000. It works with MSME infrastructure development by (i) running a startup incubator, (ii) introducing the SAP SE startup B2B accelerator;[48] and (iii) introducing an early-stage working product incubator. For MSMEs, BANA advises the government on drafting relevant laws. It also offers advice and provides documents to the Ministry of Higher Technology, helping it establish a national venture fund (in process for the past 2 years).[49]

---

48 SAP SE is a German multinational software reseller based in Walldorf, Baden-Württemberg, Germany. It develops enterprise software to manage business operations and customer relations.

49 Interview with Sona Veziryan and Grigor Hovhannisyan of BANA, March 2022.

3. Access to Finance

- The MSME credit market remains relatively small, with loans outstanding in 2021 of AMD1.2 trillion, or 31.6% of total bank loans and 16.8% of GDP. Wholesale and retail trade ranked highest (28.4%), and concentrated in the capital Yerevan (75.9%).
- The government implements MSME development mainly through Enterprise Armenia. Public credit guarantees target startups (up to the full loan amount) and existing MSMEs (up to 70% as partial guarantees). In 2020, 30 MSMEs received AMD128 million in guarantees.
- Among nonbank finance institutions, 34% are microfinance institutions, mostly universal credit organizations. In 2021, the microfinance credit market remained small (4.3% of GDP).
- Digital financial services are developing rapidly under a law that aims to promote noncash payments and limit cash transactions.
- The stock market does not have a dedicated MSME board. Currently, the "C Platform" under the Armenia Securities Exchange can be tapped by MSMEs. The government and stock exchange plan to start a MSME board.
- ACRA Credit Reporting is a private sector credit bureau. There are several financial education programs for MSMEs organized by the central bank and private sector associations. The National Strategy for Financial Education, established in 2012, is a benchmark policy framework for financial education.

Bank Credit

As of end-2021, there were 17 private commercial banks and one state-owned development financial institution—the Development and Investment Corporation of Armenia (DICA) (Table 2.3). Despite the pandemic, the credit market increased by 14.5% from AMD3,911 billion in 2019 to AMD3,698 billion in 2020. However, growth of loans outstanding slowed mostly due to deepening uncertainties and reduced opportunities for attracting new financial resources.

Commercial banks have succeeded in mitigating credit risks by offering credit reviews, credit holidays, and restructuring existing credits, even as the NPL ratio rose to 4.5% in 2020 from 3.4% in 2019. The central bank says this was mostly due to the increase in consumer NPLs rather than business NPLs. In 2021, loans outstanding fell by 5.5% compared with 2020, due to the economic slowdown, low credit demand, and currency movements. However, the NPL ratio in 2021 dropped to 1.9% in 2021 after controlling for currency revaluation.

Official statistics on MSME loans are available after 2020. The MSME credit market remains small, with AMD1.2 trillion in MSME loans outstanding in 2021—31.6% of bank lending and 16.8% of GDP—down by 0.9% from 2020 (Figure 2.8A and Table 2.3). MSME NPLs decreased sharply, with the NPL ratio dropping from 5.3% in 2020 to 2.1% in 2021.

In 2021, the largest amount of MSME credit went to wholesale and retail trade (28.4%), followed by construction (15.2%), manufacturing (14.3%), other services (11.9%), agriculture (6.6%), and transportation and communication (3.8%) (Figure 2.8B). "Others (unclassified)" accounted for 19.9%. The overall structure of MSME lending by industry has been stable and resembles the overall industry structure. By region, 75.9% of MSME loans in 2021 went to firms located in the capital Yerevan, with the remaining 24.1% for those in other regions (Figure 2.8C). Long-term loans (more than 5 year maturity) accounted for 53.9% of MSME lending in 2021, followed by medium-term (1–5 year tenors) loans (39.6%) and short-term (less than 1 year) loans (6.5%) (Figure 2.8D).

Figure 2.8: MSME Loans

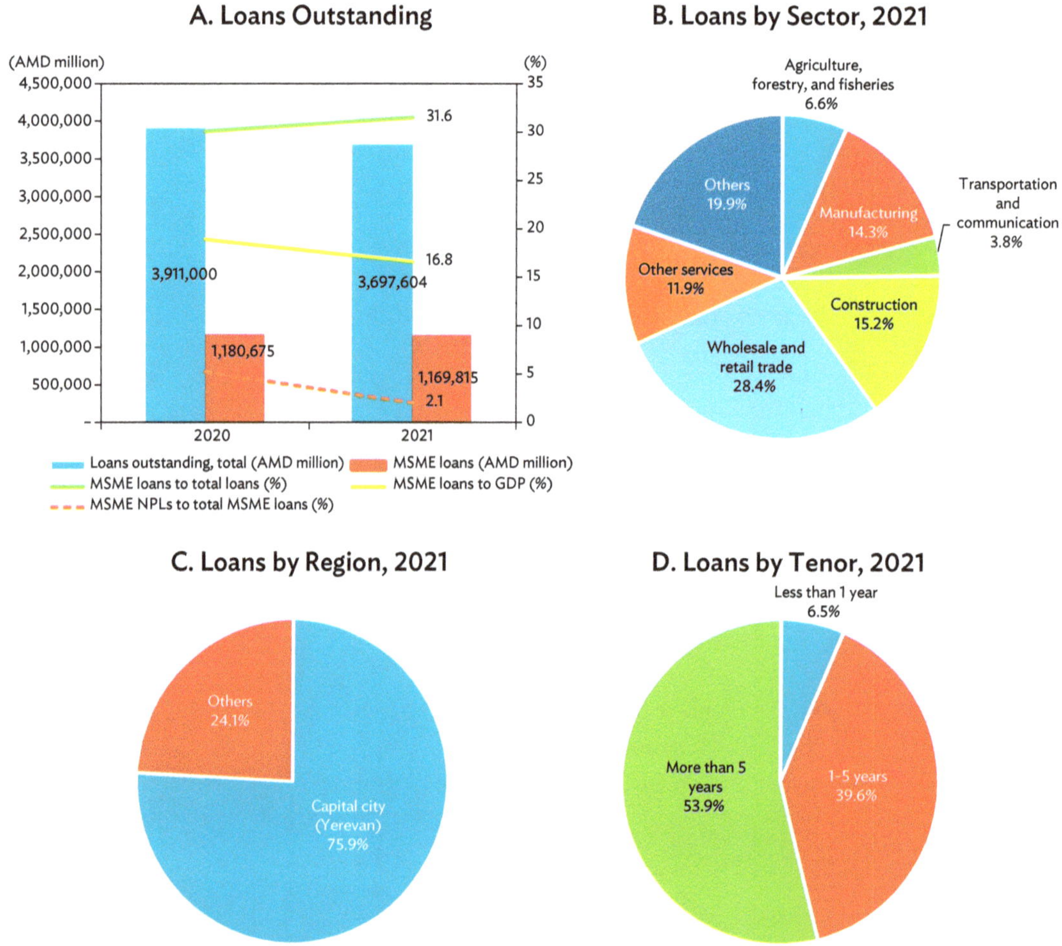

GDP = gross domestic product; MSME = micro, small, and medium-sized enterprise, NPL = nonperforming loan.

Source: ADB Asia SME Monitor 2022 database. Data from Central Bank of Armenia.

Several programs to finance MSMEs were launched to relieve the effects of the pandemic. In 2021, the Black Sea Trade and Development Bank created a $6 million MSME loan facility to DICA for domestic MSME capital expenditures and working capital loans. BSTDB's MSME lending exceeds EUR100 million. Government measures to help MSMEs withstand the pandemic were channeled through DICA, commercial banks, and credit organizations with no interest for the first 2 years and 12% for the third year.

Public Financing and Guarantees

Part of the government's financial support to MSMEs comes via the public credit guarantee program for both startups and businesses operating for over 20 years. The state programs are mainly intended for MSMEs operating in regions for more even distribution.

From 2000, the government used MSME development programs mostly through the Small and Medium Entrepreneurship Development National Center (SME DNC) Foundation. SME DNC was responsible for providing loan guarantees through its partner financial institutions. In 2019, SME DNC was renamed "Enterprise Armenia" Investment Support Center. It remains the government's main channel for boosting MSME growth.

Enterprise Armenia targets startups and mature MSMEs. For startups, the guarantee covers the entire loan amount; for existing businesses, the guarantee covers up to 70%. Enterprise Armenia also applies different strategies to boost access to finance in rural areas, specifically targeting border regions.

Enterprise Armenia's startup program provides consulting marketing, management, access to new markets, as well as offering credit guarantees. The terms for startup loan guarantees include (i) maximum amount of AMD5 million, (ii) maximum maturity of 5 years, (iii) maximum grace period of 6 months, with (iv) no collateral requirements.

As of end-2020, there were AMD136.9 million in guarantees approved for 30 MSMEs with AMD128.1 million disbursed (Figure 2.9 and Table 2.4).

Figure 2.9: Credit Guarantees

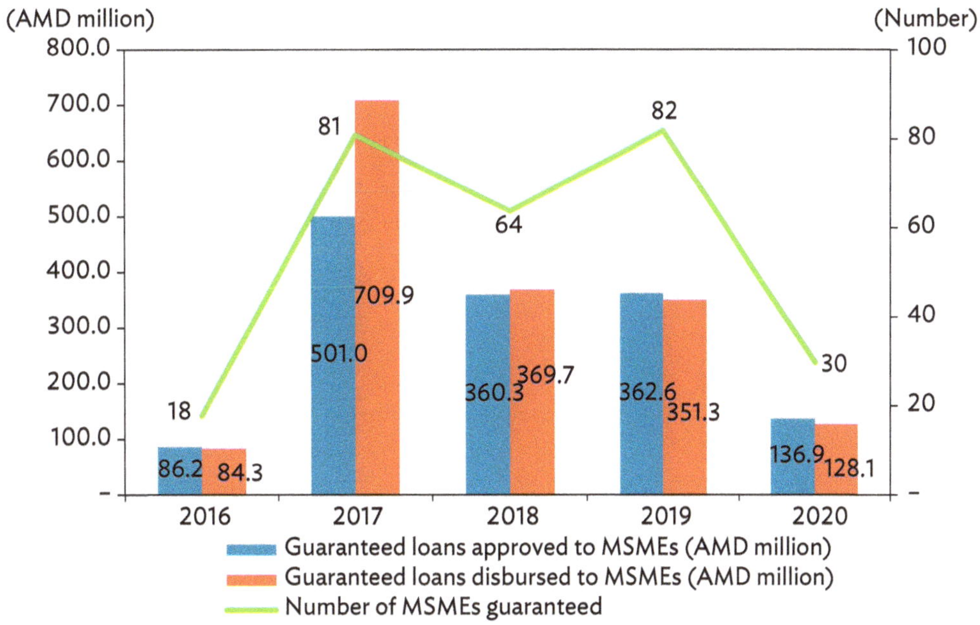

MSME = micro, small, and medium-sized enterprise.

Note: In 2020, the government allocated AMD9 billion and AMD560 million specifically to MSMEs as part of its pandemic response.

Source: ADB Asia SME Monitor 2022 database. Data from the Ministry of Economy of the Republic of Armenia.

Nonbank Financing

The financial sector is complex. It consists of banks, foreign bank representatives, liquidation organizations, credit organizations, a credit bureau, insurance companies, an insurance bureau, insurance brokers, insurance agents, pawnshops (*lombards*), currency dealers and exchange agencies, payment organizations, investment companies, investment and pension fund managers, a securities market, and investment funds. All are licensed and supervised by the Central Bank of Armenia. As of end-2021, there were 134 nonbank finance institutions (NBFIs)—46 were microfinance institutions (MFIs), 81 pawnshops, and 7 insurance companies (Figure 2.10A and Table 2.5).

NBFI assets have been growing since 2009. The average value of assets to GDP increased from 0.5% in 2009 to 1.6% in 2020.

MFIs comprise 34% of NBFIs, mainly universal credit organizations.[50] They increased from nine in 2004 to 32 in 2010. For 2010–2015, the number of MFIs did not change. Since 2016, it increased once again, reaching 46 in 2021. MFI loans outstanding amounted to AMD339 billion in 2019 (pre-pandemic)—48.8% growth from 2018—before dropping by 10.4% to AMD304 billion in 2020; it decreased only slightly to AMD303 billion in 2021 (Figure 2.10B). The MFI credit market remains small at 4.3% of GDP.

"Other services" received the most MFI loans in 2021 (36.3%), followed by agriculture (22.8%), manufacturing (7.4%), wholesale and retail trade (6.9%), construction (2.6%), and transportation and communication (1.3%). Those unclassified consumed 22.7% (Figure 2.10C).

Pawnshops partly support MSME working capital. Financing outstanding from pawnshops was AMD6.7 billion in 2021; after contracting 15.6% in 2020 and 2.7% in 2021 (Figure 2.10D).

The Union of Credit Organizations, an NGO, was founded in 2008 by six universal credit organizations. It was renamed the Association of Credit Organizations in 2021. It helps develop the financial and credit system through more complete and effective use of credit organizations. Its main objectives include (i) participating in discussions on financial initiatives; (ii) legislative initiatives in the financial sector, credit industry, and making recommendations on strategic credit issues; (iii) conducting economic analysis and research on the credit industry; (iv) organizing training programs for members and staff; and (v) introducing business rules, credit transparency, and financial literacy among customers. As of August 2022, 27 credit organizations were association members.[51]

50 The Law on Credit Organizations of Armenia, 2002. ՎԱՐԿԱՅԻՆ ԿԱԶՄԱԿԵՐՊՈՒԹՅՈՒՆՆԵՐԻ ՄԱՍԻՆ (irtek.am).

51 Interview with Mr. Khoren Kerobyan, the Executive Director of the ACORA NGO, Acora, dated on 10 August 2022.

Figure 2.10: Nonbank Finance

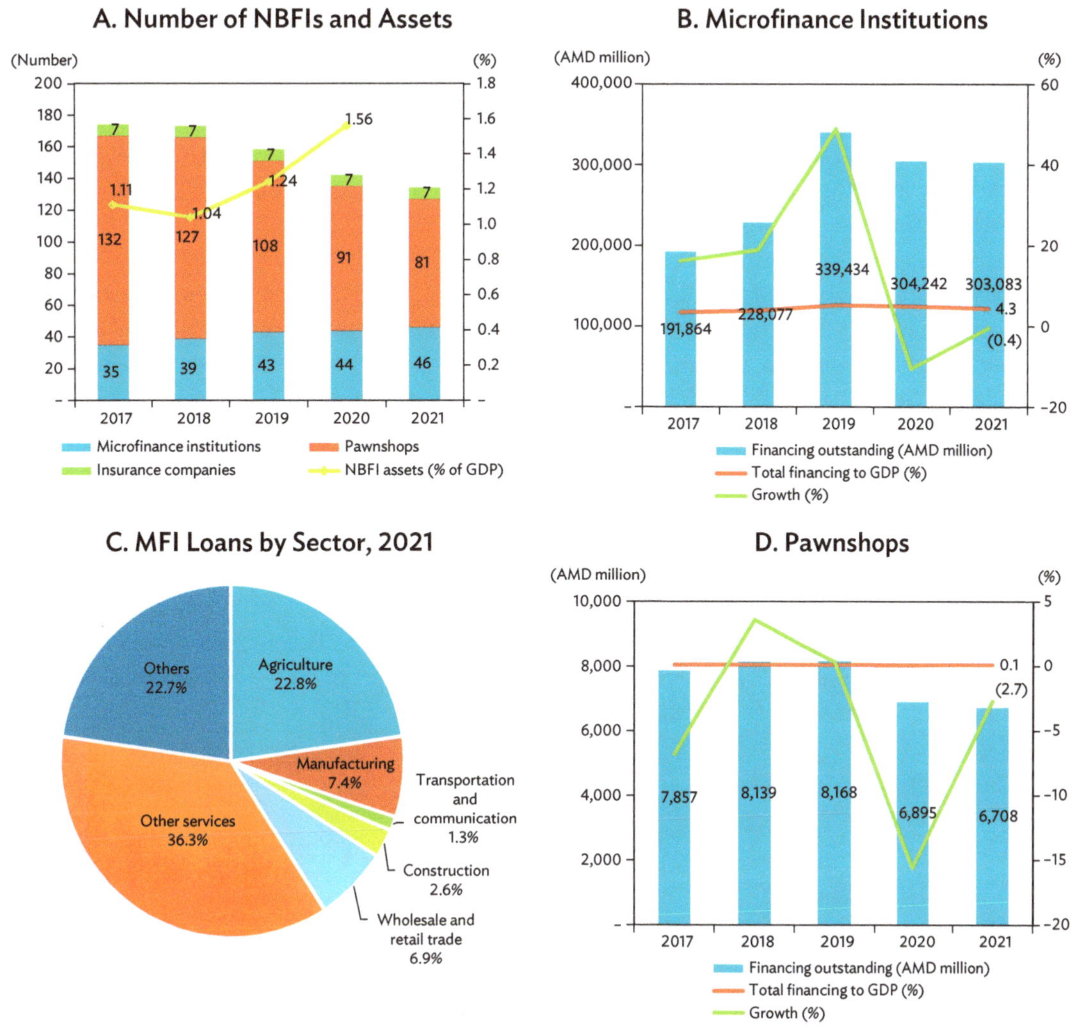

GDP = gross domestic product, MFI = microfinance institution, NBFI = nonbank financial institution.

Source: ADB Asia SME Monitor 2022 database. Data from the Central Bank of Armenia.

Digital Financial Services

Armenia has a law that promotes digital payments over cash settlements. According to Article 929 of the Republic of Armenia Civil Code of 2022, "settlements between legal persons and settlements by participation of citizens in connection with their entrepreneurial activities shall be made on a noncash basis. Payments between the aforementioned persons may also be made in cash, unless otherwise provided by law."

There are several debit and credit cards available for MSMEs to bill their customers digitally. They include MasterCard, Visa, American Express, Diners Club International, МИР, and the Japan Credit Bureau.

In 2000, the Armenian Card CJSC (ArCa) unified card payment system was launched—a joint project of the United States Agency for International Development, the Central Bank of Armenia, and commercial banks. Member banks were authorized to issue and serve ArCa cards, which expanded the card market and accelerated its growth. ArCa is responsible for overall administration and management of the payment system, processing card transactions, ATMs, merchant registration, clearing services for members, short messaging service (SMS), unstructured supplementary service data service for card transactions, and fraud monitoring and detection. It provides a 24/7 call center service.

According to the 2021 central bank annual report, transaction value increased by 32.4% over 2020, while the number of transactions increased by 54.7%.[52] Also, there was a continuous increase in the number of POS terminals available, particularly in the first half of 2021. The number of POS terminals increased by 34% to 16,535 with the number of virtual POS terminals rising by 42% to 2,911.[53]

Idram is an interoperable payment system used by registered firms or individual entrepreneurs using e-commerce. Idram can substitute for ATMs—businesses can accept payments from customers who use the Idram application if their cards are registered with the system. Merchant contracts can be signed and integrated in a few business days. Idram charges MSMEs AMD15 ($0.033) per transaction. As of March 2022, there were around 1.5 million registered users, with few hundred thousand active users monthly. There are more than 9,000 point of sales that use Idram QR codes, with around 7,000 partners. And there are around 400 services (about 300 partners)—such as utilities, mobile operators, paying road fines, tuition fees, and loan repayments that accept payments from the Idram wallet.

Tellcell is a licensed financial operator that, since 2007, offers MSMEs a full range of financial services and products. Each month, more than 1.5 million users and 3,000 partners tap the system. The number of clicks can reach up to 50 million per month. As of March 2022, there were 520,000 unique users of the Telcell payment system; in 2022, the transaction value processed by Telcell reached $754 million (Figure 2.11).

Figure 2.11: Telcell Transaction Turnover, 2019–2022

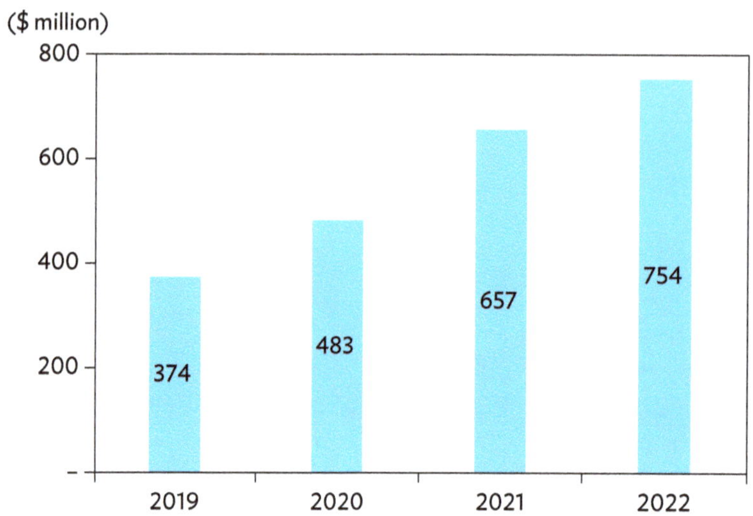

Source: Telcell (2022).

52 Central Bank of Armenia. 2021 Annual Report (in Armenian) . https://www.cba.am/AM/pperiodicals/Annual Report_2022.pdf.
53 K-061_himnavorum.pdf (parliament.am).

EasyPay was licensed in 2014. Merchants can receive payments by using EasyWallet's QR and AirPay. As of May 2022, EasyPay had over 3,000 payment terminals throughout Armenia. EasyPay earned AMD3.9 billion in revenue in 2020, around 40% more than in 2019 (AMD2.8 billion).[54] Samsung and Apple Pay entered the Armenian market in early 2022 and will operate through six banks. People can make contactless payments after adding their card to the wallet application on iPhone and Apple Watch.

Other payment systems include: (i) Yandex Money, one of the most popular online Russian payment services—the company is a joint venture between Russia's main search engine, Yandex, and one of the largest Russian banks, Sberbank—covering mobile carrier billing, cash payments, prepaid card payments, and electronic money payments; (ii) InecoPay is a simple, secure cashless mobile payment system that can be accessed via the InecoMobile application; and (iii) the QIWI payment system, the most widely used e-wallet across CIS countries, caters to large user bases.

Despite the growth of noncash payments, 64.5% of card transactions are cash withdrawals (by contrast, in the Russian Federation cash withdrawals are 43.7% of the total and in Estonia 30.6%).[55] Thus, the new law was introduced to deepen financial intermediation, create a culture accepting noncash payments, and to facilitate more efficient tax collection.

In July 2022, the Law on Cashless Payments became effective, under which payments exceeding AMD300,000 (around $600) should be cashless—via wire transfer, payment cards, or payment systems. There are also provisions that prohibit certain cash transactions regardless of amount—for example, advisory services involving accounting, auditing, legal, financial, and IT should be paid via noncash methods. Additionally, all foreign transactions should be cashless, regardless of the amount. Finally, all organizations, including MSMEs, should pay salaries and business trip expenses using noncash methods.[56]

Box 2.3: Idram&IDBank Digital Financial Ecosystem—Path to Success

Today, most people enjoy the ease of using online payments, express loans, and a cashless daily life. At the beginning of the 2000s, however, the world was just beginning to discover the potential benefits of emerging technological trends and innovations. In 2004, a group of enthusiasts had the idea to create the online payment platform Idram.am, which went on to provide its users with online wallets that could be used to make payments from utility bills to online shopping.

Idram evolved from a startup to an online platform with a complete toolkit. In 2008, Idram LLC was registered as a "payment system operator." In 2009, the central bank gave the company a license for money transfers. But Idram also needed authorization to issue electronic money. At that point, the platform had around 40,000 registered users, but only 3,000 of them were active. The company needed to advance swiftly. In 2012, it received a license to issue electronic money, the first in Armenia. The same year it introduced its application for iOS and Android operating systems. A few months later, the Idram application gained 3,000 active users. Soon the app expanded its list of services. Idram users could pay utility and state fees and transfer money abroad using a single application. In addition, the option of linking a bank card to the account was developed.

continued on next page

54 EasyPay | Reports.

55 K-061_himnavorum.pdf (parliament.am).

56 2022 Impress Article "Cash or Non-cash?" կանխիկ թե անկանխիկ (impress.am), original text of the new Law in Armenian: անկանխիկ գործառնությունների մասին (irtek.am).

Box 2.3 continued

As of July 2022, there were 1.5 million registered users in the system, with over 200,000 transactions daily. Much resulted from a strategic partnership between Idram and IDBank—a universal bank that frinds innovative and digital solutions for clients. Its partnership with Idram became a critical component of IDBank's larger plan to rebrand itself and completely digitalize. A joint digital platform was established that would include Idram's existing toolkit, adding new IDBank capacities. Starting in 2019, the platform was launched as the first open banking model in Armenia. On the Idram&IDBank digital platform, each of the more than 300 partners offer their own solutions (some 400 online services) and products via a single mobile application and web interface.

One breakthrough product was online ordering of bank cards and other products. Improved customer experience and convenience made it possible to dramatically increase the bank's active digital customer base, as well as significantly expand its registry of bank cards. IDBank is the largest issuer of bank cards for international payment systems with more than 300,000 issued international cards.

Another result of the partnership is the Rocket Line digital installment, which follows the well-known "buy now, pay later" pattern. In the 20 months since the product launch, the number of Rocket Line contracts has grown to 900,000.

Idram&IDBank is the only platform demanding complete online identification, guaranteeing 99.9% user security. There are over 9,000 stores all over Armenia receiving payments via Idram QR codes with about 850 online shops using Idram web and mobile checkouts.

According to Similarweb, the Idram&IDBank application ranks top in Armenia on Google Play and App Store in the financial category with over 1 million downloads. It is actively used by about 45% of the economically active population. More than 35% of noncash payments are done via card transaction, QR payment, and web or mobile checkout.

Source: Interview with Sergey Arakelyan, Digital Banking Director - Management Board Member at IDBank, May 2022.

Capital Markets

In 2021, the Armenian Securities Exchange (AMX) main board capitalization was around AMD174 billion with 10 listed companies. Trading volume was AMD406 million (Figure 2.12A and Table 2.6). During 2010-2021, market capitalization of the AMX grew at a compound annual growth rate of around 11%, even as institutional and legislative changes were underway. There were no initial public offerings (IPOs) during this period.

As of June 2022, the AMX did not have a designated index nor board dedicated to MSMEs. However, the AMX and the government plan to start a dedicated MSME board, though it is not clear when. The market can be characterized as passive, with equity markets under development, and the stock market focusing on fixed income stocks—mainly government bonds.

There are three types of listing venues at the AMX—A and B are normal listing venues, with C less regulated but riskier (alternative). Despite no designated board for MSMEs, the C platform can be considered a logical place for them to list.[57] The C platform trading value was AMD393 million in 2021 (Figure 2.12B).

57 Interview with Mikayel Hayrapetyan, the chief executive officer (CEO) of AMX, March 2022.

The AMX sees market development as creating designated venues, such as a micro-platform to trade stock options, or an equity crowdfunding venue—which is part of the AMX 5-year business plan—expected to open in late 2024 with the cooperation of the central bank, commercial banks, and international partners. One other designated venue may be for IT and other technology companies.

As for capital market infrastructure, investment banks remain undeveloped, and there are no specific institutions or initiatives to help MSMEs list. The AMX does not have incubators or accelerators. The only MSME support initiative planned involves cooperation with international finance institutions (IFIs) for introducing financial literacy training for MSMEs. Private accelerators and business angel networks do exist and some are active, but none within the AMX itself.

Potential capital market investors include both institutional investors (such as pension funds) and individuals (Armenia's diaspora and local high-net-worth individuals who currently rely on bank deposits).[58]

The central bank plans to initiate legislation to align current laws with Markets in Financial Instruments Regulation II and establish minimum requirements for an MSME growth market.

Figure 2.12: Equity Markets

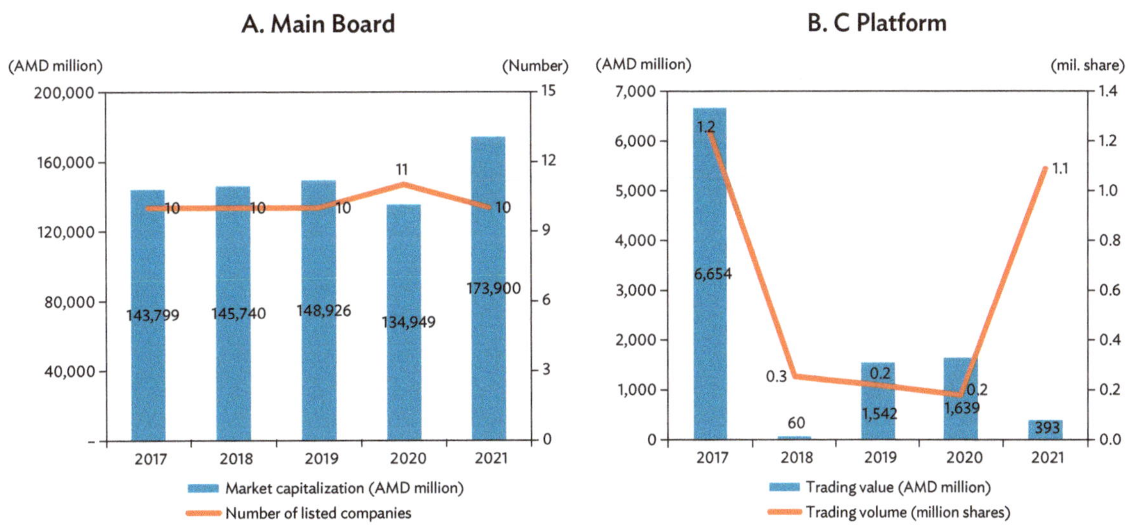

Source: ADB Asia SME Monitor 2022 database. Data from Central Depository of Armenia, Armenian Securities Exchange (AMX).

58 Interview with Mikayel Hayrapetyan, the CEO of AMX, March 2022.

Financial Infrastructure

The financial system remains dominated by the banking system, with nearly 85% of financial assets held by banks and NBFIs. Financial infrastructure remains rather limited. For example, there is only one private (no public) credit bureau.

ACRA, the private credit bureau, was founded in January 2004 and works with banks and MFIs. Its primary purpose is data gathering from banks and NBFIs, processing and updating information while providing security and confidentiality. ACRA also offers new and innovative risk assessment services and other solutions to clients in banking, finance, insurance, and business in general.

ACRA is owned by the commercial banks and the central bank. it receives capital investments, while users (banks and credit organizations) pay for services rendered. Thus, ACRA is considered a for-profit company, even as there are limits on profits set by the government to avoid misuse, moral hazard, and other risks.

ACRA products include (i) individual credit reports (one-time and subscription based) and (ii) FICO (ACRA scoring) for industry-related statistical reports and sales, along with auxiliary services (signals, push notifications, tax products, integrator function on return of income tax).

ACRA remained profitable during the pandemic, although financial institution and MSME bankruptcies reduced its bottom-line. ACRA considers itself "as advanced technologically as an IT company." It is developing its own software and offers data analysis. ACRA employs 30 people, about half are IT specialists.[59]

The central bank, in cooperation with IFIs and international donors, has taken the lead in providing consumers financial education. Since 2007, the central bank has prioritized improving financial literacy through various projects. The country participates in various financial literacy assessments conducted globally—such as the OECD International Network on Financial Education literacy survey (2010) and the World Bank's financial capability survey (2012). The government approved a 5-year National Strategy for Financial Education in 2014.[60] Coordinated with the central bank,[61] the strategy was reviewed and updated in 2019 for another 5 years (through 2024).

Since 2010, numerous institutions have worked to improve financial literacy. With these programs mostly independent, there is little consistency despite the duplications among projects. In May 2012, the Committee of National Strategy for Financial Education (NSFE) was established to unify financial education projects.

The NSFE is an interagency advisory body whose main mission is to increase financial literacy in schools, spread awareness about financial literacy among adults, and establish coordinated, monitored, and evaluated financial literacy projects throughout the country.

The initiative has succeeded, with financial literacy now offered as an elective course in most high schools.[62] It is consumer-oriented, with MSMEs involved only if they join a project.

59 Interview with Ashot Gabrielyan, CEO of ACRA Credit Reporting Agency, 11 May 2022.

60 OSCE. 2019. Roadmap for a National Strategy for Financial Education in Armenia; Financial Inclusion in Armenia: The Financial Capability Assessment Project (FCAP), 2014.

61 Central Bank of Armenia. For Consumer. https://www.cba.am/en/SitePages/fcpforconsumer.aspx.

62 Interview with Armenuhi Mkrtchyan, the Head of Consumer Protection and Financial Education Center at Central Bank of Armenia, April 2022.

A financial capability barometer (FCB) baseline survey conducted in 2014 revealed that Armenia had ample room to improve in its financial literacy. Based on survey results, only 18% of the population was financially literate.[63] About 36% of respondents took out new loans to refinance existing loans. Only 6% of the respondents held savings accounts in financial institutions, although 64% did save for unexpected events. Several projects have been implemented within the NSFE framework since 2014.

For example, Financial Education in Rural Areas was launched in 2015 in cooperation with the Ministry of Territorial Administration and Infrastructure. The program was designed to improve the financial knowledge and capabilities of the rural population through training. During 2016, 2017, and 2019, workshops were organized in 158 rural communities with 2,518 participants. These rural workshops focused on seasonality, planning, and budgeting; and better understanding of debt, savings, and other financial services for more responsible financial decision-making.

Financial Education in Schools was launched in 2014 (*Financial Inclusion, Regulation, Financial Literacy, and Financial Education in Armenia*, ADBI Working Paper Series No. 843). Based on a financial literacy curriculum, teacher manuals, and teacher training programs, the financial education topics were integrated into four subjects in primary, secondary, and high schools—*Mathematics, Me and the World, Algebra,* and *Social Sciences*. The program was piloted in 14 schools during the 2017–2018 academic year. Based on the positive feedback, a teacher training program was launched in 2018 for 2,532 teachers from 346 schools. An additional 2,419 teachers from 339 schools joined in 2019. The plan is to include all schools in the country by 2021. In 2019, the Ministry of Education and Science adopted the Finance Passport School Guideline for primary and secondary schools and a Savings Game as official school teaching material.[64]

Beginning 2013, a My Finance Month project was organized annually through the National Society of Financial Educators, focusing on personal financial management. More than 35 public and private institutions are involved each year, with more than 25 smaller educational projects targeting all population groups. The purpose of the program is to increase awareness, knowledge, and skills on financial services and on general financial literacy topics. The central bank is also involved with similar projects and initiatives, collaborating with various institutions and partners to ensure continuity among the financial education projects in the country.

A second FCB survey was conducted in 2019 to measure progress made since the 2014 baseline study and create a plan for the next 5 years. Based on the results, the current financial literacy programs will be adjusted to improve the country's Financial Capability Index (FCI). A new NSFE action plan will be developed for 2020–2024.

In 2019, the FCI increased by 2.3% percentage points over 2014—to 46.8%—though it did not affect the country's classification as "average" among financial capability groups.[65][66]

There are several financial education initiatives and support programs for MSMEs. In 2019, a "successful start" program was implemented for startup entrepreneurs, 12 programs in rural regions, and 2 in Yerevan. Participants included 167 startup entrepreneurs, 94 with developed business plans and 76 receiving financial support. In addition, Enterprise Armenia distributed loan guarantees totaling AMD180.5 million (around $400,000) to

63 The sample included 1,536 people, which ensures a 2.5% margin of error at a confidence level of 95%; The Study of The Financial Capability of Population In Armenia 2019. EV Consulting CJSC, March 2020.

64 These tools are accessible from https://abcfinance.am/.

65 The FCI measures the level of knowledge, skills, and attitudes needed to make informed judgments and effective decisions regarding the use and management of money. It is based on a questionnaire measuring three primary areas: behavior on managing money, personal characteristics relating to money management, and money relationships. A range of different types of institutions can use the financial capability index. For more info see http://www.cgap.org/p/site/c/pubs/template.rc?gbl%.

66 The Study of The Financial Capability of Population in Armenia 2019, prepared by EV Consulting, March 2020.

42 startup entrepreneurs.[67] In 2018, state-initiated and supported startup support programs were carried out in 16 regions, with 245 of 405 applicants selected to participate (128 women and 117 men). Some 188 participants presented 96 successful business plans, 65 of which received financial support.[68]

The American University of Armenia's Turpanjian Rural Development Program (AUA TRDP) was established in 2006 with a donation of $5 million to provide education and economic opportunities to people in rural areas in Armenia, Artsakh, and Javakhk (Armenian populated regions in neighboring Georgia). Under the program, entrepreneurs apply to undergo training and eventually receive a program-sponsored low-interest loan. The result is a business plan prepared by the beneficiaries. In addition to providing a practical business education, the program offers financial assistance by helping entrepreneurs obtain bank loans.

For rural residents, receiving loans is especially difficult, and interest rates can be exceedingly high, ranging from 20% to 40% annually. With AUA TRDP acting as guarantor, beneficiaries can receive loans at a 6% interest rate from the program's partner banks. After loans have been approved, AUA TRDP continues support through monitoring and mentoring. As of 2021, 549 businesses were established, 875 jobs created, and 1,545 applicants completed training.[69]

Other initiatives provide business training for MSMEs and individual entrepreneurs:

- **Green Lane NGO.** Active for 16 years, it provides training and support to 8,526 members, with 51 programs in partnership with United Nations agencies and the Austrian Development Agency, among others.
- **Shen NGO.** Created in 1988 by a group of professors and students at Yerevan Polytechnic Institute, it addresses urgent humanitarian issues. It works in over 350 rural communities providing (i) humanitarian aid; (ii) an integrated approach to rural development; (iii) physical and social infrastructure rehabilitation; (iv) asset-based community development; (iv) value chain development using a "Markets for Poor" approach; and (v) agricultural cooperative development. Almost all projects include capacity building so beneficiaries can ensure project sustainability. Shen NGO also cooperates with large companies involved with corporate social responsibility (for example, Orange and France Telecom, among others). In 2022, Shen NGO planned a micro business simulation pilot project for180 people.
- **The German Sparkassenstiftung** (German Savings Banks Foundation for International Cooperation, or DSIK). A nonprofit development agency, DSIK works worldwide on rural and MSME development, financial literacy, green finance, and institutional capacity building. It was commissioned by the German government to implement a regional program in the South Caucasus and Ukraine to promote rural entrepreneurship and finance for sustainable MSME development. In supporting the central bank on financial education, it began focusing on farmers' financial education in March 2021.[70] A survey conducted among potential beneficiaries found the vast majority (85%) of respondents or their family members have not received training on topics related to agricultural activities/business in the last 12 months.[71] For registered businesses, it was slightly below 80%. The main areas of training is on agricultural aspects of technologies, seeds, and agribusiness. Sales and marketing training is less common. Pure agricultural topics top the list (agro-processing, agro-investments and costs, and production and management technologies). Entrepreneurial skills follow—sales and marketing, financial record keeping and accounting. Legislation, taxation, and computer literacy are ranked lowest.

67 SUMMARY REPORT, 2019 Programs implemented by the National Investment Support Foundation under the treaty between Small and Medium Entrepreneurship Development National Center and the Ministry of Economy, N 114-19 of 05.09.2019.

68 SUMMARY REPORT, 2018 Programs implemented by the National Investment Support Foundation.

69 Turpanjian Rural Development Program (aua.am).

70 Interview with Eric Boettcher, Country Representative, DSIK Armenia.

71 Technical Needs Assessment among entrepreneurial households and micro/smallholder farmers in the agricultural production and processing sector in Armenia, Prepared by Civitta Armenia, March 2022.

4. Policies and Regulations

- Since 2000, the government has built a regulatory framework and tax regime to promote MSME development. The Ministry of Economy is the focal ministry for MSME development.
- The Small and Medium Entrepreneurship Development Strategy for 2020–2024 contains reforms that increase MSME competitiveness through the regulatory framework, access to resources (including finance), human capital development, market access, and business culture.
- There is no comprehensive national financial inclusion strategy, but several financial assistance programs are being implemented in cooperation with international organizations.
- In response to the pandemic, the government set more than 25 emergency measures, including assistance to businesses (mostly MSMEs) totaling more than AMD113 billion.
- The Russian invasion of Ukraine affected the economy mostly through currency appreciation; it hit MSME operating in IT. The government and central bank had no specific response measures as of end-August 2022.

MSME Development

Most businesses benefit from preferential taxes, either under the turnover tax, the micro entrepreneurship regime, or other targeted tax benefits. Only a small fraction pays VAT due to an exceptionally high VAT registration threshold. Thus, VAT does adequately contribute to government revenues, nor to the country's tax culture. Bringing VAT policy into line with regional benchmarks and simplifying its administration would allow for rebalancing tax revenues away from income taxes while expanding the taxpayer base.

MSMEs have a preferential presumptive tax regime provided through a so-called "turnover tax." This allows most MSMEs to benefit from a simplified preferential regime available to resident companies, individual entrepreneurs, and notaries. The turnover tax applies to taxpayers generating sales of up to AMD115 million. For MSMEs, it replaces the profit tax and VAT. Starting in 2020, a new micro entrepreneurship tax regime was introduced, in part to replace a patent tax, whereby micro businesses in specific activities (specified by government decree) with sales revenues below AMD24 million were exempt from turnover and profit taxes.

Despite preferential treatment, businesses producing goods subject to excise tax, as well as those importing these goods, must still charge VAT on sales. Taxpayers above the revenue threshold shift to the standard profit tax regime, and they must register for VAT. Applications for the simplified regime can be requested until 20 February each calendar year, allowing businesses some leeway in choosing the regime that best suits their economic interests.

There are many different turnover tax rates—depending on the type of business activity—ranging from 1.5% to 25% of sales revenue. Tax returns are submitted quarterly, with payments made within the following month. Turnover tax revenues have grown at an annual pre-pandemic growth rate of 25% between 2015 and 2019 (second only to excise revenues), but they remained just 2.0% of total tax revenues in 2019.

Several laws regulate MSMEs. Law No.121 of 2000 on State Support for Small and Medium Entrepreneurship (5 December) defines MSMEs, outlines state support, and the principles behind state policy.

The Tax Code No.165 of 2016 (4 October) regulates specified tax payments and defines tax principles, the concepts of tax payment, the types and scope of taxpayers, tax rates, and how to calculate tax payments.

The Law No.232 of 2001 on Joint Stock Companies (25 September) defines the legal status of joint-stock companies, how to set them up, implementing and terminating activities, shareholder rights and obligations, as well as the protection of the rights of shareholders, creditors and other legal interests.

The Law No.252 of 2001 on Companies with Limited Liability (24 October) regulates legal relations arising from the establishment, activity, reorganization and liquidation of companies.

The government has medium- to long-term MSME support strategies for MSMEs (Table 2.7). The Ministry of Economy is the focal point for MSME development. It is responsible for developing MSME strategies and submitting them to the government for approval. The ministry is also responsible for state-supported MSME programs.

In 2014, the Ministry of Economy prepared a long-term Strategic Development Plan of Armenia for 2014–2025, which outlines a general set of socioeconomic development priorities, their goals, main obstacles and constraints to development, along with the key reforms and policy tools needed, and the main risks. It prioritizes (i) providing national security for the public; (ii) boosting entrepreneurial capabilities and performance, enhancing entrepreneurial skills and capabilities, and strengthening supply chain management, (iii) enhancing various capacities to promote sustainable economic development; (iv) internationalizing high-growth firms, promoting networking and business collaboration; and (v) broadening opportunities for inclusive growth.

In 2015, the government approved a Small and Medium Entrepreneurship Development Strategy for 2016–2018. It sets a common approach to MSME development—through policies, programs and actions—for government authorities, civil society representatives, the private sector, and international organizations. These include (i) using and protecting intellectual property; (ii) increasing productivity, market access, and growth; (iii) fostering an entrepreneurial culture across society and enhancing entrepreneurship education and skills; (iv) accelerating economic growth through innovative firms, facilitating technology exchange and innovation; and (v) optimizing the regulatory environment and improving access to finance along with financial inclusion for entrepreneurs and enterprises.

In 2020, the Small and Medium Entrepreneurship Development Strategy for 2020–2024 was prepared. The strategy promotes reforms to increase MSME competitiveness in terms of regulatory framework, access to resources (including finance), human resource development, market access, and business culture. This done by (i) improving the economy's regulatory environment and public administration; (ii) promoting cooperation among MSMEs, large firms, and foreign investment; (iii) ensuring access to capital is available through capital markets; (iv) promoting use of advanced technology; and (v) developing modern information and communication technology (ICT) systems that are well suited to market growth.

There are many barriers to MSME development. Government authorities and private sector institutions that participated in the Asia SME Monitor 2022 responded to a survey on the key challenges facing MSME development (March 2022). The top five included the following:

1. **Lack of transparency.** Insufficient transparency creates information asymmetry between MSMEs and financial institutions, limiting their access to financial resources.
2. **Difficulties in entering foreign markets.** The domestic market is small; so for MSMEs to develop and expand their business, they must be able to easily and affordably enter foreign markets.
3. **Insufficient business and financial literacy.** A lack of financial management and financial literacy reduces the investment planning capacity of MSMEs, which results in many unviable loan applications and a lack of knowledge, training, and education.

4. **Poor risk assessment and data gathering.** Using new technology and advanced data collection would facilitate lending to new clients without credit histories.
5. **Use of alternative financing sources.** Aside from standard lending products, MSMEs need to tap alternative financing or liquidity mechanisms to obtain needed capital.

Respondents also ranked the top five policy priorities to promote MSME development and access to finance: (i) expand incentives for financial disclosure and formalizing MSMEs; (ii) improve export promotion tools, disseminate exporting skills, and promote internationalization; (iii) provide MSMEs access to targeted financial advisory services on business planning and marketing, financial products, and financial reporting—in partnership with the United Nations Development Program, the central bank runs a Financial Education for Women program in science, technology, engineering, mathematics or STEM, and law, along with entrepreneurial education for teenagers and other youth through the OECD International Money Week; (iv) promote the use of new technologies to improve the MSME database and risk assessment to help strengthen credit reporting and decision-making; and (v) develop and/or improve financing products such as financial leasing, factoring (with and without recourse), crowdfunding, and warehouse receipt financing, among others.

Preferential taxation regimes tailored to MSMEs aim to reduce the opportunity costs of taxation. For informal businesses, lowering taxes and compliance costs encourage MSMEs to legally register. Becoming part of the formal economy opens up new growth possibilities as well as access to social safety nets and other government incentives. Formalization strategies work with MSMEs that are growth-oriented rather than subsistence-oriented (Amin et al., 2019). MSMEs in the formal economy since inception also benefit from preferential taxation and government incentives that lower the after-tax cost of capital. Special regimes for MSMEs are thus instrumental in generating productivity gains that eventually build a larger tax base and thus larger tax revenues. These special tax regimes are usually packaged under three modalities: (i) presumptive regimes based on proxies measuring business activity (for example, revenues, assets, or others); (ii) discounted or reduced corporate income tax rates; and (iii) tax exemptions available for certain taxes, such as VAT.[72]

Financial Inclusion

Several international aid agencies support financial inclusion or MSME access to finance. An example is the MSME support program financed by Germany's KfW Development Bank. The program aims develop the country's financial sector, giving financial institutions the resources needed to make MSME lending more efficient and profitable. The program also introduces new lending technologies and supports skills development and continuing training for credit officers.

The program was established within the framework of a 1998 intergovernmental agreement on financial cooperation between Germany and Armenia, and in accordance with a loan agreement—a EUR16.8 million credit line for 40 years, with a 10-year grace period—between KfW and the central bank. Lending is primarily refinancing, where partner financial institutions (PFI) first lend using their own funds, and afterward apply to the Program Management Unit (PMU) of the "German-Armenian Fund" (GAF) for refinancing. If the loans comply with program requirements, the central bank refinances the loans. It is required that PFI loans to MSMEs are in local currency and at market rates, which are refinanced out of the GAF in local currency with maturities up to 5 years.

KfW also provides grants for financing technical assistance to PFIs. Internationale Projekt Consult GmbH (IPC) was selected as program consultant in 1999. In close cooperation with PFIs, it worked on new lending technologies implemented within 6 years. Instead of the collateral-based lending mechanisms which existed before the program,

[72] EESE Assessment of MSME trends and policies in Armenia, International Labour Office – Geneva: ILO, 2022.

IPC introduced a completely new approach in assessing MSMEs, one where collateral was not the primary criterion of creditworthiness. This helped transform business lending and boosted commercial bank development.

Since the program started through end-December 2020, PFIs provided a total of 75,723 loans amounting to AMD293 billion. Eleven PFIs participated in the program, along with 10 commercial banks and one credit organization.[73]

Based on the success of the GAF-MSME program, the government lent GAF an additional AMD15.2 billion in December 2008—within the framework of the measures taken in response to the global financial crisis to support MSMEs (GAF-MSME-Gov). Lending was done using the technology of the GAF-MSME-KfW Program under the same credit conditions. The program closed in November 2013.

Another example was the $50 million agreement between the central bank and the World Bank in February 2009—again in response to the global financial crisis. The main purpose of the "access to finance for small and medium enterprises" program (GAF-MSME-WB/AFSME) was to maintain or increase loan availability to MSMEs, thus fostering their growth. The loan was granted with a term of 26.5 years. Based on the standards set out by the World Bank, eight partner banks were selected to participate.

ADB initiated a women's MSME support program—the Women Entrepreneurship Support Sector Development Program. The January 2015 loan agreement between the central bank and ADB was for $20 million, maturing in 31.5 years. The program stimulates entrepreneurial development among women through the financial system, increasing funds available for women-owned MSMEs.[74] At least 50% of program funds should be disbursed to women-owned MSMEs. For implementation, five partner financial institutions were selected by the central bank and ADB.

There is also an agriculture and tourism finance program by the European Investment Bank. The program is implemented within the framework of a EUR50 million ($62.5 million) loan agreement signed in December 2014 between the European Investment Bank and the Central Bank of Armenia. The program finances MSMEs operating in the field of agriculture and tourism, control and management of the program implemented by the PMU GAF of the central bank. The PFI loans are disbursed in local currency with up to 7.5 years maturity with principal repayment at the end of the loan term. The loans in line with the program's eligibility criteria provided by the PFIs may be refinanced by GAF not later than 6 months after of initial disbursement. Beneficiaries include MSMEs with less than 250 employees. The loan must not greater than the equivalent of EUR1 million a maturity of not more than 7.5 years with a 2-year grace period.

For women entrepreneurs' access to finance, Figure 2.13 illustrates the reasons given as to why respondents rated "access to finance" as an obstacle—from a 2021 survey conducted by the International Finance Corporation.[75] The most common reason is high interest rates and difficult terms of loans (42.7% of respondents), followed by those who said people were not solvent (22%), and those who mentioned they lacked expense financing (10.1%). Access to finance was rated an obstacle primarily by micro businesses—those mostly women-owned (44.9% of micro businesses and 24% of large businesses). High interest rates and difficult loan terms were also mentioned. Participants in the qualitative study discussed financing challenges that occur throughout the entrepreneurial cycle, from establishment to growth.

[73] German Armenian Fund. SME Support. https://gaf.am/en/sectors-of-lending/sme-support.html.

[74] A women-owned MSME should meet at least one of the following criteria: at least 50% of the enterprise should be owned by women, at least 60% of the executive body should consist of women, or at least 50% of the employees should be women.

[75] E. Karagulyan et al. 2021. *Women Entrepreneurship Study in Armenia : Qualitative and Quantitative Study - Synthesis Report.* Washington, DC: World Bank. https://documents.worldbank.org/en/publication/documents-reports/documentdetail/911301621224449437/women-entrepreneurship-study-in-armenia-qualitative-and-quantitative-study-synthesis-report.

Figure 2.13: Major Obstacles for Business Development among Women Entrepreneurs in Armenia, 2022

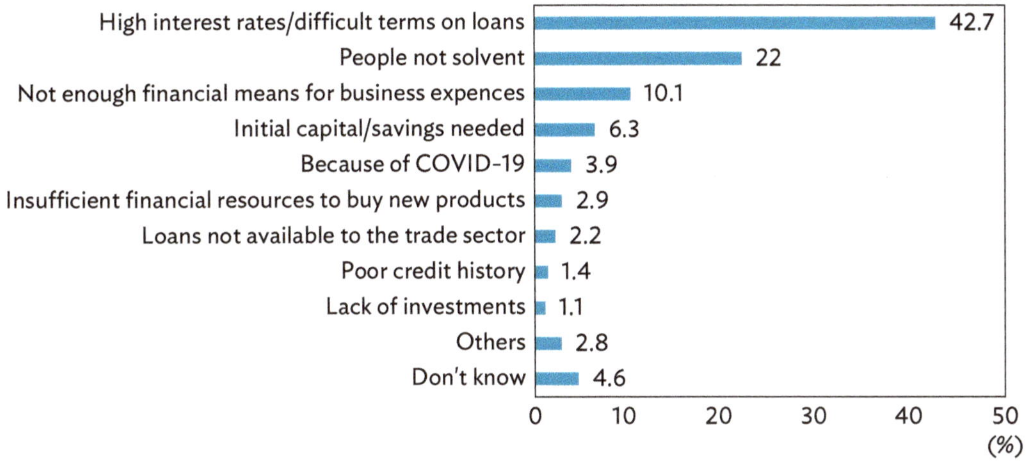

COVID-19 = coronavirus disease.

Source: IFC's Women Entrepreneurship Study in Armenia.

Bank loans are difficult to obtain due to high interest rates and the large collateral required—importantly, collateral requirements affect women entrepreneurs more due to issues such as societal inheritance practices that favor sons. Also, the privatization of land in the 1990s gave male entrepreneurs a greater advantage over women.

More than 40% of respondents to an ADB survey reported the most needed support for their businesses was interest-free financing or grants for business development, with over 20% citing membership in business chambers or participation in international business events or competitions.[76] The top training needs were related to internationalization, digitalization, global visibility, and entrepreneurship (around 50%), with women entrepreneurs citing the need to undergo training related to personal development (around 24%).

Response to COVID-19

Along with the pandemic measures taken on 16 March 2020, the government declared a state of emergency lasting until 14 April 2020 to prevent the spread of COVID-19. The emergency measures included the closure of all educational institutions, closing the borders with Georgia and Iran, banning gatherings of over 20 people, and postponing the 2020 Armenian constitutional referendum.[77]

From 25 March 2020, only medical institutions, infrastructure facilities, banks, pharmacies, supermarkets, smaller shops selling food, and food delivery services were allowed to stay open, while citizens were required to carry identification and written statements justifying the need to visit one of these establishments. From 1 April 2020, public transportation was suspended—including underground mass transit in Yerevan. However, when the government extended the state of emergency until 14 May, it modified the ban to allow farming, fishing, processing of tobacco products, production of cement and other construction materials, and open-air construction work from 13 April, and to open shops selling household appliances and mostly export-oriented textile factories from 20 April.

[76] ADB. 2021. Rapid Assessment on COVID-19 and Its Impact on Women Entrepreneurship.

[77] Breaking International News & Views | Reuters.

Also, printing companies, repair shops, real estate agencies, and some other businesses were allowed to resume operations from 23 April.[78]

The government took over 25 initiatives—worth AMD107 billion—to support MSMEs hit by the pandemic (Table 7a). Most important were measure one (individual businesses and temporary access to MSMEs), three (specifically on MSMEs), and nineteen (support for innovative, competitive businesses).

Measure one (AMD6 billion) dampened the economic consequences of the pandemic by helping individual businesses mitigate liquidity risks due to the spread of COVID-19. The assistance provided businesses with temporary access to finance to respond to changing demand, to meet external challenges, and to continue or adapt to the changing economic situation and to adjust their development strategies.

The assistance included (i) cofinancing to maintain sufficient collateral, smoothing currency risk, and partially reducing interest expenses; (ii) refinancing to completely neutralize a firm's currency risk, as well as partially reducing interest expenses; and (iii) subsidizing to significantly reduce interest expenses.

Businesses could use the assistance to finance (i) employee salaries; (ii) tax payments, duties, and other mandatory payments; (iii) purchase or import of raw materials (with conditions); (iv) purchase or import of new devices and equipment; (v) payments for public services (expenses for electricity, water, gas, and telecommunications); and (vi) food and medicine imports for some companies.

Measure one had certain conditions: (i) local currency unless a cofinancing instrument; (ii) terms up to 24 months; (iii) maximum lending amount of AMD500 million or equivalent (maximum amount of cofinancing or refinancing of AMD250 million); (iv) credit funds must be noncash or bank transfers; and (v) maximum interest rates from 0% to 6% per annum.

Measure three (AMD9.3 billion, AMD8.8 billion disbursed) supported MSMEs resolve liquidity issues caused by the COVID-19 outbreak. Sectors included processing industries; accommodation and public catering; transportation and storage; tourism services; other tertiary services; health care, preschool education (private kindergartens); sporting activities (sports clubs and swimming pools); entertainment and leisure activities (except for computer games and internet clubs); and construction of buildings, civil construction, and specialized construction activities. Loans were provided to MSMEs meeting the local currency criteria, for a maximum 36 months (6-month grace period), and with a maximum loan amount of AMD50 million (but not more than 10% of the MSME's 2019 turnover). Again, credit funds were on a noncash or bank transfer basis.

Measure nineteen supported competitive business and entrepreneurial ideas developed by beneficiaries for startups and for promoting innovative business plans. The main recipients were regional MSMEs and startups. Loan terms included (i) local currency; (ii) maximum 60-month maturity (6-month grace period); (iii) a maximum loan of AMD10 million for startups and AMD20 million for innovative development; and (iv) annual interest rate of 7%–10%.

---

[78] Heinrich Böll Foundation. 2020. The COVID-19 Pandemic in the South Caucasus. *Caucasus Analytical Digest*. No. 115. https://css.ethz.ch/content/dam/ethz/special-interest/gess/cis/center-for-securities-studies/pdfs/CAD115.pdf.

Response to the Russian Invasion of Ukraine

The invasion affects Armenia's economy of in several ways, although there is no evidence of specific damage to MSMEs. The country has relatively strong trade with the Russian Federation, while relatively weak ties with Ukraine. Over the past 10 years, the Russian Federation's share of Armenian exports averaged about 23%, while Ukraine accounted for around 1%. There are no signs that the Russian Federation markets will be closed to Armenian goods. On the contrary, many Armenian companies view the situation as an opportunity to increase their presence in the Russian Federation markets, as many foreign companies are planning or already left.

The biggest concern, especially for exporters, is the depreciation of the US dollar against the *dram*. This came about as part of the Russian Federation's IT sector relocated to Armenia as a result of sanctions. The US dollars lost almost 20% of its value during February–August 2022.

The government and central bank have not taken specific actions to stop the currency's appreciation. Central bank officials say they are concentrating on controlling inflation, which is in fact aided by the US dollar depreciation—the central bank raised its refinancing rate three times during 2022, from 8% to 9.5%.

In sum, the Russian invasion of Ukraine affected the Armenian economy mostly through its currency appreciation. It hit MSMEs in the IT sector, as those mostly engaged in outsourcing IT services to foreign companies went out of business due to the dram's appreciation.

Data Tables

Table 2.1: MSME Definitions

Item	Micro	Small	Medium
Number of employees	0–9	10–49	50–249
Revenue from the previous year	<AMD100 million	<AMD500 million	<AMD1.5 billion
Book value of assets as of the end of the previous year	<AMD100 million	<AMD500 million	<AMD1 billion

MSME = micro, small, and medium-sized enterprise.

Source: ADB Asia SME Monitor 2022 database. Data from Law No.121 of 5 December 2000 on State Support for Small and Medium Entrepreneurship (https://www.arlis.am/documentview.aspx?docID=64617).

Table 2.2: MSME Landscape

End-of-period data

Item	2004	2005	2006	2007	2008	2009	2010	2011	2012	2013	2014	2015	2016	2017	2018	2019	2020	2021
NUMBER OF ENTERPRISES																		
Number of enterprises, total*	95,936	102,170	81,469	83,797	133,045	136,008	60,477	70,084	74,791	78,787	77,378	70,061	77,538	59,575	68,780	75,180	83,164	...
Number of MSMEs	93,825	99,820	79,595	81,953	129,985	132,923	59,267	68,682	73,295	77,999	76,589	69,360	76,763	59,467	68,654	75,045	83,032	...
Micro	77,228	78,977	67,130	69,216	98,453	103,230	54,819	63,953	69,096	72,868	71,550	64,794	55,052	55,921	64,344	70,030	78,530	...
Small	12,855	16,552	10,754	10,642	24,347	22,849	3,603	3,824	3,928	4,105	4,021	3,651	3,102	3,031	3,686	4,272	3,807	...
Medium	3,742	4,291	1,711	2,095	7,184	6,800	845	905	901	1,026	1,008	913	775	515	624	743	695	...
Number of large enterprises	2,111	2,350	1,874	1,844	3,060	3,128	1,210	1,402	1,496	788	789	701	775	108	126	135	132	...
MSME to total (%)	97.8	97.7	97.7	97.8	97.7	97.7	98.0	98.0	98.0	99.0	99.0	99.0	99.0	99.8	99.8	99.8	99.8	...
MSME growth (%)	...	1.1	0.8	1.0	1.6	1.0	0.4	1.2	1.1	1.1	1.0	0.9	1.1	0.8	1.2	1.1	1.1	...
MSMEs by sector (% share)																		
Manufacturing	17.1	18.1	18.2	17.9	18.3	...	8.5	8.4	8.3	...	8.7	8.9	9.2	9.6	9.8	9.9	12.7	...
Construction	5.2	5.5	5.6	5.6	5.6	...	2.1	2.0	1.9	...	1.9	1.9	1.8	2.0	2.2	2.4	2.6	...
Wholesale and retail trade; repair of motor vehicles and motorcycles	48.1	50.9	50.5	50.3	50.0	...	60.3	59.9	59.2	...	58.7	59.3	59.2	67.5	64.2	62.5	58.1	...
Transportation and storage	2.9	3.3	3.3	3.6	3.6	...	3.2	3.6	5.1	...	3.5	1.7	1.1	1.7	2.5	2.8	4.0	...
Accommodation and food service activities	...	...	...	...	...	...	3.7	3.9	3.9	...	3.9	4.1	4.2	4.3	5.9	6.4	6.1	...
Other services**	21.0	16.3	16.3	16.6	16.5	...	20.9	21.0	21.2	...	22.3	23.1	24.0	14.4	15.0	15.6	16.2	...
Others***	5.7	5.9	6.0	5.9	6.0	...	1.2	1.2	1.2	...	1.1	1.1	0.4	0.4	0.4	0.4	0.3	...
MSMEs by region (% share)																		
Capital city (Yerevan)	48.5	48.3	49.0	46.0	47.3	46.5	...	...	53.0	51.0	52.0	53.3	51.8	52.1	51.9	52.3	51.5	...
Others	51.5	51.7	51.0	54.0	52.7	53.5	...	...	47.0	49.0	48.0	46.8	48.2	47.9	48.1	47.7	48.5	...
EMPLOYMENT																		
Number of employment, total****	535,903	551,029	562,218	657,347	691,193	682,935	379,207	411,916	425,789	...	542,916	535,575	370,624	253,939	312,005	355,429	338,998	...
Number of employment by MSMEs	365,486	375,802	383,432	448,311	471,394	465,761	258,619	280,927	290,388	...	370,269	365,262	238,311	168,185	212,963	248,069	232,955	...
Micro	121,088	121,583	124,534	170,733	99,653	105,955	96,457	108,858	115,239	...	137,268	137,354	116,722	60,999	82,585	95,930	90,917	...
Small	146,639	153,637	156,213	180,646	179,152	175,488	75,006	78,767	81,161	...	113,100	109,611	60,273	57,259	69,328	79,807	72,002	...
Medium	97,759	100,582	102,686	96,932	192,588	184,318	87,156	93,302	93,988	...	119,901	118,297	61,316	49,927	61,050	72,332	70,036	...
Number of employment by large enterprises	170,417	175,227	178,785	209,036	219,799	217,173	120,588	130,989	135,401	...	172,647	170,313	132,313	85,754	99,042	107,360	106,043	...
MSME employees to total (%)	68.2	68.2	68.2	68.2	68.2	68.2	68.2	68.2	68.2	...	68.2	68.2	64.3	66.2	68.3	69.8	68.7	...
MSME employees growth (%)*****	...	3.0	2.0	17.0	5.0	(1.0)	(44.0)	9.0	3.0	...	...	(1.0)	(35.0)	(29.0)	27.0	16.0	(6.0)	...
Share of female employees to total employees (%)	41.6	41.9	45.7	48.1	48.1	45.5	...	...	...	...	...	...	...	...	...	...	...	...

continued on next page

Table 2.2 *continued*

Item	2004	2005	2006	2007	2008	2009	2010	2011	2012	2013	2014	2015	2016	2017	2018	2019	2020	2021
Employment by MSME by sector (% share)																		
Manufacturing	8.2	...	...	4.9	5.7	18.8	13.4	13.4	13.3	...	13.7	13.6	...	20.2	20.7	21.0	22.2	...
Construction	9.9	...	...	4.8	7.5	16.2	7.5	7.5	6.9	...	7.5	7.0	...	9.6	8.1	8.1	8.9	...
Wholesale and retail trade; repair of motor vehicles and motorcycles	27.0	...	...	11.9	12.0	39.9	27.6	28.4	28.8	...	30.0	30.4	...	31.0	31.6	31.8	31.6	...
Transportation and storage	1.6	...	...	7.4	1.6	6.0	4.7	4.7	4.9	...	4.0	3.5	...	4.8	4.4	4.0	3.9	...
Accommodation and food service activities	...	...	...	...	...	...	4.5	4.8	4.9	...	6.3	6.7	...	9.7	11.8	12.0	9.9	...
Other services**	18.8	...	...	30.2	21.1	19.1	39.7	38.8	38.6	...	35.5	36.0	...	23.5	22.5	21.9	22.4	...
Others***	34.5	...	...	40.8	52.0	...	2.5	2.5	2.5	...	3.1	2.8	...	1.2	1.0	1.2	1.0	...
Employment by MSMEs by region (% share)																		
Capital city (Yerevan)	...	79.4	...	...	70.9	69.5	...	...	61.0	...	...	...	...	67.7	66.3	66.0	65.0	...
Others	...	20.6	...	...	29.1	30.5	...	...	39.0	...	...	...	...	32.3	33.7	34.0	35.0	...
CONTRIBUTION TO GROSS VALUE ADDED (GVA)																		
GVA of MSMEs (AMD million)	736,467	892,667	1,070,445	1,291,206	1,487,951	1,335,202	1,487,887	1,643,407	1,698,993	1,559,516	1,564,691	1,616,739	1,681,700	1,371,222	1,417,780	1,708,535	1,625,388	...
MSME contribution to GVA (% share)	38.6	39.8	40.3	41.0	41.7	42.5	43.0	43.5	42.5	34.2	32.4	32.0	33.1	24.6	23.6	26.0	26.3	...
MSME GVA growth (%)	...	21.2	19.9	20.6	15.2	(10.3)	11.4	10.5	3.4	(8.2)	0.3	3.3	4.0	(18.5)	3.4	20.5	(4.9)	...
MSME labor productivity (AMD million)	2.0	2.4	2.8	2.9	3.2	2.9	5.8	5.8	5.9	...	4.2	4.4	7.1	8.2	6.7	6.9	7.0	...
MSME GVA by sector (% share)																		
Manufacturing	15.2	14.5	16.8	16.1	11.4	14.3	13.3	13.0	12.3	...	...	...	...	17.8	18.6	20.8	24.1	...
Construction	17.1	30.2	41.7	43.1	48.2	24.0	11.3	11.3	9.3	...	...	...	...	17.1	13.8	11.3	12.8	...
Wholesale and retail trade; repair of motor vehicles and motorcycles	16.6	16.4					42.9	43.6	46.6	...	...	...	...	35.0	31.3	34.7	34.2	...
Transportation and storage	5.1	5.8	18.4	23.8	22.0	27.5	3.3	3.6	4.1	...	...	...	...	4.7	6.6	5.8	5.8	...
Accommodation and food service activities	...	...					2.8	2.6	3.0	...	...	...	...	5.4	6.8	5.8	2.7	...
Other services**	15.2	21.2	23.2	17.0	18.3	34.3	24.6	23.8	22.8	...	...	...	...	18.9	21.4	20.8	19.6	...
Others***	30.8	12.0	...	...	...	...	1.8	2.1	1.9	...	...	...	...	1.2	1.5	0.9	0.8	...
MSME GVA by region (% share)																		
Capital city (Yerevan)	...	...	...	...	...	...	...	...	65.0	...	...	...	...	...	...	...	...	...
Others	...	...	...	...	...	...	...	...	35.0	...	...	...	...	...	...	...	...	...
EXPORTS****																		
Total export value (AMD million)	383,137	445,481	409,778	395,000	323,435	258,456	389,203	496,916	554,505	605,705	643,633	709,716	860,718	1,078,571	1,162,777	1,271,328	1,217,760	1,450,752
Total export growth (%)	5.4	16.3	(8.0)	(3.6)	(18.1)	(20.1)	50.6	27.7	11.6	9.2	6.3	10.3	21.3	25.3	7.8	9.3	(4.2)	19.1
MSME export value (AMD million)	60,153	73,059	69,252	68,730	57,895	45,747	...	...	...	...	...	...	...	...	...	...	...	...
MSME export to total export value (%)	15.7	16.4	16.9	17.4	17.9	17.7	...	...	...	...	...	...	...	...	...	...	...	...
MSME export growth (%)	...	21.5	(5.2)	(0.8)	(15.8)	(21.0)	...	...	...	...	...	...	...	...	...	...	...	...
IMPORTS****																		
Total import value (AMD million)	715,871	824,134	911,653	1,120,178	1,354,100	1,208,616	1,401,481	1,543,780	1,711,967	1,796,552	1,840,425	1,547,776	1,572,562	1,974,802	2,398,191	2,658,048	2,199,984	2,571,264
Total import growth (%)	5.6	15.1	10.6	22.9	20.9	(10.7)	16.0	10.2	10.9	4.9	2.4	(15.9)	1.6	25.6	21.4	10.8	(17.2)	16.9
MSME import value (AMD million)	249,123	299,161	335,488	417,826	511,850	316,657	...	...	...	...	...	...	...	...	...	...	...	...
MSME import to total import value (%)	34.8	36.3	36.8	37.3	37.8	26.2	...	...	...	...	...	...	...	...	...	...	...	...
MSME import growth (%)	...	20.1	12.1	24.5	22.5	(38.1)	...	...	...	...	...	...	...	...	...	...	...	...

GVA = gross value added; MSME = micro, small, and medium-sized enterprise.

* For 2013 to 2016, the number of "active enterprises" are reflected. For these years Armstat did not provide data for MSME types separately, but used the term "active enterprises" which included micro, small, medium-sized, and large enterprises. Thus, the mention of 99% of enterprises being MSMEs is taken as the basis for calculations, with the rest of the numbers estimates. The proportion of types of enterprises mentioned in the report was applied. Source: Business Support Office for the European Bank for Reconstruction and Development (EBRD).

** Other services include electricity, gas, steam, and air-conditioning supply; water supply, sewerage, waste management and remediation activities; information and communication; real estate activities; professional, scientific, and technical activities; administrative and support service activities; repair of computers and personal and household goods.

*** Others include mining and quarrying.

**** For 2004 to 2017 Armstat provides the number of employed people, which is defined as "a person aged 15-75 who had paid or unpaid work during the researched week, regardless of whether the work was permanent, temporary or seasonal, one-time or casual, even if this work was only one hour during the researched week." For years after 2017 the methodology changes, and the statistical service has provided the number of hired people, defined as " a person who works on the basis of a contract signed with an employer, an employment order or a verbal agreement and receives monetary and/or in-kind compensation in the form of a salary." According to historical data for 2017-2020, the average number of employed people was 68.2% of total number of people employed in the real sector. The average is also applied for calculating the number of MSME employees for 2004-2017.

***** MSME Employees Growth numbers for 2010, 2016, 2017 and 2018 changed drastically. In 2010, The RA Law on Support to MSMEs was approved, which clearly defined MSMEs.

****** Imports and exports were from Armstat, with the US dollar at the average currency rate of each year; data from the central bank.

Source: ADB Asia SME Monitor 2022 database. Data from the Statistical Committee of the Republic of Armenia (Armstat).

Table 2.3: Bank Credit

End-of-period data

Item	2004	2005	2006	2007	2008	2009	2010	2011	2012	2013	2014	2015	2016	2017	2018	2019	2020	2021
OPERATING BANKS																		
Number of operating banking institutions, total	20	21	21	22	22	22	21	21	22	22	22	22	20	18	18	18	18	18
State-owned commercial banks	...	...	...	...	...	...	...	...	...	...	...	...	...	...	...	...	...	...
State-owned development financial institutions*	...	...	...	...	...	...	...	...	1	1	1	1	1	1	1	1	1	1
Private commercial banks	20	21	21	22	22	22	21	21	21	21	21	21	19	17	17	17	17	17
Foreign commercial banks	...	...	...	...	...	...	...	...	...	...	...	...	...	...	...	...	...	...
Credit																		
Loans outstanding, total (AMD million)	132,325	184,023	229,654	408,732	616,790	703,366	888,612	1,210,495	1,535,190	1,706,100	2,067,953	2,006,101	2,315,719	2,516,837	2,932,928	3,414,787	3,911,000	3,697,604
Loans outstanding in domestic currency (AMD million)	39,863	66,984	106,156	242,571	374,999	331,280	368,412	451,180	527,299	618,376	672,596	667,665	819,267	917,996	1,257,866	1,627,082	1,887,699	2,016,105
Loans outstanding in foreign currency (AMD million)	92,462	117,039	123,497	166,161	241,791	372,086	520,200	759,314	1,007,891	1,087,725	1,395,357	1,338,435	1,496,452	1,598,842	1,675,062	1,787,706	2,023,301	1,681,499
Loan growth (%)	...	39.1	24.8	78.0	50.9	14.0	26.3	36.2	26.8	11.1	21.2	(3.0)	15.4	8.7	16.5	16.4	14.5	(5.5)
Total bank loans to GDP (%)	6.9	8.2	8.6	13.0	17.3	22.4	25.7	32.0	36.0	37.5	42.8	39.8	45.7	45.2	48.7	52.2	63.3	53.0
Lending rate (%, annual average)	18.6	17.9	16.5	17.5	17.1	18.8	19.2	17.8	17.2	16.0	16.4	17.6	17.4	14.4	12.8	12.1	11.6	11.8
Gross nonperforming loans (NPLs) (AMD million)	1,512	971	2,409	4,430	6,067	21,449	17,315	25,144	31,847	38,321	77,189	91,036	111,445	105,961	98,409	124,891	188,085	74,059
Gross NPLs to total loans (%)	1.1	0.5	1.0	1.0	1.0	2.9	1.8	2.0	2.0	2.2	3.6	4.4	4.6	4.0	3.2	3.4	4.5	1.9
Deposits																		
Deposits, total (AMD million)	226,981	261,339	299,605	398,514	449,461	626,792	673,062	934,220	1,132,447	1,521,255	1,604,247	1,789,275	2,177,444	2,463,734	2,728,324	3,255,658	3,329,284	3,617,266
Deposits in domestic currency (AMD million)	49,203	84,109	130,703	230,654	218,469	164,017	204,296	292,436	336,766	441,481	439,054	513,280	700,475	916,073	1,013,820	1,310,795	1,439,038	1,691,927
Deposits in foreign currency (AMD million)	177,777	177,230	168,902	167,860	230,992	462,775	468,766	641,784	795,681	1,079,774	1,165,193	1,275,995	1,476,968	1,547,661	1,714,504	1,944,863	1,890,246	1,925,339
Deposit rate (%, annual average)**	4.9	5.8	5.8	6.3	6.6	8.7	9.0	9.3	9.6	10.2	10.4	14.2	11.6	9.0	8.7	8.5	8.1	8.2
MSME LOANS* **																		
MSME loans outstanding, total (AMD million)****	...	...	...	...	...	...	...	...	...	...	...	...	...	...	...	...	1,180,675	1,169,815
MSME loans to total loans outstanding (%)	...	...	...	...	...	...	...	...	...	...	...	...	...	...	...	...	30.2	31.6
MSME loans to GDP (%)	...	...	...	...	...	...	...	...	...	...	...	...	...	...	...	...	19.1	16.8
MSME loan growth (%)	...	...	...	...	...	...	...	...	...	...	...	...	...	...	...	...	...	(0.9)
MSME lending rate (%, annual average)	...	...	...	...	...	...	...	...	...	...	...	...	...	...	...	...	8.6	8.8
Nonperforming MSME loans (NPLs) (AMD million)	...	...	...	...	...	...	...	...	...	...	...	...	...	...	...	...	62,943	25,069
MSME NPLs to total MSME loans (%)	...	...	...	...	...	...	...	...	...	...	...	...	...	...	...	...	5.3	2.1
Number of MSME loan borrowers	...	...	...	...	...	...	...	...	...	...	...	...	...	...	...	...	...	...
MSME loan borrowers to total bank borrowers (%)	...	...	...	...	...	...	...	...	...	...	...	...	...	...	...	...	...	...
MSME loan rejection rate (% of total applications)	...	...	...	...	...	...	...	...	...	...	...	...	...	...	...	...	...	...
Number of MSME savings account in banks	...	...	...	...	...	...	...	...	...	...	...	...	...	...	...	...	...	...
Guaranteed MSME loans (AMD million)	...	...	...	...	...	...	...	...	...	...	...	...	...	...	...	...	...	...
Non-collateral MSME loans (AMD million)	...	...	...	...	...	...	...	...	...	...	...	...	...	...	...	...	...	...
MSME loans outstanding by sector (% share)																		
Agriculture, forestry, and fisheries	...	...	...	...	...	...	...	...	...	...	...	...	...	...	...	...	3.8	6.6
Manufacturing	...	...	...	...	...	...	...	...	...	...	...	...	...	...	...	...	14.1	14.3
Transportation and communication	...	...	...	...	...	...	...	...	...	...	...	...	...	...	...	...	4.6	3.8
Construction	...	...	...	...	...	...	...	...	...	...	...	...	...	...	...	...	12.6	15.2
Wholesale and retail trade	...	...	...	...	...	...	...	...	...	...	...	...	...	...	...	...	28.8	28.4
Other services	...	...	...	...	...	...	...	...	...	...	...	...	...	...	...	...	14.0	11.9
Others	...	...	...	...	...	...	...	...	...	...	...	...	...	...	...	...	22.2	19.9
MSME loans outstanding by region (% share)																		
Capital city (Yerevan)	...	...	...	...	...	...	...	...	...	...	...	...	...	...	...	...	71.7	75.9
Other	...	...	...	...	...	...	...	...	...	...	...	...	...	...	...	...	28.3	24.1
MSME loans outstanding by type of use (% share)																		
For working capital	...	...	...	...	...	...	...	...	...	...	...	...	...	...	...	...	...	...
For capital investment	...	...	...	...	...	...	...	...	...	...	...	...	...	...	...	...	...	...
MSME loans outstanding by tenor (% share)																		
Less than 1 year	...	...	...	...	...	...	...	...	...	...	...	...	...	...	...	...	5.0	6.5
1-5 years	...	...	...	...	...	...	...	...	...	...	...	...	...	...	...	...	40.5	39.6
More than 5 years	...	...	...	...	...	...	...	...	...	...	...	...	...	...	...	...	54.4	53.9

GDP = gross domestic product; MSME = micro, small, and medium-sized enterprise.

* State-owned development financial institution is DICA - Development and Investment Corporation of Armenia (see DICA.am).

** Weighted average interest rates on deposits and lending from legal entities and households by commercial banks. Average deposit and lending rates (up to 1 year, excluding demand in AMD).

*** MSME loans include only resident loans.

**** Loans outstanding includes loans of legal entities and individuals (bank-related loans of entities and individuals are also included).

Source: ADB Asia SME Monitor 2022 database. Data from the Central Bank of Armenia.

Table 2.4: Public Financing and Guarantees

End-of-period data

Item	2004	2005	2006	2007	2008	2009	2010	2011	2012	2013	2014	2015	2016	2017	2018	2019	2020	2021
SUBSIDIZED LOANS TO MSMEs																		
Number of funds	...	...	...	...	...	...	...	...	...	...	...	...	...	...	...	...	...	...
Number of subsidized loans (new approval)*	...	...	...	12	5	3	3	...	...	...	...	...	...	...	...	...	...	...
Outstanding of subsidized loans to MSMEs (AMD million)	...	...	...	...	...	...	...	...	...	...	...	...	...	...	...	...	...	...
Subsidized loans disbursed to MSMEs (AMD million)	...	...	...	2.9	1.2	0.7	1.1	...	...	...	...	...	...	...	...	...	...	...
Growth (%)	...	...	...	...	(57.6)	(46.3)	63.2	...	...	...	...	...	...	...	...	...	...	...
Number of MSMEs that accepted subsidized loans	...	...	...	12	5	3	3	...	...	...	...	...	...	...	...	...	...	...
MSME access to subsidized loans (% of total MSMEs)	...	...	...	...	...	...	...	...	...	...	...	...	...	...	...	...	...	...

MSME = micro, small, and medium-sized enterprise.

Source: ADB Asia SME Monitor 2022 database. Data from Reports of the Ministry of Finance (i) 2007-2020 https://minfin.am/hy/page/petakan_byujei_hashvetvutyun/; (ii) SME DNC reports 2004-2019 https://smednc.am/hy/files

End-of-period data

Item	2004	2005	2006	2007	2008	2009	2010	2011	2012	2013	2014	2015	2016	2017	2018	2019	2020	2021
CREDIT GUARANTEES																		
Number of guarantee schemes	1	1	1	2	2	2	2	2	2	2	2	3	2	3	3	2	1	...
Guaranteed loans outstanding to MSMEs (AMD million)	...	...	...	...	...	...	...	...	...	...	...	...	...	...	...	...	...	...
Guaranteed loans approved to MSMEs (AMD million)**	25.5	197.6	342.2	405.9	257.8	405.6	117.0	89.5	447.6	924.0	932.0	824.8	86.2	501.0	360.3	362.6	136.9	...
Guaranteed loans disbursed to MSMEs (AMD million)***	47.3	366.1	628.1	748.0	428.5	598.1	181.2	122.1	578.1	1,104.1	1,091.0	859.5	84.3	709.9	369.7	351.3	128.1	...
Growth (%)	...	674.0	71.6	19.1	(42.7)	39.6	(69.7)	(32.6)	373.5	91.0	(1.2)	(21.2)	(90.2)	742.1	(47.9)	(5.0)	(63.5)	...
Number of MSMEs guaranteed	7	56	87	129	97	122	53	28	150	243	235	176	18	81	64	82	30	...
MSME access to credit guarantees (% of total MSMEs)	...	...	...	...	...	...	...	...	...	...	...	...	...	...	...	...	...	...
Guaranteed MSME loans to total MSME loans (%)	...	...	...	...	...	...	...	...	...	...	...	...	...	...	...	...	...	...
Nonperforming guaranteed MSME loans to total guaranteed MSME loans (NPL ratio; %)	...	...	...	...	...	...	...	...	...	...	...	...	...	...	...	...	...	...

MSME = micro, small, and medium-sized enterprise; NPL = nonperforming loan.

* Starting 2011, the main state financing mechanisms for MSMEs were credit guarantees, while subsidizing programs for 2007-2010 were pilot programs, which were discontinued. The government switched back to credit guarantees and did not provide subsidies to MSMEs for those years.

** The approved guarantee amount is the amount of the guarantee provided by the relevant state fund. For startups, the guarantee covers the entire loan amount, and for existing businesses, the guarantee covers up to 70% of the loan amount.

*** The amount of the guaranteed loan provided to MSMEs is the amount provided by the relevant partner bank or financial institution for the project guaranteed by the relevant state fund.

**** In 2020, two programs for neutralizing the economic consequences of coronavirus were approved for special SMEs (third measure and 19th measure), for which AMD9 billion and AMD560 million, respectively, were provided (data are included in the COVID-19 responses file).

Source: ADB Asia SME Monitor 2022 database. Data from the Ministry of Economy of the Republic of Armenia.

Table 2.5: Nonbank Finance

End-of-period data

Item	2004	2005	2006	2007	2008	2009	2010	2011	2012	2013	2014	2015	2016	2017	2018	2019	2020	2021
NUMBER OF NONBANK FINANCE INSTITUTIONS																		
Nonbank finance institutions, total	35	33	96	93	106	156	171	178	182	188	181	190	188	174	173	158	142	134
Microfinance institutions*	9	10	17	21	24	27	32	32	32	33	32	32	34	35	39	43	44	46
Pawnshops	...	...	64	62	70	117	128	137	143	148	142	151	147	132	127	108	91	81
Insurance companies	26	23	15	10	12	12	11	9	7	7	7	7	7	7	7	7	7	7
MICROFINANCE INSTITUTIONS																		
Financing outstanding, total (AMD million)	2,393	4,848	14,677	35,820	53,461	50,296	59,654	80,788	113,244	135,674	165,821	177,707	165,179	191,864	228,077	339,434	304,242	303,083
Growth (%)	...	102.6	202.8	144.1	49.3	(5.9)	18.6	35.4	40.2	19.8	22.2	7.2	(7.0)	16.2	18.9	48.8	(10.4)	(0.4)
Total financing to GDP (%)	0.1	0.2	0.6	1.1	1.5	1.6	1.7	2.1	2.7	3.0	3.4	3.5	3.3	3.4	3.8	5.2	4.9	4.3
Annual lending rate (%, on average)	...	...	...	...	...	...	...	...	...	...	...	...	...	...	...	...	...	...
Gross nonperforming loans (NPLs) (AMD million)	...	...	...	...	...	...	...	...	...	...	...	...	...	...	...	...	...	...
Gross NPLs to total loans (%)	...	...	...	...	...	...	...	...	...	...	...	...	...	...	...	...	...	...
Savings (AMD million)	1,210	1,738	4,662	8,520	9,027	11,542	16,444	23,273	24,893	28,923	38,424	54,347	69,578	59,596	83,405	115,162	68,572	75,049
Number of customers financed, total	...	...	...	...	...	...	...	...	...	...	...	...	...	...	...	...	...	...
Financing outstanding by sector (% share)																		
Agriculture, forestry, and fisheries	...	...	...	...	...	...	24.5	28.1	26.1	28.5	30.3	33.0	30.8	28.0	26.1	20.2	23.5	22.8
Manufacturing	...	...	...	...	...	...	7.3	13.6	13.3	12.5	11.1	10.4	8.4	6.6	5.4	4.9	6.8	7.4
Transportation and communication	...	...	...	...	...	...	4.0	1.0	0.9	1.2	4.3	1.2	1.1	1.0	1.0	1.1	1.4	1.3
Construction	...	...	...	...	...	...	5.9	4.2	5.2	4.2	3.0	2.2	1.8	2.3	1.7	1.5	2.1	2.6
Wholesale and retail trade	...	...	...	...	...	...	21.7	18.6	17.3	16.3	15.1	14.1	11.9	11.5	9.6	7.2	7.7	6.9
Other services	...	...	...	...	...	...	28.7	31.3	34.0	32.8	31.7	34.4	40.7	46.7	50.9	43.4	40.2	36.3
Others	...	...	...	...	...	...	8.0	3.3	3.1	4.6	4.5	4.7	5.3	4.0	5.2	21.7	18.2	22.7
Financing outstanding by region (% share)																		
Capital city (Yerevan)	...	...	...	...	...	...	...	...	...	...	...	...	...	...	...	...	...	...
Others	...	...	...	...	...	...	...	...	...	...	...	...	...	...	...	...	...	...
PAWNSHOPS																		
Financing outstanding, total (AMD million)	...	...	1,713	2,410	3,921	5,147	9,930	12,954	15,103	14,151	8,389	8,796	8,432	7,857	8,139	8,168	6,895	6,708
Growth (%)	...	...	...	40.7	62.7	31.3	92.9	30.5	16.6	(6.3)	(40.7)	4.8	(4.1)	(6.8)	3.6	0.4	(15.6)	(2.7)
Total financing to GDP (%)	...	...	0.06	0.08	0.11	0.16	0.29	0.34	0.35	0.31	0.17	0.17	0.17	0.14	0.14	0.12	0.11	0.10
Annual financing rate (%, on average)	...	...	...	...	...	...	...	...	...	...	...	...	...	...	...	...	...	...
Gross nonperforming financing (NPFs) (AMD million)	...	...	...	...	...	...	...	...	...	...	...	...	...	...	...	...	...	...
Gross NPFs to total financing (%)	...	...	...	...	...	...	...	...	...	...	...	...	...	...	...	...	...	...
Number of customers financed, total	...	...	...	...	...	...	...	...	...	...	...	...	...	...	...	...	...	...

GDP = gross domestic product.

* Microfinance institutions are referred to in the Armenian law as credit organizations. The activity of a credit organization is defined as the business activity of borrowing and (or) concluding similar transactions and lending in the form of credits or other investments. Law regulating the activity of credit organizations can be found here: http://www.parliament.am/law_docs/220602HO359eng.pdf?lang=eng.

Source: ADB Asia SME Monitor 2022 database. Data from the Central Bank of Armenia.

Table 2.6: Capital Markets

End-of-period data

Item	2004	2005	2006	2007	2008	2009	2010	2011	2012	2013	2014	2015	2016	2017	2018	2019	2020	2021
EQUITY MARKET																		
Main Board																		
Index*	...	...	...	...	...	...	...	...	...	...	...	...	...	...	...	...	...	...
Market capitalization (AMD million)	8,796	18,877	21,872	32,090	53,991	53,097	52,621	53,847	53,333	61,698	73,001	103,771	134,305	143,799	145,740	148,926	134,949	173,900
Growth (%)	...	114.6	15.9	46.7	68.2	(1.7)	(0.9)	2.3	(1.0)	15.7	18.3	42.1	29.4	7.1	1.4	2.2	(9.4)	28.9
Trading value (AMD million)	851	605	2,150	1,517	262	98	128	200	413	1,494	28,772	4,313	20,511	12,057	2,142	2,162	1,657	406
Trading volume (million shares)	1.3	1.1	0.7	0.5	0.3	0.1	0.1	0.1	0.2	0.6	0.3	1.0	138.5	5.7	1.8	0.3	0.2	1.1
Number of listed companies	...	197	35	33	10	11	11	11	11	11	11	10	11	10	10	10	11	10
Number of IPOs	...	...	...	...	...	...	...	...	...	...	...	...	...	...	...	...	...	...
Number of delisted companies	...	1	...	...	...	...	...	...	...	...	...	...	...	...	...	...	...	1
C Platform**																		
Market capitalization (AMD million)	...	...	...	...	...	...	...	...	...	...	...	...	...	...	...	...	...	...
Growth (%)	...	...	...	...	...	...	...	...	...	...	...	...	...	...	...	...	...	...
Trading value (AMD million)	744	586	2,048	1,473	240	95	98	81	191	1,087	28,695	2,881	7	6,654	60	1,542	1,639	393
Trading volume (million shares)	1.3	1.1	0.7	0.5	0.3	0.1	0.1	0.0	0.1	0.2	0.2	0.04	0.01	1.2	0.3	0.2	0.2	1.1
Number of listed companies	...	...	...	...	...	...	...	...	...	...	...	...	...	...	...	...	...	...
Number of IPOs	...	...	...	...	...	...	...	...	...	...	...	...	...	...	...	...	...	...
Number of delisted companies	...	...	...	...	...	...	...	...	...	...	...	...	...	...	...	...	...	...
Moved to the main board	...	...	...	...	...	...	...	...	...	...	...	...	...	...	...	...	...	...
Moved from the main board	...	...	...	...	...	...	...	...	...	...	...	...	...	...	...	...	...	...

IPO = initial public offering.

* There is no Armenian Securities Exchange index.

** There is no specialized board for MSMEs, but Armenia has a C platform (free market for all) which can also be considered for MSMEs. The numbers provided in the C platform are also included in the main board. In addition, for C platform, there are no specialized listing requirements. The C platform is operating under the stock exchange.

Source: ADB Asia SME Monitor 2022 database. Data from Central Depository of Armenia (AMX).

Table 2.6a: Listing Requirements Armenia Securities Exchange

Criteria	Stock		
	Primary List (A)	Secondary List (B)	Free Market or C platform (also available for MSMEs)
Total calculation value	No less than AMD1 billion.	No less than AMD500 mjillion	None.
Issuer's period of operation	No less than 3 years.	No less than 3 years.	None.
Independent auditor and a positive net profit requirements	Issuer's financial statements for the past 3 years shall be approved by an independent auditor and shall contain a positive net profit.	None.	None.
The minimum number of registered shareholders	There must be at least 100 registered shareholders of a given class of Issuer's securities.	None.	None.
Free float	The portion of securities in public circulation shall be no less than 15% of the total number of voting shares.	The portion of securities in public circulation shall be no less than 10% of the total number of voting shares.	None.
Market makers	The issuer should ensure that the bond has at least one market maker on the exchange.	None.	None.

MSME = micro, small, and medium-sized enterprise.

Note: Other general listing requirements are stated in Article 3 of Rules on Securities Listing and Admission to Trading Regulation of AMX https://amx.am/uploads/company/documents/jA1GEDDQbJATUe2gnsdcHl10ohOFQRjWKgCfrSIS.pdf

Source: ADB Asia SME Monitor 2022 database. Data from Central Depository of Armenia (AMX).

Table 2.7: Policies and Regulations

Regulations	
Name	**Outline**
Law No.121 of 2000 on State Support for Small and Medium Entrepreneurship	The purpose of this law is to define the criteria of small and medium enterprises, the main directions of state support, the principles of implementation of state policy in that sphere.
Tax Code No.165 of 2016 of the Republic of Armenia	It regulates the relations related to the payments provided by the Tax Code, defines the principles of the tax system of the Republic of Armenia, the concepts of tax payment, types, scope of taxpayers, tax rates, tax calculation, and payments, among others.
Law No.232 of 2001 on Joint Stock Companies	The law defines the legal status of joint-stock companies, the procedure for their establishment, implementation and termination of activities, the rights and obligations of shareholders, as well as ensures the protection of the rights of shareholders, creditors and legal interests.
Law No.122 of 2008 on Consumer Credit	Law also applies to loans of up to AMD5 million and (or) credits in foreign currency equivalent to agricultural and micro economic entities up to AMD5 million and (or) in foreign currency equivalent.
Law No.252 of 2001 on Companies with Limited Liability	The law regulates the legal relations arising in connection with the establishment, activity, reorganization, and liquidation of these companies.
Prime Minister No.638 Decision of 2011 on Establishing a Small and Medium Enterprise Development Council of the Republic of Armenia	The purpose of the decision is to ensure an effective dialogue between the state and the business community on improving the business environment in the field of small and medium enterprises.

Regulators and Policymakers	
Name	**Responsibility**
Ministry of Economy	The ministry is the focal ministry for MSME development. It is responsible for developing SME strategies and submitting them to the government . The Ministry is also responsible for state-supported programs for MSMEs.
Ministry of Finance	The ministry is responsible for the provision of appropriate funding and implementation of reports for the implementation of state support programs for MSMEs.
State Revenue Committee (SRC)	The committee is responsible for tax regulation and tax collection. The State Revenue Committee implements tax and customs reforms for the development of small and medium enterprises. In particular, the SRC is responsible for the entire policy implemented to reduce the accounting costs of MSMEs. At the same time, the SRC establishes simple procedures for MSMEs by reducing the amount of information they submit to tax authorities.
Central Bank of Armenia (CBA)	Regulate and supervise banks, microfinance institutions, pawnshops, and insurance companies.
Enterprise Armenia (fromer Small and Medium Entrepreneurship Development National Center [SMEDNC])	SMEDNC was authorized to provide state support to small and medium entrepreneurship in the country. The support is provided through implementation of annual SME state support programs with resources allocated from the state budget.
Small and Medium Enterprise Development Council of the Republic of Armenia	The council is an advisory body to promote the development of the business environment for small and medium-sized enterprises through public-private sector dialogue, to identify existing barriers to MSME activities, and to propose solutions to eliminate them.

Policies		
Name	**Responsible Entity**	**Outline**
2011 State Support Program for Small and Medium Entrepreneurship (Government No.80 Decision of 2011)	Ministry of Economy	This decision envisages support mechanisms for MSMEs in 2011: 1) Create an enabling regulatory and administrative environment. 2) Enhance competitiveness. 3) Improve access to finance. 4) Enhance access to markets and enlarging markets for MSMEs.
2012 State Support Program for Small and Medium Entrepreneurship (Government No.1790 Decision of 2011)	Ministry of Economy	This decision envisages support mechanisms for MSMEs in 2012: 1) Improving access to finance. 2) Formation of new entrepreneurs. 3) Promoting the increase of productivity for upgrading the quality and standard of products and services of MSMEs. 4) Encouraging and creating favorable conditions for establishing business member organizations. 5) Enhancing entrepreneurial attitude and characteristics within society.

continued on next page

Table 2.7 *continued*

2013 Program "Support to Small and Medium Enterprises" and the Program Implementation Schedule (Government No.55 Decision of 2013)	Ministry of Economy	This decision envisages support mechanisms for MSMEs in 2013: 1) Increasing the provision of supports and business development services (BDS). 2) Creating an enabling environment. 3) Access to finance. 4) Creating and developing entrepreneurs. 5) Business development consultation. 6) Increasing productivity. 7) Market access and expansion.
2014 Program "Support to Small and Medium Enterprises" and the Program Implementation Schedule (Government No.1511 Decision of 2013)	Ministry of Economy	This decision envisages support mechanisms for MSMEs in 2014: 1) Create favorable environment to start and operate a business 2) Promote productivity, technology, and innovation. 3) Promote access to finance. 4) Access and expand markets. 5) Entrepreneurial development. 6) Providing and accessing information.
2015 Program "Support to Small and Medium Enterprises" and the Program Implementation Schedule (Government No.217 Decision of 2015)	Ministry of Economy	This decision envisages support mechanisms for MSMEs in 2015: 1) Improe the availability and sustainability of credit. 2) Strengthen village funds. 3) Promote access to business development counseling. 4) Promote advanced technology use. 5) Use and protect intellectual property.
2016 Program "Support to Small and Medium Enterprises" and the Program Implementation Schedule (Government No.403 Decision of 2016)	Ministry of Economy	This decision envisages support mechanisms for MSMEs in 2016: 1) Access to finance. 2) Access to markets. 3) Capacity development of human resources. 4) Strengthening business capacity. 5) Financial education.
Small and Medium Entrepreneurship Development Strategy 2020-2024 (Government No.1443 Decision of 2020)	Ministry of Economy	The strategy aims to promote reforms to increase MSME competitiveness in key areas such as the regulatory framework, access to resources (including finance), human capital development, market access, and business culture: 1) Improve the regulatory environment and public administration of economic activities. 2) Cooperation among MSMEs, large firms, and foreign investment firms. 3) Ensure the necessary conditions and environment required for enterprises to raise capital through capital markets. 4) Promote advanced technology use. 5) Develop modern information and communication technology systems that are well-suited to the desired level of market growth.
Small and Medium Entrepreneurship Development Strategy 2016-2018 (Government No.44 Decision of 2015)	Ministry of Economy	A common approach to the MSME policies, programs and actions developed, implemented by state structures, civil society representatives, the private sector and international organizations: 1) Use and protect intellectual property. 2) Increase producitivty and market access and expansion. 3) Foster an entrepreneurial culture across all segments of society. Enhancement of entrepreneurship education and skills. 4) Accelerate economic growth through innovation-driven enterprises. Facilitate technology exchange and innovation. 5) Optimize the regulatory environment and access to finance. Improve access to finance and financial inclusion for entrepreneurs and enterprises.
Strategic Development Plan of Armenia for 2014-2025 (Government No.442 Decision of 2014)	Ministry of Economy	The document outlines the general set of socio-economic development priorities for the country through 2025, its goals, the main obstacles to development, the constraints, key reforms needed to achieve the priorities, policy tools, and the main risks: 1) Create national security for public contentment. 2) Boost the entrepreneurial capabilities and performance. Enhance entrepreneurship skills and capabilities of companies. Strengthen supply chain management. 3) Enhance different capacities to promote constant economic development. 4) Internationalize high-growth enterprises. Promote networking and business collaboration. 5) Broaden opportunities and promote equality in society.

MSME = micro, small, and medium-sized enterprise.

Source: ADB Asia SME Monitor 2022 database. Data from https://www.arlis.am/, The Ministry of Economy of Armenia, Central Bank of Armenia.

Table 2.7a: COVID-19 Emergency Measures

	Name	Fund Size (AMD '000)	Actual Spent (AMD '000)	Performance (%)	Outline
Business Sector					
1	The first package of measures to alleviate the consequences of COVID-19 outbreak (2020)	6,047,000	6,000,000	99.2	The general objective of the program is to support separate business entities operating in the Republic of Armenia to solve possible liquidity issues resulting from by the COVID-19 outbreak.
2	The second package of measures to alleviate the consequences of COVID-19 outbreak (2020)	4,000,000	4,000,000	100.0	The aim of the measures is to support separate business entities operating in the agriculture sector to solve possible liquidity issues resulting from the COVID-19 outbreak.
3	The third package of measures to alleviate the consequences of COVID-19 outbreak (2020)	9,300,000	8,876,354	95.4	The aim of this package is to support business entities that derive from small and medium-sized entrepreneurship and meet the criteria set out in this program, to solve possible liquidity issues resulting from the COVID-19 outbreak.
4	The fifth package of measures to alleviate the consequences of COVID-19 outbreak (2020)	2,200,000	2,165,534	98.4	Beneficiaries are provided with a one-time grant in accordance with the relevant formula. Target: effective job support. Beneficiary: resident economic entity with 2–50 employees. Potential beneficiaries: more than 12,000 businesses. One-time grant, in the amount of the salary of every fifth employee.
5	The 10th package of measures to alleviate the consequences of COVID-19 outbreak (2020)	300,000	294,684	98.2	Target: support for microenterprises. Beneficiaries: economic entities registered as microenterprises. Support: one-time assistance in the amount of 10% of the turnover of goods, services provided in the first quarter of 2020, but not more than twice the minimum wage.
6	The 18th package of measures to alleviate the consequences of COVID-19 outbreak (2020)	2,114,000	2,113,997	100.0	Target: Effective job support, Beneficiary: economic entities registered in the Republic of Armenia that had 2–100 employees from 1 February 2020 to 30 April 2020; Form of Support: one-time grant; Basic Terms and Conditions: the actual income fund calculated by the economic entities has not decreased during the period, or the decrease is no more than 5%.
7	The 19th package of measures to alleviate the consequences of COVID-19 outbreak (2020)	562,500	562,500	100.0	Target: support for competitive business ideas, entrepreneurial ideas developed by beneficiaries seeking to start a business, promotion of innovative business plans Beneficiary: Armenia-registered economic entity or individual entrepreneur.
8	The 21st package of measures to alleviate the consequences of COVID-19 outbreak (2020)	2,630,000	2,614,917	99.4	Target: effective job support. Beneficiary: business entities with 2–100 employees as of 1 March 2020 through 31 May 2020. Form of assistance: one-time grant in the amount of the salary of every fifth employee.
9	The 23th package of measures to alleviate the consequences of COVID-19 outbreak (2020)	3,300,000	2,399,890	72.7	The purpose of the event is to support the continuation of activities and the maintenance of jobs in the current situation due to the difficulties encountered by the economic entities of the Republic of Armenia in certain spheres directly related to tourism due to the spread of coronavirus.

continued on next page

Table 2.7a *continued*

	Name	Fund Size (AMD '000)	Actual Spent (AMD '000)	Performance (%)	Outline
10	The 24th package of measures to alleviate the consequences of COVID-19 outbreak (2020)	350,000	274,280	78.4	The aim of the package is to support economic entities engaged in agricultural raw materials, including grape processing, as well as grape refrigeration and export in the Republic of Armenia in 2020.
11		280,000	258,714	92.4	
12	The 25th package of measures to alleviate the consequences of COVID-19 outbreak (2020)	250,000	36,135	14.5	Transport companies will be provided with support for 75% of unpaid interest from 1 April 2020, to help them fulfill their credit obligations to ensure the continuity of their activities, as well as to protect the collateral property for the development loan.
13	Other support provided by ministry of economy	5,880,979	4,962,407	84.4	Provision of accommodation for isolated persons due to COVID-19.
14	Subsidizing interest rates on coronavirus (COVID-19) economic repercussions	3,500,000	2,318,075	66.2	Provision of loans on affordable terms to neutralize the economic consequences of COVID-19.
15	Lending to the economy to neutralize the economic effects of coronavirus (COVID-19)	7,500,000	7,500,000	100.0	Ensure access to finance.
16	Providing a budget loan to the Artsakh Republic	5,100,000	5,100,000	100.0	Assistance related to the implementation of current expenses of the Republic of Artsakh.
17	Financial assistance to transport companies due to COVID-19	108,139	108,139	100.0	Assistance provided to transport companies to alleviate problems.
Education Sector					
18	Elimination of problems caused by the coronavirus in the field of education	3,187	2,723	85.4	Provision of appropriate support to education.
Health Sector					
19	Implementation of prevention, control, treatment, and other complex measures for coronavirus infection (COVID-19) in the Republic of Armenia	26,491,924	26,491,923	100.0	To eliminate the health risks of COVID-19, the state has implemented several measures. Under this assistance, both medical assistance was provided along with acquisition of vaccines and other support.
20	Implementation of diagnostic measures for coronavirus infection (COVID-19) in the Republic of Armenia	1,229,506	1,129,409	91.9	
21	Measures to obtain a vaccine for the prevention of coronavirus infection (COVID) in the Republic of Armenia	890,000	890,000	100.0	
22	Procurement of medical devices for the prevention, control and treatment of coronavirus infection (COVID-19) in the Republic of Armenia	755,782	655,782	86.8	
23	Other Support	2,885,020	2,639,135	91.5	
Social Sector					
24	Care services for people over 18 years old	54,844	37,833	69.0	Implementation of social programs by the state to mitigate the impact of the pandemic for certain groups.
25	Social Assistance to Individual Social Groups for Crisis Response, Emergency Response, Mitigation and Elimination	27,525,874	25,921,386	94.2	
Other Support					
26	Financial compensation of self-isolated persons in local self-government bodies conditioned by COVID-19	50,000	31,622	63.2	Other support provided to resolve various problems.
	Grand Total	113,308,756	107,385,439	94.8	

COVID-19 = coronavirus disease

Source: ADB Asia SME Monitor 2022 database. Data from the Government of the Republic of Armenia.

Country Review

Azerbaijan

Overview

Gross domestic product (GDP) expanded by 5.6% in 2021 to reach AZN92.9 billion. According to the Asian Development Bank (ADB), Azerbaijan`s GDP is expected to grow by 3.7% in 2022 and 2.8% in 2023.[79] The economy relies on its energy resources (crude oil and natural gas) and related exports for much of its output. In 2021, mining contributed 34.4% of GDP, followed by wholesale and retail trade (10.1%), transportation and storage (6.9%), manufacturing (6.8%), and agriculture (5.9%).

Out of a population of nearly 10.1 million, 5.3 million were economically active as of 2021. Of those employed, 36.3% worked in agriculture, forestry and fishing sector, followed by trade and transport repair (14.1%), education (7.7%), and construction (7.5%).

In 2020, micro, small, and medium-sized enterprises (MSMEs) accounted for 99.7% of enterprises and generated 348,723 jobs, or 42.1% of those employed. However, their contribution to the gross value added (GVA) remains small.80 The GVA of MSMEs amounted to AZN10.9 billion, or 16.7% of total GVA, mainly from those in wholesale and retail trade, construction, manufacturing, and transportation and storage. Although there is limited information on MSMEs in international markets and global value chains, they have actively participated in government projects and receive public tenders.

Banking is the largest source of finance for businesses. It holds nearly 95% of financial institutions' assets. MSME loans gradually expanded to AZN4.5 billion in 2021, while nonperforming loans (NPLs) to total MSME loans remained high at 6.8% (4.3% of total bank credit). To increase access to finance for MSMEs, the government introduced concessional loan programs (subsidized loans outstanding of AZN625 million in 2021 by Enterprise Development Fund). Microfinance institutions supplement MSME financing, mainly lending to agriculture. The capital market remains weak with a market capitalization of 4.7% of GDP. There is no dedicated MSME market.

Economic diversification is part of Azerbaijan`s long-term strategy toward building sustainable and resilient growth, with MSMEs playing a critical role. In December 2016, the government approved a "Strategic roadmap on the production of consumer goods on the level of small and medium entrepreneurship in Azerbaijan." It sets out a short-term, long-term, and aspirational strategic vision for MSME development. As a result, the Small and Medium Business Development Agency was established in 2018 under the Ministry of Economy to promote entrepreneurship, protect entrepreneurs, facilitate financing, provide training and consulting services, and act as a one-stop shop for MSMEs. The government adopted its "Socio-economic development strategy of the Republic of Azerbaijan for 2022–2026" in July 2022, which also specifies steps leading to the MSME development.

---

79 ADB. 2022. *Asian Development Outlook 2022: Mobilizing Taxes for Development*. Manila. https://www.adb.org/sites/default/files/publication/784041/ado2022.pdf.

80 GVA includes the total value of products and services.

As elsewhere, the coronavirus disease (COVID-19) pandemic worsened the socioeconomic environment affecting MSMEs. In response, the government adopted a package of support measures in 2020 to minimize the pandemic damage on businesses and households.

The Russian invasion of Ukraine added to the crisis for businesses engaged in trading with both countries. However, there have been no measures (such as government support programs for business) taken to directly limit the negative impact of the invasion.

1. Impact of the Global Economy on MSMEs

COVID-19 Impact

COVID-19 caused the greatest public health crisis in Azerbaijan history. The first case was diagnosed at the end of February 2020, with the country going through six waves of COVID-19 infections between March 2020 and June 2022.[81] The first wave in May–August 2020 was relatively mild, whereas the October 2020–January 2021 second wave was devasting in terms of the number of daily infected people and deaths. Three more waves of COVID-19 hit in March–May 2021, July 2021–September 2021, and October 2021–December 2021. The final sixth wave was short lived (January 2022–February 2022). As of end-July 2022, 798,838 people had been infected with 9,748 deaths.

As the number of cases surged in March 2020, the government acted quickly to impose a series of lockdown measures—including social distancing, travel restrictions, closures of non-essential shops, prohibition of public gathering, restricted public movements, and limitations on some commercial activities.[82] E-commerce for essential goods (including medicines) and restaurant delivery were allowed. Lockdown measures were eased or tightened as waves came and went. All lockdown measures were relaxed after May 2022 as the situation began to normalize.

The economy was hit hard by the pandemic soon after it started in 2020. GDP contracted by 4.3% by end-2020 compared to 2019, including a 2.6% decrease in the non-oil sector and a 6.5% drop in the share of hydrocarbons. However, in addition, Azerbaijan's economy was hit by low international oil prices as well as the relatively limited 44-day military conflict with neighboring Armenia in September–October 2020. In April 2020, the Minister of Economy reported that daily economic losses were between AZN120 million to AZN150 million ($70.6 million to $88.2 million) due to the pandemic.[83] Nonetheless, the economy recovered quickly from the crisis during 2021, withy GDP growing by 5.6% compared to 2020.

[81] For details and graphs, see https://www.worldometers.info/coronavirus/country/azerbaijan/

[82] Government introduced an SMS-based permit system for residents to leave their homes or track their current whereabouts in some cities and districts (special quarantine zones).

[83] https://news.day.az/az/economic/1228181.html

Few assessments have been conducted on the COVID-19 impact on MSMEs or business, in general. A survey study by Xu and Abbasov (2021) found around 93% of MSME business operations were either extremely damaged or otherwise negatively impacted.[84] The survey findings also found that those most negatively affected were in tourism (26.6%), restaurants and cafés (22.1%), and education (13.6%), while those delivering essential goods and services—pharmacies (0.2%), insurance (0.8%), and agriculture (1.2%)—were among the least affected by the pandemic. As in many other economies, the pandemic created two business clusters—those devastated by COVID-19 and firms nearly unaffected or benefiting from the pandemic.

Entrepreneurs were optimistic about their business operations during the recovery period. The Deloitte Business Outlook in Azerbaijan surveyed businesses and found that 65% of the respondents believed that their business would return to pre-pandemic conditions less than 1 year from the time of the survey.[85]

The United Nations Entity for Gender Equality and the Empowerment of Women and the United Nations Population Fund conducted telephone interviews in Azerbaijan to assess the impact of COVID-19 on the lives and livelihood of men and women.[86] They found that self-employed men and women (microenterprises) were most affected by lockdown measures compared to those working as employees.

Impact of the Russian Invasion of Ukraine

As the lockdown measures were gradually being relaxed, business owners in Azerbaijan were resuming operations, looking forward to at least partially recovering pandemic-related losses. Those hopes were dashed, however, as inflation and disrupted supply chains continued as the crisis shifted to the Russian invasion of Ukraine.

Given that both the Russian Federation and Ukraine are among Azerbaijan's main trading partners (ranked third and seventh, respectively), the invasion damaged non-oil trade. In January–June 2022, exports to the Russian Federation dropped by 6.8% compared to the same period in 2021. The largest decrease was in potatoes, persimmon, and preformed polypropylene products, among others. As for imports from Ukraine, imports during January–June 2022 decreased by 39.7% compared to the same period in 2021—driven by tobacco, paper and paper products, and medicines, among others.

The Russian Federation's share of Azerbaijan's agricultural and food imports was 35% ($773.4 million) with Ukraine's share 11% ($236.5 million). Thus, a long invasion could seriously dent the supply of food.

Beyond trade, the invasion also affected individual remittances from the Russian Federation and Ukraine to Azerbaijan, where they account for almost 56% of total remittances. According to estimates of the Central Bank of Azerbaijan, private remittances received from the Russian Federation and Ukraine declined by 16.9% and 26.7%, respectively, in first quarter of 2022 compared to the same period in 2021. Sanctions against the Russian Federation also hit migrant employment and their ability to send remittances. The short-term depreciation of the Russian *ruble* also contributed to the drop in remittances during the first months of the invasion.

---

84 Q. Xu and S. Abbasov. 2021. Impact of Covid-19 Pandemic on Small and Medium-Sized Enterprises (SMEs) in Azerbaijan. *Open Journal of Business and Management*. Vol. 9, No.6. pp. 2759-2771. https://www.scirp.org/journal/paperinformation.aspx?paperid=112945.

85 Deloitte. 2022. *Business outlook in Azerbaijan, 2021 Results*. https://www2.deloitte.com/content/dam/Deloitte/az/Documents/risk/BO%20in%20Azerbaijan%202022.pdf.

86 UN Women. Azerbaijan: The impact of COVID-19 on women's and men's lives and livelihoods. https://eca.unwomen.org/sites/default/files/Field%20Office%20ECA/Attachments/Publications/2020/07/Factsheet-Azerbaijan-FIN-min.pdf.

2. MSME Development

- In 2020, MSMEs accounted for 99.7% of Azerbaijan enterprises. Microenterprise workers dominate the MSME labor pool. Most MSMEs work in traditional personal-contact-based businesses such as wholesale and retail trade, as well as transportation and storage. The geographic spread of MSMEs is uneven, with nearly half operating in the capital, Baku.
- MSMEs accounted for 42.1% of the labor force in 2020, a significant increase from the 5.4% in 2004. Average nominal monthly wages for MSME employees are lower than those for the overall economy.
- Although the MSME contribution to GVA has grown to 16.7% (in 2020), its share remains small. Nearly 44.5% of this value added was generated by medium-sized enterprises with 40.7% by microenterprises.
- Access to international markets remains a major challenge. Due to regulatory reform, however, a significant share of government tenders now go to MSMEs.
- E-commerce is growing swiftly as more of the population has access to the internet. Growth accelerated during the mobility restrictions in response to the pandemic. Research and development (R&D) expenditures by MSMEs remain small.
- Several government authorities provide networking, capacity building, government-to-business (G2B) and business-to-business (B2B) services to MSMEs and startups, along with incubation and acceleration opportunities either individually or in collaboration with international development agencies.

Scale of MSMEs

Between 2004 and 2020, the definition of MSMEs in Azerbaijan was changed four times. Through 2017, only small enterprises were classified, based on the number of employees and annual revenue. From 2004 to 2009, small enterprises were defined on criteria approved by the Cabinet of Ministers of the Republic of Azerbaijan (April 2004). Small firms in industry and construction had to have fewer than 40 employees and annual revenue less than AZN200,000; scientific, technical, and consulting services had limits of 20 employees and AZN150,000 in revenue; agriculture, 15 workers and revenues below AZN100,000; wholesale trade, 10 employees and AZN300,000 in revenue; while firms in retail trade, transport, services, and other economic activities were limited to 5 employees and AZN100,000 in revenues.

In December 2009, the Cabinet of Ministers raised limits to qualify as a small enterprise—industry and construction (fewer than 50 employees and AZN500,000 in annual revenue); agriculture (25 employees and AZN250,000);. wholesale trade (15 employees and AZN1 million); and retail trade, transport, services and other economic activities (10 employees and AZN250,000).

A unified definition was introduced in June 2015 for small and medium-sized enterprises (SMEs). Small enterprises were those with fewer than 25 employees and up to AZN200,000 annual revenue. Medium-sized enterprises were firms with 25–125 employees and annual revenues of AZN200,000–AZN1.25 million.

In December 2018, a new classification system was again introduced, this time removing disparities between different government agencies. Microenterprises were introduced as firms with up to 10 employees and annual revenues up to AZN200,000; small enterprises had 11–50 employees and annual revenues more than AZN200,000 but less than AZN3 million; and medium-sized enterprises had 51–250 employees and annual revenues from AZN3 million to AZN30 million (Table 3.1).

As of end-2020, Azerbaijan had 316,370 operating MSMEs (Figure3.1A and Table 3.2). They grew between 2004 and 2020 at a 4% compound annual growth rate (CAGR). However, as the definitions of MSMEs changed, so did the number of MSMEs. The new definitions allowed the government to shrink or expand MSME coverage—a remarkable reduction in 2011 and surge in 2018. Interestingly, the number of MSMEs increased by 16.6% in 2020 over 2019 even during the COVID-19 pandemic, mostly the result of new microenterprises, as many previously unregistered microenterprises registered to qualify for support, particularly in health and social works (up 110%), information and communication (69%), education (64%), and transportation and storage (54%). By firm size, microenterprises accounted for 97% of MSMEs in 2020, with small enterprises (1.9%) and medium-sized enterprises (0.9%) holding small fractions.

Most MSMEs are engaged in businesses requiring personal contact. As of end-2020, 32.8% of MSMEs operated in wholesale and retail trade, followed by transportation and storage (20.9%), manufacturing (3.9%), and construction (3.7%) (Figure 3.1B).[87] Other services such as accommodation and food, information and communication, and real estate accounted for 35.0%.

In 2020, the vast majority of MSMEs had no state participation (99.4%), while the remaining 0.6% were state-owned. Among non-state-owned enterprises, 99.0% were privately owned, 0.8% foreign-owned, and 0.2% joint ventures.

Geographically, the distribution of MSMEs is uneven. Nearly half operate in the capital city, Baku (47.5% in 2020), which is both the most populated city and main economic center—due to the oil and gas industries—followed by regions such as Absheron-Khizi (9.0%), Lankaran-Astara (5.4%), and Shak-Zagatala (5.0%) (Figure 3.1C). In general, the data show huge regional disparities in MSME activities despite the fact that enterprises registered in regions qualify for tax concessions.

87 There are no further statistics are available to breakdown manufacturing sector.

Figure 3.1: Number of MSMEs

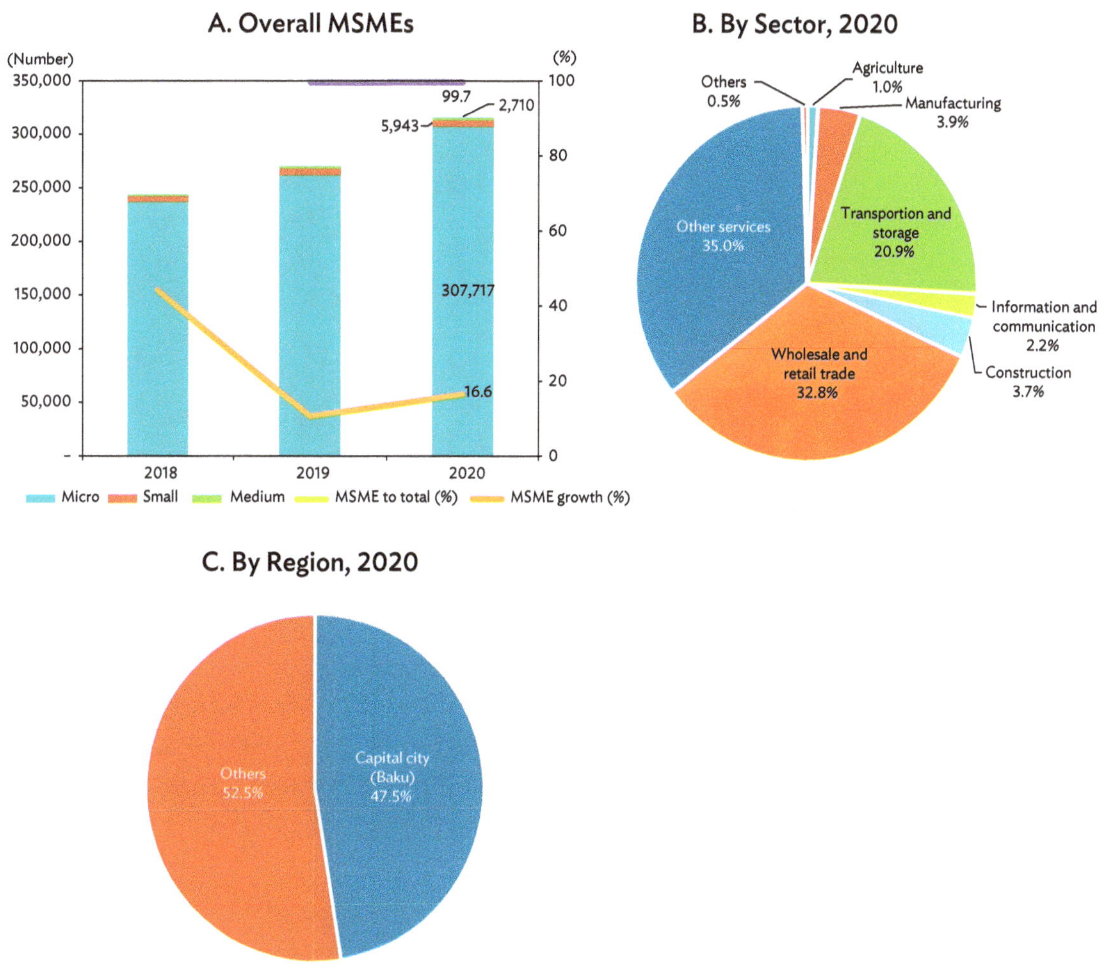

MSME = micro, small, and medium-sized enterprise.

Source: ADB Asia SME Monitor 2022 database. Data from State Statistical Committee of the Republic of Azerbaijan.

Employment

State Statistical Committee data indicates MSMEs generated 348,723 jobs (or 42.1% of the labor force) in 2020 (Figure 3.2A and Table 3.2). Tine-series data indicate that between 2004 and 2020, MSME employment increased significantly at 10% CAGR. Due to the changes in MSME definitions, a remarkable rise in employment was reported in 2015. Medium-sized enterprises held the largest share at 61.9%, followed by small enterprises (26.4%) and microenterprises (11.7%) in 2020.

The largest share of MSME employees work in construction (16.8%), followed by wholesale and retail trade (15.9%); manufacturing (13.6%); others (mining and quarrying, electricity, gas and steam supply, water supply, sewerage, waste management, and remediation activities) (9.5%); transportation and storage (6.6%); agriculture (5.2%); and information and communication (4.4%) (Figure 3.2B). About 28% of MSME employees work in other services that include accommodation and food services, human health and social work, real estate, and education, among others.

Available data also indicate that a significant share of the MSME employment is concentrated in Baku (62.6%) (Figure 3.2C). This is expected, as almost half of MSMEs operating are in Baku city. Other regions include Absheron-Khizi (6.7%) and the Nakhchivan Autonomous Republic (4.7%). The share of other economic regions in total MSME employment ranges between 0.5% and 3.4%. The vast regional gap in MSME employment certainly shows there are less economic opportunities as well as underutilized labor across these regions.

The statistics show that women made up a quarter of MSMEs employees in 2020, suggesting that female labor force participation in MSMEs is relatively low. Microenterprises absorbed the largest share of women employees (29.7%), followed by small (26.9%) and medium-sized (24.1%) enterprises. There is an obvious need to attract more female labor into the job market as well as encourage female businesses, especially female-led MSMEs.

Figure 3.2: Employment by MSMEs

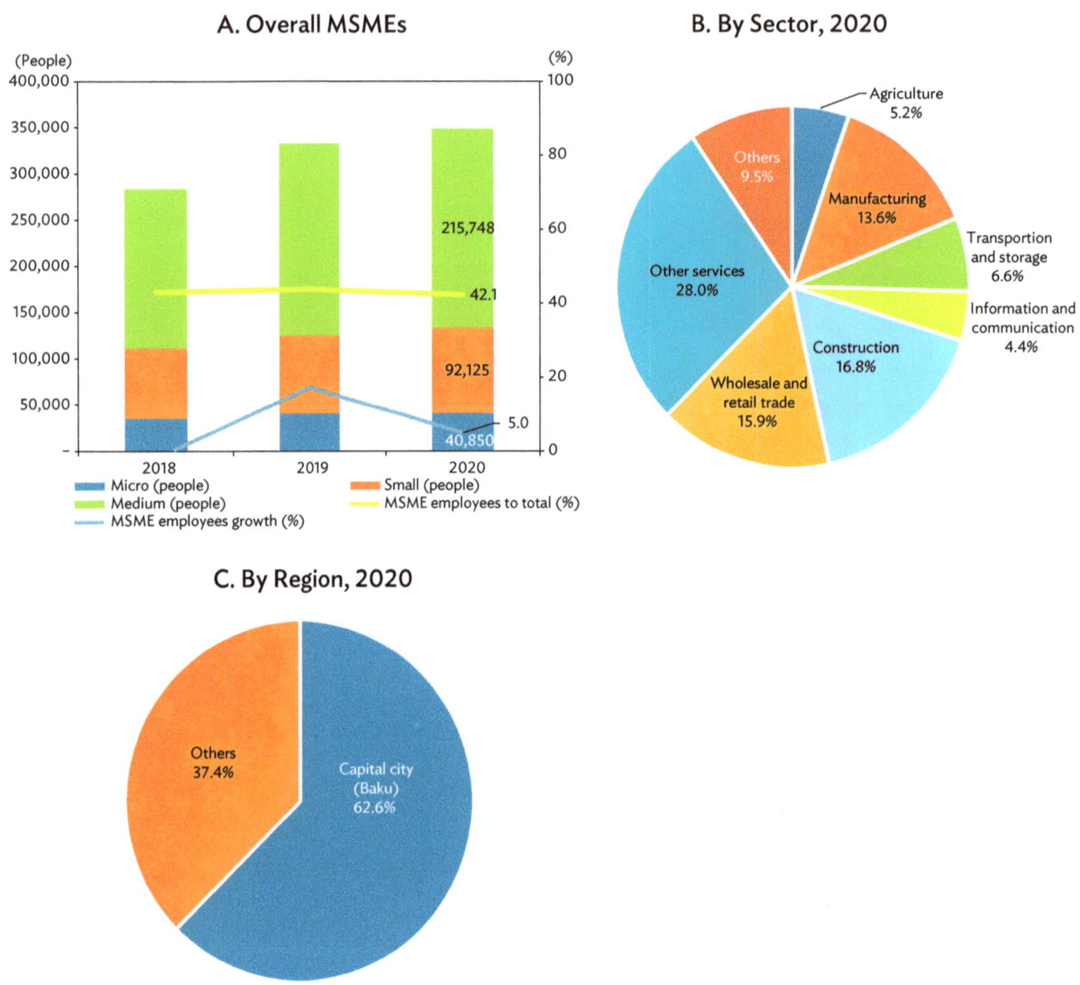

MSME = micro, small, and medium-sized enterprise.

Source: ADB Asia SME Monitor 2022 database. Data from State Statistical Committee of the Republic of Azerbaijan.

The average monthly nominal wage in MSMEs was AZN612.3 ($360.2) in 2020, 15.3% higher from the average nominal wage in 2019.[88] This was below the average monthly wage across all economic activities (AZN707.7 or $416.3). Average nominal wages were higher in medium-sized enterprises (AZN714.4 or $420.2), followed by small enterprises (AZN533.8 or $314) and microenterprises (AZN359.4 or $211.4) in 2020.

Business Productivity

There are no available data on MSME contributions to GDP. However, time-series data exist for GVA. Between 2004 and 2020, MSME GVA grew steadily, following the impressive economic growth driven by oil and gas development (Figure 3.3A and Table 3.2). The GVA of MSMEs increased significantly after 2018, largely explained by changes in defining MSMEs coupled with MSME growth. New definitions added more enterprises under the MSME umbrella, which contributed to the expansion in GVA. In 2020, MSME GVA reached AZN10.9 billion, about 11.2% more than in 2018. In 2020, almost 44.5% of value added came from medium-sized enterprises, with 40.7% from microenterprises. Small enterprises contributed 14.8%.

MSMEs' GVA as a share of total GVA rose from 1.8% in 2004 to 16.7% in 2020, still significantly lower than most developed countries. For instance, in the OECD, MSMEs are the major contributors to value creation, generating between 50% and 60% of GVA,[89] and in the European Union (EU), MSMEs contribute 52.4%.[90]

Based on available data, wholesale and retail trade was the largest contributor to GVA in 2020 (29.4%) (Figure 3.3B). This was followed by construction (14.5%), manufacturing (13.5%), transportation and storage (7.1%), and information and communication (4.3%), similar to the ranking in 2019.

Figure 3.3: MSME Contribution to Gross Value Added

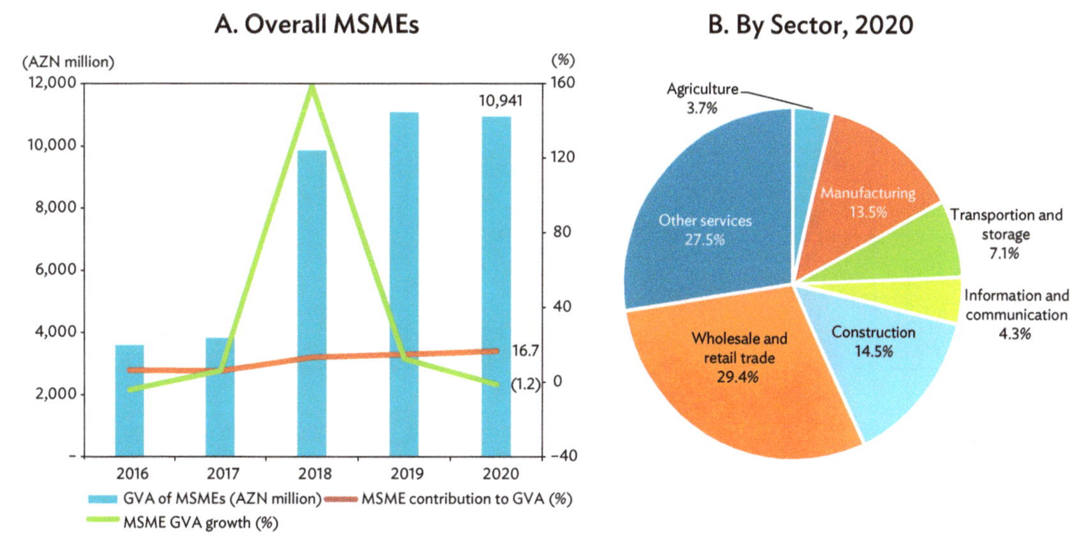

GVA = gross value added; MSME = micro, small, and medium-sized enterprise.

Note: GVA data across the economic sectors are available from 2019.

Source: ADB Asia SME Monitor 2022 database. Data from State Statistical Committee of the Republic of Azerbaijan.

88 As of September 2022, $1=AZN1.7.

89 OECD. 2016b. Entrepreneurship at a Glance 2016. Paris: OECD Publishing.

90 Eurostat. 2022. EU small and medium-sized enterprises: an overview. 27 June. https://ec.europa.eu/eurostat/de/web/products-eurostat-news/-/edn-20220627-1.

Market Access

Although there are no specific data on MSME trade, data for exports and imports are available for businesses in general. According to Aliyev (2019), however, the share of MSME exports does not exceed 5%-6%,[91] meaning there remains great potential for MSMEs to trade internationally and to join global value chains.

Total exports reached $13.7 billion in 2020, almost triple the amount in 2004 (8.2% CAGR) (Figure 3.4 and Table 3.2). Most of this growth derived from crude oil exports. In 2008, the volume of crude oil using the Baku–Tbilis–Ceyhan pipeline (constructed in 2006) was double that exported in 2007. International oil prices were also high. However, due to the 2007–2008 global financial crisis (which affected the global oil market and reduced prices), exports fell in 2009. The same occurred in 2014.

Overall, about 90% of Azerbaijan's export revenues come from oil. There is thus an obvious need to diversify export products. Given that the main exporters in Azerbaijan are large enterprises such as the State Oil Company of Azerbaijan Republic, MSMEs are excluded from hydrocarbon exports. Diversification is needed to internationalize MSMEs.

Figure 3.4: Exports and Imports

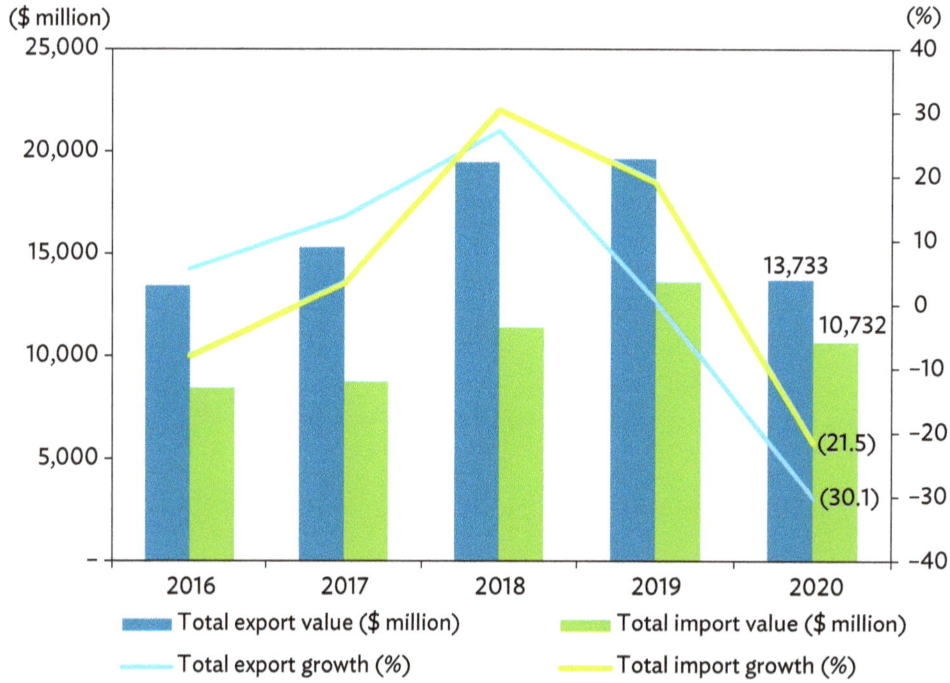

Source: ADB Asia Monitoring 2022 database. Data from the State Statistical Committee of the Republic of Azerbaijan.

[91] S. Aliyev. 2019. Problems and Opportunities for Leveraging SME Finance through Value Chains in Azerbaijan. *ADBI Working Paper Series*. No. 973. Tokyo: ADB Institute. https://www.adb.org/sites/default/files/publication/511266/adbi-wp973.pdf

Imports rose from $3.5 billion in 2004 to $10.7 billion in 2020 (6.8% CAGR) (Table 3.2), largely driven by increased domestic demand, with imports of machinery and equipment for mining leading the way. In general, between 2004–2020, Azerbaijan posted a trade surplus.

The Azerbaijan Export and Investment Promotion Foundation (AZPROMO) under the Ministry of Economy was established in 2003 to promote non-oil exports and attract foreign investment. AZPROMO holds a variety of international events to help develop non-oil business, promote products internationally, facilitate networking with local companies, support foreign companies interested in gathering information about the investment climate, and provide services to interested investors.

There are also opportunities to develop MSME access to the domestic market through government regulatory reforms to increase MSME participation in government tenders. As a result, MSMEs won 90% of government tenders in 2020.[92]

Technology and Innovation

Information and communication technology (ICT) is growing rapidly. The number of internet users per 100 people increased sharply from 46 people in 2010 to 85 in 2020, well above the global average of 60 people and equal to the EU average.[93]

In 2020, the entire population (100%) lived in areas covered by mobile communications. Mobile cellular subscriptions as per 100 people was 102 in 2020, slightly below the global average of 106 people.

E-commerce is growing rapidly as more people access the internet. According to the central bank, e-trade reached AZN7.2 billion in 2020, a more than 20 times increase from 2015 (the first year for which the data are available). The large increase in e-commerce in 2020 may be also attributed to the lockdowns during the pandemic.

B2C dominates e-commerce. Platforms such as tap.az and lalafo.az (marketplaces for private posts), umico.az (selling all types of goods), turbo.az (buying and selling automobiles), bina.az (for real estate), and azexport.az (a government-led digital marketplace for exports) are among the largest e-commerce platforms.

Azerbaijan's Digital Trade Hub is a cutting-edge government startup built on public-private partnerships.[94] It offers various services such as electronic and mobile access to facilitate e-trade and economic activity while reducing transaction costs. Foreign and local entrepreneurs can create and sign documents online, as well as execute real-time electronic services.

R&D expenditures by MSMEs amounted to AZN15.6 million in 2020, 67.2% lower than 2019, again largely due to the pandemic. Most R&D spending went to construction (14%), mining (13.5%), manufacturing (5%), trade and transport repair (4.9%), and transportation and storage (4.1%). In 2020, 49.6% of MSME spending for R&D was in medium-sized enterprises, 42.2% in small enterprises, with the remaining 8.2% in microenterprises. Countrywide, MSME R&D was 9.6% of total R&D.

---

92 Center for Analysis of Economic Reforms and Communication of the Republic of Azerbaijan. 2021. Rashad Huseynov: "Public Procurement Is Being Further Improved. News release. 23 June. https://ereforms.gov.az/en/media/xeberler/resad-huseynov-dovlet-satinalmalari-daha-da-tekmillesdirilir-111.

93 World Bank. Individuals using the Internet (% of population) - Azerbaijan. https://data.worldbank.org/indicator/IT.NET.USER.ZS?locations=AZ

94 Digital Trade Hub of Azerbaijan. https://dth.az.

Box 3.1: The Government's Green Energy Development Initiative

Several renewable energy projects are being implemented in Azerbaijan. One is the pilot "Knowledge Exchange and Technical Assistance for the Development of Floating Solar Systems," funded by the Ministry of Energy and the Asian Development Bank. It will construct a floating solar station with a total capacity of 100 kilowatts (kW) (95 kW on water, 5 kW on land) on Lake Boyukshor. To implement the project, a trilateral agreement was signed between the Ministry of Energy, the State Committee for Urban Planning and Architecture, and Provitaz—an MSME subcontractor providing the reinforced poles to hold the solar panels in place and related technical work. Another example of MSME involvement in clean energy is the "Promotion of Decentralized Renewable Energy Solutions in Azerbaijan" project. EcoEnergy Consulting LLC worked with DENA (German Energy Agency) and the Ministry of Energy. The project identified and analyzed potential local market opportunities and applications for decentralized energy supply from renewable sources. A list of recommendations was drawn up to establish specific support mechanisms.

Source: Ministry of Energy of the Republic of Azerbaijan.

Networking and Support

There are several government agencies for MSMEs. They include (i) the Small and Medium Business Development Agency (SMBDA) under the Ministry of Economy, (ii) the Simplified Support to Family Businesses (ABAD) under the State Agency for Public Services and Social Innovations, (iii) the Incubation and Acceleration Center (INNOLAND) of the State Agency for Citizen Services and Social Innovations, (iv) the Center for Fourth Industrial Revolution Analysis and Coordination under the Ministry of Economy, and (v) the Innovation and Digital Development Agency under the Ministry of Digital Transformation and Transport. There is also EnterpriseAzerbaijan.com—under the Center for Economic Analysis and Communication—which provides networking, capacity building, G2B and B2B services, as well as incubation and acceleration opportunities for MSMEs and startups, either individually or in collaboration with international development agencies.

As a unit of the SMBDA, "SME Houses" was established in 2018, offering one stop shops that deliver G2B and B2B services to MSMEs. Currently, there are two SME Houses operating in Azerbaijan regions. The goal is to establish two SME Houses each year between 2022 and 2024 and one between 2025 and 2026 under the "Socio-economic development strategy of the Republic of Azerbaijan for 2022–2026."[95]

Since 2018, SMBDA has organized "SME Development Centers" (www.kobim.az) that operate in nearly all regions. They assist and guide MSMEs by providing various business development services for MSMEs, including training, advisory services, and business networking activities.

"SME Friends" is a flagship project of the SMBDA. SME Friends are assigned in administrative districts and cities to work closely with businesses in providing comprehensive support. It aims to both create new MSMEs and expand existing ones, in part by identifying investment projects to assist investors. SME friends collects information about the development needs of MSMEs through meetings, surveys, and monitoring.

Established in 2016, ABAD provides business planning, marketing, branding and design, financial accounting, and legal services to family businesses in arts and agriculture to ensure active participation of people in the socioeconomic life of the country.

[95] https://static.president.az/upload/Files/2022/07/22/5478ed13955fb35f0715325d7f76a8ea_3699216.pdf

INNOLAND was established in 2018 as an incubation, acceleration, and research facility that provides co-working space, accelerator and incubator programs, and training for startups.

The Innovation and Digital Development Agency was established in 2021 to assist businesses obtain modern technologies and technological solutions, enable innovation-oriented scientific research and innovative projects (also startups) through financial and innovation initiatives.

The Center for Fourth Industrial Revolution Analysis and Coordination was established in 2021 to attract innovative technologies, promote environmentally friendly solutions, conduct research in artificial intelligence and machine learning while contributing to the growth of the digital economy.

Operated by the Center for Analysis of Economic Reforms and Communication, Enterprise Azerbaijan is a portal designed to attract investment and increase access to alternative funding for business development.

The Azerbaijan Chamber of Commerce and Industry supports local businesses in dealing with foreign chambers, disseminating commercial offers to international organizations and chambers, providing information about foreign companies looking to collaborate with local businesses, organizing international B2B meetings and organizing seminars and conferences.

Although not specifically designed for MSMEs, there are several nonprofit business associations. The National Confederation of Entrepreneurs (Employers) Organizations is among the oldest and largest associations. It protects the rights, property and other interests of entrepreneurship entities with state authorities, municipalities and other organizations; participates in collective bargaining with government and trade unions to regulate labor relations; and helps build permanent business relations between members, assists businesses in finding partners within and outside the country.

There are sector associations such as the Azerbaijan Packaging Industry Association, the Machinery and Equipment Manufacturers Association, the Pomegranate Producers and Exporters Association, the Egg Producers and Exporters Association, the Azerbaijan Hazelnut Producers and Exporters Association, among others. These organizations advocate for their businesses with government and conduct various networking activities.

Finally, there are many foreign trade chambers operating within Azerbaijan—such as the American Chamber of Commerce, Türkiye–Azerbaijan Chamber of Commerce and Industry, German-Azerbaijani Chamber of Commerce, Azerbaijan-France Chamber of Commerce and Industry, Italy Azerbaijan Chamber of Commerce, and Israel Azerbaijan Chamber of Commerce and Industry. They facilitate dialogue with government bodies, organize high-level networking events and offer various business services, including market research, help in finding partners, and organizing B2B meetings, among other services.

Box 3.2: Support Mechanism to Attract Private Investment for Business Development

An "Investment Promotion Certificate" is a legislative document that supports entrepreneurial activities of small and medium-sized businesses and provides grounds for obtaining benefits under the "Tax Code" and the "Law of the Republic of Azerbaijan on Customs Tariffs." Enterprises can apply to the Ministry of Economy to obtain the certificate, which grants entrepreneurs the following benefits:

- 50% reduction of income tax for individual entrepreneurs;
- 50% reduction of profit tax for legal persons;
- value-added tax (VAT) and customs duties exemptions on imports of machinery, technological equipment and installations;
- property tax exemptions; and
- land tax exemptions.

All of the above benefits are restricted to 7 years of the date of the issuance of the certificate.

The government adopted a new order "On certain measures to accelerate economic development in the liberated territories" in December 2021. It also approved "Support for investors applying environmentally friendly technologies, creating green growth, and using renewable energy sources in the liberated territories."

Source: Ministry of Economy of the Republic of Azerbaijan.

3. Access to Finance

- The government supports the MSME credit market, especially through the pandemic. Bank loans to MSMEs have increased considerably, to AZN4.4 billion in 2021, a 29.4% increase from 2020. MSME loans to total loans increased to 26.7% in 2021, rising to 4.8% of GDP. MSME nonperforming loans (NPLs) to total MSME loans fell to 6.8% in 2021, but still above the overall NPL ratio.
- The government offers soft loan programs with interest rate subsidies and credit guarantees to supplement the financial needs of business, including MSMEs. The Mortgage and Credit Guarantee Fund, Agrarian Credit and Development Agency, and Entrepreneurship Development Fund are the main conduits.
- The nonbank finance industry has yet to meet the financial demand of enterprises. Microfinance institutions, credit unions, leasing, and pawnshops are nonbank financing options for businesses, although they do not specifically target MSMEs.
- Digital financial services have yet to emerge, though a newly adopted Digital Payment Strategy for 2021–2023 will support its development. The Azerbaijan Fintech Association was established in 2021, with 25 fintech companies providing services in financial markets.
- The capital market is weak in Azerbaijan, with market capitalization at 4.7% of GDP. There is no dedicated MSME equity market.
- The Azerbaijan Credit Bureau (privaté credit bureau) and the State Register of Encumbrances of Movable Property were established in 2018 as part of reform measures outlined in the Strategic Roadmap for the Development of Financial Services.

Bank Credit

Azerbaijan has a two-tier banking system. The first tier is the Central Bank of the Republic of Azerbaijan with the second tier comprising commercial banks and nonbank credit institutions. As of June 2022, there were 26 banks operating, of which two were state-owned. There are several other financial institutions—nonbanking credit institutions and credit unions—that offer limited banking services. Other financial institutions such as insurance companies, the stock exchange, and leasing firms are small and thus have limited influence on the nationwide financial system.

The banking sector has faced several challenges since 2014. The 2014–2015 oil price shock led to a sharp drop in foreign currency earnings, leading to two *manat* devaluations in 2015 (February and December). The number of NPLs increased substantially and there was a high degree of dollarization. Subsequent reforms improved overall sector stability. Between 2015 and 2017, 15 banks were closed mainly due to high NPLs, poor asset quality, and liquidity shortages. In 2020, an additional four banks were closed for similar reasons. Compared with 2016, the number of bank branches and divisions also fell from 700 to 576 in 2021. Latest available statistics show the share of regional branches to total bank branches dropped from 53.9% in 2018 to 47.6% in 2020. By contrast, the number of nonbank finance institution branches rose from 228 to 266 during 2019–2021. There is a large territorial imbalance between Baku and outside regions in terms of banking service coverage. Baku and the Absheron region represent 52.4% of the banking service network.

The banking industry is thus highly concentrated. Five banks control 73.2% of the banking market share by asset size (in 2021). The largest bank is the state-owned Bank ABB Open Joint Stock Company with a 29.9% market share by asset size. Foreign ownership is in the form of foreign bank subsidiaries from the Russian Federation (Bank VTB) and Türkiye (Ziraat Bank and Yapi Kredi Bank) along with bank branches from Iran and Pakistan.

As of end-2021, banks held assets of AZN38.5 billion, liabilities of AZN33.5 billion, and AZN5 billion in balance capital. Banks' credit portfolio covered 43.3% of banking assets. Deposits covered 80.4% of liabilities (AZN26.9 billion). Bank credits increased from AZN0.9 billion in 2004 to AZN16.7 billion in 2021—a CAGR of 17.8%. Of total loan outstanding in 2021, 74% were in domestic currency with the remaining 26% in foreign currency (mainly US dollars). In general, Azerbaijan has a lower bank-credit-to-GDP ratio than the regional average, with the ratio declining by more than half since 2015, falling to 17.9% in 2021 (Table 3). Although the annual average lending rate dropped by more than 33.2 percentage points between 2004 and 2021, it remains relatively high at 11.8% (2021). Gross NPLs to total loans increased from 2.5% in 2004 to 4.3% in 2021.

Bank deposits increased significantly from 2004 to 2021 with (19.9% CAGR). However, the devaluation in February 2015 was accompanied by a dollarization of deposits, with the second decreasing the deposit base. As a result of measures taken by the government and central bank (changes in deposit regulations, state interventions to stabilize the *manat* exchange rate, among others) and stabilizing oil prices, bank deposits began to increase again by 2017. Since then, the volume of total deposits increased by almost 60% to AZN26.9 billion in 2021. The share of local currency deposits hit a low of 21.2% in 2015, rising to 52.4% in 2021, largely due to the higher annual returns on local currency deposits compared to foreign currency deposits. Annual average deposit rates were 4.8% in 2021, significantly lower than the 9.3% rate in 2004.

Banks allocate more funds to consumer loans for individuals than to the real sector of the economy. In 2021, 49.9% of banking credit was allocated to households, a more than 77-percentage-point increase since 2004. Among firms in 2021, the largest borrowers were in trade and services (17.9%), industry and manufacturing (5.8%), and building and construction (5.4%).

Information on MSME loans is unavailable. Yet, according to the OECD SME Policy Index 2020, Azerbaijan lags behind in terms of MSME access to finance among Eastern Partnership countries with score of 3.12 (against the 3.57 average).[96] Nonetheless, Azerbaijan has shown good progress in facilitating MSME finance in recent years. According to The Global Competitiveness Report 2019, the financial system ranked 24th among the 96 countries included in terms of financing MSMEs.[97] In 2020, investments for fixed capital formation in MSMEs was AZN2.7 billion. About 80% of MSME investment in fixed assets came from local sources with the remaining 20% financed externally. Relatively high interest rates (the annual average MSME interest rate was 11.5% during 2018–2021) along with strict lending terms and conditions led MSMEs to continue to rely on internal funding or personal loans. Compared with 2019, MSME investments in fixed capital fell by 21.9% in 2020 as a result of the pandemic.

Government support for the MSME credit market increased during the COVID-19 crisis. Bank loans to MSMEs increased significantly from 2018 to 2021.[98] The amount of MSME loans rose by 54.7% from AZN2.9 billion to AZN4.4 billion (Figure 3.5A and Table 3.3). However, in 2020, due to the pandemic, MSME loans dropped by almost 8% compared with 2019. MSME loans to total loans outstanding increased by 17.1 percentage points from 22.8% in 2018 to 26.7% in 2021. MSME loans to GDP also increased from 3.6% to 4.8% during the period.

MSME NPLs to total MSME loans fell substantially from 33.4% in 2018 to 6.8% in 2021. Nonetheless, it remains above the gross NPLs to total loan ratio (4.3% in 2021).

Because most MSMEs operate in Baku, it is not surprising MSME credit is concentrated there (73.7% in 2021) with the remaining 26.3% in other regions (Figure 3.5B). However, the gap narrowed somewhat between 2018 and 2021.

Figure 3.5: MSME Loans

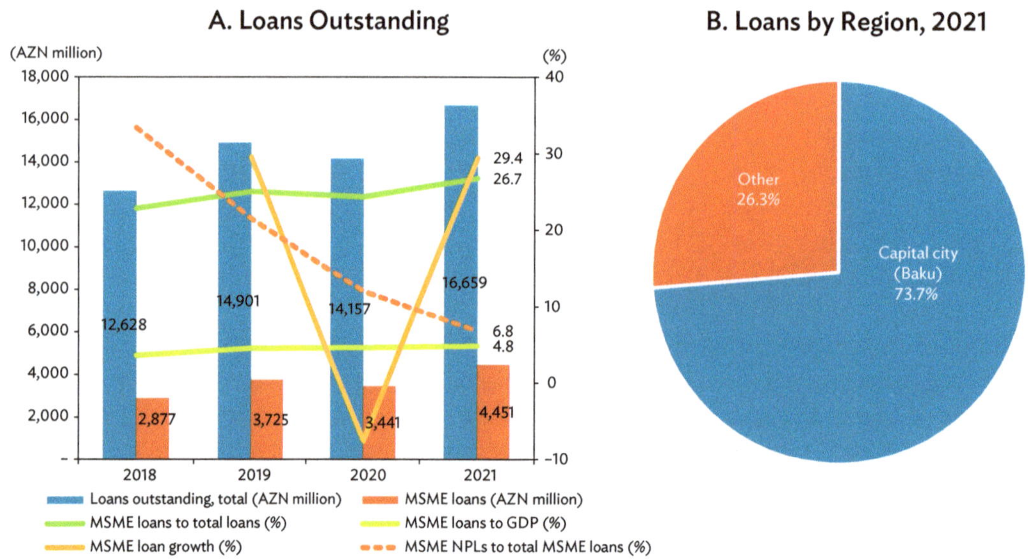

GDP = gross domestic product, MSME = micro, small, and medium-sized enterprise, NPL = nonperforming loan.

Source: ADB Asia SME Monitor 2022 database. Data from Central Bank of the Republic of Azerbaijan.

96 OECDiLibrary. SME Policy Index. https://www.oecd-ilibrary.org/development/sme-policy-index-eastern-partner-countries-2020_8b45614b-en.

97 K. Schwab, ed. 2019. *The Global Competitiveness Report 2019*. Geneva: World Economic Forum. https://www3.weforum.org/docs/WEF_TheGlobalCompetitivenessReport2019.pdf.

98 Statistics on MSME loans are available from 2018.

Public Financing and Guarantees

To supplement the financial needs of businesses, including MSMEs, the government provides soft loan programs with interest rate subsidies and credit guarantees. The Mortgage and Credit Guarantee Fund, the Agrarian Credit and Development Agency (AKIA) under the Ministry of Agriculture, and the Entrepreneurship Development Fund (EDF) under the Ministry of Economy mainly finance businesses, including MSMEs.

EDF supports entrepreneurial development, including MSMEs, through subsidized loans. It was launched in 2018 as successor to the National Fund for Entrepreneurship Support. The number of subsidized loans (new approval) increased over 2004–2021 at 2% CAGR. The subsidized loans disbursed to MSMEs amounted to AZN115 million in 2021, 7.7% higher than 2020 (Table 4). Compared with 2020, the number of MSMEs receiving subsidized loans more than doubled in 2021 from 903 to 1,895. Subsidized loans to MSMEs have increased substantially by reducing the average loan size per MSME. Total outstanding subsidized loans increased from AZN394.4 million in 2018 to AZN625.2 million in 2021, an increase of 58.5% (Figure 6). By fund size, the EDF is the largest government-led fund, with AZN868 million available as of 2020.

AKIA has had several names since 2004. Farmers and small agricultural firms benefit from AKIA's subsidized financing. It subsidizes credits for agricultural production, processing, storage and sales, along with innovative projects related to agrarian development. Discounted loans to purchase agricultural machinery, equipment and animals; microcredits; and other low-interest agricultural loans are the main focus of AKIA loans. Also, it provides microcredits to agricultural producers (at a maximum AZN15,000) with repayment periods of up to 3 years. In 2021, AKIA allocated AZN97 million in credits to purchase agricultural machinery and equipment (82.5%), and to purchase animal stock (17.5%).[99] To improve its provision of microcredit to producers during the pandemic the government allocated additional funds worth AZN30 million.[100]

The Mortgage and Credit Guarantee Fund, which specializes in loans to businesses, was established in 2017 (as a legal successor of the Azerbaijan Morgage Fund) and for the first time issued guarantees. Guaranteed loans more than tripled during 2019–2021 to reach AZN138.6 million (Figure 3.6). As of end June 2022, guaranteed total loans to enterprises amounted to AZN312.4 million, with guarantee to credit ration of 60.7%.

Still, there remains huge unmet MSME market demand for subsidized lending. Only 0.3% of MSMEs in the country gained access to EDF loans in 2020. Commercial banks and nonbank finance institutions must narrow this demand gap for inexpensive loans. They must constantly work with MSMEs to increase their financial literacy, transparency, and project preparation skills.

99 https://report.az/ask/akia-oten-il-texnika-ve-heyvan-alisi-ucun-97-milyon-manat-kredit-verib/
100 https://president.az/az/articles/view/36524

Figure 3.6. Public Financing

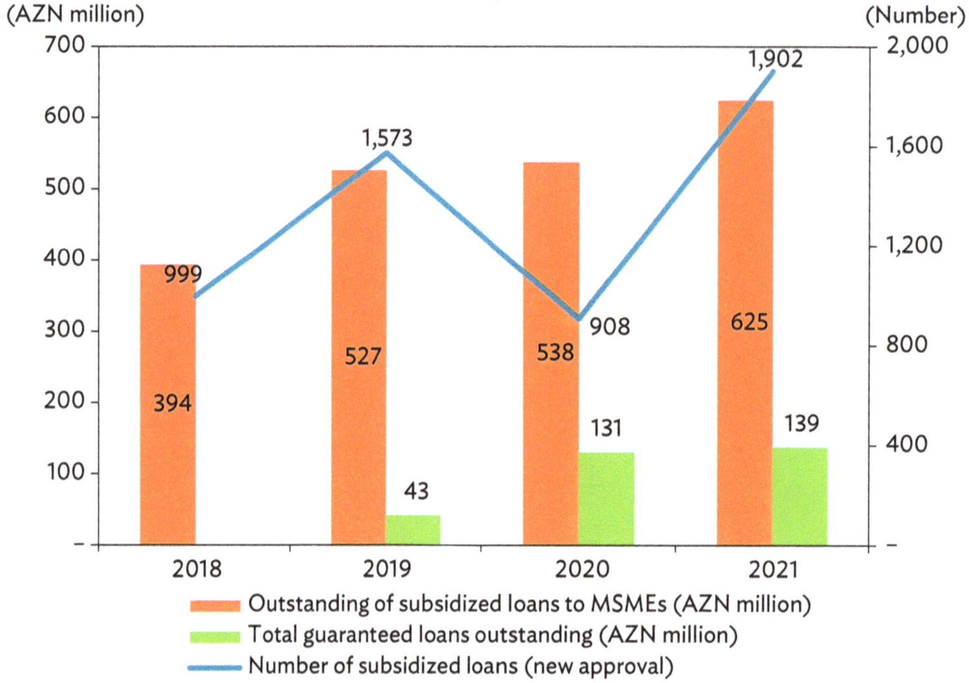

MSME = micro, small, and medium-sized enterprise.

Note: Only the Entrepreneurship Development Fund under the Ministry of Economy. Loan breakdown by MSME size is unavailable.

Source: ADB Asia SME Monitor 2022 database. Data from Central Bank of the Republic of Azerbaijan.

Nonbank Financing

Nonbank finance remains modest. Microfinance institutions, credit unions/cooperatives, leasing companies, and pawnshops are the main options available, although they do not specifically target MSMEs. Microfinance institutions and credit unions/cooperatives are regulated and supervised by the central bank, whereas leasing companies, factoring, pawnshops, and other nonbank financing are not.

Detailed statistical data on MSME loans provided by nonbank financial institutions are unavailable. The number of nonbank financial institutions increased from 70 in 2004 to 99 in 2021 (14 financed with foreign capital) (Figure 3.7A and Table 3.5). The increase is due to a rise in microfinance institutions, which grew from 15 in 2004 to 56 in 2021. Some 21% of nonbank financial institutions were microfinance institutions in 2004, rising to 57% in 2021. However, the number of credit unions/cooperatives decreased between 2004 and 2021 their share dropping from 79% to 43% in the same period.

The 43 credit unions/cooperatives lend mainly to members. Their loan assets increased between 2004 and 2015, reaching AZN86 million in 2015. Afterward they began to decrease, amounting to just AZN14 million in 2021. Lending contracted during 2012–2021. (Figure 3.7B). Similar to microfinance institutions, credit unions/cooperatives also play a limited financing role, contributing just 0.02% of GDP by 2021.

While an important source of funding among nonbank financial institutions, microfinance suffered during the economic slowdown and pandemic, largely focusing on consumer lending. As they do not use electronic payments, they are dependent on banks (24.6% of microfinance liabilities are bank credits) and other payment systems. Nevertheless, during 2004–2021, their assets increased by a factor of 17 (a CAGR of 17.2%). Microfinance institutions had their highest value in 2015 (AZN607 million), dropping to AZN343 million in 2019. Microfinance credit fluctuated over 2012–2021, reaching AZN498 million in 2015, up 65.6% from 2012, decreasing to AZN333.3 million in 2021 (Figure 3.7C).

The number of customers financed via microfinance fluctuated over 2017–2021. It fell dramatically from 150,438 in 2017 to 108,163 customers in 2018 (down 28.1%). It increased to 273,000 customers in 2021. The annual average lending rate was 27%, significantly higher than the average bank lending rate. Gross NPLs to total loans dropped from 42.1% to 21.0% during 2018–2021, with microfinance lending to GDP just 0.4% in 2021. There is obviously room to grow.

Agriculture, forestry, and fisheries held 13% of microfinance lending in 2021, followed by wholesale and retail trade (8%) (Figure 3.7D). The remaining 79% of lending was unclassified or under other services. Clients in Baku received most microfinance credit (60% in 2021).

Azerpost LLC (Azerbaijan`s state postal operator) has an extensive branch network outside the capital (1,176 branches and divisions) and provides some financial inclusion for the majority of the population, including services such as currency exchange, money transfers, settlement, and cash operations, all regulated by the central bank. While Azerpost does not have authority to conduct credit operations, recent reforms under the State Program for the expansion of digital payments in 2018-2020 aims to expand the role of Azerpost in lending. Therefore, the central bank, Azerpost LLC, and Access Bank have launched agent banking in the country in partnership with international financial institutions. As a result, it is expected that the access to banking services will expand, especially in remote areas.[101]

Leasing is currently regulated by the "Civil Code" as there is no separate law.[102] According to the State Tax Service information in 2017–2018, 174 leasing companies and about 700 pawnshops were operating in the country.[103]

[101] https://e-cbar.az/News/Info/6512224

[102] American Chamber of Commerce in Azerbaijan. White Paper 2021. Baku: AmCham https://amcham.az/uploads/publication/44f683a841 63b3523afe57c2e008bc8c.pdf?v=1646311157.

[103] https://vergiler.az/news/economy/155.html

Figure 3.7: Nonbank Finance

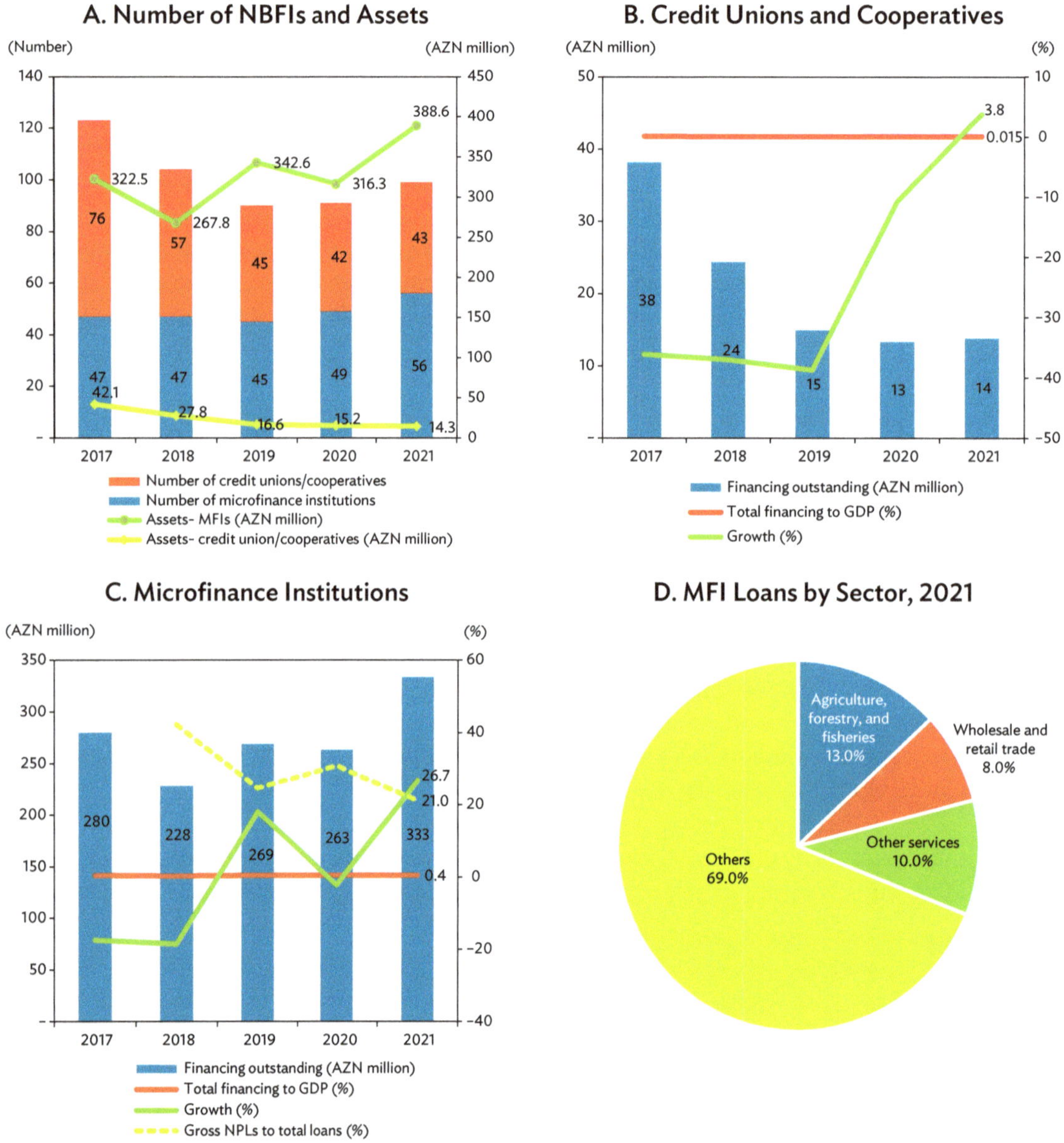

GDP = gross domestic product, MFI = microfinance institution, NBFI = nonbank financing institution, NPL = nonperforming loan.

Source: ADB Asia SME Monitor 2022 database. Data from Central Bank of the Republic of Azerbaijan.

Digital Financial Services

The use of financial technology continues to grow as individual companies, especially banks and insurance companies, upgrade their systems. Mobile and digital banking is now a part of nearly all credit organizations. Software using artificial intelligence, chatbots carrying out customer services are also given to customers by some banks (Pashabank, Rabitabank, and VTB, among others). Fintech solutions can provide online loans for paying utility bills, for example.

Nevertheless, a legislative framework is needed to regulate e-money and payment companies. The central bank prepared a law on payment systems in 2016 and announced it will prepare a financial literacy strategy to incorporate digital financial services. As of August 2022, neither has been approved.

The share of card payments increased from 9.5% to 22.7% between 2017 and 2021, while the share of contactless noncash payments using POS terminals grew from 0.2% in 2016 to 39% in 2020. In 2020, 75.2% of current account transfers by number (up by 47.6 percentage points since 2016) and 61.6% by value (up 57 percentage points) were conducted using internet or mobile e-banking services. As of end-2020, there were on average 72 POS terminals per 10,000 people. However, it is significantly lower in many regions—in 58 regions there were less than 50 POS terminals and less than 10 POS terminals in 20 regions. Only Baku, Shirvan, Naftalan, Gakh, Lankaran, and Nakhchivan had more.

The digital banking reforms of recent years include the creation of an Instant Payment System, use of quick response (QR) codes, and a blockchain-based Digital Identification System. The Instant Payment System uses QR codes for MSMEs to accept non-cash payments. The central bank's Digital Payment Strategy allows businesses to access more affordable financial services by expanding use of digital payment services.[104] The Azerbaijan Fintech Association was established in 2021, with 25 fintech companies now providing services in financial markets.

Peer-to-peer (P2P) lending and crowdfunding for financing startups and MSMEs are rare in Azerbaijan, where there is no legal definition of "crowdfunding." Nonetheless, enterpriseazerbaijan.com (2018) and toxum.org (2021) platforms are used to find investors for innovative startups, including MSMEs. More alternative financial mechanisms for MSMEs and startups are needed.

Capital Markets

Capital market development remains in its infancy. The central bank-regulated Baku Stock Exchange—a closed joint-stock company with 20 shareholders—has been the sole authorized stock exchange since 1997. Updated listing and trading rules were approved in 2020 and 2021. Listing requirements for the standard market segment are as follows:

- the issuer must be an open joint-stock company;
- the issue of shares must be carried out by way of public offering or accepted for public trading;
- the term of validity of the issuer must be at least 1 year;
- the authorized capital of the issuer must be at least AZN200,000;
- the issuer's financial statements shall be prepared in accordance with International Financial Reporting Standards, and annual financial statements for the most recent financial year must be audited by an external (independent) auditor; and
- the issuer must have a regularly updated website that covers its activities.

While the central bank approved a fee schedule for stock exchange services in December 2020, it has also been trying to promote public awareness through events, online platforms and the media to help create a more favorable environment for issuers and financial intermediaries.

[104] https://uploads.cbar.az/assets/semiannual%20report%20-%2003.08%20last_FO_03_eng.cleaned_01_v02_PSD_FIN1.pdf

Still, market capitalization remains low compared to markets in similar economies. Developing better corporate governance standards, boosting transparency, increasing public awareness, and further developing financial intermediation could help the securities market become more attractive. The basic problem is that it is easier obtaining bank financing than it is listing of the exchange.

In 2021, market capitalization was AZN4.4 billion (8.5% CAGR between 2016 and 2021) (Figure 3.8 and Table 3.6). Market capitalization was about 4.7% of GDP, far lower than upper middle-income economies (78.6% of GDP in 2020).[105] Trading values have also been highly volatile. Annual trading value dropped by more than 73% in 2021 compared with 2016, while trading volume more than tripled—from 1.9 billion shares to 6.2 billion. Listed companies grew from just five in 2016 to 28 by 2021. Delisted companies also increased from seven to 11 during 2016–2021.

As of June 2022, there was no dedicated MSME board on the Baku Stock Exchange, a barrier to MSME participation. Establishing an MSME board could help successful, innovative MSMEs better access the market as a funding source.

Figure 3.8: Equity Markets

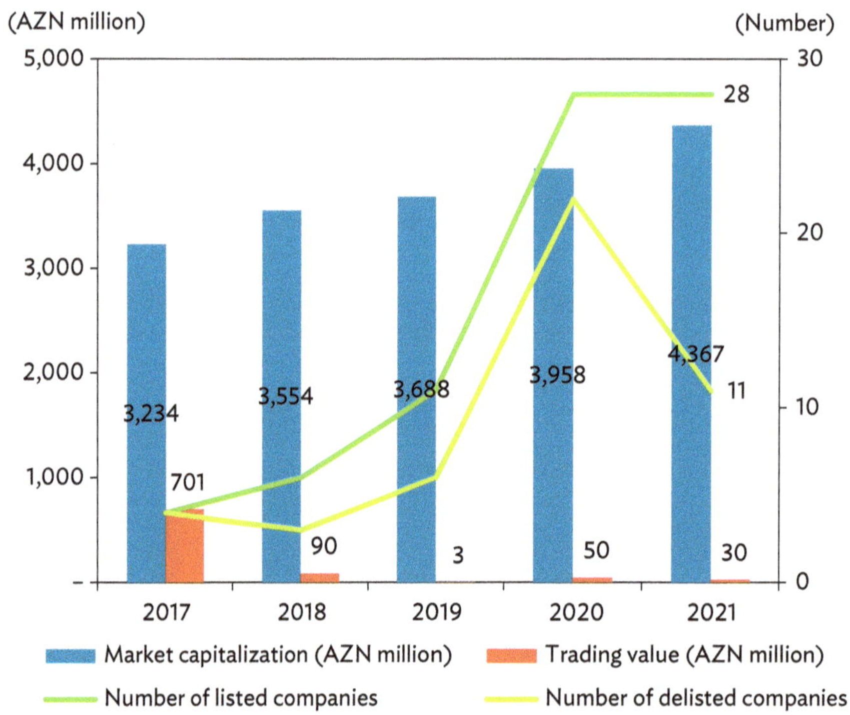

Source: ADB Asia SME Monitor 2022 database. Data from Baku Stock Exchange.

[105] World Bank. Market capitalization of listed domestic companies (% of GDP). https://data.worldbank.org/indicator/CM.MKT.LCAP.GD.ZS (accessed 31 August 2022).

Financial Infrastructure

Financial literacy in the country is relatively low. A 2021 OECD survey conducted across the Commonwealth of Independent States (CIS) members—Armenia, Azerbaijan, Belarus, Kazakhstan, the Kyrgyz Republic, Tajikistan, and Uzbekistan)—gave Azerbaijan an average financial literacy score of 45.9%, the lowest among CIS members, which averaged 55.8%.[106] However, young adults had average scores above the CIS average. Improving financial literacy is a key element of the government's strategic roadmap to foster entrepreneurship and MSME growth. Since 2016, the central bank has conducted financial literacy programs and offered training to the public, including children, youth, and teachers in preschool education. Under the Azerbaijan Banks Association, the Azerbaijan Banking Training Center offers financial training to entrepreneurs. Banks and microfinance institutions also provide basic financial education to their clients, especially those operating in rural areas and those owned and managed by women. Although the Association of Fintech in Azerbaijan was launched under the digital payment state program (2018–2020), fintech use remains several years in the future.

To strengthen financial inclusion, a private credit bureau and the "State Register of Encumbrances of Movable Property" were established in 2018. The state register allows borrowers to obtain loans by mortgaging real estate and movable assets. Registering allows financial institutions to receive information on business collateral, including MSMEs.

As of September 2021, the Azerbaijan Credit Bureau LLC (ACB) had 3.4 million files on borrowers in their database (3.2 million individuals, 18,668 legal entities, and 108,937 microenterprises).[107] Of these, 1.9 million borrowers (1.8 million individuals, 6,965 legal entities, and 80,296 microenterprises) had active loans. In 2021, ACB received 33.5 million inquiries, including 200,000 requests from credit institutions. And as of June 2019, 13,827 people had applied and received credit reports. ACB is expanding operations and is expected to play an increasingly important role in expanding MSME access to credit—including from microfinance institutions—in less time and cost. Although services provided remain limited, ACB covers around 44% of the adult population (compared with 28.7% on the public credit registry in 2014). As of March 2022, ACB had signed contracts to exchange information with 198 organizations—including the Central Bank, the Ministry of Justice, the Mortgage and Credit Guarantee Fund, 26 banks, 56 nonbank credit organizations, 35 credit unions, 5 leasing companies, 22 insurance companies, 3 mobile service operators, 3 utility services operators, and 17 retail companies, among others. The ACB database includes detailed borrower information on loan amounts, type of loans, past-due amounts, collateral and credit guarantees, and credit scores. Borrowers can access their own credit data, and lenders can update incorrect data. MSMEs, particularly informal, small, and microenterprises, are unaware about loan assessment procedures. They lack documentation, business records, and proper business plans. This makes it difficult for financial institutions to assess a borrower's creditworthiness.

Venture capital and business angel networks have yet to be developed due to infrastructure, regulatory, and financial constraints. However, in June 2022, the Innovation and Digital Development Agency under the Ministry of Digital Development and Transport—along with private company Pasha Holding—announced the creation of a joint venture capital fund as an incentive for innovation.

To ensure information from credit reporting systems follow international best practices, the Association of Credit Information Providers of Eurasia was established in 2018. Credit registries and bureaus representing Azerbaijan, Belarus, Georgia, Kazakhstan, the Kyrgyz Republic, Tajikistan, Ukraine, and Uzbekistan are members.

---

[106] OECD. 2021. *Financial Literacy Levels in the Commonwealth of Independent States in 2021*. https://www.oecd.org/daf/fin/financial-education/Financial-literacy-levels-in-the-commonwealth-of-independent-states-in-2021.pdf

[107] ACB was established by Azerbaijan's eight largest banks.

4. Policies and Regulations

- The Small and Medium Business Development Agency, established in 2017 under the Ministry of Economy, is responsible for the development of MSMEs.
- The Strategic Road Map for MSME entrepreneurs to produce consumer goods sets out short, long, and aspirational visions for MSME development to benefit the country.
- The Socio-economic Development Strategy for 2022–2026—adopted in 2022—identifies the policies best able to develop MSMEs.
- As there is no specific national financial inclusion strategy, one should be crafted that creates an effective and efficient process of promoting inclusive growth.
- The country's comprehensive emergency assistance program included economic and social measures to support enterprises and households during the pandemic, with several supporting affected MSMEs.
- While there are no specific government support mechanisms for businesses—including MSMEs—to minimize the harm from the Russian invasion of Ukraine, the government is planning subsidies to help the economy, for example, increasing wheat production.

MSME Development

MSME development is among the government's non-oil sector priorities. The July 2022 Socio-economic development strategy for 2022-2026 underscores the importance of MSME development to ensure a steadily growing competitive economy (Table 3.7). The strategy aims to create new financing mechanisms for new entrepreneurs, startups, and those expanding existing businesses. Some 20%–30% of financial resources will be spent on supporting microenterprises, 35%–45% on small firms, and 25%–35% on medium-sized enterprises. Based on the success of similar programs in other countries, startups and incubators will be supported along with export-oriented producers of goods and services will also be improved. Increasing MSME access to knowledge and information is also critical.[108]

A Strategic Road Map for [M]SME production of consumer goods was adopted in 2016, covering 2017–2020. The roadmap identified five strategic targets: (i) improve the business climate and regulatory framework for [M]SME operations; (ii) ensure cost-effective, efficient [M]SME access to financial resources; (iii) internationalize [M]SMEs and increase their access to foreign markets; (iv) increase [M]SME knowledge and skills while accelerating their adoption of best practices; and (v) promote innovation and expanding R&D for [M]SMEs. The roadmap also sets a strategic vision for 2020, a long-term vision for 2025, and an aspirational vision afterward. It states that "Azerbaijan's long-term vision for 2025 is to further improve competitiveness of [M]SMEs, achieve supply of daily consumer products by [M]SMEs and give rise to significant [M]SME contribution to the country's GDP and employment." Its aspirational vision after 2025 is "to generate at least 60% of its GDP through [M]SMEs and establish a strong network of local [M]SMEs that integrate into global value chains."[109]

SMBDA, established in 2017 under the Ministry of Economy, provides assistance and a range of services to MSMEs. It also coordinates and regulates public services for MSMEs. It issues a startup certificates for MSMEs, which exempt them from paying income/profit taxes for up to 3 years. SMEDA also provides small-scale grants to innovative startups. The Entrepreneurship Development Fund under the Ministry of Economy and the Agrarian Credit and Development Agency under the Ministry of Agriculture support MSME access to finance and offers soft loans.

[108] https://static.president.az/upload/Files/2022/07/22/5478ed13955fb35f0715325d7f76a8ea_3699216.pdf

[109] https://static.president.az/pdf/38542.pdf

Several line ministries and government bodies support MSME development either directly or indirectly. Sabah.lab, for example, is a startup accelerator center under the Education Institute and supported by the Ministry of Education and Science. The State Employment Agency under the Ministry of Labor and Social Security offers support for micro and small businesses under its 2017 "Self-Employment Program." The program distributes assets (equipment, machinery, tools, and materials, among others) to the self-employed. It also designs and conducts business training for self-employed people.

Financial Inclusion

The government lacks a specific national financial inclusion strategy. Yet, its 2016 Strategic Roadmap for Development of Financial Services sets out a vision and action plan for 2017–2020. The roadmap had five strategic targets: (i) establish a financial system of dynamic and sound institutions, (ii) develop financial markets, (iii) strengthen infrastructure, (iv) improve regulations and control mechanisms, and (v) improve financial literacy. It too defined visions for 2020, 2025, and after. It said that "... development of Azerbaijan's financial sector by 2020 is to establish a financial system with a development potential that is sustainable against internal and external shocks, deeply focused on risk management processes and covered by strong infrastructure elements." The long-term vision for 2025 is "to have a robust, resilient and balanced financial system that is enabled by a well-established regulatory legal framework and that provides a wide range of financial services for all customer segments." Its aspirational vision post-2025 is "to establish a financial sector that attracts foreign investors and is competitive on a regional scale."[110]

It is widely recognized that improving digital financial services certainly helps increase financial inclusion by (i) increasing access to finance, (ii) reaching the unserved and underserved population especially in rural areas, and (iii) allowing more people to participate in the formal financial system. Because payments are often the entry point for accessing the services of banks and nonbank financial institutions, improving their access is a critical first step in achieving universal access to finance. The government's 2018–2020 State Program on Expansion of Digital Payments, implemented by the central bank, aimed to (i) eliminate institutional factors blocking the development of a digital payment systems, (ii) improve financial intermediation, (iii) introduce innovative payment systems, and (iv) strengthen financial inclusion.

Response to COVID-19

In February 2020, an Operational Headquarters (Task Force) of officials from government agencies and institutions was established by the Cabinet of Ministers. It monitors the evolving situation, prevents the threat of COVID-19, and coordinates and develops pandemic response measures. The government adopted an action plan in April 2020 to lessen the harm caused by the pandemic on economy as a whole, its sectors, and maintain population welfare. The plan is constructed on three broad pillars:

- **Support for economic growth and entrepreneurs.** This pillar incorporates several government support measures: (i) temporary tax relief provided for affected businesses, including MSMEs; (ii) a credit guarantee and interest subsidy scheme to support the financial stability of affected enterprises, with additional resources allocated to provide AZN90 million ($52.9 million) in preferential mortgage loans; (iii) AZN280 million ($164.7 million) to provide financial support for public transport—the largest share going to air transportation; (iv) partial salary support for affected businesses, with AZN215 million ($126.5 million) allocated for 300,000 contracted employees; (v) some AZN80 million ($47.1 million) to support about 300,000 affected microenterprises; (vi) affected entrepreneurs were exempt from

[110] https://static.president.az/pdf/38542.pdf

rents on state property and government-owned land until end-2020; and (vii) reduced or exempt custom duties for essential food and medical products.

- **Support for employment and social welfare.** Aside from supporting businesses, the government included social protection measures to assist the most vulnerable. These included creating 50,000 paid public jobs during May–April 2020, lump-sum payments of AZN190 ($111.8) per month (April, May, June, and August 2020)—or AZN333 million ($195.6 million) in total—to those officially registered as unemployed (about 600,000 people).[111] Also, AZN40 million ($23.5 million) was allocated for the payment of annual tuition fees for students from socially vulnerable families. To reduce household costs, the government increased monthly discount limits for electricity during April–May 2020, allocating AZN10 million ($5.9 million). About 5 million people benefited from these social support programs.[112]
- **Macroeconomic and financial stability.** Under this pillar, the Ministry of Economy, the Ministry of Finance, and the central bank were asked to develop a macroeconomic policy framework reflecting the new economic realities. The central bank was also asked to (i) expand the size of its sterilization portfolio depending on the monetary situation, (ii) grant a regulatory holiday to credit institutions so they could regulate liabilities of pandemic-affected businesses during lockdowns, and (iii) strengthen control of capital flows and currency exchange.

And to support agricultural producers during the pandemic, the government set aside AZN30 million ($17.6 million) mostly used as microcredits to farmers.

In March 2020, a "Fund to Support the Fight Against Coronavirus" was established to contain the spread of COVID-19 and offer financial support for initiatives to prevent the spread of infection.[113] The fund compensated medical professionals, offered material assistance, enhanced the facilities and technical capabilities of medical institutions, established medical institutions under special regulations, organized and implemented control and monitoring, funded medical research, trained medical specialists, conducted awareness activities, and other measures to contain infections.

The country also contributed to the global fight against the pandemic, pledging about $5 million to the World Health Organization.

Response to the Russian Invasion of Ukraine

There are no specific government support measures to businesses—including MSMEs—to minimize the economic damage caused by the invasion. The crisis mainly affected Azerbaijan's food supply, especially wheat. In July 2022, the government announced it would offer additional subsidies to increase wheat production.[114] Farmers, including micro, small, and medium-sized firms, can tap these funds from 2023 through 2028.

---

111 The minimum living cost was set at AZN190 in 2020.

112 OECD. COVID-19 crisis response in Eastern Partner countries (updated 13 October 2020). https://www.oecd.org/coronavirus/policy-responses/covid-19-crisis-response-in-eu-eastern-partner-countries-7759afa3/.

113 https://e-qanun.az/framework/44792

114 Above current crop subsidies.

Data Tables

Table 3.1: MSME Definitions

A. MSME Definition after 2018

Item	Micro	Small	Medium
Annual revenue (I) (AZN)	I ≤ 200 000	200 000 < I ≤ 3 000 000	3 000 000 < I ≤ 30 000 000
Number of employees	1–10	11–50	51–250

Source: ADB Asia SME Monitor 2022 database. Micro, small, and medium-sized enterprises (MSMEs) are defined in accordance with the criteria approved by the Cabinet of Ministers of the Republic of Azerbaijan on 21 December 2018 № 556. (https://e-qanun.az/framework/41048).

B. SME Definition, 2015–2017

Item	Small	Medium
Annual revenue (I) (AZN)	≤ 200 000	200 000 < I ≤ 1 250 000
Number of employees	< 25	25-125

Source: ADB Asia SME Monitor 2022 database. Small and medium-sized enterprises (SMEs) are defined in accordance with the criteria approved by the Cabinet of Ministers of the Republic of Azerbaijan on 5 June 2015 № 215 (https://e-qanun.az/framework/30115).

C. Small Enterprises Definition, 2010–2014

Item	Industry and Construction	Agriculture	Wholesale trade	Retail trade, transport, services and other economic activities
Annual revenue (AZN)	≤ 500 000	≤ 250 000	≤ 1 000 000	≤ 250 000
Number of employee	< 50	< 25	< 15	< 10

Source: ADB Asia SME Monitor 2022 database. Small enterprises are defined in accordance with the criteria approved by the Cabinet of Ministers of the Republic of Azerbaijan on 18 December 2009 № 192 (https://e-qanun.az/framework/18857).

D. Small Enterprises Definition before 2009

Item	Industry and Construction	Scientific, technical and consulting service	Agriculture	Wholesale trade	Retail trade, transport, services and other economic activities
Annual revenue (AZN)	< 200 000	< 150 000	< 100 000	< 300 000	< 100 000
Number of employees	< 40	< 20	< 15	< 10	< 5

Source: ADB Asia SME Monitor 2022 database. Small enterprises are defined in accordance with the criteria approved by the Cabinet of Ministers of the Republic of Azerbaijan on 20 April 2004 № 57 (https://e-qanun.az/framework/6110).

Table 3.2: MSME Landscape

End-of-period data

Item	2004	2005	2006	2007	2008	2009	2010	2011	2012	2013	2014	2015	2016	2017	2018	2019	2020
NUMBER OF ENTERPRISES*																	
Number of enterprises, total	...	...	...	...	...	...	...	...	...	...	...	...	...	...	...	272,295	317,299
Number of MSMEs	161,434	178,540	184,281	196,972	204,960	205,028	207,120	135,353	141,422	165,277	186,898	187,375	191,695	169,603	244,883	271,304	316,370
Micro	...	...	...	...	...	...	...	...	...	...	...	...	...	...	237,815	262,622	307,717
Small	161,434	178,540	184,281	196,972	204,960	205,028	207,120	135,353	141,422	165,277	186,898	183,271	187,598	165,386	4,930	5,956	5,943
Medium	...	...	...	...	...	...	...	...	...	...	...	4,104	4,097	4,217	2,138	2,726	2,710
Number of large enterprises	...	...	...	...	...	...	...	...	...	...	...	...	...	...	...	991	929
MSME to total (%)	...	...	...	...	...	...	...	...	...	...	...	...	...	...	...	99.6	99.7
MSME growth (%)	...	10.6	3.2	6.9	4.1	0.0	1.0	(34.6)	4.5	16.9	13.1	0.3	2.3	(11.5)	44.4	10.8	16.6
MSMEs by sector (% share)																	
Agriculture, forestry, and fisheries	2.5	2.2	2.1	1.9	2.0	2.0	1.9	2.9	2.8	2.4	1.8	2.0	1.9	1.9	1.3	1.2	1.0
Manufacturing	2.2	2.1	2.5	2.5	2.3	2.3	2.2	3.3	3.1	3.1	3.4	2.4	3.1	3.6	3.4	3.5	3.9
Transportion and storage	10.5	10.1	10.4	10.1	10.1	10.7	10.7	16.7	17.7	16.9	15.1	15.3	15.1	17.2	16.3	15.8	20.9
Information and communication**	...	...	0.2	0.2	0.2	0.1	0.1	0.2	0.2	0.2	0.2	0.4	0.4	0.5	1.4	1.5	2.2
Construction	0.9	0.7	1.1	1.1	1.1	1.1	0.7	1.1	1.2	1.2	1.2	1.4	1.5	1.7	1.6	2.3	3.7
Wholesale and retail trade	72.6	70.5	67.7	65.0	64.4	64.2	64.6	50.8	50.3	52.9	49.1	52.1	51.0	43.0	31.4	31.3	32.8
Other services	11.3	14.4	16.0	19.2	19.9	19.6	19.8	25.0	24.7	23.3	29.2	26.0	26.6	31.7	44.2	43.9	35.0
Others***	...	...	...	...	...	...	...	...	...	...	...	0.4	0.4	0.4	0.4	0.5	0.5
MSMEs by region (% share)																	
Capital city (Baku)	37.9	36.8	34.3	35.9	36.4	38.3	36.8	35.2	35.4	35.3	37.6	41.9	39.2	41.4	45.4	47.9	47.5
Others	62.1	63.2	65.7	64.1	63.6	61.7	63.2	64.8	64.6	64.7	62.4	58.1	60.8	58.6	54.6	52.1	52.5
EMPLOYMENT****																	
Number of employment, total	...	...	...	...	...	...	...	...	...	...	...	...	...	...	660,180	760,478	827,520
Number of employment by MSMEs	68,565	73,447	87,524	92,108	103,246	105,902	93,205	90,182	95,503	108,976	115,035	284,066	281,099	290,132	283,432	332,255	348,723
Micro	...	...	...	...	...	...	...	...	...	...	...	...	...	...	35,014	40,233	40,850
Small	68,565	73,447	87,524	92,108	103,246	105,902	93,205	90,182	95,503	108,976	115,035	87,626	100,957	101,898	76,052	85,072	92,125
Medium	...	...	...	...	...	...	...	...	...	...	...	196,440	180,142	188,234	172,366	206,950	215,748
Number of employment by large enterprises	...	...	...	...	...	...	...	...	...	...	...	...	...	...	376,748	428,223	478,797
MSME employees to total (%)	5.4	5.6	6.5	6.7	7.3	7.6	6.7	6.5	6.4	7.9	7.6	6.3	20.4	20.8	42.9	43.7	42.1
MSME employees growth (%)	...	7.1	19.2	5.2	12.1	2.6	(12.0)	(3.2)	5.9	14.1	5.6	146.9	(1.0)	3.2	(2.3)	17.2	5.0
Share of female employees to total employees by MSME (%)	...	...	...	...	...	...	...	...	...	...	...	33.2	34.9	34.4	25.9	26.7	25.5
Employment by MSME by sector (% share)																	
Agriculture, forestry, and fisheries	13.3	11.6	9.6	8.3	8.1	8.0	5.8	5.6	5.5	5.1	5.1	5.5	5.0	5.1	4.6	5.0	5.2
Manufacturing	31.5	26.3	29.9	30.5	27.3	20.2	20.8	18.3	18.7	18.5	15.1	6.2	5.7	5.8	14.5	14.3	13.6
Transportion and storage	1.3	1.2	2.0	1.7	1.5	1.3	1.6	1.8	1.7	2.0	2.2	4.3	4.0	3.8	6.6	6.5	6.6
Information and communication**	...	...	2.7	3.6	1.1	0.8	1.8	1.5	2.0	2.2	2.7	3.4	3.0	2.7	4.9	4.5	4.4
Construction	14.8	13.9	18.8	20.0	18.9	14.4	11.0	10.4	12.6	14.2	10.9	5.9	6.7	7.0	15.9	14.6	16.8
Wholesale and retail trade	22.9	30.6	14.6	16.6	21.3	33.6	38.0	41.2	38.9	34.5	33.6	32.1	35.5	37.7	13.8	17.4	15.9
Other services	16.2	16.4	22.4	19.3	21.8	21.7	21.0	21.2	20.6	23.5	30.4	38.2	35.8	34.1	29.6	27.8	28.0
Others***	...	...	...	...	...	...	...	...	...	...	...	4.4	4.3	3.8	10.1	9.9	9.5
Employment by MSMEs by region (% share)																	
Capital city (Baku)	49.6	48.5	44.2	46.4	52.1	54.9	62.4	63.0	64.6	64.9	66.8	45.8	43.3	42.2	59.2	60.3	62.6
Others	50.4	51.5	55.8	53.6	47.9	45.1	37.6	37.0	35.4	35.1	33.2	54.2	56.7	57.8	40.8	39.7	37.4

continued on next page

Table 3.2 *continued*

Item	2004	2005	2006	2007	2008	2009	2010	2011	2012	2013	2014	2015	2016	2017	2018	2019	2020
CONTRIBUTION TO GROSS VALUE ADDED (GVA)*****																	
GVA of MSMEs (AZN million)	143	203	365	449	719	845	1,120	1,692	2,081	2,453	2,363	3,735	3,587	3,808	9,837	11,072	10,941
MSME contribution to total GVA (% share)	1.8	1.6	1.9	1.6	1.8	2.6	2.8	3.5	4.1	4.5	4.3	7.5	6.4	5.9	13.4	14.9	16.7
MSME GVA growth (%)	...	42.4	79.7	23.2	60.0	17.5	32.6	51.1	23.0	17.9	(3.7)	58.1	(4.0)	6.1	158.3	12.6	(1.2)
MSME labor productivity (AZN million)	...	...	...	...	...	...	...	...	...	...	...	...	...	...	...	...	...
MSME GVA by sector (% share)																	
Agriculture, forestry, and fisheries	...	...	...	...	...	...	...	...	...	...	...	...	...	...	...	2.8	3.7
Industry (NACE sections B,C,D,E)	...	...	...	...	...	...	...	...	...	...	...	...	...	...	...	12.3	13.5
Transportion and storage	...	...	...	...	...	...	...	...	...	...	...	...	...	...	...	9.1	7.1
Information and communication	...	...	...	...	...	...	...	...	...	...	...	...	...	...	...	4.9	4.3
Construction	...	...	...	...	...	...	...	...	...	...	...	...	...	...	...	12.2	14.5
Wholesale and retail trade	...	...	...	...	...	...	...	...	...	...	...	...	...	...	...	23.9	29.4
Other services	...	...	...	...	...	...	...	...	...	...	...	...	...	...	...	34.8	27.5
Others	...	...	...	...	...	...	...	...	...	...	...	...	...	...	...	...	...
MSME GVA by region (% share)																	
Capital city (Baku)	...	...	...	...	...	...	...	...	...	...	...	...	...	...	...	...	...
Others	...	...	...	...	...	...	...	...	...	...	...	...	...	...	...	...	...
EXPORTS																	
Total export value ($ million)	3,616	4,347	6,372	6,058	47,756	14,701	21,360	26,571	23,908	23,975	21,829	12,729	13,458	15,320	19,489	19,635	13,733
Total export growth (%)	39.6	20.2	46.6	(4.9)	688.3	(69.2)	45.3	24.4	(10.0)	0.3	(9.0)	(41.7)	5.7	13.8	27.2	0.7	(30.1)
MSME export value ($ million)	...	...	...	...	...	...	...	...	...	...	...	...	...	...	...	...	...
MSME export to total export value (%)	...	...	...	...	...	...	...	...	...	...	...	...	...	...	...	...	...
MSME export growth (%)	...	...	...	...	...	...	...	...	...	...	...	...	...	...	...	...	...
IMPORTS																	
Total import value ($ million)	3,516	4,211	5,267	5,714	7,170	6,123	6,601	9,756	9,653	10,713	9,188	9,217	8,489	8,783	11,466	13,668	10,732
Total import growth (%)	33.9	19.8	25.1	8.5	25.5	(14.6)	7.8	47.8	(1.1)	11.0	(14.2)	0.3	(7.9)	3.5	30.5	19.2	(21.5)
MSME import value ($ million)	...	...	...	...	...	...	...	...	...	...	...	...	...	...	...	...	...
MSME import to total import value (%)	...	...	...	...	...	...	...	...	...	...	...	...	...	...	...	...	...
MSME import growth (%)	...	...	...	...	...	...	...	...	...	...	...	...	...	...	...	...	...

MSME = micro, small, and medium-sized enterprise; NACE = Nomenclature of Economic Activities.

* Active enterprises.
** In 2004–2005, communication activities were part of the "Transport and storage" section.
*** Includes mining and quarrying; electricity, gas, and water supply.
**** Excludes the number of private enterprises without a legal entity and its employees.
***** GVA is defined as output at basic prices minus intermediate consumption at purchaser prices.
Note: The classification of enterprises was frequently amended: different definitions were used in data before 2009, 2010–2014, 2015–2017, and after 2018 (see Table 1: MSME Definition).

Source: ADB Asia SME Monitor 2022 database. Data from the State Statistical Committee of the Republic of Azerbaijan.

Table 3.3: Bank Credit

End-of-period data

Item	2004	2005	2006	2007	2008	2009	2010	2011	2012	2013	2014	2015	2016	2017	2018	2019	2020	2021
OPERATING BANKS																		
Number of operating banks, total	44	44	44	46	46	46	45	44	43	43	45	43	32	30	30	30	26	26
State-owned commercial banks	2	2	2	2	1	1	1	1	1	1	2	2	2	2	2	2	2	2
Private commercial banks (domestic)	27	24	22	23	22	22	22	20	20	20	20	20	15	13	13	14	12	12
Foreign commercial banks*	15	18	20	21	23	23	22	23	22	22	23	21	15	15	15	14	12	12
Credit																		
Loans outstanding, total (AZN million)	871	1,372	2,272	4,555	7,027	8,238	8,039	9,493	11,357	14,865	17,876	20,882	15,938	11,338	12,628	14,901	14,157	16,659
Loans outstanding in domestic currency (AZN million)	256	482	1,098	2,421	3,562	4,821	4,833	6,304	7,809	10,796	13,085	10,566	8,309	6,651	7,772	9,646	9,880	12,296
Loans outstanding in foreign currency (AZN million)	615	890	1,173	2,134	3,464	3,417	3,206	3,189	3,547	4,069	4,791	10,316	7,629	4,687	4,856	5,255	4,277	4,363
Loan growth (%)	58.6	57.5	65.6	100.5	54.3	17.2	(2.4)	18.1	19.6	30.9	20.3	16.8	(23.7)	(28.9)	11.4	18.0	(5.0)	17.7
Total bank loans to GDP (%)	10.2	11.0	12.1	16.1	17.5	23.1	18.9	18.2	20.7	25.5	30.3	38.4	26.4	16.1	15.8	18.2	19.5	17.9
Lending rate (%, annual average)	17.7	16.4	16.8	16.6	16.0	16.5	16.7	16.5	15.4	14.2	13.6	13.1	10.4	11.8	11.9	11.1	11.1	11.8
Gross nonperforming loans (NPLs) (AZN million)	22	14	78	100	160	304	493	634	749	793	976	1,508	1,473	1,627	1,585	1,273	893	719
Gross NPLs to total loans (%)	2.5	1.0	3.4	2.2	2.3	3.7	6.1	6.7	6.6	5.3	5.5	7.2	9.2	14.3	12.6	8.5	6.3	4.3
Deposits																		
Deposits, total (AZN million)	1,029	1,381	2,233	3,438	4,055	4,293	5,165	6,673	7,711	8,879	11,106	16,998	16,410	16,895	18,590	21,327	20,723	26,938
Deposits in domestic currency (AZN million)	205	257	819	1,671	1,953	1,836	2,716	3,641	4,345	5,481	6,548	3,596	4,833	5,205	7,152	9,120	9,692	14,111
Deposits in foreign currency (AZN million)	824	1,123	1,414	1,767	2,102	2,457	2,449	3,032	3,366	3,398	4,557	13,401	11,577	11,689	11,439	12,206	11,031	12,828
Deposit rate (%, annual average)	9.3	10.1	11.3	11.9	9.0	11.0	11.4	10.8	10.1	9.2	8.8	8.0	5.1	5.2	4.7	4.3	4.2	4.8
MSME LOANS																		
MSME loans outstanding, total (AZN million)	...	...	...	...	...	...	...	...	...	...	...	...	...	...	2,877	3,725	3,441	4,451
MSME loans to total loans outstanding (%)	...	...	...	...	...	...	...	...	...	...	...	...	...	...	22.8	25.0	24.3	26.7
MSME loans to GDP (%)	...	...	...	...	...	...	...	...	...	...	...	...	...	...	3.6	4.5	4.6	4.8
MSME loan growth (%)	...	...	...	...	...	...	...	...	...	...	...	...	...	...	...	29.5	(7.6)	29.4
MSME lending rate (%, annual average)	...	...	...	...	...	...	...	...	...	...	...	...	...	...	11.2	11.5	11.3	11.8
Nonperforming MSME loans (NPLs) (AZN million)**	...	...	...	...	...	...	...	...	...	...	...	...	...	...	960	800	412	300.7
MSME NPLs to total MSME loans (%)	...	...	...	...	...	...	...	...	...	...	...	...	...	...	33.4	21.5	12.0	6.8
Number of MSME loan borrowers	...	...	...	...	...	...	...	...	...	...	...	...	...	...	...	...	...	...
MSME loan borrowers to total bank borrowers (%)	...	...	...	...	...	...	...	...	...	...	...	...	...	...	...	...	...	...
MSME loan rejection rate (% of total applications)	...	...	...	...	...	...	...	...	...	...	...	...	...	...	...	...	...	...
Number of MSME savings account in banks	...	...	...	...	...	...	...	...	...	...	...	...	...	...	...	...	...	...
Guaranteed MSME loans (AZN million)	...	...	...	...	...	...	...	...	...	...	...	...	...	...	...	...	...	...
Non-collateral MSME loans (AZN million)	...	...	...	...	...	...	...	...	...	...	...	...	...	...	...	...	...	...
MSME loans outstanding by sector (% share)																		
Agriculture, forestry, and fisheries	...	...	...	...	...	...	...	...	...	...	...	...	...	...	...	...	...	...
Manufacturing	...	...	...	...	...	...	...	...	...	...	...	...	...	...	...	...	...	...
Transportation and communication	...	...	...	...	...	...	...	...	...	...	...	...	...	...	...	...	...	...
Construction	...	...	...	...	...	...	...	...	...	...	...	...	...	...	...	...	...	...
Wholesale and retail trade	...	...	...	...	...	...	...	...	...	...	...	...	...	...	...	...	...	...
Other services	...	...	...	...	...	...	...	...	...	...	...	...	...	...	...	...	...	...
Others	...	...	...	...	...	...	...	...	...	...	...	...	...	...	...	...	...	...
MSME loans outstanding by region (% share)																		
Capital city (Baku)	...	...	...	...	...	...	...	...	...	...	...	...	...	...	81.0	78.5	77.8	73.7
Other	...	...	...	...	...	...	...	...	...	...	...	...	...	...	19.0	21.5	22.2	26.3
MSME loans outstanding by type of use (% share)																		
For working capital	...	...	...	...	...	...	...	...	...	...	...	...	...	...	...	...	...	...
For capital investment	...	...	...	...	...	...	...	...	...	...	...	...	...	...	...	...	...	...
MSME loans outstanding by maturity (% share)																		
Less than 1 year	...	...	...	...	...	...	...	...	...	...	...	...	...	...	...	...	...	...
1-5 years	...	...	...	...	...	...	...	...	...	...	...	...	...	...	...	...	...	...
More than 5 years	...	...	...	...	...	...	...	...	...	...	...	...	...	...	...	...	...	...

GDP = gross domestic product; MSME = micro, small and medium-sized enterprise..

* Banks with foreign capital included here. Particularly, (i) banks with 50% to 100% foreign capital, of which local branches of foreign banks and (ii) bank with less than 50% of the foreign capital included here.

** Overdue (+30 days).

Source: ADB Asia SME Monitor 2022 database. Data from Central Bank of the Republic of Azerbaijan.

Table 3.4: Public Financing and Guarantees

End-of-period data

Item	2004	2005	2006	2007	2008	2009	2010	2011	2012	2013	2014	2015	2016	2017	2018	2019	2020	2021
SUBSIDIZED LOANS TO MSMEs																		
Number of funds	1	2	2	2	2	2	2	2	3	3	3	3	3	3	3	3	3	3
Number of subsidized loans (new approvals)	1,338	2,203	1,771	882	797	2,101	1,430	1,643	2,419	4,468	5,560	5,243	2,477	1,953	999	1,573	908	1,902
Outstanding of subsidized loans to MSMEs (AZN million)		...	...	...	...	...	...	...	...	...	...	...	...	...	394	527	538	625
Growth (%)	...	...	...	...	...	...	...	...	...	...	...	...	...	...	...	33.5	2.1	16.2
Subsidized loans disbursed to MSMEs (AZN million)	...	...	...	...	...	...	...	...	...	...	...	...	...	...	...	...	107	115
Number of MSMEs that accepted subsidized loans	...	...	...	...	...	...	...	...	...	...	...	...	...	...	...	...	903	1,895
MSME access to subsidized loans (% of MSMEs)	...	...	...	...	...	...	...	...	...	...	...	...	...	...	...	...	0.3	...

MSME = micro, small, and medium-sized enterprise.

Note: Entrepreneurship Development Fund under the Ministry of Economy of the Republic of Azerbaijan.

End-of-period data

Item	2004	2005	2006	2007	2008	2009	2010	2011	2012	2013	2014	2015	2016	2017	2018	2019	2020	2021
CREDIT GUARANTEES																		
Number of guarantee schemes	...	...	...	...	...	...	...	...	...	...	...	...	...	1	1	1	1	1
Guaranteed loans outstanding to MSMEs (AZN million)	...	...	...	...	...	...	...	...	...	...	...	...	...	...	...	...	...	...
Growth (%)	...	...	...	...	...	...	...	...	...	...	...	...	...	...	...	...	...	...
Guaranteed loans approved to MSMEs (AZN million)	...	...	...	...	...	...	...	...	...	...	...	...	...	...	...	...	...	...
Guaranteed loans disbursed to MSMEs (AZN million)	...	...	...	...	...	...	...	...	...	...	...	...	...	...	...	...	...	...
Number of MSMEs guaranteed	...	...	...	...	...	...	...	...	...	...	...	...	...	...	...	...	...	...
MSME access to credit guarantees (% of MSMEs)	...	...	...	...	...	...	...	...	...	...	...	...	...	...	...	...	...	...
Guaranteed MSME loans to total MSME loans (%)	...	...	...	...	...	...	...	...	...	...	...	...	...	...	...	...	...	...
Nonperforming guaranteed MSME loans to total guaranteed MSME loans (NPL ratio; %)	...	...	...	...	...	...	...	...	...	...	...	...	...	...	...	...	...	...
Total guaranteed loans outstanding (AZN million)	...	...	...	...	...	...	...	...	...	...	...	...	...	...	...	42.7	131.2	138.6

MSME = micro, small, and medium-sized enterprise.

Note: Loan breakdown by MSME size is not available.

Source: ADB Asia SME Monitor 2022 database. Data from Central Bank of the Republic of Azerbaijan.

Table 3.4a: Refinancing Schemes for MSMEs

Name of the Fund	Year of the launch	Fund Size (AZN million)	Taget Beneficiaries	Amount of Refinance (AZN million)*	Number of MSMEs benefitted*	Status (ongoing/ closed)
1. Entrepreneurship Development Fund under the Ministry of Economy of the Republic of Azerbaijan	1992	868 (as of 2020)	Agriculture, manufacturing, services, tourism, logistics, digital economy, telecommunications, startups, renewable energy, etc. (excluding oil and trade)	...	...	ongoing
2. Agrarian Credit and Development Agency (AKIA) under the Ministry of Agriculture of the Republic of Azerbaijan	2004	37 (as of 2019)	Production, processing, storage and sale of agricultural products, and financing of innovative projects related to agrarian development in the regions.	...	...	ongoing
3. State Fund for Development of Information Technologies (SFDIT) under the Ministry of Transport, Communications and High Technologies	2012	...	Enterpreneurs in ICT sector.	...	...	ongoing
Grand Total (AZN million)		...		...		

ICT = information and communication technology; MSME = micro, small, and medium-sized enterprise.

Source: ADB Asia SME Monitor 2022 database. Data from Central Bank of the Republic of Azerbaijan.

Table 3.5: Nonbank Finance

End-of-period data

Item	2004	2005	2006	2007	2008	2009	2010	2011	2012	2013	2014	2015	2016	2017	2018	2019	2020	2021
NUMBER OF NONBANK FINANCE INSTITUTIONS																		
Nonbank Finance Institutions, total	70	85	94	96	94	96	101	125	133	148	157	157	144	123	104	90	91	99
Microfinance institutions	15	17	17	19	19	19	19	28	29	37	48	48	47	47	47	45	49	56
Credit unions/cooperatives	55	68	77	77	75	77	82	97	104	111	109	109	97	76	57	45	42	43
MICROFINANCE INSTITUTIONS																		
Assets, total (AZN million)	22.3	38.4	59.0	127.9	174.9	185.8	193.0	251.4	329.3	457.5	550.7	607.4	342.8	322.5	267.8	342.6	316.3	388.6
Financing outstanding, total (AZN million)	...	...	...	...	...	...	...	...	301.0	402.0	477.0	498.4	339.0	280.0	228.0	269.0	263.0	333.3
Growth (%)	...	...	...	...	...	...	...	...	...	33.6	18.7	4.5	(32.0)	(17.4)	(18.6)	18.0	(2.2)	26.7
Total financing to GDP (%)	0.262	0.307	0.315	0.451	0.436	0.522	0.454	0.483	0.601	0.786	0.933	1.117	0.567	0.459	0.334	0.418	0.436	0.418
Annual lending rate (%, on average)	...	...	...	...	...	...	...	...	...	...	...	...	...	...	...	24.0	28.0	27.0
Gross nonperforming loans (NPLs) (AZN million)	...	...	...	...	...	...	...	...	...	...	...	...	...	...	96.0	66.0	81.0	70.0
Gross NPLs to total loans (%)	...	...	...	...	...	...	...	...	...	...	...	...	...	...	42.1	24.5	30.8	21.0
Savings (AZN million)*	...	...	...	...	...	...	...	...	...	...	...	...	...	...	...	...	...	...
Number of customers financed, total	...	...	...	...	...	...	...	...	...	...	...	...	...	150,438	108,163	155,865	154,174	273,000
Financing outstanding by sector (% share)																		
Agriculture, forestry, and fisheries	...	...	...	...	...	...	...	...	...	...	...	...	...	...	...	...	...	13.0
Wholesale and retail trade	...	...	...	...	...	...	...	...	...	...	...	...	...	...	...	...	...	8.0
Other services	...	...	...	...	...	...	...	...	...	...	...	...	...	...	...	...	...	10.0
Others	...	...	...	...	...	...	...	...	...	...	...	...	...	...	...	...	...	69.0
Financing outstanding by region (% share)**																		
Capital city (Baku)	...	...	...	...	...	...	...	...	...	...	...	...	...	...	...	...	...	60.0
Others	...	...	...	...	...	...	...	...	...	...	...	...	...	...	...	...	...	40.0
CREDIT UNIONS AND COOPERATIVES																		
Assets, total (AZN million)	3.9	6.7	8.8	12.7	15.6	22.6	31.7	38.2	45.6	53.8	69.7	86.4	59.2	42.1	27.8	16.6	15.2	14.3
Financing outstanding, total (AZN million)	...	...	...	...	...	...	...	...	42.3	51.1	62.0	79.6	59.5	38.1	24.3	14.9	13.3	13.8
Growth (%)	...	...	...	...	...	...	...	...	...	20.6	21.3	29.0	(24.6)	(36.1)	(37.0)	(38.7)	(10.7)	3.8
Total financing to GDP (%)	...	...	...	...	...	...	...	...	...	0.088	0.105	0.146	0.098	0.054	0.030	0.018	0.018	0.015
Annual lending rate (%, on average)	...	...	...	...	...	...	...	...	...	...	...	...	...	...	...	...	...	...
Gross nonperforming loans (NPLs) (AZN million)	...	...	...	...	...	...	...	...	...	...	...	...	...	...	...	...	...	...
Gross NPLs to total loans (%)	...	...	...	...	...	...	...	...	...	...	...	...	...	...	...	...	...	...
Number of customers financed, total	...	...	...	...	...	...	...	...	...	...	...	...	...	...	...	...	...	...
Financing outstanding by sector (% share)																		
Agriculture, forestry, and fisheries	...	...	...	...	...	...	...	...	...	...	...	...	...	...	...	...	...	...
Manufacturing	...	...	...	...	...	...	...	...	...	...	...	...	...	...	...	...	...	...
Transportation and communication	...	...	...	...	...	...	...	...	...	...	...	...	...	...	...	...	...	...
Construction	...	...	...	...	...	...	...	...	...	...	...	...	...	...	...	...	...	...
Wholesale and retail trade	...	...	...	...	...	...	...	...	...	...	...	...	...	...	...	...	...	...
Other services	...	...	...	...	...	...	...	...	...	...	...	...	...	...	...	...	...	...
Others	...	...	...	...	...	...	...	...	...	...	...	...	...	...	...	...	...	...
Financing outstanding by region (% share)																		
Capital city (Baku)	...	...	...	...	...	...	...	...	...	...	...	...	...	...	...	...	...	...
Others	...	...	...	...	...	...	...	...	...	...	...	...	...	...	...	...	...	...

GDP = gross domestic product.

* Microfinance institutions are not allowed to take deposits.

** In calculating regional distribution, "Aqrarkredit" Closed Joint Stock Company, which provides microcredits for businesses, was excluded.

Source: ADB Asia SME Monitor 2022 database. Data from Central Bank of the Republic of Azerbaijan.

Table 3.6: Capital Markets

End-of-period data

Item	2016	2017	2018	2019	2020	2021
EQUITY MARKET						
Main Board						
Market capitalization (AZN million)	2,681	3,234	3,554	3,688	3,958	4,367
Growth (%)	...	20.6	9.9	3.8	7.3	10.3
Trading value (AZN million)	113	701	90	3	50	30
Trading volume (million shares)	1,863	1,575	2,120	2,069	2,087	6,219
Number of listed companies	5	4	6	11	28	28
Number of IPOs	...	...	...	...	...	...
Number of delisted companies	7	4	3	6	22	11

IPO = initial public offering.
Source: ADB Asia SME Monitor 2022 database. Data from Baku Stock Exchange.

Table 3.6a: Listing Requirements—Baku Stock Exchange

Criteria	Stock
	Main Board
The requirements for the inclusion of shares in the premium market segment are as follows:	The issuer must be an open joint-stock company. The issue of shares must be carried out by way of public offering or admitted to public trading. Bankruptcy proceedings must not be initiated or the financial stability of the issuer must not be compromised within 1 year prior to the submission of application. The term of activity of the issuer must be at least 3 (three) years and must operate with a net profit of at least 1 year for the last 3 financial years. The issuer's authorized capital must be at least AZN2.5 million. At least 10% of the issuer's listed shares, and in case of nonpayment of this condition, the volume of free-float in the equivalent of at least AZN500,000 shall be provided. (https://www.bfb.az/en/view-file/listing-rules-eng-final.pdf)
The requirements for the inclusion of shares in the standard market segment are as follows:	The issuer must be an open joint-stock company. The issue of shares must be carried out by way of public offering or accepted for public trading. The term of validity of the issuer must be at least 1 year. The authorized capital of the issuer must be at least AZN200,000. The issuer's financial statements shall be prepared in accordance with IFRS requirements. Annual financial statements for the last financial year must be audited by an external (independent) auditor. The issuer must have a website that is regularly updated and covers important areas of its activities. (https://www.bfb.az/en/view-file/listing-rules-eng-final.pdf)

IFRS = International Financial Reporting Standards.
Source: ADB Asia SME Monitor 2022 database. Data from Baku Stock Exchange.

Table 3.7: Policies and Regulations

Regulations	
Name	**Outline**
Decree of the President of the Republic of Azerbaijan on ensuring the activities of the Small and Medium Business Development Agency of the Republic of Azerbaijan, № 148 of 2018	The decree ensures activities of the Small and Medium Business Development Agency of the Republic of Azerbaijan.
Decree of the President of the Republic of Azerbaijan on the approval of the "Guidelines on providing state support for internal market research for the purpose of stimulating the competitive production of micro, small and medium-sized enterprises", № 713 of 2019	The decree sets guidelines on providing state support for internal market research for the purpose of stimulating the competitive production of micro, small, and medium-sized enterprises (MSMEs).
Decision of the Cabinet of Ministers of the Republic of Azerbaijan on the approval of the "criteria for determining the startup", № 20 of 2021	This decision makes possible startup certification for MSMEs.
Decree of the President of the Republic of Azerbaijan on the approval of the "Regulations on the "e-KOB evi" (e-SME house) portal", № 1415 of 2021	The decree identifies the guidelines of e-KOB evi web page.
Decree of the President of the Republic of Azerbaijan on the approval of the "Rule of support for the expansion of the sale of products produced by micro and small business entities using the trade networks", № 1482 of 2021	The decree sets the rules on support for expanding the sales in trade networks by micro and small business entities.
Decree of the President of the Republic of Azerbaijan on further improvement of management of small and medium enterprises, № 1771 of 2017	The decree aims to further improve the management in the field of small and medium-sized enterprises.
Decision of the Cabinet of Ministers of the Republic of Azerbaijan on approval of the "Regulation on the financing of education, science, research and support projects related to the development of micro, small and medium entrepreneurship", № 364 of 2020	The decision regulates financing of education, science, research and support projects related to the development of micro, small, and medium entrepreneurship.
Decree of the Cabinet of Ministers on the approval of the "criteria for the division of micro, small, medium and large business entities", № 556 of 2018.	The regulation identifies criteria for MSMEs in Azerbaijan.
Law of the Republic of Azerbaijan On Suspension of Inspections of Entrepreneurial Activities, № 1410-IVQ of 2015	Inspections in the field of entrepreneurship in the territory of the Republic of Azerbaijan are suspended until 1 January 2023.
Law of the Republic of Azerbaijan On State Support to Small Business, № 673-IQ of 1999	The law aims to implement the right of everyone to engage in entrepreneurial activity and other types of economic activity not prohibited by law, as defined by the Constitution of the Republic of Azerbaijan, and defines the economic, legal, organizational basis, forms and methods of state assistance to small businesses in the Republic of Azerbaijan.
Tax Code of the Republic of Azerbaijan, № 905-IQ of 2000	The code defines fundamental taxation principles and establishes procedures for tax calculation, payment, and collection in Azerbaijan, lists the duties and rights of tax payers and tax authorities, and lists penalties for breaking the law on taxes.
Customs Code of the Republic of Azerbaijan, 164-IVQ of 2011	The customs code establishes the legal, economic, and organizational foundation for customs in the country. It specifies the general procedures and rules that apply to goods and vehicles that are imported into, exported from, or transit through the country's customs area, as well as the rights and responsibilities of individuals in relation to these matters.
Law on State Registration and the State Register of Legal Entities, № 560-IIQ of 2003	Conducting state registration and the state register of legal entities in the territory of the Azerbaijan Republic.
Law of the Republic of Azerbaijan on investment activity, №551-VIQ of 2022	The law defines the legal and economic bases of investment activities in the Republic of Azerbaijan in accordance with the 1st, 10th, 11th, 13th and 26th clauses of Part I of Article 94 of the Constitution of the Republic of Azerbaijan, provides protection of the rights and legal interests of investors.
Law on Public Procurement, № 245-IIQ of 2001	The law determines the economic, legal, and organizational basis of public procurement in the Republic of Azerbaijan; the principles and rules of efficient and economical use of public funds during procurement; and the creation of an equal competitive environment for all consignors (contractors) based on competition and transparency.
Law on Privatization of State Property in Azerbaijan, № 878-IQ of 2000	The program introduced privatization checks (vouchers) that could be sold or redeemed in exchange for assets subject to privatization.

continued on next page

Table 3.7 *continued*

Law of the Republic of Azerbaijan on Banks, № 590-IIQ of 2004	The law defines the principles, rules and standards for organization, internal management, regulation of activities and liquidation of banks with the purpose of alignment of the legal framework of the banking system to international standards, increasing the role of banking services in the economy, enforcement of the protection of bank depositors and creditors, and overall maintenance of stable and safe performance of the banking system.
Law of the Republic of Azerbaijan on Non-Bank Credit Institutions, № 933-IIIQ of 2009	The law defines the rules on establishment, management and regulation of nonbank credit institutions with an aim to better meet demand of legal entities and individuals in the Republic of Azerbaijan for financial resources and create suitable conditions for access to financial services.
Law of the Republic of Azerbaijan on Credit Unions, № 876-IQ of 2000	The law determines economic, legislative and organizational basis for establishment and operation of credit unions in the Republic of Azerbaijan.
Law of the Republic of Azerbaijan on Securities Market, № 1284-IVQ of 2015	The law was adopted pursuant to sections 11 and 15 of Part I of Article 94 of the Constitution of the Republic of Azerbaijan and sets forth the principles and rules for issue, state registration, public offering of investment securities, depository and post-trading systems, market for securities and derivative instruments, organization, management and liquidation of persons holding licenses in the securities market and central depository, and sets forth the legal and economic grounds for relations relating to protection of investor rights and for regulation and oversight by the state of the securities market.
Law of the Republic of Azerbaijan on Investment Funds, № 1101-IIIQ of 2010	The law defines the principles and rules of organization, management, and liquidation of investment funds in the Republic of Azerbaijan, as well as the legal and economic basis of regulation and control in the field of investment fund activity.
Regulators and Policymakers	
Name	**Responsibility**
Small and Medium Business Development Agency (SMBDA), Ministry of Economy	The objective is to support micro, small, and medium-sized enterprise (MSME) business development in the country; strengthen the role of MSMEs in the national economy; increase their competitiveness and contribution to national development indicators; participate in protection of MSMEs interests and problem resolution; facilitate MSMEs institutional support mechanisms; and coordinate activities of government agencies and private institutions in this area. SMBDA provides government-to-business and business-to-business platforms, and performs coordinating, supervision, monitoring and evaluation functions.
Export and Investment Promotion Agency of the Republic of Azerbaijan (AZPROMO), Ministry of Economy	AZPROMO aims to stimulate the export of non-oil sector products, attract foreign investments to the national economy, expand cooperation between local and foreign business communities, and organize large-scale events in Azerbaijan and abroad for businesses.
Entrepreneurship Development Fund, Ministry of Economy	Offers loans to MSMEs, small farmers, and agricultural companies at preferential rates.
State Agency for Public Service and Social Innovations (under the President of the Republic of Azerbaijan)	The agency carries out socially oriented projects aimed at ensuring the active participation of citizens in the socioeconomic life of the Republic of Azerbaijan, developing small and medium entrepreneurship, raising the employment rate of the population and supporting the formation of competitive family businesses in the country. Agency's "ABAD" (Simplified Support to Family Businesses) centers implement assistance projects for family businesses engaged in arts and agriculture.
Central Bank of the Republic of Azerbaijan (CBAR)	Regulate and supervise commercial banks, nonbank finance institutions, and capital markets. To supervise capital markets, the Financial Market Supervisory Authority was established in 2016 by presidential decree; however, it was liquidated in 2019 and its functions were transferred to the CBAR.
Mortgage and Credit Guarantee Fund of the Republic of Azerbaijan	Provides guarantees and subsidies to enterprises operating in the non-oil sector (excluding the financial sector).
Agrarian Credit and Development Agency under the Ministry of Agriculture	The executive body that ensures the involvement and use of loans for state support of individuals and legal entities engaged in entrepreneurial activity in the agrarian sector.

continued on next page

Table 3.7 *continued*

Policies		
Name	**Responsible Entity**	**Outline**
Socio-Economic Development Strategy of the Republic of Azerbaijan for 2022–2026	Government	The five national priorities for the socioeconomic development of the country are as follows: 1. sustainably growing a competitive economy; 2. society based on dynamic, inclusive and social justice; 3. competitive human capital and space for modern innovations; 4. great return to the liberated territories; 5. clean environment and "green growth" country.
Azerbaijan 2030: National Priorities for Socio-Economic Development		
Strategic Road Map for the Production of Consumer Goods at the level of SMEs (SME Roadmap)	Ministry of Economy	The following strategic directions are included in the MSME roadmap: 1. improving the business environment and regulatory framework for MSMEs; 2. ensuring access to finance for MSMEs; 3. increasing internationalization of MSMEs; 4. promoting MSME innovations; 5. increasing MSME skills.
State Program on Socio-Economic Development of Regions of the Republic of Azerbaijan for 2019–2023	Ministry of Economy	The main goal of the program is to ensure sustainable and balanced development of regions in Azerbaijan, including a competitive economy based on the principles of sustainable development, social welfare meeting high standards, efficient use of natural resources and creating a favorable environment that allows for the formation of an ecologically safe system that ensures reliable protection of the environment. Under the State Program following (direclty) MSME development related tasks are expected to be performed: 1. accelerating the development of entrepreneurship, including MSMEs, strengthening their financial stability; 2. provision of services (including necessary mobile services) by state institutions in the field of MSME development to entrepreneurs in a one-stop shop with better quality, convenience, and applying modern innovations; 3. to support the realization of the development potential of the regions, the creation of new MSMEs, the development of existing MSMEs, the formation and efficient operation of the MSME Friends network across the country, which will ensure the convenient access of MSMEs to state support mechanisms.
State Program on the Development Production of Citrus between 2018–2025	Ministry of Agriculture	The sector-level state programs aim to develop specific agriculture subsectors in the country. The common aim is to ensure the sustainable development of subsectors in the country by increasing state support, introducing modern technologies and raising interest in the production and export of final products.
State Program on the Development Production of Winemaking between 2018–2025		
State Program on the Development Production of Cocoon and Silk between 2018–2025		
State Program on the Development Production of Rice between 2018–2025		
State Program on the Development Production of Cotton between 2017–2022		
State Program on the Development Production of Tobacco between 2017–2022		

Sources: ADB Asia SME Monitor 2022 database. Data from www.e-qanun.az (an electronic database for legislative acts developed by the Mnistry of Justice of the Repiblic of Azerbaijan), Central Bank of the Republic of Azerbaijan, Small and Medium Business Development Agency (SMBDA), and Ministry of Agriculture of the Republic of Azerbaijan.

Table 3.7a: COVID-19 Emergency Measures

Name	Fund Size (AZN million)	Outline
Action Plan adopted by the Cabinet of Ministers for the Implementation of Clause 10.2 of Presidential Decree "On a number of measures related to reducing the negative impact of the coronavirus disease (COVID-19) pandemic and the resulting sharp fluctuations in the world energy and stock markets on the economy of the Republic of Azerbaijan, macroeconomic stability, employment issues, and business entities in the country"	1,000	• Partial coverage of wages for those who worked in areas affected by the pandemic. • Provide financial support to micro entrepreneurs operating in areas affected by the pandemic. • Review of capital and property amnesty in the country in order to expand financial sources of economic growth and investment. • Provide tax concessions for enterprises operating in areas affected by the pandemic. • Providing state guarantees for bank loans in the amount of AZN500 million for enterprises operating in areas affected by the pandemic. • Allocation of additional funds to the Entrepreneurship Development Fund. • Subsidize loan interest on the existing loan portfolio in the amount of AZN1 billion for enterprises operating in areas affected by the pandemic. • Increase the amount of funds allocated for concessional mortgage loans. • Provide financial support to the vital passenger transport sector. • Provide temporary employment of unemployed persons through the creation of a public workplace for 50,000 persons. • Provide a one-time payment in the amount of minimum living wage (AZN190) to persons registered as unemployed in the State Employment Service. • Reimbursement of tuition fees for students who are members of families belonging to socially vulnerable groups. • Increasing the concessional electricity limit for the population by 100 kilowatt-hours in April-May 2020.
Grand Total	1,000	

Source: ADB Asia SME Monitor 2022 database. Data from Cabinet of Ministers of the Republic of Azerbaijan (https://nk.gov.az/az/document/4367/).

Country Review

Georgia

Overview

Like most of the world, the coronavirus disease (COVID-19) pandemic hit Georgia's economy hard. Economic growth contracted by 6.8% in 2020.[115] Closing borders, lockdowns, and other mobility restrictions—like curfews—were imposed from March to May 2020. Lighter restrictions continued through the rest of 2020 and throughout 2021. The restrictions reduced business across the country, cutting revenues and causing many enterprises to close. The unemployment rate rose to 18.5% in 2020, up from 17.6% in 2019.[116] Government economic stimulus packages coincided with the gradual lifting of restrictions from the second quarter of 2021. This, along with the resumption of international trade, eased the pandemic impact on private businesses. The economy recovered, growing by 10.4% in 2021, higher than the pre-pandemic 5.0% in 2019.[117] Nonetheless, unemployment continued to increase—to 20.6% in 2021.

Small and medium-sized enterprises (SMEs) are crucial to Georgia's economy, accounting for 99.7% of all enterprises. In 2020, they employed more than 440,000 people, or 62.8% of the total workforce. Gross value added (GVA) of SMEs equaled 13.5 billion *Georgian lari* (GEL), a 2.0% decrease from 2019 (GEL13.8 billion). SMEs gradually increased their share of Georgia's total GVA in 2020 to 60.8%. They were responsible for more than half of both export and import values, as Georgia's international trade continues to develop. It is clear how strengthening SMEs can boost the national economy.

Access to finance is essential. Yet, it is one of the most difficult problems SMEs face. The 2019 World Bank Enterprise Survey indicated that access to finance is the second-largest obstacle after political instability. SME bank loans have grown over the years, with loans outstanding amounting to GEL8.5 billion in 2021, well above the GEL7.1 billion in pre-epidemic 2019. The national SME development strategy for 2016–2020 aimed to improve SME access to finance. SME loans to gross domestic product (GDP) grew from 10.6% in 2015 (before the national strategy) to 14.1% in 2021. However, the share of SME loans to total bank credit has fallen since 2018 (19.8% in 2021), as the SME credit market remains small. Lending was almost evenly split in 2021 between SMEs operating in the capital of Tbilisi and those in rural areas. The national SME development strategy also introduced several refinancing schemes to allow SMEs and women entrepreneurs quicker and easier access to finance.

The nonbank finance industry is less developed as the financial system remains dominated by commercial banks (holding more than 90% of financial institution assets). The most popular nonbank finance comes from microfinance institutions (MFIs). They have expanded across the country. But the pandemic led to a gradual decrease in number (38 MFIs in 2021 from 48 in 2019). To help SMEs and agribusinesses obtain loans, the central bank enacted a Law on Micro Banks in March 2022 (effective September 2022). Georgia does not have a dedicated equity market for SMEs.

[115] Ministry of Finance of Georgia. GDP and Economic Growth. https://www.mof.ge/en/4553.

[116] National Statistics Office of Georgia: https://www.geostat.ge/en/modules/categories/683/Employment-Unemployment

[117] Preliminary data for 2021.

Georgia's latest SME Development Strategy (2021–2025) targets increasing the GVA of SMEs by 20%, boosting SME employment by 10%, and raising SME labor productivity by 20%. The government sees SMEs as vital for sustainable growth. Its priorities for SME development are multifaceted. They aim to improve SMEs operational environment, access to finance, skill development, market access (including international markets), Information and communication technology, and innovation. They emphasize promoting women entrepreneurship and developing the green economy. Georgia has yet to develop a national financial inclusion strategy.

1. Impact of the Global Economy on SMEs

COVID-19 Impact

In 2020, growth momentum was stunted by COVID-19. Controlling the spread of the virus, border closures, and lockdowns hampered trade and significantly reduced SME business and economic activity.

The Georgian Chamber of Commerce and Industry (GCCI) conducted two surveys to assess how COVID-19 affected business. The first was done in March 2020 (prior to the imposition of the state of emergency and economic constraints), with the second conducted in June 2020 (after the state of emergency and economic constraints were lifted). The second survey interviewed 1,553 businesses across 50 sectors. Eighty-nine percent of respondents were local businesses with 97% SMEs. The initial findings showed that 66% of the total suffered revenue losses. Among those, 37% lost revenue between GEL5,000–20,000, while only 1% lost more than GEL500,000 (Figure 4.1).

The survey found that 76% of businesses had reduced turnover, 21% about the same, and 3% saw turnover increase. Most respondents stressed the serious direct effects of COVID-19 on their business. The critical impacts included (i) reduced sales, (ii) weaker *Georgian lari* exchange rates, (iii) logistics/supply chain disruptions, (iv) reduced availability of raw materials (at higher price), and (v) delayed costumer payments.

The survey results showed that COVID-19 also had a significant impact on a firm's employment. More than half of the respondents (53%) said they would maintain their current employee level for the 6 months from the time of the survey, 31% found it difficult to respond, 9% would reduce the number of employees, with 7% intending to hire more. Nearly half of those surveyed found it difficult to pay their employees, 43% said they had reduced salaries, and 32% said they could maintain salaries at same level. One-fifth of the respondents (20%) indicated that employees were fully or partially on unpaid leave with 5% or partially laying off employees.

PricewaterhouseCoopers conducted a follow-up survey in October 2020. Most businesses surveyed said that declining aggregate demand was the most serious negative impact of the pandemic. As a result, 68% indicated that revenues have fallen by at least 50% since May 2020.The pandemic hit the hotels and restaurants hardest (84% of firms saw revenues fall by at least 50%), followed by agriculture (59%), construction (36%), and wholesale and retail trade (34%). Three-quarters of those surveyed resumed operations after restrictions were lifted.[118]

Preliminary 2020 data from the National Statistics Office of Georgia confirmed a significant decline in turnover, output, and employment among SMEs, with turnover down by 8%, output by 9%, and employment by 22%, as compared with the SME data for 2019.

[118] Annual reports of SME Development Strategy for 2021–2025.

The pandemic, quarantine measures, and mobility restrictions—such as air and land traffic suspensions, restrictions on economic activity, and curfews—damaged the financial condition of most businesses. The restrictions on economic activities imposed in March 2020 were exceptionally severe. Any activity tied to social interaction and people's mobility proportionally increased the risk of spreading virus infections. Thus, the government decided to temporarily restrict economic activities, except for essential services. E-commerce and delivery services for groceries, food, and medicine could continue to operate. All retail outlets were closed, except for groceries and pharmacies. All those still functioning had to operate in accordance with recommendations issued by the Ministry of Healthcare.

SMEs were hit hardest. Government and central bank assistance to private sector businesses focused on helping maintain liquidity, both by writing off or deferring existing tax liabilities and by delivering liquidity directly. Government financial support programs were modified frequently with changing cofinancing terms and limits, while businesses qualifying for assistance expanded. New financial support was added, such as GEL330 million credit guarantee scheme.

Figure 4.1: COVID-19 Impact on Businesses

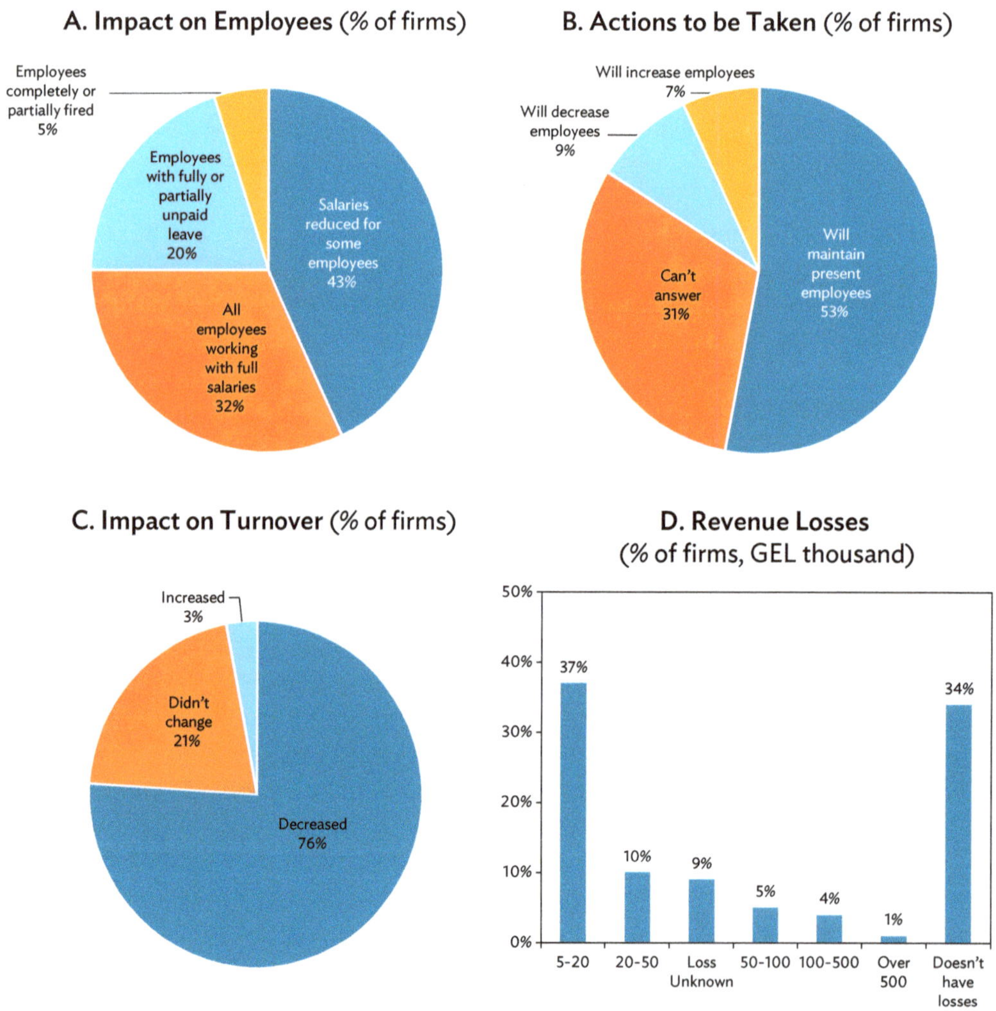

Source: ADB Asia SME Monitor 2022 database. Data from the survey conducted by Georgian Chamber of Commerce and Industry (GCCI) in June 2020.

Impact of the Russian Invasion of Ukraine

The Russian invasion of Ukraine beginning February 2022 has affected the global economy and economic outlook. It had raised prices for food, energy and other commodities, contributing to supply shocks and shortages. It has damaged Georgia's economy, particularly on trade.

Trade with Ukraine slowed considerably since the invasion began. According to the National Statistics Office of Georgia, imports from Ukraine (tobacco or substitute cigar, cigarettes, and related products; medicinal products; and other solid residues from extracted soybean oil; and ferroalloys, among others) were valued at $35.2 million in February 2022, but decreased sharply in March 2022, by 68.1% ($11.2 million). Exports to Ukraine (mostly automobiles; mineral or chemical fertilizers; other nitrogenous products; ferroalloys; mineral and fresh water; and wine, among others) also decreased significantly. In February 2022, these exports amounted to $15.9 million, but fell by 88.5% ($1.8 million) 1 month later.

Similarly, trade with the Russian Federation dropped. Imports (petroleum and petroleum oils, coke and semi-coke of coal/lignite/peat; wheat or meslin flour; margarine; and electricity, among others) amounted to $95.9 million in February 2022, falling to $91.6 million in March 2022. Exports to the Russian Federation (ferroalloys; wine and spirits; natural or artificial water; and fresh or dried fruit, among others) totaled $50.2 million in February, decreasing by 66.2% ($16.9 million) in March.

The trend was similar during January–June 2022 for SME trade. Exports from Georgian SMEs decreased for both Ukraine and the Russian Federation—to $24.8 million for Ukraine, a 40.4% drop from January to June 2021 ($41.6 million); and $94.0 million to the Russian Federation, a 13.5% decline ($108.6 million).

The invasion also hurt Georgia's trade with other Commonwealth of Independent States (CIS) members—which includes both the Russian Federation and Ukraine. Imports from CIS countries (petroleum and petroleum products, natural gas and other gaseous hydrocarbons; ores and copper concentrates, among others) decreased by 18.1% in March 2022 compared with February. Exports (automobiles; ferroalloys; wine; medicinal products; and mineral and fresh water, among others) decreased by 35.9%. By contrast, trade with the European Union (EU) was mixed. While imports (oil and oil products; medical supplies; automobiles and trucks; vaccines, blood and immune products, among others) increased by 4.3% over the same period. Exports to the EU (ores and copper concentrates; nuts; ferroalloys; and wine, among others) fell 4.1%.

While exports of Georgia's SMEs fell in Ukraine and the Russian Federation, they increased to both the CIS and EU. In January–June 2022, SME exports to the CIS amounted to $384.3 million, or a 6.3% increase from the same period in 2021 ($361.5 million). SME exports to the EU reached $292.9 million, a 49.8% increase ($195.5 million).

The impact of the Russian invasion of Ukraine contributed to high inflation as well. Since the beginning of 2022, inflation has been edging downward—from 13.9% in January to 11.8% in March—but rose again in April (12.8%) and May (13.3%). Fuel price increases affected business logistics and manufacturers.[119] Residential property prices in Georgia were affected along with commercial rents for business offices.[120] These increased costs, coupled with the impact of the pandemic, put additional pressure on SME operations.

There are several predictions and scenarios assessing how the invasion could affect Georgia's overall economy. A report from TBC Capital (February 2022) took a scenario-based approach. If it had been over within 3 months, the report estimated Georgia's GDP growth would decrease from 6% to 4% with a 5% GEL depreciation by the

119 For example, according to Socar Georgia Petroleum, "nano super fuel" cost GEL3.26 prior to the invasion, rising 28.8% to GEL4.10 as of 11 May 2022 (SOCAR Georgia Petroleum. https://www.sgp.ge/en/price?start_date=2022-01-01&end_date=2022-05-11).

120 According to the National Statistics Office of Georgia, the Residential Property Price Index (2020 average=100) rose to 113.1 in the first quarter of 2022 from 108.5 in the fourth quarter of 2021.

end of 2022. There would be moderate central bank intervention and fiscal stimulus financed externally. Inflation would be slightly above the 3% target for 2022, with the GEL policy rate falling to about 9.0% (from 10.5% in 2021).

However, the report also presented a "delayed solution scenario" (the invasion continuing for more than 3 months), it estimated losses in net inflows in 2022 would reach $110 million compared with 2021, and $740 million compared to an earlier 2022 baseline. With a currency depreciation of 5%–10%, the GDP growth in 2022 would drop to around 0.5%. It expected the drop in net inflows to be compensated by central bank interventions and government external borrowings. It suggested a risk that people and firms would switch to foreign currency deposits and GEL loans, which in fact occurred during the pandemic, causing an estimated 50% loss in net inflows.

2. SME Development

- SMEs comprise 99.7% of all enterprises. Most operate in distributive trade, manufacturing, transportation, and construction. Around half or more SMEs operate outside the capital, Tbilisi.
- In 2020, SMEs employed more than 440,000 people, or 62.8% of total workforce. Around 30% of those employed by SMEs work in wholesale and retail trade. The COVID-19 pandemic badly affected SME employment, which lost 10% of employees in 2020.
- Despite the pandemic, SMEs generated 60.8% of the country's GVA in 2020. Since 2009, they contributed a relatively high 50% or more to GVA.
- Many SMEs are involved in international trade. Their exports and imports recovered quickly from the pandemic impact. SMEs have contributed over 50% of exports and imports by value since 2015.
- While most SMEs use the internet for business, e-commerce has yet to fully develop due to a lack of appropriate infrastructure for online transactions and poor innovation.
- Both government authorities (Enterprise Georgia and GITA) and the private sector (the GCCI and SME Development Association) support industrializing SMEs, along with developing business cluster and infrastructure through advisory and training services, grants and other funding sources.

Scale of SMEs

SMEs are defined based on the size of employment and business turnover, which is used for official statistics. There is no microenterprise category in Georgia. Definitions were initially developed in 2002, based on the average annual number of employees according to EU definitions. They were updated under the SME Development Strategy for 2016–2020. However, the criteria did not comply with current EU criteria. It was again updated under the SME Development Strategy for 2021–2025—small enterprises have fewer than 50 employees annually or an annual turnover of less than GEL12 million; medium-sized enterprises have from 50 to 250 employees or turnover of GEL12 million–GEL60 million (Table 4.1).

While the official definition does not separate micro and small businesses, there are institutions that define them for different purposes. For example, the Ministry of Finance splits micro and small businesses for special tax treatment. A micro business can be a person who does not use hired labor and works independently, with gross income not exceeding GEL30,000. While small businesses pay taxes under special tax treatments, micro businesses are exempt from personal income tax and withholding tax upon payment of service fees.[121]

According to the National Statistics Office, in 2020 there were 129,268 SMEs operating in Georgia, or 99.7% of all enterprises. Most were small firms (127,371 or some 99% of the total). Medium-sized enterprises comprised

121 Legislative Herald of Georgia. Tax Code of Georgia. https://www.matsne.gov.ge/ka/document/view/1043717?impose=translateEn&publication=118.

just 1% (1,897 enterprises) (Figure 4.2A and Table 4.2). Since 2013, the number of SMEs has been increasing, more pronounced for small firms; but the growth has been decelerating since 2018. By sector, 39.5% were in wholesale and retail trade (including repair of motor vehicles and motorcycles), followed by manufacturing (8.9%), transportation and storage (7.1%), and construction (6.6%) (Figure 4.2B).[122] By region, 45.2% were based in the capital city of Tbilisi, with the remaining 54.8% outside the capital or in rural areas (Figure 4.2C). Importantly, in 2014–2020 more than half of SMEs were permanently registered in rural areas.

The government recognizes the rights, knowledge, and potential of women working in SMEs, as well as the disadvantages they face in business opportunities and access to finance. In 2020, the share of women employed in business was 41.5% of total employment (58.5% for men). The nominal average monthly salary was GEL864.7 for women and GEL1,380.5 for men in 2019—a woman earned 62.6% of a man's salary, a 37% pay gap. The inequity occurs more in small enterprises, where the gender pay gap is 43%, while in large enterprises the gap is 34%.[123]

Figure 4.2: Number of SMEs

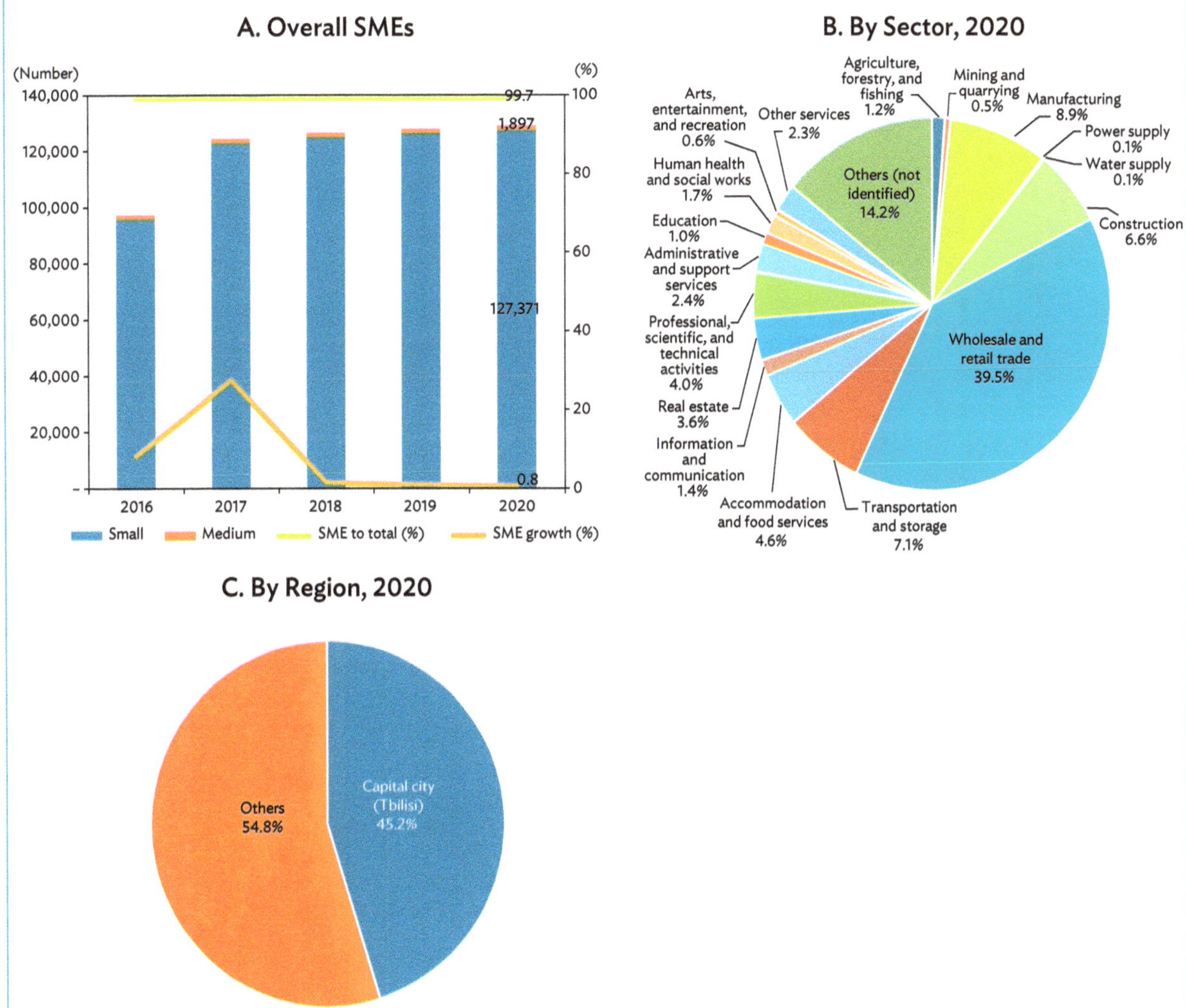

SME = small and medium-sized enterprise.

Source: ADB Asia SME Monitor 2022 database. Data from National Statistics Office of Georgia.

[122] Economic activities are classified under the Nomenclature of Economic Activities rev.2.

[123] SME Development Strategy of Georgia for 2021–2025.

Employment

SMEs employed 442,164 people in 2020, or 62.8% of total employment. Small enterprises absorbed 289,706 workers (65.5% of SME employment), followed by medium-sized enterprises (152,458 workers, or 34.5%) (Figure 4.3A and Table 4.2). Employment in SMEs has been growing steadily since 2009—after the 2008–2009 global financial crisis, with an average 7.6% growth in 2009–2019. However, it decreased by 10.1% in 2020 due to the pandemic impact.

Wholesale and retail trade held the largest number of jobs, (29.8%), followed by manufacturing (12.7%), construction (11.6%), human health and social work (7.0%), transportation and storage (6.1%), and accommodation and food services (5.8%) (Figure 4.3B). SMEs in Tbilisi generated the most jobs (52.9% in 2020), with the remaining 47.1% outside the capital or in rural areas (Figure 4.3C).

Figure 4.3: Employment by SMEs

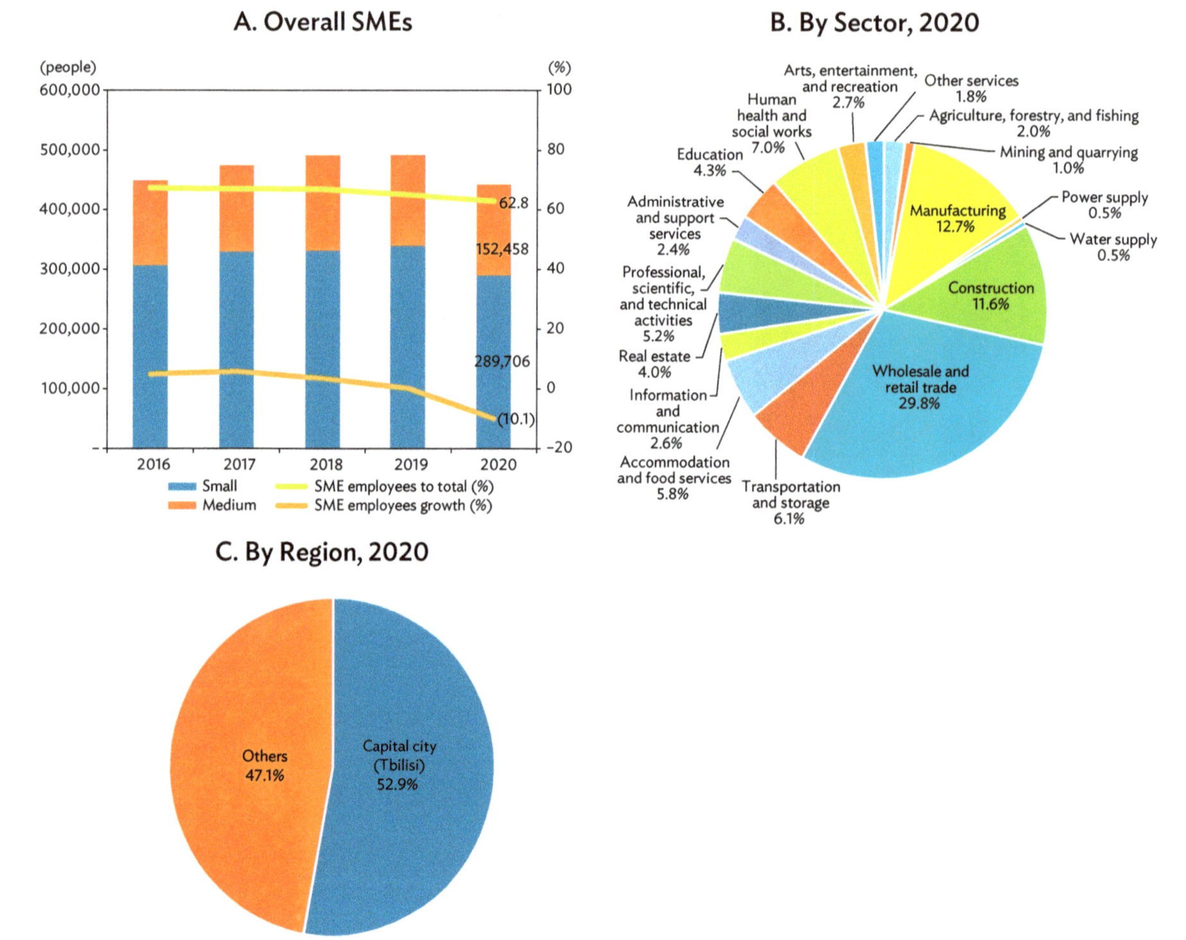

SME = small and medium-sized enterprise.

Source: ADB Asia SME Monitor 2022 database. Data from National Statistics Office of Georgia.

In 2019, the average pay of workers in business was GEL1,161.7, with those in medium-sized enterprises earning a bit more (GEL1,416.8). This was also higher than the average for those in large enterprises. Those working in small enterprises earned and average GEL893.5.

Business Productivity

Time-bound comparisons of SME contributions to GDP are unavailable. SME contributions to gross value added (GVA)[124] is tracked annually. SME GVA growth has recorded high increase since 2007 at the peak in 2011 (52.1%). However, it decreased by 2.0% in 2020 or GEL13.5 billion, affected by the pandemic and mobility restrictions. Yet, SME contribution to GVA remained high at 60.8%, which constantly shows more than half of the total GVA after 2019 or the global financial crisis (Figure 4.4A and Table 4.2). The average growth of SME GVA during 2009–2020 was 16.4%. By sector, wholesale and retail trade contributed the most (26.5% in 2020), followed by construction (20.9%) and manufacturing (12.3%) (Figure 4.4B). By region, 62.9% of SMEs' GVA were generated in the capital Tbilisi in 2020 (Figure 4.4C).

The COVID-19 pandemic and nationwide lockdown immediately hurt private business. But SMEs showed their resilience during the pandemic. Their contribution to GVA increased 1.5 percentage points in 2020 from 2019, when SME labor productivity reached GEL28,077—medium-sized enterprises adding GEL38,728 and small enterprises GEL23,287.[125, 126] In 2020, during the pandemic, it increased to GEL30,596. Europe's Deep and Comprehensive Free Trade Area (DCFTA), the introduction of new business technologies, and the creation of clusters all played a major role in increasing labor productivity.

One of the government's priorities is to ensure high productivity among SMEs. The "Clusters4Development (C4D)" project gave the Ministry of Economy and Sustainable Development (MESD) and the Entrepreneurship Development Agency (Enterprise Georgia) the opportunity to develop and implement a framework for business clusters. A National Cluster Development Program can help local SMEs become more competitive over the long term. Enterprise Georgia uses a cluster-based policy approach to enhance a firm's productivity, drive innovation and stimulate new business opportunities for SMEs. The Georgian Construction Materials Cluster—registered in December 2020 with support of the EU-GIZ project C4D—brings together SMEs operating in construction. The cluster helps local companies increase productivity, improve quality and safety, and optimize management and processes.[127]

C4D helped establish the Georgian Apparel and Fashion Association (registered in December 2020), which covers local apparel factories, fashion designers, and ateliers. Most of the 200 companies in the apparel sector are SMEs.[128] Cluster members are introduced to buyers with access to wider business networks. They increasingly work together and promote each other's products to maximise reach, bolster their stature, and increase productivity.

The United Nations Industrial Development Organization conducted a survey in December 2019, mapping out 53 emerging and potential clusters focusing on manufacturing and agribusiness (such as winemaking, marine fishing, food processing, beverages, tobacco products, textiles, wearing apparel, paper and paper products, among others). This was carried out in Tbilisi and nine of Georgia's 11 regions (Abkhazia and Tskhinvali were excluded due to the

124 GVA in basic prices is calculated on the basis of output, to which the subsidies on products are added, and purchasing of goods and services are subtracted (except products, that are bought for as-is-resale), and also changes in stocks of materials and supplies are added or subtracted. This is estimated according to the cost of various factor expenses of industrial activities of the economic entities.

125 SME labor productivity was calculated as GVA of SMEs divided by the number of SME employees.

126 National Statistics Office of Georgia.

127 Georgian Construction Materials Cluster. https://gcmc.ge/en/about-gcmc/.

128 Georgian Apparel and Fashion Association. https://gafa.org.ge/en/contact-us.

lack of data).[129] Clusters were identified according to UNIDO's cluster methodology of qualitative and quantitative assessments.[130] The clusters were ranked according to different criteria (export competitiveness, export value per firm, number of employees, value added per employee, and regional competitiveness of the sector, among others). The highest-scoring clusters hold the greatest potential for future employment, export/import substitution, and collaboration. The top 10 clusters were (i) beverages (wine) (Kakheti region), (ii) pharmaceuticals (Tbilisi), (iii) poultry (Kvemo-Kartli), (iv) wine (Racha Lechkhumi-Kvemo Svaneti), (v) furniture (Tbilisi), (vi) beverages (wine) (Kvemo-Kartli), (vii) jewelry (Tbilisi), (viii) marine fishing (Samegrelo-Zemo Svaneti), (ix) apparel (Tbilisi), and (x) processing and preserving of fruit and vegetables (Samegrelo-Zemo Svaneti).

Figure 4.4: SME Contribution to Gross Value Added

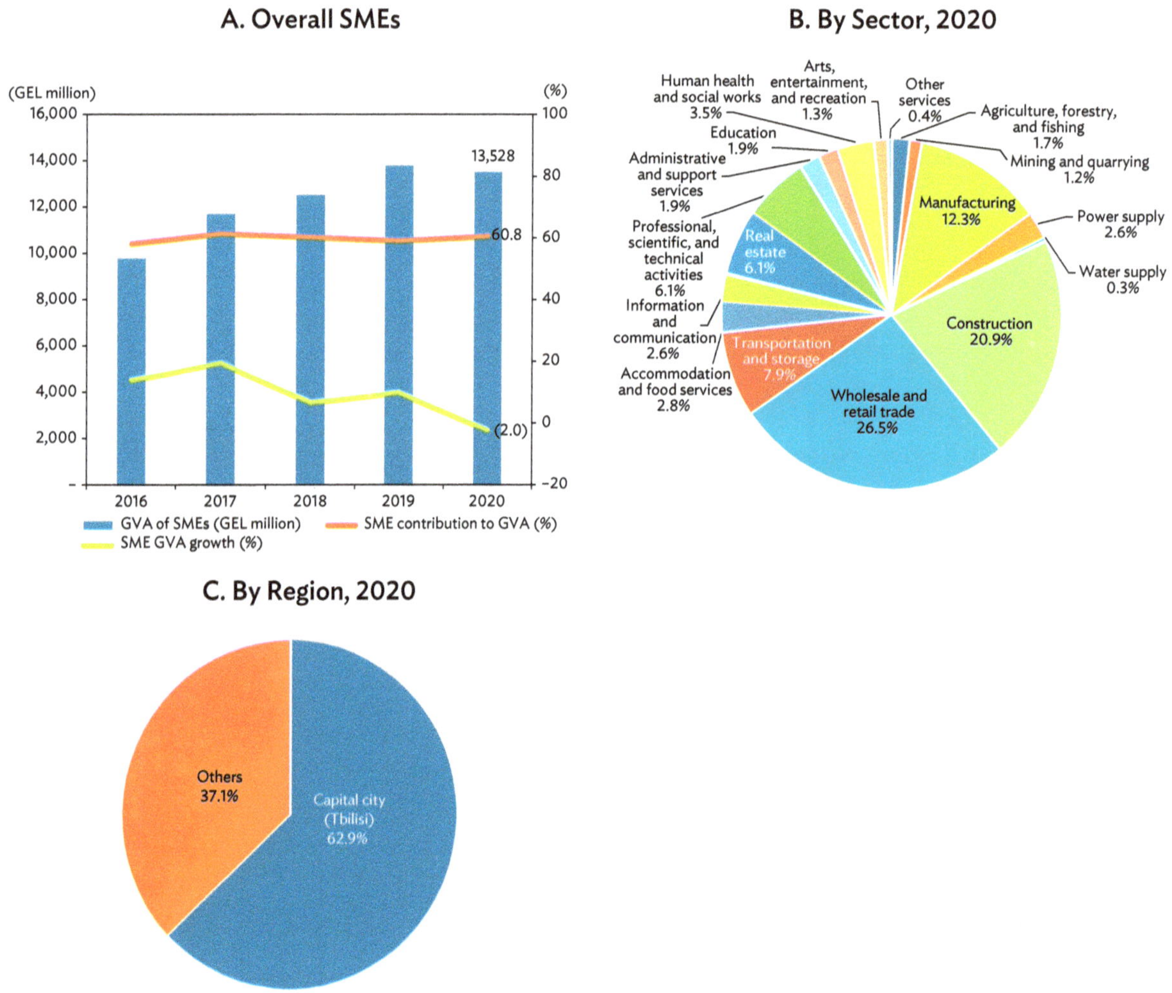

GVA = gross value added, SME = small and medium-sized enterprise.

Source: ADB Asia SME Monitor 2022 database. Data from National Statistics Office of Georgia.

[129] UN Industrial Development Organization. 2019. *Mapping Emerging and Potential Manufacturing and Agri-Business Clusters in Georgia.* https://www.gda.ge/shared/userfiles/images/UNIDO_Final%20cluster%20mapping%20report%20in%20Georgia.pdf.

[130] http://backonline.apswiss.ch/6001/cluster_approach_print.pdf

Market Access

Market access and internationalizing SMEs are part of the core strategies under the national SME policy as well as the Georgia's long-term development plan. It is critical that strong SMEs can access global markets. Participating in global value chains help develop SME trade, both exports and imports. It also strengthens their competitiveness, which helps the government make SMEs more inclusive.

Exports grew from 2017–2019, but fell by 12.0% in 2020 (GEL3,343 million) due to the pandemic and mobility restrictions. They recovered in 2021 to GEL4,242 million (up 26.9%) as borders reopened with the EU, CIS countries, and Türkiye) and mobility restrictions were gradually lifted. Similarly, SME exports decreased by 5.9% in 2020 to GEL1,864 million, recovering rapidly in 2021 to GEL2,372 million (27.2% growth) (Figure 4.5A and Table 4.2). Since 2015, SME exports have accounted for more than 50% of total export value (55.9% in 2021), although still below the 63.8% peak in 2016. SME exports drove the recovery of the overall export industry in 2021 (Figure 4.5B).

Imports have been growing since 2016, but declined by 15.4% in 2020 (GEL8,053 million) due to the pandemic. Imports also recovered rapidly in 2021, growing 25.5% (GEL10,104 million). SME imports decreased by 13.2% in 2020 (GEL4,705 million) and recovered quickly in 2021 by 22.7% (GEL5,775 million). SME imports have continued to account for more than 50% of total import value (since 2015).

The government sees large potential for developing SME exports further through the DCFTA. The pact allows Georgia to gradually use three of the four "freedoms" within the EU internal market—the free movement of goods, services, and capital. The fourth freedom—the free movement of people—will come through a visa liberalization process.[131] The DCFTA negotiation began in 2009 and was concluded on 27 June 2014 in Brussels. The agreement was ratified by the Parliament of Georgia on 18 July 2016.[132] The DCFTA opened Georgia's largest market with

Figure 4.5: SME Exports and Imports

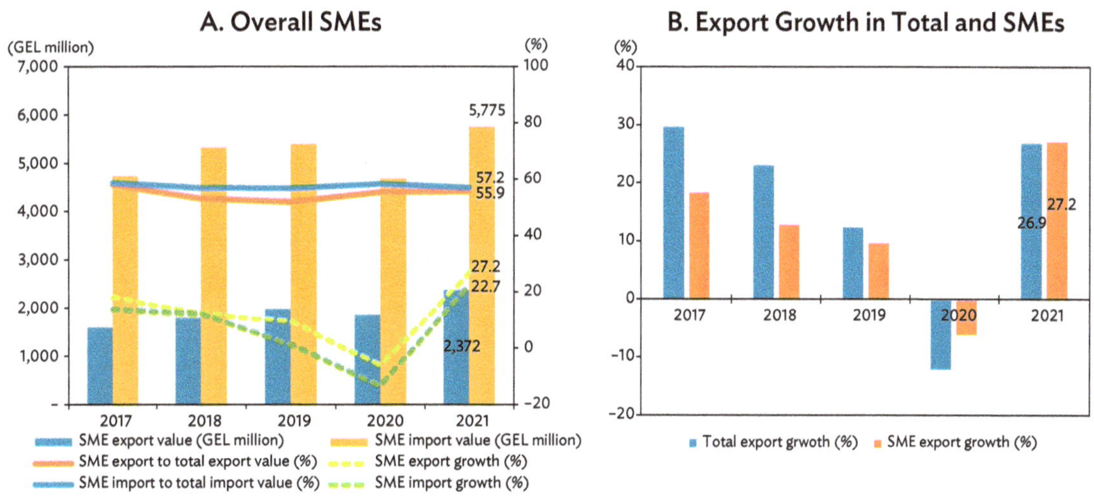

SME = small and medium-sized enterprise.

Source: ADB Asia SME Monitor 2022 database. Data from National Statistics Office of Georgia.

131 Ministry of Economy and Sustainable Development of Georgia.

132 DCFTA. Agreement. https://dcfta.gov.ge/en/agreement.

28 countries and more than 500 million potential customers. It provides an incentive for more SMEs to export, create new jobs, and make the country more attractive for investors. Because of the DCFTA, foreign trade turnover with the EU increased by 49% in January–February 2022 ($537 million). The share in total trade turnover grew to 21%, with exports to the EU growing by 57% ($159 million), and imports from the EU increasing by 46% ($378 million). In particular, agricultural exports to the EU grew by 7% ($26.8 million), as SMEs could tap the EU market, selling nuts, wine, and spirits, among others.[133]

Technology and Innovation

Georgia enjoys high internet access but uses it more for mobile phones than personal or business computers. Internet access was 83.8% in 2020, (13.8 percentage points higher than 2016–2020). This was above the CIS average and close to the average in Europe. Access varies by region, with the highest rates in Tbilisi and Adjara (more than 90% in 2020) and the lowest in the Racha-Lechkhumi and Kvemo Svaneti region (53%). Computer access, however, remains comparatively low (62% in 2020)—above the global average but below the 79% reported in developed countries.[134]

As of 2019, revenue for those authorized in the electronic communications was GEL1.2 billion, a 16.2% increase from 2012. Fixed broadband internet subscribers totaled 941,000, up by 94.7% from 2012, with 3.2 million mobile internet users. There were 5.38 million mobile subscribers in 2019 with the density per 100 inhabitants reaching 156%.[135]

According to the National Statistics Office of Georgia, more than 90% of enterprises had internet access over the past 5 years (2016–2020). The pandemic merely accelerated the trend. For example, the share of firms with access to the internet was 93% in 2019, increasing to 95% in 2021 (Figure 4.6). There are also more businesses with a dedicated web page—19.7% in 2021 from 18.4% in 2019.

Figure 4.6: Internet Access

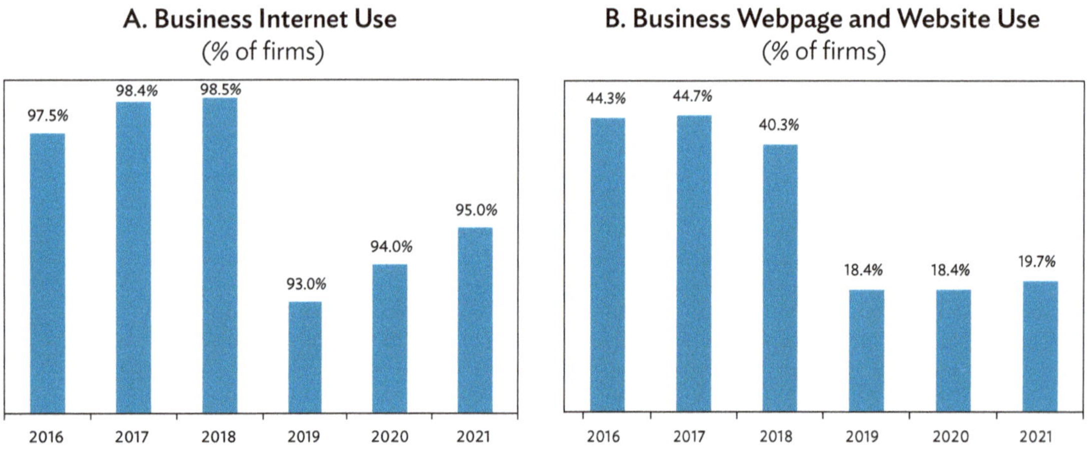

Note: In some cases, large variations in time series were due to sampling changes in 2018, when all companies with employees were included in the survey, unlike the previous methodology where all companies with 10 employees or more were included in the survey.

Source: ADB Asia SME Monitor 2022 database. Data from National Statistics Office of Georgia.

133 DCFTA. Tariffs. https://dcfta.gov.ge/en/dcfta-for-businness?id=56.

134 Galt and Taggart. 2021. *E-commerce in Georgia.* 20 July. https://api.galtandtaggart.com/sites/default/files/2021-07/report/e-commerce-in-georgia_july-2021_eng.pdf.

135 National Statistics Office of Georgia.

However, e-commerce and online sales remain low. By 2020, only 4.1% of businesses had web sales (Figure 4.7A),[136] with most (66.0%) domestic, followed by sales to the EU (14.1%), CIS (10.1%), and the US (5.7%) (Figure 4.7B). The share of SMEs using online sales of goods and services is low given the lack of appropriate infrastructure for online transactions and payments, and a lack of innovation. In 2020, 96.8% of SMEs reported no online sales, though it fell slightly to 96.1% in 2021.[137]

Figure 4.7: E-commerce

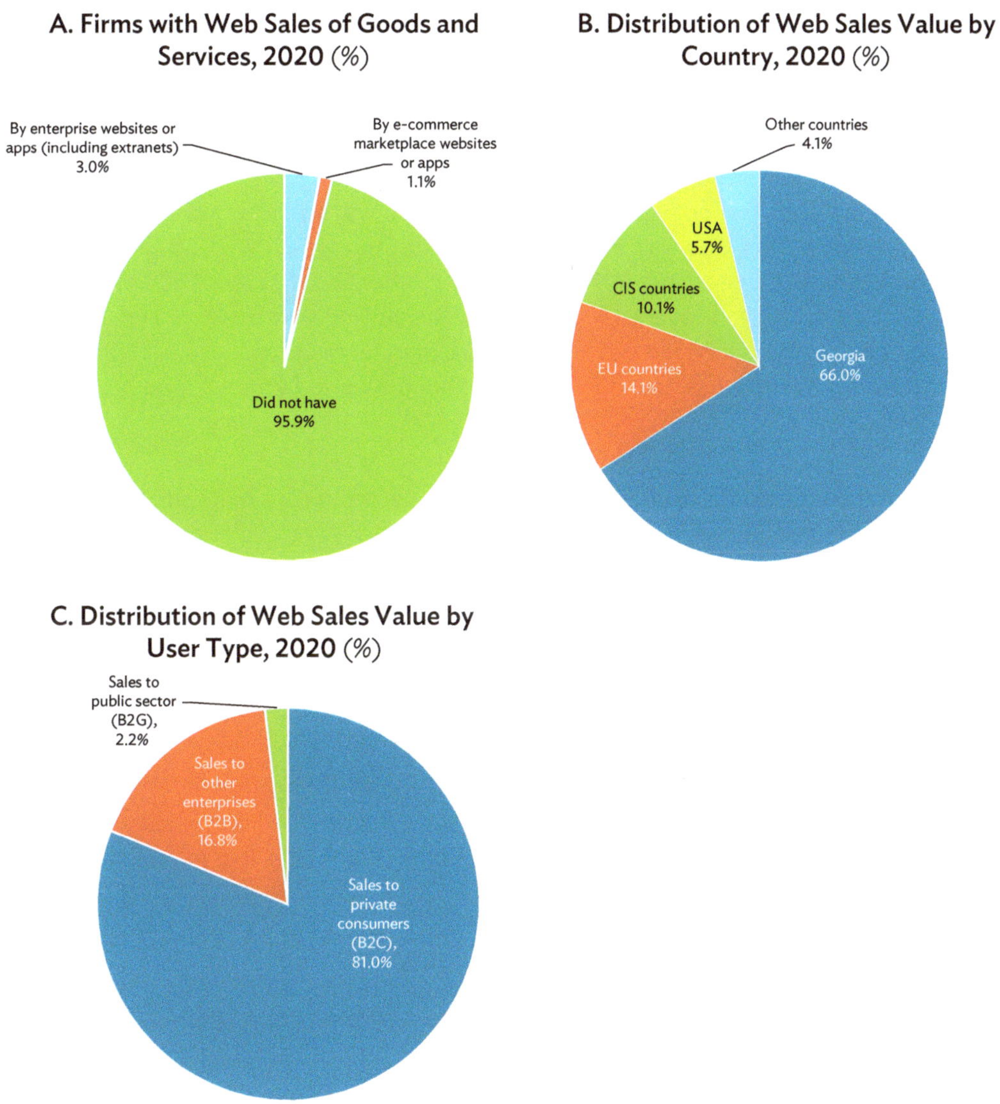

S B2B = business-to-business, B2C = business-to-consumer, B2G = business-to-government ME = small and medium-sized enterprise.

Source: ADB Asia SME Monitor 2022 database. Data from National Statistics Office of Georgia.

136 The percentage is calculated only for those enterprises with internet access during the relevant period.

137 National Statistics Office of Georgia.

Business-to-business (B2B), business-to-commerce (B2C), consumer-to-consumer (C2C), and business-to-government (B2G) transactions are all used, with B2C most common with an 81.0% share in 2020. This was followed by B2B (16.8%) and B2G (2.2%) (Figure 4.7C).

Despite various international assessments of progress, innovation and technology remains a major challenge. According to the 2019 Global Competitiveness Report, Georgia ranked 91st in opportunities for innovation. According to the INSEAD 2020 Global Innovation Index, Georgia ranked 63rd out of 131 countries (31.78 points) and 79th in terms of business technology.[138]

In 2021, to promote innovation, the government gave 31 firms small grants (up to GEL15,000), 40 startups cofinancing grants (GEL100,000), and 10 startups awarded innovation cofinancing grants (GEL650,000). To support the development and commercialization of innovative products, the Georgia National Innovation Ecosystem (GENIE) Project provided GEL100,000 cofinancing grants for startups and GEL650,000 cofinancing innovation grants for startups. In 2021, 140 startups were funded.[139]

The Georgia Innovation and Technology Agency (GITA) supports startups and innovative businesses by providing grants or training. The Georgia's Rural Development Strategy 2017–2020 received a GEL7 million budget from GITA for 2020. During 2017–2020, at least 2,050 beneficiaries received entrepreneurial training in rural areas supported by public funds, with at least 350 developing new business and 25 establishing new SMEs.[140] GITA implements the Integrated Development Program for Pilot Regions 2020–2022 with EU grants in the regions of Imereti, Kakheti, Guria, and Racha-Lechkhumi-Kvemo Svaneti.[141] The program included two categories for grants:

(i) A GEL30,000 grant to SMEs to introduce, test or improve innovations that can be commercialized, internationally as well.
(ii) An Innovative Entrepreneurship Grant of GEL100,000 to finance business projects with innovative and/or technological aspects with a high potential for commercialization.

[138] Cornell University, INSEAD, and WIPO. 2020. *Global Innovation Index 2020: Who Will Finance Innovation?* Geneva: World Intellectual Property Organization.

[139] Ministry of Economy and Sustainable Development of Georgia. http://www.economy.ge/uploads/files/2017/ek__politika/sme_strategy/2022/sme_strategy_2021_2.pdf.

[140] Georgia's Innovation and Technology Agency. 2020 Report of the Action Plan for the Rural Development Strategy 2017-2020. https://gita.gov.ge/uploads/2022/4/6/1649499414596.pdf.

[141] Georgia's Innovation and Technology Agency. https://gita.gov.ge/news/sapilote-regionebis-integrirebuli-ganvitarebis-programis-parglebshi-gita-s-sagranto-programebis-gamarjvebulebi-tsnobilia-yKkp5o1A2.

Box 4.1: Developing E-commerce to Support Market Access and Business Expansion for SMEs

During the early phase of the pandemic, the Georgian Chamber of Commerce and Industry (GCCI) conducted a countrywide business survey on current and prospective challenges. The results showed that most businesses, especially small and medium-sized enterprises (SMEs), had great interest and required support to integrate e-commerce in their activities. GCCI shared its findings with the government and initiated its own support mechanisms. The pandemic clearly showed that modern business requires successful e-commerce, with Georgia's entrepreneurs expressing their readiness to integrate. As in many other countries, the pandemic greatly accelerated e-commerce development in Georgia.

In 2021, with the support of Academy of Munich and Upper Bavaria IHK, the GCCI implemented a "free e-commerce training for entrepreneurs" project to explain how e-commerce works, from the basics to intermediate level.

Training curriculum was tailored to the Georgia's business needs, but included international best practices. The project team worked with many participants individually, examining their e-commerce platforms and providing various requests for assistance with technical support and additional information. The team provided online or telephone consultancy for training program participants.

The training programs cover the following topics:

- Introduction to e-commerce;
- Business models and platforms;
- Social networks and their importance;
- How to create a Facebook page;
- International e-commerce platforms; and
- Local e-commerce platforms, among others.

The training programs were conducted over 7 months, from February to August 2021, with more than 600 entrepreneurs participating. The training cycle included online as well as face-to-face training formats and in the three major cities of Georgia–Kutaisi, Telavi, and Zugdidi.

The training programs also included guest speakers from major e-commerce outlets in Georgia, discussing success stories and sharing experience across various fields. During the project preparation phase, GCCI staff underwent intensive training and consulting on the current e-commerce systems available.

The GCCI carefully analyzed participant feedback and developed two extension projects: "Free Webpages for Entrepreneurs" and an "E-Commerce guidebook." These were logical "next steps" of the training. Participants had stressed a lack of finance for building individual web pages, as well as the need for relevant literature on e-commerce in Georgian.

The "Free Webpages for Entrepreneurs" project provided 100 beneficiaries web pages with built in e-commerce and online payment systems. An open call for applicants was posted on the GCCI webpage, social media, and other outlets. The 100 beneficiaries were identified by a special commission to assess their applications, evaluating an applicant's motivation and long-term goals. Web pages were created by developers contracted by GCCI, also providing technical support and training on website management.

The digital "E-Commerce guidebook" is in Georgian and available for free download, with a printed version available as well.

Source: Georgian Chamber of Commerce and Industry (GCCI).

Networking and Support

Enterprise Georgia and GITA were established in February 2014 under the Ministry of Economy and Sustainable Development (MESD) supervision to promote the SME creation and development and help enhance competitiveness through innovation.

Enterprise Georgia: It is the main state institution supporting entrepreneurship, including SME entrepreneurship. The agency aims to increase private sector competitiveness by using tools to support entrepreneurship, exports, and encourage foreign direct investment. For example, the "Produce in Georgia" program provides (i) cofinancing for loans approved by commercial banks or leasing interest rates issued by leasing companies; (ii) advice to hotels and tourism services, enabling entrepreneurs develop their hotel business and create new jobs; and (iii) technical assistance, where beneficiaries are reimbursed for information-consulting service expenses within a set limit. In addition, the micro and small grants program helps develop SME business, establish a modern entrepreneurial culture, and create new jobs. The program provides financial support and technical assistance needed to start a business and/or re-equipping an existing one. The credit guarantee scheme also improves SMEs access to finance for that otherwise cannot meet loan requirements. Due to the COVID-19 pandemic, Enterprise Georgia has developed several programs to support several of the most affected industries in the country.

GITA: It is the main government agency supporting economic development based on knowledge and innovative technologies. Among its goals are to (i) coordinate the process of creating and developing an innovative ecosystem; (ii) stimulate innovation, modern technologies, and research and development (R&D); (iii) promote commercialization; and (iv) create innovative startups and increase their competitiveness. GITA also provides financial support as well as the appropriate services an innovative startup needs.

Aside from the government, private sector organizations also support SME development—such as the GCCI and SMEDA:

GCCI: Established as an independent private sector agency, GCCI (i) provides information and consulting services to businesses, (ii) helps businesses raise professional education levels and their qualifications for advancement, (iii) promotes exports, (iv) helps firms attract investments, (v) facilitates dispute resolution between entrepreneurial businesses, and (vi) creates alternative dispute resolution. Membership is voluntary. In 2021, GCCI had 1,536 members, 97% of which were SMEs. It operates eight regional offices nationwide.

SMEDA: Established in 2021 during the pandemic, it is a membership-based and independent nonprofit organization that promotes the sustainability, growth and development of SMEs through advocacy, innovative approaches tailored to their needs, consulting, and training. SMEDA works digitally as well as through direct, physical contact. Digitalization allows SMEDA to deal online with its SME members, originally to reduce the risk of COVID-19 infections. To help women in business, SMEDA launched the "STARTA" (digital accelerator for women entrepreneurs) pilot project from January–August 2022. The 20 female entrepreneurs selected went through training, a mentoring program, and networking. Training was combined with the mentoring program so the knowledge acquired could be practiced on the job with experienced mentors. The project was financed by the USAID Economic Governance Program.[142]

[142] For more information about STARTA, see https://sme.org.ge/en/starta.

Box 4.2: Axel—Georgian Business Angel Network

Launched in June 2021, Axel is the first Business Angel Network in Georgia. A joint initiative by Startup Büro and Kedari Ventures, they bring important expertise for technology entrepreneurship, ecosystem building, investing, and access to venture capital. Axel hopes to accelerate development of Georgia's tech startup ecosystem by facilitating Smart Money investments for the most promising entrepreneurs. Within 8 months, Axel already networked over 50 local and foreign angel investors, some based in Estonia, Poland, Germany, and the United Kingdom.

Axel, with support from the Tbilisi City Hall, hosted two international conferences, bringing together Business Angel Network investors and network managers from six Baltic and Nordic countries—Latvia, Lithuania, Estonia, Norway, Denmark, and Finland. Axel is also a member of the European Business Angel Network (EBAN) and EBAN CEE community.

Axel helps connect business founders with potential investors, who not only provide financial resources but invest time and energy to mentor and guide entrepreneurs through their startup journey. From an investor's perspective, Axel helps with deal flow and provides investment services such as due diligence, pro bono legal consulting, and managing a syndicate, among others.

For example, OMOFOX, one of Axel's portfolio startups, is a global digital freight forwarding platform founded by Georgian entrepreneurs. It allows customers to quote, book, and track shipments in real time. It provides a single end-to-end platform to streamline communications between the various parties involved in the shipping process. OMOFOX holds a competitive edge over existing freight forwarders given its ability to not only offer a digital product, but more importantly to share its digital company culture of radical innovation and flexible approach to work. It offers the best synthesis of digital products with logistics experts.

OMOFOX tries to resolve several logistic pain points: it provides (i) instant transportation rates for customers—both small and large—that need goods shipped globally; (ii) transparency and access to operational data; (iii) a liquidity network for customer requests— a platform that allows OMOFOX team members to add their carriers and partners to one unified network (the network currently has 700 members worldwide; (iv) interface and technology—the average customer can spend 2.5 hours less per day coordinating shipments and making sure import flows move smoothly; (v) geographical advise—it will first expand services to Armenia and Azerbaijan, and then Kazakhstan, Uzbekistan, Tajikistan, the Kyrgyz Republic, Bulgaria, and Türkiye, where they expect a first mover advantage as digital freight forwarders. OMOFOX projects to have a 3%–4% share of the regional market over the next 2 years.

In its first year, OMOFOX had more than 20 employees, gross merchandise volume of over $1.5 million, and more than 250 customers. Going forward, it intends to maximize efficiency in digitalizing the freight forwarding industry.

Source: Axel (Georgian Business Angel Network).

3. Access to Finance

- Bank lending to SMEs continued to grow even during the pandemic. Credit grew by 9%-10% in 2020 and 2021, exceeding the pre-pandemic levels. But the SME credit market remains small.
- There are several public financing programs for SMEs and agriculture using grants, subsidized loans, and credit guarantees. Enterprise Georgia channels public financing to SMEs. Credit guarantees offer portfolio and partial (80%) guarantees.
- The nonbank finance industry consists of microfinance institutions (MFIs), but remains small in scale (2.3% of GDP for MFI lending in 2021). The Law on Micro Banks was enacted in 2022 to help finance SMEs and entrepreneurs.
- Digital finance solutions remain underdeveloped. The planned Capital Market Development Strategy (CMDS) will address the feasibility of P2P lending and equity crowdfunding platforms for SMEs, among others.
- There is no dedicated equity market for SMEs and no corporate bond issuance by SMEs under the Georgian Stock Exchange. The government is exploring the use of standard practices for SME capital market financing, attract investors, and reduce the regulatory burden in general.
- Developing credit data infrastructure is crucial to improve SME access to finance. CreditInfo Georgia is Georgia's sole credit bureau, offering credit information reports and credit scoring. The central bank began collecting credit registry data as a test in 2021.

Bank Credit

The National Bank of Georgia—the central bank—supervises commercial banks to maintain financial stability. The Organic Law of Georgia on the National Bank of Georgia, and the Law of Georgia on the Activities of Commercial Banks, stipulate supervision and regulation of commercial banks. These are based on international best practices and include EU legislation and standards, along with the principles developed by the Basel Committee on Banking Supervision.[143] In 2021, there were 14 banks operating in the country—1 bank is 100% domestically owned, 2 banks have foreign capital participation of less than 50%, and 11 banks have foreign capital participation of more than 50% (Table 4.3).

Access to finance has been one of the major obstacles to SME development over the years. The financial system is dominated by commercial banking (more than 90% of financial institution assets). Nonbank and market-based financing remain underdeveloped. Bank lending to SMEs continued to grow even during the pandemic. SME loans outstanding was GEL7.9 billion in 2020, a 10.3% increase from the GEL7.1 billion 2019. It increased another 9.3% in 2021, to GEL8.5 billion (Figure 4.8A and Table 4.3). Although growing, the SME credit market remains small. SME loans accounted for 14.1% of GDP in 2021, compared with 10.6% in 2015, before the national SME development strategy (2016–2020) was implemented. The share of SME loans to total loans outstanding was also small at 19.8% in 2021, down gradually from its 2017 peak of 23.6%.

By sector, loans were approved for SMEs in wholesale and retail trade (18.8% of SME loans in 2021—down from 34.1% in 2015), followed by other services (14.0%); manufacturing (8.8%); construction (7.2%); agriculture, forestry, and fisheries (4.6%); and transportation and communication (2.5%) (Figure 4.8B). The largest group was unclassified as "others" (44.2%).

Geographically, the share of SME loans outstanding is gradually increasing in regions outside of the capital. In 2015, 59.1% of SME loans were issued in Tbilisi, with 40.9% for SMEs in other regions. In 2021, 50.9% were in Tbilisi with the remaining 49.1% for other regions (an 8.2-percentage-point increase from 2015) (Figure 4.8C).

[143] National Bank of Georgia. Banking Supervision. https://nbg.gov.ge/en/page/banking-supervision.

The SME Development Strategy 2016–2020 helped strengthen the SME environment in rural areas, which also increased bank interest in SME lending nationwide.

SME loans outstanding are categorized as short-term loans (less than 1 year), medium-term loans (1–5 years), and long-term loans (more than 5 years). In recent years the share of long-term loans increased significantly (to 45.7% in 2021, up from 34.6% in 2015)—the share fell in 2020 (48.2%) due to the pandemic (Figure 4.8D). Medium-term loans to SMEs followed a similar pattern (56.3% in 2015 to 45.1% in 2021), with the share up slightly from 2020 (43.5%). Short-term loans to SMEs have been less than 10% since 2018 (9.2% in 2021). The increasing trend toward long-term SME lending can be the result of the positive aspects of SME business performance—SMEs have more forward-looking, longer-term business plans, making it easier to access long-term financing.

Figure 4.8: SME Loans

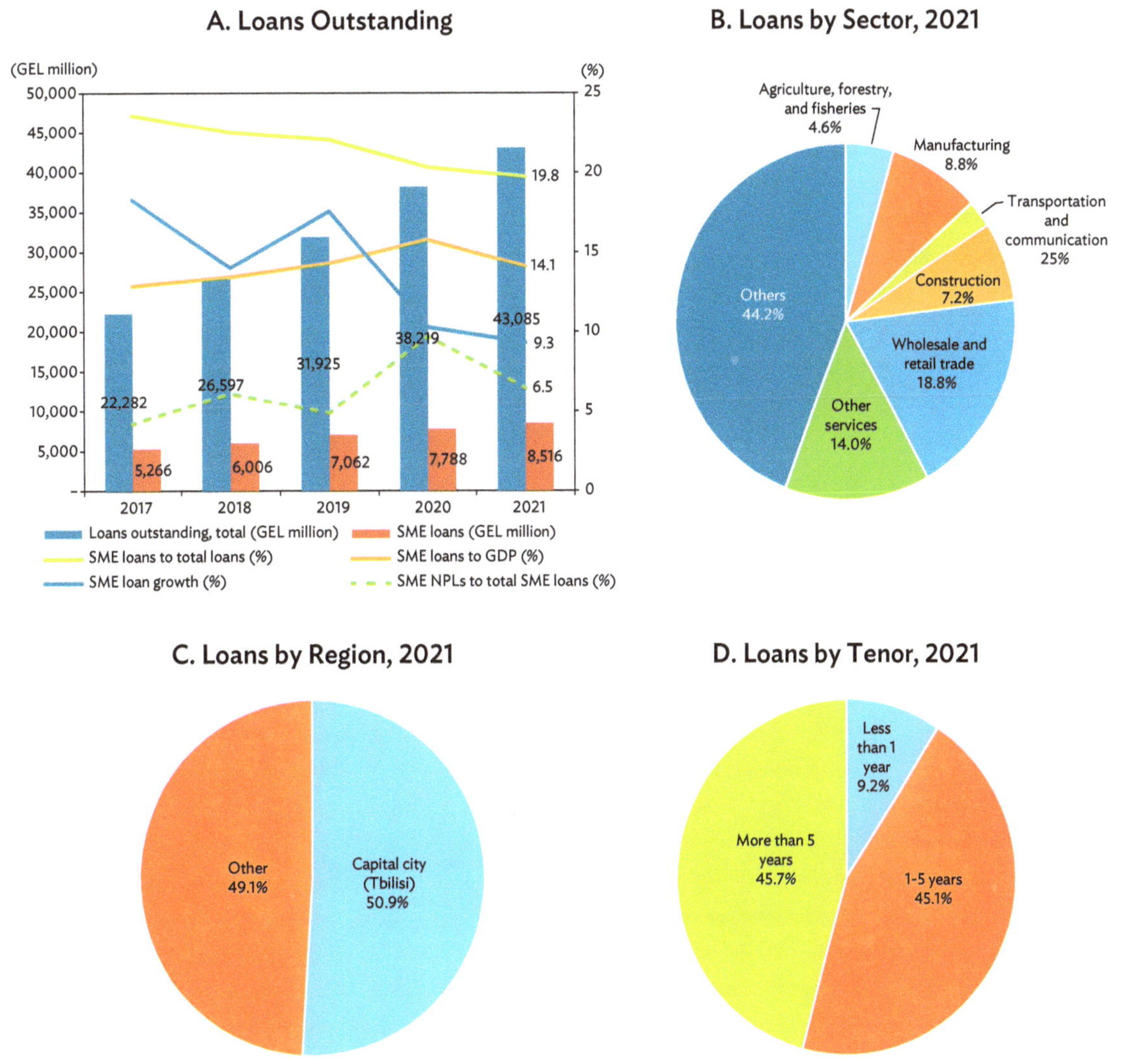

SME = small and medium-sized enterprise, NPL = nonperforming loan.

Note: SME NPLs to total SME loans (%) is derived from supervisory reporting. Microenterprise loans are included under SME or retail lending.

Source: ADB Asia SME Monitor 2022 database. Data from National Bank of Georgia.

Both collateralized and non-collateral SME loans continue to rise, even during the pandemic. Collateralized SME loans equaled GEL6.7 billion in 2020, an 8.8% increase from GEL6.2 billion in 2019. These loans increased by another 7.9% in 2021, reaching GEL7.2 billion. Collateralized SME loans, 85% of the total, remains the traditional way to lend to SMEs. Non-collateral SME loans (15%) are a small fraction but growing. They amounted to GEL1.1 billion in 2020, up 20.7% from GEL899 million in 2019. They continued to grow by 18.2% in 2021, reaching GEL1.3 billion.

Public Financing and Guarantees

The government offers SMEs various programs providing grants and other forms of funding. New subsidized loans increased dramatically in 2021 (439 loans, from 141 in 2020). They amounted to GEL1.5 billion in 2021, a 78.9% increase from 2020 (GEL828 million) (Figure 4.9A and Table 4.4). The share of subsidized loans to total MSME loans increased rapidly from 3.8% in 2015 to 17.4% in 2021.

Enterprise Georgia uses guaranteed loans to channel financing to SMEs. Guaranteed SME loans disbursed amounted to GEL235.7 million in 2021, up 84.2% from the GEL128.0 million in 2020. The guaranteed loans outstanding to SMEs amounted to GEL101.1 million in 2020 and GEL204.7 million in 2021. Although increasing, guaranteed loans are just a small share of SME bank loans—3.6% in 2021 and 2.1% in 2020. Guaranteed loans to SMEs more than doubled to 318 in 2021 from 133 in 2020, but number remains small.

Figure 4.9: Public Financing

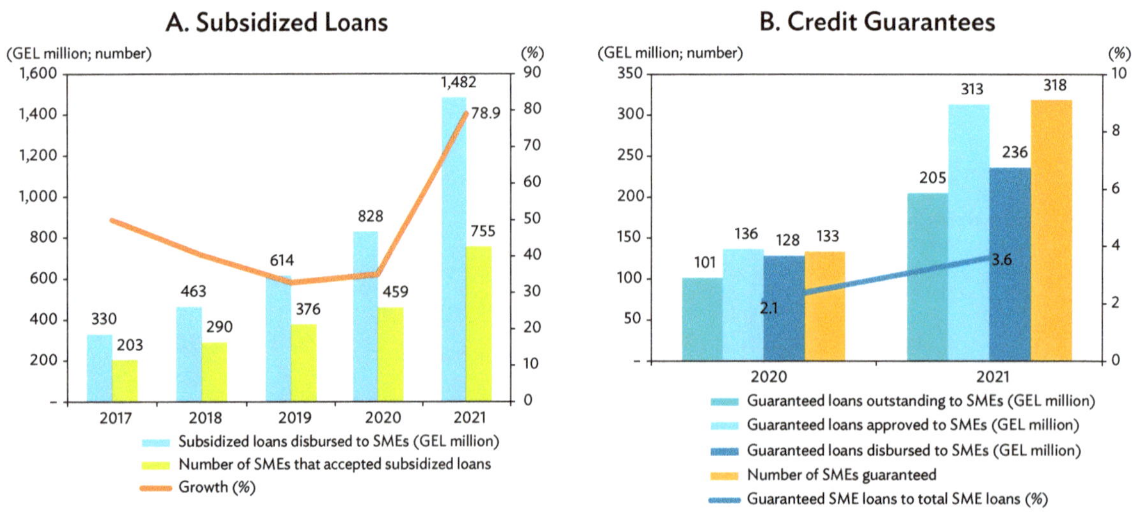

SMEs = small and medium-sized enterprises.

Note: Cumulative amounts and numbers.

Source: ADB Asia SME Monitor 2022 database. Data from Enterprise Georgia.

Enterprise Georgia provides portfolio guarantees for those evaluated by commercial banks and microfinance institutions. Under this program, a credit guarantee is issued for not more than 80% of the loan principal amount and not more than 35% of the loan portfolio allowed for each financial institution. For commercial banks, the minimum loan is GEL50,000 with a maximum of GEL5 million. For microfinance institutions, the minimum loan amount is GEL20,000 with a maximum of GEL5 million. The maximum loan guarantee term is 10 years.[144] Total loan liabilities cannot exceed GEL12 million at the time a firm joins the program. The beneficiary may apply for multiple loans so long as the total amount under the program does not exceed GEL5 million. Loans are available for production and processing, the hotel industry, electricity generation, education, training centers, services exports, and high-tech medical laboratories.

Under the Government Resolution No.163 on Credit Guarantee Scheme, Enterprise Georgia also offers the program specifically to SME loans, guaranteeing up to 80% of the principal loan amount. The loans must be between GEL20,000 and GEL10 million and can be issued by either commercial banks or microfinance institutions. Under Government Resolution No.365, Enterprise Georgia subsidizes SME loan and lease interest payments for SMEs. The cofinancing rate is the central bank refinancing rate minus 3 percentage points for loans and 5 percentage points for leases. Enterprise Georgia provides cofinancing for the first 36 months after the date of loan disbursement. Loan/lease amounts are between GEL50,000 and GEL10 million. In addition, under the EU Pilot Regions Program, in case the loan is between GEL50,000 and GEL1.5 million, beneficiaries from pilot regions receive a grant from 10% to 20% of the loan amount.[145]

To support micro and small enterprises, the Enterprise Georgia disburses micro grants (under the program "Micro and Small Business Support 2022") to the winners of the competition conducted under its program. The program covers several stages: business ideas competition, training, and business plans competition. The winning entrepreneurs receive grants up to GEL30,000 (GEL40,000 for 3 specific regions selected for pilot project).

Public guaranteed loans outstanding to SMEs amounted to GEL204.7 million in 2021, a 102.5% increase from 2020 (GEL101.1 million) (Figure 4.9B). Credit guarantee programs benefited 318 SMEs.

Georgia's Ministry of Environment Protection and Agriculture began a Preferential Agrocredit Project through the Rural Development Agency in March 2013. Under this project, agrocredits are granted by commercial banks and financial institutions in compliance with the terms and conditions set by the Rural Development Agency.[146] The project is designed to improve primary agricultural production, processing, storage, and sales by providing inexpensive, affordable, long-term, and preferential funding.

144 Enterprise Georgia. Credit Guarantee Mechanism. https://www.enterprisegeorgia.gov.ge/en/business-development/Credit-guarantee-mechanism.

145 Pilot regions in clude Imereti, Guria, Kakheti, Racha-Lechkhumi, and Lower Svaneti.

146 Rural Development Agency of Georgia. Partners. https://rda.gov.ge/partners/.

Box 4.3: Success Stories of Georgian Companies Cofinanced in 2021–2022

Georgia offers diversified exports, ranging from food and beverages to apparel and fashion. Even during the pandemic, exports enjoyed double digit growth and reached historic highs. There have been interesting, relatively new sector success stories that stand out.

For example, with support from Enterprise Georgia, NUTSGE, a company producing hazelnuts and hazelnut paste products, attended the Anuga 2021 exhibition, during which the company signed five agreements worth around €500,000. The company Georeg also exhibited its liquorice extract at Anuga 2021 and signed five agreements worth nearly $500,000 with firms in Germany, Denmark, and the Netherlands. One of its largest blueberry producers, Agrolane, exhibited at Gulfood 2021 and signed agreements worth more than $150,000, exporting to the Middle East. Georgia also exports a wide assortment of fresh juices and concentrates to a variety of markets to the European Union, United States, the Middle East, and Canada, among others. For example, Campa joined Gulfood 2021 signing six agreements worth $400,000.

Success stories are common in apparel and fashion. Enterprise Georgia analysis shows the industry is growing steadily, with export values increasing and markets diversified. For example, the brand KEBURIA, after participating in the XY SHOWROOM in 2021, signed agreements worth €520,000. The SITUATIONIST brand joined the RITUAL PROJECT showroom in 2022, resulting in signed contracts worth over €100,000. The Georgian brand MORE IS LOVE was featured in the RSVP Showroom in Singapore in 2022 for the first time and signed contracts worth tens of thousands of US dollars. As a result, the brand was featured in Forbes and Herworld magazines and other major publications.

Children's clothing is relatively new to Georgia's apparel industry and is growing rapidly. As a result of work with Enterprise Georgia, donor organizations, and the private sector, recent success stories show much promise. For example, brands Rko and Spillow exhibited at the Playtime Paris 2022, with Rko signing nine agreements to markets in Germany, Denmark, Japan, the United Kingdom, and France. Spillow signed four agreements with markets in Austria, Australia, Canada, and Greece.

Source: Ministry of Economy and Sustainable Development.

Nonbank Financing

The central bank supervises and regulates nonbank finance institutions (NBFIs) to ensure (i) they are stable, reliable, and sustainable; and (ii) reduce potential risks and protect creditors. Under current legislation, the supervision of NBFIs includes microfinance institutions, loan-issuing entities, currency exchange units, credit unions, and pawnshops.[147] Microfinance institutions have declined in recent years (from a peak of 81 in 2016 to 38 in 2021) (Figure 4.10A and Table 4.5). The number of credit unions has also decreased since 2004 (from 53 in 2004 to just one in 2021). Pawnshops have also decreased in number, from 204 in 2019 (when the central bank began their registration) to 183 in 2021.

NBFI assets total about GEL2 billion, with microfinance holding the largest share (GEL1.6 billion).[148] As of 2021, 38 microfinance institutions were registered with 385 branches and service centers, employing 4,041 people.[149] Despite their decreasing number, loans outstanding increased even during the pandemic—they rose 4.9% in

[147] National Bank of Georgia. Non-Bank Supervision. https://nbg.gov.ge/en/page/non-banking-supervision.
[148] National Bank of Georgia Annual Report 2021.
[149] National Bank of Georgia. Consolidated Data of Microfinance Organizations. https://nbg.gov.ge/en/page/consolidated-data-of-microfinance-organizations.

2020 from 2019 to GEL1.2 billion, and to GEL1.4 billion in 2021, up 14.9% (Figure 4.10B). However, microfinance remains small, contributing 2.3% of GDP in 2021. There are fewer nonperforming loans (NPLs), with the NPL ratio for microfinance lending falling from 8.3% in 2019 (pre-pandemic) to 7.5% in 2020 and 5.9% in 2021. Microfinance institutions financed 451,862 firms in 2021.

More than one-fifth (21.9% in 2017) of MFI loans were for wholesale and retail trade; followed by agriculture, forestry, and fisheries (10.4%) (Figure 4.10C). "Other services" accounted for 59.1% in 2017. Manufacturing, construction, and transportation and communication all held shares of less than 1% as of 2017. MFI loans are used more in rural areas or outside the capital (62.2% in 2021, with the remaining 37.8% to borrowers in Tbilisi) (Figure 4.10D).

Figure 4.10: Nonbank Finance

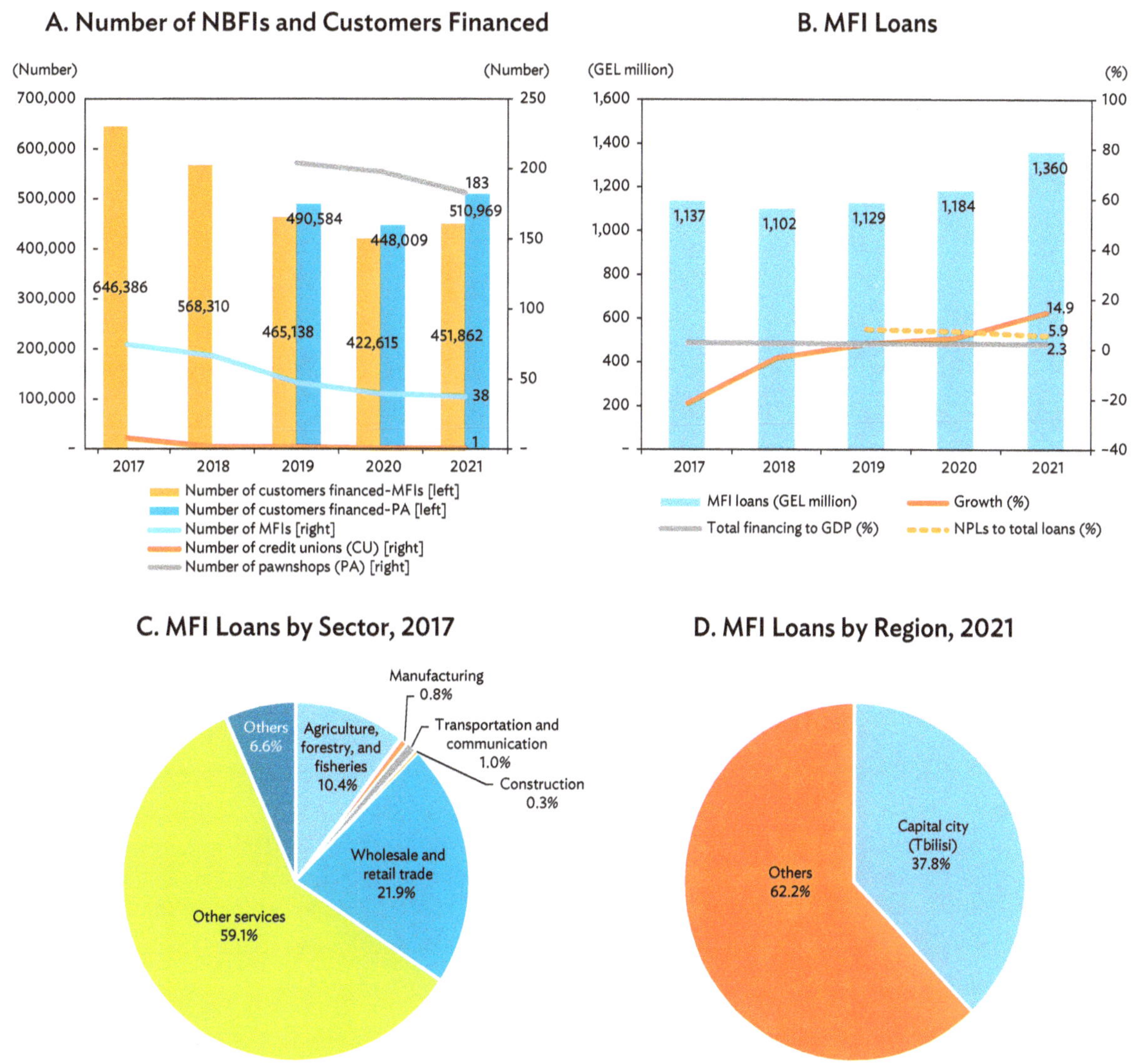

MFI = microfinance institution, NPL = nonperforming loan, NBFI = nonbank financing institution.

Source: ADB Asia SME Monitor 2022 database. Data from National Bank of Georgia.

The central bank defines an NBFI as an entity (person or firm) having disbursed more than 20 loans. According to the Order of the President of the National Bank of Georgia, the rule on registration and/or cancellation and the regulation on loan issuing entities became effective in January 2019.[150] As of 2021, there were 183 head offices and 162 branches and service centers operating, employing 2,479 people.

For pawnshops—which are also considered loan-issuing entities—outstanding finance in 2021 amounted to GEL947 million for 510,969 customers. Interestingly, 30% of pawnshop financing was conducted online in 2021.

To helps SMEs and entrepreneurs better access finance, the central bank is reforming micro banks, with the draft Law on Micro Banks still under discussion and not yet finalized. It aims to legally regulate the activities of micro banks, create a healthy environment for development, and ensure free competition in the market. According to the law, a micro banks is a legal entity established as a joint-stock company licensed by the National Bank of Georgia. It can lend to entrepreneurs, including those earning income from agriculture.

Digital Financial Services

The pandemic disrupted the use of debit and credit cards, particularly in April–June 2020, when their use and new issuance fell significantly. The average monthly growth rate in payment cards issued was 9% in 2021. By end-2021, there were 6.9 million payment cards issued by commercial banks—93% international cards—or 1.8 per capita.[151] Issuers of electronic money instruments are mainly nonbank payment service providers.[152] In 2021, there were 507 million card transactions from cards issued in Georgia worth GEL45.3 billion, with 93% performed domestically. Mobile applications were used for 29% of the transactions. The pandemic impact led to a rise in digital use—in 2021, 70 million payment transactions (GEL134 billion) were made through internet banking (up 23%from 2020) and mobile banking (up 42%).[153]

Peer-to-peer (P2P) lending and equity crowdfunding have not yet developed in Georgia and there is no regulatory legislation. The government is working on a Capital Market Development Strategy (CMDS) which addresses P2P lending and equity crowdfunding.

Banking reforms also deal with digital finance. A new framework hopes to attract fintech companies, leverage commercial bank databases and promote competition among financial service products for retail clients and merchants. The draft law on open banking is being prepared (as of end-August 2022).

Capital Markets

Georgia is still developing its stock exchange system. Major amendments in 2020 to the Securities Market Law of 1998 deal with transparency (as prescribed in the 2004 EU Transparency Directive) and newly defined insider trading prohibitions (as prescribed in the 2014 EU Market Abuse Regulation). Prospectus filing rules were simplified and can be done incrementally through a preliminary registration of the prospectus.[154] The Georgian Stock Exchange (GSE) is the only organized securities market and remains small. As of end-2021, market capitalization amounted to GEL2.4 billion with just eight listed companies (Figure 4.11 and Table 4.6). Trading value was only (GEL100,000 in 2021), below the GEL58.8 million traded in 2006. There is no dedicated equity market for SMEs and no SME corporate bond issuance under the GSE.

150 Legislative Herald of Georgia. Order of the President of the National Bank of Georgia. https://matsne.gov.ge/en/document/view/4334433?publication=0.
151 National Bank of Georgia Annual Report 2021.
152 Payment service providers registered with the National Bank of Georgia.
153 National Bank of Georgia Annual Report 2021.
154 Legislative Herald of Georgia. Law of Georgia on Securities Market: https://matsne.gov.ge/en/document/view/18196?publication=35.

Due to relatively high listing fees and requirements, the GSE does not find creating a dedicated SME market feasible, given the difficulty in attracting investors. SMEs can list, but they have little interest in capital markets and tend to seek bank credit or alternative finance. The CMDS (under review as of August 2022) tries to (i) identify the challenges SMEs face in accessing nonbank financing, and (ii) allows SMEs to tap capital through equity crowdfunding, P2P working capital loans through factoring, and financing through investment funds.

CMDS in its current form touches on these issues by using a logframe (logical framework). Provisions that exempt certain SMEs from stringent securities requirements, easing regulations for SMEs to go public and attracting investment funds to participate, and proper supporting legislative reforms should help unlock the financing potential for SMEs. The government is exploring, with international partners, ways to introduce standard practices, based on the Simple Agreement for Future Equity, or SAFE, to decrease the cost of finance between startups and investors and to simplify negotiating terms.

To increase market depth, the Ministry of Economy and Sustainable Development is working on a securitization framework to create a legal basis for establishing and managing special purpose vehicles (SPVs) and issuing securitized debts. It is expected to enact the new law by end-2022. The government is discussing with international partners to possibly include SME-oriented strategies, including syndicating issuance through a common SPV, to reduce issuance costs. This remains under discussion.

Figure 4.11: Equity Markets

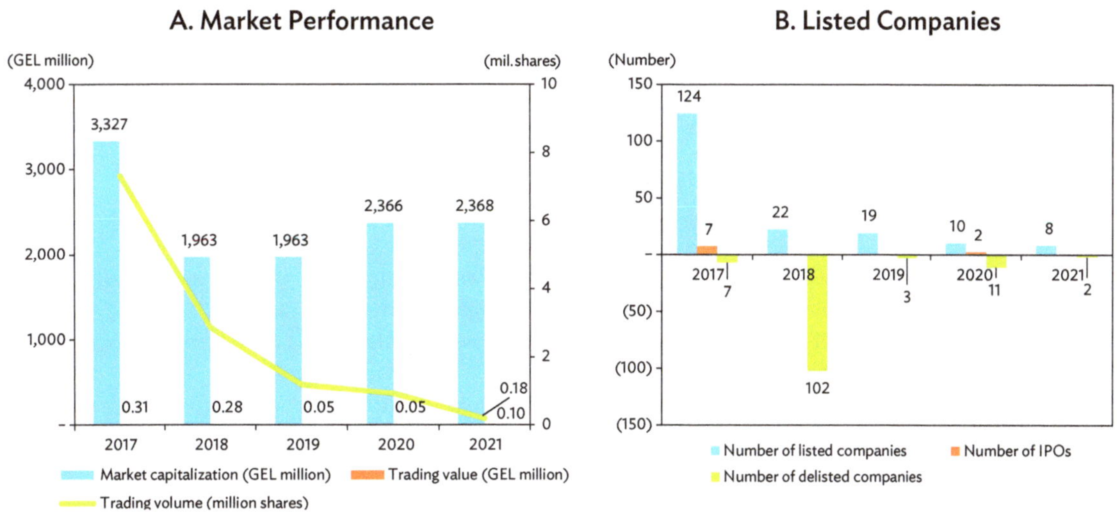

IPO = initial public offering.

Source: ADB Asia SME Monitor 2022 database. Data from Georgian Stock Exchange.

Financial Infrastructure

An amendment to the Organic Law on the National Bank of Georgia was approved at the end of 2017 and became effective in January 2018.[155] It authorizes the central bank to regulate and supervise the activities of a Credit Information Bureau, which collects, stores, processes, and shares credit, noncredit and other relevant information. The bureau also works in related fields, whether selling software, creating and using statistical and behavioral models, or offering analytical and educational activities. As of end-2021, 224 lending organizations and 29 noncompliant organizations cooperate with the Credit Bureau. The number of participating lending institutions in the bureau's data collection process may differ, as those joining or leaving affect the bureau's database.[156]

In the second half of 2021, the bureau underwent institutional reform, providing a strong authentication rule when remotely obtaining consent from a data subject, requiring new reporting on income from remittances, among others. In 2021, the central bank began collecting credit registry data as a test. The Credit Registry is designed as a database allowing the collection of comprehensive credit risk information. The central bank requires data submitted monthly, including data on credit details, refinancing loans, investments, and rejected credit applications.

Established in 2005, CreditInfo Georgia is the only credit bureau in Georgia, regulated by the central bank. It specializes in credit information and transmission of information to help the decision-making process for banks, leasing companies, and other finance institutions that lend money, provide services, or sell products on credit. CreditInfo Georgia provides credit reports on existing and closed loans. An integral part of the report is payment history and information related to overdue loans. The report also contains some personal data.[157] Data processing is connected with financial institutions' online systems, updated daily. In 2011, Creditinfo Georgia launched a scoring system "Creditinfo Predictor," with ranging from 0 to 400. These scores help credit institutions determine the probability of timely repayment. It also helps businesses improve access credit, as the higher the score, the less likely a business will default.[158]

4. Policies and Regulations

- The government has a national SME development strategy. Following the success of the strategy for 2016–2020, the strategy for 2021–2025 includes numeric targets such as increasing gross value added of SMEs by 20%, SME employment by 10%, and SME labor productivity by 20%. The strategy addresses the development of women entrepreneurships and a green economy.
- Georgia has yet to create a national financial inclusion strategy. But the central bank built a national strategy on financial education in 2016, leading to several initiatives for SMEs, entrepreneurs, and focused groups like agribusiness. The financial education portal "Finedu" was established in 2020.
- In response to the pandemic, the government created an anti-crisis plan so people and businesses, including SMEs, could receive financial and nonfinancial support. For example, it provided for online showrooms and online training for export-oriented firms. The central bank also offered liquidity support to commercial banks to promote SME financing.
- Enterprise Georgia launched an Export Assistance Program to promote the growth of export-oriented SMEs during the pandemic recovery and the Russian invasion of Ukraine.

155 National Bank of Georgia Annual Report 2018.
156 National Bank of Georgia Annual Report 2021.
157 CreditInfo Georgia. Credit Report. https://ge.creditinfo.com/en/products-list/credit-report/.
158 CreditInfo Georgia. Scoring Report. https://ge.creditinfo.com/en/products-list/scoring-report/.

SME Development

Georgia has an SME Development Strategy which aims to promote, popularize, and develop SMEs (Table 4.7). Based on the principle of "Think Small First," the 2016–2020 strategy improved the competitiveness of SMEs, providing a solid basis for inclusive and long-term economic growth. The strategy established goals for 2020, and identified SME strengths and weaknesses. The main barriers to SME development were:

- lack of business skills and experience;
- low competitiveness;
- low productivity;
- limited access to finance, especially long term;
- low levels of innovation and R&D, insufficient collaboration between public R&D institutions and SMEs, and limited capacities to adopt new technology;
- insufficient human resources; and
- low capacity for exports, internationalization, and a lack of knowledge on foreign markets.

The numeric targets for 2020 were to (i) increase SME output by an average 10% annually, (ii) increase SME jobs by 15%, (iii) expand SME labor productivity by 7%, and (iv) support SMEs modernize and upgrade technology. It also aimed to strengthen SMEs though increased competitiveness in domestic and international markets. There were several strategic priorities:

- further improve legislative, institutional framework, and operational environment for SMEs,
- develop SME skills and promote an entrepreneurial culture,
- promote SME exports internationalization, and
- facilitate SME innovation and R&D.

The strategy also dealt with improving access to finance, the biggest structural problem preventing SMEs from growing and entering international markets. The 2019 World Bank Enterprise Survey found financial access was second—after political instability—among the top 10 constraints for bettering the business environment. The strategy helped improve SME access through legal reforms that allowed grants to commercial entities and supported many financial education initiatives.

According to the 2020 assessment of the SME Development Strategy 2016–2020, the targets were met as follows: (i) 13.2% average annual growth of SME output during 2014–2019, (ii) 32% growth in employment in 2019, and (iii) 14.2% growth in SME labor productivity in 2019. The iInvestment environment also improved for both SMEs and the national economy as a whole. In 2019, foreign direct investment in SMEs reached $488.4 million, 6.6% more than in 2018.

GITA continues as a major contributor to R&D and business innovation. During 2016–2017, Micro Grants, Startup Georgia, and the Matching Grants program were initiated. The Micro Grants Program, launched in 2016, offers up to GEL5,000 to support entrepreneurs in developing business prototypes. Since its inception, GITA had received 350 applications, with grants distributed to more than 200 applicants during 2016–2017. Startup Georgia, with a budget of GEL35 million, disbursed GEL11 million in 2016 for the first round of the project. The program issues grants up to GEL100,000 to develop business models and go-to-market strategies for SME products.[159]

[159] Midterm Evaluation Georgia's SME Development Strategy 2016–2020.

GITA complements financial support with training, coaching, mentoring, and consulting for program beneficiaries. Training on coding, robotics, intellectual property, digital marketing, and export-oriented information and communication technology skills are also regularly conducted at various regional innovation centers—registering over 1,000 participants during 2016. In 2016, Georgia joined Horizon 2020, the EU's program for research and innovation, which provides funding for developing scientific and innovation capacity to research institutes, universities, individual researchers, and SMEs.

The SME Development Strategy for 2021–2025 aims to minimize the impact of the pandemic on the business environment and, similar to the previous strategy, sets targets for 2025 based on a 2019 baseline: increase (i) value added of SMEs by 20%, (ii) SME employment by 10%, and (iii) SME labor productivity by 20%. The strategy will (i) refine existing laws, strengthen institutions, and improve the operating environment for SMEs; (ii) improve access to finance; (iii) develop SME skills and promote an entrepreneurial culture; (iv) promote SME export growth, improve international market access; and (v) improve electronic communications, information technology, innovation, and R&D. Great attention is paid to promoting the development of women entrepreneurs and the green economy.

Financial Inclusion

Georgia has yet to formulate a national financial inclusion strategy. However, the central bank developed a national strategy on financial education in 2016—which continues today—designed to expand financial education, ultimately the prerequisite for improving financial well-being and protecting the consumer rights.

Under the strategy, the financial education portal "Finedu" was created in 2020 to disseminate information needed to make financial decisions for potential borrowers of financial institutions. It provides consultations, calculators, publications, brochures, thematic guidelines, and blogs.[160] The portal also offers webinars, online meetings, and competitions held for various groups including children, youth, adults, teachers, and entrepreneurs. As of end-2021, Finedu had more than 95,000 users with 277,000 page views during more than 130,000 sessions. Finedu's Facebook page reached 800,000 unique users in 2021 and gained 9,800 subscribers. Instagram and LinkedIn pages were launched in the second half of 2021, with 1,100 subscribers.[161]

In cooperation with the International Financial Education Network of the Organization for Economic Co-operation and Development (OECD/INFE), Georgia joined the 2021 International Survey on Financial Education for Micro, Small and Medium Entrepreneurs. The survey was conducted using OECD/INFE methodology and involved 14 countries. The survey received responses from 1,000 MSME owners across the country—firms with an annual turnover of up to GEL1.5 million and up to 50 employees were selected. The survey found Georgia's overall financial education score was 10.3 out of a 17-point scale (60%), lower than the average of the countries surveyed. Financial literacy rated 3.1 out of 5.0, financial behavior rated 5.6 out of 9.0, and financial dependency rated 1.6 out of 3.0. Businesses located in the capital rated higher than those in rural areas in all categories.

Various projects support SMEs financial education. The National Bank of Georgia, with support from the European Fund for South-East Europe Development program (EFSE/DF) and the Export Development Association, developed a financial education program for micro and small entrepreneurs in 2018. An online training module was created with two online training programs conducted in 2020, delivering online materials to 250 registered participants.

160 Finedu. https://www.finedu.gov.ge/.

161 National Bank of Georgia Annual Report 2021.

The central bank also developed a financial education program in 2020 to support agribusiness development. The project was implemented in cooperation with EFSE/DF with help from the Civil Development Agency. The goal of the program was to help entrepreneurs in agriculture select the best financial products for their business needs and capacities, and to make the better financial decisions. A manual and training modules were developed. A practical guide specifically for farmers "Make Better Financial Decisions" was also published. The National Bank of Georgia continues to provide financial education programs and webinars continued to support micro and small entrepreneurs remotely during the pandemic (2020).

Response to COVID-19

Georgia, along with international organizations, created several assistance packages for businesses during the COVID-19 pandemic, especially for SMEs. Enterprise Georgia established support mechanisms for export-oriented firms during 2020-2021, which included cofinancing online showrooms and online training for potential exporters. Enterprise Georgia supported the apparel sector, introducing "cofinancing of online showrooms" for apparel producing companies and fashion designers, which served as a substitute for physical showrooms for business matching. The mechanism became popular and feedback from those using the service was positive. Enterprise Georgia also launched an online training course for potential exporters with support of USAID's "Governing for Growth (G4G)" program. The course offered remote learning for existing and potential export-related companies. The course covers the full export cycle and introduces relevant topics of interest to companies considering exporting. The program, particularly popular during the pandemic, is free and available on four different platforms, including the Enterprise Georgia website.

In June 2020, the central bank launched its third liquidity instrument to reduce the pandemic's damage to the economy and to support SMEs. The new finance was designed to support SMEs with 1 month of assistance, renewable monthly. In 2021, eight commercial banks used this new liquidity, with volume fluctuating over the months—from GEL473.7 million to GEL632.0 million at the end of 2021.[162]

In December 2020, the European Investment Bank, a lending arm of the EU, provided €10 million to the ProCredit Group for a new credit line for SMEs and midcaps to support a faster recovery from the pandemic.[163] It also invested €25 million to expand credit for SMEs and midcaps at TBC Bank JSC.[164]

Promoting rural development and strengthening the rural economy are among the top priorities in Georgia. Support for people in rural areas and local businesses was critical during the pandemic. Lockdowns, closed markets, and the ensuing economic slowdown severely affected vulnerable rural communities. In response, the EU and United Nations Development Programme, together with the Rural Development Agency of the Ministry of Environment and Agriculture, launched a GEL9 million joint rural development grants program in 2020.

Aside from these international assistance measures, the government supported small-scale farmers in line with its Anti-Crisis Economic Plan. It subsidized up to GEL37 million in agricultural goods and services for landowners with registered landholdings of from 0.25 hectares (ha) to 10 ha. About 200,000 farmers received this assistance

162 National Bank of Georgia Annual Report 2021.

163 Delegation of the European Union to Georgia. 2020. Team Europe: EIB and ProCredit to support faster recovery of Georgia`s SMEs from the COVID-19 crisis with €10 million. News release. 21 December. https://www.eeas.europa.eu/delegations/georgia/team-europe-eib-and-procredit-support-faster-recovery-georgias-smes-covid-19_en.

164 EIB. 2020. Georgia: Team Europe - EIB to invest €25 million to aid recovery of enterprises from COVID-19 pandemic and expand a credit line with TBC Bank JSC. News release. 21 December. https://www.eib.org/en/press/all/2020-396-team-europe-eib-to-invest-eur25-million-to-aid-recovery-of-georgian-enterprises-from-covid-19-pandemic-and-expand-a-credit-line-with-tbc-bank-jsc#:~:text=The%20European%20Investment%20Bank%20.

as of 2020.[165] Also, the GEL9.7 million State Program for Support of Agricultural Production in 2020 funded 50% of the agricultural machinery, greenhouses, and the purchase and installation of irrigation systems for annual crops.

Prior to the pandemic, tourism was a rapidly growing industry, contributing 11.5% of GDP and employing more than 150,000 people in 2019. To help tourism overcome the crisis impact and restart operations, the government provided several measures:

- In 2020, tourism-related businesses were exempt from the property tax, while income tax was postponed until end-2020. GEL45 million was allocated to cover property taxes, with GEL90 million to cover the postponed income taxes.
- The government subsidized 80% of interest payments for hotels with less than GEL20 million in turnover for 6 months. About 3,000 hotels qualified for the GEL60 million budget program.
- Public catering facilities could qualify for the credit guarantee scheme help liquidity shortages and finance operations.
- It subsidized bank guarantee interest payments for travel agencies and tour operators for 6 months.
- Special measures were offered to get tourism services back on track. The government co-funded GEL200 million for tourism businesses to join tourism expos, with GEL5 million allocated to support travel agencies and guides.[166]

Response to the Russian Invasion of Ukraine

The invasion, which started in February 2022, reduced foreign trade and created new barriers for exporters. Georgia launched an Export Assistance Program (applications were accepted from 7 April to 10 May) to help SME exporters. The program provides technical assistance to exporting companies to eliminate export barriers for beneficiaries and introduce export incentives for diversifying export markets, products, and services; identify sectors and products with high export potential; and stimulate international sales.

The program has several components. The first is a GEL20,000 fund for product licensing and certification. This includes applying international auditing standards and obtaining international quality certificates and licensing. The second is a GEL20,000 fund for branding. This includes branding development strategy, rebranding, and product packaging (according to the brand book). The third is a €10,000 equivalent fund for stimulating international sales, providing financial assistance in national currencies to help exports join international trade networks in target markets—the Middle East, the EU, the United Kingdom, the United States, Canada, and Japan.[167] The is available across the country, especially in pilot regions such as Imereti, Kakheti, Guria, Racha-Lechkhumi, and Kvemo Svaneti.

[165] https://stopcov.ge/Content/files/COVID_RESPONSE_REPORT__ENG.pdf

[166] https://stopcov.ge/Content/files/COVID_RESPONSE_REPORT__ENG.pdf

[167] Enterprise Georgia. Export Promotion and Development. https://www.enterprisegeorgia.gov.ge/en/export-support.

Data Tables

Table 4.1: SME Definitions

A. Definition after 2017

Item	Small	Medium
Number of employees	Fewer than 50 employees per year	More than 50 but not exceed 250 employees per year
Annual turnover	Less than GEL12 million	More than GEL12 million but not exceed GEL60 million per year

Note: There is no definition of microenterprises in Georgia.

Source: ADB Asia SME Monitor 2022 database. Data from the SME Development Strategy of Georgia for 2021-2025.

B. Definition before 2017

Item	Small	Medium
Number of employees	Fewer than 20 employees per year	More than 20 but not exceed 100 employees per year
Annual turnover	Less than GEL500,000	More than GEL500,000 but not exceed GEL1.5 million per year

Note: There is no definition of microenterprises in Georgia.

Source: ADB Asia SME Monitor 2022 database. Data from the SME Development Strategy of Georgia for 2016-2020.

Table 4.2: SME Landscape

End-of-period data

Item	2004	2005	2006	2007	2008	2009	2010	2011	2012	2013	2014	2015	2016	2017	2018	2019	2020	2021
NUMBER OF ENTERPRISES																		
Number of enterprises, total	27,338	34,935	33,512	33,229	33,127	38,167	42,549	57,559	54,673	59,028	70,759	90,403	97,960	124,982	127,153	128,623	129,659	...
Number of SMEs*	27,217	34,783	33,374	33,072	32,961	37,990	42,365	57,325	54,418	58,761	70,491	90,092	97,627	124,614	126,770	128,204	129,268	...
Small	26,380	33,780	32,355	31,840	31,834	36,842	41,216	56,000	53,149	57,337	69,041	88,462	95,950	122,858	124,926	126,323	127,371	...
Medium	837	1,003	1,019	1,232	1,127	1,148	1,149	1,325	1,269	1,424	1,450	1,630	1,677	1,756	1,844	1,881	1,897	...
Number of large enterprises	121	152	138	157	166	177	184	234	255	267	268	311	333	368	383	419	391	...
SME to total (%)	99.6	99.6	99.6	99.5	99.5	99.5	99.6	99.6	99.5	99.5	99.6	99.7	99.7	99.7	99.7	99.7	99.7	...
SME growth (%)	...	27.8	(4.1)	(0.9)	(0.3)	15.3	11.5	35.3	(5.1)	8.0	20.0	27.8	8.4	27.6	1.7	1.1	0.8	...
SMEs by sector (% share)**																		
Agriculture, forestry, and fishing	...	...	...	...	...	...	...	...	...	...	1.1	1.2	1.3	1.1	0.9	1.0	1.2	...
Mining and quarrying	...	...	...	...	...	...	...	...	...	...	0.7	0.6	0.6	0.5	0.5	0.5	0.5	...
Manufacturing	...	...	...	...	...	...	...	...	...	...	10.9	9.3	9.7	7.9	7.4	7.8	8.9	...
Electricity, gas, steam, and air-conditioning supply	...	...	...	...	...	...	...	...	...	...	0.1	0.1	0.1	0.1	0.1	0.1	0.1	...
Water supply; sewerage, waste management, and remediation	...	...	...	...	...	...	...	...	...	...	0.1	0.1	0.1	0.1	0.1	0.1	0.1	...
Construction	...	...	...	...	...	...	...	...	...	...	8.5	6.6	7.3	5.5	5.0	5.7	6.6	...
Wholesale and retail trade; repair of motor vehicles and motorcycles	...	...	...	...	...	...	...	...	...	...	46.2	49.5	50.1	38.2	37.1	37.3	39.5	...
Transportation and storage	...	...	...	...	...	...	...	...	...	...	4.0	5.7	6.1	5.4	5.4	5.7	7.1	...
Accommodation and food services	...	...	...	...	...	...	...	...	...	...	6.3	4.9	5.5	4.6	4.1	4.4	4.6	...
Information and communication	...	...	...	...	...	...	...	...	...	...	1.8	1.4	1.4	1.2	1.1	1.2	1.4	...
Real estate	...	...	...	...	...	...	...	...	...	...	4.1	3.4	3.7	3.4	3.2	3.4	3.6	...
Professional, scientific, and technical activities	...	...	...	...	...	...	...	...	...	...	5.3	4.1	3.9	3.7	3.4	3.6	4.0	...
Administrative and support services	...	...	...	...	...	...	...	...	...	...	3.0	2.7	2.8	2.4	2.1	2.2	2.4	...
Education	...	...	...	...	...	...	...	...	...	...	1.8	1.2	1.1	1.0	0.9	0.9	1.0	...
Human health and social works	...	...	...	...	...	...	...	...	...	...	2.5	1.9	1.6	1.6	1.5	1.6	1.7	...
Arts, entertainment, and recreation	...	...	...	...	...	...	...	...	...	...	0.7	0.7	0.7	0.6	0.5	0.5	0.6	...
Other services	...	...	...	...	...	...	...	...	...	...	1.9	1.6	1.4	1.9	1.9	2.0	2.3	...
Others (not identified)	...	...	...	...	...	...	...	...	...	...	1.0	5.0	2.4	20.9	24.7	22.1	14.2	...
SMEs by region (% share)																		
Capital city (Tbilisi)	...	...	...	...	...	...	...	...	...	...	52.1	47.6	49.6	47.3	46.6	46.9	45.2	...
Others	...	...	...	...	...	...	...	...	...	...	47.9	52.4	50.4	52.7	53.4	53.1	54.8	...
EMPLOYMENT																		
Number of employment, total	322,779	388,946	360,987	361,209	349,250	387,463	397,806	503,236	534,397	550,885	592,147	626,739	666,790	708,165	734,215	756,852	703,874	...
Number of employment by SMEs	205,685	253,481	246,516	244,953	226,064	257,776	265,939	349,993	364,953	372,463	405,637	428,153	448,990	474,576	490,897	491,668	442,164	...
Small	125,649	159,093	148,975	135,801	121,348	151,430	161,665	231,305	246,931	246,538	279,205	290,982	306,543	329,112	330,803	339,152	289,706	...
Medium	80,036	94,388	97,541	109,151	104,716	106,346	104,274	118,688	118,022	125,925	126,432	137,171	142,447	145,463	160,095	152,516	152,458	...
Number of employment by large enterprises	117,094	135,465	114,471	116,256	123,186	129,686	131,867	153,243	169,444	178,422	186,510	198,586	217,800	233,589	243,318	265,184	261,710	...
SME employees to total (%)	63.7	65.2	68.3	67.8	64.7	66.5	66.9	69.5	68.3	67.6	68.5	68.3	67.3	67.0	66.9	65.0	62.8	...
SME employees growth (%)	...	23.2	(2.7)	(0.6)	(7.7)	14.0	3.2	31.6	4.3	2.1	8.9	5.6	4.9	5.7	3.4	0.2	(10.1)	...
Share of female employees to total employees (%)	...	...	37.5	37.7	39.3	39.1	39.0	36.9	36.6	37.9	39.3	39.3	39.8	39.8	40.2	41.4	41.5	...
Employment by SME by sector (% share)**																		
Agriculture, forestry, and fishing	1.5	1.4	1.5	1.6	1.5	2.2	2.2	1.6	1.6	1.6	1.6	1.6	1.7	1.8	1.8	1.9	2.0	...
Mining and quarrying	0.9	0.7	0.8	0.7	0.7	1.2	1.0	0.9	1.0	0.8	0.9	1.1	1.0	0.9	0.9	0.8	1.0	...
Manufacturing	16.3	15.9	15.8	15.2	15.2	15.3	16.4	14.8	14.6	13.7	13.6	13.5	13.5	12.5	12.2	11.7	12.7	...
Electricity, gas, steam, and air-conditioning supply	1.8	1.6	1.5	1.4	1.4	1.2	1.0	0.7	0.8	0.7	0.6	0.5	0.5	0.5	0.5	0.4	0.5	...
Water supply; sewerage, waste management, and remediation	3.3	2.4	2.6	2.6	2.6	1.3	1.1	1.0	0.6	0.7	0.3	0.8	0.6	0.7	0.5	0.5	0.5	...
Construction	8.2	11.4	14.3	17.3	13.2	13.6	12.2	13.9	14.8	14.9	14.1	13.2	12.3	12.3	12.2	11.3	11.6	...
Wholesale and retail trade; repair of motor vehicles and motorcycles	24.2	21.5	19.0	18.2	18.9	21.0	20.1	24.9	25.4	25.6	26.7	28.0	28.6	29.2	29.4	30.1	29.8	...
Transportation and storage	5.8	5.1	5.1	4.4	4.9	4.8	4.6	3.7	4.6	4.6	4.5	4.6	5.4	5.8	5.9	6.3	6.1	...

continued on next page

Table 4.2 *continued*

Item	2004	2005	2006	2007	2008	2009	2010	2011	2012	2013	2014	2015	2016	2017	2018	2019	2020	2021
Accommodation and food services	3.5	4.2	4.6	4.4	4.3	4.4	4.9	5.8	6.8	7.1	6.7	6.8	7.1	7.3	7.6	8.0	5.8	...
Information and communication	2.6	2.6	2.3	2.5	2.9	2.8	3.0	2.8	2.8	2.6	2.3	2.3	2.5	2.8	2.7	2.7	2.6	...
Real estate	3.5	3.7	3.5	3.7	4.1	3.6	3.7	4.6	3.8	3.9	3.9	3.7	3.7	3.6	3.6	3.7	4.0	...
Professional, scientific, and technical activities	3.1	3.6	3.5	3.2	3.5	3.8	3.8	5.3	5.7	5.2	5.7	5.4	5.3	5.2	5.3	5.4	5.2	...
Administrative and support services	1.6	2.0	2.7	2.5	2.6	2.4	3.1	3.2	3.3	3.6	3.3	3.0	2.9	3.0	3.3	3.4	2.4	...
Education	5.7	5.9	5.1	5.5	5.9	5.1	5.5	4.7	4.4	4.8	4.8	4.5	4.4	4.1	4.0	4.0	4.3	...
Human health and social works	15.6	14.9	15.9	14.8	16.4	14.9	15.2	9.1	6.8	7.5	7.5	7.3	7.1	6.5	6.5	6.1	7.0	...
Arts, entertainment, and recreation	1.0	1.3	0.8	0.9	1.1	1.4	1.2	1.8	1.9	1.7	1.9	1.9	1.9	2.2	2.0	2.0	2.7	...
Other services	1.4	1.4	1.0	0.9	0.9	1.0	1.0	1.0	1.1	1.1	1.6	1.4	1.6	1.6	1.6	1.7	1.8	...
Employment by SME by region (% share)																		
Capital city (Tbilisi)	...	...	45.3	46.8	47.4	52.5	53.3	56.9	53.5	53.2	52.6	56.9	54.1	53.1	53.8	51.5	52.9	...
Others	...	...	54.7	53.2	52.6	47.5	46.7	43.1	46.5	46.8	47.4	43.1	45.9	46.9	46.2	48.5	47.1	...
CONTRIBUTION TO GROSS VALUE ADDED (GVA)																		
GVA of SMEs (GEL million)	...	...	1,608	2,228	2,342	2,857	3,379	5,140	6,203	6,794	7,357	8,578	9,795	11,722	12,534	13,805	13,528	...
SME contribution to GVA (% share)	...	...	46.2	49.1	45.4	52.3	50.4	55.5	55.4	56.0	57.3	56.1	58.4	61.6	60.5	59.3	60.8	...
SME GVA growth (%)	...	...	...	38.6	5.1	22.0	18.3	52.1	20.7	9.5	8.3	16.6	14.2	19.7	6.9	10.1	(2.0)	...
SME labor productivity (GEL)***	...	...	6,521	9,097	10,361	11,082	12,706	14,685	16,996	18,241	18,138	20,034	21,815	24,700	25,532	28,077	30,596	...
SME GVA by sector (% share)**																		
Agriculture, forestry, and fishing	...	...	0.5	0.6	0.5	0.9	0.8	1.1	1.0	1.0	0.9	1.0	1.0	1.0	1.0	1.5	1.7	...
Mining and quarrying	...	...	0.9	0.8	0.7	1.6	1.8	1.5	1.2	1.1	1.2	1.4	1.1	1.3	1.1	1.1	1.2	...
Manufacturing	...	...	15.4	15.4	15.9	14.4	15.8	13.9	13.5	13.3	13.9	13.0	12.4	12.3	11.0	10.8	12.3	...
Electricity, gas, steam, and air-conditioning supply	...	...	4.9	3.3	2.5	2.4	2.3	1.9	1.5	1.5	2.1	2.4	2.3	2.3	2.5	2.4	2.6	...
Water supply; sewerage, waste management, and remediation	...	...	1.1	1.0	0.9	0.4	0.4	0.5	0.4	0.4	0.3	0.4	0.3	0.4	0.3	0.3	0.3	...
Construction	...	...	18	20.0	14.8	15.7	13.6	15.2	18.0	19.7	16.4	18.1	17.8	19.4	20.6	19.1	20.9	...
Wholesale and retail trade; repair of motor vehicles and motorcycles	...	...	23.3	25.2	27.5	25.7	26.7	28.2	26.9	25.3	26.5	25.9	25.1	24.3	24.8	25.3	26.5	...
Transportation and storage	...	...	8.4	6.2	7.2	7.3	7.2	6.5	7.2	7.2	7.4	7.1	7.3	8.9	7.5	8.1	7.9	...
Accommodation and food services	...	...	2.6	2.6	2.3	2.5	3.1	3.0	3.5	3.6	3.3	3.8	5.1	4.3	4.4	5.6	2.8	...
Information and communication	...	...	4.3	4.4	4.5	4.6	3.9	3.1	3.0	2.4	2.4	2.8	2.4	2.7	2.8	2.8	2.6	...
Real estate	...	...	4.1	4.3	6.6	6.8	5.9	6.2	4.4	6.0	6.7	6.2	7.0	6.4	6.9	7.0	6.1	...
Professional, scientific, and technical activities	...	...	5.6	5.1	4.5	5.2	5.4	6.4	7.8	6.0	6.7	6.7	7.0	6.7	6.9	6.3	6.1	...
Administrative and support services	...	...	2.3	2.6	2.1	2.2	2.2	2.8	2.6	2.6	2.6	2.5	3.0	2.8	2.7	3.1	1.9	...
Education	...	...	2.1	2.3	2.5	2.4	2.6	1.9	1.7	2.0	2.0	1.8	1.9	1.6	1.7	1.6	1.9	...
Human health and social works	...	...	5.4	5.0	5.8	6.3	6.7	4.6	3.6	4.1	5.0	4.5	4.4	3.7	3.7	3.3	3.5	...
Arts, entertainment, and recreation	...	...	0.5	0.7	1.3	1.1	1.5	3.9	3.3	3.4	2.3	1.9	1.2	1.3	1.4	1.3	1.3	...
Other services	...	...	0.3	0.3	0.4	0.4	0.4	0.4	0.4	0.4	0.5	0.5	0.5	0.5	0.6	0.5	0.4	...
SME GVA by region (% share)																		
Capital city (Tbilisi)	...	...	62.1	66.9	67.1	68.6	67.5	70.6	68.5	67.4	66.3	65.2	66.4	62.4	64.2	63.2	62.9	...
Others	...	...	37.9	33.1	32.9	31.4	32.5	29.4	31.5	32.6	33.7	34.8	33.6	37.6	35.8	36.8	37.1	...
EXPORTS																		
Total export value (GEL million)	647	866	937	1,232	1,495	1,134	1,677	2,186	2,377	2,910	2,861	2,204	2,117	2,746	3,380	3,798	3,343	4,242
Total export growth (%)	40.2	33.8	8.2	31.6	21.4	(24.2)	48.0	30.4	8.7	22.5	(1.7)	(23.0)	(3.9)	29.7	23.1	12.4	(12.0)	26.9
SME export value (GEL million)	...	...	...	...	...	...	...	...	...	...	...	1,355	1,352	1,601	1,806	1,982	1,864	2,372
SME export to total export value (%)	...	...	...	...	...	...	...	...	...	...	...	61.5	63.8	58.3	53.4	52.2	55.8	55.9
SME export growth (%)	...	...	...	...	...	...	...	...	...	...	...	...	(0.3)	18.4	12.9	9.7	(5.9)	27.2
IMPORTS																		
Total import value (GEL million)	1,844	2,488	3,675	5,212	6,302	4,476	5,236	7,072	8,056	8,023	8,602	7,304	7,342	8,057	9,362	9,519	8,053	10,104
Total import growth (%)	61.9	34.9	47.7	41.8	20.9	(29.0)	17.0	35.1	13.9	(0.4)	7.2	(15.1)	0.5	9.7	16.2	1.7	(15.4)	25.5
SME import value (GEL million)	...	...	...	...	...	...	...	...	...	...	...	3,944	4,170	4,759	5,345	5,421	4,705	5,775
SME import to total import value (%)	...	...	...	...	...	...	...	...	...	...	...	54.0	56.8	59.1	57.1	57.0	58.4	57.2
SME import growth (%)	...	...	...	...	...	...	...	...	...	...	...	...	5.7	14.1	12.3	1.4	(13.2)	22.7

SME = small and medium-sized enterprise.

* There is no classification of microenterprises in Georgia.

** Based on the classification of NACE (Nomenclature générale des Activités économiques dans les Communautés Européennes) rev.2. NACE is the statistical classification of economic activities developed since 1970 in the European Union.

*** SME labor productivity = gross value added of SMEs (GEL)/number of employees by SMEs.

Source: ADB Asia SME Monitor 2022 database. Data from Annual Statistical Survey of Enterprises (https://www.geostat.ge/en/modules/categories/195/business-statistics; https://www.geostat.ge/en/modules/categories/93/regional-statistics; https://www.geostat.ge/en/modules/categories/35/external-trade).

Table 4.3: Bank Credit

End-of-period data

Item	2004	2005	2006	2007	2008	2009	2010	2011	2012	2013	2014	2015	2016	2017	2018	2019	2020	2021
OPERATING BANKS																		
Number of operating banks, total	21	19	17	19	20	19	19	19	19	21	21	19	16	16	15	15	15	14
Domestic banks (100% capital control)	9	7	5	5	3	4	3	1	2	1	2	1	2	1	1	1	1	1
Foreign-invested banks (capital investment by less than 50%)	4	1	...	...	1	1	3	5	3	4	3	2	2	2	3	3	2	2
Foreign-invested banks (capital investment by more than 50%)	6	9	10	12	14	12	11	11	11	14	14	15	11	13	11	11	12	11
Foreign banks' branches	2	2	2	2	2	2	2	2	3	2	2	1	1	...	...	...	...	...
Credit																		
Loans outstanding, total (GEL million)	915	1,691	2,637	4,505	5,823	5,021	6,082	7,519	8,489	10,239	12,714	16,013	18,907	22,282	26,597	31,925	38,219	43,085
In domestic currency (GEL million)	129	396	691	1,408	1,544	1,145	1,567	2,337	2,714	3,820	4,946	5,671	6,533	9,558	11,415	14,246	16,939	21,167
In foreign currency (GEL million)	785	1,295	1,946	3,097	4,279	3,876	4,515	5,182	5,776	6,419	7,768	10,342	12,374	12,723	15,182	17,679	21,280	21,919
Loan growth (%), exclude foreign exchange effect	38.4	87.4	61.3	79.8	25.0	(14.5)	16.7	28.8	13.5	17.1	19.0	8.2	10.8	18.6	17.8	16.2	9.0	18.2
Loan growth (%), include foreign exchange effect	23.8	84.9	56.0	70.8	29.3	(13.8)	21.1	23.6	12.9	20.6	24.2	26.0	18.1	17.9	19.4	20.0	19.7	12.7
Total bank loans to GDP (%)	9.3	14.5	19.1	26.5	30.5	27.9	27.9	29.5	31.2	35.8	40.8	47.2	52.8	54.7	59.6	64.8	77.6	71.5
Lending rate, total (%, annual weighted average)	20.3	17.5	18.4	18.8	21.6	22.1	19.0	18.3	18.6	17.0	15.8	14.7	14.2	13.1	12.4	11.7	12.1	12.1
Lending rate, local currency (%, annual weighted average)	24.0	20.4	19.6	20.8	22.7	23.8	22.0	21.8	21.6	20.1	19.8	19.7	19.3	16.6	16.1	15.0	15.5	15.6
Lending rate, Foreign Currency (%, annual weighted average)	19.4	16.2	17.4	17.5	20.8	21.1	17.2	15.3	15.4	13.5	11.3	10.3	9.5	8.3	7.8	7.0	6.6	6.4
Gross nonperforming loans (NPLs) (GEL million)*	...	65	68	121	766	926	784	667	810	791	988	1,200	1,380	1,337	1,480	1,414	3,203	2,255
Gross NPLs to total loans (%)*	...	3.8	2.5	2.6	12.8	17.9	12.5	8.6	9.3	7.5	7.6	7.5	7.3	6.0	5.6	4.4	8.4	5.2
Deposits																		
Deposits, total (GEL million)	971	1,310	2,097	3,209	3,568	3,950	5,488	6,745	7,650	9,665	11,605	14,386	16,998	19,851	23,053	26,257	34,628	37,240
In domestic currency (GEL million)	265	396	686	1,179	961	1,243	1,759	2,703	2,748	3,880	4,629	4,440	4,902	6,890	8,499	9,460	13,368	14,922
In foreign currency (GEL million)	706	914	1,411	2,030	2,607	2,707	3,729	4,042	4,902	5,784	6,976	9,946	12,096	12,961	14,554	16,798	21,259	22,317
Deposit rate, total (%, annual weighted average)	4.3	4.0	5.6	6.7	6.5	6.5	6.1	6.7	6.7	5.5	4.7	4.4	4.6	4.5	4.7	4.6	5.5	5.2
Deposit rate, local currency (%, annual weighted average)	3.2	3.7	5.7	6.9	7.0	6.9	7.0	7.7	7.6	6.4	5.7	5.5	6.5	6.7	6.6	6.3	7.5	7.5
Deposit rate, foreign currency (%, annual weighted average)	4.7	4.1	5.5	6.4	5.9	6.0	5.2	5.4	5.5	4.2	3.5	3.2	2.6	2.0	1.9	1.8	1.7	1.0
SME LOANS*																		
SME loans outstanding, total (GEL million)	...	...	...	...	...	...	...	...	...	...	...	3,612	4,451	5,266	6,006	7,062	7,788	8,516
SME loans to total loans outstanding (%)	...	...	...	...	...	...	...	...	...	...	...	22.6	23.5	23.6	22.6	22.1	20.4	19.8
SME loans to GDP (%)	...	...	...	...	...	...	...	...	...	...	...	10.6	12.4	12.9	13.5	14.3	15.8	14.1
SME loan growth (%), exclude foreign exchange effect	...	...	...	...	...	...	...	...	...	...	...	...	23.3	18.3	14.0	17.6	10.3	9.3
SME loan growth (%), include foreign exchange effect	...	...	...	...	...	...	...	...	...	...	...	...	15.4	19.2	12.6	14.1	0.4	14.6
SME lending rate, total (%, annual average)	...	...	...	...	...	...	...	...	...	...	...	...	14.2	13.1	12.4	11.7	12.1	12.1
SME lending rate, local currency (%, annual average)	...	...	...	...	...	...	...	...	...	...	...	...	19.3	16.6	16.1	15.0	15.5	15.6
SME lending rate, foreign currency (%, annual average)	...	...	...	...	...	...	...	...	...	...	...	...	9.5	8.3	7.8	7.0	6.6	6.4
Nonperforming SME loans (NPLs) (GEL million)	...	...	...	...	...	...	145	134	111	102	101	161	206	221	407	400	974	748
SME NPLs to total SME loans (%)	...	...	...	...	...	...	10.3	8.7	6.4	5.0	4.2	4.4	5.2	4.3	6.1	4.9	9.8	6.5
Number of SME loan borrowers	2,359	4,468	6,612	9,418	11,172	12,164	13,204	22,952	9,243	9,604	10,719	11,341	13,427	15,620	10,699	13,140	13,332	...
SME loan borrowers to total bank borrowers (%)	...	...	...	...	...	...	...	...	...	...	...	...	...	...	...	...	...	...
SME loan rejection rate (% of total applications)	...	...	...	...	...	...	...	...	...	...	...	...	...	...	...	...	...	...
Number of SME savings account in banks**	57,718	81,838	134,412	187,445	212,330	229,690	229,256	240,946	145,890	146,398	165,934	164,980	177,458	126,277	150,688	160,880	154,037	...
Collateralized SME loans (GEL million)	...	...	...	...	...	...	...	...	...	...	...	3,209	4,050	4,677	5,292	6,164	6,704	7,234
Non-collateral SME loans (GEL million)	...	...	...	...	...	...	...	...	...	...	...	403	401	590	714	899	1,084	1,282

continued on next page

Table 4.3 *continued*

Item	2004	2005	2006	2007	2008	2009	2010	2011	2012	2013	2014	2015	2016	2017	2018	2019	2020	2021
SME loans outstanding by sector (% share)																		
Agriculture, forestry, and fisheries	...	...	...	...	...	...	...	...	...	...	...	4.2	4.7	4.0	3.5	3.3	3.7	4.6
Manufacturing	...	...	...	...	...	...	...	...	...	...	...	9.4	10.5	8.9	7.8	9.6	7.8	8.8
Transportation and communication	...	...	...	...	...	...	...	...	...	...	...	1.3	1.4	1.6	2.2	1.9	2.5	2.5
Construction	...	...	...	...	...	...	...	...	...	...	...	4.3	5.4	5.5	5.5	6.2	6.1	7.2
Wholesale and retail trade	...	...	...	...	...	...	...	...	...	...	...	34.1	30.2	25.0	23.1	21.0	19.0	18.8
Other services	...	...	...	...	...	...	...	...	...	...	...	10.3	12.1	10.2	11.6	12.3	15.2	14.0
Others	...	...	...	...	...	...	...	...	...	...	...	36.4	35.9	44.8	46.4	45.7	45.7	44.2
SME loans outstanding by region (% share)																		
Capital city (Tbilisi)	...	...	...	...	...	...	...	...	...	...	...	59.1	58.1	54.5	52.1	52.8	51.3	50.9
Other	...	...	...	...	...	...	...	...	...	...	...	40.9	42.0	45.5	47.9	47.2	48.7	49.1
SME loans outstanding by type of use (% share)																		
For working capital	...	...	...	...	...	...	...	...	...	...	...	...	...	...	...	...	...	...
For capital investment	...	...	...	...	...	...	...	...	...	...	...	...	...	...	...	...	...	...
SME loans outstanding by tenor (% share)																		
Less than 1 year	...	...	...	...	...	...	...	...	...	...	...	9.1	12.4	10.5	8.6	6.3	8.3	9.2
1-5 years	...	...	...	...	...	...	...	...	...	...	...	56.3	48.5	48.9	49.7	49.7	43.5	45.1
More than 5 years	...	...	...	...	...	...	...	...	...	...	...	34.6	39.1	40.6	41.7	44.0	48.2	45.7

GDP = gross domestic product, SME = small and medium-sized enterprise.

* Data include principal amounts of overdue loans.

** Data collected once a year.

Source: ADB Asia SME Monitor 2022. Data from the the National Bank of Georgia.

Table 4.4: Public Financing and Guarantees

End-of-period data

Item	2014	2015	2016	2017	2018	2019	2020	2021
SUBSIDIZED LOANS TO SMEs								
Number of funds	...	...	...	...	...	...	...	...
Number of subsidized loans (new approval)	23	46	73	86	115	130	141	439
Outstanding of subsidized loans to SMEs (GEL million)	...	...	...	...	...	...	...	...
Subsidized loans disbursed to SMEs (GEL million)*	53.2	135.5	220.3	330.1	462.9	614.0	828.2	1,481.5
Growth (%)	...	154.8	62.6	49.8	40.2	32.6	34.9	78.9
Number of SMEs that accepted subsidized loans*	23	67	131	203	290	376	459	755
SME access to subsidized loans (% of total SMEs)	...	...	...	0.2	0.2	0.3	0.4	0.4
CREDIT GUARANTEES								
Number of guarantee schemes	...	...	...	...	...	...	...	...
Guaranteed loans outstanding to SMEs (GEL million)**	...	...	...	...	...	...	101.1	204.7
Growth (%)	...	...	...	...	...	...	...	102.5
Guaranteed loans approved to SMEs (GEL million)*	...	...	...	...	...	...	136.3	312.7
Guaranteed loans disbursed to SMEs (GEL million)*	...	...	...	...	...	...	128.0	235.7
Number of SMEs guaranteed *	...	...	...	...	...	...	133	318
SME access to credit guarantees (% of total SMEs)	...	...	...	...	...	...	0.1	0.2
Guaranteed SME loans to total SME loans (%)	...	...	...	...	...	...	2.1	3.6
Nonperforming guaranteed SME loans to total guaranteed SME loans (NPL ratio; %)	...	...	...	...	...	...	...	...

NPL = nonperforming loan, SME = small and medium-sized enterprise.

* Cumulative amounts and numbers.

** Balance amount of guaranteed loans to SMEs at the end of the year.

Source: ADB Asia SME Monitor 2022 database. Data from Enterprise Georgia, Ministry of Economy and Sustainable Development.

Table 4.5: Nonbank Finance

End-of-period data

Item	2004	2005	2006	2007	2008	2009	2010	2011	2012	2013	2014	2015	2016	2017	2018	2019	2020	2021
NUMBER OF NONBANK FINANCE INSTITUTIONS																		
Nonbank finance institutions, total	53	40	41	39	45	56	67	80	80	84	87	85	92	83	69	254	239	222
Microfinance institutions	...	...	3	15	27	38	49	62	62	67	70	70	81	75	67	48	40	38
Credit unions/cooperatives	53	40	38	24	18	18	18	18	18	17	17	15	11	8	2	2	1	1
Pawnshops	...	...	...	...	...	...	...	...	...	...	...	...	...	...	...	204	198	183
MICROFINANCE INSTITUTIONS																		
Loans outstanding, total (GEL million)	...	...	2	55	113	130	230	349	519	620	852	1,198	1,444	1,137	1,102	1,129	1,184	1,360
Growth (%)	...	...	...	2,617.0	105.6	15.1	76.9	51.9	48.7	19.6	37.4	40.5	20.6	(21.2)	(3.1)	2.5	4.9	14.9
Total loans to GDP (%)	...	...	0.01	0.3	0.6	0.7	1.1	1.4	1.9	2.2	2.7	3.5	4.0	2.8	2.5	2.3	2.4	2.3
Annual lending rate (%, on average)	...	...	...	...	...	...	...	...	...	...	...	...	...	...	29.3	24.1	23.7	23.9
Gross nonperforming loans (NPLs) (GEL million)	...	...	...	...	...	...	...	...	...	...	...	...	...	...	...	93.7	89.4	79.7
Gross NPLs to total loans (%)	...	...	...	...	...	...	...	...	...	...	...	...	...	...	...	8.3	7.5	5.9
Savings (GEL million)	...	...	...	...	...	...	...	...	...	...	...	...	...	...	...	...	...	...
Number of customers financed, total	...	...	...	...	...	...	...	...	...	...	...	...	...	646,386	568,310	465,138	422,615	451,862
Loans outstanding by sector (% share)																		
Agriculture, forestry, and fisheries	...	...	...	17.2	20.9	22.5	27.1	26.5	27.6	23.5	22.0	21.3	19.4	10.4	...	...	...	...
Manufacturing	...	...	...	...	3.0	2.1	2.2	1.2	1.0	0.2	0.2	0.3	0.3	0.8	...	...	...	...
Transportation and communication	...	...	...	0.0	1.2	1.3	1.5	1.8	1.4	0.1	0.1	0.2	0.2	1.0	...	...	...	...
Construction	...	...	...	...	0.8	0.5	0.4	0.4	0.4	0.4	0.4	0.7	0.5	0.3	...	...	...	...
Wholesale and retail trade	...	...	...	46.9	39.1	35.0	31.5	30.1	26.9	21.2	20.0	22.5	20.3	21.9	...	...	...	...
Other services	...	...	...	8.0	29.9	31.6	30.1	30.7	35.2	45.3	50.8	47.7	52.9	59.1	...	...	...	...
Others	...	...	...	27.8	5.1	7.1	7.3	9.3	7.5	9.2	6.4	7.4	6.5	6.6	...	...	...	...
Trade and service	...	...	...	...	...	...	...	...	...	...	...	...	...	...	17.0	18.6	16.9	13.0
Custom loans	...	...	...	...	...	...	...	...	...	...	...	...	...	...	30.6	23.8	22.4	24.8
Agriculture	...	...	...	...	...	...	...	...	...	...	...	...	...	...	8.6	9.2	8.4	6.6
Online loans	...	...	...	...	...	...	...	...	...	...	...	...	...	...	9.6	2.6	0.1	0.0
Pawning	...	...	...	...	...	...	...	...	...	...	...	...	...	...	27.2	38.3	43.9	48.4
Installments	...	...	...	...	...	...	...	...	...	...	...	...	...	...	2.9	3.2	4.1	4.0
Other	...	...	...	...	...	...	...	...	...	...	...	...	...	...	2.2	1.2	0.8	0.7
Loans issued to legal entities	...	...	...	...	...	...	...	...	...	...	...	...	...	...	1.9	3.1	3.5	2.5
Loans outstanding by region (% share)																		
Capital city (Tbilisi)	...	...	...	...	...	...	...	...	...	...	...	...	...	...	...	28.8	24.9	37.8
Others	...	...	...	...	...	...	...	...	...	...	...	...	...	...	...	71.2	75.1	62.2
CREDIT UNIONS AND COOPERATIVES																		
Loans outstanding, total (GEL thousand)	1,484	1,623	1,629	1,122	1,375	1,535	2,139	3,556	4,879	5,370	5,626	6,884	6,576	5,768	1,857	465	480	476
Growth (%)	39.7	9.4	0.4	(31.1)	22.5	11.6	39.3	66.3	37.2	10.1	4.8	22.4	(4.5)	(12.3)	(67.8)	(75.0)	3.2	(0.9)
Total loans to GDP (%)	0.002	0.001	0.001	0.001	0.001	0.001	0.001	0.001	0.002	0.002	0.002	0.002	0.002	0.001	0.004	0.001	0.001	0.001
Annual lending rate (%, on average)	...	...	...	...	...	...	...	...	...	...	...	...	...	...	...	...	...	...
Gross nonperforming loans (NPLs) (GEL thousand)	...	...	...	...	...	...	...	...	...	...	...	...	...	...	...	...	...	...
Gross NPLs to total loans (%)	...	...	...	...	...	...	...	...	...	...	...	...	...	...	...	...	...	...
Number of customers financed, total	...	...	...	...	...	...	...	...	...	...	...	...	...	...	...	...	...	...

continued on next page

Table 4.5 *continued*

Item	2004	2005	2006	2007	2008	2009	2010	2011	2012	2013	2014	2015	2016	2017	2018	2019	2020	2021
PAWNSHOPS																		
Financing outstanding, total (GEL million)	...	...	...	...	...	...	...	...	...	...	...	...	...	...	...	415	412	947
Growth (%)	...	...	...	...	...	...	...	...	...	...	...	...	...	...	...	...	(0.6)	129.7
Total financing to GDP (%)	...	...	...	...	...	...	...	...	...	...	...	...	...	...	...	0.8	0.8	1.6
Annual financing rate (%, on average)	...	...	...	...	...	...	...	...	...	...	...	...	...	...	...	...	...	...
Gross nonperforming financing (NPFs) (GEL million)	...	...	...	...	...	...	...	...	...	...	...	...	...	...	...	...	...	...
Gross NPFs to total financing (%)	...	...	...	...	...	...	...	...	...	...	...	...	...	...	...	...	...	...
Number of customers financed, total	...	...	...	...	...	...	...	...	...	...	...	...	...	...	...	490,584	448,009	510,969
Financing outstanding by sector (% share)																		
Pawnshop loans	...	...	...	...	...	...	...	...	...	...	...	...	...	...	...	67.8	65.9	29.5
Consumer loans	...	...	...	...	...	...	...	...	...	...	...	...	...	...	...	8.5	7.7	27.7
Business loans	...	...	...	...	...	...	...	...	...	...	...	...	...	...	...	0.1	0.1	0.0
Real estate loans	...	...	...	...	...	...	...	...	...	...	...	...	...	...	...	2.3	1.6	0.4
Auto loans	...	...	...	...	...	...	...	...	...	...	...	...	...	...	...	0.1	0.1	0.1
Trade and service loans	...	...	...	...	...	...	...	...	...	...	...	...	...	...	...	2.0	2.6	1.9
Loans online	...	...	...	...	...	...	...	...	...	...	...	...	...	...	...	8.5	10.2	30.0
Agricultural industry loans	...	...	...	...	...	...	...	...	...	...	...	...	...	...	...	0.1	0.1	2.8
Other loans	...	...	...	...	...	...	...	...	...	...	...	...	...	...	...	3.2	1.0	1.4
Loans to legal entities	...	...	...	...	...	...	...	...	...	...	...	...	...	...	...	7.5	10.8	6.2
Financing outstanding by region (% share)																		
Capital city (Tbilisi)	...	...	...	...	...	...	...	...	...	...	...	...	...	...	...	...	...	...
Others	...	...	...	...	...	...	...	...	...	...	...	...	...	...	...	...	...	...

GDP = gross domestic product.
Source: ADB Asia SME Monitor 2022 database. Data from the the National Bank of Georgia.

Table 4.6: Capital Markets

End-of-period data

Item	2004	2005	2006	2007	2008	2009	2010	2011	2012	2013	2014	2015	2016	2017	2018	2019	2020	2021
EQUITY MARKET																		
Main Board																		
Index [GSX]	...	...	164.6	207.2	72.8	74.7	121.7	78.8	80.0	116.9	103.4	95.5	108.8	222.0	140.6	92.5	85.2	108.5
Market capitalization (GEL million)	...	...	...	...	...	...	...	...	1,462	2,074	2,152	1,324	1,729	3,327	1,963	1,963	2,366	2,368
Growth (%)	...	...	...	...	...	...	...	...	...	41.9	3.7	(38.5)	30.6	92.4	(41.0)	(0.0)	20.5	0.1
Trading value (GEL million)	46.4	62.4	58.8	38.2	10.6	3.1	5.1	2.5	8.9	0.5	0.9	0.8	0.5	0.3	0.3	0.1	0.1	0.1
Trading volume (million shares)	30.0	32.4	17.2	14.6	12.5	12.7	41.6	12.1	10.0	27.2	12.1	6.2	3.6	7.3	2.9	1.2	0.9	0.2
Number of listed companies	276	250	242	161	157	145	138	135	133	129	129	124	124	124	22	19	10	8
Number of IPOs*	...	1	3	2	1	...	...	...	...	...	1	...	9	7	...	...	2	...
Number of delisted companies	1	27	11	83	5	12	7	3	2	4	1	5	9	7	102	3	11	2

IPO = initial public offering.

* Data refer to the number of new listings.

Note: There are no dedicated SME equity market and corporate bond issuance by SMEs.

Source: ADB Asia SME Monitor 2022 database. Data from Georgian Stock Exchange.

Table 4.7: Policies and Regulations

Regulations	
Name	**Outline**
Government Resolution No.365 of 2014 on Establishment of Enterprise Georgia	Enterprise Georgia was established in 2014 and is the main state institution supporting entrepreneurship, including small and medium entrepreneurship. Enterprise Georgia offers the following services: 1. Loan/lease interest payment subsidies for small and medium-sized enterprises (SMEs). In addition to the interest payment subsidies, the agency offers partial guarantees for loans up to 60% of the principal loan amount. Also, the beneficiaries can receive grants if certain terms are satisfied. 2. Partial guarantees for loans up to 60% of the principal loan amount. Beneficiaries can receive grants if certain terms are met. 3. Supporting micro and small enterprises: the agency disburses micro grants to the winners of competitions conducted within the scope of the program. 4. Film in Georgia: the agency disburses cash rebates on qualifying expenses to companies that produce media content in Georgia.
Government Resolution No.163 of 2019 on Credit Guarantee Scheme	The program is a partial guarantee scheme for SME loans. The agency guarantees up to 80% of the principal loan amount. The loans must in the range of GEL20,000 to GEL10 million and can be issued by both commercial banks and microfinance organizations.
Decree No.51/04 of 2014 of the Governor of NBG on the approval of the "Regulation on Assets Classification and the Creation and Use of Reserves for Losses by Commercial Banks"	The regulation ensures commercial banks develop and the implement internal procedures and reporting requirements for classifiying assets and provisioning obligations. Asset classification shall be applied to all assets in all currencies, including items on balance sheets, as well as all of those off-balance-sheet items established as such by International Accounting Standards.
Decree No.44/04 of 2020 of the Governor of NBG on the approval of the "Regulation on Lending to the Individuals"	The regulation promotes a stable and sustainable functioning of the financial system and encourages responsible lending to individuals by the loan-issuing organization. The requirements apply to all types of loans/guarantees/claims on collateral issued by loan-issuing organizations to individuals (including individual entrepreneurs).
Law of Georgia on Security Market No.1745 of 1998	The law helps develop the securities market to protect the interests of investors, to ensure transparency of issuer information at the time of public offerings, ensures transparency in public trading of securities, and establishes fair rules and free competition in the public trading of securities.
Stock Exchange Licensing, Financial Reporting, and Minimum Capital Requirement Rule, 169/01 of 2010	Sets licensing requirements, reporting transparency and audit requirements, minimum equity capital, and cash requirements.
Rule of Financial Instruments Trading System Recognization as Organized Market, 33/04 of 2018	Organizes the market to benefit listed companies with tax relief, impacting the business enviroment, including SMEs.
Tax code of Georgia, No.3591 of 2011 (with subsequent amendments)	VAT - Within the framework of Association agreement between Georgia and the European Union, Georgian tax legislation was harmonized with Council Directive 2006/112/EC of 28 November 2006 on the common system of the value added tax. As a result of amendments, which came into force 1 January 2021, new VAT legislation was adopted. Changes were also introduced to relevant secondary legislaton. While positively affecting taxpayers, the new VAT system introduces new regulatory provisions, including new rules related to the place of supply of services, international cargo, VAT taxable amounts, taxation of vouchers, principles of taxable persons and economic activity.
Minister of Finance Order on Administration of Taxes, No.996 of 2010 (with subsequent amendments)	Special tax regimes for individuals—Individuals may obtain the special status of micro business or fixed taxpayer and individual entrepreneurs—status of small businesses. Micro businesses are exempt from personal income tax. They are also exempt from the obligation to withhold tax at the source upon payment of service fees. Small businesses are liable for personal income tax at 1%. The applicable personal income tax rate increases to 3% if gross income of a small business received from economic activities exceeds GEL500,000. A 3% rate applies from the beginning of the month in which a small business exceeded the GEL500,000 threshold until the end of a calendar year.
Law of Georgia on Microfinance Organizations No.3482 of 2006	Legal regulation of the activities of microfinance organizations and creation of a healthy environment for their development.

continued on next page

Table 4.7 *continued*

Law of Georgia on Investment Funds No.6805 of 2020	The purpose of this law is to develop the investment funds market, to ensure free competition in the market, and to protect the interests of investors. This law applies to a) investment funds established in Georgia, as well as foreign investment funds offered in Georgia; b) asset management companies of investment funds; c) asset management companies established in Georgia, irrespective of whether or not an investment fund under its management is established in Georgia; and d) other natural and legal persons involved in activities related to the investment, management, safekeeping, administration, and record keeping and registration of investment fund assets.
Resolution No.1-1/66 of 2014 on the approval of the regulations of the Agency for Innovations and Technologies of Georgia	The Agency for Innovations and Technologies of Georgia is the main government agency supporting development of an economy based on knowledge and innovative technologies. Among the goals of the agency are to coordinate the process of creating and developing an innovative ecosystem in the country, to stimulate innovation, modern technologies, research and development (R&D), to promote their commercialization and use, to create innovative startups and increase their competitiveness, among others. The agency's tasks include financial support as well as the acquisition and supply of appropriate services for innovative startups.
Law of Georgia on Public Procurement No.1388 of 2005	This law determines the general legal, organizational, and economic principles for conducting public procurement. The purpose of this law is to: a) ensure rational spending of monetary funds designated for public procurement; b) promote effective competition in the area of production of goods, performance of services and construction works necessary for the state; c) ensure a fair and nondiscriminatory approach to participants of a procurement when performing public procurement; d) ensure publicity of public procurement; and e) create a Unified Electronic System of Public Procurement and build public confidence in the system.
Law of Georgia on Accounting, Reporting, and Auditing No.5386 of 2016	The law sets the legal framework according to internationally recognized standards for accounting, preparing and filing financial and management reports, reports on payments to government, professional certification, auditing and quality assurance, public oversight and enforcement. The law aims to facilitate financial transparency and economic growth through approximating or meeting the requirements of respective European Union directives regulating accounting and the audit of entities.
Regulators and Policymakers	
Name	**Responsibility**
Ministry of Economy and and Sustainable Development (MESD)	The MESD is responsible for the development, planning, monitoring of implementation and evaluation of the country's economic policy related to SMEs.
Enterprise Georgia, MESD	Implement SME development policies and strategies under the MESD. The main goal of the agency is supporting entrepreneurship, including small and medium entrepreneurship. The agency aims to increase private sector competitiveness by using tools that support entrepreneurship, as well as support export growth and encourage foreign direct investment.
National Bank of Georgia (NBG)	Georgia's central bank strives for financial sector stability and promotes long-term economic growth; develops and implements monetary and exchange rate policies; ensures the functioning of the monetary system; and facilitates secure, sustainable and effective payment systems. The functions of the central bank affect the overall business environment, including SMEs.
Ministry of Environmental Protection and Agriculture (MEPA)	Responsible for managing and fostering environmental protection, agriculture, and rural development, including the promotion of agribusiness. i) Implements state policy in environmental protection, agriculture, and rural development. ii) Manages and oversees natural resource developmnent (apart from natural deposits such as oil and gas). iii) Fosters sustainable development and green economic principles. iv) Monitors and managest the reduction of environmental pollution.

continued on next page

Table 4.7 *continued*

Rural Development Agency (RDA), MEPA	Established under Ministry of Environmental Protection and Agriculture, the main goal of the RDA is to develop agriculture in the country and for this purpose to plan and implement various programs and activities. RDA supports both startups and SME rural enterprises and focuses exclusively on agriculture-related activities.
Ministry of Finance of Georgia (MOF), Department of Tax and Customs Policy	The department is responsible for tax and customs policy design. The MOF separates micro and small businesses and applies Special tax treatments differently, in particular, the status of micro business may be granted to a natural person who does not use hired labor, and conducts business independently, and whose gross receivable income during the calendar year does not exceed GEL30 000. If small businesses pay taxes under special tax treatments, micro businesses are exempt from personal income tax. They are exempt from obligations to withhold tax at source upon payment of service fees.
Revenue Service of Georgia (GRS), MOF	The GRS is responsible for tax and customs administration. It also covers phytosanitary, veterinary and sanitary border-quarantine control. Revenues mobilized as a result of joint work and cooperation of the GRS, individuals, and legal entities carrying out economic activities account for more than 90% of Georgia's budget.
Service for Accounting, Reporting and Auditing Supervision (SARAS)	SARAS enhances the reliability of financial and management information for making effective economic decisions by implementing international standards—increasing SMEs' access to finance.

Policies

Name	Responsible Entity	Outline
National Strategy of Financial Education, 2016	National Bank of Georgia	The strategy aims to raise the level of financial education across Georgia, ultimately a prerequisite for improving financial well-being and protecting the rights of consumers. The strategy created FinEdu, the first Georgian educational webportal fully dedicated to financial education that offers educational resources such as publications and blogs, brochures, manuals and other printed and supporting material, video and audio content. FinEdu's educational and informational activities also target SMEs.
SME Development Strategy of Georgia 2016-2020	Government of Georgia	The SME Development Strategy for Georgia aims to create a favourable environment for SME developmnt, enhancing their competitiveness and innovative capacity leading to higher income and more jobs, resulting in more inclusive and sustainable economic growth. The strategy will: 1) Further improve legislative, institutional framework and operational environment for SMEs, 2) Improve access to finance, 3) Develop and promote SME skills and entrepreneurial culture, 4) Promote SME exports and internationalization, 5) Facilitate SME innovation and R&D.
SME Development Strategy of Georgia 2021-2025	Government of Georgia	To promote further development of small and medium entrepreneurship and restore the positive trends that existed before the pandemic. This strategy includes two new strategic directions: (i) promoting women entrepreneurship and (ii) promoting green economic development. The target indicators for 2025 (2019 base year) include 1) Increasing added value of SMEs by 20%. 2) Increasing SME employees by 10%. 3) Increasing SME productivity by 20%.
Agriculture and Rural Development Strategy of Georgia 2021-2027 and its Action Plan 2021-2023	Rural Development Agency	Based on sustainable development principles, the strategy will diversify/develop economic opportunities in rural areas, improve social conditions and the quality of life. Strategy goals are to build 1) Competitive agricultural and non-agriculture sectors. 2) Sustainable use of natural resources, retain the ecosystem, and adapt to climate change. 3) Effective systems for food/feed safety, veterinary and plant protection.

Source: ADB Asia SME Monitor 2022 database. Data from the following sources:

Legislative Herald of Georgia; Ministry of Economy and and Sustainable Development (MESD); Ministry of Environmental Protection and Agriculture (MEPA); Georgian Stock Exchange; Enterprise Georgia; National Bank of Georgia; Ministry of Finance of Georgia; Service for Accounting, Reporting and Auditing Supervision (SARAS); Revenue Service of Georgia.

Table 4.7a: COVID-19 Emergency Measures

Name	Fund Size (GEL and EUR)	Outline
Cofinancing Mechanism to Support Small and Family Hotel Industry (Government Resolution No.177 of 2020)*	61,614,807	Cofinancing loan interest payments of small and family hotels (must be small and medium-sized enterprises [SMEs]).
Mechanism of Subsidising Bank Guarantees Presented by Enterprises for Operating in the Scopes of Co-operating with International Air Transport Association (IATA) and Activities of General Sales Agent (GSA) (Government Resolution No.425 of 2020)		Subsidizes guarantee fees of enterprises for cooperating with the International Air Transport Association (IATA) and activities of general sales agents (GSA).
Cofinancing Mechanism to Support Restaurant Industry (Government Resolution No.728 of 2020)		Cofinancing loan/lease interest payments of restaurants (must be SMEs).
Cofinancing Mechanism to Support Sports Facilities and Kindergartens (Government Resolution No.50 of 2021)		Cofinancing loan interest payments of sports facilities and kindergartens (must be SMEs).
Cofinancing Mechanism to Support Event Organisers (Government Resolution No.678 of 2020)		Cofinancing loan interest payments of support event organizers (must be SMEs).
Support Mechanism for Mortgage Loans (Government Resolution No.387 of 2020)**	34,071,534	1) Cofinancing interest payments of mortgage loans of natural persons purchasing newly built/building houses/apartments. 2) Guaranteeing mortgage loans of natural persons purchasing newly built/building houses/apartments. 1 and 2 are not mutually exclusive.
Preferential Agrocredit for Financing Annual Crops (2020)	4,419,012	To finance harvesting costs of annual crops, the state fully covers 6-month interest rates.
State Program for Support of Agricultural Production (2020)	9,651,127	Funding was set at 50% for agricultural machinery, greenhouses, and the purchase/installation of irrigation systems for annual crops.
State Programme of Dairy Modernization and Market Access (DiMMA) (2020)	12,000,000 (EUR)	Envisages cofinancing for the dairy industry, the start of new activities, as well as the expansion/modernization/re-equipment. Veterinary and artificial insemination is country-wide, With others prioritizing the regions of Imereti, Samegrelo-Zemo Svaneti, Samtskhe-Javakheti, Racha-Lechkhumi and QvemoSvaneti, Kakheti, Qvemo kartli.
State Program for Incentives for Agricultural Land Owners (2020)	33,306,118	The goal is to facilitate primary production of agricultural products for owners of agricultural land registered with the LEPL National Agency of Public Registry. The subsidy is determined by calculating 200 points per hectare (ha), for land between 0.25 ha to 10 ha. Points can be used in agricultural stores and/or plowing.
Credit guarantee scheme	330,000,000	On 24 June 2020, GEL330 million was allocated for a credit guarantee scheme to help businesses cope with the pandemic.
Forex operations***	3,524,208,689	National Bank of Georgia sold $916 million in 2020 and $243 million in 2021 on the foreign exchange market to prevent a disorderly depreciation.
Asian Development Bank (various programs)	1,679,001,132	Financing and cofinancing programs, supporting Georgia in fighting against the pandemic, including guarantees and loans under ADB's Trade Finance Program; Regional Support to Address the Outbreak of COVID-19 and Potential Outbreaks of Other Communicable Diseases; COVID-19 Pandemic Response Option (CPRO) under ADB's Countercyclical Support Facility, among others.
Grand Total	GEL 5,676,272,419 EUR 12,000,000	

* The fund size (amounts) covers GEL51,614,807 for 2020 and GEL10,000,000 for 2021.
**The fund size (amounts) covers GEL10,964,559 for 2020 and GEL23,106,975 for 2021.
*** No special name of the program.

Source: ADB Asia SME Monitor 2022 database. Data from the following: Ministry of Economy and Sustainable Development (MESD); Ministry of Environmental Protection and Agriculture (MEPA); ADB COVID-19 Policy Database.

Country Review
Kazakhstan

Overview

Due to the coronavirus disease (COVID-19) pandemic, Kazakhstan's economy contracted by 2.5% in 2020. Micro, small, and medium-sized enterprises (MSMEs) were hardest hit from government mobility restrictions. However, the economy quickly recovered, growing by 4.1% in 2021, backed by a series of government assistance programs which in part benefited MSMEs.[168] Then came the Russian invasion of Ukraine in early 2022, deepening global economic uncertainty, particularly across the European Union (EU) and Central and West Asia. Prices rose rapidly for most commodities, including metals, grains, and energy. Inflationary pressures intensified beyond those due to stimulus packages. Kazakhstan was not immune. The Russian invasion of Ukraine threatens MSME operations as high inflation increases operating costs.

In Kazakhstan, nearly all (99.9%) registered firms are MSMEs. They operate nationwide, with many in services, including distributive trade or low-tech industries, and typically focus on domestic markets. Most have yet to tap global marketplaces or join global value chains. MSMEs do not contribute much to creating quality jobs—over the past decade, they absorbed less than 40% of the total workforce. In 2021, they contributed 33.5% of gross value added (GVA), which is also relatively small. Nonetheless, it has been growing gradually, especially in the capital Astana and Almaty. While MSMEs have generally remained low-tech, the pandemic likely accelerated digitalization. The government is also promoting MSME participation in e-commerce. Both government and private sector associations such as chambers of commerce offer a wide range of business development support, including training and educational programs.

Bank credit to MSMEs remains small, accounting for 4.6% of gross domestic product (GDP) and 20.0% of total bank lending in 2021. Limited access to formal financial services remains a major barrier to MSME development. Government financial assistance during the pandemic helped MSME credit grow. The government's Damu Entrepreneurship Development Fund JSC (DAMU) has supported MSME development since 1997. It offers interest subsidies, credit guarantees, and concessional loans to MSMEs. The National Fund, a refinancing scheme started in 2014, also supports MSME financing. Nonbank finance is provided by microfinance institutions and credit unions, yet it remains small as well. While microfinance loans have been increasing, their nonperforming loans have also been rising beyond pre-pandemic levels. The pandemic underscored the importance of digital finance to MSMEs, with the central bank responding by promoting digitalization across financial system. Internet and mobile banking is growing in popularity. As an alternative finance option, the Kazakhstan Stock Exchange created the Alternative Board dedicated for MSMEs in 2017. Since its establishment, this new board has steadily expanded with 89 listed companies as of end-2021. MSMEs can also issue corporate bonds under the new board.

[168] ADB. 2022. *Key Indicators for Asia and the Pacific 2022*. Manila; Ministry of National Economy of the Republic of Kazakhstan. 2021. MNE summed up the results of socio-economic development of Kazakhstan for 7 months of 2021. News release. 11 August. https://www.gov.kz/memleket/entities/economy/press/news/details/240491?lang=en.

Kazakhstan's long-term National Development Plan (through 2025) established 10 national priorities, including the formation of a diversified and innovative economy by developing entrepreneurship and increasing the competitiveness of domestic firms. The National Project on Entrepreneurship Development for 2021–2025 promotes entrepreneurs and MSMEs to create more jobs, diversify the economy, and boost competition. MSMEs should hold a 35% share of GDP, according to project targets (as mentioned, MSME GVA reached 33.5% of GDP in 2021). While there is no national financial inclusion policy covering financial access for all, including MSMEs, DAMU in effect is applying financial inclusion strategies.

In response to the pandemic's impact, the government set out a Comprehensive Plan on Recovery of Economic Growth until 2021, identifying 10 directions needed for recovery and 172 systemic and sector measures to boost business activities (May 2020). The central bank and Agency for Regulation and Development of Financial Markets (ARDFM) created a Program of Concessional Lending to businesses, including MSMEs, during the pandemic. In response to the Russian invasion of Ukraine, the government established an anti-crisis command center in March 2022 to mitigate the impact of anti-Russian sanctions on Kazakhstan's economy.

1. Impact of the Global Economy on MSMEs

COVID-19 Impact

On 26 January 2020, sanitary and epidemiological control at checkpoints on the border of Kazakhstan was strengthened, and people arriving from the People's Republic of China (PRC) began being medically monitored. The next day, an Interdepartmental Commission was created for the prevention of the spread of COVID-19, coordinated by the Deputy Prime Minister, to manage measures to prevent the emergence and spread of infections. Kazakhstan's first case was detected 13 March 2020. The government called a state of emergency between 16 March and 15 April 2020, extended until 11 May, and applied strict containment measures—including restrictions on entry and exit to and from the country, prohibition against large gatherings, and closing a wide range of nonfood establishments.

From 11 May to 1 June 2020, the Interdepartmental Commission decided to ease quarantines selectively. However, due to the increase in infections, strict isolation measures were introduced between 5 July and 17 August 2020, with 80% of employees told to work remotely, public transport suspended, and other restrictions on mass gatherings. A day of national mourning for those who died from COVID-19 was declared on 13 July 2020. On 26 August 2020, Kazakhstan and the Russian Federation signed an agreement on the supply of the latter's "Sputnik V" vaccine. In September 2020, the Research Institute for Biological Safety Problems of the Ministry of Education and Science began clinical trials of the national vaccine "QazVac."

In June 2020, Ernst&Young consulting conducted a survey of 285 MSMEs. It found that microbusinesses with 10 or fewer employees were hurt most. Even though the government provided many support measures, around 15% of survey respondents reported they were unable to use state support as they were outside their field of activities, with more than half (51%) of respondents noted various barriers encountered in obtaining assistance—such as a lack of information, bureaucracy, negligence, and a lack of proper communication by support operators. The survey results showed that, among the measures provided, most MSMEs took advantage of (i) tax deferment, (ii) taxes exemptions from payroll contributions, and (iii) suspending loan repayments to financial institutions due to liquidity problems.

Survey respondents listed what they needed in terms of assistance: (i) interest-free loans and allocating financial subsidies directly; (ii) reimbursement of rent and utility payments as direct financial support; (iii) public guarantees for loans; (iv) loan restructuring by lowering interest rates or extending maturities; (v) additional deferrals of loan repayments to expand access to liquidity; (vi) simplifying import and export procedures; (vii) cancelling forfeits, penalty interest, and extending deadlines for completing government contracts; (viii) support for inclusion in the supply chains of large international and domestic companies to increase demand for goods and services; (ix) discounting prices or providing free personal protective equipment; (x) workplace disinfection services; (xi) subsidized purchases of equipment and services needed for employees to work remotely; (xii) training and advice on accessing financial assistance; (xiii) support to revise credit conditions; (xiv) creating a support hotline to receive complaints or appeals; (xv) support for shifting to digital platforms; and (xvi) obtaining expert support on a wide range nonfinancial support measures. The study reflected the need for continuously monitoring MSMEs on required policy support, especially on expanding financial and nonfinancial assistance using online instruments, as well as introducing flexible regional support programs to MSMEs based on socioeconomic factors.[169]

A KPMG survey conducted in July 2020 elicited 60 responses from both MSMEs and large firms, banks, development institutions, and business associations. The study found several key issues of concern: (i) the lack of a central information portal for government support and limited staff to implement government programs (one operator for each state program) as the main barrier to participating in government support programs; (ii) the need to expand industry criteria and "reengineer" business support programs; and (iii) a central platform for a constructive, transparent dialogue among government, business, and experts.

Survey respondents saw the quality of government support measures as below average (4.7 on a 10-point scale (Figure 5.1). KPMG used sufficiency, effectiveness, and timeliness when estimating satisfaction of government support measures. The "sufficiency" criterion was lowest, with respondents highlighting various systemic barriers and poor coverage by industry and type of activity. Also, 42% of the respondents mentioned the establishment of a "one-stop window," enhancing communication, and consolidating government programs as a way to improve the quality of state support.

Figure 5.1: Assessment of Government COVID-19 Support Measures

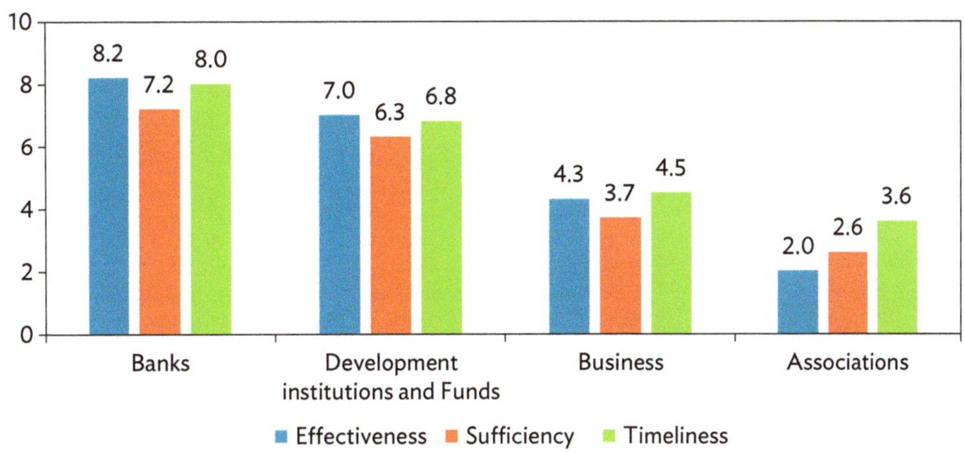

COVID-19 = coronavirus disease.

Source: ADB Asia SME Monitor 2022 database. Data from KPMG study survey "COVID-19 pandemic: are state business support measures effective in Kazakhstan?"

169 https://assets.ey.com/content/dam/ey-sites/ey-com/ru_kz/topics/advisory/ey-sme-resultst-and-recommendations.pdf

The average rating differed by category. Banks highly rated the quality of government support measures. As main barriers, banks said the small number of good borrowers in the credit market and the poor quality of financial information. In contrast, respondents from business mostly spoke negatively about working with second-tier banks.

Among shortcomings, entrepreneurs noted limited financing, high requirements for loan collateral, and little desire to lend to certain types of companies. Among respondents from development institutions, opinions were divided. Some highly appreciated the quality of existing support mechanisms, while others were more critical, emphasizing the need for improvement. Respondents from businesses wanted more government support measures—due to the limitation by type, size, amount of funding available, and the short period for receiving benefits. Respondents from business associations saw several problems with the quality of government support mechanisms: problems in legislation, the reluctance of banks to lend to investment projects, the delay in support measures given the urgency of containing COVID-19, administrative and bureaucratic barriers, the lack of thought out government programs, and the need for a central coordinator for implementation.[170]

"Fusion Lab" was hired by Visa to conduct a survey of 350 MSMEs from seven cities, including capital Astana, in July–August 2020. About 82% cited the damage from COVID-19 on their business, 69% highlighted loss of revenue, with 23% suspending their business. More than 50% of MSME respondents placed at least some of their employees on unpaid leave or cut wages. A majority had reduced orders/sales due to decreased consumption or customer business, late or interrupted deliveries, store closures, and restrictions on employee mobility. Digitalization accelerated, with 42% of respondents reporting better opportunities for sales, with 18% exclusively selling their products online. By payment format, 67% provided customers the opportunity to pay electronically, with 8% accepting only noncash payments.[171]

In general, the survey results dealt with government support measures, but did not fully cover employment and wages.

Impact of the Russian Invasion of Ukraine

The first quarter of 2022 found macroeconomic conditions worsening due to a "tragic January" in Kazakhstan and the Russian invasion of Ukraine. The *tenge* depreciated against the US dollar from KZT434/USD1 to KZT497.2/USD1 between December 2021 and March 2022, while inflation rose from 8.4% to 12.0%. According to the Growth at Risk quarterly report of the ARDFM,[172] higher food prices were primarily behind the rise in inflation.

On 2 March 2022, the government launched an anti-crisis command center to mitigate the possible impact of anti-Russian sanctions on Kazakhstan, including executive agencies from economic blocs, representatives of business communities and industry experts.

Kazakhstan is a member of the Eurasian Economic Union (EAEU), which includes Russia. Around 42% of Kazakhstan's imports come from Russia. Thus, the sanctions worsened the macroeconomic situation, especially on financial stability. During January–June 2022, the *tenge* lost almost 50% of its *ruble* value—from KZT5.82 to KZT8.75/RUB—which increased costs of imports and added inflationary pressure. Most MSMEs suffered and sought alternative imports from other countries such as the PRC or Türkiye.

[170] https://assets.kpmg/content/dam/kpmg/kz/pdf/2020/07/covid-pandemic-report.pdf
[171] https://kapital.kz/business/89697/kak-chuvstvuyet-sebya-mikro-malyy-i-sredniy-biznes-v-kazakhstane.html
[172] https://www.gov.kz/memleket/entities/ardfm/documents/details/304535?lang=ru

On 24 February 2022, the National Bank of Kazakhstan (NBK), the central bank, increased its base rate from 10.25% to 13.5% to reduce pressure on currency and inflation rates.[173] The NBK increased marginal rates on household *tenge* deposits, as recommended by the Kazakhstan Deposit Guarantee Fund. On 25 April and 25 July 2022, NBK again increased its base rate to 14.0% and 14.5%, the annual inflation rate continued to rise.

With the increased uncertainty in foreign markets—and to prevent further impact of the increased volatility of the *ruble*—the NBK decided to conduct Kazakhstan tenge to US dollar trading on the Frankfurt auction. As of 25 February 2022, gross external reserves were $87.7 billion, including assets of the National Fund ($54 billion) and the gold and currency reserves ($33.7 billion). By 30 April, reserves had dropped by $1.7 billion (assets of the National Fund fell by $1.5 billion with gold and currency reserves down by $0.2 billion).[174] Transfers from the National Fund grew from KZT264 billion to KZT577.5 billion (up 118.8%) between February and June 2022.

On 6 April 2022, the Office of Foreign Assets Control of the United States Department of the Treasury added three Russian banks—Sberbank, Alfa-Bank, VneshTorgBank (VTB)—and their branches in Kazakhstan to the list of banks banned from using SWIFT.

The sanctions on Alfa-Bank suspended transfers in US dollars and Euros for individuals and legal entities. Visa and MasterCard credit cards outside of their own network of ATMs and POS terminals were suspended. The bank temporarily placed limits on cash withdrawals and transfers, and stopped loan approvals. Card payments at POS terminals for cards of other banks were also suspended.[175]

To attract new *tenge* liquidity, Alfa-Bank Kazakhstan sold a portion of its loan portfolio to second-tier banks. An overhaul of the shareholder structure could lead to the withdrawal of Alfa-Bank Kazakhstan from the sanctions list.[176] On 3 May 2022, the ARDFM approved the application of Bank Center Credit (BCC) to purchase 100% shares of Alfa-Bank Kazakhstan. On 23 May 2022, BCC completed the purchase and reissued its license as "Eco Center Bank", a subsidiary of BCC.

SberBank Kazakhstan negotiated with "Baiterek" National Managing Holdings to sell 100% of its shares, whereas VTB announced plans to transform its subsidiary to retain the local bank instead of having to sell.

Most MSMEs rushed to transfer their bank accounts with the sanctioned banks to second-tier banks.

Another major impact involved the Caspian Pipeline Consortium (CPC). CPC is the largest international oil transportation project with the Russian Federation, Kazakhstan, and leading oil companies building a 1,500-kilometer.[177] The pipeline moves oil from large fields in Western Kazakhstan, as well as from Russian Federation producers to a port near Novorossiysk. The share of Kazakhstan shippers accounts for around 80% of the volume. Present capacity of the pipeline is 67 million tons of oil per year. It was planned to increase volume up to 83 million tons of oil annually. expected changes will definitely lower export income. Much of Kazakhstan's economic development and macroeconomy depends on oil prices and export volume. Thus, the Russian invasion of Ukraine and the lack a CPC alternative for oil transportation will weaken the national economy. MSMEs will likely

[173] Official Information Source of the Prime Minister of the Republic of Kazakhstan. 2022. To ensure stability and protection of financial market, Government, together with National Bank of Kazakhstan, is implementing a program to protect tenge deposits. News release. 1 March. https://primeminister.kz/en/news/dlya-obespecheniya-stabilnosti-i-zashchity-finrynka-pravitelstvo-sovmestno-s-nacbankom-rk-realizuet-programmu-zashchity-tengovyh-vkladov-1246.

[174] National Bank of Kazakhstan. International Reserves and Assets of the National Oil Fund of Republic of Kazakhstan. https://nationalbank.kz/en/international-reserve-and-asset/mezhdunarodnye-rezervy-i-aktivy-nacionalnogo-fonda-rk (accessed 31 August 2022).

[175] https://www.gov.kz/memleket/entities/ardfm/press/news/details/353345?lang=ru

[176] https://www.gov.kz/memleket/entities/ardfm/press/news/details/355815?lang=ru

[177] Caspian Pipeline Consortium. General Information. https://www.cpc.ru/en/about/pages/general.aspx.

suffer from possible budget deficits, a rise in import costs, reduced amounts of state support, access to finance, and other macroeconomic factors.

There is also a growing trend to relocate some companies from the Russian Federation and Belarus to Kazakhstan. This may be to avoid sanctions and re-export goods to the Russian Federation and Belarus. There is also a concern that countries and international organizations that imposed sanctions against the Russian Federation and Belarus may expand them to include Kazakhstan.

One positive aspect of relocating companies is the potential inflow of technology and human resources. According to sources at the Ministry of Digital Development, Innovation, and Aerospace, its subsidiary—International IT-Technopark "Astana Hub"—is helping 468 information technology (IT) companies relocate from neighboring countries. However, they did not provide details.[178]

In March 2022, the Ministry of Trade and Integration launched a website (www.sanction2022.kz) to collect and regularly update a list of sanctions and restrictions—using Foreign Economic Activity Commodity Nomenclature for products prohibited for export and import to the Russian Federation and Belarus. As the government wants to avoid secondary sanctions and mitigate the impact of existing sanctions, it is against re-exports so as not to be fined by its Western partners.

Nevertheless, Kazakhstan's EAEU partners are also preparing joint anti-crisis measures coordinated by the Council of Eurasian Economic Commission (EEC). The EEC expanded the list of goods qualifying for equal access for public procurement. The EEC also introduced changes to the Rules for Registration and Expertise of Medicinal Products for Medical Use to support domestic pharmaceutical manufacturers. Three types of procedures were introduced for simplified and accelerated access to highly effective drugs in the EAEU market, as well as drugs that can meet the increased needs of healthcare systems. On Kazakhstan's initiative, the EEC Board suspended anti-dumping measures against European herbicides until 30 September 2022 and against graphite electrodes until 1 October 2022. These were aimed to support Kazakh consumers in agro-industries and metallurgical enterprises. In addition, the duty-free limit for importing goods for individuals was increased to €1,000 for goods transported by post. And from 27 March 2022, "conditional" registration of medicines was allowed throughout the EAEU—"conditional" meaning it applies to drugs whose benefits far outweigh any possible risks and are intended for the treatment, prevention, or diagnosis of disabling or life-threatening diseases. The measure should make it possible to bring innovative medicines to markets and patients faster.[179] However, the Russian Federation continues to play a dominant role in decision-making between EAEU members on all types of regulations.

To sum up, there are numerous consequences of anti-Russian sanctions on the Kazakhstan economy. However, the main impacts include (i) logistical barriers on raw material costs and supply chains, (ii) the drop in trade between Kazakhstan and Ukraine, (iii) contract violations due to the failure to meet transportation deadlines, (iv) the search for new suppliers due to import restrictions on some goods from the Russian Federation, (v) accelerating inflation, (vi) the drop in exports from local businesses—including MSMEs—due to a lack of components and increased transportation costs, and (vii) obsolete infrastructure of the along alternative transportation routes.

[178] https://kapital.kz/tehnology/104121/astana-hub-konsul-tiruyet-468-zarubezhnykh-kompaniy-po-relokatsii-v-rk.html
[179] https://atameken.kz/ru/news/46975-prinyaty-klyuchevye-resheniya-kasayushiesya-predprinimatel-skoj-deyatel-nosti

2. MSME Development

- Almost all (99.9%) registered firms actively operating are MSMEs. More than half are engaged in services like distributive trade, followed by agriculture. They are spread nationwide, with about 10% operating in the capital.
- MSMEs, however, account for just a relatively small share of the labor force (39.3% of the workforce in 2021). The share has been gradually increasing in the capital, Astana.
- MSME contribution to gross value added is also relatively small (33.5% in 2021), although it has been gradually increasing. Much comes from Astana and Almaty.
- Most MSME businesses focus on domestic markets. They are not well connected with global markets or global value chains.
- MSMEs are in an early stage of technological development. But the pandemic accelerated MSME digitalization, with the government supporting participation in e-commerce.
- The international technopark Astana Hub promotes startups and provides a wide range of business and educational programs. The National Chamber of Entrepreneurs supports MSMEs and local entrepreneurs through its small and medium business development committee.

Scale of MSMEs

MSMEs are defined by annual average income and number of employees in accordance with the Entrepreneurial Code of 2015 (Table 5.1). A microenterprise is a legal entity—including individual entrepreneurs and farms—with fewer than 15 employees and/or income of less than 30,000 times the Monthly Calculation Index index (MCI), which was KZT3,063 as of 1 January 2022, and KZT3,180 as of 1 April.[180] A small enterprise is a legal entity with fewer than 100 employees and/or income of less than 300,000 times the MCI. A medium-sized enterprise is a legal entity with more than 100 but fewer than 250 employees, and/or income more than 300,000 times but less than 3,000,000 times the MCI. For national statistics, only the criterion of the annual average number of employees is used, and microenterprises are included in the category of small enterprises in accordance with the Bureau of National Statistics (dated 5 February 2015 Order No.27).

There are two types of statistics for the number of MSMEs: registered and operating enterprises. In 2021, there were 1.7 million registered MSMEs, of which 1.4 million were operating, or 84.5% of those registered (Figure 5.2 and Table 5.2). The share of operating MSMEs to those registered has increased consistently since 2017 (74.4%).

Over the past 10 years, there has been generally more moderate growth in the number of registered MSMEs (5.2% in 2021). It declined sharply in 2015 (by 10.5%) due to new tax and civil codes which simplified liquidation proceedings of legal entities. For instance, before 2015, this procedure might take about 6 months, whereas currently entrepreneurs may complete liquidation proceedings in less than 20 days (assuming no legal violations). Despite these changes, the share of MSMEs to total enterprises remained almost constant (99.9% in 2021).

Operating MSMEs increased more steadily than registered MSMEs during 2017 (3.6%) and 2021 (5.5%)—likely due to digitalizing tax report processes.

[180] MCI is established by the Law on the Republican Budget (No.77-VII as of 2 December 2021, approved triennially) and effective as of 1 January of the corresponding calendar year; see https://adilet.zan.kz/rus/docs/Z2100000077.

Figure 5.2: Number of MSMEs

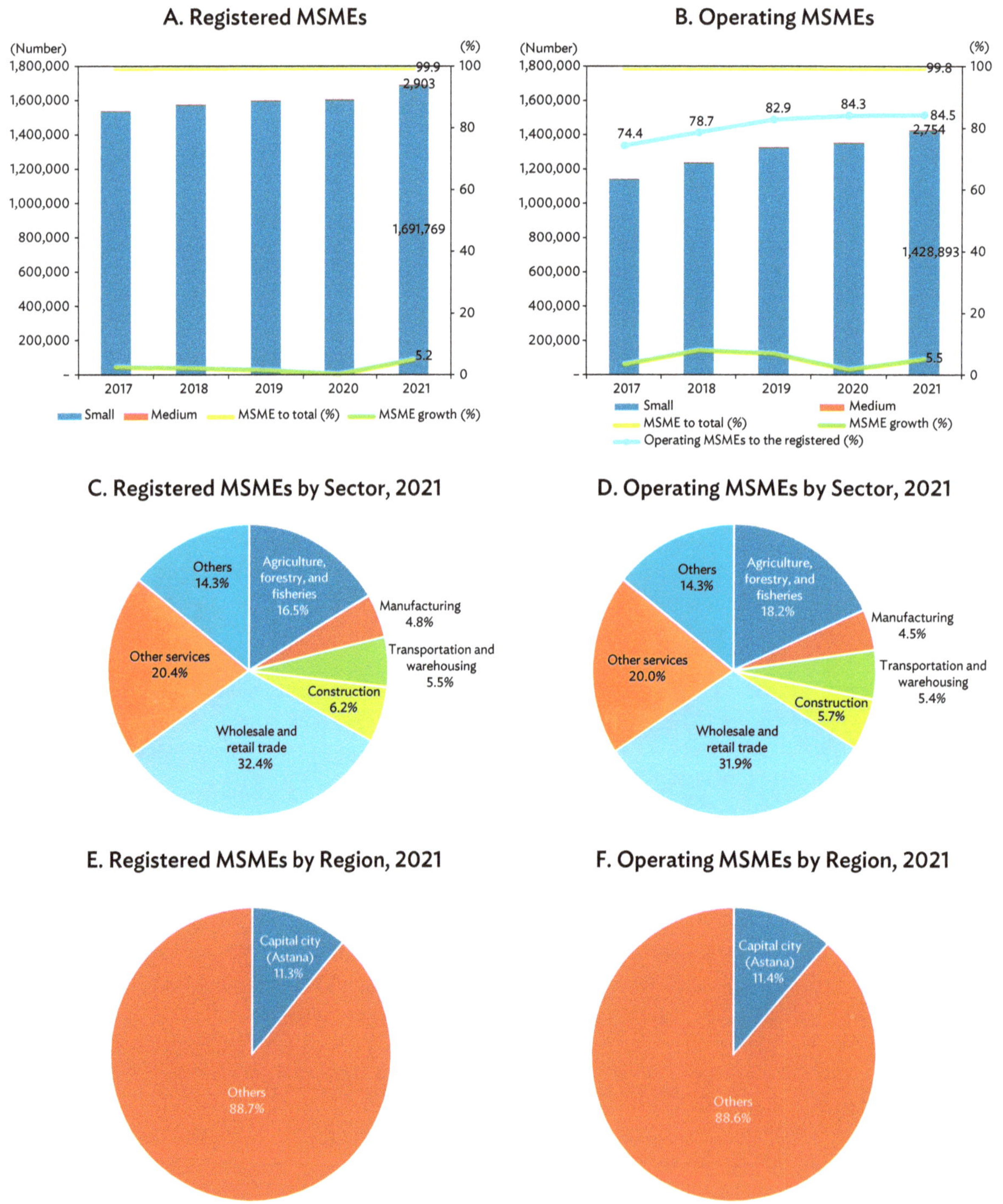

MSME = micro, small, and medium-sized enterprise.

Source: ADB Asia SME Monitor 2022 database. Data from Bureau of National Statistics.

For registered MSMEs, one-third (32.4%) were engaged in wholesale and retail trade in 2021, followed by other services (20.4%) and agriculture/forestry/fisheries (16.5%). The structure was similar for operating MSMEs (31.9% for trade, 20.0% for other services, and 18.2% for agriculture/forestry/fisheries).

Geographically, a small fraction of MSMEs were located in the capital city Astana (11.3% of registered and 11.4% of operating MSMEs), while the majority (88.7% of registered and 88.6% of operating) were based in other provinces.

Business registration was simplified beginning 26 July 2022, when the E-gov.kz portal opened for remote registration). This may boost the future number of registered MSMEs.

Employment

MSMEs employed 3.5 million people in 2021, accounting for 39.3% of the total workforce, a relatively small share of the labor force (Figure 5.3 and Table 5.2). This has been almost unchanged over the decade, suggesting that MSMEs have yet to provide adequate employment. Despite the growing number of MSMEs, the number of employees has been 4.1% growth in 2019 to 0.7% growth in 2020, and a 0.3% contraction in 2021. Due to the pandemic impact, it suggests that MSMEs likely laid off workers to manage operating and administration costs.

In 2021, more than a quarter (28.5%) MSMEs employees worked in wholesale and retail trade, followed by other services (26.3%) and agriculture/forestry/fisheries (13.0%). While similar in structure to the number of MSMEs, those in manufacturing held a relatively higher share (10.0% in 2021). Geographically, the share of those working in the capital Astana reached 12.0% in 2021, the share increasing gradually since 2010 (5.8%) or after the 2008–2009 global financial crisis.

In 2021, the share of female employees to total employees remained low at 16.0%, with a similar ratio over the decade. Females accounted for 63.9% of working aged females, lower than the ratio of male workers (75.4%). The unemployment rate for women (5.5% in 2021) remains higher than for men (4.2%). There is no relevant data for MSMEs, but female labor participation is likely limited to MSMEs given their small share in labor absorption.

The government acknowledges the harsh employment environment for MSMEs. The MSME Development Concept for 2030 endorsed in April 2022 says that entrepreneurship is often forced, creating poor quality jobs. It also says that changes in labor code practices shifting the tax burden to employers and easing the tax processes for entrepreneurs led to an artificial rise in the number of entrepreneurs. This implies that statistically increasing the number of MSMEs is not correlated to their level of job creation. How MSMEs can generate quality jobs would thus be a critical area for policy support.

Figure 5.3: Employment by MSMEs

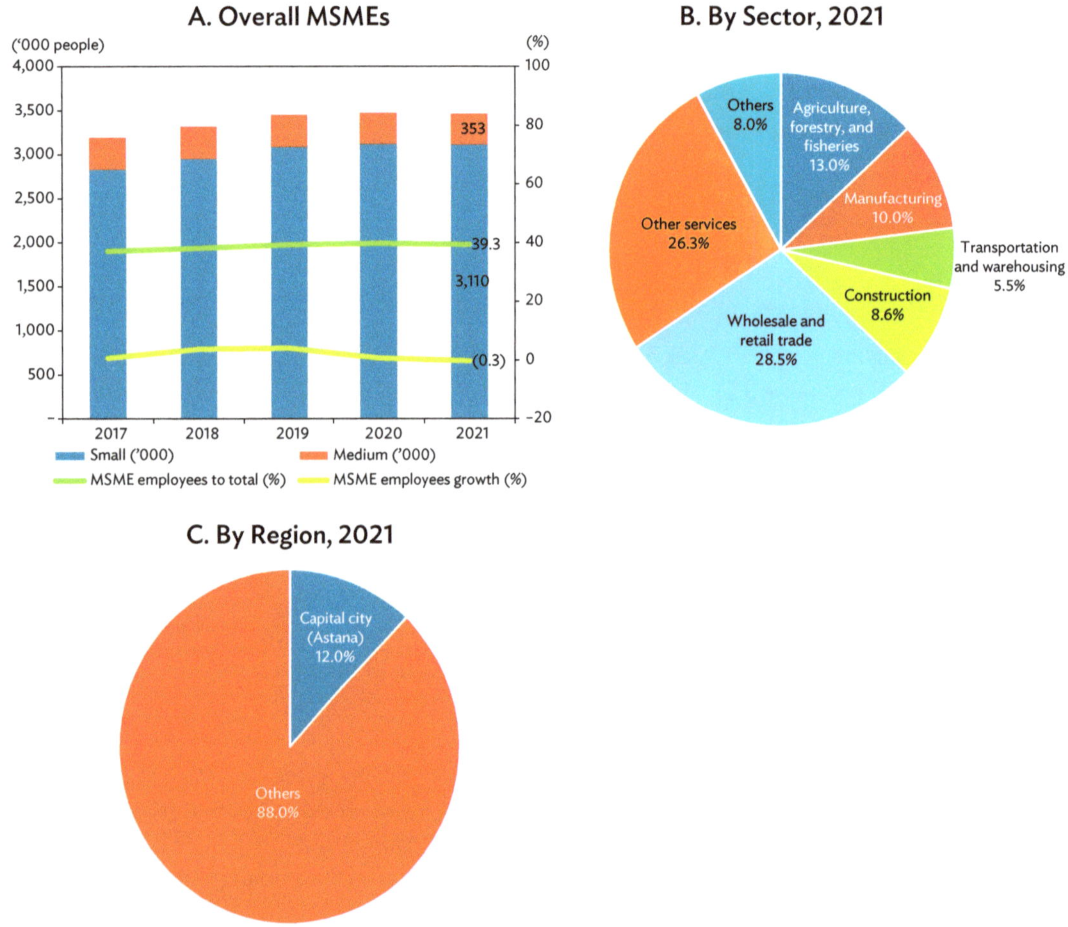

MSME = micro, small, and medium-sized enterprise.

Source: ADB Asia SME Monitor 2022 database. Data from Bureau of National Statistics.

Business Productivity

With no data on MSME contributions to GDP available, gross value added (GVA) is used to measure MSME productivity. GVA is calculated as the difference between output and intermediate consumption expenditures. The GVA for MSMEs is the sum of MSMEs, individual entrepreneurs, and farms. It amounted to KZT28.1 trillion in 2021, a 21.2% increase from 2020 (KZT23.2 trillion) (Figure 5.4 and Table 5.2). Growth sharply decelerated by 5.3% in 2020 from 25.4% in 2019, seriously affected by the pandemic and mobility restrictions, and then increased in 2021. MSME productivity remains small. Their contribution to total GVA was 33.5% in 2021, though it has been growing gradually since 2016 (26.8%).

There is no available data on the GVA of MSMEs classified by sector, but by region, the largest and most stable contribution was in Astana and Almaty (Figure 4B). In Astana, MSME GVA accounted for 59.0% of the region's GVA in 2021. In Almaty, it was 47.5%. The overall geographical distribution of MSME GVA is unavailable.

Labor productivity has fluctuated over the decade with sharp declines in 2015 (–12.6%) and 2021 (–20.4%) associated with a sharp drop in oil prices in 2015 and the impact of the pandemic in 2021. Labor productivity is calculated as the ratio of the volume of manufactured products, work performed, and services rendered to the number of employees. MSME labor productivity was KZT5.3 million in 2021.

The government approved a comprehensive action plan to counter the informal economy for 2021–2023 and to reduce the informal sector's share of GDP to 15% by 2025. Although official statistics do not provide the share of MSMEs in the informal economy, the MSME Development Concept until 2030 indicates high MSME participation in the informal economy. As it is not reflected in the statistics, MSME contribution to economic development is likely underestimated.

Figure 5.4: MSME Contribution to Gross Value Added

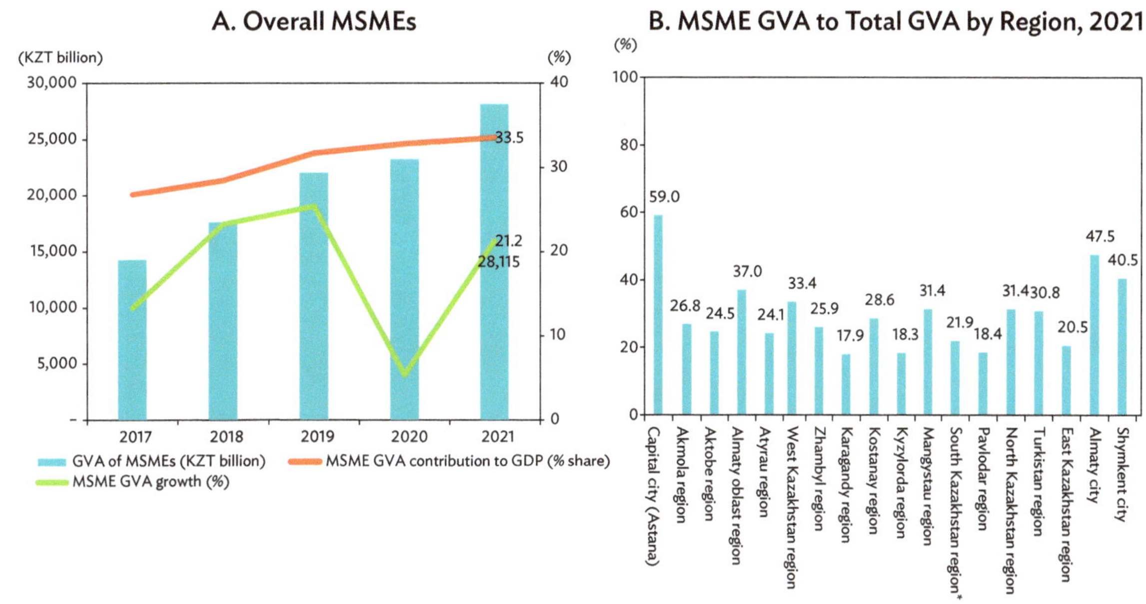

GDP = gross domestic product; GVA = gross value added; MSME = micro, small, and medium-sized enterprise.

* Data in 2021 for Figure 4B.

Source: ADB Asia SME Monitor 2022 database. Data from Bureau of National Statistics.

Market Access

Most MSMEs focus on domestic markets. They have yet to tap global markets and global value chains. The government is considering policy measures to support MSME exporters through Baiterek and its subsidiaries—DAMU, the Development Bank of Kazakhstan (DBK), and Kazakh Export. In 2021, KZT220 billion was allocated for financing export-oriented projects from previously allocated funds through the DBK and DAMU. KZT100 billion of this was allocated for interbank financing to MSME exporters through DAMU, which, through second-tier banks, allocated KZT34.3 billion to support 82 MSME exporters in 2020. In 2021, KZT30.7 billion went to support 61 MSME exporters.[181] Kazakh Export plays a key role in assisting non-commodity exports. It has supported 301 export-oriented firms in 21 sectors with the largest share going to food processing (148 firms).

There are no data on MSME exports and imports. The country's exports—largely mineral resources—began to decrease in 2019 (–5.0%) and further fell due to the pandemic in 2020 (–18.1%). However, it recovered sharply in 2021 to $60.3 billion, a 26.9% increase from 2020 (Figure 5.5 and Table 5.2). In 2020, exports of mineral resources were 66% of the total, followed by metals and components (16%). imports were also hurt by the pandemic in 2020 ($38.9 billion, or –2.0%) but recovered in 2021 ($41.2 billion, up 5.8%). In 2020, almost half of imports (46.5%) was for machinery, equipment, vehicles, instruments, and apparatus.

[181] https://baiterek.gov.kz/ru/o-kholdinge/otchetnost-kholdinga/?SECTION_ID=212

International trade has largely remained unchanged in Kazakhstan as its economy has relied on oil and gas exports for the 3 decades since independence. This why MSME participation in export markets is likely limited. But there is potential in the parts and components industry and agricultural products for MSMEs as material/product suppliers in global value chains. Business cluster development and MSME participation in global value chains are need critical policy support to boost MSME exports.

Figure 5.5: Exports and Imports

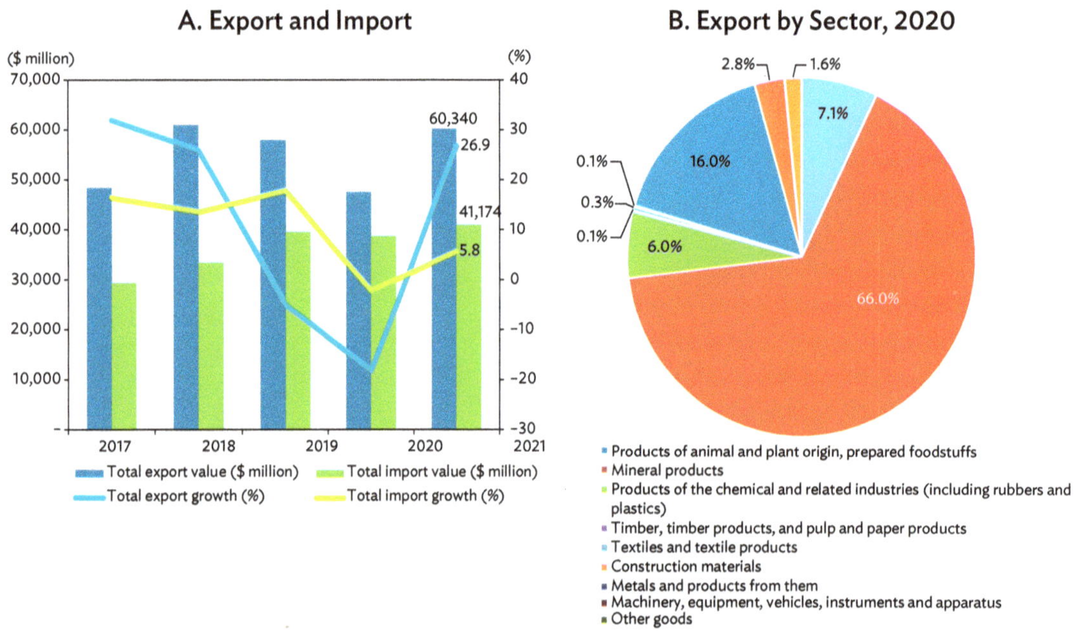

Source: ADB Asia SME Monitor 2022 database. Data from Bureau of National Statistics.

Technology and Innovation

The pandemic accelerated the ongoing trend to digitalize business—including MSMEs—and adopt new technologies. High demand for fast, quality services and products are leading MSMEs to boost their competitiveness. Quasi-public technoparks and development institutions regularly organize a wide range of "acceleration" and "incubation" programs. In April 2022, the international IT-technopark Astana Hub and Google for Startups launched a joint Silkway Accelerator Program for Central Asian startups to match products with markets. Fifteen startups were selected for the first group. They include, for example, a popular marketplace—Naimi.kz—for finding self-employed personal service professionals for home and office .

Kazakhstan is at an early stage of MSME technology development as it strives to create "unicorns." Most MSMEs are in low-technology industries like distributive trade. To help MSMEs access technology, QazIndustry JSC subsidizes up to 40% of the costs for purchasing IT products by MSMEs. If IT solutions are successful, the subsidy will cover up to 50% of the cost. However, as of 27 June 2022, it supported just 10 MSMEs nationwide.

The government offers several types of assistance to technology-based startups, centered on digitalization. "Smart Parking" is an example MSME technology, in which car parking spaces are managed using license plate recognition technology (Box 5.1).

Box 5.1: Smart Parking

The Smart Parking Technologies project is a system for managing parking spaces using license plate recognition technology. The idea came up when founder Amirkhan Omarov worked at Mercury Properties, which focused on commercial real estate—shopping centers, business centers, hotels, and warehouses. He noticed that efficiently organizing and automating parking was too costly, and there were too few parking experts worldwide. He tried setting up "co-working spaces" using "SmArt.Point" at the Almaty Towers Business Center; testing for the first time a smart parking system based on license number recognition technology.

Technology

A smart parking system applies state-of-the-art technology using car number recognition algorithms with 99% accuracy. This eliminates paper or plastic tickets, and the barrier is controlled by a camera that records entry and exit. The software integrates payment systems within the application (app). For example, customers can pay for parking through Kaspi bank, Qiwi, Halyk Homebank, Sberbank, and Rakhmet apps, SMS messages, and shopping center apps. The software can easily integrate with shopping center marketing campaigns. For example, a mall visitor makes a purchase for $300 and gets 3 hours of free parking as an incentive. The software also gives the user access to direct payments. The project allows parking owners to analyze performance: occupancy by the hour and free spaces in real time. Another advantage is that the system works on almost any equipment and eliminates dependence on a specific brand or vendor, dramatically reducing equipment costs. Often, companies bear the capital cost of refurbishing parking spaces instead of the parking lot owner, offsetting costs with a share of future parking revenues. This allows owners to increase parking revenues, reduce operating costs for operators, security guards, and tickets, and significantly increase customer convenience at no cost. The technology is used sporadically in the United States (US), Australia, and the United Kingdom, but is new to Kazakhstan.

Company portfolio and clients

As of April 2022, the company had about 50 clients, including shopping centers and buildings (Esentai Mall, MFC Globus, Promenade, MEGA Silk way, Trade House Eurasia, Trade House Aimaktau, and Green Mall); business centers (Almaty Towers business center); and residential complexes (BI Family Village in Astana and the Baisal residential complex planned in Almaty). They work with all major construction companies and property owners (Mercury Properties, BI Group, and Basis-A, RAMS, among others). They also have clients in Kyiv, Ukraine's capital—the multifunctional complex InterGal City, LCD Sonyachna Brama, and the Unit City complex. It also operates at Cornish City Garage in New York, US. Each month it adds 5-10 clients. The company contacts shopping center owners and managers in Ukraine, the US, Malaysia, and United Arab Emirates. Many express interest.

Project team and financial conditions

The company employs about 35-40 people and is operationally self-sustaining. As of April 2022, revenues were $50,000–$60,000 a month, and monthly growth of 15%-20%.

Cited by Startup Accelerator Y-Combinator

The company was in the top 7% of US startup accelerator Y-Combinator and noted by other accelerators in the US and Europe—MassChallenge, WiseGuys, Pi Labs, Plug & Play.

Source: Interview with Amirkhan Omarov, project manager of Smart Parking Technologies (https://astanahub.com/article/umnaia-parkovka-amirkhan-omarov-o-proekte-smart-parking-dokhodakh-kompanii-i-vykhode-na-eksport), 7 April 2022.

The government works to promote MSME participation in e-commerce through international trade platforms like Alibaba. In April 2022, the Ministry of Trade and Integration, together with its subsidiary QazIndustry, offered "gold supplier" access for 12 months to Alibaba for 48 local trading firms and manufacturers. By end-2022, it will add 22 more companies. During 2019–2022 (24 June), around 200 companies received government support for launching e-commerce sites on Alibaba's B2B platform. According to the Ministry of Trade and Integration, total sales of those using the Alibaba platform reached $167.7 million. In June 2022, Kazakhstan opened a National Pavilion on Alibaba to promote e-commerce for more MSMEs.

The largest local e-commerce markets are Kaspi.kz, Halyk Market, Mechta.kz, and Ozon Marketplace. According to joint research of PwC Kazakhstan and the Association of Digital Kazakhstan, retail e-commerce trade increased from KZT327 million in 2019 to KZT1 trillion in 2021. The number of completed e-commerce transactions increased by 45%, to 37 million in 2021, with the average transaction value increasing 20% in 2021 (to KZT28,200) from 2020. By end-2021, the share of e-commerce in retail trade volume was 11%. Small businesses like e-commerce as an opportunity to promote sales, whereas customers find it convenient to purchase household goods and electronic devices.

Networking and Support

The Ministry of National Economy is responsible for implementing policy measures to support and develop MSMEs. There are also several interconnected agencies and companies working for MSME development—such as DAMU, JSC QazTechVentures, Kazakh Export, and its mother company Baiterek. DAMU supports MSME development through policy measures broadening access to finance, increasing cost-effectiveness, and increasing the number of MSMEs covered by its assistance. DAMU, in cooperation with the business school at Nazarbayev University, conducts free professional MSME management training wuith financial support of the Ministry of National Economy. Over the past years, DAMU worked toward providing support for women-owned businesses, including work with ADB and other international financial institutions.

QazTechVentures supports technology-based entrepreneurship with venture financing, consultancies, and business incubation tools. During 2020–2022, it helped MSMEs join the Kazakhstan Digital Accelerator program—up to 3 months with a $50,000 investment for up to a 9% share in the startup. Kazakh Export supports export growth of non-commodity goods and services in priority sectors regardless of company size. There is also QazIndustry, a national think tank that promotes exports, labor productivity, and technological development in manufacturing.

IT and digitalization are also a government priority. Since 2018, it operates the Astana Hub international technopark to promote local and international startups. It offers a wide range of business and educational programs for IT-exports, incubation, and accelerator programs as well as courses for no-code development platforms and other means of support. Astana Hub also provides exemptions from corporate income tax, value-added tax (VAT) for nonresidents, VAT for imports based on goods listed, royalty tax, individual income and social taxes for residents. From April 2019 to end-2021, members saved KZT23,4 billion on taxes. Most of the participants are from Astana (337 firms), Almaty (268), and Karaganda region (16).[182]

There is also a state-owned Innovation Park branded as a "Tech Garden" to provide venture capital for the Tech Garden Venture Fund. It supports IT-startups under the international acceleration program Startup Kazakhstan. Some private and international venture funds—like the MOST Ventures Fund—offer financial and nonfinancial support to technology-based entrepreneurs.

[182] Astana hub. About us. https://astanahub.com/en/l/h/about-us.

There is also the National Chamber of Entrepreneurs "Atameken" (NCE) representing interests of small, medium-sized, and large enterprises to the government. It is an umbrella organization for different types of small associations and unions. A special small and medium business development committee analyses and develops unified positions on MSME development issues for government negotiations. The NCE has branches in all Kazakhstan for regional entrepreneurial development. NCE has 196 accredited associations (unions) covering various industries including MSMEs. In general, there is a tendency for several entrepreneurs to join together as unions or associations to represent their common interests.

3. Access to Finance

- MSME bank credit remains small, with loans outstanding 4.6% of GDP and 20.0% of total bank lending in 2021. Newly introduced government financial assistance programs should help MSME credit growth.
- DAMU is a main operator of MSME development and distributes interest subsidies, credit guarantees, and soft loans by distributing public funds. There are refinancing schemes available for MSMEs through the National Fund.
- The microfinance institution (MFI) industry remains small. While MFI loans have increased, so too have nonperforming loans (NPLs), above pre-pandemic levels. However, credit union financing has grown sharply, coupled with a drop in NPLs.
- The COVID-19 pandemic accelerated the shift to digital finance for individuals and MSMEs. Internet and mobile banking, together with instant payment systems, are spreading widely. The central bank plans to create a national digital currency—the "digital tenge."
- In 2017, the Kazakhstan Stock Exchange created a new board—the Alternative Board—dedicated to MSMEs with simplified listing requirements. The Alternative Board has steadily grown with 89 listed companies as of end-2021. MSMEs can also issue corporate bonds on the new board.
- There are two credit bureaus in Kazakhstan (one public, one private). There is also an active collateral registry.

Bank Credit

The NBK, Kazakhstan's central bank, is responsible for financial stability, monetary policy, and supervises commercial banks. Other banks are called second-tier banks except the Development Bank of Kazakhstan (DBK) which holds special legal status. The Agency for Regulation and Development of Financial Markets (ARDFM) protects consumer rights and controls financial markets and other financial organizations. In 2020, the NBK asked ARDFM to regulate and supervise the nonbank finance industry as well. As of end-2021, there were 31 commercial banks, including 1 state-owned bank (the Housing Construction Bank Otbasy), 8 development financial institutions, 10 private commercial banks, and 12 foreign commercial banks.

MSME access to finance is central to inclusive development. Yet, MSME bank credit remains small. MSME loans outstanding was KZT3.8 trillion in 2021, or 4.6% of GDP (Figure 5.6 and Table 5.3). MSME loans accounted for 20.0% of total bank loans outstanding in 2021. The MSME credit market fell sharply during 2017–2019 (down 7.1% in 2017, 15.2% in 2018, and 10.8% in 2019). The central bank tightened regulations and the introduction of new rules based on International Financial Reporting Standard 9 (IFRS 9), resulting in the liquidation of several second-tier banks. However, due to newly introduced government financial assistance programs in response to the pandemic (easing MSME loan application requirements under the Business Roadmap 2025), MSME credit increased sharply—by 19.3% in 2020 and another 50.0% in 2021. The annual average MSME lending rate was 12.9% in 2021. But emergency financial assistance brought the lending rate for MSMEs down to 6% as restrictions were lifted and processing time reduced—significantly expanding lending to MSMEs. The emergency financial assistance raised the maximum lending amount to KZT7 billion for subsidized loans and up to KZT1 billion for guaranteed loans.

Support for small businesses—including microenterprises—was strengthened under the Business Roadmap 2025. It included portfolio subsidies and partial guarantees for micro credits.

Non-collateral MSME loans remain small, accounting for 5.3% to 8.4% of MSME loans between 2016–2020. However, it grew to 15.7% in 2021. Guaranteed loans are more popular, however, accounting for 84.3% of MSME loans in 2021. Long-term (over 5-year tenors) credit was 82.2% of MSME loans, while 17.8% were short-term (less than 1 year). NPL data for MSMEs is unavailable. Gross NPLs (over 90 days) to total bank loans fell to 3.3% in 2021 from 6.9% in 2020), below pre-pandemic levels (8.1% in 2019).

In 2021, MSME loans covered "other services"—including accommodation and food services—(23.9%), followed by agriculture (24.1%). Loans to wholesale and retail trade was a small fraction (1.8%), given their limited access to bank credit. Unclassified ("others") loans accounted for 32.1%. MSME loans were spread nationwide; with 16.2% for firms located in the capital Astana and the remaining 83.8% widely disbursed to other regions and rural areas.

Figure 5.6: MSME Loans

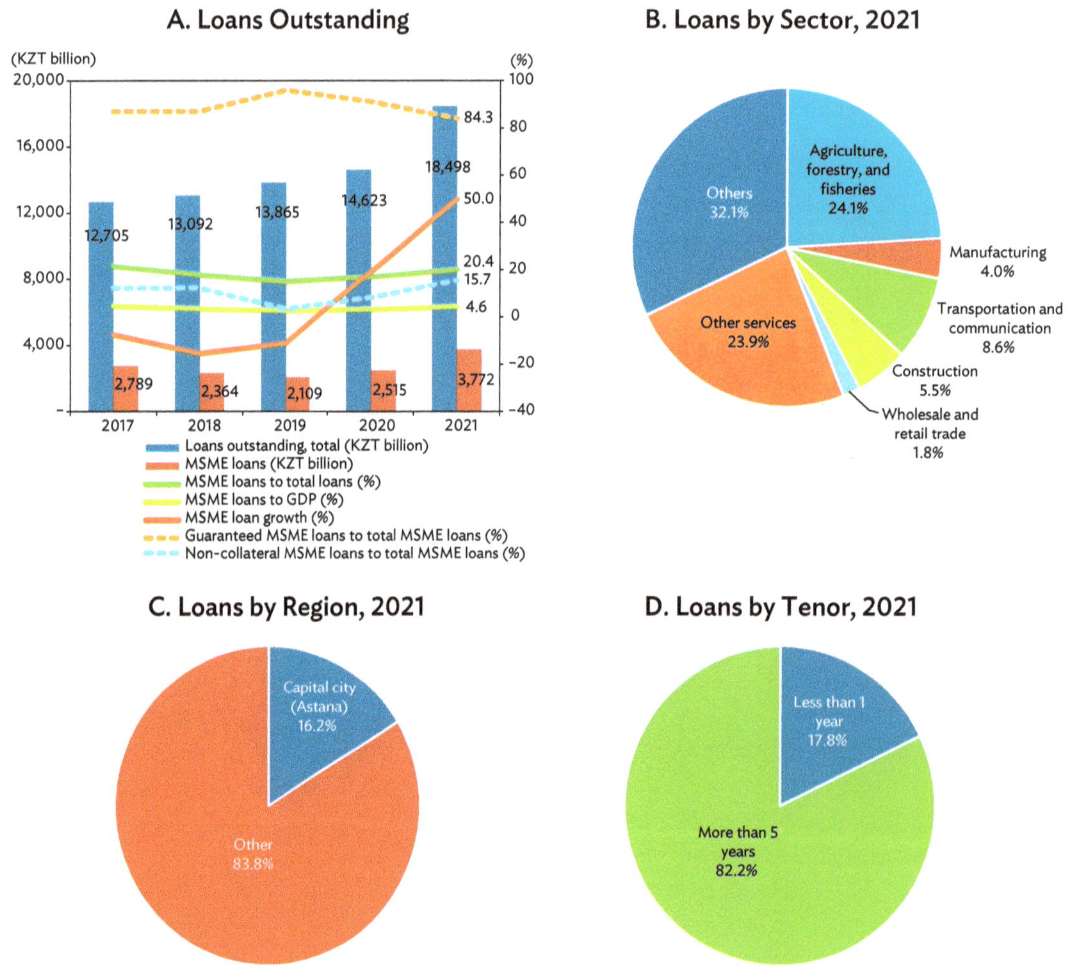

GDP = gross domestic product, MSME = micro, small, and medium-sized enterprise.
Source: ADB Asia SME Monitor 2022 database. Data from National Bank of Kazakhstan.

Public Financing and Guarantees

DAMU distributes public funds to MSMEs using subsidies and guarantees as well as soft loans. In 2021, KZT734 billion in subsidized loans went to MSMEs (up 83.6% from 2020 and 158.2% from 2019), due to the emergency financial support amid the pandemic (Figure 5.7 and Table 5.4). These loans reached 7,269 MSMEs in 2021, nearly double (98.5%) the number in 2020 (3,662 firms). Still, MSME access to subsidized loans remains limited, as they service just 0.5% of operating MSMEs.

Guaranteed loans to MSMEs have increased sharply since 2017, especially during the pandemic. It reached KZT275 billion in 2020, a 168.1% increase from 2019, and KZT365 billion in 2021, a 32.6% increase from 2020. The number of MSMEs guaranteed also increased steadily—7,347 firms in 2020 (up 174.9% from 2019), and 17,219 firms in 2021 (up 134.4%). The sharp growth was largely due to a 10-day limit on approving guarantees and lifting constraints by industry. However, MSME credit guarantees were just 1.2% of guarantees approved in 2021 (although well above the 0.1% and 0.5% during the previous 5 years).

One problem is insufficient dissemination of information about government support measures; the lack of adequate incentives for second-tier banks to work with MSMEs; and insufficient MSME documentation, including financial statements, for them to apply for government support measures.

An Accounts Committee report 2020 indicated that KZT270 billion was allocated for the Business Roadmap 2020 from 2015 to 2019. The largest share (71%) went to expenditures on interest subsidies, loan guarantees, state grants and microcredit. However, just 19,600 MSMEs, or 3,900 firms annually, were able to use the subsidies or guarantees—or 0.3% of the average annual number of operating MSMEs. Budget expenditures for developing industrial infrastructure accounted for 22% of the total, with 6% going to nonfinancial instruments. The Accounts Committee said, "the impact of the invested budgetary funds and provided state support measures (in the form of interest rate subsidies and credit guarantees) on the increase in active MSMEs is negligible."

Figure 5.7: Public Financing

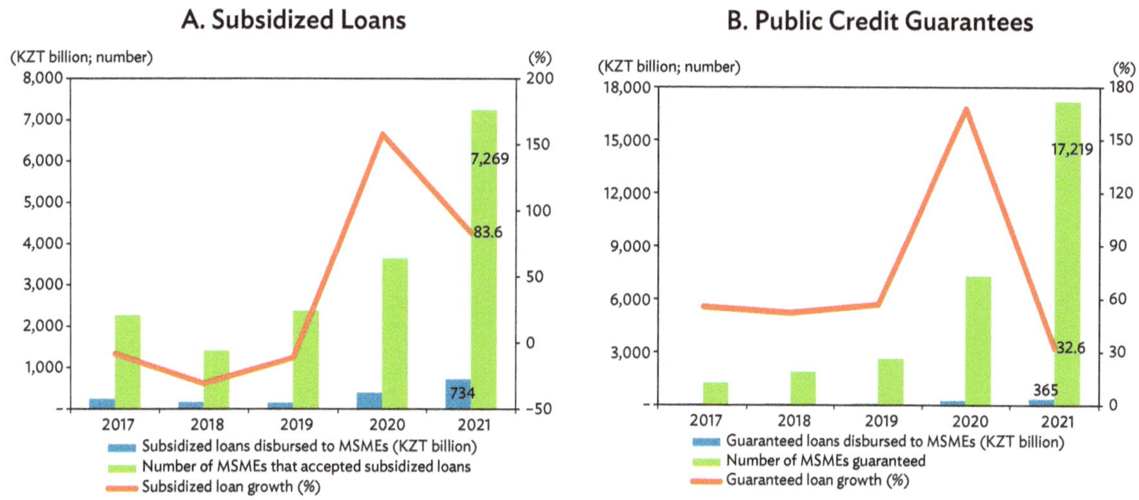

MSME = micro, small, and medium-sized enterprise.

Source: ADB Asia SME Monitor 2022 database. Data from Entrepreneurship Development Fund "DAMU."

There are refinancing schemes available for MSMEs through the National Fund in three tranches. They began in 2014 and are continuing, targeting MSME manufacturers. As of end-2021, KZT820.8 billion was disbursed, benefiting 2,791 MSMEs. In 2020, during the State of Emergency, the central bank launched a refinancing scheme to provide concessional loans through second-tier banks as a temporary emergency measure. They had an annual lending rate of 8% for up to 12 months (large firms and MSMEs). It disbursed KZT1,123 billion, benefiting 1,503 entrepreneurs. It was closed in 2021.

Nonbank Financing

Nonbank finance is also important part of MSME finance. As of end-2021, 1,100 nonbank finance institutions (NBFIs) were operating in Kazakhstan, including 242 microfinance institutions (MFIs), 219 credit unions, 7 finance companies, 605 pawnshops, and 27 insurance companies (Figure 5.8 and Table 5.5). Since 2019, the number of MFIs has been increasing, exceeding the number of credit unions—the increase due to easier registration requirements.

In January 2020, MFI supervision moved from the NBK to the ARDFM. Thus, for microcredit lending, MFIs must register with the ARDFM under specific prudential standards and requirements—such as joining as credit bureau and reporting on borrowers' credit records. MFI loans outstanding have expanded rapidly, increasing by 70.3% in 2021 (KZT743 billion) from 2020 (KZT437 billion). But total financing remains small at less than 1% of GDP. While MFI loans have been increasing, NPLs are also above pre-pandemic levels (4.0% in 2019, 6.1% in 2020, and 6.9% in 2021). Maximum loans cannot exceed 20,000 times the MCI for individuals and registered firms.

MFI loans are popular among individual entrepreneurs and MSMEs for working capital. Although MFIs have faced funding problems in many cases, they can tap external funding sources from international financial institutions. For example, in June 2022, ADB and a leading microfinance organization—KMF Limited Liability Company (KMF)—signed a loan for up to $15 million or its *tenge* equivalent to expand access to credit for MSMEs.[183]

Credit unions have grown rapidly since 2012. Total financing outstanding reached KZT241.5 billion in 2021, a 13.0% increase from 2020 KZT213.8 billion. The NPL ratio to total financing fell from 2.7% in 2019 (pre-pandemic) to 1.7% in 2021. Credit unions provide financing only to members, meaning there are relatively few NPLs. The financing covers about 20% of Kazakhstan's farmers. ARDFM requires credit unions to register in cities such as Astana, Almaty, and Shymkent. Credit unions are not allowed to take deposits, limiting their funding options.

Other finance companies and pawnshops held outstanding loans worth KZT1,399 billion in 2020 and KZT132 billion in 2021, respectively, recording 4.6% and 16.8% growth from 2020. The nonperforming financing rate was relatively high at 5.5% for finance companies and 4.6% for pawnshops in 2021.

[183] ADB. 2022. ADB and KMF Sign $15 Million Loan to Improve Access to Finance for MSMEs in Kazakhstan. News release. 13 June. https://www.adb.org/news/adb-and-kmf-sign-15-million-loan-improve-access-finance-msmes-kazakhstan.

Figure 5.8: Nonbank Finance

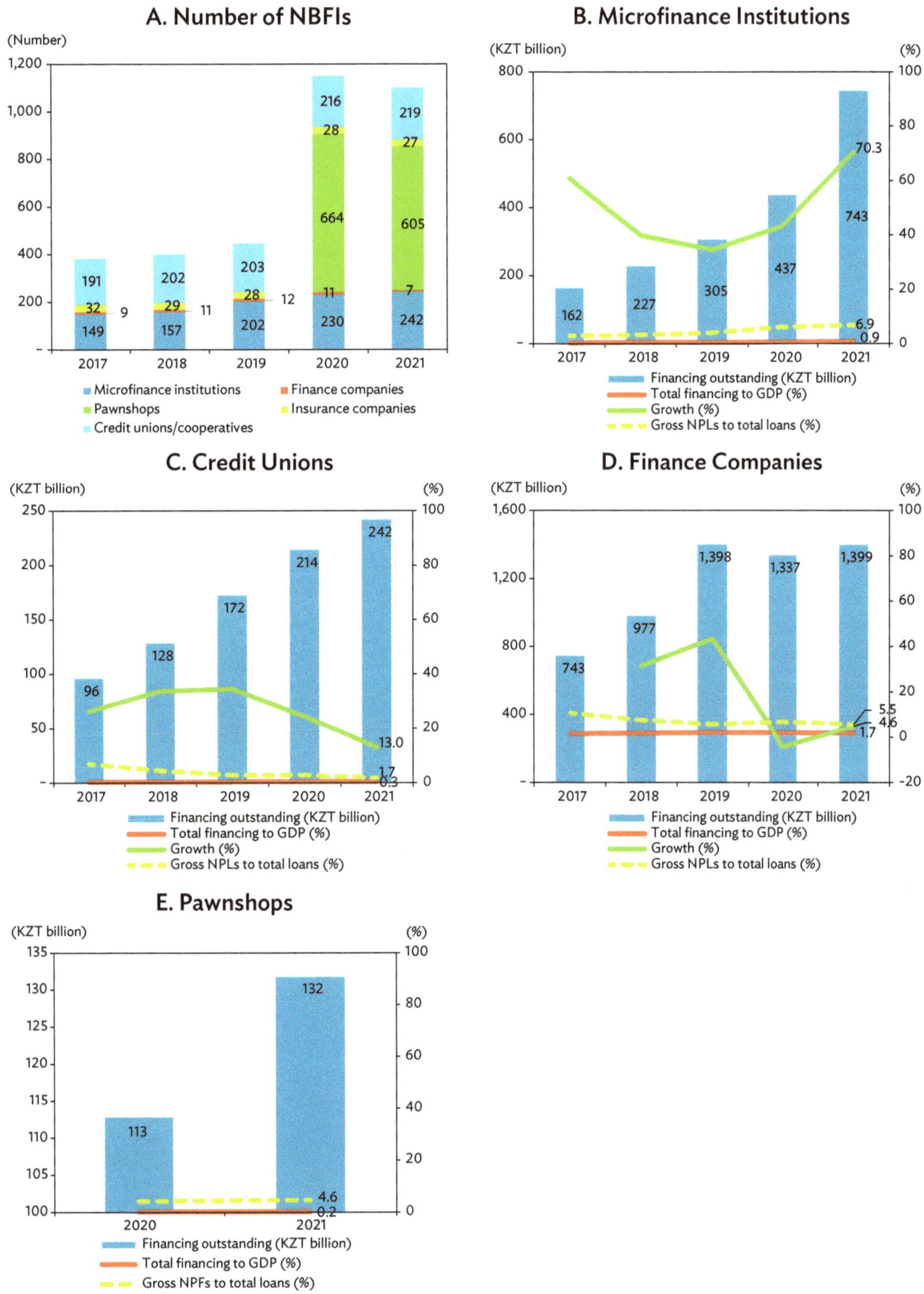

GDP = gross domestic product, NBFI = nonbank financing institution, NPF = nonperforming financing, NPL = nonperforming loan.

Source: ADB Asia SME Monitor 2022 database. Data from Agency for Regulation and Development of the Financial Market (for A and B, D and E); Association of Credit Unions (C);

Digital Financial Services

Card payments have grown. According to the NBK, as of April 2022, payment cards are issued by 19 banks and Kazpost JSC. They issue international payment cards like VISA, Mastercard, UnionPay, and American Express, while local banks issue domestic payment cards such as the Altyn Card (Halyk Bank of Kazakhstan), local Citibank Kazakhstan cards, and Kaspi.kz payment cards (Kaspi Bank). As of 1 April, 2022, there were 57.7 million payment cards in circulation. The most common were debit cards (77.8% of the total) and credit cards (19.0%). There were also debit cards with payment limits and prepaid cards (3.2%). In March 2022, there were 680.9 million transactions (worth KZT9.9 trillion), up 3.3% from 658.9 million transactions in 2021 and 23.8% in value (KZT8.0 trillion).

Internet and mobile banking accounted for 66.0% of transactions and 84.1% of the value of noncash payments and money transfers, with POS terminals covering 33.9% in number and 15.7% in value. Cash withdrawals were made through ATMs (98.7% in number and 86.9% in value.[184]

The pandemic accelerated digital finance for individuals and MSMEs. Local second-tier banks offer digital services for financing, purchasing goods, and some public services. During 2020, Halyk Bank, one of the largest banks in the country, launched its "Halyk Market" and "Halyk Investment" applications. In 2020, it updated an application for small businesses using IOS and Android platforms, so customers transact payments using their smartphones. By the end of 2020, there were 88,000 monthly users on the web and 66,000 using its mobile version.[185]

Kaspi Bank's digital service reaches about 11 million people, with 6 million using their application daily. On Kaspi.kz, clients can pay for more than 5,000 different services and transfer money without commission. As of 2021, more than 1.2 million goods were solod on its marketplace, with payments in installments and on credit. The Kaspi.kz marketplace has over 80,000 businesses registered—the majority are MSMEs. It offers several tech services in cooperation with government agencies. For example, every third transaction of automobile sales in the country are transacted online using the Kaspi.kz application.[186]

The NBK is exploring the creation of a "digital tenge," with a decision likely by the end of 2022.

In June 2022, the NBK launched an upgraded platform for its instant payment system between customers of various second-tier banks. It allows transfers using a mobile phone number and payments using a QR code between clients of different banks. Nine second-tier banks have concluded agreements on using the system, with four already providing access to their customers.[187]

Capital Markets

The limited sources of MSME financing means funding options need to be diversified for both working capital and growth capital. Capital markets open to MSMEs is thus critical. In June 2017, the Kazakhstan Stock Exchange (KASE) opened an Alternative Board catering to MSMEs. It offers simplified listing requirements to encourage them to use the stock market for financing.

The government hopes to make MSMEs the backbone for economic diversification. Aside from finance, the Alternative Board is expected to improve MSME corporate governance, promote better disclosure of information,

[184] National Bank of Kazakhstan. Statistics of payment cards. https://www.nationalbank.kz/en/news/elektronnye-bankovskie-uslugi.

[185] Annual Report of Halyk Bank for 2020 financial year.

[186] https://forbes.kz/finances/finance/mihail_lomtadze_kaspikz_sdelano_v_kazahstane/ *over 80 thousand of business entities in Kaspi.kz marketplace.

[187] National Bank of Kazakhstan. 2022. National Bank of Kazakhstan launches the Instant Payment System into operation. News release. 20 June. https://www.nationalbank.kz/en/news/novosti/13765.

and deepen their corporate values. According to the law establishing the board, MSMEs are not taxed on income (dividends and coupon interest) from securities listed and income from the increase in a stock's value through open trading. To issue securities on the Alternative Board, the issuer must meet the following basic requirements: (i) financial statements must be prepared in accordance with IFRS accounting standards and must be confirmed by an audit organization included in the List of Audit Organizations recognized by KASE; and (ii) issuer documents must not contain restrictions on the free transfer of securities.

Since its opening, the Alternative Board has steadily expanded, except in 2020 due to the pandemic. Market capitalization reached KZT528 billion in 2021, 13.7% higher than 2020 (KZT464 billion), when it contracted 45.5% from 2019 due to the pandemic) (Figure 5.9 and Table 5.6). From 43 firms in 2017, there were 89 firms listed as of end-2021. During 2019–2021, eight companies moved to the Main Board. According to KASE, companies on the Alternative Board have a diversified investor base both in terms of buying and selling securities. If issuers on the Alternative Board have a rating score of at least "BB-" by Standard&Poor's and/or an equivalent rating from "Fitch" and/or "Moody's Investors Service", the listed company will be transferred to the Main Board.

Individuals and legal entities (brokers, other legal entities, banking organizations, and insurance organizations) dominate buying and selling on the Alternative Board. Corporate bonds are traded less by individuals and more by legal entities.

Aside from equity, MSMEs can issue corporate bonds on the Alternative Board to support and attract financing for MSME investment projects. Most corporate bonds have 1–5 years maturity (2018–2021) and are increasingly popular among MSMEs (particularly medium-sized firms). In 2021, corporate bonds issued by MSMEs totaled KZT53 billion (KZT39.5 billion for *tenge*-denominated bonds and KZT13.5 billion for foreign currency bonds). Government incentives for MSMEs to raise funds through KASE include the corporate bond option. The coupon rate on bonds issued by medium-sized firms can be subsidized under the National Project on Entrepreneurship Development for 2021–2025 (NPED), with DAMU providing bond guarantees up to 5 years up to KZT2.5 billion.

Figure 5.9: Capital Markets

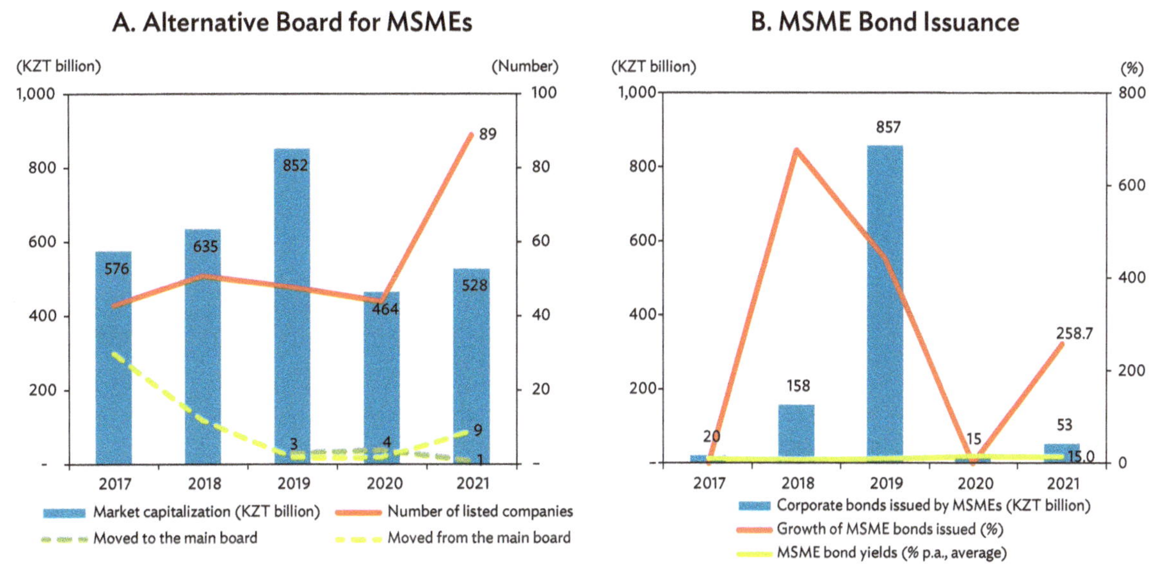

MSME = micro, small, and medium-sized enterprise.
ADB Asia SME Monitor 2022 database. Data from Kazakhstan Stock Exchange.
Source: ADB

The cost of financial advisory services, auditing, listing, and annual fees is the main barrier for MSMEs seeking to list on the exchange. Also, MSME financial statements often do not comply with IFRS or Generally Accepted Accounting Principles (GAAP) international standards.

Aside from the stock exchange, MSMEs can attract loan and equity financing from crowdfunding platforms. Since June 2019, the Astana International Financial Centre (AIFC) introduced a regulatory framework for loan- and equity-investment-based crowdfunding platforms. The framework carries prudential standards for operators, including requirements on anti-money laundering and counter terrorism financing, fundraising limits, risk disclosure, conflict of interest, and due diligence of firms using crowdfunding. Based on AIFC public register, the licensed crowdfunding platforms include Ikapitalist, Proportunity, VentureRocket Eurasia, GoCrowd, and Crowdest. However, there remains a general lack of understanding of how crowdfunding works, both by potential investors and the few reliable borrowers.

Financial Infrastructure

There are two credit bureaus in Kazakhstan: JSC State Credit Bureau (SCB) and First Credit Bureau LLP (FCB). They act in accordance with the Law on Credit Bureaus and the Formation of Credit Histories in the Republic of Kazakhstan dated 6 July 2004.

As of end-2021, more than 500 organizations report credit histories to the SCB, which include (i) second-tier banks, (ii) microfinance institutions, (iii) organizations carrying out certain types of banking operations, (iv) monopoly utility services, (v) other credit organizations, (vi) cellular operators (information about individuals that received communication facilities on credit or in installments), and (vii) collection agencies. They are mandated to report and update the SCB, whereas reporting to the the FCB is optional. Since January 2020, pawnshops, credit unions, and organizations providing loans, including online (remotely via the internet) must submit and update their credit histories. The SCB also houses an insurance database, where insurance (reinsurance) companies must keep their information updated. Since 2019, insurance policies for vehicles can be issued online.

There are some general conditions related to credit bureau activities: (i) when applying for a loan, the bank must request written permission from the applicant to access their credit report from the bureau; (ii) each bank has their own lending decision-making policy, and credit bureaus do not participate or influence decisions; (iii) the credit bureau does not adjust, correct, or delete items on a credit history; and (iv) a personal credit report can be obtained free of charge once a year from the credit bureau or online through the e-government portal.[188]

The FCB is a private credit bureau established by BCC, Jusan Bank, Halyk Bank, Forte Bank, Astana Finance JSC, and Credit Info. It has more than 650 suppliers-recipients of information, an up-to-date database of credit histories and more than 40 services that provide data for credit and noncredit processes, statistics, and predictive analytics for financial markets. It also provides corporate credit reports with complete information on loan issuance and repayments.

In 2017, FCB launched a service—"The Strongest"—to assess the creditworthiness, reliability, and payment discipline of MSMEs. The service is aimed at companies for which there is no mandatory rating or audit but where the competitive market benefits from an objective independent assessment. The Strongest can also be used for tenders, as a certified assessment of the credit report of a counterparty or for public relations purposes. In addition, in 2021 the ARDFM developed an Agency's Rating Estimation System (ARES) to run a rating model of corporate borrowers. ARES estimates a borrower's credit risk, predicts the probability of default, and more accurately credit losses based on borrower financial statements. It uses adjustment factors to consider the effect of an economic shock.

[188] https://fingramota.kz/ru/post/kak-rabotayut-kreditnye-byuro-v-kazahstane.

In the future, ARES estimates will not only determine the level of borrower's risk but also assess loan rates of corporate borrowers and analyze their marketability. This will be used to determine how much additional lending a borrower can absorb without threatening its overall financial condition. This will allow ARDFM to conduct deeper analyses and refine government incentive programs.

The nonprofit JSC state corporation "Government for Citizens" registers collateral for both individuals and legal entities as a "one-stop shop" for registering movable and immovable collateral. It is integrated with a database for all public agencies and generates online public services through the e-gov portal. Depending on the type of collateral, Government for Citizens issues a certificate of collateral registration within 1–2 working days.

4. Policies and Regulations

- A long-term National Development Plan through 2025 set 10 priorities—to develop a diversified, innovative economy through entrepreneurship and more competitive domestic enterprises.
- The National Project on Entrepreneurship Development for 2021–2025 promotes entrepreneurships, develops small firms to create more jobs, supports medium-sized firms to diversify the economy, and builds an inclusive competitive environment.
- In 2022, the government approved the Development Concept of Small and Medium-sized Enterprises until 2030, which identified key challenges for MSME development.
- There is no national financial inclusion policy covering financial access for MSMEs. But in effect DAMU implements financial inclusion strategies.
- The government approved a Comprehensive Plan on Recovery of Economic Growth through 2021, with 10 "directions" and 172 systemic or sectoral measures to keep businesses operating during the pandemic (May 2020).
- The central bank and ARDFM initiated a Program of Concessional Lending to businesses, including MSMEs, in response to the pandemic.
- The government provided local anti-crisis measures including financial and nonfinancial support for MSMEs (from July 2020).
- The government established an anti-crisis command center in March 2022 to mitigate the impact of anti-Russian sanctions on Kazakhstan's economy.

MSME Development

In February 2021, Kazakhstan's President approved the National Development Plan through 2025 (NDP), the main state planning document supporting the long-term (2050) Development Strategy of Kazakhstan. The NDP supplanted the 2018 strategic plan in response to the economic slowdown due to the pandemic and uncertainty in the capital and commodity markets.

One of the 10 NDP priorities is creating a diversified and innovative economy through the development of entrepreneurship and increasing domestic competitiveness. There are 17 tasks defined by the NDP covering issues such as simplifying procedures for starting a business, increasing access to finance through government support, reforms in agriculture, transport and logistics, developing domestic tourism, digitalization of basic industries, and development of venture financing for MSMEs.

The Ministry of National Economy developed the National Project on Entrepreneurship Development for 2021–2025 (NPED) to ensure reforms were qualitative, small businesses developed to boost jobs, medium-sized businesses supported to help drive economic diversification, and that competition was equal. The NPED during

5-year budget is KZT8.5 trillion, including a national budget of KZT1.03 trillion, municipal budgets of KZT124 billion, and extra-budgetary funds of KZT7.3 trillion. These will provide financial support to entrepreneurs, including MSMEs, for increasing access to finance for businesses (KZT705 billion), or 8.3% total funding.

In April 2022, the government approved the Development Concept of Small and Medium-sized Enterprises until 2030, highlighting the key challenges that facing MSMEs, which currently have to deal with legal issues, favoritism, and a high risk of the confiscation of property. There is still favoritism in markets due the intervention from state-owned enterprises, direct export/import bans, and direct/indirect intervention to government price setting.

MSMEs and entrepreneurship must also build on currently underdeveloped human capital and create an environment conducive to entrepreneurs. Pressure from inspection agencies constrains MSME development as well, along with interference from law enforcement and attempts to take over firms. In addition, most MSMEs complain about lengthy approval times for government support as many processes have not yet digitized. Access to finance, tax policy and its administration, along with excessive bureaucracy are frequently cited as barriers. Other problems faced by entrepreneurs include acquiring company premises, availability of raw materials and liquidity, high rental costs, and information gaps on state programs for entrepreneurial development.[189]

Risk avoidance and overcoming institutional barriers also hold entrepreneurship development back. A complicated and unpredictable business climate works against steady MSME development, accompanied by a growing regulatory burden and resistance against reducing administrative barriers.

MSME development both increasing financial support and non-financial measures that improve entrepreneurial skills and competence. The Entrepreneurial Code of the Republic of Kazakhstan is the main regulatory act for MSME development, but other laws and regulations can intervene—such as tax and civil codes, laws implementing new regulatory policies for entrepreneurs, and similar documents. In June 2021, statutory regulations defining social entrepreneurship and categorizing beneficiaries was approved.

Financial Inclusion

There is no national financial inclusion policy related to financial access for all—including MSMEs. In effect, DAMU, following the NPED, implements financial inclusion strategies.

DAMU provides guarantees and interest rate subsidies for MSMEs. NPED targets the following priority sectors for financial support: (i) agriculture, including cereals (excluding rice), legumes, and oilseeds; (ii) mining; (iii) light industry and furniture manufacturing; (iv) manufacturing construction materials and other non-metallic manufacturing products; (v) metallurgy, metalworking, mechanical engineering; (vi) transportation and warehousing; (vii) tourism; (viii) information and communication; (ix) renting and operating of owned or leased real estate; (x) professional, scientific, and technical activities; (xi) rental and leasing; (xii) education; (xiii) arts, entertainment, and recreation; (xiv) health care and social services; and (xv) other services.

Aside from financial support under the NPED (guarantee amount up to 85% of the loan amount), DAMU offers guarantees on microcredits under the "Economy of Simple Things" program—no more than 50% of the loan amount. Loan guarantees are the most popular type of financial support requested by MSMEs. There are also portfolio subsidies, subsidies for "Economy of Simple Things" projects and for low-carbon development of sustainable cities. There are also subsidies under a United Nations Development Programme (UNDP)-Global Environment Facility project to reduce investment risk on renewable energy. And there are subsidies for from 6% to 10% of the interest rate for all subsidy support. DAMU also provides leasing opportunities and loan provisions

[189] https://www.gov.kz/memleket/entities/economy/documents/details/226792?lang=ru draft of decree.

through second-tier banks and microfinance institutions, as well as MSME loans based on principles of Islamic financing.

MSMEs mainly obtain finance through second-tier banks. As an alternative, there are capital market instruments through the Alternative Board. As mentioned, listing costs, especially those for meeting disclosure requirements under international standards like IFRS and GAAP, are a critical barrier for MSMEs tapping capital markets, even as KASE helps develop programs to prepare MSMEs for stock market listing. The program will offer an opportunity to attract needed funding as well as help MSMEs be more transparent while improving corporate governance.

Response to COVID-19

On 23 March 2020 at a meeting on establishing a state of emergency, the President ordered the Ministry of Labor and Social Care to pay monthly amounts of KZT42,500 (the minimum wage) for those who lost their regular income due to the crisis. He also allowed MSMEs to delay tax payments and other payments required for 3 months without accruing fines and penalties. More than 1.6 million people and 11,500 MSMEs received loan deferral equivalent to more than KZT360 billion. Also, on 1 September 2020, the President reduced the rate on MSME loans to 6% in the most-affected sectors of the economy.[190]

On 20 May 2020, the government approved a Comprehensive Plan on Recovery of Economic Growth through 2021, consisting of 10 "directions" and 172 systemic and sector measures to stimulate business, support employment, and increase people's income.

The NBK, together with the ARDFM, adopted a Program of Concessional Lending to businesses. The program, funded by the NBK, ran until 31 December 2021 with a KZT800 billion budget with the possibility of using funds through a revolving mechanism. The program supported entrepreneurs affected during the state of emergency by issuing soft loans through banks for up to 12 months with 8% annual interest. The funds were used to replenish working capital, including payments for goods, works, services, taxes, and other payments like wages. Concessional lending was provided to both MSMEs and large firms. As of end-2021, second-tier banks accepted 3,615 applications for KZT833.2 billion. A total of 11,785 loans were issued totaling KZT1.1 trillion to 1,551 entrepreneurs (of which 1,270 were MSMEs, 233 individual entrepreneurs, and 48 large firms). Some 6,798 loans worth KZT510.7 billion went for repayment of previously issued loans.

In July 2020, the government said the total package of anti-crisis measures, excluding tax preferences and local government support, reached KZT5.9 trillion, of which KZT3.5 trillion was from the national budget and KZT2.5 trillion from extra-budgetary funds. Specifically, KZT1 trillion was provided for financing the "Employment Roadmap," with KZT300 billion from the national budget and KZT700 billion from extra-budgetary funds. KZT1 trillion of extra-budgetary funds were provided for the "Economy of Simple Things" program for concessional lending to at 8% interest and to expand preferential lending to investment projects at 6% per annum. To compensate for the losses of small businesses, KZT237 billion was provided for tax and fee exemptions for MSME salaries and for large businesses in affected sectors. KZT240 billion went for the expansion of state programs: (i) KZT50 billion helped subsidize the agro-industrial complex, (ii) KZT50 billion helped develop the labor market under the "Enbek" State Program, (iii) KZT84.5 billion subsidized interest rates and guaranteed loans under the State Program "Business Road Map 2025," and (iv) KZT55 billion went develop social and engineering infrastructure in rural areas under the "Auyl-El Besigi" project. KZT66.9 billion was allocated from government reserves to contain COVID-19, with KZT46.6 billion going to the Ministry of Health.[191]

190 Information received from annual report of DAMU on SME statement on 2020.

191 https://primeminister.kz/ru/news/reviews/antikrizisnye-mery-pravitelstva-vozobnovlenie-rosta-ekonomiki-i-podderzhka-msb-862620

Response to the Russian Invasion of Ukraine

On 2 March 2022, the government established an anti-crisis command center to mitigate the possible impact of anti-Russian sanctions on Kazakhstan. Heads of economic ministries and agencies, representatives of the business community, and other experts were included. The government, together with NCE, AIFC, and industry representatives, formulated a sanctions scenario defining specific risks and their economic impact, as well as possible countermeasures to limit any damage.

Several new support measures were proposed to help domestic companies and reduce the administrative burden. Under the framework for public procurement, for example, mechanisms were proposed to exclude suppliers affected by the closure of logistics corridors and other supply disruptions. It was also proposed to increase the size of state subsidies for insurance premiums to support agricultural producers. In addition, support to expand preferential leasing of agricultural machinery for domestic production was proposed. The Ministry of Agriculture planned to extend its quota for the export of flour and wheat until 1 October 2022, setting limits of 550,000 tons of wheat and meslin and 370,000 tons of wheat and rye flour.[192]

On 16 March 2022, measures were taken to assure farmers they would access to necessary fuels and lubricants, prevent shortages and food price inflation, including forward purchases of agricultural products from state stabilization funds.

Media and social networks reported an alleged mass opening of bank accounts by citizens of the Russian Federation and Belarus in Kazakhstan banks, which could lead secondary sanctions imposed on Kazakhstan. In response, the ARDFM notified second-tier banks to conduct due diligence of foreign applicants before opening bank accounts in accordance with know-your-customer standards. Sources of origin of a client's money, the legal status of its counterparty, and the conditions and economic purpose of transactions were included. In general, measures related to the Russian invasion of Ukraine remain under review by the anti-crisis command center, coinciding with the recovery action plan after what is called Kazakhstan's "Tragic January."

[192] https://www.export.gov.kz/news/detail/1435?showType=EXPORT

Data Tables

Table 5.1: MSME Definition*

Type	Item	Micro	Small	Medium
Legal entity and individual entrepreneurs	Annual average income	Less than 30,000 times the Monthly Calculation Index (MCI).***	More than 30,000 but less than 300,000 times the MCI.	More than 300,000 but less than 3,000,000 times the MCI.
	Annual average number of employees**	Fewer than 15.	More than 15 but fewer than 100.	More than 100 but fewer than 250.

MSME = micro, small, and medium-sized enterprise.

Note: For the purposes of state support and application of other norms of Kazakhstan legislation, small businesses as well as microenterprises cannot be individual entrepreneurs and legal entities engaged in trafficking narcotics, psychotropic substances and precursors,production and/or wholesale of excisable products, grain storage activities at grain receiving points,organizing a lottery, gambling,circulation of radioactive materials,banking activities (or certain types of banking operations) and activities in the insurance market (except for the activities of an insurance agent),audit, professional activity in the securities market, activities of credit bureaus,security activity, circulation of civilian and service weapons and cartridges for them.

* For the purposes of providing state support and applying other norms of Kazakhstan legislation, two criteria are used: the average annual number of employees and the average annual income.

** For the purposes of state statistics, only the criterion of the annual average number of employees is used (microenterprises are included in the number of small firms in accordance with dimension classifier of Bureau of National Statistics dated 5 February 2015 order N27).

*** MCI established by the law on the republican budget and effective as of 1 January of the corresponding calendar year (MCI for 2022 calendar year is equivalent to KZT3,180).

Source: ADB Asia SME Monitor 2022 database. Data from Entrepreneurial Code of the Republic of Kazakhstan dated by 29 October 2015 (with amendments as of 1 January 2022).

Table 5.2: MSME Landscape

End-of-period data

Item	2005	2006	2007	2008	2009	2010	2011	2012	2013	2014	2015	2016	2017	2018	2019	2020	2021
NUMBER OF REGISTERED ENTERPRISES																	
Number of registered enterprises, total	744,839	842,154	940,435	1,028,627	937,063	1,199,154	1,386,077	1,402,119	1,538,416	1,657,861	1,483,940	1,500,679	1,542,975	1,580,235	1,606,241	1,612,901	1,697,133
Number of MSMEs	742,785	840,000	938,155	1,026,255	934,691	1,196,725	1,383,727	1,399,787	1,535,983	1,655,386	1,481,454	1,498,243	1,540,592	1,577,747	1,603,839	1,610,496	1,694,672
Micro*	...	...	...	...	...	...	...	...	...	...	...	...	...	...	...	...	...
Small	739,047	836,231	934,102	1,022,485	923,667	1,184,854	1,371,068	1,387,634	1,523,373	1,649,329	1,478,365	1,495,227	1,537,633	1,574,789	1,601,081	1,607,830	1,691,769
Medium	3,738	3,769	4,053	3,770	11,024	11,871	12,659	12,153	12,610	6,057	3,089	3,016	2,959	2,958	2,758	2,666	2,903
Number of large enterprises	2,054	2,154	2,280	2,372	2,372	2,429	2,350	2,332	2,433	2,475	2,486	2,436	2,383	2,488	2,402	2,405	2,461
MSME to total (%)	99.7	99.7	99.8	99.8	99.7	99.8	99.8	99.8	99.8	99.9	99.8	99.8	99.8	99.8	99.9	99.9	99.9
MSME growth (%)	...	13.1	11.7	9.4	(8.9)	28.0	15.6	1.2	9.7	7.8	(10.5)	1.1	2.8	2.4	1.7	0.4	5.2
Registered MSMEs by sector (% share)																	
Agriculture, forestry, and fisheries	26.8	24.6	22.0	20.1	22.1	16.6	15.3	22.3	20.4	19.3	15.5	15.3	15.7	15.8	16.7	17.3	16.5
Manufacturing	3.5	3.4	3.4	3.3	3.6	3.2	3.0	3.2	3.1	3.3	3.7	3.8	3.9	3.9	4.1	4.4	4.8
Transportation and warehousing	7.6	8.0	8.6	8.7	7.1	8.2	7.8	8.1	8.0	8.1	7.6	7.3	6.8	6.5	6.1	5.8	5.5
Construction	3.5	3.8	4.2	4.3	4.9	4.1	3.9	4.1	4.2	4.3	4.8	5.1	5.3	5.4	5.6	5.9	6.2
Wholesale and retail trade	40.2	40.6	40.5	41.0	40.9	46.1	48.6	38.4	39.7	39.2	39.9	38.8	37.4	36.2	33.9	32.7	32.4
Other services	9.6	10.4	11.5	12.2	12.9	14.8	14.1	15.7	15.7	16.2	17.7	18.2	19.0	19.4	19.9	20.2	20.4
Others	8.7	9.2	9.8	10.4	8.6	7.0	7.3	8.0	8.9	9.7	10.9	11.5	11.9	12.7	13.5	13.7	14.3
Registered Number of MSMEs by region (% share)																	
Capital city (Astana)	5.1	5.6	6.1	6.3	6.0	6.5	6.5	6.7	7.0	7.5	8.4	9.1	9.6	10.3	10.4	10.8	11.3
Others	94.9	94.4	93.9	93.7	94.0	93.5	93.5	93.3	93.0	92.5	91.6	90.9	90.4	89.7	89.6	89.2	88.7
NUMBER OF OPERATING ENTERPRISES																	
Number of enterprises, total	509,250	574,718	645,465	710,027	665,597	663,864	848,369	812,001	890,588	929,241	1,244,998	1,108,715	1,148,296	1,243,735	1,332,589	1,359,668	1,434,057
Number of MSMEs	507,365	572,738	643,376	707,821	663,374	661,598	846,111	809,750	888,233	926,844	1,242,579	1,106,353	1,145,994	1,241,328	1,330,244	1,357,311	1,431,647
Micro*	...	...	...	...	...	...	...	...	...	...	...	...	...	...	...	...	...
Small	504,824	570,060	640,900	703,802	659,214	652,886	837,083	801,362	879,921	922,285	1,239,682	1,103,642	1,143,376	1,238,708	1,327,742	1,354,825	1,428,893
Medium	2,541	2,678	2,476	4,019	4,160	8,712	9,028	8,388	8,312	4,559	2,897	2,711	2,618	2,620	2,502	2,486	2,754
Number of large enterprises	1,885	1,980	2,089	2,206	2,223	2,266	2,258	2,251	2,355	2,397	2,419	2,362	2,302	2,407	2,345	2,357	2,410
MSME to total (%)	99.6	99.7	99.7	99.7	99.7	99.7	99.7	99.7	99.7	99.7	99.8	99.8	99.8	99.8	99.8	99.8	99.8
MSME growth (%)	...	12.9	12.3	10.0	(6.3)	(0.3)	27.9	(4.3)	9.7	4.3	34.1	(11.0)	3.6	8.3	7.2	2.0	5.5
Operating MSMEs by sector (% share)																	
Agriculture, forestry, and fisheries	31.9	29.5	27.1	24.6	26.4	26.5	22.2	21.0	18.4	17.1	17.1	18.9	19.4	18.6	19.0	19.2	18.2
Manufacturing	2.8	2.6	2.6	2.6	2.4	2.8	2.6	2.9	2.8	3.0	3.4	3.7	3.7	3.7	3.9	4.2	4.5
Transportation and warehousing	6.8	7.3	7.8	7.6	6.8	6.0	6.1	6.4	6.6	6.7	7.1	6.5	6.0	6.2	6.0	5.7	5.4
Construction	2.2	2.1	2.6	2.3	2.6	2.9	2.5	2.6	2.6	2.8	4.0	4.4	4.5	4.7	4.9	5.3	5.7
Wholesale and retail trade	36.5	37.6	37.3	39.0	37.9	41.5	45.6	41.3	42.9	42.0	39.7	36.5	35.6	35.0	33.3	32.1	31.9
Other services	12.5	13.2	14.5	14.8	15.1	13.7	13.8	16.1	16.5	17.2	17.1	18.2	18.9	19.0	19.4	19.7	20.0
Others	7.3	7.8	8.1	9.1	8.8	6.6	7.3	9.7	10.2	11.1	11.4	11.7	11.8	12.8	13.7	13.7	14.3
Operating MSMEs by region (% share)																	
Capital city (Astana)	4.2	4.0	4.5	4.6	3.9	5.3	5.9	6.4	6.6	7.0	8.0	8.4	8.5	10.0	10.1	10.7	11.4
Others	95.8	96.0	95.5	95.4	96.1	94.7	94.1	93.6	93.4	93.0	92.0	91.6	91.5	90.0	89.9	89.3	88.6
EMPLOYMENT																	
Number of employment, total ('000)	7,261	7,404	7,631	7,857	7,903	8,114	8,302	8,507	8,571	8,510	8,433	8,553	8,585	8,695	8,781	8,732	8,813
Number of employment by MSMEs	1,876	1,952	2,121	2,153	2,297	2,631	2,427	2,383	2,577	2,811	3,184	3,167	3,190	3,312	3,449	3,473	3,463
Micro*	...	...	...	...	...	...	...	...	...	...	...	...	...	...	...	...	...
Small	1,610	1,685	1,862	1,755	1,892	1,882	1,738	1,708	1,865	2,294	2,832	2,814	2,829	2,948	3,084	3,117	3,110
Medium	265	267	259	398	405	748	689	675	712	517	352	353	361	365	365	356	353
Number of employment by large enterprises	1,327	1,391	1,467	1,576	1,563	1,537	1,557	1,599	1,670	1,707	1,745	1,725	1,734	1,777	1,853	1,822	1,817
MSME employees to total (%)	25.8	26.4	27.8	27.4	29.1	32.4	29.2	28.0	30.1	33.0	37.8	37.0	37.2	38.1	39.3	39.8	39.3
MSME employees growth (%)	...	4.1	8.7	1.5	6.7	14.5	(7.7)	(1.8)	8.1	9.1	13.3	(0.5)	0.7	3.8	4.1	0.7	(0.3)
Share of female employees to total employees (%)	19.4	19.1	18.5	18.0	17.9	17.4	17.0	16.6	16.5	16.6	16.7	16.5	16.4	16.2	16.1	16.2	16.0

continued on next page

Table 5.2 *continued*

Item	2005	2006	2007	2008	2009	2010	2011	2012	2013	2014	2015	2016	2017	2018	2019	2020	2021
Employment by MSME by sector (% share)																	
Agriculture, forestry, and fisheries	33.5	31.7	30.7	26.0	27.2	23.5	22.1	19.6	16.9	14.5	12.9	12.7	13.1	12.6	13.0	13.0	13.0
Manufacturing	8.9	8.6	7.8	8.9	8.7	10.4	10.3	10.4	9.8	9.8	9.7	9.7	10.1	10.3	9.9	9.9	10.0
Transportation and warehousing	4.8	5.0	5.2	5.5	5.3	4.8	5.0	5.6	5.5	5.7	6.1	6.0	5.6	5.9	5.5	5.5	5.5
Construction	7.7	8.1	8.4	7.8	8.5	11.7	9.1	8.4	8.5	8.5	8.8	9.3	8.9	8.8	8.7	9.8	8.6
Wholesale and retail trade	26.5	27.9	28.2	28.4	27.0	26.0	27.8	27.7	29.8	30.8	30.9	29.8	29.1	29.4	28.9	27.9	28.5
Other services	13.7	14.1	14.6	17.5	19.6	21.1	22.2	23.5	24.0	24.7	24.5	25.4	26.0	25.3	25.8	25.7	26.3
Others	4.8	4.8	5.0	5.8	3.7	2.5	3.6	4.8	5.4	6.1	6.9	7.1	7.2	7.6	8.3	8.2	8.0
Employment by MSMEs by region (% share)																	
Capital city (Astana)	5.3	5.7	6.5	5.5	5.3	5.8	6.2	6.8	7.7	9.0	9.1	10.3	10.3	11.3	11.2	11.5	12.0
Others	94.7	94.3	93.5	94.5	94.7	94.2	93.8	93.2	92.3	91.0	90.9	89.7	89.7	88.7	88.8	88.5	88.0
CONTRIBUTION TO GROSS VALUE ADDED (GVA)**																	
GVA of MSMEs (KZT million)	797,576	1,003,032	1,370,578	2,673,017	3,002,660	4,498,009	4,890,986	5,303,593	6,027,426	10,294,709	10,196,652	12,584,004	14,257,284	17,569,900	22,029,151	23,189,145	28,115,260
MSME contribution to GVA (% share)	10.5	9.8	10.7	16.7	17.7	20.6	17.3	17.1	16.7	25.9	24.9	26.8	26.8	28.4	31.7	32.8	33.5
MSME GVA growth (%)	...	25.8	36.6	95.0	12.3	49.8	8.7	8.4	13.6	70.8	(1.0)	23.4	13.3	23.2	25.4	5.3	21.2
MSME labor productivity (KZT thousand/people)	425	514	646	1,242	1,307	1,710	2,015	2,225	2,339	3,662	3,203	3,974	4,469	5,304	6,388	6,678	5,315
MSME GVA to total GVA of the region (% share)																	
Capital city (Astana)	13.1	11.1	15.1	27.2	32.2	28.9	31.5	28.6	29.1	61.8	46.0	57.4	54.4	48.6	55.1	56.8	59.0
Akmola region	19.9	17.2	13.5	19.2	20.3	24.0	23.4	20.1	19.5	23.1	25.6	26.1	25.1	30.8	28.6	27.1	26.8
Aktobe region	6.9	6.4	7.3	11.6	10.6	17.7	13.8	14.1	13.5	17.8	22.1	19.4	18.3	20.7	21.2	23.8	24.5
Almaty oblast region	18.5	21.2	16.9	19.4	27.8	33.1	25.9	24.9	23.7	27.0	25.1	26.9	26.4	32.0	33.6	32.4	37.0
Atyrau region	4.0	4.9	5.0	10.3	10.2	8.1	6.9	7.3	5.8	8.8	14.2	11.8	16.8	18.7	22.0	19.5	24.1
West Kazakhstan region	7.5	8.5	7.8	12.4	26.9	32.3	12.6	11.0	13.6	38.7	39.9	41.9	40.1	36.0	37.3	34.1	33.4
Zhambyl region	15.3	16.3	18.1	27.2	17.6	21.0	18.1	16.9	19.3	20.1	19.9	19.8	18.8	20.9	20.9	26.5	25.9
Karagandy region	5.5	5.6	5.7	7.7	7.6	10.7	10.7	11.1	11.1	12.4	12.7	12.1	12.7	17.2	16.8	17.9	17.9
Kostanay region	13.4	13.7	14.6	21.5	17.4	21.0	20.2	17.7	17.6	23.3	21.8	23.2	25.1	29.4	32.8	31.5	28.6
Kyzylorda region	9.3	8.3	8.5	8.3	11.2	14.3	8.7	11.3	10.6	12.0	13.5	13.2	14.2	16.9	17.8	17.6	18.3
Mangystau region	4.9	4.5	5.5	7.7	9.1	16.1	10.7	10.2	9.7	17.6	19.9	22.9	15.6	16.8	22.9	29.4	31.4
South Kazakhstan region	15.0	16.3	17.5	17.0	14.8	21.2	18.7	16.6	16.1	19.7	20.2	22.9	21.9	...	...	...	...
Pavlodar region	8.8	9.1	10.5	6.9	9.3	13.3	11.8	11.9	12.1	18.5	19.7	15.1	17.4	16.2	18.6	18.8	18.4
North Kazakhstan region	18.5	18.6	19.6	22.2	22.6	25.0	25.3	25.6	25.6	25.2	23.9	24.4	25.4	29.7	30.3	31.5	31.4
Turkistan region	...	...	...	...	...	...	...	...	...	...	...	...	...	19.5	23.1	24.4	30.8
East Kazakhstan region	11.3	9.6	9.8	13.7	13.7	16.2	16.7	15.4	14.6	14.2	15.4	16.9	15.7	18.0	19.5	20.0	20.5
Almaty city	12.7	10.1	11.3	27.8	25.4	30.2	25.8	25.4	22.3	33.9	29.1	33.7	35.3	40.1	44.8	49.2	47.5
Shymkent city	...	...	...	...	...	...	...	...	...	...	...	...	...	25.6	34.1	31.8	40.5
EXPORTS																	
Total export value ($ million)	27,849	38,250	47,755	71,184	43,196	60,271	84,336	86,449	84,700	79,460	45,956	36,737	48,503	61,111	58,066	47,541	60,340
Total export growth (%)	38.6	37.3	24.8	49.1	(39.3)	39.5	39.9	2.5	(2.0)	(6.2)	(42.2)	(20.1)	32.0	26.0	(5.0)	(18.1)	26.9
MSME export value ($ million)	...	...	...	...	...	...	...	...	...	...	...	...	...	...	...	...	...
MSME export to total export value (%)	...	...	...	...	...	...	...	...	...	...	...	...	...	...	...	...	...
MSME export growth (%)	...	...	...	...	...	...	...	...	...	...	...	...	...	...	...	...	...
IMPORTS																	
Total import value ($ million)	17,352	23,677	32,756	37,889	28,409	31,127	36,906	46,358	48,806	41,296	30,568	25,377	29,600	33,659	39,709	38,929	41,174
Total import growth (%)	35.8	36.4	38.3	15.7	(25.0)	9.6	18.6	25.6	5.3	(15.4)	(26.0)	(17.0)	16.6	13.7	18.0	(2.0)	5.8
MSME import value ($ million)	...	...	...	...	...	...	...	...	...	...	...	...	...	...	...	...	...
MSME import to total import value (%)	...	...	...	...	...	...	...	...	...	...	...	...	...	...	...	...	...
MSME import growth (%)	...	...	...	...	...	...	...	...	...	...	...	...	...	...	...	...	...

MSME = micro, small, and medium-sized enterprise.

* There is no microenterprise category in the national statistics. Only the criterion of the annual average number of employees is used for the statistics. Microenterprises are included in the category of small firms in accordance with the dimension classifier of the Bureau of National Statistics dated on 5 February 2015 Order No.27.

**GVA of MSMEs is calculated as a sum of small, medium-sized enterprises, individual entrepreneurs and farms GVA (GVA is defined as difference between output and intermediate consumption expenditure)

Source: ADB Asia SME Monitor 2022 database. Data from Bureau of National Statistics under Agency on Strategic Planning and Reforms of the Republic of Kazakhstan.

Table 5.3: Bank Credit

End-of-period data

Item	2004	2005	2006	2007	2008	2009	2010	2011	2012	2013	2014	2015	2016	2017	2018	2019	2020	2021
OPERATING BANKS																		
Number of operating banks, total	34	33	33	35	37	38	38	38	38	55	55	52	51	49	45	44	40	31
State-owned commercial banks*	1	1	1	1	1	1	1	1	1	1	1	1	1	1	1	1	1	1
State-owned development financial institutions**	...	...	...	...	...	...	...	...	...	17	17	17	17	17	17	17	14	8
Private commercial banks	18	18	18	22	23	24	23	22	22	22	23	20	20	18	14	13	12	10
Foreign commercial banks	15	14	14	12	13	13	14	15	15	15	14	14	13	13	13	13	13	12
Credit																		
Loans outstanding, total (KZT million)	1,484,010	2,592,090	4,690,998	7,258,369	7,460,281	7,644,036	7,591,593	8,811,248	9,958,040	11,291,548	12,105,684	12,674,245	12,708,324	12,705,352	13,091,764	13,864,890	14,623,065	18,497,653
Loans outstanding in domestic currency (KZT million)	714,071	1,255,882	2,421,943	4,158,399	4,162,074	3,944,283	4,383,014	5,682,129	7,041,296	7,936,659	8,565,052	8,401,114	8,578,859	9,366,787	10,094,320	11,560,763	12,726,647	16,588,156
Loans outstanding in foreign currency (KZT million)	769,939	1,336,208	2,269,055	3,099,970	3,298,207	3,699,754	3,208,578	3,129,119	2,916,744	3,354,890	3,540,632	4,273,131	4,129,465	3,338,565	2,997,444	2,304,127	1,896,418	1,909,497
Loan growth (%)	...	74.7	81.0	54.7	2.8	2.5	(0.7)	16.1	13.0	13.4	7.2	4.7	0.3	(0.02)	3.0	5.9	5.5	26.5
Total bank loans to GDP (%)	25.3	34.1	45.9	56.5	46.5	44.9	34.8	31.2	32.1	31.4	30.5	31.0	27.1	23.4	21.2	19.9	20.7	22.5
Lending rate (%, annual average)	13.1	13.3	13.2	13.6	15.3	14.5	13.7	12.7	12.8	12.9	12.1	14.3	15.4	14.3	13.5	13.8	13.2	14.1
Gross nonperforming loans (NPLs) (KZT million)	...	...	...	...	476	2,040	2,153	3,226	3,473	4,158	3,340	1,237	1,042	1,265	1,016	1,200	1,082	669
Gross NPLs to total loans (%)	...	...	...	...	5.2	21.2	23.8	30.8	29.8	31.2	23.6	8.0	6.7	9.3	7.4	8.1	6.9	3.3
Deposits																		
Deposits, total (KZT million)	1,270,843	1,653,536	3,076,729	3,890,142	5,409,359	6,573,863	7,334,340	8,386,537	8,994,735	10,085,857	11,679,177	15,888,902	18,049,782	17,509,992	18,553,214	19,021,565	22,089,738	27,101,567
Deposits in domestic currency (KZT million)	721,461	960,758	1,993,770	2,645,750	3,492,693	3,699,522	4,776,648	5,756,881	6,311,613	6,314,138	5,195,426	4,949,628	8,219,707	9,160,880	9,568,984	10,820,833	13,855,690	17,337,508
Deposits in foreign currency (KZT million)	549,382	692,778	1,082,959	1,244,392	1,916,666	2,874,341	2,557,692	2,629,656	2,683,122	3,771,720	6,483,751	10,939,274	9,830,074	8,349,112	8,984,230	8,200,731	8,234,049	9,764,059
Deposit rate (%, annual average)	2.8	3.4	4.0	5.1	4.7	4.3	3.5	3.6	3.5	4.4	4.8	8.8	9.9	7.9	6.8	6.8	7.0	6.8
MSME LOANS																		
MSME loans outstanding, total (KZT million)	288,367	470,168	861,045	1,505,487	1,570,734	1,708,189	1,384,956	1,341,578	1,412,005	1,283,441	1,788,059	2,060,455	3,002,974	2,788,589	2,363,861	2,108,945	2,515,308	3,772,244
MSME loans to total loans outstanding (%)	19.4	18.1	18.4	20.7	21.1	22.3	18.2	15.2	14.2	11.4	14.8	16.3	23.6	21.9	18.1	15.2	17.2	20.4
MSME loans to GDP (%)	4.9	6.2	8.4	11.7	9.8	10.0	6.3	4.8	4.6	3.6	4.5	5.0	6.4	5.1	3.8	3.0	3.6	4.6
MSME loan growth (%)	...	63.0	83.1	74.8	4.3	8.8	(18.9)	(3.1)	5.2	(9.1)	39.3	15.2	45.7	(7.1)	(15.2)	(10.8)	19.3	50.0
MSME lending rate (%, annual average)	15.0	14.7	14.1	14.3	15.7	14.0	13.3	12.5	12.1	12.5	11.5	12.9	14.0	13.7	12.7	12.7	11.6	12.9
Nonperforming MSME loans (NPLs) (KZT million)	...	...	...	...	...	...	...	...	...	...	...	...	...	...	...	...	...	...
MSME NPLs to total MSME loans (%)	...	...	...	...	...	...	...	...	...	...	...	...	...	...	...	...	...	...
Number of MSME loan borrowers	...	...	...	...	...	...	...	...	...	...	...	...	...	...	...	...	...	...
MSME loan borrowers to total bank borrowers (%)	...	...	...	...	...	...	...	...	...	...	...	...	...	...	...	...	...	...
MSME loan rejection rate (% of total applications)	...	...	...	...	...	...	...	...	...	...	...	...	...	...	...	...	...	...
Number of MSME savings account in banks	...	...	...	...	...	...	...	...	...	...	...	...	...	...	...	...	...	...
Guaranteed MSME loans (KZT million)	281,101	459,967	815,956	1,439,563	1,547,544	1,693,113	1,300,949	1,292,633	1,363,022	1,237,482	1,740,191	1,946,651	2,844,644	2,441,602	2,069,238	2,032,762	2,303,766	3,181,582
Non-collateral MSME loans (KZT million)	7,266	10,201	45,089	65,924	23,190	15,076	84,007	48,945	48,983	45,959	47,868	113,804	158,330	346,987	294,623	76,183	211,542	590,662
MSME loans outstanding by sector (% share)																		
Agriculture, forestry, and fisheries	14.3	9.9	8.4	7.4	10.5	9.7	9.0	14.3	13.2	11.9	12.8	15.6	12.9	13.3	14.7	13.6	13.4	24.1
Manufacturing	10.4	10.7	9.6	7.3	6.2	5.6	4.9	4.6	3.8	3.3	4.5	4.1	6.9	13.0	8.4	4.6	3.6	4.0
Transportation and communication	13.8	17.7	15.6	20.3	17.6	15.9	14.0	17.4	16.3	10.4	13.0	13.0	13.5	11.8	10.5	12.5	11.0	8.6
Construction	1.8	2.9	2.9	2.4	2.5	2.5	3.8	3.0	3.5	4.5	4.7	6.6	4.9	5.4	6.3	5.7	4.8	5.5
Wholesale and retail trade	0.5	0.2	0.2	0.9	1.0	1.1	0.9	1.4	1.5	1.7	1.2	0.8	0.5	0.4	0.7	0.4	0.4	1.8
Other services	41.6	40.4	39.5	41.2	41.0	40.9	38.0	30.9	32.6	30.6	33.7	32.2	37.0	26.8	23.0	25.8	26.4	23.9
Others	17.7	18.2	23.8	20.5	21.1	24.3	29.4	28.4	29.1	37.7	29.9	27.6	24.3	29.2	36.4	37.4	40.3	32.1
MSME loans outstanding by region (% share)																		
Capital city (Astana)	9.0	9.9	7.8	7.2	5.8	5.7	10.7	7.7	12.1	8.7	14.4	15.1	27.3	25.5	16.3	12.9	13.9	16.2
Other	91.0	90.1	92.2	92.8	94.2	94.3	89.3	92.3	87.9	91.3	85.6	84.9	72.7	74.5	83.7	87.1	86.1	83.8
MSME loans outstanding by type of use (% share)																		
For working capital	...	...	...	...	...	...	...	...	...	...	...	...	...	...	...	...	...	...
For capital investment	...	...	...	...	...	...	...	...	...	...	...	...	...	...	...	...	...	...
MSME loans outstanding by tenor (% share)																		
Less than 1 year	33.8	30.1	27.7	19.7	19.0	13.8	14.7	16.3	19.6	15.5	21.9	18.9	24.4	14.8	16.4	15.9	17.9	17.8
1-5 years	...	...	...	...	...	...	...	...	...	...	...	...	...	...	...	...	...	...
More than 5 years	66.2	69.9	72.3	80.3	81.0	86.2	85.3	83.7	80.4	84.5	78.1	81.1	75.6	85.2	83.6	84.1	82.1	82.2

GDP = gross domestic product; MSME = micro, small, and medium-sized enterprise.

* One state-owned bank is the housing construction bank Otbasy.

** Eight institutions are Baiterek subsidiaries.

Source: ADB Asia SME Monitor 2022 database. Data from National Bank of Kazakhstan.

Table 5.4: Public Financing and Guarantees

End-of-period data

Item	2010	2011	2012	2013	2014	2015	2016	2017	2018	2019	2020	2021
SUBSIDIZED LOANS TO MSMEs												
Number of funds*	...	...	...	...	...	...	...	...	...	...	...	7
Number of subsidized loans (new approval)	135	744	1,451	1,455	1,814	1,595	2,121	2,287	1,470	2,647	14,262	...
Outstanding of subsidized loans to MSMEs (KZT million)	...	...	...	...	...	...	...	...	...	...	...	...
Subsidized loans disbursed to MSMEs (KZT million)	83,081	275,124	511,857	361,163	338,005	270,131	270,436	248,641	173,157	154,894	399,993	734,224
Growth (%)	...	231.2	86.0	(29.4)	(6.4)	(20.1)	0.1	(8.1)	(30.4)	(10.5)	158.2	83.6
Number of MSMEs that accepted subsidized loans	143	634	1,521	1,185	1,767	1,595	2,121	2,287	1,432	2,401	3,662	7,269
MSME access to subsidized loans (% of total MSMEs)**	0.02	0.1	0.2	0.1	0.2	0.1	0.2	0.2	0.1	0.2	0.3	0.5

MSME = micro, small, and medium-sized enterprise.

* Based on DAMU website (number of offered subsidy programs).

** Calculated based on the number of operating MSMEs and the number of MSMEs that accepted subsidized loans.

Note: Entrepreneurship Development Fund "DAMU" begun to prepare annual reports on SME development since 2009, but information available only since 2010.

End-of-period data

Item	2010	2011	2012	2013	2014	2015	2016	2017	2018	2019	2020	2021
CREDIT GUARANTEES												
Number of guarantee schemes	1	1	1	1	1	1	2	3	3	3	4	4
Guaranteed loans outstanding to MSMEs (KZT million)	...	...	...	...	...	...	...	...	...	...	...	...
Guaranteed loans approved to MSMEs (KZT million)	...	...	...	...	...	...	...	...	...	...	...	...
Guaranteed loans disbursed to MSMEs (KZT million)	677.2	4237.6	10,991	7,090	15,448	26,964	27,474	42,846	65,348	102,748	275,466	365,286
Growth (%)	...	525.7	159.4	(35.5)	117.9	74.5	1.9	55.9	52.5	57.2	168.1	32.6
Number of MSMEs guaranteed	3	24	87	143	443	941	979	1,317	1,944	2,673	7,347	17,219
MSME access to credit guarantees (% of total MSMEs)*	0.000	0.003	0.01	0.02	0.05	0.1	0.1	0.1	0.2	0.2	0.5	1.2
Guaranteed MSME loans to total MSME loans (%)**	0.05	0.3	0.8	0.6	0.9	1.3	0.9	1.5	2.8	4.9	11.0	9.7
Nonperforming guaranteed MSME loans to total guaranteed MSME loans (NPL ratio; %)	...	...	...	...	...	...	...	...	...	...	...	...

MSME = micro, small, and medium-sized enterprise.

* Calculated based on the number of operating MSMEs.

** Calculated based on guaranteed loans disbursed to MSMEs.

Source: ADB Asia SME Monitor 2022 database. Data from National Bank of Kazakhstan, DAMU JSC, and its public annual reports.

Table 5.4a: Refinancing Schemes for MSMEs

Name of the Fund	Year of the launch	Fund Size (KZT million)	Target Beneficiaries	Amount of Refinance (KZT million)*	Number of MSMEs benefitted*	Status (ongoing/closed)
1. National Fund of the Republic of Kazakhstan (1 tranche)	2014	100,000	MSMEs in manufacturing.	255,191	1,188	Ongoing
2. National Fund of the Republic of Kazakhstan (2 tranche)	2014	50,000	MSMEs in manufacturing.	281,869	767	Ongoing
3. National Fund of the Republic of Kazakhstan (3 tranche)	2015	50,000	MSMEs in manufacturing.	283,720	836	Ongoing
4. National Bank of Kazakhstan soft loan program (up to 12-month bank loans at 8% per annum).	2020	800,000	Entrepreneurs (large and MSMEs) amid the state of emergency.	1,123,200	1,503	Closed
Grand Total (KZT million)				1,943,981	4,294	

MSME = micro, small, and medium-sized enterprise.

* Data as of end-2021.

Source: ADB Asia SME Monitor 2022 database. Data from National Bank of Kazakhstan, DAMU JSC, and its public annual reports.

Table 5.5: Nonbank Finance

End-of-period data

Item	2004	2005	2006	2007	2008	2009	2010	2011	2012	2013	2014	2015	2016	2017	2018	2019	2020	2021
NUMBER OF NONBANK FINANCE INSTITUTIONS																		
Nonbank Finance Institutions, total	132	216	211	228	239	218	216	213	208	217	230	286	363	381	399	445	1,149	1,100
Microfinance institutions*	...	...	...	...	...	...	...	...	...	5	15	71	136	149	157	202	230	242
Finance Companies	45	48	26	34	34	16	15	14	11	10	11	11	11	9	11	12	11	7
Pawnshops	...	...	...	...	...	...	...	...	...	...	...	...	...	...	...	...	664	605
Insurance companies	...	37	39	41	44	41	40	38	35	34	34	33	32	32	29	28	28	27
Credit unions/cooperatives	87	131	146	153	161	161	161	161	162	168	170	171	184	191	202	203	216	219
MICROFINANCE INSTITUTIONS																		
Financing outstanding, total (KZT million)**	...	...	...	...	...	...	...	...	...	...	...	64,560	101,044	162,397	226,766	304,950	436,521	743,339
Growth (%)	...	...	...	...	...	...	...	...	...	...	...	...	56.5	60.7	39.6	34.5	43.1	70.3
Total financing to GDP (%)***	...	...	...	...	...	...	...	...	...	...	...	0.2	0.2	0.3	0.4	0.4	0.6	0.9
Annual lending rate (%, on average)	...	...	...	...	...	...	...	...	...	...	...	...	...	...	...	...	...	...
Gross nonperforming loans (NPLs) (KZT million)	...	...	...	...	...	...	...	...	...	...	...	...	...	4,575	7,215	12,053	26,826	51,243
Gross NPLs to total loans (%)	...	...	...	...	...	...	...	...	...	...	...	...	...	2.8	3.2	4.0	6.1	6.9
Savings (KZT million)****	...	...	...	...	...	...	...	...	...	...	...	...	...	...	...	...	...	...
Number of customers financed, total	...	...	...	...	...	...	...	...	...	...	...	...	...	...	...	...	...	...
CREDIT UNIONS AND COOPERATIVES*****																		
Financing outstanding, total (KZT million)	4,400	9,200	12,500	18,000	22,000	22,600	19,100	17,900	25,300	36,500	50,400	62,900	75,900	95,800	128,000	172,000	213,800	241,500
Growth (%)	175.0	109.1	35.9	44.0	22.2	2.7	(15.5)	(6.3)	41.3	44.3	38.1	24.8	20.7	26.2	33.6	34.4	24.3	13.0
Total financing to GDP (%)***	0.1	0.1	0.1	0.1	0.1	0.1	0.1	0.1	0.1	0.1	0.1	0.2	0.2	0.2	0.2	0.2	0.3	0.3
Annual lending rate (%, on average)	...	...	...	...	...	...	...	...	...	...	...	...	...	...	...	...	...	...
Gross nonperforming loans (NPLs) (KZT million)	...	...	...	...	...	...	...	...	...	...	...	...	...	...	...	...	...	...
Gross NPLs to total loans (%)	...	...	...	...	...	...	...	...	...	...	...	...	...	6.9	4.4	2.7	2.7	1.7
Number of customers financed, total	1,473	2,850	3,905	5,505	3,565	2,624	1,438	1,395	2,505	2,974	2,898	2,053	3,210	4,406	5,800	5,900	7,200	6,500
FINANCE COMPANIES																		
Financing outstanding, total (KZT million)	...	...	...	...	...	...	...	...	...	...	...	...	...	743,300	976,700	1,398,400	1,336,700	1,398,600
Growth (%)	...	...	...	...	...	...	...	...	...	...	...	...	...	...	31.4	43.2	(4.4)	4.6
Total financing to GDP (%)	...	...	...	...	...	...	...	...	...	...	...	...	...	1.4	1.6	2.0	1.9	1.7
Annual lending rate (%, on average)	...	...	...	...	...	...	...	...	...	...	...	...	...	...	...	...	...	...
Gross nonperforming financing (NPFs) (KZT million)	...	...	...	...	...	...	...	...	...	...	...	...	...	78,700	72,700	76,500	89,700	77,300
Gross NPFs to total financing (%)	...	...	...	...	...	...	...	...	...	...	...	...	...	10.6	7.4	5.5	6.7	5.5
Number of customers financed, total	...	...	...	...	...	...	...	...	...	...	...	...	...	...	...	...	...	...
PAWNSHOPS																		
Financing outstanding, total (KZT million)	...	...	...	...	...	...	...	...	...	...	...	...	...	...	...	...	112,744	131,672
Growth (%)	...	...	...	...	...	...	...	...	...	...	...	...	...	...	...	...	...	16.8
Total financing to GDP (%)	...	...	...	...	...	...	...	...	...	...	...	...	...	...	...	...	0.2	0.2
Annual lending rate (%, on average)	...	...	...	...	...	...	...	...	...	...	...	...	...	...	...	...	...	...
Gross nonperforming financing (NPFs) (KZT million)	...	...	...	...	...	...	...	...	...	...	...	...	...	...	...	...	4,720	6,097
Gross NPFs to total financing (%)	...	...	...	...	...	...	...	...	...	...	...	...	...	...	...	...	4.2	4.6
Number of customers financed, total	...	...	...	...	...	...	...	...	...	...	...	...	...	...	...	...	...	...

GDP = gross domestic product.

* Microfinance organizations are regulated by the National Bank until 2015; they are regulated by the Agency on Financial Market Regulation since 2016.
** Data for 2017-2021 has been revised by the Agency for Regulation and Development of the Financial Market.
*** Data for 2021 is tentative.
**** Microfinance institutions are not allowed to take savings.
***** Credit union/cooperatives data is for the agriculture sector.

Source: ADB Asia SME Monitor 2022 database. Data from the Agency for Regulation and Development of the Financial Market and Association of Credit Unions ([https://www.gov.kz/memleket/entities/ardfm/press/article/details/72515?lang=ru]).

Table 5.6: Capital Markets

End-of-period data

Item	2004	2005	2006	2007	2008	2009	2010	2011	2012	2013	2014	2015	2016	2017	2018	2019	2020	2021
EQUITY MARKET																		
Main Board																		
KASE Index*	213.4	646.4	2,418.1	2,634.5	898.3	1,766.1	1,715.8	1,104.1	968.1	930.9	944.0	878.3	1,355.9	2,158.3	2,322.1	2,394.7	2,674.1	3,672.3
Market capitalization (KZT million)**	512,287	1,407,419	7,189,648	6,475,829	3,853,313	8,506,238	8,959,446	6,425,940	5,363,455	4,351,085	4,542,276	12,382,405	14,271,471	16,565,407	14,852,007	16,368,545	18,585,732	28,233,280
Growth (%)	...	174.7	410.8	(9.9)	(40.5)	120.8	5.3	(28.3)	(16.5)	(18.9)	4.4	172.6	15.3	16.1	(10.3)	10.2	13.5	51.9
Trading value (KZT million)	...	...	...	...	...	...	...	...	...	...	...	...	...	...	...	...	...	...
Trading volume (million shares)*	2,028	2,739	2,077	1,540	2,090	1,499	4,701	1,152	1,410	978	1,727	327	181	1,592	2,437	1,805	1,915	3,184
Number of listed companies	54	62	68	69	74	72	65	67	78	81	76	85	98	61	59	74	77	58
Number of IPOs	...	...	2	...	...	...	1	...	2	...	1	1	1	2	1	...	...	...
Number of delisted companies	...	...	...	...	...	...	...	...	...	...	...	...	...	...	...	...	...	...
Alternative Board for MSMEs**																		
Market capitalization (KZT million)***	...	...	...	...	...	...	...	...	...	...	...	...	...	576,252	635,411	852,494	464,369	528,080
Growth (%)	...	...	...	...	...	...	...	...	...	...	...	...	...	...	10.3	34.2	(45.5)	13.7
Trading value (KZT million)	...	...	...	...	...	...	...	...	...	...	...	...	...	...	...	...	...	...
Trading volume (million shares)*	...	...	...	...	...	...	...	...	...	...	...	...	...	1	587	275	189	8
Number of listed companies	...	...	...	...	...	...	...	...	...	...	...	...	...	43	51	48	44	89
Number of IPOs	...	...	...	...	...	...	...	...	...	...	...	...	...	...	...	2	...	...
Number of delisted companies	...	...	...	...	...	...	...	...	...	...	...	...	...	...	...	...	...	...
Moved to the main board	...	...	...	...	...	...	...	...	...	...	...	...	...	...	...	3	4	1
Moved from the main board	...	...	...	...	...	...	...	...	...	...	...	...	...	30	12	2	2	9
BOND MARKET																		
Corporate Bonds Issued by MSMEs																		
Corporate bonds issued by MSMEs, total (KZT million)	...	...	...	...	...	...	...	...	...	...	...	...	...	20,331	157,900	857,400	14,807	53,107
In local currency denominated (KZT million)	...	...	...	...	...	...	...	...	...	...	...	...	...	20,331	157,900	857,400	10,600	39,553
In foreign currency enominated (KZT million)	...	...	...	...	...	...	...	...	...	...	...	...	...	...	...	...	4,207	13,554
Growth (%)	...	...	...	...	...	...	...	...	...	...	...	...	...	...	676.6	443.0	(98.2)	258.7
Number of MSME that issued bonds	...	...	...	...	...	...	...	...	...	...	...	...	...	...	...	...	...	...
MSME bond yields (% per annum, on average)****	...	...	...	...	...	...	...	...	...	...	...	...	...	11.3	9.3	11.3	16.8	15.0
MSME bonds by maturity (% share)																		
Less than 1 year	...	...	...	...	...	...	...	...	...	...	...	...	...	...	...	...	...	...
1-5 years	...	...	...	...	...	...	...	...	...	...	...	...	...	40.0	70.0	53.3	100.0	100.0
5-10 years	...	...	...	...	...	...	...	...	...	...	...	...	...	60.0	20.0	46.7	...	...
More than 10 years	...	...	...	...	...	...	...	...	...	...	...	...	...	...	10.0	...	...	...

IPO = initial public offering; KASE = Kazakhstan Stock Exchange; MSME = micro, small, and medium-sized enterprise.

* KASE Index is the ratio of included into the representative list shares market prices at the list development date to this list shares prices at a certain date, weighted on capitalization considering free-floating shares. KASE Index value is recalculated after each deal concluded on shares, included into the index representative list.

** Excluding unlisted securities.

*** Since 10 June 2017, KASE's official list began to be divided into the main board, intended for large issuers, and an alternative board, which was established for small and medium-sized enterprises.

**** Coupon rate (% per annum, on average).

Source: ADB Asia SME Monitor 2022 database. Data from Kazakhstan Stock Exchange (KASE).

Table 5.6a: Listing Requirements—Kazakhstan Stock Exchange

Criteria	Stock	
	Main Board	Alternative Board for MSMEs
1. Lifetime of an issuer	at least 3 years	not required
2. Balance sheet total (the total amount of the report on the financial position of the issuer on the asset)	at least 2,550,000 times monthly calculation index (MCI) for each of the last 3 years	not required
3. Sales volume (revenue, operating income) of the issuer	at least 3,000,000 times the MCI for each of the last 3 years	not required
4. The current rating score of the issuer (this criterion is separate, if the issuer fulfills the criteria specified in rows 1-3 of this table, the fulfillment of this criterion is optional)	Not lower than "BB-" according to the international scale of S&P Global Ratings and/or Fitch Ratings and/or Moody's Investors Service	not required
5. Annual financial statements of the issuer (in the presence of subsidiaries - consolidated financial statements), prepared in accordance with IFRS or US GAAP	for the last 3 completed financial years	for the last 1 completed financial year
6. Interim financial statements (in the presence of subsidiaries - consolidated interim financial statements), prepared in accordance with IFRS or US GAAP, must be supported by an auditor's report or a report on the review of these financial statements, from the date of which no more than 6 months must pass before the date of filing with the Exchange of the relevant application for listing securities	Provided if: 1) an application for the inclusion of securities was submitted within the first 4 months from the date of the end of the last completed financial year, and there is no annual financial statement, confirmed by an audit report, for the last completed financial year; 2) the application for inclusion of securities was submitted after August 31 of the current year.	It is provided if the application for the inclusion of securities is submitted within the first 4 months from the date of the end of the last completed financial year, and there is no annual financial statement, confirmed by an audit report, for the last completed financial year.
7. Audit organization	included in the list of audit organizations recognized by the Exchange at the first level (https://kase.kz/files/normative_base/list_audit.pdf)	included in the list of audit organizations recognized by the Exchange (https://kase.kz/files/normative_base/list_audit.pdf)
8. Discount of securities is carried out (to be carried out after their issue/listing) by Central securities depositary	required	required
9. For an issuer established in the organizational and legal form of a joint-stock company - the presence of a corporate governance code approved by the general meeting of shareholders	required	required
10. Absence in the issuer's charter and/or securities issue prospectus of provisions that infringe or restrict the rights of securities owners to alienate (transfer) them	required	required
11. Number of declared ordinary shares	at least 100 000 shares	at least 100,000 shares
12. Number of authorized preferred shares	at least 10 000 shares	at least 10,000 shares

Criteria	Bonds		
	Main Board	Alternative Board for MSMEs	Private Placement Platform*
1. Lifetime of an issuer	at least 3 years	not required	not required
2. Balance sheet total (the total amount of the report on the financial position of the issuer on the asset)	at least 2,550,000 times Monthly calculation index (MCI) for each of the last 3 years	not required	not required
3. Sales volume (revenue, operating income) of the issuer	at least 3,000,000 times the MCI for each of the last 3 years	not required	not required
4. The current rating score of the issuer (this criterion is separate, if the issuer fulfills the criteria specified in rows 1-3 of this table, the fulfillment of this criterion is optional)	Not lower than "BB-" according to the international scale of S&P Global Ratings and/or Fitch Ratings and/or Moody's Investors Service	not required	not required

continued on next page

Table 5.6a *continued*

5. Annual financial statements of the issuer (in the presence of subsidiaries - consolidated financial statements), prepared in accordance with IFRS or US GAAP	for the last 3 completed financial years	for the last 1 completed financial year	for the last 1 completed financial year
6. Interim financial statements (in the presence of subsidiaries - consolidated interim financial statements), prepared in accordance with IFRS or US GAAP, must be supported by an auditor's report or a report on the review of these financial statements, from the date of which no more than 6 months must pass before the date of filing with the Exchange of the relevant application for listing securities	Provided if: 1) an application for the inclusion of securities was submitted within the first 4 months from the date of the end of the last completed financial year, and there is no annual financial statement, confirmed by an audit report, for the last completed financial year; 2) the application for inclusion of securities was submitted after August 31 of the current year.	It is provided if the application for the inclusion of securities is submitted within the first 4 months from the date of the end of the last completed financial year, and there is no annual financial statement, confirmed by an audit report, for the last completed financial year.	not required
7. Audit organization	included in the list of audit organizations recognized by the Exchange at the first level (https://kase.kz/files/normative_base/list_audit.pdf)	included in the list of audit organizations recognized by the Exchange (https://kase.kz/files/normative_base/list_audit.pdf)	included in the list of audit organizations recognized by the Exchange at the first level (https://kase.kz/files/normative_base/list_audit.pdf)
8. Discount of securities is carried out (to be carried out after their issue/listing) by central securities depositary	required	required	required
9. For an issuer established in the organizational and legal form of a joint-stock company - the presence of a corporate governance code approved by the general meeting of shareholders	required	required	not required
10. Absence in the issuer's charter and/or securities issue prospectus of provisions that infringe or restrict the rights of securities owners to alienate (transfer) them	mandatory	mandatory	not required
11. Presence of market maker	required if , provided that the number of holders of these bonds is 10 or more persons	not required	not required
12. Absence of defaults, unsettled situations of non-fulfillment of obligations to holders of previously issued securities for the payment of the principal debt and / or coupon interest	mandatory	mandatory	not required
13. Availability of other securities of the issuer in the official list of the Exchange	required only for the category "Commercial bonds" (with a maturity of not more than 12 months)	required only for the category "Commercial bonds" (with a maturity of not more than 12 months)	not required

GAAP = Generally Accepted Accounting Principles; IFRS = International Financial Reporting Standards; MSME = micro, small, and medium-sized enterprise; US = United States.

* For bonds subject to private placement in accordance with the requirements of the law on the securities market.

Source: ADB Asia SME Monitor 2022 database. Data from Kazakhstan Stock Exchange (KASE).

Table 5.7: Policies and Regulations

Regulations	
Name	**Outline**
Entrepreneurial Code of the Republic of Kazakhstan dated 29 October 2015 No.375-V	Defines the legal, economic, and social conditions and guarantees that ensure the freedom of entrepreneurship; regulates relations arising in connection with the interaction of business entities and the state, including government regulation and support for entrepreneurship.
Tax Code of the Republic of Kazakhstan dated 25 December 2017 No.120-VI	Establishes the fundamental principles of taxation; regulates power relations in establishing, introducing, changing, canceling, the procedure for calculating and paying taxes and other obligatory payments to the budget.
Civil Code of the Republic of Kazakhstan dated 27 December 1994 No.268-XIII	Regulates goods-money and other property relations based on the equality of participants, as well as personal non-property relations related to property. Participants of relations regulated by civil law are citizens, legal entities, the state, as well as administrative-territorial units.
Labor Code of the Republic of Kazakhstan dated 23 November 2015 No.414-V	Defines the legal regulation of labor relations.
Law of the Republic of Kazakhstan "On Microfinance activities" dated 26 November 2012 No.56-V	Establishes the features of the establishment of organizations engaged in microfinance activities and determines the features of state regulation.
Law of the Republic of Kazakhstan "On state regulation of the development of the agro-industrial complex and rural areas" dated 8 July 2005 No.66-III	Defines the legal, organizational, economic, and social foundations for the implementation of state regulation of the development of the agro-industrial complex and rural areas.
Law of the Republic of Kazakhstan "On agricultural cooperatives" dated 29 October 2015 No.372-V	Defines the legal status, rights, and obligations of members of agricultural cooperatives, as well as the legal status, procedure for the establishment, operation, reorganization and liquidation of agricultural cooperatives and its associations (unions).
Law of the Republic of Kazakhstan "On the securities market" dated 2 July, 2003 No.461-II	Regulates public relations arising in the process of issuing, placing, circulation, and redemption of emissive securities and other financial instruments; the specifics of the creation and activities of securities market entities; determines the procedure for regulating, controlling and supervising the securities market.
Law of the Republic of Kazakhstan "On Joint Stock Companies" dated 13 May, 2003 No.415-II	Determines the legal status, procedure for the establishment, operation, reorganization and liquidation of a joint-stock company; rights and obligations of shareholders.
Law of the Republic of Kazakhstan "On Limited and Additional Liability Partnerships" dated 22 April, 1998 No. 220-1	Determines the legal status of partnerships with limited and additional liability, the rights and obligations of their participants, the procedure for the establishment, operation, reorganization and liquidation of partnerships.
Law of the Republic of Kazakhstan "On investment and venture funds" dated 7 July, 2004 No.576-II	Defines the legal status, features of the establishment, operation, reorganization and liquidation of a joint-stock investment fund, the conditions and procedure for the establishment,operation and termination of the existence of a unit investment fund, the features of the legal status and activities of venture funds.
Law of the Republic of Kazakhstan "On state procurement" dated 4 December 2015 No.434-V	Defines state procurement regulations.
Law of the Republic of Kazakhstan "On accounting and financial reporting" dated 28 February 2007 No.234-III	Establishes the principles, basic qualitative characteristics and rules for accounting and financial reporting.
Law of the Republic of Kazakhstan "On financial leasing" dated 5 July 2000 No.78-II	Regulates relations arising in the process of financial leasing.
Law of the Republic of Kazakhstan "On complex entrepreneurial license (franchising)" dated 24 June, 2002 No.330-II	Regulates relations related to the implementation of a complex entrepreneurial license (franchising), determines the content of the complex entrepreneurial license agreement and is aimed at the development and state support of franchising activities.
Law of the Republic of Kazakhstan "On Copyright and Related Rights" dated 10 June, 1996 No.6-I	Regulates relations in the field of intellectual property arising in connection with the creation and use of works of science, literature and art (copyright), productions, performances, phonograms, broadcasts of broadcasting and cable broadcasting organizations (related rights).
Regulators and Policymakers	
Name	**Responsibility**
Ministry of National Economy	Responsible for development of entrepreneurship and introducing state support measures.
Ministry of Agriculture	Responsible for increasing the competitiveness of the agro-industrial complex and land administration.
Ministry of Digital Development, Innovations and Aerospace industry	Responsible for the formation and implementation of state policy in the field of digital development, innovation, communications, provision of public services, electronic industry.

continued on next page

Table 5.7 *continued*

State Revenue Committee of the Ministry of Finance	Responsible for regulatory, implementation and control functions in the field of customs affairs and ensuring the completeness and timeliness of tax receipts, customs and other obligatory payments to the state budget, calculation, deduction, transfer of social payments.
National Bank of Kazakhstan (NBK)	Responsible for price stability, conduct monetary policy, and supervise commercial banks.
Agency for Regulation and Development of Financial Markets	Responsible for stability of financial system, protection of the rights of financial services consumers as well as control of financial market and financial organizations (established on 1 January 2020).
Ministry of Trade and Integration	Responsible for development and promotion of exports of non-primary goods and services; development and regulation of domestic trade, improvement of trade infrastructure, development of exchange and electronic trade.
Ministry of Industry and Infrastructure Development	Responsible for policy measures in the field of industrial and innovative development, transport and logistics, scientific and technological development, mining and metallurgical complex,mechanical engineering, coal, chemical, pharmaceutical and medical industries, light construction industry.
"Baiterek" National Managing Holding JSC (parent company of "DAMU")	Responsible for diversification, support for innovations, exports development, increase in labor productivity. It plays role of the key national development institution and financial operator for implementation of state programs/ national projects.
"DAMU" JSC Entrepreneurship Development Fund	Responsible for promotion of the high-quality development of private entrepreneurship by providing financial support measures.

Policies		
Name	**Responsible Entity**	**Outline**
Development concept of small and medium-sized enterprises until 2030	Ministry of National Economy	The concept formulates the state policy for the development of MSMEs, which defines the basic principles and approaches for the allocation of state resources aimed at the development of MSMEs.
National project on entrepreneurship development for 2021-2025 (instead of state program "Business Road Map-2025")	Ministry of National Economy	Developed for the purpose of ensuring progressive changes in the structure of entrepreneurship by prioritizing the following aspects: (i) development of small businesses to increase employment of the population, (ii) reliance on medium-sized businesses as a driver for diversification of the economy, and (iii) comprehensive development of competition through equal conditions for business entities.
National project for the development of the agro-industrial complex for 2021–2025	Ministry of Agriculture	Developed for the purpose of enhancing of a competitive agro-industrial complex by increasing labor productivity by 2.5 times, doubling the export of agro-industrial complex products, and providing domestically produced socially significant food products.
"Business Road Map-2025" state program	Ministry of National Economy	Ensuring sustainable and balanced growth of regional entrepreneurship, as well as maintaining existing and creating new permanent jobs.
"Enbek" State Program for the Development of Productive Employment and Mass Entrepreneurship for 2017–2021 (closed)	Ministry of Labor and Social Protection	Promoting productive employment of the population and involving citizens in entrepreneurship.
"Economy of Simple Things"	National Bank of Kazakhstan	Expansion of production in manufacturing and the agro-industrial complex; saturation of the domestic market with goods and services of domestic producers. The NBK, using its own funds and funds placed under its management, purchases bonds of second-tier banks (STB) and the ACC worth up to KZT1 trillion with a loan maturity of up to 10 years at a final rate of return of up to 11% per annum. STB and ACC utilize these funds to finance priority projects in manufacturing, services, and agro-industrial complex.
Development Strategy of the Damu Fund for 2014-2023	"DAMU" Entrepreneurship Development Fund	Developed for the purpose to provide MSMEs with a wide range of financial instruments, increase the share of financial support and the amount of funding under the state programs for MSMEs, developing and introducing performance criteria to MSME projects, diversification of raising fund sources for programs.

MSME = micro, small, and medium-sized enterprise.

Source: ADB Asia SME Monitor 2022 database. Data from National Bank, Kazakhstan Stock Exchange, Ministry of National Economy, Ministry of Agriculture, Ministry of Investment and Infrastructure Development, Ministry of Trade and Integration, "Baiterek" National Managing Holding, "DAMU" Entrepreneurship Development Fund, and Ministry of Labor and Social Protection.

Table 5.7a: COVID-19 Emergency Measures

Name	Fund Size (KZT billion)	Outline
1. Comprehensive plan on recovery of economic growth for 2020–2021	n/a	10 directions: (i) attracting investments, (ii) real sector of economy, (iii) service economy, (iv) MSMEs, (v) macroeconomic stability, (vi) labor market, (vii) digitilization of economy, (viii) social sector, (ix) regional development, and (x) strategic planning. 172 systemic and sector measures to stimulate business activity, support employment, and increase the income of the population.
2. Program of concessional lending to business entities for 2020–2021	800	Aimed at supporting entrepreneurs affected during the state of emergency by issuing soft loans by banks for up to 12 months at 8% rate per annum. Funds were provided to entrepreneurs to replenish working capital, including payments for goods, works, services, taxes and other payments to the budget, wages. Concessional lending was provided to both large businesses and medium and small businesses.
3. Funding for expansion of the state programs	240	(i) Subsidizing the agro-industrial complex – T50 billion. (ii) Development of the labor market under the "Enbek" State Program – T50 billion. (iii) Subsidizing the interest rate and guaranteeing loans under the State Program "Business Road Map - 2025" – T84.5 billion. (iv) Development of social and engineering infrastructure in rural areas under the project "Auyl - El Besigi" – T55 billion.
4. Funding of "Employment Road Map" program	1,000	(i) Ensuring employment and preventing the growth of unemployment. (ii) Creation of jobs through the development of the infrastructure of settlements and ensuring the income of the population. (iii) Development and expansion of the entrepreneurial initiative of citizens to create new permanent jobs.
5. Funding of tax exemption for business entities	237	To compensate for the losses of small businesses, associated with the provision of exemptions from taxes and fees on the salary fund for MSMEs and large businesses in the affected sectors of the economy.
6. "Economy of Simple Things" program	1,000	Expansion of production in manufacturing and the agro-industrial complex; saturation of the domestic market with goods and services of domestic producers.
7. Financing working capital of SMEs	600	Measure was aimed to help SMEs finance working capital.
8. "Economy of Common Goods" program	100	Providing loans to farmers (dated 14 May 2020).
Grand Total	**3,977**	

MSME = micro, small, and medium-sized enterprise, SME = small and medium-sized enterprise.

Source: ADB Asia SME Monitor 2022 database. Data from ADB COVID-19 Policy Database and official website Primeminister.kz (https://primeminister.kz/ru/news/reviews/antikrizisnye-mery-pravitelstva-vozobnovlenie-rosta-ekonomiki-i-podderzhka-msb-862620).

Country Review

Kyrgyz Republic

Overview

In 2021, gross domestic product (GDP) grew by 3.6% to KGS723 billion.[193] GDP is expected to grow by 4.2% in 2022 to KGS 835 billion, the slowdown due to the impact of economic sanctions against the Russian Federation over its invasion of Ukraine.[194] The 2020 unemployment rate was 5.8%.

Micro, small, and medium-sized enterprises (MSMEs) play an important role in economic development. According to the National Statistical Committee of the Kyrgyz Republic, there are 17,050 MSMEs, employing 93,000 people. MSMEs accounted for 42.8% of GDP and 27.3% of exports in 2021.

Access to finance is one of the serious problems faced by MSMEs in the Kyrgyz Republic. The Cabinet of Ministers considers MSME development a priority. In recent years it has increased the capital held by state banks, recommending they allocate these funds for MSME lending in priority sectors, to export-oriented companies, and for cluster development.

Despite the growth in loans from the banking and nonbanking systems, interest rates remain high while maturities remain short. Business loans accounted for 76.8% of commercial bank loans outstanding in 2021. The credit guarantee system is being successfully developed, which helps MSMEs obtain needed credit in case they lack collateral, while also helping reduce bank credit risk.

Nonbank financial institutions, including microfinance institutions, are viable alternative sources of MSME financing—although they remain small in scale. The Kyrgyz stock market is in its infancy, yet MSMEs can raise funds by issuing bonds, though they have just started to develop.

The Ministry of Economy and Commerce is responsible for coordinating MSME policies. In 2016, the National Bank of the Kyrgyz Republic (NBKR)—the country's central bank—launched a National Financial Literacy Program, and in March 2022, the Cabinet of Ministers approved a Financial Inclusion Strategy for 2022–2026, which will help improve financial literacy among MSMEs and assist increasing their access to formal financial services.

---

193 Bulletin of the National Bank of the Kyrgyz Republic. www.nbkr.kg.

194 Report of the National Bank of the Kyrgyz Republic "On money-credit policy 2 quarter, 2022" www.nbkr.kg.

1. Impact of the Global Economy on MSMEs

COVID-19 Impact

The coronavirus disease (COVID-19) pandemic damaged the Kyrgyz economy as it did to countries worldwide. In 2020, GDP decreased by 8.6%, inflation grew to 9.7% (3.1% in 2019), the budget deficit reached 3.3% of GDP (0.1% of GDP in 2019). The country dealt with widespread isolation, as both public and private organizations switched to remote operations.

A JIA Business Association survey described some of the impact the pandemic had on MSMEs.[195] It reported that 50.1% of MSME respondents said nothing had changed workwise; 21.2% indicated that operations temporarily stopped at the time of the outbreak but resumed gradually; a quarter said work was stopped and had yet to resume (10.9% due to COVID-19 infections among employees, 7.8% due to reduced orders, and 4.8% by government order). At the same time, 2.2% of respondents said they closed operations.

More than half of the respondents reported some impact on revenue and product/service orders—12.7% said they faced a serious drop (50% to 100%) in revenue, 12.3% on orders, and 10.1% said their employees were affected. Some (8.3%) saw their income grow (14.3% felt no impact); orders grew for 9.6% (12.7% saw no change); and 10.1% hired new labor (20.1% reported no change).

The study found that 50% of respondents expected their MSME operations in 2021 would show some improvement (but not dramatic): (i) 12% expected growth or no impact on revenue, 12%–13% on orders, and 10%–17% on labor; (ii) 33%–50% expected a drop in revenue (9% said it would be significant—from 50% to 100%), 8% expected a drop in orders, with another 8% expecting a significant decrease in employment; and (iii) over 30% said they were unable to predict what might happen in 2021.

Given that many MSMEs are borrowers, the central bank adopted three resolutions in 2020 offering support during the pandemic:[196]

- Banks and nonbank financial institutions were instructed (i) not to charge or collect commissions and fines, (ii) to reconsider payments on loans and grant deferrals of payments for at least 3 months, and (iii) not to lower MSME ratings.
- General terms and procedures for granting commercial bank credit were defined so they would meet central bank standards and pay interest to depositors on time.
- Simplify requirements for MSMEs to obtain credit by eliminating the need for tax and social service certificates.

Despite the support, MSMEs still suffered, although probably less than otherwise:

- The number of MSMEs in 2020 and 2021 remained stagnant, growing just 0.2% both years.
- There were fewer people employed by registered MSMEs—49.3% of the total nationwide in 2021, down 3.3 percentage points from 2020 (52.6%).
- The MSME share of GDP dropped from 42.8% in 2019 to 40.6% in 2020, before recovering to 42.8% in 2021.

195 JIA Association "Assessing the impact of the COVID-19 pandemic on businesses in Kyrgyzstan."

196 "On provisional rules for the regulation of financial and credit institutions in connection with the pandemic COVID 19" dated 18 March 2020, № 2020-P-12/13-1-(BS); "On the provision of loans by the National Bank of the Kyrgyz Republic to commercial banks to mitigate the negative impacts of the COVID-19 pandemic in the Kyrgyz Republic" dated 24 March 2020 № 2020-P-09\15-9-(NLA); "On Provisional Rules for Classification of Assets and Making Appropriate Allocations to the Reserve for Covering Potential Losses and Losses by Commercial Banks and Certain Non-Banking Organizations" dated 29 April 2020, #2020-P-12/25-7-(NLA).

- While gross MSME income fell by 8% in 2020 compared with 2019, it increased by 50.0% in 2021 to KGS203 billion. During 2016–2019, gross income grew by an average 14%—by sector, gross 2020 MSME income was
  - up 26% for agriculture (since 2016),
  - down 4% for industry (2019),
  - down 23% for extractive products (2019),
  - down 20% for construction (2019), and
  - down 7.4% for services (2019)—hotels and restaurants fell by 42%, entertainment and recreation by 60%, and education by 30.
- Foreign direct investment (FDI) inflows to MSMEs in 2020 decreased by 46% compared with 2019:
  - industry was unchanged from 2019;
  - mining received 22.0% less FDI than in 2019;
  - manufacturing saw FDI inflows significantly increase to $27.5 million, up 78.6% from 2019;
  - FDI in trade fell 12.0% from 2019; and
  - FDI in construction was 57.0% lower than 2019.
- MSME exports dropped by 30% in 2020, recovering rapidly (up 52.8% in 2021).

For households and businesses affected by the pandemic, bank loans increased by 11.0% in 2020, expanding further by 11.8% in 2021.[197] This was associated with a 15.6% increase in banking assets in 2021 compared with 2020. The weighted average interest rate for 2020 dropped from 14.8% in 2019 to 13.9% in 2020, but increased to 14.2% in 2021. The growth in the weighted average interest rate was in response to an increase in the central bank discount rate to 8% in 2021 from 5% in 2020.

In 2021, GDP grew by 3.6% despite the pandemic, but inflation remained high at 11.6%. After the restrictions in 2020, the economy gradually stabilized with MSMEs recovering in share of GDP, gross income, and exports .

Impact of the Russian Invasion of Ukraine

The Kyrgyz economy is closely interconnected with the economies of the Russian Federation and Ukraine. According to World Bank forecasts, the invasion's impact will be significant: (i) GDP will decrease by 5% in 2022; (ii) inflation will rise to an annual 15%; (iii) remittances from Kyrgyz workers in the Russian Federation will decline by 33%; and (iv) an unknown number of migrants working in the Russian Federation will likely return, increasing unemployment.[198] The impact from the Russian Federation is expected to be far greater:

Russian Federation. Kyrgyz trade with the Russian Federation in 2021 totaled $2.3 billion—with exports valued at $393.3 million (23.7% of all exports) and imports at $1.9 billion (34.2%). Economic sanctions imposed on the Russian Federation affect its financial system, imports of high-tech and dual-use products, civil aviation, and energy. Several large Russian banks were disconnected from the SWIFT system. Access of Russian companies and banks to capital markets has been nearly shut. The United States (US) and Canada also imposed a ban on imports of oil and other energy products along with steel products. Several countries have banned visas to Russian citizens. The Kyrgyz Republic has already felt their impact. For example, Kyrgyz migrant workers face significant difficulties sending money home, exporters have trouble receiving payment for delivered goods, and importers have problems paying for Russian products. The number of flights has been cut significantly. Also, a supplier that normally transit goods through the Russian Federation before arriving in the Kyrgyz Republic must look for alternative routes. The Russian Federation has banned grain and sugar exports to other Eurasian Economic Union (EAEU) members (Armenia, Belarus, Kazakhstan, and the Kyrgyz Republic). More than 100 product categories—including technology, telecommunications, medical equipment, vehicles, agricultural machinery, electrical equipment,

197 NBKR Bulletin, www.nbkr.kg
198 Global Economic Prospects, World Bank, https://www.vsemirnyjbank.org/ru/publication/global-economic-prospects.

railway cars and locomotives, containers, turbines, and machine tools—are only allowed into other EAEU countries with special permission.

Ukraine. Total trade between the Kyrgyz Republic and Ukraine in 2021 was $61.1 million—exports amounted to $6.5 million (0.2% of total exports) and imports worth $54.6 million (1.0% of total imports). Nevertheless, Ukraine plays a significant role in certain commodities such as medicines and food products. Representatives of Kyrgyz pharmaceutical companies have said they cancelled all orders placed in Ukraine. It is uncertain when supplies can resume. Ukraine is not a significant transit route for Kyrgyz carriers (as of August 2022).

The Kyrgyz economy has felt the invasion's impact in several ways:

- in February 2022, as the *som* devalued by more than 20%, the central bank increased its discount rate to 14%—subsequently, the exchange rate stabilized and then strengthened;
- interest rates on loans have gradually increased;
- the central bank restricted the export of US dollar cash; and
- prices rose for fuel and lubricants, sugar, vegetable oil, and flour, even as there was no shortage of goods.

In September 2022, the central bank forecast GDP to grow by 4.2% with inflation rising to 15.5%. The impact of a prolonged Russian invasion of Ukraine will likely include further supply chain disruptions for international trade along with inflationary pressure on commodities and energy. This could seriously impact MSME operations sly in 2022, delaying the pandemic recovery in MSME productivity and international trade.

2. MSME Development

- There were 17,050 MSMEs operating in 2021, or 98.2% of all Kyrgyz enterprises. More than half are in services and concentrated in the capital city of Bishkek.
- The number of MSME employees has been declining since the COVID-19 outbreak in 2020. As of end-2021, MSMEs employ 93,000 people, or 49.3% of the labor force. While many work in services like wholesale and retail trade, about one-third work in manufacturing.
- MSMEs provided 42.8% of GDP in 2021, mainly from trade and agriculture. Promoting growth-oriented MSMEs is critical to boost national productivity.
- Most MSME operations target domestic markets and highly rely on imported goods for production. Those participating in global value chains account for over 25% of total export value.
- The government's High Technology Park of the Kyrgyz Republic (High-Tech Park) in Bishkek offers several benefits such as value-added tax (VAT) exemptions for imported equipment and technology. The government is promoting higher technology and quality control for agri-businesses.
- E-commerce and digitalization are expanding as online transactions and infrastructure expand along with e-payment systems. MSMEs increasingly use e-commerce for retail sales.
- MSME associations and the Chamber of Commerce and Industry—through consulting and training services—support MSME development and industrialization as well as business clusters and infrastructure development.

Scale of MSMEs

MSMEs are divided into two groups by type of activity. They are defined by annual turnover and the number of employees by sector (Table 6.1). Group 1 includes MSMEs in agriculture, fishing, mining, manufacturing, and power supply (electricity, gas, and water). Group 2 includes MSMEs in services. A microenterprise has (i) up to 14 employees and an annual turnover of up to KGS150,000 for Group 1 and (ii) up to seven employees and turnover of up to

KGS230,000 for Group 2. A small enterprise has (i) 15 to 50 employees and an annual turnover of KGS150,001–KGS500,000 for Group 1 and (ii) eight to 15 employees and turnover of KGS230,001–KGS500,000 for Group 2. A medium-sized company (i) employs 51 to 200 people with an annual turnover of KGS500,001–KGS2 million for Group 1 and (ii) employs 16 to 50 employees with turnover of KGS500,001–KGS2 million for Group 2.

A total of 17,050 MSMEs operated in 2021—or 98.2% of all enterprises. Most—16,252 firms—were small enterprises with 798 medium-sized enterprises (Figure 6.1A and Table 6.2). More than half of MSMEs are in services—28.0% for wholesale and retail trade, 5.3% for transport and communication, and 36.6% for other services—followed by manufacturing (14.6%), construction (12.2%), and agriculture (3.3%) (Figure 6.1B). The growth of MSMEs by number decelerated sharply during the COVID-19 pandemic in 2020 and 2021, stagnating at a 0.2% annual increase.

By region, most MSMEs (62.5%) are concentrated in Bishkek, the capital city, with the remaining 37.5% spread across the regions (Figure 6.1C). The number of MSMEs is lower in rural areas as work as farmers and individual entrepreneurs with no legal identity. The geographical distribution has not changed in a decade.

Figure 6.1: Number of MSMEs

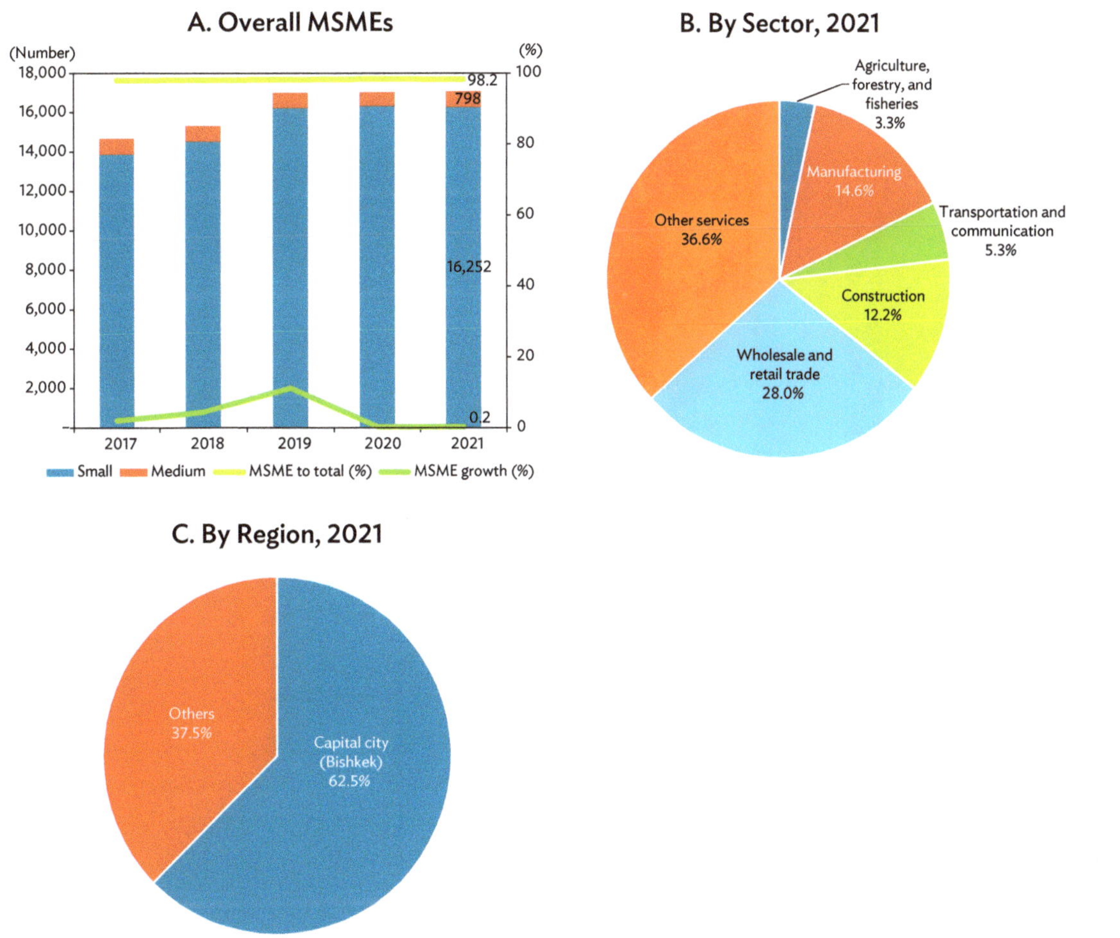

MSME = micro, small, and medium-sized enterprise.

Source: ADB Asia SME Monitor 2022 database. Data from the National Statistics Committee.

Employment

Over the past decade, MSMEs absorbed up to half of the labor force. After the COVID-19 outbreak in 2020, employment has gone down. In 2019, before the pandemic, MSMEs employed around 108,000 workers or 53.0% of the labor force. But as the pandemic spread in 2020, MSME employment contracted by 6.5% to 101,000 workers (52.6% share), and dropped a further 7.8% in 2021, to 93,000 workers (49.3% share) (Figure 6.2A and Table 6.2).

By sector, 32.4% worked in manufacturing, followed by other services like accommodations and food services (29.1%), wholesale and retail trade (17.7%), construction (12.7%), agriculture (4.2%), and transportation and communications (3.9%) (Figure 6.2B). Many MSME workers were in services.

In 2021, around half (49.9%) of the MSME labor force worked in Bishkek, with the remaining half (50.1%) scattered across the regions (Figure 6.2C). Since 2013, there have been slightly more working in the capital (over 50%) than in other regions. This reversed slightly in 2021, suggesting that rural MSMEs now tend to hire more employees than those in Bishkek—even with the large number (62.5%) of MSMEs operating there. Small enterprises employed 63.4% of workers and medium enterprises 36.6%.

Figure 6.2: Employment by MSMEs

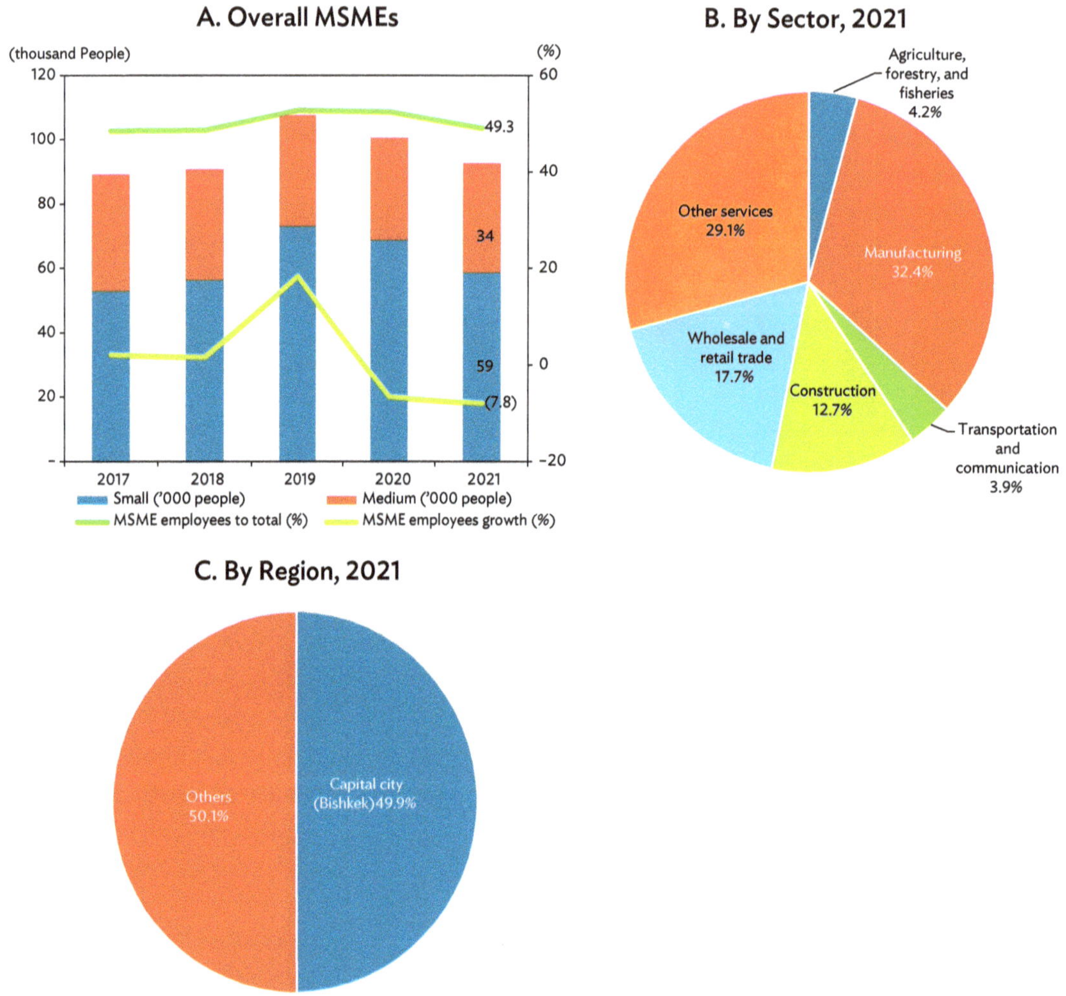

MSME = micro, small, and medium-sized enterprise.

Source: ADB Asia SME Monitor 2022 database. Data from the National Statistics Committee.

Business Productivity

MSMEs productivity recovered sharply in 2021. In pre-pandemic 2019, MSMEs accounted for 42.8% of the country's GDP (KGS265.4 billion, a 9.5% increase from the previous year). As the pandemic took hold in 2020, the MSME share of GDP dropped sharply to 40.6% (KGS244.4 billion, down by 7.9%). However, in 2021 it recovered quickly, back to the 2019 42.8% GDP share (KGS309.5 billion, up by 26.7% from 2020 and well above the 2019 level). The recovery was driven by renewed exports (Figure 6.3A and Table 6.2).

More than one-third (39.3%) of MSME output in 2021 came from wholesale and retail trade, followed by agriculture (20.8%), manufacturing (14.7%), construction (10.3%), transportation and communications (4.9%), and other services (3.0%) (Figure 6.3B). MSMEs in domestic trade and agriculture have remained a solid pillar and main driver of MSME contributions to GDP. However, they tend to be stability-oriented—growth-oriented MSMEs that boost productivity through innovation, or actively expand into global markets, remain few and far between.

Figure 6.3: MSME Contribution to GDP

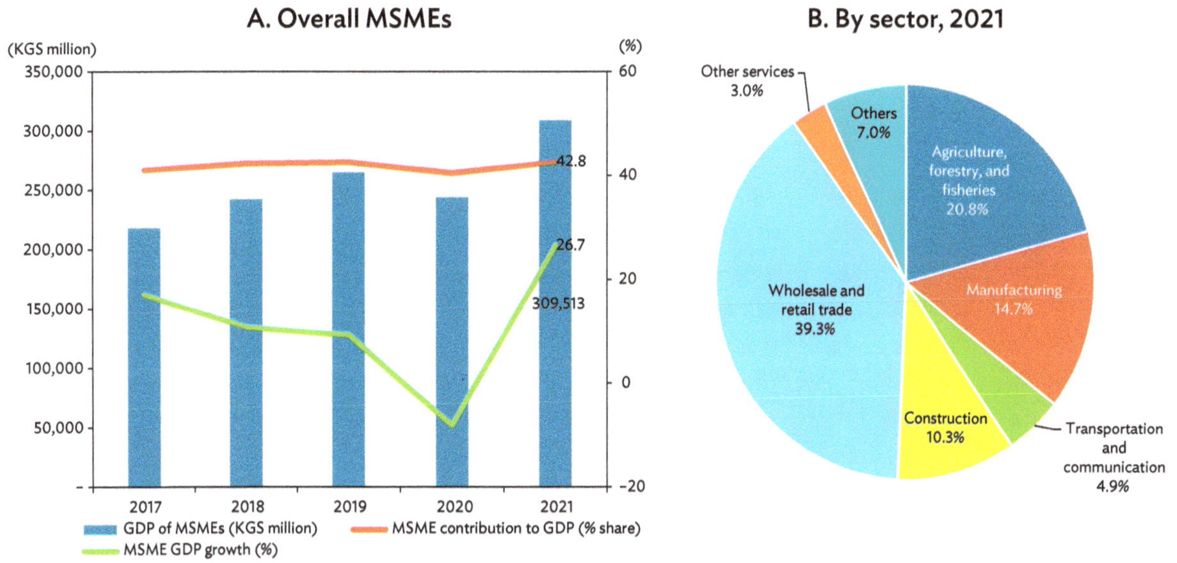

GDP = gross domestic product, MSME = micro, small, and medium-sized enterprise.

Source: ADB Asia SME Monitor 2022 database. Data from the National Statistics Committee.

Market Access

The majority of MSMEs supply the domestic market. Yet, they rely a great deal on imported goods for production and sales. MSME imports accounted for more than half of the country's total import bill over the past decade. In 2021, they amounted to $3.2 billion (56.7% of total imports), up 56.3% from pandemic-plagued 2020 (when MSME imports contracted by 38.0%) (Figure 6.4A and Table 6.2). MSMEs mainly import (i) electronic communications equipment from the People's Republic of China (PRC) and Viet Nam; (ii) rods, wire rods, and corner pieces from the Russian Federation, Kazakhstan, and the PRC; (iii) medicines from the Russian Federation, India, and Türkiye; and (iv) fabrics from the PRC.

MSME access to global markets and their participation in global value chains has grown slowly. Exports reached $752 million in 2021 (27.3% of total exports). They grew by 52.8% in 2021, recovering from the 30.0% contraction in 2020 (Figure 6.4A and 6.4B). MSME exports are volatile and react sharply to external shocks like the pandemic or the Russian invasion of Ukraine. MSME exports fell far more rapidly than non-MSME exports in 2020 (total exports contracted just 0.7% in 2020), and they recovered faster than non-MSME exports in 2021—helped by government support measures (Figure 6.4B). Although the share of MSME exports to total exports has fallen since 2019, they still contribute significantly to overall exports (the share peaked at 39.3% in 2018). MSMEs mainly export (i) vegetables and fruit to the Russian Federation and Kazakhstan; (ii) milk and dairy products, primarily to Kazakhstan; (iii) cotton, mainly to the Russian Federation; and (iv) sewing products to the Russian Federation and Kazakhstan.

Figure 6.4: MSME Exports and Imports

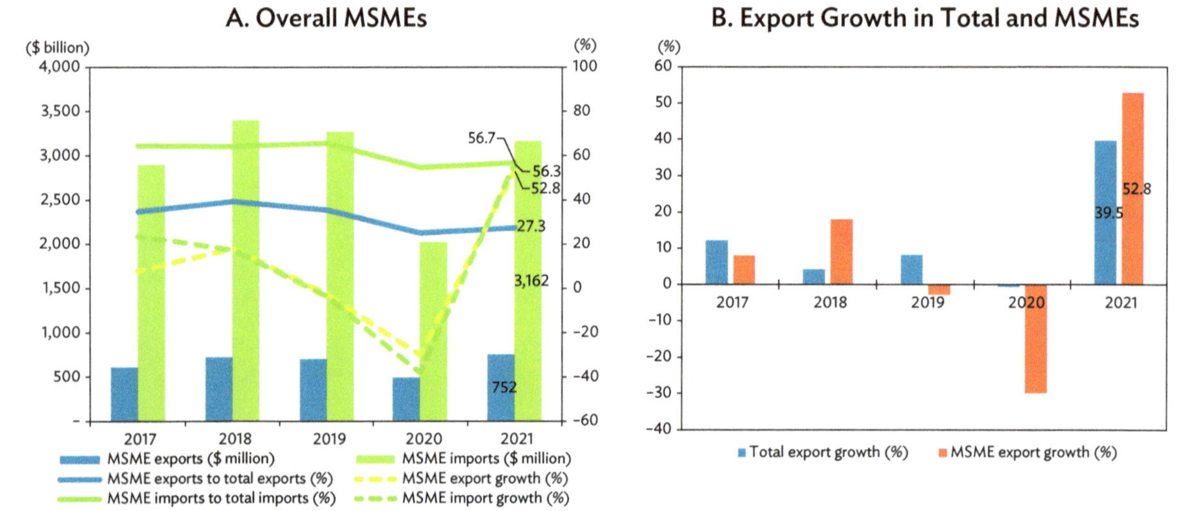

MSME = micro, small, and medium-sized enterprise.

Source: ADB Asia SME Monitor 2022 database. Data from the National Statistics Committee.

Technology and Innovation

With few exceptions, MSMEs use mostly low-technology production. Bishkek's High-Tech Park (established 2011) clusters about 100 companies, including MSMEs. In 2021, High-Tech Park revenues increased by 81.0% compared to 2020, with the number of employees up by 52.0%. Manufactured products (software and information technology) are exported mainly to the United States (38.2% of the 2021 exports, nearly three times the 2020 value); followed by the Russian Federation (16.6%, up 253%); and Kazakhstan (15.8%, up 118%).

One major development in technology and innovation is e-commerce. As in many countries, e-commerce and digitalization are expanding rapidly. The Kyrgyz Republic has its own Association of E-commerce, with members such as tech-based local firms Lalafo, Svetofor, Kivana, Namba market, and Wildberries, among others.

The Ministry of Economy and Commerce and Ministry of Agriculture support environment-friendly cultivation of agricultural crops, and applying new technologies for processing. The introduction of International Organization for Standardization (ISO) 22000 (food safety management) and ISO 9001 (quality management) should increase competitiveness and greater international market access.

Box 6.1: Business Cluster Development in the Kyrgyz Republic—High-Tech Park

The government's High Technology Park of the Kyrgyz Republic (High-Tech Park) in Bishkek was created in 2011 with special benefits for resident information technology (IT) firms. These include exemption from taxes and benefits for insurance premiums, exemptions from profit, sales, and value-added taxes. As the largest expenditure in IT is salaries, the government also reduced income tax (to 5.0% of the national average monthly wage) and social contributions (to 12.0%). The tax benefits will expire in 2026 (15 years after the park opened).

To become a High-Tech Park resident, a firm must meet three requirements:

(i) it must be IT-related,
(ii) it must receive at least 80.0% of its revenues from exports (within 18 months), and
(iii) it must contribute 1.0% of revenues to the High-Tech Park.

As of end-2021, there were 97 resident firms (employing more than 1,000 people) collectively earning KGS2.1 billion in revenues—with 93.5% derived from exports.

Source: High-Tech Park website: http://htp.kg/

Networking and Support

There are about 100 business associations in the Kyrgyz Republic. The Chamber of Commerce and Industry is one of the largest organizations promoting MSME development. It has branches in all regions and more than 1,000 members. It offers opportunities for networking and business services—such as international exhibitions, finding partners, organizing meetings between buyers and sellers, and consulting.

There are other MSME development associations offering consultations, information, knowledge, and networking support. They conduct research on MSME development and help identify and resolve vulnerabilities.

In addition to private sector initiatives to support MSME business networks, the Ministry of Economy and Commerce, the Agency for Development and Investment, and other government agencies offer support. Together with international development agencies, they design and conduct capacity development programs for MSMEs.

Several ministries and agencies contribute to startup development. For example, the Ministry of Economy and Commerce created an "Entrepreneurs Service Center" single window for MSMEs. The State Service of Intellectual Property and Innovation (Kyrgyzpatent), the Ministry of Environment, and commercial banks promote green technology, organic food production, waste recycling, and other areas MSMEs may want to explore.

Box 6.2: Business Communities Support Private Sector Development for MSMEs

The Kyrgyz Republic has many associations representing interests of entrepreneurs, farmers, and investors.

The Chamber of Commerce and Industry. The Chamber of Commerce and Industry of the Kyrgyz Republic (CCI) is a nongovernment organization designed to advocate and protect the interests of entrepreneurs; promote the development of the national economy; and represent industrial, scientific, technical and trade relations with other countries. It had 1,006 members as of 2022. The Law "On the Chamber of Commerce and Industry of the Kyrgyz Republic" defines the general legal, economic, and social basis of its activities and state relations. The CCI protects the rights and interests of entrepreneurs in international trade and intellectual property; provides assistance to enterprises operating in foreign markets; and develops new forms of cooperation, assists in finding partners, business contacts, and assists in resolving conflicts.

It organizes economic and trade missions and delegations, international exhibitions and fairs, and promotes better interaction between entrepreneurs and government agencies. It also confirms certificates on the origin of goods and issues documents related to the mutual trade of goods and services, trains specialists for entrepreneurial activities and offers other types of training. The CCI also helps members meet standards and quality control.

The JIA Business Association. JIA was created in 2006 as an initiative for entrepreneurs from different regions of the country. It brings together more than 1,000 representatives of MSMEs, with almost 70% engaged in trade, services, manufacturing, and construction. JIA is the only Kyrgyz association that is a member of the International Organization of Employers. It works with government institutions, international organizations, and embassies to help entrepreneurs develop their business through various events, information and consulting support. It also works with government on regulatory reforms that improve the business climate.

With support from the Organization for Security and Cooperation in Europe, JIA opened a Business Support Center (BSC) to provide information and consulting support to entrepreneurs. Experts provide services to entrepreneurs covering, for example, marketing, sales, strategic and financial management, information technology tools for business development, human resource management, and legal services, among others. The BSC provided 3,437 consultations in 2019–2020, especially during the pandemic. The association also organizes various business and study tours, business camps to learn and share experiences on business development, discovering new markets, visits to successful firms, and promote partnerships among participants.

Source: Chamber of Commerce and Industry website: https://cci.kg/; Business Association JIA website: https://jia.kg/ru/

3. Access to Finance

- MSME credit data are unavailable in the Kyrgyz Republic. Commercial bank business loans include those to MSMEs. A large portion of these loans go to wholesale and retail trade and agriculture—typically MSMEs. And they are growing.
- The government provides concessional loans with interest rate subsidies to agriculture-based MSMEs. The Guarantee Fund supports MSME access to bank credit, offering a 50% partial credit guarantee.
- The nonbank finance industry remains small but is increasingly used for MSME financing through microfinance institutions and credit unions.
- Financial technology (fintech) and digital finance are making great strides in expanding MSME access to finance. Digital infrastructure such as digital wallets and a unified payments system (ELcard) is a key factor in promoting more inclusive MSME financing.
- MSMEs are not listed on equity markets; but some issue corporate bonds to raise growth capital. Improving financial literacy and regulatory compliance for potential issuers is key for more small firms to tap capital markets.
- There are two private credit bureaus and a centralized collateral registry. The government also uses a state credit registry to improve MSME access to credit.

Bank Credit

The National Bank of the Kyrgyz Republic (NBKR) is the central bank and regulates the activities of banks and nonbank finance institutions (microfinance institutions, credit unions, and guarantee funds). Banks provide loans largely based on available collateral, guarantees from the Open Joint Stock Company (OJSC) Guarantee Fund, and personal guarantees. Other forms of lending remain limited, cash-flow-based based lending, trade financing, project-based lending, and structured finance. There were 23 commercial banks as of end-2021, of which 2 were state-owned, 5 private sector banks, and 16 foreign banks (Table 6.3).

MSME credit data are unavailable. Data on commercial bank business loans cover all loans to enterprises, including MSMEs. Since 2017, business loans increased from KGS87.2 billion to KGS139.6 billion in 2021 (Figure 6.5A and Table 6.3). This rapid growth is attributed to newly digitized businesses, greater use of digital finance, and formalizing more MSMEs due to the introduction of a goods and services tax in July 2017. Also, business loan growth during the pandemic was helped by government interest rate subsidies, emergency credit guarantee programs, capital injections to commercial banks, and central bank deregulation on lending. Loan growth has tempered more recently, decelerating from 15.5% in 2017 to 9.2% in 2021.

Loans for wholesale and retail trade—mostly MSMEs—were highest (36.7% of business loans outstanding in 2021), followed by agriculture (23.8%), manufacturing (11.6%), construction (9.7%), other services such as accommodation and food services (4.8%), and transportation and communications (3.1%) (Figure 6.5B). Unclassified (others) accounted for 10.4% in 2021.

Business loans are spread nationwide from small-holder farmers to MSMEs handling domestic trade—55% of loans outstanding are for firms in Bishkek, with the remaining 45% covering those in rural areas (Figure 6.5C). Business loans include short-term loans (tenors of less than 1 year) and medium-term loans (tenors of 1–5 years). In 2021, short-term loans accounted for 10.2% of business loans outstanding, with 89.8% medium-term loans (Figure 6.5D). The share of medium-term loans has gradually grew from 43.8% in 2005. The weighted average lending rate of business loans fell from 12.6% in 2018 to 11.9% in 2020, but rose slightly to 12.2% in 2021.

Figure 6.5: Business Loans

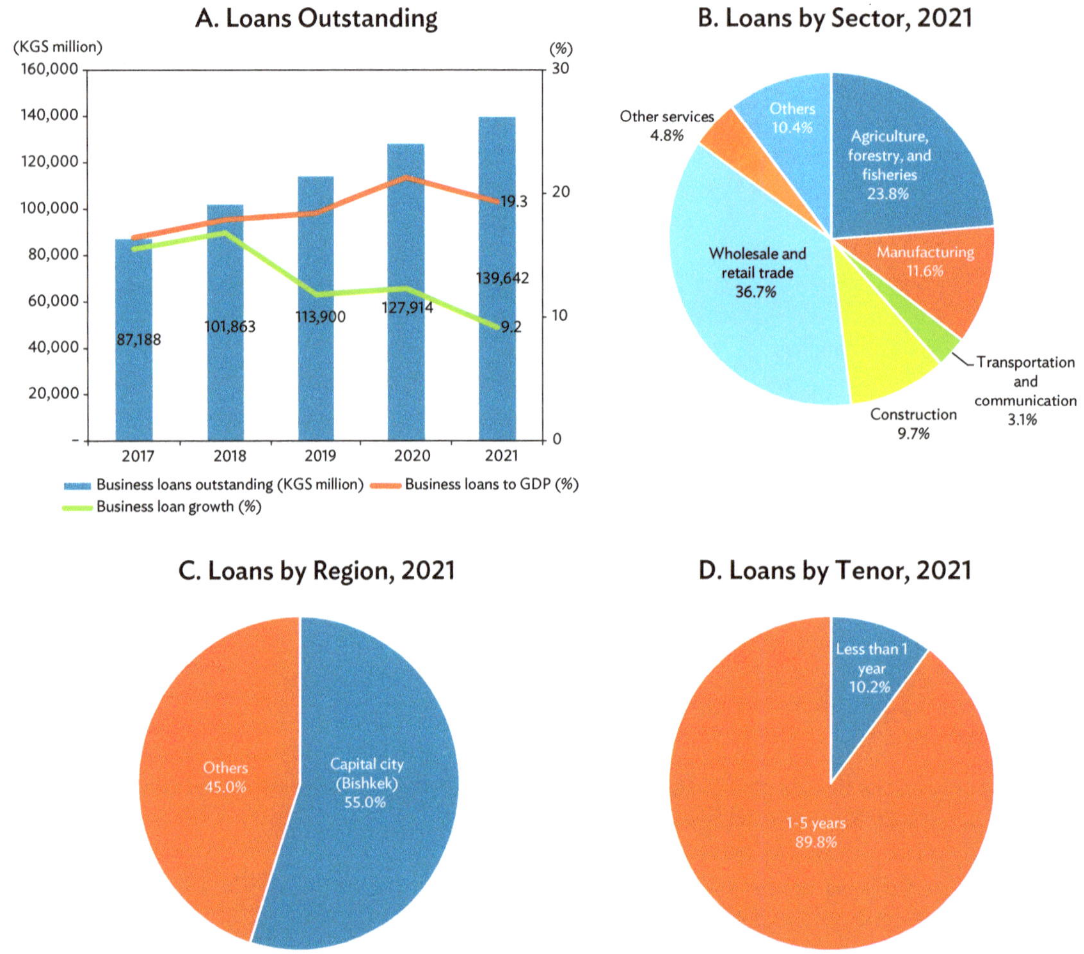

GDP = gross domestic product, MSME = micro, small, and medium-sized enterprise.

Source: ADB Asia SME Monitor 2022 database. Data from the National Bank of the Kyrgyz Republic.

Despite the growth of business loans, limited access to finance remains a major obstacle. The average share of business loans to GDP in 2015–2021 was 18.1%. While it increased from 17.6% in 2015 to 19.3% in 2021, in total they remain small. One reason behind the poor access to bank credit is risk—such as the inability to repay due to business uncertainties, such as volatile consumer demand. The lack of standard documentation also makes it difficult for lenders to assess the MSME creditworthiness. While coverage is adequate in large urban areas, access to credit in remote areas remains limited.

Public Financing and Guarantees

a. Subsidized loans

Since 2013, the government has been implementing a "Financing of Agriculture" program to subsidize interest on agricultural loans covering crops, livestock, agricultural processing, and related businesses including MSMEs. Lending is done mainly through two state-owned banks. As of end-2021, the program set a maximum loan amount for crops and livestock of KGS1 million, with no limit set on loans for agricultural processing. The annual interest rate for all sectors was 6.0%.

Subsidized loans from banks to agri-based MSMEs amounted to KGS6.2 billion in 2021, the same as those issued in 2020 (also KGS6.2 billion) (Figure 6.6A and Table 6.4). There were 10,407 MSME borrowers receiving subsidized loans, down by 13.1% from 2020 (11,979). The average amount of subsidized loan for MSMEs appears higher, however. In the 9 years of the project (2013 to 2021), KGS5.2 billion in subsidized lending went to farmers and agricultural processors. Over the same period, 112,500 loans totaling KGS46.9 billion were issued to agri-based MSMEs. The annual average amount of subsidies was KGS588 million.

To use government funds more effectively, the Cabinet of Ministers plans to gradually transfer all subsidized loans to state banks increasing their capitalization. In 2022, for example, the capitalization of the two state banks was to be increased by KGS10 billion, bringing their capitalization to the equivalent of $100 million.

b. Credit guarantees

Credit guarantees help MSMEs get the loans they need when collateral is insufficient. The funds reduce bank credit risks. In 2016, the OJSC Guarantee Fund was established as part of ADB's Investment Climate Improvement Program-2 with KGS282 million ($4.1 million)[199] as initial capital—ADB contributed $3 million in financial support. By end-2021, the capital had reached KGS6.6 billion ($78.2 million). Shareholders of the Guarantee Fund include the central bank (91.2%) and the government (8.8%). The Guarantee Fund operates based on the central bank supervised Law "On Guarantee Funds in the Kyrgyz Republic."

The maximum guaranteed amount is no more than 50% of the loan and no more than 10% of the capital, or KGS660 million ($7.8 million). The fund provides (i) individual guarantees, (ii) portfolio guarantees, (iii) guarantees based on Islamic principles, and (iv) mixed types of guarantees. There were regional guarantee funds available from 2011 to 2019.

In 2021, guaranteed loans outstanding to MSMEs amounted to KGS5.8 billion, a 14.8% increase from 2020 (Figure 6.6B and Table 6.4). The growth of guaranteed loans has slowed since 2018 (when it increased by 121.7%). In 2021, 977 MSMEs received guarantees, well above the 291 MSMEs in 2017.

Although guaranteed loans have grown rapidly, their use remains limited for MSME credit—just 2.5% of all MSME loans in 2021. Since the COVID-19 outbreak in 2020, nonperforming guaranteed loans have been rising. The ratio of nonperforming guaranteed MSME loans to total guaranteed MSME loans increased sharply to 2.2% in 2020 from 0.4% in 2019, and jumped to 4.6% in 2021.

The World Bank—together with the Ministry of Finance—implemented a project to introduce portfolio guarantees, adding $32 million to the Guarantee Fund. In addition, the fund developed a methodology and software for its guarantee operations and under IFRS-9 (financial instruments) and ISO 9001:2015 (quality management). It also introduced a corporate governance system for MSMEs and a guarantee instrument following Islamic principles. The demand for MSME guarantees has been increasing yearly.

199 Exchange rates of local currency to US dollar refer to end-of-year currency rates from the International Monetary Fund/International Financial Statistics (IMF/IFS) in designated years.

Figure 6.6: Public Financing

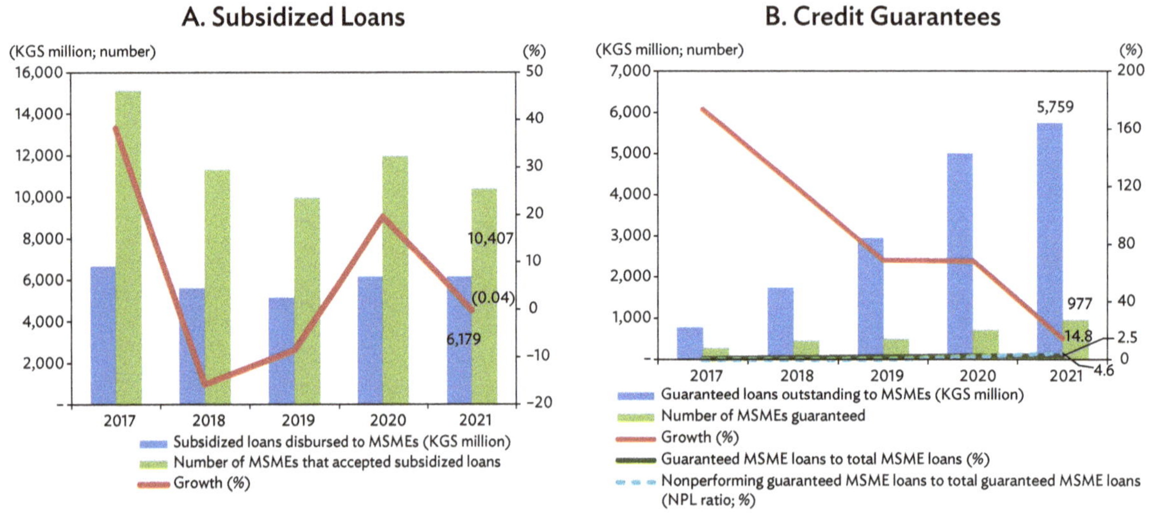

MSME = micro, small, and medium-sized enterprise, NPL = nonperforming loan.

Source: ADB Asia SME Monitor 2022 database. Data from the Ministry of Finance of the Kyrgyz Republic.

Source: ADB Asia SME Monitor 2022 database. Data from the National Bank of the Kyrgyz Republic.

Nonbank Financing

Nonbank finance institutions (NBFIs) are playing an increasingly important role in providing MSMEs with access to finance. They have more coverage and are more flexible than banks. NBFIs include microfinance institutions (MFIs), credit unions, the JSC Financial Company on Credit Unions, and OJSC Guarantee Fund. MFIs are divided into three categories: (i) microfinance companies, (ii) microcredit companies, and (iii) microcredit agencies. The central bank supervises NBFIs, which must have a license or certificate of registration for operations and satisfy a minimum capital requirement—supplied by the initial shareholders. In 2021, NBFIs had capital of KGS11.9 billion, 29.3% more than in 2020. Of the total, 55.5% was for the Guarantee Fund. There were 620 NBFIs operating as of end-2021, including 133 MFIs (including 10 microfinance companies, 86 microcredit companies, and 37 microcredit agencies), 88 credit unions, 1 Financial Company for Credit Unions, 1 Guarantee Fund, 12 leasing companies, 17 insurance companies, and 369 other nonbank finance institutions (Figure 6.7A and Table 6.5).

Microfinance institutions. MFI loans for MSMEs more than doubled from KGS8.2 billion in 2017 to KGS17.5 billion in 2021, an average annual growth rate of 53.5% (Figure 6.7B). In 2021, MFI lending grew 21.9% mainly due to emergency credit guarantees in response to the pandemic. Although MFI loans expanded, loans outstanding remained relatively small (3.7% of GDP in 2021). NPLs have decreased gradually since 2016—from an exceptionally high 31.4% of MFI loans in 2016 to 29.1% in 2021. In 2021, MFI helped finance 644,552 clients, down from 706,610 in 2020. MFI loans are most popular in agriculture (39.5% of MFI loans to MSMEs in 2021), followed by wholesale and retail trade (18.9%), construction (18.4%), other services like accommodations and food services (13.8%), transportation and communication (2.4%), and manufacturing (1.2%) (Figure 6.7C). Unclassified (others) accounted for 5.7%. The share of MFI loans to MSMEs grew in construction and wholesale and retail trade as the economy began to recover from the pandemic.

Credit unions. Credit union financing to MSMEs in 2021 dropped to KGS918 million, down 8.1% from KGS 999 million in 2017 (Figure 6.7B). Credit unions are legally obliged to lend only to members. Similar to MFIs, agriculture is the most popular credit union borrower (27.3% of the 2021 total), followed by wholesale and retail trade (20.9%), construction (20.4%), transport and communication (1.6%), manufacturing (1.3%), and other services (0.8%) (Figure 6.7D). Unclassified "others" was 27.7% in 2021.

Finance company. JSC Financial Company on Credit Unions lends to credit unions. The company was established in 1997 with the help of ADB and was subsequently privatized. JSC's loan portfolio has been declining—in 2021, it was KGS315 million, 6.5% down from 2020 (KGS336 million).

Leasing companies. Leasing companies leased out KGS1.7 billion in 2021, up 34.9% from 2020. MSME demand for leasing is growing as an alternative financing option, although the leasing market remains small (0.2% of GDP in 2021).

Figure 6.7: Nonbank Finance

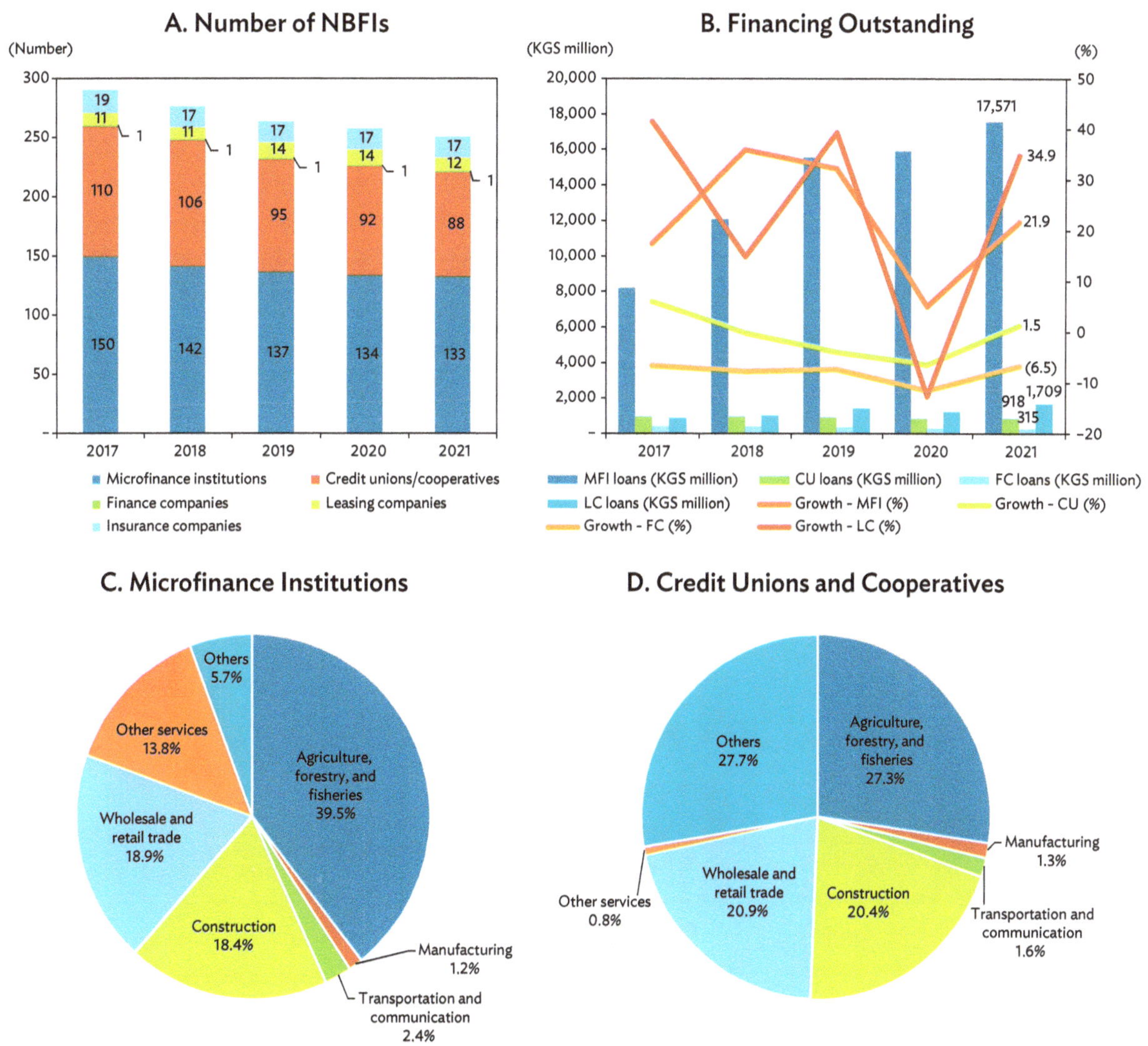

CU = credit union, FC = finance company, LC = leasing company, MFI = microfinance institution, NBFI = nonbank financing institution.

Source: ADB Asia SME Monitor 2022 database. Data from National Statistical Committee, National Bank of the Kyrgyz Republic, and Financial Market Regulation and Supervision Service under the Ministry of Economy and Commerce.

Digital Financial Services

Mobile device penetration reached the relatively high rate of 1,102 units per 1,000 people, or 7.3 million subscribers in 2020.[200]

About 63% of the population aged 15 years and above use the internet. The most active are those aged 15–28 years.[201] The high penetration of mobile communications and internet use, especially among those most active, helps drive the development of digital financial services across the country. Demand is increasing, particularly for e-wallets and mobile banking. Thus, mobile operators and financial and credit institutions are introducing or improving digital financial services. In 2014, 18.5% of adults owned an account at a financial institution or mobile money service provider; by 2017, it had increased to 39.9%.[202]

A major indicator of financial services is the number of bank cards issued by commercial banks. By end-2021, banks had issued 3.6 million cards, with more than 60% part of the national payment system "Elcard." Since 2018, Elcard issuance has grown 83%, or 2.2 million cards. The number of transactions increased from 18 million transactions in 2018 to 57 million in 2021, with the value of transactions reaching KGS199 billion, a 2.5 times increase over 2018 (Figure 6.8A). Since 2018, annual payments nearly doubled to KGS375 billion in 2021 (Figure 6.8B). More than 53% of the payment value came via the national payment system Elcard.

The Elcard payment system works with other systems. For example, direct money transfers from the Russian Federation's "Mir" cards to Elcard began in 2020. From 15 June 2020 to 20 October 2021, there were 121,030 transactions worth KGS700.3 million.

Kyrgyz payment systems continue to develop. By end-2021, more than 20 organizations were licensed to operate a payment system. In 2018, payments amounted to KGS29 billion. In 2021, it reached KGS92 billion, more than three times the transaction value. However, the actual number of payments fell from 174 million to 157 million as the value of individual payments increased.

Figure 6.8: Bank Cards

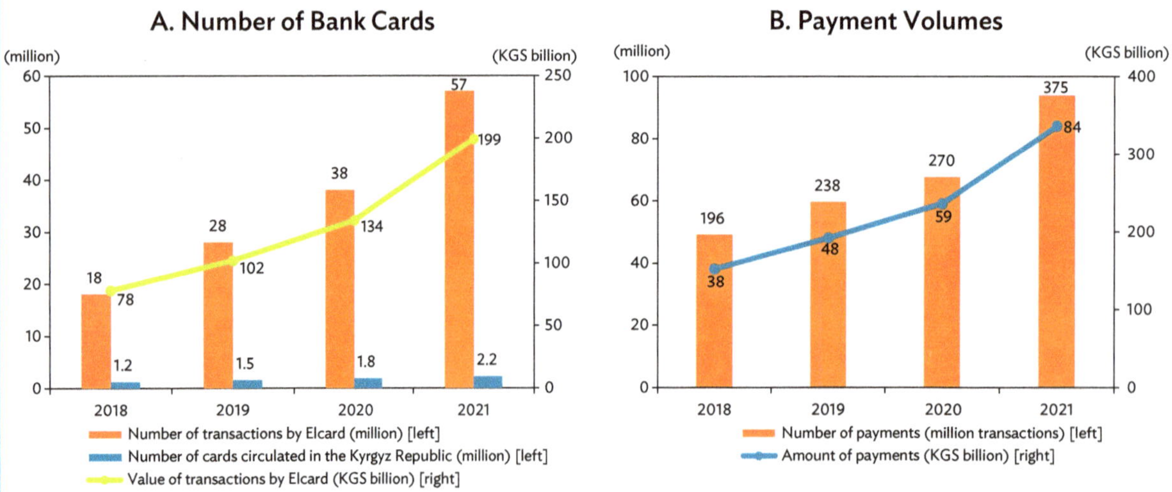

Source: ADB Asia SME Monitor 2022 database. Data from the National Bank of the Kyrgyz Republic.

200 National Statistical Committee of the Kyrgyz Republic. The number of telephone sets and subscriber devices of mobile (cellular) communication. http://www.stat.kg/en/opendata/category/3902/ (accessed 31 August 2022).

201 http://www.stat.kg/ru/news/den-interneta-99-kyrgyzstancev-ohvacheny-mobilnymi-setyami/

202 World Bank. World Development Indicators. https://databank.worldbank.org/source/world-development-indicators (accessed 31 August 2022).

More people and MSMEs are using digital financial services. For example, in 2021, the number of electronic wallets increased by 40.8% over 2020, or more than 4.4 million wallets.[203]

The use of e-money continues to grow:

- The value of money transfers between electronic wallets almost doubled between 2020 and 2021 to KGS12.7 billion. The number of money transfers also increased 2.6 times, or 5.1 million transactions.
- The value of redemption (cashing out) transactions for electronic money increased by 35.0% to KGS26.8 billion in 2021. The number of transactions doubled to 6.1 million.
- The value of e-money transactions for buying goods and services rose 39.8% between 2020 and 2021, amounting to KGS10 billion, while the number of transactions fell by 17.0% to 13.1 million transactions.
- The value of newly issued electronic money increased by 32.2% in 2021 to KGS36.4 billion, while the number of transactions decreased by 43.1%, to 7.5 million.

Capital Markets

The Kyrgyz Stock Exchange (KSE) remains in its infancy. Stock market capitalization of the main board was KGS51.1 billion as of end-2021, a 53.8% increase from 2020 (KGS33.2 billion) (Figure 6.9A and Table 6.6). However, trading value fell from KGS11.8 billion in 2020 to KGS9.7 billion in 2021, largely due to the pandemic. Securities of 26 issuers were traded over the same period. Most deals involved financial sector stocks. MSMEs are not listed on the KSE, but some issue bonds to raise funds to develop their business. Three MSMEs have issued corporate bonds, valued at KGS169 million (for manufacturing, agri-processing, and sewing and trade) (Figure 6.9B).

The main problems MSMEs face in tapping capital markets include low levels of financial literacy, poor institutional structures, inadequate corporate governance, and the fear of diluting the value of MSME owners' shares. In addition, the high cost of compliance, especially related to KSE rules and compliance with the Joint Stock Company Law, is a significant financial burden for MSMEs.

Figure 6.9: Capital Markets

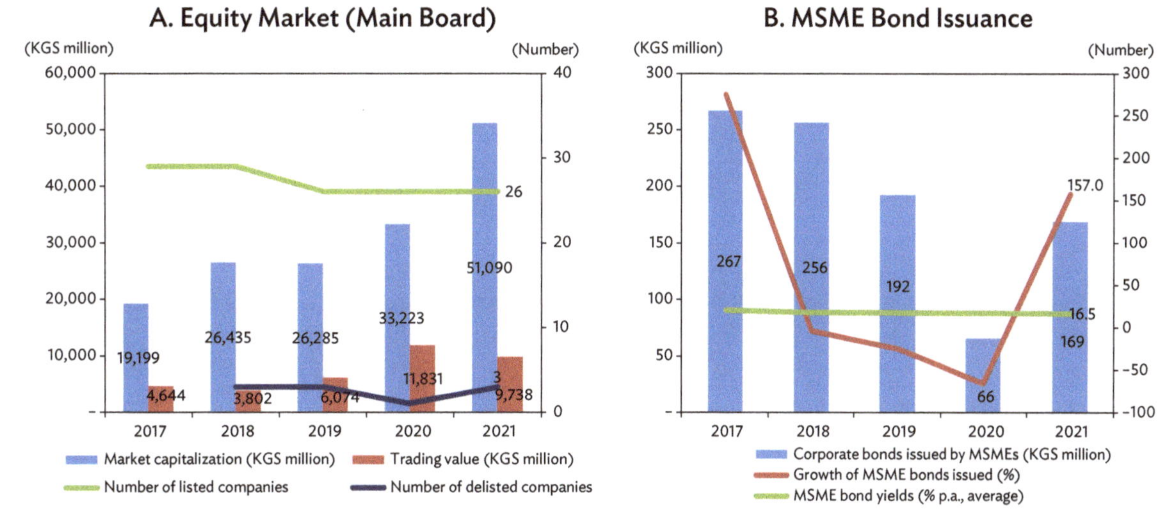

MSME = micro, small, and medium-sized enterprise.

Source: ADB Asia SME Monitor 2022 database. Data from the Kyrgyz Stock Exchange.

[203] https://nbkr.kg/DOC/15012022/000000000057944.pdf

Financial Infrastructure

As of end-2021, there were two active credit bureaus: (i) Credit Bureau "Ishenim" Close Joint Stock Company (CJSC), established in 2003; and (ii) Credit Bureau "CRIF KG" CJSC, established in 2018. To collect credit information, they partner with of more than 240 financial-credit institutions. Ishenim manages a constantly growing database of credit histories, with 5.5 million credit histories, including MSMEs, stored as of end-March 2022. Ishenim prepares credit reports for individuals and legal entities and make scoring assessments (such as expert scoring, IFRS-9 scoring, and application scoring), based on the results it assigns ratings to creditors.

A unified state register registers movable property as collateral for the right of claim for obligations under credit agreements. Until 2019, these functions were carried out by the Central Registration Office of the Ministry of Justice. In February 2019, it was liquidated, with its functions transferred to the Pledge Registration Department of the Ministry of Justice.

4. Policies and Regulations

- The Ministry of Economy and Commerce is responsible for the development of MSMEs in the country. The law on State Support for Small Business of 2007 provides a framework and governing principles for MSME development and support.
- The National Development Strategy through 2040 set priority MSME sectors for support; including agriculture, manufacturing, energy, and tourism.
- The government launched several thematic assistance programs addressing MSME development such as the Financing of Agriculture Program, the Export Development Program, and women entrepreneurs support program.
- State and local governments play a crucial role in promoting rural MSME development, for instance, through the "One Village One Product" program.
- The 2016–2020 Financial Literacy Program provided staged support to improve financial literacy for children, adults, and MSMEs.
- The government approved a Strategy for Improving Financial Inclusion for 2022–2026 in 2022 to improve and expand access to finance for all, addressing digital finance, infrastructure, financial product diversification, consumer protection, and financial literacy.
- During the pandemic, the government provided comprehensive emergency assistance to businesses and households, including financial support programs including credit guarantees.
- The government is taking several measures in response to the impact of the Russian invasion of Ukraine, for example, an anti-crisis plan for 2022 and financial assistance for MSMEs.

MSME Development

In 2007, the Law "On State Support for Small Business" was adopted to develop MSMEs. Following the law, national MSME support programs have been developed, MSME development funds were established, and strategic directions set for the development of MSMEs. The Ministry of Economy and Commerce coordinates MSME support and development, and formulates medium- to long-term MSME development policies.

The National Development Strategy through 2040 identifies strategic priority sectors and the role MSMEs play in implementing the strategy. The priority sectors for MSME development include agriculture and agri-processing, manufacturing, energy, and tourism, among others. The Development and Investment Agency helps MSMEs attract investments for products and services. The Ministry of Foreign Affairs promotes exports of goods produced by MSMEs.

In addition to legislative and institutional support for MSMEs, the government has consistently provided financial support to support MSMEs:

- The Financing of Agriculture Program has been operating since 2013 and allocates funds to subsidize interest payments on loans and promote development of agricultural MSMEs. In 2022, the interest rate for agricultural MSMEs is 6.0% as opposed to the average commercial bank interest rate of 16.4% (the average subsidy is just over 10%).
- Programs that subsidize interest rates for exporters appear every few years—the schemes are similar to those of the Financing of Agriculture Program.
- The central bank provides funds to commercial banks for MSME lending at credit auctions.
- The Export Development Program for 2019–2022 was approved in 2018. It (i) ensures a favorable regulatory environment to develop competitive and high-quality domestic products, (ii) provides financial support for exporters, and (iii) encourages entrepreneurs to produce competitive products for foreign markets.
- Development funds targeting regions have been disbursed since 2021 to support and develop local MSMEs. The funds come from the national budget and annual contributions of firms engaged in mining (gold and others).
- A program to support MSME cluster development was started in 2021. The annual program has thus far created nine agricultural clusters through KGS9 billion in concessional loans.

In terms of thematic assistance, the government supports the development of women-led MSMEs. A program to support women entrepreneurs for 2022–2026 was adopted in 2021. It defines the principles of support for women entrepreneurs and the sources of funding to support their businesses (also using credit guarantees to help provide necessary credit). The program (i) improves and optimizes legislation regulating women entrepreneurship; (ii) supports and forms state and public institutions to assist in boosting their expertise and business potential; and (iii) provides women entrepreneurs accessible information, consulting, production, technological, and educational services.

The Strategy for Sustainable Development of Industry for 2019–2023 aims to (i) develop industries in regions based on their comparative advantage (in resources, among others); (ii) expand high-tech and competitive export industries; (iii) promote the transition of the economy from the currently dominant raw material exports to more industrial and innovative exports; and (iv) create an effective management system and a business climate that attracts investments.

There are also support programs run by international organizations along with finance and credit organizations. These projects include the "One Village One Product" program (supported by the Japan International Cooperation Agency) and "One Region One Enterprise" project (OJSC Guarantee Fund), among others.[204]

MSMEs face three major types of problems and challenges:

(i) For entrepreneurs:
  - low level of financial literacy;
  - low level of institutional development;
  - high interest rates on loans;

[204] The main goal of the One Region One Enterprise project is to help entrepreneurs open new enterprises or new product lines for existing enterprises.

- limited long-term lending;
- issues of corporate management and quality standards (ISO 9001, ISO 22000, among others); and
- develop export potential.

(ii) For the financial and banking system:
- the need to boost capital;
- a need to attract investment in capital and assets of financial credit organizations;
- increase the share of the loan portfolios to GDP from 23%–25% to 45%–50%, basically doubling existing loan portfolios, decrease interest rates, while lengthening maturities; and
- activate unused or poorly used financial instruments such as factoring, leasing, syndicated loans, warehouse receipt financing, trade and structured finance, investment lending, and insurance.

(iii) For government entities:
- establish a development bank to support medium-sized and large enterprises;
- create conditions for expanding exports such as setting up an "Export Center;"
- support startup projects through, for example, a startup project support bank;
- promote venture capital funds;
- create factoring companies;
- establish investment funds to help capitalize new firms; and
- more actively support Islamic banking.

Financial Inclusion

The central bank, established in 1992, is responsible for maintaining price stability and financial system stability. It regulates and supervises banks and nonbank financial institutions through licensing. In 2016, it became the executive agency for implementing the 2016–2020 Financial Literacy Program, the first to increase financial literacy for both people and MSMEs.[205]

The program was done in three stages, each with its own action plan: Action Plan for the Stage 1 of the Program (2016–2017), Stage 2 of the Program (2018–2019), and Stage 3 of the Program (2020). The program targeted three objectives—the first covered financial education for children and youth, the second to improve financial literacy of adults, and the third to ensure access to financial information and financial services. The central bank, banking and microfinance system, ministries and departments, along with other government organizations and the private sector all participated in implementing the program.

One result was the preparation and publication of books and textbooks for children and adults along with introducing financial literacy as proper subject for school and university curricula. The program conducted training for adults and entrepreneurs, as well as provided access to financial information and information about the services offered by financial institutions. There remain many unresolved issues related to access to finance for both MSMEs and the general population.

To further expand MSME access to finance, the government approved a Strategy for Improving Financial Inclusion for 2022–2026.[206] The goal is to improve financial inclusion of MSMEs by creating the financial infrastructure and mechanisms that provide a wide range of high quality, secure, affordable, and responsive financial services, both traditionally and digitally. The strategy has five main components: (i) digital finance and products, (ii) infrastructure, (iii) financial product diversification, (iv) consumer protection, and (v) financial literacy.

205 Decree of the Government of the Kyrgyz Republic, No. 319 of 15 June 2016.

206 Resolution of the Cabinet of Ministers of the Kyrgyz Republic, No.119-p of 18 March 2022.

The strategy builds on the results of previous programs to improve financial access and literacy and other strategic documents for 2018–2021, which cover the (i) development of the banking system, (ii) development of the microfinance system, and (iii) development of payments systems.

The roadmap for implementing the strategy assumes specific results are met:

- **Digital finance and products.** It will increase the number of (i) payment terminals, including ATMs; (ii) issued bank cards and transaction values; (iii) digital payment transactions, improved payment systems; and (iv) companies investing in the stock market, among others.
- **Infrastructure.** The development of reliable physical, financial, digital, and payments infrastructure to ensure effective and efficient financial services are available to MSMEs and the general population.
- **Diversification of financial products.** The number of banking and nonbanking services available to MSMEs and individuals will be increased. Particular attention will be paid to resolving problems in (i) green finance, (ii) special products for women, (iii) agricultural finance, (iv) savings and remittance-based products, and (v) Islamic finance.
- **Consumer protection.** The level of consumer protection will broaden, including information disclosure and transparency, fair treatment of consumers and the market behavior of financial institutions, protecting data privacy, as well as introducing mechanisms for out-of-court dispute settlement.
- **Financial literacy.** Improve the financial literacy of all stakeholders, including MSMEs and the general population.

Response to COVID-19

The COVID-19 pandemic hit the Kyrgyz economy and business operations hard in 2020. Many MSMEs faced reduced income, production and sales, and their workforce. Logistics and supply chains for goods and services were disrupted. The government responded by taking anti-crisis measures, financed by the budget and internationally sourced funds, which made it possible to provide rapid assistance to MSMEs.

The government adopted six main measures:

(i) An Anti-Crisis Response Plan for Coronavirus Infection and Early Recovery on Interaction between the Government of the Kyrgyz Republic and the Emergency Response Coordination Unit helped identify funding sources for its response.
(ii) The Decree of the Government of the Kyrgyz Republic No.162-p dated 6 May 2020 was adopted to restore economic activity and support MSMEs with an initial funding of KGS14 billion and additional funding of KGS12.5 billion.
(iii) The Decree of the Government of the Kyrgyz Republic No. 272-p dated 13 August 2020 to ensure the social stability, sustainability of the economy, and maintenance of the population's income.
(iv) The Decree of the OJSC Guarantee Fund dated 8 August 2020 No.39/1 to increase MSME access to finance during 2020–2022 with initial funding of KGS1.0 billion.
(v) The "Emergency Assistance to MSMEs affected by COVID-19" program with World Bank support will support interest-free loans and help implement portfolio guarantees.
(vi) To reduce poverty, increase the wage of social workers by 50.0% in 2022.

During the pandemic, many MSMEs were unable to repay loans due to the serious difficulty in selling goods and services. Bank loan portfolios were in danger of deteriorating, and disputes between MSMEs and banks increased. The central bank thus took several measures to ease requirements for delayed loan repayments, recommended commercial banks to restructure loans, cancel fines and penalties, ease documentary requirements for obtaining loans, and maintain loan classifications despite delayed repayments.

The central bank also took several measures:

(i) Banks and nonbanking financial-credit institutions are instructed (a) not to charge and collect fees and penalties, (b) reconsider the timing of payments on loans and grant deferred payments for at least 3 months, and (c) not to worsen loan classifications ("On temporary regulations of financial-credit institutions in connection with the pandemic COVID-19" of 18.03.03.2020 №2020-P-12/13-1-(BS)).
(ii) The general conditions and procedures for granting central bank loans to commercial bank should comply with central bank economic standards, then timely fulfillment of obligations to depositors ("On the provision by the National Bank of the Kyrgyz Republic of loans to commercial banks in order to mitigate the negative impacts of the COVID-19 pandemic in the Kyrgyz Republic" dated 24 March 2020 No.2020-P-09\15-9- [NPA]).
(iii) Ease the requirements for MSMEs to obtain a loan by cancelling the requirement to obtain certificates from tax and social services ("On temporary rules for the classification of assets and the implementation of appropriate allocations to the reserve to cover potential losses and damages by commercial banks and individual nonbank organizations" dated 29 April 2020 No.2020-P-12/25-7-[NPA]).
(iv) Conduct credit auctions for commercial banks.

All these measures contributed to stabilize the economy and the financial and economic condition of MSMEs. The quality of the loan portfolio did not deteriorate, and the value of MSME lending increased despite the pandemic.

Response to the Russian Invasion of Ukraine

The Kyrgyz economy is closely connected with the Russian Federation's economy. In 2021, 23.7% of Kyrgyz exports went to the Russian Federation, and 34.2% of imports came from the Russian Federation. Supply chains of goods and services gradually broke down. The sanctions initially affected the US dollar exchange rate with Kyrgyz *som*, which depreciated sharply from KGS85/$1 to KGS106/$1, gradually improving to KGS81/$1. Inflation is expected to reach 15.5% by end-2022. Despite the invasion's impact on the Kyrgyz economy, the central bank raised its estimate of GDP growth to 4.2% in September 2022. Exports in several sectors have grown—for example, the apparel industry increased the value of its exports to the Russian Federation. The government is taking the following measures that should help growth opportunities for MSMEs:

(i) It adopted an anti-crisis plan for 2022 worth KGS126 billion.
(ii) A Development Bank of the Kyrgyz Republic is being created to finance large projects involving medium-sized and large enterprises.
(iii) A Central Asian Guarantee Fund is under consideration, which will help increase trade between Central Asian countries.
(iv) A capital increase of $100 million (in local currrency) is being considered for each of the two state-owned banks and OJSC Guarantee Fund.
(v) To ensure food security, KGS9 billion has been allocated to create nine agricultural and agricultural processing clusters.
(vi) Fields under cultivation are expanding to meet demand for agricultural products.

(vii) To reduce coal imports and develop the local coal industry, "Kavak" JSC was established with a KGS1 billion capital allocation, with the state coal enterprise "Kyrgyzkomur" provided with needed equipment.
(viii) The construction of the 1,860 megawatts Kambarata HPP-1 dam will increase power supply.
(ix) "Kyrgyzindustry" JSC was established with initial capital of KGS1 billion to develop industry (manufacturing).
(x) The OJSC Tourism Development Support Fund was created with initial capital of KGS1 billion.

The invasion and associated sanction against the Russian Federation seriously affected Kyrgyz financial markets. Russian banks banned from usinmg the SWIFT system initially created problems for Kyrgyz banks—which were gradually resolved. One of the problems was a shortage of US dollars in cash, which led to export restrictions. To help stabilze the banking system, the central bank is considering increasing the minimum capital requirements for banks and microfinance organizations. The central bank has taken and is taking the following measures:

(i) the discount rate has been increased to 14.0%;
(ii) measures to curb inflation and provide price stability are underway;
(iii) an increase in the minimum authorized capital of banks to KGS1 billion (KGS600 million as of end-August 2022) is under consideration;
(iv) as part of a "regulatory sandbox," new financial instruments are being introduced to promote and facilitate MSMEs by easing credit terms, reducing the number of documents required, and using digitalization and bank cards when granting loans; and
(v) the Kyrgyz Union of Banks has begun upgrading the country's financial markets.

Data Tables

Table 6.1: MSME Definition

Item	Micro	Small	Medium
I. **Group 1**: Agriculture, hunting and forestry; fishing, fish farming; mining; manufacturing; production and distribution of electricity, gas, and water; construction.			
Number of employees	Up to 14 employees	15 - 50 employees	51 - 200 employees
Annual revenue	Up to KGS150,000	KGS150,001 - KGS500,000	KGS500,001 - KGS2,000 000
II. **Group 2**: Trade; repair of cars, household goods and personal items; hotels and restaurants; transport and communication; financial activities; real estate operations, renting and services to consumers; education; health care and social services; provision of public, social, and personal services.			
Number of employees	Up to 7 employees	8 - 15 employees	16 - 50 employees
Annual revenue	Up to KGS230,000	KGS230,001 - KGS500,000	KGS500,001 - KGS2,000,000

MSME = micro, small, and medium-sized enterprise.

Source: ADB Asia SME Monitor 2022 database. Data from Resolution No.78 of the Government of the Kyrgyz Republic, 17 February 1998.

Table 6.2: MSME Landscape

End-of-period data

Item	2004	2005	2006	2007	2008	2009	2010	2011	2012	2013	2014	2015	2016	2017	2018	2019	2020	2021
NUMBER OF ENTERPRISES*																		
Number of enterprises, total	8,863	8,850	9,654	10,223	12,371	12,557	12,466	12,514	12,228	12,839	13,797	14,311	14,663	14,967	15,594	17,294	17,315	17,361
Number of MSMEs	8,485	8,471	9,267	9,852	11,988	12,221	12,161	12,211	11,931	12,549	13,505	14,027	14,368	14,653	15,289	16,978	17,019	17,050
Micro	...	...	...	...	...	...	...	...	...	...	...	...	...	...	...	...	...	...
Small	7,729	7,689	8,424	9,002	11,103	11,374	11,338	11,371	11,127	11,749	12,712	13,232	13,592	13,858	14,520	16,199	16,302	16,252
Medium	756	782	843	850	885	847	823	840	804	800	793	795	776	795	769	779	717	798
Number of large enterprises	378	379	387	371	383	336	305	303	297	290	292	284	295	314	305	316	296	311
MSME to total (%)	95.7	95.7	96.0	96.4	96.9	97.3	97.6	97.6	97.6	97.7	97.9	98.0	98.0	97.9	98.0	98.2	98.3	98.2
MSME growth (%)	4.9	(0.2)	9.4	6.3	21.7	1.9	(0.5)	0.4	(2.3)	5.2	7.6	3.9	2.4	2.0	4.3	11.0	0.2	0.2
MSMEs by sector (% share)*																		
Agriculture, forestry, and fisheries	4.2	3.9	3.6	3.0	3.0	3.1	3.1	3.3	4.0	3.6	3.5	3.2	3.2	2.9	3.0	3.0	3.1	3.3
Manufacturing	20.8	19.6	18.8	18.6	18.4	18.4	18.2	18.0	17.7	16.8	16.5	16.2	14.9	14.7	15.3	15.2	15.1	14.6
Transportation and communication	8.6	9.0	8.7	8.3	8.5	8.5	8.5	8.5	8.8	5.8	5.7	5.7	5.4	5.6	5.4	5.1	5.1	5.3
Construction	9.7	10.4	9.9	10.5	10.6	10.4	10.6	10.7	10.2	10.5	11.1	10.9	11.1	11.6	11.9	11.9	12.1	12.2
Wholesale and retail trade	33.1	32.6	31.0	29.9	30.0	28.8	28.0	27.7	26.2	25.9	25.3	25.5	26.3	26.3	26.1	26.7	27.4	28.0
Other services	23.6	24.5	28.0	29.7	29.5	30.8	31.6	31.8	33.0	37.2	38.0	38.5	39.1	38.9	38.2	38.1	37.3	36.6
MSMEs by region (% share)*																		
Capital city (Bishkek)	60.8	63.8	63.3	66.6	67.9	65.9	65.8	65.9	64.7	66.5	68.6	69.4	69.4	67.9	67.2	68.0	66.9	62.5
Others	39.2	36.2	36.7	33.4	32.1	34.1	34.2	34.1	35.3	33.5	31.4	30.6	30.6	32.1	32.8	32.0	33.1	37.5
EMPLOYMENT*																		
Number of employment, total ('000)	197	194	202	205	213	197	184	182	181	182	182	181	181	184	186	203	192	189
Number of employment by MSMEs	87	84	88	91	97	93	89	86	87	88	89	88	87	89	91	108	101	93
Micro	...	...	...	...	...	...	...	...	...	...	...	...	...	...	...	...	...	...
Small	42	39	45	48	53	52	50	46	50	51	52	52	52	53	57	73	69	59
Medium	45	45	43	43	44	41	38	40	37	37	37	36	35	36	34	34	32	34
Number of employment by large enterprises	110	110	114	114	116	104	95	96	94	94	94	93	94	94	95	96	91	96
MSME employees to total (%)	44.1	43.4	43.6	44.2	45.6	47.2	48.2	47.2	48.3	48.5	48.5	48.8	48.2	48.7	48.9	53.0	52.6	49.3
MSME employees growth (%)	(1.9)	(3.2)	4.4	3.3	6.6	(4.0)	(4.6)	(2.9)	1.6	0.7	0.6	(0.2)	(1.0)	2.3	1.8	18.5	(6.5)	(7.8)
Share of female employees to total employees (%)	28.8	31.5	33.0	34.0	19.5	20.3	33.3	33.0	33.1	33.5	33.1	23.2	32.1	32.0	32.7	31.1	30.6	30.8

continued on next page

Table 6.2 *continued*

Item	2004	2005	2006	2007	2008	2009	2010	2011	2012	2013	2014	2015	2016	2017	2018	2019	2020	2021
Employment by MSME by sector (% share)																		
Agriculture, forestry, and fisheries	9.5	9.5	8.9	7.6	7.4	5.9	6.0	6.4	6.4	6.2	5.9	5.3	4.8	4.3	4.1	4.5	4.1	4.2
Manufacturing	38.7	37.1	35.7	35.6	34.1	35.6	35.4	36.2	34.7	34.5	33.9	34.5	33.5	33.7	32.8	36.4	38.3	32.4
Transportation and communication	5.7	6.1	6.1	5.8	5.7	6.1	6.1	6.0	5.8	3.7	4.8	3.7	3.6	3.5	3.5	4.6	4.9	3.9
Construction	19.5	19.3	17.1	18.1	17.7	16.5	14.7	14.7	14.5	13.7	14.1	13.4	14.1	14.1	13.8	11.9	11.2	12.7
Wholesale and retail trade	14.6	14.4	14.5	14.2	14.1	14.2	14.5	13.6	14.1	14.3	14.4	15.2	15.4	15.6	15.7	14.5	15.1	17.7
Other services	12.0	13.6	17.7	18.7	20.9	21.7	23.2	23.1	24.5	27.6	26.9	28.0	28.6	28.8	30.1	28.1	26.3	29.1
Employment by MSMEs by region (% share)																		
Capital city (Bishkek)	43.5	45.6	46.8	48.8	50.8	48.8	48.7	48.7	49.3	50.2	50.1	50.3	50.8	50.4	51.4	52.4	50.6	49.9
Others	56.5	54.4	53.2	51.2	49.2	51.2	51.3	51.3	50.7	49.8	49.9	49.7	49.2	49.6	48.6	47.3	49.4	50.1
CONTRIBUTION TO GDP																		
GDP of MSMEs (KGS million)	40,825	44,397	51,505	60,433	85,319	85,635	90,763	113,131	124,072	138,043	161,264	173,292	186,602	218,608	242,499	265,441	244,373	309,513
MSME contribution to GDP (% share)	43.3	44.0	45.2	42.6	45.5	42.6	41.2	39.5	39.9	38.9	40.3	40.3	39.1	41.2	42.5	42.8	40.6	42.8
MSME GDP growth (%)	...	8.8	16.0	17.3	41.2	0.4	6.0	24.6	9.7	11.3	16.8	7.5	7.7	17.2	10.9	9.5	(7.9)	26.7
MSME labor productivity (KGS million)	...	...	...	...	...	...	...	...	...	...	...	...	...	...	...	...	...	...
MSME GDP by sector (% share)																		
Agriculture, forestry, and fisheries	...	...	...	...	33.6	25.4	29.2	28.9	25.8	24.7	21.8	23.1	19.9	18.7	16.7	16.8	20.7	20.8
Manufacturing	...	...	...	...	11.4	12.2	11.8	13.4	12.3	12.9	10.9	10.7	11.0	10.7	9.9	10.0	13.5	14.7
Transportation and communication	...	...	...	...	5.7	6.6	6.7	6.8	7.3	6.4	6.5	5.7	5.6	5.6	5.9	6.1	4.9	4.9
Construction	...	...	...	...	6.2	7.5	6.1	5.6	6.0	6.4	6.5	6.7	8.7	14.1	14.8	11.4	10.8	10.3
Wholesale and retail trade	...	...	...	...	33.8	37.3	35.6	35.2	37.3	38.3	42.2	42.7	41.9	39.1	37.3	40.1	38.7	39.3
Other services	...	...	...	...	2.6	2.8	1.6	2.3	3.0	3.6	4.2	5.2	4.9	4.4	4.2	4.2	3.2	3.0
Others	...	...	...	...	6.6	8.2	9.1	7.8	8.3	7.7	7.9	6.0	7.9	7.5	11.0	11.2	8.1	7.0
MSME GDP by region (% share)																		
Capital city (Bishkek)	...	...	...	...	...	...	...	...	...	...	...	...	...	...	...	...	...	...
Others	...	...	...	...	...	...	...	...	...	...	...	...	...	...	...	...	...	...
EXPORTS																		
Total export value ($ million)	721	674	891	1,321	1,856	1,673	1,756	2,242	1,928	2,007	1,884	1,483	1,573	1,764	1,837	1,986	1,973	2,752
Total export growth (%)	23.7	(6.5)	32.2	48.3	40.5	(9.8)	5.0	27.7	(14.0)	4.1	(6.1)	(21.3)	6.1	12.1	4.1	8.1	(0.7)	39.5
MSME export value ($ million)	223	218	361	386	773	430	454	626	676	578	465	541	568	613	723	703	492	752
MSME export to total export value (%)	30.9	32.3	40.5	29.3	41.7	25.7	25.9	27.9	35.0	28.8	24.7	36.5	36.1	34.7	39.3	35.4	24.9	27.3
MSME export growth (%)	...	(2.3)	65.8	7.1	100.0	(44.4)	5.6	37.9	7.9	(14.4)	(19.5)	16.2	5.1	7.9	17.9	(2.8)	(30.0)	52.8
IMPORTS																		
Total import value ($ million)	947	1,189	1,931	2,789	4,072	3,040	3,223	4,261	5,576	5,987	5,735	4,154	4,000	4,495	5,292	4,989	3,719	5,580
Total import growth (%)	31.2	25.5	62.5	44.4	46.0	(25.3)	6.0	32.2	30.9	7.4	(4.2)	(27.6)	(3.7)	12.4	17.7	(5.7)	(25.5)	50.1
MSME import value ($ million)	550	739	1,141	1,139	2,837	2,001	2,048	2,588	3,216	3,178	3,054	2,524	2,343	2,896	3,398	3,266	2,024	3,162
MSME import to total import value (%)	58.1	62.2	59.1	40.8	69.7	65.8	63.5	60.5	57.3	52.1	53.3	60.8	58.6	64.4	64.2	65.5	54.4	56.7
MSME import growth (%)	...	34.4	54.4	(0.2)	149.2	(29.5)	2.3	26.4	24.3	(1.2)	(3.9)	(17.4)	(7.2)	23.6	17.3	(3.9)	(38.0)	56.3

GDP = gross domestic product; MSME = micro, small, and medium-sized enterprise.

* Data are presented including individual entrepreneurs and rural (farmer) households.

Source: ADB Asia SME Monitor 2022 database. Data from the National Statistic Committee of the Kyrgyz Republic.

Table 6.3: Bank Credit

End-of-period data

Item	2004	2005	2006	2007	2008	2009	2010	2011	2012	2013	2014	2015	2016	2017	2018	2019	2020	2021
OPERATING BANKS																		
Number of operating banks, total	19	20	21	22	22	22	22	22	22	23	24	24	25	25	25	24	23	23
State-owned commercial banks	1	1	1	2	2	2	2	2	2	2	2	2	2	2	2	2	2	2
State-owned development financial institutions	...	...	...	...	...	...	...	...	...	...	...	...	...	...	...	...	...	...
Private commercial banks	6	7	8	8	8	8	8	8	7	7	8	7	7	7	7	6	5	5
Foreign commercial banks	12	12	12	12	12	12	12	12	13	14	14	15	16	16	16	16	16	16
Credit																		
Loans outstanding, total (KGS million)	5,805	7,712	11,350	20,851	25,608	25,214	26,382	31,217	40,105	53,962	78,756	93,954	93,499	108,325	127,882	146,439	162,550	181,783
Loans outstanding in domestic currency (KGS million)	1,724	2,207	3,469	7,848	9,024	9,545	11,665	13,969	18,558	25,037	33,363	42,215	51,875	67,206	79,366	94,977	109,010	131,034
Loans outstanding in foreign currency (KGS million)	4,081	5,505	7,881	13,002	16,584	15,669	14,717	17,248	21,547	28,924	45,393	51,738	41,624	41,119	48,516	51,462	53,540	50,750
Loan growth (%)	100.6	32.8	47.2	83.7	22.8	(1.5)	4.6	18.3	28.5	34.5	45.9	19.3	(0.5)	15.9	18.1	14.5	11.0	11.8
Total bank loans to GDP (%)	6.2	7.6	10.0	14.7	13.6	12.5	12.0	10.9	12.9	15.2	19.7	21.8	19.6	20.4	22.5	23.7	27.0	25.1
Lending rate (%, annual average)	...	...	...	...	...	...	...	...	...	...	...	...	...	...	15.0	14.8	13.9	14.2
Gross nonperforming loans (NPLs) (KGS million)	...	...	...	...	723	1,205	3,041	2,155	2,109	2,031	2,325	3,620	5,070	4,654	5,143	6,793	9,703	12,459
Gross NPLs to total loans (%)	...	...	...	...	...	...	...	...	...	...	...	...	...	...	...	...	...	...
Deposits																		
Deposits, total (KGS million)	8,206	13,052	16,807	23,443	29,558	39,604	34,065	38,675	50,651	67,334	82,535	102,878	107,079	121,597	133,118	150,954	180,928	242,947
Deposits in domestic currency (KGS million)	2,461	3,540	5,771	11,230	12,527	14,832	16,330	19,299	26,928	34,486	36,034	35,383	52,427	63,839	74,634	93,286	103,364	142,961
Deposits in foreign currency (KGS million)	5,745	9,512	11,036	12,212	17,031	24,773	17,735	19,376	23,724	32,848	46,501	67,494	54,652	57,758	58,484	57,668	77,564	99,986
Deposit rate (%, annual average)	...	...	...	...	...	...	...	...	...	...	...	...	...	...	4.1	4.2	3.8	3.7
BUSINESS LOANS*																		
Business loans outstanding, total (KGS million)	5,056	6,550	8,814	16,194	19,894	20,099	21,647	25,483	32,466	43,563	63,778	75,922	75,471	87,188	101,863	113,900	127,914	139,642
Business loans to total loans outstanding (%)	87.1	84.9	77.7	77.7	77.7	79.7	82.1	81.6	81.0	80.7	81.0	80.8	80.7	80.5	79.7	77.8	78.7	76.8
Business loans to GDP (%)	5.4	6.5	7.7	11.4	10.6	10.0	9.8	8.9	10.5	12.3	15.9	17.6	15.8	16.4	17.9	18.4	21.3	19.3
Business loan growth (%)	95.1	29.6	34.6	83.7	22.8	1.0	7.7	17.7	27.4	34.2	46.4	19.0	(0.6)	15.5	16.8	11.8	12.3	9.2
Lending rate (%, annual average)	...	...	...	...	...	...	...	...	...	...	...	...	...	...	12.6	12.6	11.9	12.2
Nonperforming business loans (NPLs) (KGS million)	...	...	...	...	...	...	...	...	...	...	...	...	...	...	...	...	...	...
NPLs to total business loans (%)	...	...	...	...	...	...	...	...	...	...	...	...	...	...	...	...	...	...
Number of business loan borrowers	...	...	...	...	...	...	...	...	...	...	...	...	...	...	...	...	...	...
Borrowers to total bank borrowers (%)	...	...	...	...	...	...	...	...	...	...	...	...	...	...	...	...	...	...
Loan rejection rate (% of total applications)	...	...	...	...	...	...	...	...	...	...	...	...	...	...	...	...	...	...
Number of business savings account in banks	...	...	...	...	...	...	...	...	...	...	...	...	...	...	...	...	...	...
Guaranteed business loans (KGS million)	...	...	...	...	...	...	...	...	...	...	...	...	...	...	...	...	...	...
Non-collateral business loans (KGS million)	...	...	...	...	...	...	...	...	...	...	...	...	...	...	...	...	...	...
BUSINESS loans outstanding by sector (% share)																		
Agriculture, forestry, and fisheries	2.2	2.4	4.2	15.7	14.8	15.3	15.5	15.6	18.7	21.5	22.6	23.3	25.7	24.7	23.2	24.3	23.8	23.8
Manufacturing	25.0	21.4	15.6	9.5	8.0	7.4	7.0	6.8	7.2	10.3	10.9	11.1	12.0	13.0	12.6	11.9	12.5	11.6
Transportation and communication	2.1	1.4	3.0	1.7	2.0	1.3	1.5	1.6	3.2	2.8	2.4	2.2	2.1	2.3	2.5	2.9	3.0	3.1
Construction	5.6	7.1	7.5	8.8	12.2	9.7	9.4	6.9	6.8	7.2	7.6	7.1	7.6	8.9	11.1	11.5	10.7	9.7
Wholesale and retail trade	53.5	50.5	52.7	48.8	46.4	52.0	52.4	52.5	49.4	45.5	43.9	41.0	37.2	35.6	34.3	32.7	32.6	36.7
Other services	0.3	0.2	0.1	0.2	0.6	0.2	0.4	0.8	2.0	1.8	2.3	4.0	4.7	4.4	5.0	4.5	5.0	4.8
Others	11.2	17.1	17.0	15.3	16.0	14.1	13.7	15.8	12.8	10.9	10.3	11.3	10.7	11.1	11.3	12.3	12.3	10.4
Business loans outstanding by region (% share)																		
Capital city (Bishkek)	60.0	60.0	60.0	60.0	60.0	67.0	65.0	63.0	57.0	57.0	59.0	58.0	55.0	56.0	58.9	57.0	56.0	55.0
Others	40.0	40.0	40.0	40.0	40.0	33.0	35.0	37.0	43.0	43.0	41.0	42.0	45.0	44.0	41.1	43.0	44.0	45.0
Business loans outstanding by type of use (% share)																		
For working capital	...	...	...	...	...	...	...	...	...	...	...	...	...	...	...	...	...	...
For capital investment	...	...	...	...	...	...	...	...	...	...	...	...	...	...	...	...	...	...
Business loans outstanding by tenor (% share)																		
Less than 1 year	38.7	56.2	48.8	36.4	32.5	31.0	28.6	24.8	25.1	18.6	17.3	22.1	18.8	13.2	12.2	11.3	10.2	10.2
1-5 years	61.3	43.8	51.2	63.6	67.5	69.0	71.4	75.2	74.9	81.4	82.7	77.9	81.2	86.8	87.8	88.7	89.8	89.8
More than 5 years	...	...	...	...	...	...	...	...	...	...	...	...	...	...	...	...	...	...

GDP = gross domestic product.

* Business loans cover all enterprises including micro, small, medium-sized, and large enterprises.

Source: ADB Asia SME Monitor 2022 database. Data from the National Bank of the Kyrgyz Republic, Bulletin (https://www.nbkr.kg/index1.jsp?item=137&lang=RUS).

Table 6.4: Public Financing and Guarantees

End-of-period data

Item	2011	2012	2013	2014	2015	2016	2017	2018	2019	2020	2021
SUBSIDIZED LOANS TO MSMEs											
Number of funds	...	...	6	6	6	5	6	11	9	7	7
Number of subsidized loans (new approval)	...	...	14,839	15,525	9,980	13,246	15,163	11,343	9,976	11,979	10,407
Outstanding of subsidized loans to MSMEs (KGS million)	...	...	...	...	...	...	...	...	...	...	...
Subsidized loans disbursed to MSMEs (KGS million)	...	...	3,171	5,300	3,801	4,833	6,684	5,640	5,164	6,181	6,179
Growth (%)	...	...	...	67.1	(28.3)	27.1	38.3	(15.6)	(8.4)	19.7	(0.04)
Number of MSMEs that accepted subsidized loans	...	...	14,839	15,525	9,980	13,246	15,163	11,343	9,976	11,979	10,407
MSME access to subsidized loans (% of total MSMEs)	...	...	2.0	2.1	1.3	1.6	1.8	1.3	1.1	1.3	1.2

MSME = micro, small, and medium-sized enterprise; NPL = nonperforming loan.

Source: ADB Asia SME Monitor 2022 database. Data from the Ministry of Finance of the Kyrgyz Republic.

End-of-period data

Item	2011	2012	2013	2014	2015	2016	2017	2018	2019	2020	2021
CREDIT GUARANTEES											
Number of guarantee schemes	2	2	5	5	6	6	6	6	6	1	1
Guaranteed loans outstanding to MSMEs (KGS million)	5	16	43	75	55	41	790	1,752	2,967	5,015	5,759
Growth (%)	...	245.0	165.8	74.2	(25.7)	(26.6)	174.0	121.7	69.3	69.1	14.8
Guaranteed loans approved to MSMEs (KGS million)	5	16	43	75	55	44	1,012	1,836	2,909	3,645	4,224
Guaranteed loans disbursed to MSMEs (KGS million)	5	16	43	75	55	41	910	1,641	2,555	2,941	3,935
Number of MSMEs guaranteed	16	36	106	159	98	64	291	469	515	732	977
MSME access to credit guarantees (% of total MSMEs)	0.003	0.005	0.015	0.021	0.013	0.008	0.03	0.05	0.06	0.08	0.11
Guaranteed MSME loans to total MSME loans (%)	0.01	0.04	0.07	0.09	0.07	0.04	0.9	1.4	2.0	2.5	2.5
Nonperforming guaranteed MSME loans to total guaranteed MSME loans (NPL ratio; %)*	...	...	...	...	...	...	0.1	0.2	0.4	2.2	4.6

MSME = micro, small, and medium-sized enterprise; NPL = nonperforming loan.

* Nonperforming guaranteed MSME loans with ≥ 90 days overdue are used for calculation.

Source: ADB Asia SME Monitor 2022 database. Data from National Bank of Kazakhstan, DAMU JSC, and its public annual reports

Table 6.5: Nonbank Finance

End-of-period data

Item	2004	2005	2006	2007	2008	2009	2010	2011	2012	2013	2014	2015	2016	2017	2018	2019	2020	2021
NUMBER OF NONBANK FINANCE INSTITUTIONS																		
Nonbank Finance Institutions, total	798	866	909	1,032	1,126	1,301	1,419	1,600	1,515	799	699	668	717	701	701	675	652	620
Microfinance institutions	75	106	147	232	291	359	397	454	320	277	215	172	162	150	142	137	134	133
Credit unions/cooperatives	305	320	308	272	248	238	217	197	183	153	135	125	116	110	106	95	92	88
Finance companies	1	1	1	1	1	1	1	1	1	1	1	1	1	1	1	1	1	1
Pawnshops	116	141	145	180	196	284	475	633	669	...	...	...	...	...	...	...	...	...
Leasing companies	12	12	15	14	8	8	7	8	8	5	9	11	11	11	11	14	14	12
Insurance companies	12	11	12	16	18	19	19	16	16	18	17	17	19	19	17	17	17	17
Others*	277	275	281	317	364	392	303	291	318	345	322	342	408	410	424	411	394	369
MICROFINANCE INSTITUTIONS																		
Loans outstanding, total (KGS million)	785	1,488	2,055	4,052	6,196	7,525	9,335	13,247	12,720	16,116	18,853	11,595	7,629	8,216	12,085	15,555	15,906	17,571
Growth (%)	81.0	89.6	38.1	97.1	59.4	22.8	25.4	45.7	(3.0)	25.5	23.5	(35.6)	(29.0)	17.6	36.1	32.4	5.2	21.9
Total loans to GDP (%)	0.8	1.5	1.8	2.9	3.4	3.9	4.5	5.1	4.5	5.0	5.4	3.3	2.1	2.2	2.8	3.4	3.7	3.7
Annual lending rate (%, on average)	28.0	33.5	33.5	32.9	32.5	34.5	31.7	38.3	34.9	31.0	30.0	32.2	31.4	31.2	30.4	30.0	29.8	29.1
Gross nonperforming loans (NPLs) (KGS million)	...	...	...	...	...	...	...	...	...	...	...	...	...	...	...	...	...	...
Gross NPLs to total loans (%)	...	...	...	...	...	...	...	...	...	...	...	...	...	...	...	...	...	...
Savings (KGS million)	...	...	...	...	...	...	...	...	...	...	...	...	...	...	...	...	...	...
Number of customers financed, total	140,934	146,633	172,702	188,166	311,126	412,290	484,921	579,687	528,654	513,494	456,587	333,658	239,413	307,997	481,895	624,460	706,610	644,552
Financing outstanding by sector (% share)																		
Agriculture, forestry, and fisheries	12.0	17.2	25.0	29.2	36.7	43.2	48.2	47.6	48.8	45.6	42.4	47.0	36.3	35.1	37.4	37.5	39.6	39.5
Manufacturing	3.5	5.0	3.8	2.9	2.7	2.4	2.2	1.9	1.6	1.2	1.1	1.4	1.5	1.8	1.6	1.3	1.3	1.2
Transportation and communication	...	...	...	...	2.3	0.1	1.0	1.5	0.8	1.2	1.9	1.3	1.4	1.7	1.6	2.0	2.1	2.4
Construction	6.6	9.8	3.6	3.2	2.5	2.3	1.8	2.6	2.6	3.6	4.6	7.0	9.2	12.3	10.5	13.8	13.6	18.4
Wholesale and retail trade	66.1	52.9	55.9	50.8	41.5	36.8	30.4	29.8	22.8	22.3	22.7	20.6	21.1	20.2	17.4	17.1	16.7	18.9
Other services	4.1	3.9	...	...	5.5	6.3	5.8	3.7	4.1	7.2	7.5	12.2	15.9	15.9	25.0	22.3	20.3	13.8
Others	7.8	11.2	11.7	13.8	8.8	8.9	10.6	13.0	19.2	18.9	19.7	10.5	14.6	13.0	6.4	6.0	6.4	5.7
Financing outstanding by region (% share)																		
Capital city (Bishkek)	...	...	...	...	...	...	...	...	...	...	...	...	...	...	...	...	...	...
Others	...	...	...	...	...	...	...	...	...	...	...	...	...	...	...	...	...	...
CREDIT UNIONS AND COOPERATIVES																		
Loans outstanding, total (KGS million)	449	580	674	768	882	959	1,140	1,232	1,345	1,456	1,153	934	941	999	1,000	964	904	918
Growth (%)	55.3	29.4	16.1	13.9	14.9	8.7	18.9	8.1	9.2	8.3	(20.9)	(19.0)	0.8	6.2	0.1	(3.7)	(6.2)	1.5
Total loans to GDP (%)	0.5	0.6	0.6	0.5	0.5	0.5	0.5	0.4	0.4	0.4	0.3	0.2	0.2	0.2	0.2	0.2	0.2	0.1
Annual lending rate (%, on average)	28.7	26.8	25.9	25.8	28.0	29.6	30.7	29.0	29.1	27.3	25.6	27.9	27.8	25.9	27.4	26.6	26.5	25.3
Gross nonperforming loans (NPLs) (KGS million)	...	...	...	...	...	...	...	...	...	...	...	...	...	...	...	...	...	...
Gross NPLs to total loans (%)	...	...	...	...	...	...	...	...	...	...	...	...	...	...	...	...	...	...
Number of customers financed, total	...	...	...	...	...	...	...	...	...	...	...	...	...	...	...	...	...	...
Financing outstanding by sector (% share)																		
Agriculture, forestry, and fisheries	56.7	59.1	55.7	50.8	50.6	50.3	49.0	48.4	46.2	43.3	46.9	50.9	47.5	40.3	35.7	30.8	30.4	27.3
Manufacturing	5.0	3.0	2.9	2.2	2.2	1.5	1.9	1.7	1.0	1.2	1.2	1.1	1.9	1.8	1.7	1.4	2.1	1.3
Transportation and communication	0.9	1.1	1.7	1.1	0.6	0.5	0.4	0.4	0.5	0.3	0.5	0.7	0.5	0.8	1.0	1.4	1.4	1.6
Construction	3.0	4.6	4.2	4.9	4.0	3.8	3.8	3.6	3.3	3.2	3.9	5.7	10.2	15.3	16.8	19.5	18.8	20.4
Wholesale and retail trade	25.6	25.8	29.7	33.5	33.2	33.1	32.3	33.8	35.5	37.0	33.5	24.9	22.9	22.9	24.9	23.7	22.6	20.9
Other services	...	...	...	...	0.3	0.4	0.4	0.3	0.5	4.4	1.1	1.6	1.0	1.0	1.0	0.9	1.0	0.8
Others	8.7	6.4	5.8	7.5	9.1	10.4	12.2	11.7	13.1	10.6	12.9	14.9	15.9	17.8	18.9	22.2	23.6	27.7

continued on next page

Table 6.5 *continued*

Item	2004	2005	2006	2007	2008	2009	2010	2011	2012	2013	2014	2015	2016	2017	2018	2019	2020	2021
Financing outstanding by region (% share)																		
Capital city (Bishkek)	...	...	...	...	...	...	...	...	...	...	...	...	...	...	...	...	...	...
Others	...	...	...	...	...	...	...	...	...	...	...	...	...	...	...	...	...	...
FINANCE COMPANIES																		
Loans outstanding, total (KGS million)	...	...	...	...	...	427	460	434	408	407	399	472	475	444	411	379	336	315
Growth (%)	...	...	...	...	...	...	7.6	(5.7)	(11.3)	(0.4)	(2.1)	18.4	0.4	(6.4)	(7.5)	(7.1)	(11.4)	(6.5)
Total loans to GDP (%)	...	...	...	...	...	0.21	0.21	0.15	0.13	0.11	0.10	0.11	0.10	0.08	0.07	0.06	0.06	0.04
Annual lending rate (%, on average)	...	...	...	...	...	14.6	15.5	15.8	15.9	15.4	15.9	16.5	16.6	16.5	15.7	15.2	15.0	14.8
Gross nonperforming loans (NPLs) (KGS million)	...	...	...	...	...	...	...	...	...	...	...	...	...	...	...	...	...	...
Gross NPLs to total loans (%)	...	...	...	...	...	...	...	...	...	...	...	...	...	...	...	...	...	...
Number of customers financed, total	...	...	...	...	...	...	...	...	...	...	...	...	...	...	...	...	...	...
Financing outstanding by sector (% share)																		
Agriculture, forestry, and fisheries	...	...	...	...	...	...	...	...	...	7.5	3.4	0.7	...	1.5	0.7	...	...	...
Manufacturing	...	...	...	...	...	...	...	...	...	...	...	...	...	...	...	...	...	...
Transportation and communication	...	...	...	...	...	...	...	...	...	...	...	...	...	...	...	...	...	...
Construction	...	...	...	...	...	1.0	1.2	1.0	0.9	0.6	1.9	2.1	7.3	12.7	15.1	18.1	14.9	15.5
Wholesale and retail trade	...	...	...	...	...	...	...	...	...	...	...	...	...	...	...	...	...	...
Other services	...	...	...	...	...	...	...	...	...	...	...	...	...	...	...	...	...	...
Others	...	...	...	...	...	99.0	98.8	99.0	99.1	92.0	94.8	97.3	92.7	85.8	84.2	81.9	85.1	84.5
Financing outstanding by region (% share)																		
Capital city (Bishkek)	...	...	...	...	...	...	...	...	...	...	...	...	...	...	...	...	...	...
Others	...	...	...	...	...	...	...	...	...	...	...	...	...	...	...	...	...	...
PAWNSHOPS																		
Financing outstanding, total (KGS million)	11	14	20	31	45	48	62	86	115	...	...	...	...	...	...	...	...	...
Growth (%)	37.0	25.8	42.9	57.5	45.9	6.4	28.4	39.6	32.8	...	...	...	...	...	...	...	...	...
Total financing to GDP (%)	...	...	...	...	...	...	...	...	...	...	...	...	...	...	...	...	...	...
Annual financing rate (%, on average)	162.1	153.6	149.5	167.9	129.9	122.8	...	...	...	...	...	...	...	...	...	...	...	...
Gross nonperforming financing (NPFs) (KGS million)	...	...	...	...	...	...	...	...	...	...	...	...	...	...	...	...	...	...
Gross NPFs to total financing (%)	...	...	...	...	...	...	...	...	...	...	...	...	...	...	...	...	...	...
Number of customers financed, total	...	...	...	...	...	...	...	...	...	...	...	...	...	...	...	...	...	...
LEASING COMPANIES																		
Financing outstanding, total (KGS million)	...	45	56	70	68	101	14	260	372	663	615	627	638	904	1,039	1,449	1,267	1,709
Growth (%)	...	...	22.2	26.4	(3.7)	49.2	(86.4)	1,798.6	42.8	78.3	(7.2)	1.9	1.8	41.6	15.0	39.4	(12.6)	34.9
Total financing to GDP (%)	...	0.05	0.05	0.05	0.04	0.05	0.01	0.09	0.12	0.19	0.15	0.15	0.13	0.17	0.18	0.23	0.21	0.24
Annual financing rate (%, on average)	...	...	...	...	...	...	...	...	...	...	...	...	...	...	...	...	...	...
Gross nonperforming financing (NPFs) (KGS million)	...	...	...	...	...	...	...	...	...	...	...	...	...	...	...	...	...	...
Gross NPFs to total financing (%)	...	...	...	...	...	...	...	...	...	...	...	...	...	...	...	...	...	...
Number of customers financed, total	...	...	...	...	...	...	...	...	...	...	...	...	...	...	...	...	...	...

* Including stock exchanges, pension funds, OJSC Guarantee Fund, exchange bureaus, credit bureau.

GDP = gross domestic product.

Source: ADB Asia SME Monitor 2022 database. Data from National Statistical Committee, National Bank of the Kyrgyz Republic, and Financial Market Regulation and Supervision Service under the Ministry of Economy and Commerce.

Table 6.6: Capital Markets

End-of-period data

Item	2004	2005	2006	2007	2008	2009	2010	2011	2012	2013	2014	2015	2016	2017	2018	2019	2020	2021
EQUITY MARKET																		
Main Board - KSE																		
Index	74.2	69.5	87.2	90.2	96.3	90.9	107.3	220.1	224.4	259.8	259.3	343.0	499.9	550.9	758.6	754.3	953.4	1,466.1
Market capitalization (KGS million)	4,000	3,750	4,705	4,865	3,697	3,168	3,740	7,671	7,820	9,052	9,037	11,953	17,422	19,199	26,435	26,285	33,223	51,090
Growth (%)	...	(6.2)	25.4	3.4	(24.0)	(14.3)	18.1	105.1	1.9	15.8	(0.2)	32.3	45.7	10.2	37.7	(0.6)	26.4	53.8
Trading value (KGS million)	2,209	1,246	3,916	5,189	4,182	2,951	460	1,511	1,169	1,648	1,634	4,008	9,969	4,644	3,802	6,074	11,831	9,738
Trading volume (million shares)	2,204	1,235	3,916	5,187	4,080	2,921	419	1,300	1,067	1,215	1,273	3,722	9,510	3,997	3,371	5,624	11,659	9,372
Number of registered companies (listing)	...	...	10	10	9	9	11	13	18	20	21	23	26	29	29	26	26	26
Number of IPOs	...	...	...	...	...	...	...	...	...	...	...	...	...	...	...	...	1	...
Number of companies excluded from the quotation (delisted)	...	...	...	...	4	1	...	1	...	...	...	1	...	...	3	3	1	3
BOND MARKET																		
Corporate Bonds Issued by MSMEs																		
Corporate bonds issued by MSMEs, total (KGS million)	6	11	...	...	...	30	41	61	102	187	260	39	71	267	256	192	66	169
In local currency denominated (KGS million)	6	11	...	...	...	30	41	61	102	187	260	39	71	267	256	192	66	169
In foreign currency denominated (KGS million)	...	...	...	...	...	...	...	...	...	...	...	...	...	...	...	...	...	...
Growth (%)	...	88.9	...	...	...	...	33.5	49.3	67.9	83.9	39.0	(84.8)	80.8	274.6	(4.1)	(24.9)	(65.8)	157.0
Number of MSME that issues bonds	2	1	...	...	...	1	2	2	2	4	4	4	3	2	4	3	4	3
MSME bond yields (% per annum, on average)	17.3	13.0	...	...	...	20.0	20.0	18.5	18.5	19.3	18.2	18.5	18.6	20.5	17.8	17.5	17.4	16.5
MSME bonds by maturity (% share)																		
Less than 1 year	...	...	...	...	...	...	...	...	...	...	...	...	...	...	...	...	...	...
1-5 years	100.0	100.0	...	...	...	100.0	100.0	100.0	100.0	100.0	100.0	100.0	100.0	100.0	100.0	100.0	100.0	100.0
5-10 years	...	...	...	...	...	...	...	...	...	...	...	...	...	...	...	...	...	...
More than 10 years	...	...	...	...	...	...	...	...	...	...	...	...	...	...	...	...	...	...

IPO = initial public offering, KSE = Kyrgyz Stock Exchange.

Note: There is no specialized market for MSMEs.

Source: ADB Asia SME Monitor 2022 database. Data from Kyrgyz Stock Exchange.

Table 6.6a: Listing Requirements—Kyrgyz Stock Exchange

Criteria	Stock		
	Category A	Category B	Category C
Issuer	Open Joint Stock Company	Open Joint Stock Company	Open Joint Stock Company
Free float	Required	Not required	Not required
Independent board of commissioner	Required	Required	Required
Corporate secretary	Required	Required	Required
Operating period	not less than 3 years	not less than 3 years	...
Operating profit	Must have been at least breakeven for the most recent reporting year or the sum of the three most recent years. A foreign issuer must have been breakeven for each of the last 3 years.	Must be at least breakeven for the last reporting year or the sum of the last 3 years.	Must be at least breakeven for the last reporting year or by the sum of the last 3 years. This requirement applies after the third year of the Issuer's existence.
Audited financial report	The Issuer's 3-year annual financial statements must be provided with the auditor's report of an independent auditing organization (company) recognized by the Exchange.	The Issuer's 3-year annual financial statements must be provided with the auditor's report of an independent auditing organization (company) recognized by the Exchange.	The requirement to provide an auditor's report applies from the second year of existence or being on the Official List of the Exchange of this category.
Capital requirement	Not less than KGS400 million	Not less than KGS50 million	Not less than KGS10 million
Minimum offering price	Not less than KGS20 million	Not less than KGS10 million	...
Ratio of current liquidity	Not less than 100.0%	...	...
Ratio of debt and equity	Not less than 100.0%	...	...

Source: ADB Asia SME Monitor 2022 database. Data from Kyrgyz Stock Exchange.

Table 6.7: Policies and Regulations

Regulations	
Name	**Outline**
MSME Development	
Government Resolution No.78 of 1998	MSMEs are defined by economic group in the number of employees and annual revenue.
Law on State Support for Small Business, 2007	The legal basis for the activity, regulation, and state support of small businesses.
Law on Public-Private Partnership, 2007	Legal basis for the operation and regulation of public-private partnership projects.
Presidential Decree on State Support for Small Businesses, 2021	State support for small business, creating a favorable tax and customs climate.
Presidential Decree on Protecting Property and Supporting Entrepreneurs and Investors, 2021	Defines conditions for the protection of property and support for entrepreneurs and investors.
Banking	
Law on Banks and Banking Activities, 2016	Regulation of national and commercial banks.
Law on Pledge, 2005	Legal basis on granting collateral for MSME credit.
National Bank of the Kyrgyz Republic (NBKR) Regulation on the minimum requirements for credit risk management in commercial banks and other financial institutions, 2010	Credit risk reduction requirements for lending to MSMEs.
NBKR Instructions on Limitations of Credit, 2004	Instruction on limiting MSME credit to reduce risks.
NBKR requirements to Banks and Other Financial and Credit Institutions when Granting Loans to Individual Clients, 2017	Requirements for banks when issuing loans to consumers.
Nonbank finance	
Law on Microfinance Organizations, 2002	Regulation of microfinance organizations.
Law on Credit Unions, 1999	Regulation of credit unions.
Law on Exchange of Credit Information, 2014	Regulation of credit bureaus.
Capital market	
Law on Joint Stock Companies, 2003	Regulation of joint-stock companies.
Law on Securities Market, 2009	Regulation of capital market activities.
Code of Corporate Governance, 2020	Regulates corporate relations in MSMEs.
Public finance and guarantees	
Law on Guarantee Funds, 2019	Regulation of guarantee funds.

continued on next page

Table 6.7 *continued*

Regulators and Policymakers		
Name		**Responsibility**
Ministry of Economy and Commerce (MEC)		Coordination of MSMEs.
Service for Regulation and Supervision of the Financial Market, Ministry of Economy and Commerce		Supervision of capital market, joint-stock companies, insurance companies, pawnshops, and auditing companies.
Ministry of Foreign Affairs		Assistance in attracting investment in MSMEs and in exporting MSME products.
Development and Investment Agency		Assistance in attracting investment in MSMEs.
National Bank of the Kyrgyz Republic (NBKR)		(i) Conducting monetary policy; (ii) supervising the activities of banks, microfinance organizations, credit unions, and guarantee funds.
Policies		
Name	**Responsible Entity**	**Outline**
National Strategy "On the Development of the Kyrgyz Republic for 2018–2040" (2018)	Government	The strategy provides a long-term vision for developing the national economy and entrepreneurship for 2018-2040. It identifies priority sectors for MSME development, including agriculture and agri-processing, manufacturing, energy, and tourism.
Strategy for Sustainable Development of Industry of the Kyrgyz Republic for 2019–2023	Government	(i) Development of industry, taking into account the specialization of regions of the Kyrgyz Republic; (ii) expansion of a high-tech, competitive export industry, the transition of the economy from an export-raw material to industrial-innovative development; (iii) creation of an effective industrial management systems and conditions for attracting investments.
Program to support and develop women's entrepreneurship of the Kyrgyz Republic for 2022–2026	Cabinet of Ministers	(i) Improve and optimize legislation regulating women entrepreneurial activities; (ii) support and formation of state and public institutions that provide assistance in increasing the expert and analytical potential of women entrepreneurs; (iii) providing women entrepreneurs with accessible information, consulting, production, technological and educational services.
Export Development Program of the Kyrgyz Republic for 2019–2022	Government	(i) Ensuring favorable regulatory conditions for technical regulation, contributing to the development and production of competitive and high-quality domestic products; (ii) providing exporters with access to finance to build competitive export potential of enterprises for sustainable economic and export growth; (iii) encouraging entrepreneurs to produce competitive products and sell them on foreign markets.
Strategy for Improving Financial Inclusion for 2022–2026	Cabinet of Ministers	(i) Provide expanded access to financial services, (ii) expanding the use of financial instruments, (iii) providing reliable and comprehensive mechanisms to protect the rights of consumers of financial services, and (iv) improving financial literacy.
Government Program on Financial Literacy 2016–2020 (2016)	Cabinet of Ministers	This aims to improve the financial literacy among population and the access to financial information and financial services. The financial inclusion of MSMEs targets creating the financial infrastructure and mechanisms that provide a wide range of high-quality, secure, affordable, and responsive financial services, both traditionally and digitally. The program has five main components: (i) digital finance and products, (ii) infrastructure, (iii) financial product diversification, (iv) consumer protection, and (v) financial literacy.
Financing of Agriculture Program (2022)	Cabinet of Ministers	Subsidize interest rates on loans to the agriculture sector. The program is the 10th and is being realized since 2013. The main goal of the program is subsidizing interest rates on crop production, livestock, and processing of agricultural products loans.

MSME = micro, small, and medium-sized enterprise.

Source: ADB Asia SME Monitor 2022 database. Data from the Ministry of Justice of the Kyrgyz Republic (www.cbd.minjust.kg); legal Information portal (www.toktom.kg).

Table 6.7a: COVID-19 Emergency Measures

Name	Fund Size (KGZ million)	Outline
1. Restoration of economic activity and support of MSME activities, 2020 (Government Order)	14,000	(i) Formation of Anti-Crisis Fund with KGZ14 billion; (ii) emergency MSME aid for KGZ8.5 billion (World Bank project) implemented by OJSC Guarantee Fund and the Ministry of Finance for 2021–2027; and (iii) preferential funding for MSMEs. Sources of funds are the national budget, the World Bank, the European Investment Bank, the Islamic Development Bank, and the counter funds.
2. Priority measures of the Government of the Kyrgyz Republic for 2020 (Government Order)*	12,549	To reduce the negative impact on economic and social stability due to the spread of COVID-19: (i) social support of the population and food security; (ii) support for MSMEs through tax exemptions and deferrals, limit planned and unplanned inspections of MSMEs; (iii) financial measures to support MSMEs [(a) NBKR (the central bank) to conduct credit auctions and ease prudential standards and (b) commercial banks to conduct prolongation of MSME loans for at least 3 months, if necessary]; and (iv) support the stability of the state budget.
3. Ensure social stability, economic stability and maintenance of the population's income, 2020 (Government Order)	n/a	(i) Protection of public health, (ii) support for socially vulnerable segments of the population and education, (iii) ensuring economic stability and support for business development; (iv) providing MSMEs with preferential financing and guarantees from the Guarantee Fund.
4. Increasing SMEs' access to financing to mitigate the effects of COVID-19 on entrepreneurs, 2020 (OJSC Guarantee Fund Resolution)	1,000	OJSC Guarantee Fund provided seven banks with funds at 2% interest. Banks financed MSMEs with an interest rate not exceeding 10%. The term of financing is 3 years.
5. Emergency Assistance to MSMEs affected by COVID-19, 2022 (Government of the Kyrgyz Republic and the World Bank Agreement)	4,250	(i) Increase in the volume of portfolio guarantees (executing agency: JSC "GF"); (ii) increase in the provision of interest-free loans (executing agency: Ministry of Finance).
6. Credit auctions of the National Bank of the Kyrgyz Republic, 2019–2020	5,510	Providing funds to commercial banks to finance MSMEs.
Total	**37,309**	

COVID-19 = coronavirus disease; MSME = micro, small, and medium-sized enterprise, NBKR = National Bank of the Kyrgyz Republic.

* Benefits for taxes and social payments to the budget.

Source: ADB Asia SME Monitor 2022 database. Data from the Ministry of Finance of the Kyrgyz Republic.

Country Review

Tajikistan

Overview

Small and medium-sized enterprises (SMEs) are a critical driver of the Tajikistan economy, accounting for over 98% of enterprises, generating over 20% of the labor force and around 60% of gross domestic product (GDP). SMEs are mostly engaged in services, and are spread nationwide. Most SME employees also work in services, followed by agriculture. SME operations are influenced by the Russian Federation's economy. The 2014–2016 Russian financial crisis contributed to a reduction in SMEs and decelerating GDP growth. However, during the first year of the coronavirus disease (COVID-19) pandemic (2020), the number of SMEs and their workforce grew, with output remaining robust.

Most SMEs operate in small domestic markets, with a few operating internationally. The export market in Tajikistan remains small, with several barriers limiting SMEs expansion globally. E-commerce is in the early stage of the development, but has high growth potential. Most SMEs have yet to digitalize, but the digital transformation is underway and will likely expand. The state business incubator and private sector associations such as the Chamber of Commerce and Industry support SMEs and entrepreneurships through advisory and training services.

Limited access to finance is a critical factor impeding SME development. Bank credit to SMEs accounted for only 16% of total bank loans outstanding and less than 3% of GDP. The SME bank credit market is prone to external shocks like the Russian financial crisis, the pandemic, and Russian invasion of Ukraine. More than one-third of loans are approved for SMEs involved with international trade, so external shocks keep the credit market volatile. However, SME nonperforming loans (NPLs) have dropped sharply since 2017, with their 4.6% NPL ratio in 2021 far below the ratio for all bank credit (16.2%). The government offers several incentives for banks to lend to SMEs through interest rate subsidies and credit guarantees, leading to the sharp rise SME bank loans in 2021 (31.7%).

The microfinance industry is also small and exposed to external shocks. Microfinance institutions (MFIs) offer savings, credit, and remittance services for individuals and SMEs, targeting rural and areas, but they do not substitute for bank credit. Electronic money transfers have expanded. Since 2018, financial institutions have accepted noncash payments, but digital financial services remain underdeveloped and are not yet a funding option for SMEs. There are two registered stock exchanges—the Central Asian Stock Exchange (CASE) and Asian Stock Exchange (ASE). The CASE has a specialized SME board, with three firms issuing bonds in 2021. The ASE is not yet in operation. Financial infrastructure remains at an early stage of development. There are two credit bureaus—the Credit Information Bureau of Tajikistan (CIB) and the Bureau of Credit Histories Somoniyon (BCHS). The CIB has 3-4 million records, including SMEs, and shares these with banks and nonbank financing institutions (NBFIs). A credit registry is planned.

The National Development Strategy for 2030 (NDS) covers long-term socio economic development and outlines priorities for SME development including job creation. To improve the investment climate, the NDS aims to reduce administrative barriers to SME operations and build the needed infrastructure to facilitate SME growth. A new Tax

Code went into effect in early 2022. It simplifies government tax administration and reduces the tax burden on individuals and businesses, including SMEs (reducing corporate income tax). To accelerate inclusive growth, the government adopted in July 2022 a National Strategy for Financial Inclusion for 2022–2026, which will diversify financial products, and strengthen consumer protection and financial literacy.

The government adopted several emergency measures in response to the COVID-19 pandemic and the Russian invasion of and Ukraine. At the early stages of the pandemic, the government implemented a set of financial and nonfinancial assistance measures for farmers and SMEs—including subsidies, tax relief, and liquidity support for financial institutions to continue lending to affected groups. The government also adopted an anti-crisis program in March 2022 to counter the impact of the Russian invasion of Ukraine. It created an Interdepartmental Headquarters to reduce risks to the national economy and to develop an action plan.

The outlook for SMEs remains challenging as they recover from the pandemic. The sector may be small, but SMEs are growing steadily both in terms of value added and share of employment—even as access to finance remains relatively weak and financial literacy is low. One of the biggest challenges is increasing affordable access to broadband services. It is both expensive and slow, and with current sanctions against the Russian Federation—which supplies most of Tajikistan's bandwidth—congestion is a common problem. The country remains near the bottom globally in terms of internet speed.

It suggests that, unless the business climate, digital infrastructure, entrepreneurial skills, and finance improve, the ability of SMEs to withstand future economic shocks will weaken further. The government is undertaking much needed reforms—creating the stock exchange and credit bureau, strengthening regulations, and improving the ease of doing business—but a shallow financial sector and underdeveloped capital markets risk reversing these gains. The private sector's emerging comparative advantage in niche sectors will require the development of value chains. SMEs need sufficient support to use asset-based finance. A special fund could subsidize 50% of interest rates on SME loans and create export insurance and crowdfunding platforms. The existing financial architecture needs to be more transparent, with financial literacy and corporate governance standards improved if value chains are to develop.

Over the past decade, Tajikistan has made steady progress in reducing poverty and growing its economy. Between 2000 and 2018, the poverty rate fell from 83% of the population to 27.4%, while the economy grew an average 7% annually. Real GDP growth rebounded to 9.2% in 2021, after slowing to 4.5% in 2020 due to the pandemic. A sharp increase in precious metal exports, a recovery in remittance inflows, and a pickup in private investment and consumption supported the rebound. Overall, services expanded by 32.9% in 2021, agriculture by 6.6%, while construction fell by 9.6%. Remittances from the Russian Federation increased by 20.1% in 2021 from 2020. But the process has become more complicated due to sanctions against Russian banks that use the SWIFT system. The expectation that weaker remittances will moderate private consumption later in 2022 is lowering some economic forecasts. As of end-2021, 53.6% of the adult population was fully vaccinated against COVID-19. Yet there remains uncertainty over another wave of the virus. Other factors include the Rogun hydropower project proceeding more slowly than expected due to a lack of finance. As a result, GDP is forecast to grow by 2% for 2022 and 3% for 2023—largely in line with the NDS "industrial" (or moderate)[207] scenario.[208] Job creation has not kept pace with the growing working age population, leaving the economy again vulnerable to external shocks. The private sector's role in the economy remained limited. Non-monetary poverty indicators in rural areas remains high, for example, with only 36% of the rural population having access to safe drinking water.

[207] ADB. 2022. *Asian Development Outlook 2022: Mobilizing Taxes for Development*. Manila. https://www.adb.org/sites/default/files/publication/784041/ado2022.pdf.

[208] In particular, the 'industrial' scenario anticipates growth rates to be at least 6.7 % in 2020, 6.9 % in 2025, and 7.8 % in 2030.

Social and economic well-being severely deteriorated following the COVID-19 outbreak. The economy recovered quickly in 2021. However, the labor market remains weak and food insecurity more prevalent compared to pre-pandemic levels. In addition, the economy faced a new set of challenges in 2022 due to the Russian invasion of Ukraine.

Tajikistan's high vulnerability to climate change and natural hazards is an additional challenge to successful economic management. Between 1992 and 2016, climate-related disasters caused GDP losses of around $1.8 billion, affecting almost 7 million people.[209] The NDS targets increasing domestic incomes by up to 3.5 times by 2030 and reducing poverty by half. This can happen if Tajikistan transforms its current growth model and gives the private sector more opportunities to invest, create jobs, and contribute to innovation and growth.

1. Impact of the Global Economy on SMEs

COVID-19 Impact

The first confirmed case of COVID-19 in Tajikistan was on 1 May 2020. Authorities set up a high-level task force and took measures to contain the spread of the virus—including border closures, travel restrictions, suspending mosque prayers, and closing schools until 10 May 2020. The President issued a decree "On counteracting the socio-economic impact of COVID-19" on 5 June 2020.

The pandemic had a severe human and economic impact. Trade and transportation disruptions led to a sharp drop in remittances and government revenues, creating balance of payments and fiscal problems. No COVID-19 cases have been registered in Tajikistan since January 2021.

On 6 June 2020, the government issued a plan that included reopening bazaars, cafés, beauty and hairdressing salons, and barber shops, among others on 15 June. All businesses had to follow regular disinfection procedures, social distancing, with schools reopening after 4 months under COVID-19 prevention measures.

The Prevention Commission of Tajikistan prohibited holding celebrations, including cultural, festive, and other public events. It was the first country to make COVID-19 vaccines mandatory.[210]

The United Nations Development Programme (UNDP), in partnership with the government, assessed the impact of the pandemic on the lives, livelihoods,[211] and micro, small, and medium-sized enterprises (MSMEs).[212] The surveys were conducted between 25 June and 27 July 2020, focusing on the more at-risk population—vulnerable households, women, youth, and MSMEs. The surveys covered agriculture, light industry, personal services, and tourism—sectors most affected by the pandemic and major contributors or emerging drivers of economic growth. The findings included operations and commercial viability, disruptions in supply or value chains, cross-border trade, employment, informal businesses, and finance.

[209] World Bank. The World Bank in Tajikistan-Overview. https://www.worldbank.org/en/country/tajikistan/overview.

[210] ADB COVID-19 Policy Database. Tajikistan. https://covid19policy.adb.org/policy-measures/TAJ (Accessed 31 August 2022).

[211] UNDP. 2020. Impact of COVID-19 on Lives, Livelihoods and Micro, Small and MSMEs in Tajikistan. https://tajikistan.un.org/sites/default/files/2020-12/Impact-of-COVID-19-on-lives-livelihoods-and-MSMEs-Assessment-Report.pdf. UNDP definition of MSMEs includes micro, small, and medium-sized enterprises, individual entrepreneurs, and *dekhan* (individual or family farms).

[212] MSMEs in this chapter include individual entrepreneurs and *dekhkan*, which are not included in the legal definition of SMEs. Microenterprises are also not specifically defined in Tajikistan.

The sample contains significantly more MSMEs in the top 10 subsectors: (i) restaurants and cafeterias (170 MSMEs; or 24.3%); (ii) processing agricultural products (83; 11.9%); (iii) beauty industry (74; 10.6%); (iv) production of crops (61; 8.7%); (v) textiles and clothing (60; 8.6%); (vi) horticulture (46; 6.6%); (vii) accommodation and lodging (31; 4.4%); (viii) home products (24; 3.4%); (ix) home improvement (21; 3%); and (x) booking services and event management (tied at 19 MSMEs or 2.7% of the sample).

On average, MSMEs employ 13.2 workers (3.4 workers in microenterprises, 14.5 workers in small enterprises, and 55.1 workers in medium-sized enterprises). Based on government registries of legal commercial entities and individual entrepreneurs, the sample included 217 MSMEs in Khatlon oblast (31.0% of the sample), 212 in Soghd oblast (30.3 %), 148 in the capital Dushanbe (21.1%), 109 in the central government-controlled Districts of Republican Subordination around Dushanbe (15.6%), and 14 in the Gorno-Badakhshan Autonomous Region (2%).

The findings confirmed that (i) 63.1% of MSMEs were hurt by the pandemic, with variations by economic sector and size; (ii) those in rural areas were hurt more than urban MSMEs—in ease of access to business advisory services and markets; (iii) 83.1% in small-scale, cross-border trade saw a drop in sales due to border closures and travel restrictions; (iv) almost 25% closed temporarily; (v) a drop in wages were larger among employees in smaller firms and younger employees; (vi) the informal sector included a large share of women and girls; (vii) the proportion of non-registered (informal) employees varied by sector (with agriculture the largest); (viii) 85.2% saw a decrease in sales; (ix) outstanding loans pushed some further into debt; and (x) 33% said they would like the government to defer tax payments nationwide for all private businesses.

Impact of the Russian Invasion of Ukraine

Businesses worldwide, including Tajikistan, are feeling the consequences of the Russian invasion of Ukraine. The World Bank conducted a business survey on 21 July 2022 to assess the likely impact of the invasion on business activities.[213] Since February 2022, 53% of firms surveyed report they face increasing production costs with increases more widespread among firms that source inputs from the Russian Federation. Overall, 48% of those surveyed said rising costs decreased profitability, while 64% said they increased product prices.

Since the February 2022 invasion began, businesses reported increasing financial difficulties due to declining profitability and difficulty accessing new loans. About one-quarter of those surveyed (i) were under increased financial stress, (ii) needed to adjust their credit obligations, and (iii) needed to reduce their debt payments. The invasion affected businesses in other ways:

- reduced disposable income led to a decrease in demand for SME products;
- less income from remittances decreased demand for SME products/services;
- importing equipment, including electronics, from or through the Russian Federation became impossible due to sanctions and foreign company closures, which disrupted supply chains and logistics—prior to the invasion, logistics were managed by foreign companies in the Russian Federation;
- SMEs could not or were delayed in paying for goods and services and making other transfers, as most used correspondent accounts with now-sanctioned Russian banks; and
- inflation became another factor affecting SMEs as prices rose for vegetable oil, oil products, and flour—the cost of delivery trucks soared 300%.

[213] M. Iootty and M. Melecky. 2022. Taking the pulse of business in Central Asia following the Russian invasion of Ukraine. *World Bank Blogs*. 21 July. https://blogs.worldbank.org/europeandcentralasia/taking-pulse-business-central-asia-following-russian-invasion-ukraine.

In sum, businesses are being squeezed by rising production costs and worsening access to credit. Productivity and competitiveness will likely suffer, leading to closures, job losses, and slower economic growth. In response to these challenges, the government is considering assistance to

- help redirect trade affected by sanctions on the Russian Federation and identify alternative markets for imports and exports;
- tackle transport and logistics problems as well as resolve trade payment challenges;
- improve targeted financial and nonfinancial support to businesses to ensure only those in need receive support so fiscal resources are not drained unnecessarily; and
- ensure bankruptcy protection is time-bound and transparent.

2. SME Development

- Over 98% of enterprises in Tajikistan are SMEs, with most in services. They are spread nationwide. Business is strongly influenced by the Russian Federation's economy. The 2014–2016 Russian financial crisis helped lead to a reduction in SMEs.
- SMEs employed 252,719 workers or 20.4% of labor force in 2021. The share of SME employees has decreased slightly over time. As with the firms themselves, SME employees primarily work in services.
- SMEs contributed to 59.4% of GDP in 2021, up by 19.8% from 2020. While the 2014–2016 Russian financial crisis decelerated GDP growth, output generally remained robust during the COVID-19 pandemic in 2020.
- Most SMEs operate in small domestic markets, with a few involved in international markets. The small-scale export market limits the role SMEs can play in the global marketplace.
- E-commerce remains at an early stage of development, but shows high growth potential. Most SMEs have yet to digitize, but this will change as the digital economy further develops.
- The state Business Incubator and private sector associations such as the Chamber of Commerce and Industry support SMEs and entrepreneurial development through advisory and training services.

Scale of SMEs

SMEs play a crucial role in building a sustainable national economy, providing new jobs, and improving living standards. The formal SME definition has been revised several times. SMEs were defined in Law No.1107 on Government Protection and Support of Entrepreneurship that was enacted in July 2014 to promote and support entrepreneurship. The law was amended on 2 January 2020 with a revised SME definition (Table 7.1). In Tajikistan, there is no official category for microenterprises. Aggregate SME figures do not include *dekhkan* farms (individual and/or family-owned farms common across Central Asia).

According to the 2020 amendment, small enterprises are individual entrepreneurs or legal entities with annual gross income not exceeding TJS1 million and with no more than 30 employees (50 employees for agricultural producers). The law prohibits small enterprises from (i) manufacturing products subject to excise tax—for example, pharmaceuticals, spirits, and perfume; (ii) suppling primary aluminum—products from raw material or ingots; (iii) banking and insurance; (iv) managing investment funds; and (v) stock market activities. Medium-sized enterprises are defined as legal entities with an annual gross income between TJS1 million and TJS2.5 million with from 30 to 100 employees (50 to 200 employees for agricultural producers).

As of end-2021, there were 29,555 SMEs, or 98.6% of all enterprises (Figure 7.1 and Table 7.2). These figures fluctuated due to the changes in the formal SME definition and registration system, along with external shocks. From 2009 to 2010, the number decreased sharply due to a new one-stop service window that was unable to initially register all SMEs (and the change in legislation that excluded *dekhkan* farms). The number began to grow again from 2011 to 2015, expanding 1.4 times to reach 38,907. As the Russian Federation is the country's main trading partner, its financial crisis and initial sanctions imposed over the annexation of Crimea drove the number of SMEs down in 2017. But the number of SMEs has been growing steadily since 2018 (rising 6.9% in 2021).

SMEs operate unevenly across sectors. In 2021, the largest share was in services: wholesale and retail trade (13.3%), transportation and communications (4.3%), and other services (52.4%) (Figure 7.1B).[214] This was followed by agriculture (15.2%), manufacturing (7.9%), and construction (6.9%). The share of agricultural SMEs dropped sharply (from 24.7% in 2010), while manufacturing (6.1%) and transport (6.5%) grew after a one-stop shop was provided by the Tax Committee for registering enterprises and individual entrepreneurs.

The geographical spread of SMEs is uneven, but less so than in other countries. In 2021, 21.9% were in the capital city Dushanbe, with 78.1% located in other regions—with special industrial developments in the Sughd and Khatlon regions (Figure 7.1C). Tajikistan is largely agrarian with about 70% of its population in rural areas—the share of SMEs in Dushanbe has been growing slowly.

Figure 7.1: Number of SMEs

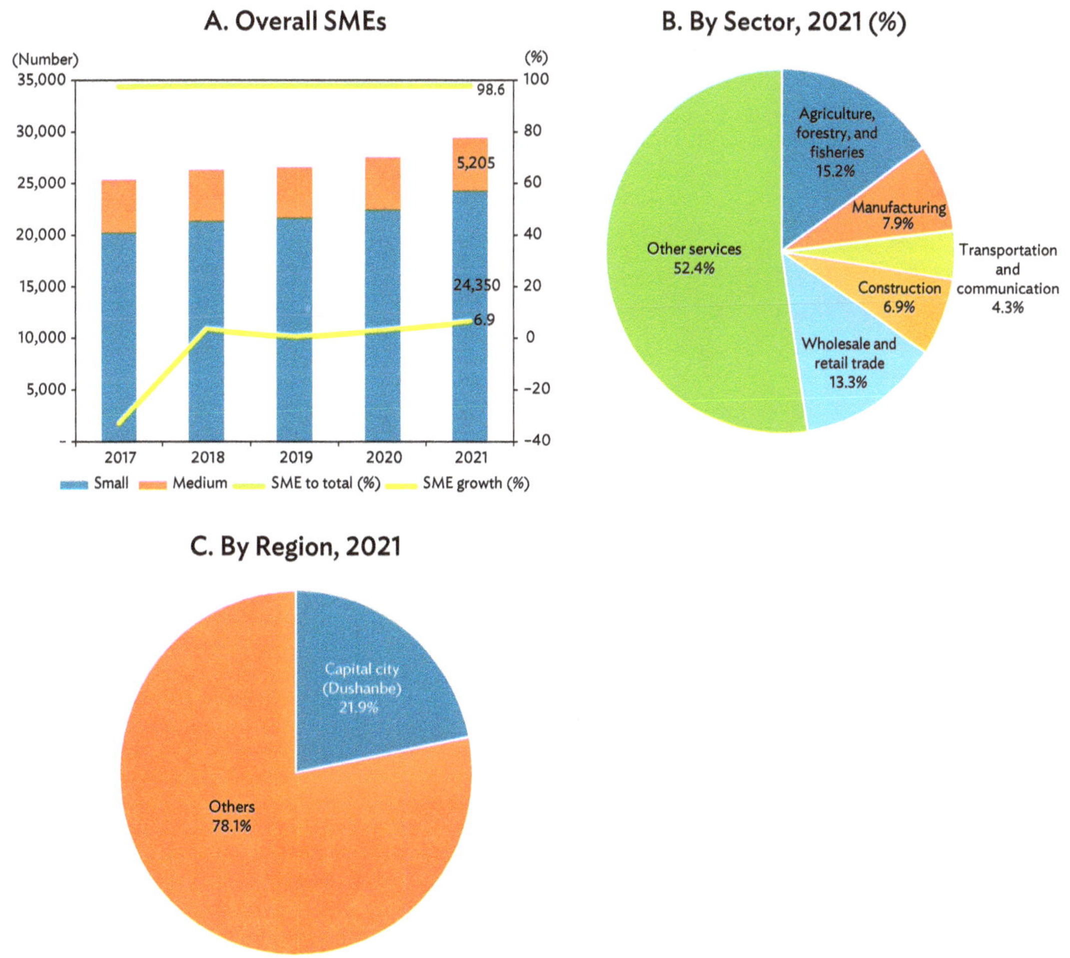

SME = small and medium-sized enterprise.

Source: ADB Asia SME Monitor 2022 database. Data from Agency on Statistics under President of the Republic of Tajikistan 2021.

214 "Other services" includes health and social services, education, public administration and defense, real estate, financial intermediation, recreation and entertainment, culture and sports, as well as other community, social, and personal services.

Data compiled by the Agency on Statistics shows that in 2021, Dushanbe had a higher concentration of small firms (82.5%) than medium-sized firms (14.9%) and large firms (2.6%). Dushanbe is both the most populated city in the country and main economic center—with a relatively well-developed SME ecosystem and available technology. It has a more economically active and educated population, with people migrating to the city searching for jobs and economic opportunities. Besides being the center of government, Dushanbe is also headquarters for almost all financial institutions and business houses. The share of small enterprises in the Sughd and Gorno-Badakhshan Autonomous Regions is 80.7%, more than the Khatlon region (1.2%) and the Republican Subordination (RRS) regions (1.5%).

Employment

SMEs employed around 252,719 workers, or 20.4% of labor force as of end-2021, with 158,900 (62.8%) in small enterprises and 93,900 (37.2%) in medium-sized enterprises (Figure 7.2A and Table 7.2). Annual growth has been less than 1% since 2019. During the pandemic in 2020, there was almost no change (a 0.2% increase from 2019 to 2020). Annual growth in 2021 was 0.6%. The share of SME employees has remained almost unchanged (around 20%) but slightly down from 21.3% in 2018.

By sector, SMEs in "other services" hired the largest number of SME employees (66.1% of the total SME labor force in 2021), followed by agriculture (13.6%), manufacturing (7.2%), wholesale and retail trade (6.0%), construction (4.9%), and transportation and communications (2.2%) (Figure 7.2B). There has been a correlation the growth in SME workers and number of SMEs during 2018–2021.

Figure 7.2: Employment by SMEs

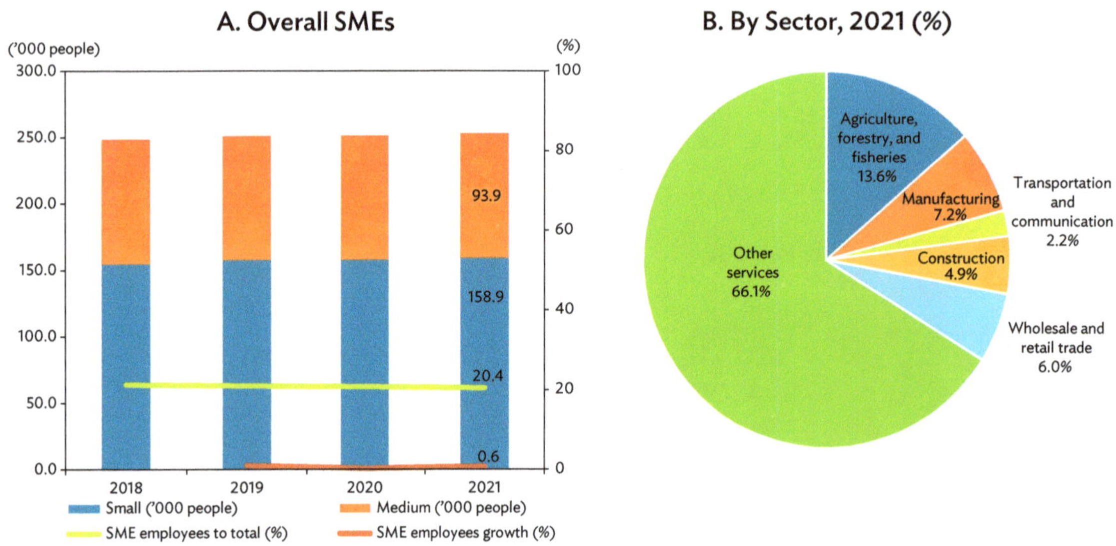

SME = small and medium-sized enterprise.

Source: ADB Asia SME Monitor 2022 database. Data from Agency on Statistics under President of the Republic of Tajikistan 2021.

Business Productivity

The Agency on Statistics report for 2021 gave figures for GDP derived from private sector businesses—statistically regarded as the GDP contributed by SMEs. Using this, SMEs contributed 59.4% of GDP in 2021, a 19.8% increase from 2020 (Figure 7.3 and Table 7.2). SME output remained robust even during pandemic-affected 2020 (58.4% share and 4.2% increase from 2019).

Figure 7.3: SME Contribution to GDP

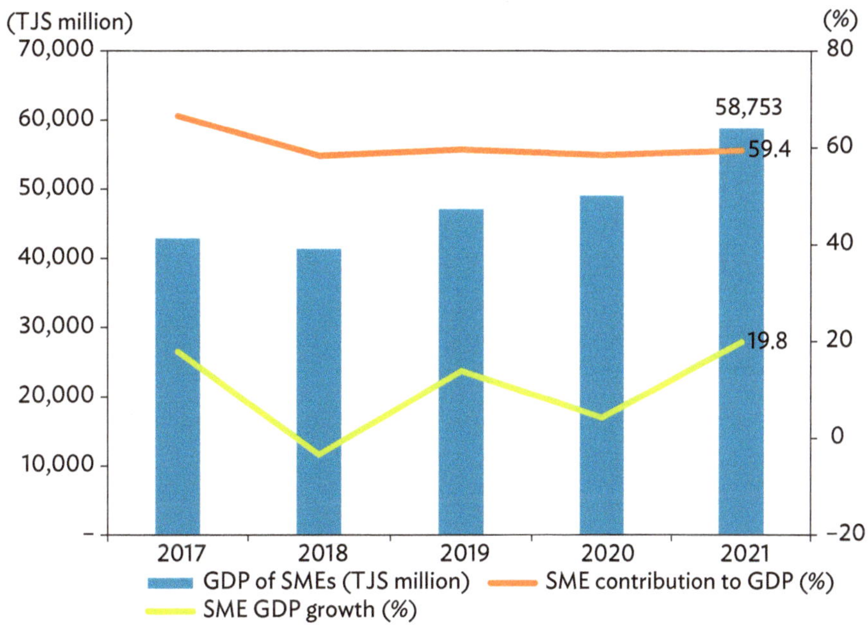

GDP = gross domestic product, SME = small and medium-sized enterprise.
Source: ADB Asia SME Monitor 2022 database. Data from Agency on Statistics under President of the Republic of Tajikistan.

Over the long term, the GDP contribution from SMEs grew steadily from TJS8.3 trillion in 2008 2008 to TJS58.8 trillion in 2021—a robust compound annual growth rate (CAGR) of 16.3. The SME share of GDP growth increased steadily from 18.2% in 2009 to 28.7% in 2014. It has been somewhat volatile since due to the impact of the Russian 2014–2016 financial crisis and other external events.

Market Access

Market access is a major problem for SMEs, both for domestic and international markets. According to a 2021 Agency on Statistics report, Tajikistan had a high export-to-import ratio of 1:2. Exports amounted to TJS24.3 trillion in 2021 (up by 52.8% from 2020, which increased by 39.7% over 2019), while imports reached TJS47.6 trillion (up 33.6% compared with a 9.7% increase in 2020) (Figure 7.4 and Table 7.2). However, exports remain small and exposed to external shocks. For example, the 2008–2009 global financial crisis cut economic growth given the sharp decline in world prices for cotton and aluminum, causing a deterioration in trade. For similar reasons, exports also fell in 2013 and 2018. Low export values suggest SMEs play a limited role in the global marketplace. The domestic economy is largely driven by private consumption and investment.

Figure 7.4: Exports and Imports

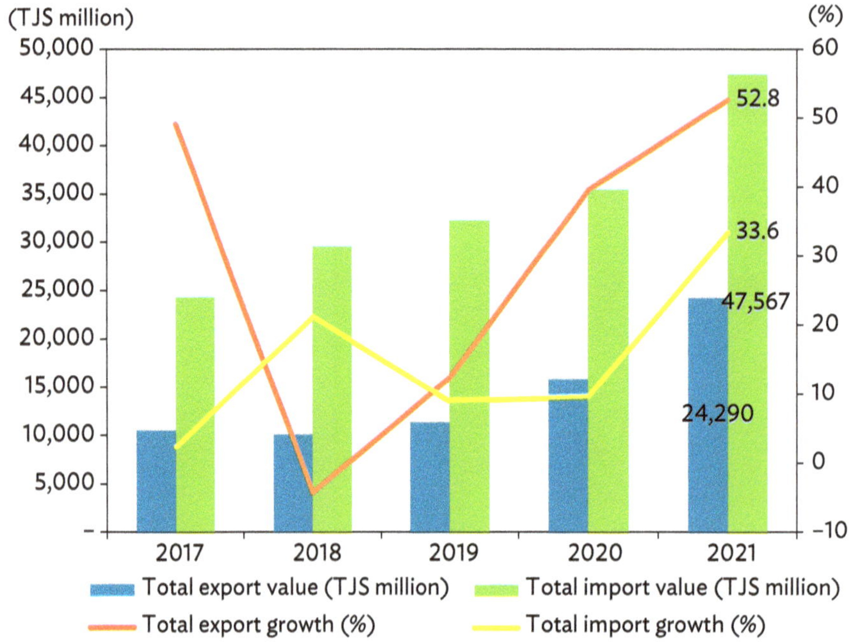

Source: ADB Asia SME Monitor 2022 database. Data from Agency on Statistics under President of the Republic of Tajikistan.

Technology and Innovation

Like much of Asia, the use of digital devices has grown rapidly. Mobile cellular subscriptions jumped from 6.5 million in 2020 (82.9 per 100 people) to 11.5 million in 2021 (121.5 per 100 people) (World Development Indicators 2021). Nonetheless, individual internet use remains limited, reaching just 26% of the population in 2020. But it continues to grow rapidly. According to the State Communications Service, in 2021 one-third of the population (or around 3.3 million people) used mobile phones or the internet. Available since 1992, it has taken well over a decade for internet infrastructure to take shape. By 2009, internet service providers had replaced satellite-based connections to allow for more widespread internet access.

One of the key challenges for developing e-commerce is insufficient and costly digital connectivity—a prerequisite for any online transaction—not just for consumers and producers, but for farmers in remote rural regions as well. Digital connectivity must be universal, affordable, and reliable. According to the GSM Association, Tajikistan had 44 unique mobile broadband subscriptions per 100 inhabitants in 2021.

According to the International Telecommunications Union, in 2021 the cost of a mobile broadband subscription (with at least 1.5 gigabytes of data) was the most expensive in the region (on average 7.5% of monthly gross national income per capita and as much as 15.3% for poor households). Broadband download speed is low, at a median 7.8 megabits per second, leaving Tajikistan 137th out of 140 countries in the Ookla Global Speedtest in August 2022.[215]

[215] Speedtest. Speedtest Global Index - Tajikistan Median Country Speeds. https://www.speedtest.net/global-index/tajikistan.

Sanctions on the Russian Federation for its invasion of Ukraine have worsened the situation. Most of Tajikistan bandwidth is sourced from the Russian Federation with primary upstream providers including the state Kazakhstan operator Transtelecom, the state Russian operator Rostelecom, and private Russian operator MegaFon. Also, US-based Cogent Communications—one of the world's largest intercontinental internet backbone providers—has cut ties with Russian customers, including Rostelecom and MegaFon. This has led to network congestion in the Russian Federation, leading to disruptions for clients elsewhere.

This partially explains Tajikistan's small e-commerce footprint. According to KPMG International Limited, $54.7 million was transacted via e-commerce in 2020. Over the past decade, a group of local startups, including Alif Sarmoya, developed an electronic mobile payment market, Somon.tj. E-commerce venture capitals and accelerators, such as 55Startups, invested in early-stage e-commerce businesses. Yet, it remains a niche market. According to the 2017 Findex, only 7.6% of the population shopped online.

The government should discuss with international financial institutions a broad digitalization program, including diversifying international connectivity transit routes to Tajikistan to boost digital resiliency and capacity, as well enhancing cybersecurity and data protection.

Fintech companies such as Alif Sarmoya are working to make online payment systems more easily accessible. Mobile payment subscribers reached 2.2 million in 2021 from a zero base in 2017. In terms of internet users, 30% shop online compared with three-quarters in the PRC, where online shopping is even more popular than in the European Union (EU).[216] The share of firms owning a website in 2019 was 28%—small enterprises (22%), medium-sized enterprises (36%), and large enterprises (59%) (ADB 2022).

Continually upgrading information and communication technology (ICT) infrastructure is critical. Tojiktelecom, Tajikistan's main fixed-line operator, has upgraded most of the backbone of its analog telephony infrastructure to fiber optics and converted more than 90% of the system to digital. Nine mobile telephony operators provide services in Code-Division Multiple Access (CDMA) or Global System for Mobile (GSM) communications to 3G or 3.5G standards. Tajikistan was the first country in Central Asia to introduce 3G services.

Despite recent progress, however, Tajikistan lags behind comparator countries in fixed lines, mobile phone subscriptions, and in internet penetration It ranked 111th among 130 countries in the World Economic Forum's Networked Readiness Index 2021 (World Economic Forum 2021).[217] Mobile phones and the internet were slow to take off, but growth accelerated as the number of migrant workers and demand for long-distance calls increased rapidly. Despite mobile subscriptions increasing from 70,000 in 2004 to more than 10.4 million by January 2020, mobile tele-density remains below the Commonwealth of Independent States and world average. The number of mobile connections in January 2020 was equivalent to 107% of its population.[218]

The high cost of mobile phones compared with average income is one of the main reasons why tele-density is lower than in other countries. There were 3.4 million internet users in January 2021, an increase of 948,000 (39%) from 2020, while internet penetration was 34.9%.

Most SMEs have yet to digitalize, but this should change rapidly as the digital economy develops.

---

216 ADB. 2022. *E-Commerce in CAREC Countries: Infrastructure Development*. Manila. https://www.adb.org/sites/default/files/publication/781526/e-commerce-carec-countries-infrastructure-development.pdf.

217 Network Readiness Index. Tajikistan. https://networkreadinessindex.org/country/tajikistan/

218 S. Kemp. 2020. Digital 2020: Tajikistan. Datareportal. https://datareportal.com/reports/digital-2021-tajikistan.

Networking and Support

There are several initiatives to develop businesses—especially SMEs and entrepreneurships—led by the government and private sector groups such as the Chamber of Commerce and Industry of the Republic of Tajikistan. The government (State Committee on Investments and State Property Management) established a state enterprise Business Incubator of Tajikistan in 2018, to promote local entrepreneurships and to develop small businesses and young startups (Box 7.1). The business incubator offers regular consultations, incubation programs, training, and other educational activities for individual entrepreneurs and SMEs. The Chamber of Commerce and Industry offers tailor-made support to individual SMEs through its "hot line," which helped SMEs survive the COVID-19 pandemic through customized advice to the SME and individual entrepreneur (Box 7.2).

Box 7.1: Business Incubator of Tajikistan Supports SME Development and Entrepreneurial Business Culture

Small and medium-sized enterprises (SMEs) are major drivers of economic development worldwide. But they face many barriers in developing their businesses. Targeted government support for businesses is critical to building an efficient market economy.

A business incubator creates the most favorable conditions for small startups by providing a set of services and resources—including preferential terms, communication facilities, offices and equipment, personnel training, and consulting, among others.

The complex of services—secretarial, accounting, legal, educational, and consulting—is extremely important as startups need comprehensive support as they build their small enterprise.

In his annual message to Tajikistan's Majlisi Oli on 26 December 2018, the President stressed the need for specific measures to organize service centers for entrepreneurs in cities and districts—centers that could act as business incubators to improve the legal, financial and economic knowledge of entrepreneurs, assist in developing business projects and finding ways to get them up and running.

A state enterprise, Business Incubator of Tajikistan, was established to help a wide range of SMEs and young people in entrepreneurial activities across the country, including the cities of Dushanbe, Bokhtar, Kulyab, Khujand, and Khorog, where it organizes various events, holds regular consultations, incubation programs, training, and other educational activities are held. The incubator's central office opened in September 2020

The Business Incubator helps many aspiring and established entrepreneurs with programs run jointly with international organizations. The story of 32-year-old Zoirjon, one of the Business Incubation Project's grantees, is a good example.

Zoirjon lives in the village of Shaydon, Asht District. In 2015–2020, he was a migrant worker in Yekaterinburg, where he worked as an assistant in a barber shop. There he learned all the subtleties of barbering. Due to pandemic restrictions, he lost his job and had to return home in late 2020. When he applied to the Business Incubator, he joined the Business Incubation Project training program—supported by the Japan International Cooperation Agency. After successfully completing the course, he received financial support to open his own hairdressing salon and purchase necessary equipment which contributed to the success of his salon.

continued on next page

Box 7.1 *continued*

There are many other personal success stories, for example, in Istaravshan, Sughd Region (with United Nations Development Programme representatives) helping Business Incubator monitor projects:

- Sanginov Nasimdzhon organized a small sewing workshop and, with his family and relatives, began sewing children's pajamas with significant results. They sew up to 30 sets of children's clothes every day and sell them on the local market.
- Salimova Dilrabo and her family started baking a variety of scones, sweets and cookies, distributing them to nearby stores.
- Makhmudov Raboniddin opened a "Rus-China" translation bureau that mainly translates from Russian into Chinese and from Chinese into Russian and Tajik. The project gave Raboniddin a special program and working computer.
- Rustamova Shakhzoda received a project-supported new "Hot Scissors" device, never seen in Khujand before, for women's makeup rooms, adding a modern flair to serving clients.

The Business Incubator has held more than 400 events, with more than 10,000 participants attending at no cost.

The Business Incubator also helps publicize the benefits of entrepreneurship across the country. As a state institution, it can both teach business techniques and promote entrepreneurship with the support of state and international programs.

Source: Interview with the International Department of the state enterprise Business Incubator of Tajikistan and presentation during ADB virtual mission held on 13 April 2022.

Box 7.2: Chamber of Commerce and Industry Offers Tailor-Made SME Support in Tajikistan

To assist entrepreneurs and members of the Chamber of Commerce and Industry of the Republic of Tajikistan during the coronavirus disease (COVID-19) pandemic, the chamber worked with the United States Agency for International Development's "Competitiveness Trade and Job Activity in Central Asia" project to launch a "Hot Line" on its website and Facebook page starting in March 2020. The Hot Line offered business advice, both orally and in written form, to help businesses resolve problems. Chamber experts and experts from agencies such as the Customs Service, Tax Committee, and others could both clarify issues and monitor the evolving business climate during the pandemic. The "Hot Line" was active from 8 a.m. to 10 p.m., 7 days a week, and could link up with regional branches of the chamber.

The Hot Line received over 300 telephone inquiries and more than 200 requests via e-mail (members.tpptj@gmail.com), with results monitored monthly and published on the Facebook platform.

Questions and requests for assistance spanned many topics, most related to the global pandemic, logistics, taxes, customs, finding business partners abroad, participating in international online exhibitions, attracting business investment, as well as on how to comply with technical regulations, standards, and sanitary and phytosanitary measures in foreign markets.

continued on next page

Box 7.2 *continued*

Written applications were processed based on consultations of chamber specialists. In matters outside the chamber's purview, Hot Line operators redirected them to the relevant ministries and agencies. To provide answers as quickly as possible, the operators directly contacted specialists from the Customs Service and specialists from regional chambers to best serve entrepreneurs during the crisis.

Frequently asked questions were on

- restrictions on bringing technological devices and equipment into Tajikistan via the People's Republic of China (PRC) or other countries;
- finding partners both domestically and abroad;
- currency transactions;
- issues related to searching for international online exhibitions;
- distribution of commercial proposals;
- checkpoint regimes and new rules affecting transportation to particular countries; and
- requests to find grants to open workshops to produce medicines and protective equipment.

There were many beneficiaries from using the Hot Line:

- Zardolu & Co., a Chamber member, was assisted in getting its dried fruit exports across the border;
- the Kazakhstan embassy was consulted and provided contacts for registering information technology companies in Tajikistan;
- OOO "Shafqat" was assisted in acquiring free personal protection equipment (PPE), organized jointly with the partner OBO "Peshraft";
- Umed Karimov, a private entrepreneur, consulted the chamber and other experts on which businesses might be less risky during the pandemic—the chamber supported his new business plan and helped look for sponsors;
- the chamber provided advice on paperwork required for exporting dried fruit to Kazakhstan and the Russian Federation;
- an employee of "Kongress Servis" rendered assistance in searching companies-manufacturers of PPE and textiles;
- the director of development of t/c Dobrotsen in the Russian Federation provided advice on transit and transportation of goods from Tajikistan to the Russian Federation—then advice was provided by a representative of the Association of Customs Brokers of Tajikistan and chamber staff;
- Kombinati Ordi Dushanbe" Ltd offered advice on filling in documents for product exports;
- Tadjero RT Company provided legal advice on contract disputes through a chamber lawyer;
- JSC "Oriyonfarm" RT-Contract with the PRC company Qingdao Hiseeking Enterprises Co.Ltd, on the purchase and delivery of medical goods: medicines and medical products—assistance was given through a chamber request to the Office of the Advisor on Trade and Economic Affairs to resolve the allocation of wagons by the PRC's transport company; and
- OOO "Usmon-D" RT Issues received advice on product exports and new markets.

Source: Interview with the vice-president of the Chamber of Commerce and Industry of the Republic of Tajikistan and presentation during the ADB virtual mission on 12 April 2022.

3. Access to Finance

- SME loans are a small fraction of the bank credit market. Bank credit to SMEs accounted for 16.0% of bank loans outstanding, or 2.5% of GDP in 2021.
- The SME bank credit market is fragile, easily affected by external shocks. More than one-third of SME loans are approved for those conducting international trade.
- SME nonperforming loans (NPLs) have fallen sharply (4.6% in 2021), far below the NPL ratio for overall bank credit (16.2%).
- The government offers several incentives for banks to lend to SMEs—interest rate subsidies and credit guarantees contributed to the sharp increase of bank loans to SMEs in 2021.
- Microfinance institutions (MFIs) offer savings, credit, and remittance services for individuals and SMEs, most targeting remote areas.
- Electronic money transfers have expanded. Since 2018, financial institutions accept noncash payments; but digital financial services remain underdeveloped, and have yet to become a funding option for SMEs.
- There are two registered stock exchanges: the Central Asian Stock Exchange (CASE) and Asian Stock Exchange (ASE), the latter not yet open. CASE has a specialized SME board, where three firms issued bonds in 2021.
- There are also two credit bureaus: (i) Credit Information Bureau (CIB) of Tajikistan and (ii) Bureau of Credit Histories Somoniyon. The CIB has a database of 3-4 million borrowers, including SME loans with banks and nonbank finance institutions (NBFIs). There are plans to open a credit registry.

The financial system is split into five sectors—banking, microfinance, nonbank credit institutions, insurance, and the capital market. Banks dominate, accounting for 84.4% of financial sector assets in 2021, followed by microfinance institutions (MFIs) (14.4%) and insurance firms (1.2%). The capital market is relatively quiet, with market capitalization at 11.6% of GDP in 2021.

As of end-2021, there were 63 financial lending institutions—14 banks (1 Islamic bank) and 49 MFIs (18 microcredit deposit organizations, 4 microcredit organizations, and 27 microcredit funds).[219] During 2020 and 2021, a license was newly issued to LLC MDO Payvand Guruh, while licenses were revoked from five banks (CJSC Bank Asia, OJSC Agroinvestbank, OJSC Tojiksodirotbonk, CJSC NBP Pakistan Subsidiary Bank in Tajikistan, and CJSC Kafolatbank) and three MFIs (MCF Fayzi Surhob, LLC MCO Madina va Hamcoron, and CJS MDO SMT-Sarmoya). During the period, 83 offices closed, leaving 1,852 operating.

As of end-2021, total assets of these lending institutions were TJS22.4 trillion, down by 14.8% from 2020 mainly due to repossessed collateral and securities. Loans outstanding reached TJS12.0 billion, up by 10% due to an increase in loans to individuals.

NPLs (overdue for more than 30 days) at end-2021 was TJS1 billion (13.4% of credit outstanding), down 10 percentage points from end-2020. Provisions for NPLs was TJS1.5 billion, or 92.5% of NPLs, 2.3 percentage points higher than in 2020. As of end-2021, the net amount of NPLs of the (less loan-loss provisions) made up TJS120.5 million, or 1.1% of the credit portfolio (net).

219 Review of Banking System of the Republic of Tajikistan on 31 December 2021. https://www.nbt.tj/upload/iblock/7af/%D0%9D%D0%B8%D0%B7%D0%BE%D0%BC%D0%B8%20%D0%B1%D0%BE%D0%BD%D0%BA%D0%B8_2021.12%20-%20ENG.pdf

Bank Credit

As of end-2021, there were 14 banks—two state-owned, seven private, and five foreign—accounting for more than 80% of financial assets (Table 7.3). The remaining 20% were NBFIs, including MFIs. The National Bank of Tajikistan (NBT), the country's central bank, regulates and supervises licensed commercial banks and NBFIs. The NBT classifies loans by economic sector and type of ownership, including SMEs. Banks typically distinguish between state-owned enterprises, SMEs, and individual entrepreneurs. By sector, loans are classified as commercial, agricultural, leasing, and "others".

Bank loans outstanding have steadily increased—even during the pandemic due to government financial assistance (subsidized loans and credit guarantees). Loans outstanding reached TJS9,437 million in 2021, up by 7.1% from TJS8.8 billion in 2020, which rose 16.2% over pre-pandemic 2019. However, bank credit remains small—10.3% of GDP, and NPLs are high (16.2%), even if it had dropped steadily since 2017 (42.5%). Lending rates of commercial banks remain high as well (annual average 20.6%).

SME loans are a small fraction of the credit market, with bank credit to SMEs accounting for 16.0% of total bank loans outstanding (2.5% of GDP) as of end-2021 (Figure 7.5A and Table 7.3). SME loans outstanding mimicked the rise and fall of crises and shocks. In 2014 and 2016, for instance, SME credit dropped sharply (by 34.1% and 53.6%, respectively), set off by the *ruble* devaluation starting from the second quarter of 2014. As the Russian Federation is Tajikistan's primary trading partner, its economic performance directly impacts the Tajik economy and businesses, especially SMEs. In 2016, the drop in SME credit was also affected by the insolvency of two systemically important banks (Agroinvestbank and Tajiksodirotbank).

Figure 7.5: SME Loans

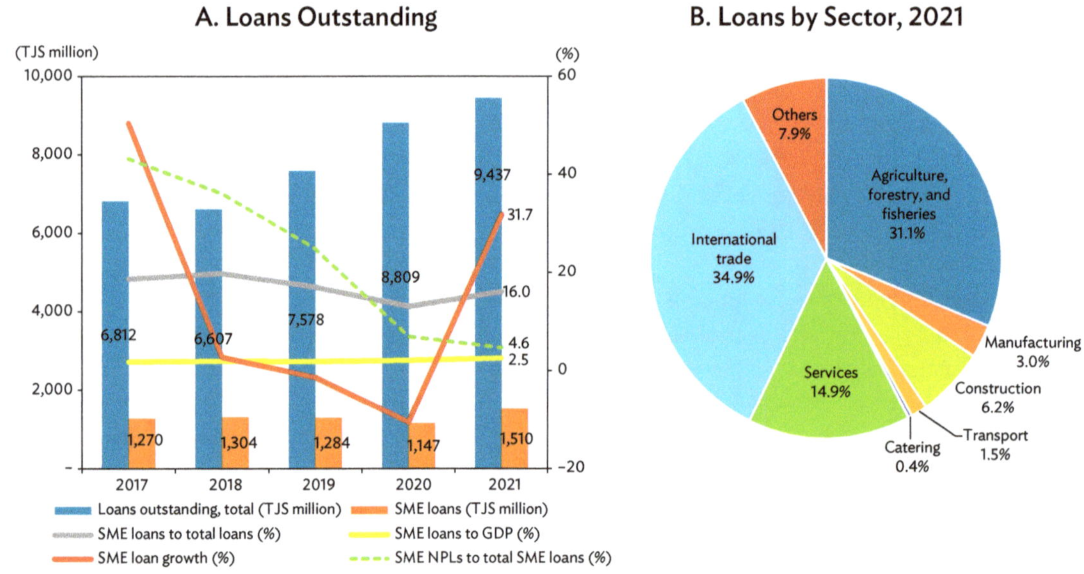

GDP = gross domestic product, NPL = nonperforming loan, SME = small and medium-sized enterprise.

Source: ADB Asia SME Monitor 2022 database. Data from National Bank of Tajikistan 2021.

The pandemic and mobility restrictions also hit SMEs hard, limiting their funding options. Supply chain disruptions, travel bans (particularly tourists), temporary business closures, and decreased investment and remittances from migrant workers all led to lower incomes. SME loans outstanding decreased from TAJ1.3 billion in 2019 (pre-pandemic) to TAJ1.1 billion in 2020, a 10.7% contraction. It recovered rapidly to TJS1.5 billion in 2021 (up by 31.7%) due to government and central bank assistance. NPLs fell sharply, with the SME NPL ratio falling from 43.2% in 2017 to 4.6% in 2021, far below the ratio for overall bank credit (16.2%).

SME loans go primarily to those involved with international trade (34.9% of total SME loans in 2021) and agriculture-based SMEs (31.1%), followed by services (14.9%), construction (6.2%), and manufacturing (3.0%) (Figure 7.5B). While SME data are unavailable, overall, 37.4% of bank lending was in the capital city Dushanbe, with the remaining 62.6% in other local regions.

The government aims to continue transforming the economy from one based on agriculture to industry. New capacities are being developed for the production of electricity, mining, modernizing food processing, domestic metallurgy (both ferrous and nonferrous), and construction materials. Nonetheless, poverty remains persistent, with many adding to their family's income as migrant workers, especially in the Russian Federation and Kazakhstan.

Public Financing and Guarantees

The government offers several incentives to encourage lending to priority sectors or groups. It has two credit programs with subsidized interest and one loan guarantee scheme (Table 7.4). They vary considerably by loan size, interest concession, collateral requirements, tenure, loan guarantees, documentation requirements, and target groups.

Subsidized loans outstanding to SMEs has increased sharply; from TJS17.3 million in 2013 to TJS217.2 million in 2021, up by a factor of 12.5 (Figure 7.6A and Table 7.4). Growth decelerated in pandemic-affected 2020, contracting by 6.2% before rebounding by 47.4% in 2021. The number of SMEs with subsidized loans increased from 12 in 2013 to 263 in 2021.

Figure 7.6: Public Financing

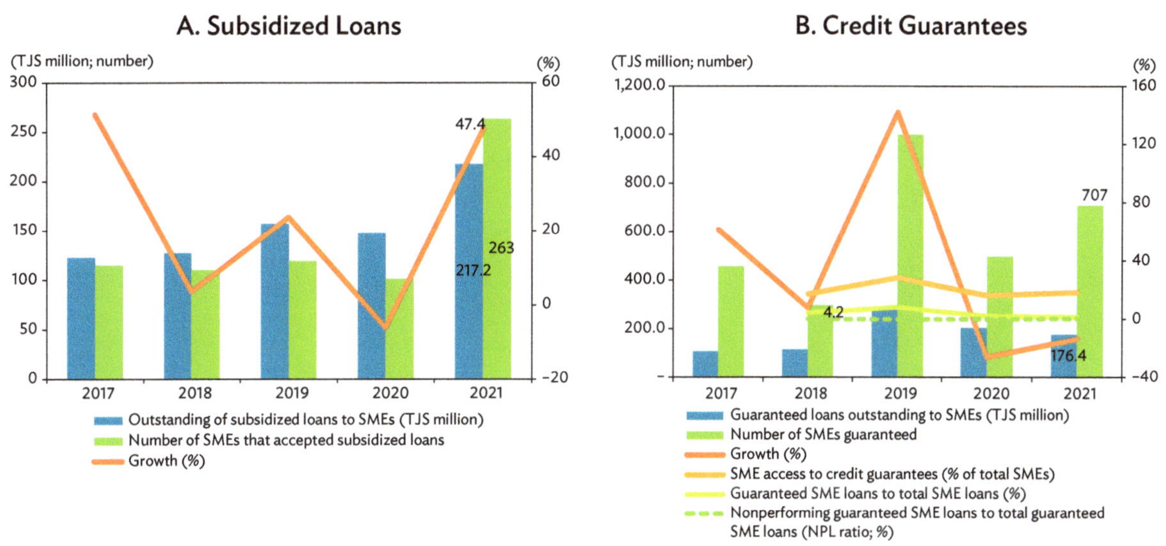

NPL = nonperforming loan, SME = small and medium-sized enterprise.

Source: ADB Asia SME Monitor 2022 database. Data from SUE Sanoatsodirotbank, Microcredit Fund "Refinancing Fund" and Credit Guarantee Fund Tajikistan.

The Credit Guarantee Fund Tajikistan (CGFT), with seven partner financial institutions, began operations in 2015. The fund guaranteed loans outstanding to SMEs was TJS176.4 million in 2021—TJS171.6 million or 97.3% was disbursed (Figure 7.6B). Although credit guarantees were used as financial assistance to businesses in response to the pandemic impact, guaranteed loans to SMEs fell in 2020 (TJS204.3 million in 2020 from TJS277.1 million in 2019, a 26.3% decrease) and in 2021 (a 13.6% decrease from 2020). Guaranteed loans were provided to 707 firms as of end-2021. SME access to credit guarantees remains limited (only 1.5% of total SME loans).

Nonbank Financing

NBFIs in Tajikistan include nonbank credit institutions and noncredit financial institutions.[220,221] Nonbank credit institutions include MFIs and insurance companies. Credit cooperatives operated until 2013, when they were closed by the central bank. Leasing companies, pawnshops, factoring, and financial companies are not regulated by the central bank but are important institutions for financing SMEs.

In 2004, the Parliament enacted Tajikistan's first microfinance law (Law of the Republic of Tajikistan dated 17 May 2004 "On microfinance organizations"). It was replaced in 2012 by the Law "On microfinance organizations" of No.816 dated 16 April 2012. The law created three types of MFIs: (i) microcredit deposit organizations (MDOs) for loans up to TJS250,000 for individuals and not exceeding TJS500,000 for SMEs and other legal entities—the amount issued to other credit organizations should not exceed TJS1.5 million; (ii) microcredit organizations (MCOs) for loans not exceeding TJS250,000 for individuals and TJS400,000 for SMEs; and (iii) microcredit funds (MCFs) for loans up to TJS250,000 for individuals and TJS350,000 for SMEs.[222]

MFIs give the vulnerable and SMEs access to savings, credit, remittances, and facilitate self-employment and other income-generating activities. MFIs collect small deposits, provide micro-loans, and practice group-based lending and group savings. In addition, they target remote areas where other financial institutions have little or no penetration. The finance is diversified, and provides quick repayment, close monitoring, and simple credit terms/conditions (with no collateral in many cases).

As of end-2021, under the 2012 law on microfinance organizations, the central bank regulated 49 MFIs—including 18 MDOs, 4 MCOs, and 27 MCFs.[223] Their major funding came from equity, term deposits (at least 12 months), other financial institution credit facilities, and call money.

From 2005–2012, the industry expanded rapidly, from 21 MFIs in 2005 to 125 in 2021. Over the same period, MFIs' aggregate loan portfolio increased almost 44 times—from TJS21 million to TJS 934 million, with the number of borrowers growing to 232,656 (Table 7.5). This was made possible by the relatively easy availability of credit for the largest MFIs, all of which were well managed and were financially self-sustainable with high rates of return. Credit was provided by foreign lenders and investors (ADB provided loans to Oxus and 13 smaller MFIs, not all of which had achieved were financially sustainable).[224] With few exceptions, almost all foreign loans were denominated in US dollars and euros. Demand for credit increased as the economy grew during this period, partly the result of

220 Nonbank credit institutions include MFIs and are licensed by the central bank.

221 Noncredit financial institutions, licensed by the central bank, are not formal credit institutions but comply with Islamic principles (Law No.1548 of 2018).

222 MDOs can sell shares or take deposits, MCOs can sell shares but cannot take deposits, while MCF can neither sell shares nor take deposits.

223 WWW,NBT.TJ, Banking statistics bulletin, #320, 2022.

224 ADB. 2013. *Report and Recommendation of the President to the Board of Directors: Proposed Grant and Administration of Technical Assistance Grant Republic of Tajikistan: Access to Green Finance Project.* Microfinance Sector Analysis (accessible from the list of linked documents in Appendix 2). Manila. https://www.adb.org/sites/default/files/linked-documents/45229-001-taj-oth-01.pdf.

higher world prices for commodity exports and partly due to increasing remittances from the Russian Federation and Kazakhstan.

Strict central bank regulation since 2015, however, led to a decrease in the number of MFIs from 106 in 2015 to 49 in 2021 (Figure 7.7A and Table 7.5). It initially led to a decrease in MFI lending but since 2018 has been growing steadily. SMEs and small farms, especially those in rural areas, likely shied away from credit due to the poor financial situation and high cost of lending.

As with much of the economy, MFIs are affected by external shocks. For example, loans outstanding fell to TJS1.7 million in 2016, down by 14.6% from 2015 (TJS2.0 million), due to the 2014–2016 Russian financial crisis and its impact on remittances. The MFI market was also hit by the COVID-19 pandemic, with loans outstanding dropping to TJS2.1 million in 2020, a 3.2% contraction from 2019. It recovered to TJS2.5 million in 2021, a 21.3% increase, with 329,220 customers receiving MFI financing (Figure 7.7B and Table 7.5). The MFI market remains small, equivalent to 2.1% of GDP (down from its 4.2% peak in 2014).

The NPL ratio surged to 12.3% in 2016, again likely due to the 2014–2016 Russian financial crisis. Since 2017, however, the NPL ratio has been improving steadily, reaching 3.3% in 2019. It jumped to 5.0% in 2020 due to the pandemic before falling back to 3.2% in 2021.

MFI performance indicators (return on assets and return on equity) and the quality of the loan portfolio is much better than for banks. Total MFIs savings, a source of lending, was TJS1.2 billion in 2021, a 58.4% CAGR between 2006 and 2021, which shows their relatively sound funding condition.

MFI loans were used mostly for individual consumption (31.3% of MFI lending in 2021), followed by agriculture (31.1%), services (16.0%), manufacturing (11.8%), international trade (3.4%) and construction (3.0%) (Figure 7.7C). Unclassified loans accounted for 2.3%. By region, 15.1% went to borrowers in the capital Dushanbe with the remaining 84.9% used in other regions (Figure 7.7D).

There were 28 banks in 1999, when the central bank raised capital requirements. Those that could not meet the requirement were transformed into credit cooperatives. After the law on microfinance organizations was adopted in 2004, the three types of MFIs (MDOs, MCOs, and MCFs) were created. As financing demand shifted from credit cooperatives to MFIs, credit cooperatives were gradually eliminated by 2013.

By January 2004, one of the constituent parts of OJSC Agroinvestbank was separated to create a separate independent NBFI CJSC Credit-Invest, which is a specialized institution providing pre-export loans to cotton-growing farms through foreign investment.

The number of nonbank credit institutions fell sharply from 12 (11 were credit cooperatives and one Credit Invest) in 2004 to 1 in 2013, with that closed in 2014 in connection with their transformation into MFIs. Due to the closure of the Credit Invest in 2009, financing outstanding of NBFIs decreased sharply from TJS1.8 billion in 2009 to TJS15.4 million in 2010.

Figure 7.7: Microfinance Institution Loans

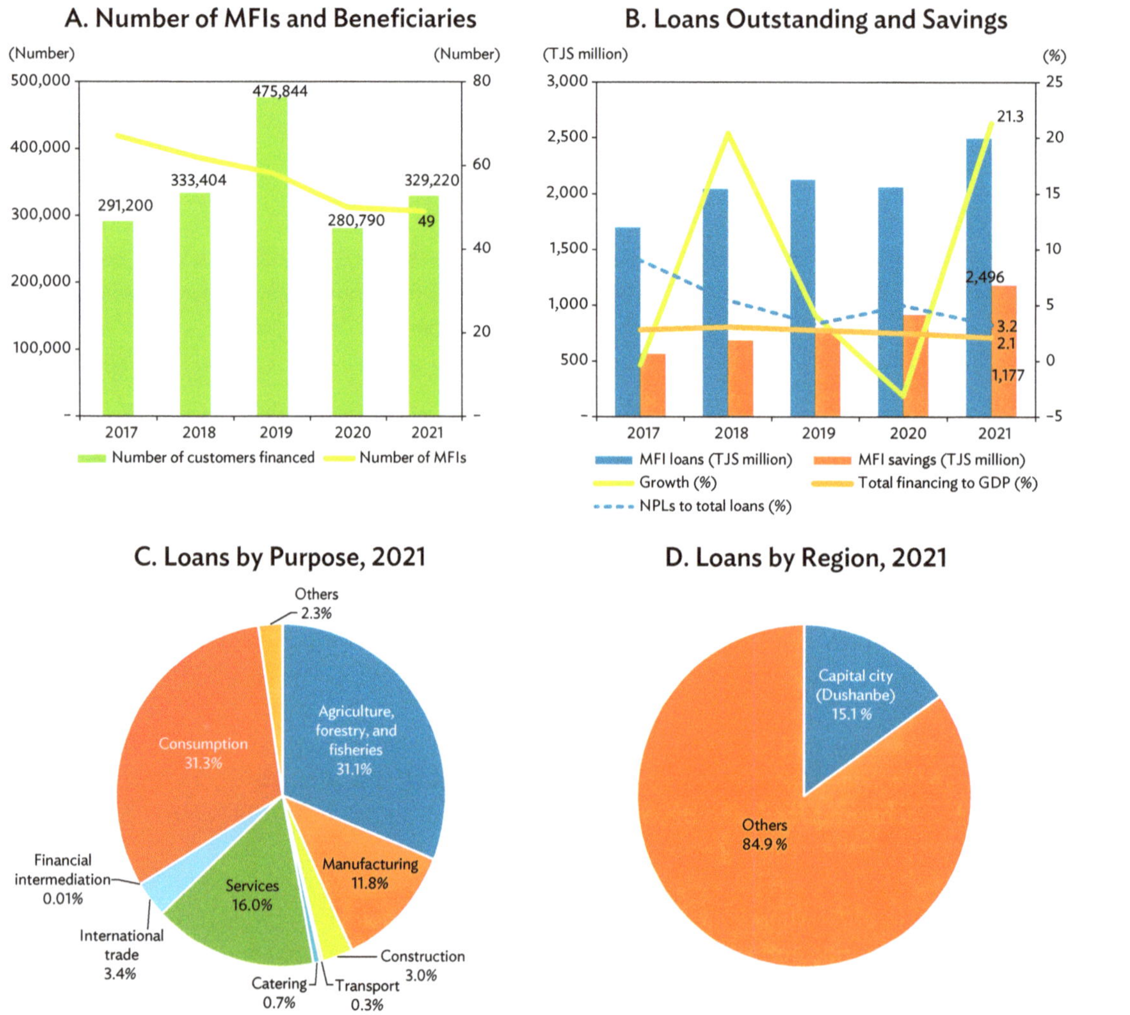

MFI = microfinance institution, NPL = nonperforming loan.

Note: Nonbank credit institutions are credit institutions entitled to implement certain banking operations. The list of banking operations for nonbank credit institutions was determined by the National Bank of Tajikistan.

Source: ADB Asia SME Monitor 2022 database. Data from National Bank of Tajikistan and Association of Microfinance Organizations of Tajikistan.

According to the Association of Banks of Tajikistan, as of end-2021, there were seven leasing companies registered but only four active. Some MFIs are developing leasing products, which would supply more medium-term finance for SMEs, especially those in agriculture and manufacturing. Leasing deals usually range from 2 months to a maximum 5 years in local currency, and from 1 year to 5 years in foreign currency. Annual interest rates range from 26% to 30% in local currency, and from 18% to 22% in foreign currency. Trade finance products have been offered by Bank Eskhata, Orienbank, Commerce Bank, and Spitamen. They provide import financing and guarantees, advise and authenticate guarantees issued by foreign banks. There are currently no factoring instruments provided by banks or independent firms.

Digital Financial Services

The introduction of electronic money transfer technologies in Tajikistan is relatively new to the domestic banking system. Since 2018, credit financial institutions have begun to actively provide their customers the option of non-cash payments.

According to the provision of part 1 of article 8 of the Law "On payment services and the payment system," only the payment service provider, which is a credit financial institution, is allowed to carry out electronic money transfers. As of June 2022, 17 credit financial institutions provided electronic wallet services. The number of electronic wallets of credit financial institutions amounted to 4.9 million the same period, an increase of 39.1% over 2021 (Figure 7.8A).

Figure 7.8: E-wallet Transactions and Value

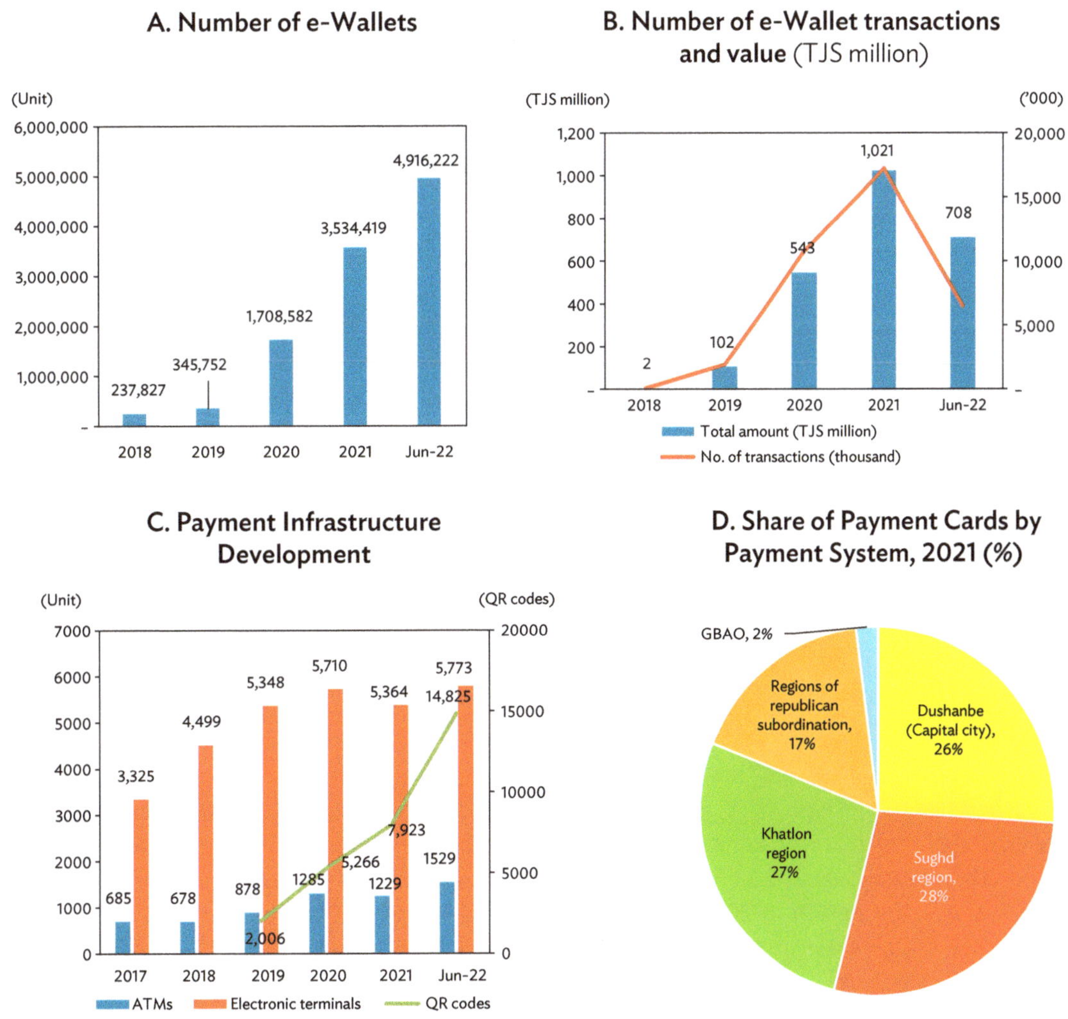

Source: ADB Asia SME Monitor 2022 database. Data from National Bank of Tajikistan.

During 2021, 17.2 million noncash transactions (up 60.9% from 2020) worth TJS1.0 billion (88.0%) were made using e-wallets (Figure 7.8B). As of June 2022, credit financial institutions had installed 1,529 ATMs and 5,773 electronic terminals for servicing bank payment card holders (Figure 7.8C). Of this total, 1,975 were installed at cash points (4.7% more than in 2021) and 3,798 in trade and service enterprises (9.2%). The use of quick response (QR) codes has expanded as well (7,923 transactions in 2021 to (14,825 transactions in June 2022, 87.1% more than June 2021).

There remain several barriers to developing SME digital financial services: taxes and the high tax burden for SMEs, high costs and low internet speed, insufficient geographic accessibility and underdeveloped financial services infrastructure in remote regions, SMEs lack a fast payment system and platform for business-to-business (B2B) and peer-to-peer (P2P) lending, and the low level of financial literacy in general.

Capital Markets

There are two registered stock exchanges, CASE (established in 2015) and ASE (2018), which in part target SMEs. Operations in ASE never began due to the pandemic and lack of highly qualified specialists (as of end-August 2022).

CASE provides a unique platform for organized securities trading. It has partnered with GMEX Technologies Limited (part of the GMEX Group), a leading provider of multi-asset exchange and post-trade technology using a business-enabling partnership approach. One of the main shareholders of GMEX Group is Deutsche Borse AG (a leading stock exchange in Europe). CASE aims to provide a convenient, transparent, reliable investment environment for local and foreign investors—to build a platform for investors and companies to trade financial instruments in compliance with international standards.

For SME financing, diversifying sources of finance would give SMEs a mechanism for providing working capital. As an alternative to bank lending, CASE allows financing through stock market instrument: by issuing shares or bonds. Since 2015, CASE has had the main board, intended for large issuers, and a specialized board created for SMEs, with simplified listing requirements to encourage them to list.

The government intends to make SMEs a reliable engine for economic diversification. One purpose of the specialized SME board is to drive the improvement of corporate governance and information disclosure by SMEs. Raising financing through the luisting of shares has several advantages, such as the ability to maintain control over the business, reduce lending rates, increase liquidity, create additional jobs, and measure the company's market value. Financing a business by issuing equity and placing bonds offers several advantages, including tax benefits: (i) income (dividends and coupon interest) on listed securities and (ii) income from the increase in value from the sale of securities in open trading.

To list securities on the "specialized" board, the issuer must meet the following basic requirements: (i) authorized capital must be at least TJS100,000, (ii) a business plan, and (iii) the number of listed shares is not more than 20% of total equity (Table 6a). Market capitalization of listed domestic companies on the main board was TJS2.6 billion in 2021, a 44.1% increase over 2020 (TJS1.8 billion). Market capitalization of listed domestic companies on the SME board was TJS40.1 million in 2021, 0.2% more than 2020 (TJS40.0 million) (Figure 7.9 and Table 7.6). As of end-2021, there were 41 listed companies on CASE, of which 38 issued shares on the main board and three issued bonds in the specialized board.

Figure 7.9: Equity Markets—Central Asian Stock Exchange

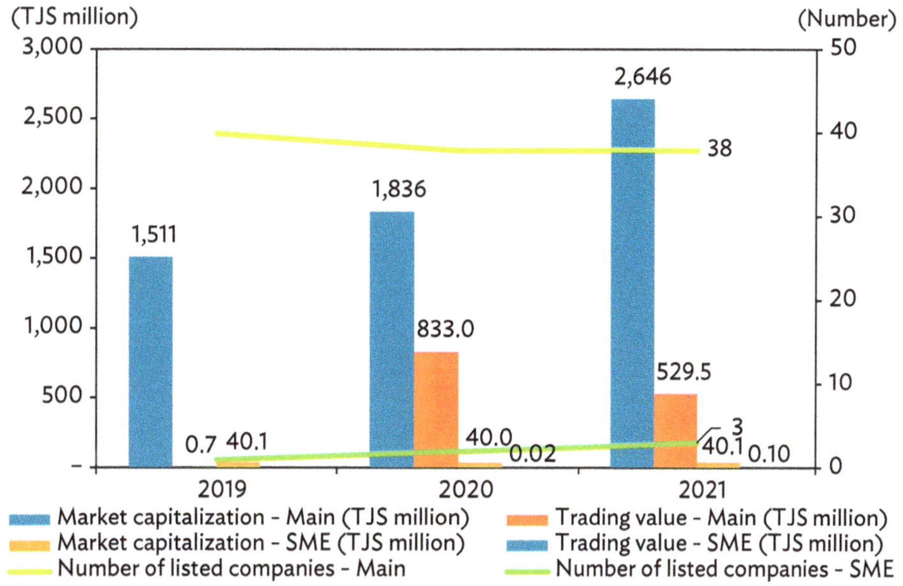

SME = small and medium-sized enterprise.
Source: ADB Asia SME Monitor 2022 database. Data from Agency for the Development of Securities and Specialized Registration of the Ministry of Finance of the Republic of Tajikistan and Central Asian Stock Exchange.

There is an unorganized securities market supervised by the Agency for the Development of Securities and Specialized Registration under the Ministry of Finance. As of end-2021, market capitalization was TJS11.5 billion, a 70.7% increase from 2020 due to additional shares issued for construction of the Rogun dam (2028 targeted completion) and new shares issued by manufacturing firms.

Financial Infrastructure

The current financial market needs to be strengthened to secure financial stability and broaden access to finance. One important step is the development of effective credit information-sharing. Credit bureaus help banks and NBFIs protect themselves from fraud and increase the competitiveness of financial institutions while simultaneously helping entrepreneurs reduce their credit risk by offering advice on loan repayments. There is no public credit registry, but one is being planned.

As of end-2021, there were two credit bureaus: (i) LLC credit histories bureau Credit-information Bureau of Tajikistan (CIBT), and (ii) LLC Bureau of Credit Histories Somoniyon (BCHS). These bureaus act in accordance with the law of the Republic of Tajikistan “On credit histories” dated 26 March 2009.

CIBT was registered as a commercial entity in April 2010 and started operating in 2013. CIBT specializes in credit information systems and credit management solutions and provides financial institutions qualified support at each stage of its customer relationship.

CIBT collects information on all borrowers in the country to reduce lending risks for both lenders borrowers. The largest local banks and microfinance organizations are CIBT shareholders, and in 2012, CRIF (a global company specializing in the development and management of credit reporting, business information, and decision support systems) joined CIBT by purchasing 49% of its shares.

CIBT's database contains more than 4 million files on individuals, individual traders, and companies. As of end-2021, 94 financial institutions had submitted credit history reports to CIBT of the following types: (i) banks; (ii) microfinance institutions; (iii) State National Energy Company "Barki Tojik" covering utilities; (iv) other nonbank organizations (except pawnshops), leasing companies; and (v) mobile operators (information on those using facilities on credit or installment). CIBT uses advanced security technology from Microsoft, Checkpoint Inc., Symantec, Cisco and SSL certificates.

CIBT can share credit information on over 3-4 million clients (including individuals and SMEs). There are more than 800 active users, including banks and microfinance institutions, with some 1.3-1.6 million requests per month. Only 70% of SMEs are covered out of those registered with the tax committee.

The BCHS database contains more than 1 million files on individuals, individual traders, and companies. As of end-2021, 27 financial institutions had submitted credit history reports of the following types: (i) banks; (ii) MFIs; and (iii) other nonbanking organizations (except pawnshops), leasing companies. BCHS uses advanced security technology from Microsoft, Cisco, and SSL certificates from famous security policy vendors.

The BCHS can share credit information on over 4.6 million clients (including individuals and SMEs). More than 320 users, including banks and MFIs, actively use the BCHS system, handling around 3,000-4,000 requests per month. Only 60% of SMEs are covered out of those registered with the tax committee.

4. Policies and Regulations

- The National Development Strategy for 2030 (NDS) sets out long-term socioeconomic development priorities for SME development, including the creation of new productive jobs.
- To improve the business and investment climate, the NDS intends to reduce administrative barriers for SMEs and develop needed infrastructure—particularly digital infrastructure—for SME growth across the country.
- The new Tax Code that started in early 2022 simplifies tax administration and reduces the tax burden (corporate income tax) on individuals and businesses, including SMEs.
- The government adopted a National Strategy for Financial Inclusion for 2022–2026 in July 2022, addressing digital financial services, diversified financial products, consumer protection, and financial literacy.
- The government took several policy measures in response to the COVID-19 pandemic, together with fiscal and financial assistance measures for farmers and SMEs—including subsidies, tax relief, and liquidity support for financial institutions to promote lending to affected individuals and businesses.
- The government adopted an anti-crisis program in March 2022 to manage the effects of the Russian invasion of Ukraine. It created an Interdepartmental Headquarters to prevent possible risks to the national economy and to develop an action plan.

SME Development

The NDS was adopted through a resolution of Parliament dated 1 December 2016, and was developed based on the Law "On state forecasts, concepts, strategies and programs of socio-economic development of the Republic of Tajikistan" and in line with the country's long-term development goals and priorities.

It sets strategic goals to expand productive employment and support for developing urban and rural SMEs as a means to boost jobs and help solve social issues. One of the five NDS priorities is to support SMEs create employment in high-tech innovative industries, including empowering youth and women.[225]

In deepening financial sector reforms, the NDS provides for strengthening SME assessments through independent auditors.

There are several barriers to creating a better business and investment climate:

- the limited domestic market and weak international trade and economic integration— the need to better access major international consumer markets and major trade and transport routes;
- insufficient industrial and digital infrastructure, assuring reliable electricity and internet bandwidth, for example;
- administrative barriers to business development and the lack of self-financing mechanisms (credit unions, mutual insurance companies, among others);
- insufficient investment infrastructure (banking, information and analytical, consulting, and others) along with mechanisms to secure property rights and contractual relations;
- an underdeveloped tax incentive system and mechanisms for financial and lending support, insurance against business risks, foreign exchange volatility, and inflation;
- ineffective state support mechanisms and business regulations both nationally and regionally;
- complex procedures (tariff and nontariff barriers) for imports and exports and the lack of regional cooperation in trade and in sharing environmental information; and
- the need for more external assistance projects aligned with national and sectoral strategies along with regional development programs.

Developing a more attractive business and investment climate will require

- creating a sustainable and efficient competitive environment for attracting private investment also includes entrepreneurship that promotes exports of domestic products;
- creating an ombudsman to protect the rights of entrepreneurs;
- developing the financial market, secondary securities market, and a liberalized, diversified insurance market;
- creating a sovereign credit market; and
- implementing an effective regulatory system for the economy, making it easier to attract investment in priority sectors.

The list of specific challenges for improving the investment climate remains long:

- improving legislation covering investment, international trade, and the introduction of international quality standards and product safety;
- attracting more and targeted external assistance to address national, sectoral and regional priorities through better use of foreign aid management information systems;

[225] The five priorities include (i) stimulating the creation of productive jobs, (ii) developing a competitive domestic labor market, (iii) increasing the impact of vocational education, (iv) increasing the share of formal employment in the economy, and (v) diversifying external labor migration.

- increasing financing through the rebranded Entrepreneurship Support Fund (ESP) to attract women entrepreneurs and provide capacity building, new investment, more efficiency at the Public-Private Partnership (PPP) Council and the PPP Projects Implementation Unit;
- developing and implementing programs and strategies to expand entrepreneurship, considering gender, investment and exports;
- developing a multi-level institutional system to support entrepreneurship according to regional and sector clusters, specialized funds and support for establishing infrastructure agencies;
- implementing policies to encourage foreign direct investment to support industrial (and innovative) economic development;
- improving the protection of the rights of entrepreneurs, both legally and by establishing an Ombudsman Institute;
- consistently implement policies that reduce the requirements for creating a business and providing a system of administrative support for medium and large-scale private investment projects, using a "single window" approach;
- developing small businesses in rural and mountainous regions by using local raw materials and integrating agricultural processing;
- further developing capital markets, including the stock exchanges;
- creating and attracting more environmentally friendly businesses;
- improving and strengthening the Investment Activity Management Institute nationally and regionally;
- introducing installments for paying value-added tax (VAT) on machinery and technological equipment, and significantly expand the list of imported industrial goods that are VAT-exempt;.
- developing PPPs by providing clear goals, objectives and priority areas for development, along with a regulatory framework that integrates of the Law "On concessions" with the Law "On PPPs";
- developing ways to track PPP projects and indicators to monitor projects;
- providing incentives for local authorities to initiate and implement PPP projects;
- establishing a PPP development fund (preparation and support), including extra-budgetary sources;
- setting tariffs for transport services and other infrastructure related to PPPs;
- creating clear procedures for investment agreements;
- arranging public offerings of projects to investors; and
- protecting socially vulnerable groups within the framework of PPP project implementation.

The Parliament adopted a new Tax Code on 3 November 2021 which became effective at the start of 2022. The purpose was to sustain economic development by creating a favorable business and investment climate, primarily for manufacturing, to promote digital technology, and ensure new sources of taxation would increase state revenues.

The new Tax Code, developed by international partners in consultation with the private sector, aims to reduce the tax burden, eliminate inconsistencies that allow for ambiguous interpretations or arbitrary application, and encourage informal enterprises to register. For manufacturing, the corporate income tax rate was set at 13%, for financial institutions and mobile companies the rate was reduced from 23% to 20%, and for other types of activities from 23% to 18%. The social tax rate for insurers was reduced from 25% to 20%.

Taxes on road usage were excluded from the new code, with the total number of taxes reduced from 10 to seven types. VAT was reduced from 18% to 15% and is expected to drop to 13% by 2027.

The State Committee on Investment and Property Management was launched in 2012 with an action plan until 2020. The program identified several long-term policy measures: (i) reforming legislation governing entrepreneurial activity, (ii) modernizing production and technological processes, (iii) attracting foreign and local investments, (iv) strengthening the institute for PPPs, (v) enhancing access to SME finance, and (vi) providing SMEs government subsidies and guarantees (Table 7.7).

The 2013 ESF provided loans to SMEs at a subsidized interest rate of 12%, focusing on startups and projects in areas where entrepreneurship was least developed. The ESF was reorganized and rebranded as the State Unitary Enterprise Industrial and Export Bank "Sanoatsodirotbank" (SUE IEB) (Resolution No.390 dated on 25 June 2020). According to the Government Order No.106-F dated 18 December 2020 on the provision of concessional loans to individual entrepreneurs affected by the pandemic, TJS180 million was transferred to SUE IEB "Sanoatsodirotbank" on 30 December 2020 to provide additional concessional loans to SMEs.

Financial Inclusion

The government adopted a National Strategy for Financial Inclusion for 2022–2026 (NSFI) on 1 July 2022, covering four key areas:

- delivery channels and digital financial services,
- variety of financial products,
- protection of consumer rights, and
- financial literacy.

The financial inclusion strategy will build a financial system where every adult and legal entity can access, learn about, and use a wide range of high-quality financial services (including savings, payments, remittances, loans, insurance, and investments) that meet demand and protect consumer rights.

To do this, the NSFI outlines three goals:

(i) Access to financial services:
  a. provide a stable, reliable and authorized structure to financial institutions;
  b. create a mail interface for banking and nonbanking products, as well as delivery channels;
  c. use digital financial technologies and other innovations to reach people otherwise outside service coverage, especially youth and women; and
  d. provide remote financial products and services tailored to market demand, as well as create customer awareness of using remote services;

(ii) Structure financial services:
  a. make available a wide range of specially designed financial resources along with simple products and services to serve the variety of market segments;
  b. ensure proper use of financial resources in serving customers, especially young people, women, and SMEs; and
  c. implement measures that stimulate consumption.

(iii) Ensure financial product and service quality:
  a. guarantee that financial products and services are properly designed, rated, and tailored to target markets;
  b. ensure comprehensive protection of consumers using financial services; and
  c. educate and build sufficient consumer literacy and confidence in making financial decisions.

The main targets for achieving these goals include

(i) Access to financial services:
   a. increase the number of credit financial institutions and subdivisions from 32.1 to 33.7 per 100,000 adult population;
   b. increase the number of ATMs per 100,000 adults from 20.5 in 2020 to at least 26.4; and
   c. increase the number of terminals at points of sale and service (PPO) from 61.0 per 100,000 adults to 87.7—and QR code users from 84.3 per 100,000 adults to 96.9.

(ii) Use of financial services:
   a. increase the number of account holders in credit financial institutions to cover 95% of the adult population;
   b. increase the volume of noncash transactions using electronic wallets by a factor of 2.4;
   c. ensure at least 60% of the adult population can effectively use digital payment services;
   d. increase the use of financial services (savings, loans, insurance) by at least 50%;
   e. ensure the quality of financial products and services used remotely;
   f. develop standard disclosure sheets for at least five types of financial products for easy comparison using common tools and open-source programming interfaces (for example, application programming interface).
   g. ensure complaint procedures covering financial service providers meet central bank requirements; and
   h. increase financial literacy by at least 10%.

Tajikistan lags most other Central Asian countries in SME access to finance through the banking system. An analysis of the drivers of SME lending in the country helps identify the main obstacles to financially integrating SMEs into the economy. Aside from the general level of economic development, these obstacles include management, availability of credit information, the level of competition, and the quality of the business environment.

Access to finance is low due to the following factors:

(i) **Macroeconomic stability and vulnerability to external shocks.** The economy relies on remittances, exports, development assistance, and foreign direct investment as sources of income. The remittance shock associated with the 2014–2016 Russian financial crisis highlighted the macroeconomic factors—especially the *somoni* exchange rate—that are highly sensitive to external shocks. The sharp devaluation of the *somoni* against the US dollar led to a full-blown banking crisis and increase in NPLs. In 2022, as a result of the Russian invasion of Ukraine, the initial sharp devaluation due to sanctions led to the opening of new local currency deposits in banks (the *somoni* has since appreciated to its early 2020 level)—emphasizing the economy's continued dependence on the Russian Federation as main trading partner.

(ii) **Inadequacy of domestic bank deposits and credit resources.** The low level of GDP per capita leads to a lack of domestic savings to meet the resource needs of banks. Thus, many financial institutions rely on foreign sources for funding, which is a financial risk for a country with a relatively low credit rating. When lending, banks are exposed to both credit and foreign exchange risk, as they are forced to lend to customers in foreign currencies (primarily US dollars). The capital of financial and credit organizations remains small, which does little to attract new credit resources. The high cost of these resources—along with high inflationary expectations and the limited transparency of lenders and administrative payments—leads to high interest rates and strict collateral requirements. Many clients, especially households and SMEs, cannot afford a loan or meet the required criteria and collateral.

(iii) **Low level of financial literacy.** Clients with low financial literacy and a lending culture with weak corporate governance create significant credit, liquidity, and potential risks.

(iv) **Lack of innovation in using new technology-based financial products.** A regulator's understanding of market developments is prerequisite to designing proper regulations. The experience of other countries shows that regulators allow innovation to be introduced on a pilot basis, provided that market participants are fully transparent. For example, the introduction of electronic services in Tajikistan is impossible without the close interaction of mobile operators and financial institutions when conducting payment transactions. Current legislation requires operators to be licensed by a credit institution, which tends to block any significant progress in this direction.

(v) **Low financial institution transparency and lack of customer confidence.** Although the central bank requires financial institutions to regularly publish financial statements, the corresponding legal document has yet to comply with the requirements of the Basel Committee on Banking Supervision. This leaves clients without the necessary information to have confidence in the system. Although a deposit insurance scheme has been tested with Agroinvestbank, Tajiksodirotbank, Tajprombank, and Fononbank, it has not increased the system's credibility.

(vi) **Another barrier is the lack of geographic access and an underdeveloped financial services infrastructure.** To reduce transaction costs, various types of products and services are offered to individuals, households, and SMEs through credit institutions' banking service centers—usually located in urban and administrative centers. Thus, these services are not sufficiently accessible to most of the population in rural or remote areas. Increased mobile banking use will help if transaction security is guaranteed, but the payment infrastructure remains poorly developed—with a smaller number of ATMs, POS terminals, and users of internet and mobile banking compared with other Central Asian countries.

ADB has proposed several measures to promote private sector growth—such as improving the investment climate and reducing dependence on external borrowings through domestic capital market development. It also recommended that regular reports of the Ministry of Finance on public debt be published, including audited annual reports of the 15 largest state-owned enterprises.

Response to COVID-19

Tajikistan's COVID Country profile outlines the government's policy responses as well as fiscal, monetary, financial, trade, SME, and other policy measures.[226] The main fiscal policy measure on 30 June 2021 was a request for disbursements under the International Monetary Fund's (IMF) Rapid Credit Facility. Earlier, on 6 May 2020, the IMF approved $189.5 million in budgetary support. Development partners, including the World Bank and ADB, also provided financial support of around $150 million. The government provided VAT exemptions on essential imports, lump-sum assistance equivalent to the minimum wage to vulnerable households and other vulnerable groups. It extended coverage of targeted social assistance to all 68 districts of the country. Health workers received supplemental pay, while tariff increases on electricity, water, and communal services were postponed until end-2020. The government also provided free medical care to COVID-19 patients along with sick leave and compensation benefits. The government provided grain, seed, and fuel to farms to boost food security, and time-bound tax holidays and relief to targeted industries and small businesses until 1 September 2020. Anti-COVID-19 measures also included subsidized food for the population and financial support to SMEs (which was made available in 2020). Tajikistan also was granted debt relief of around $50 million under the G20 Debt Service Suspension Initiative. These funds were included as supplementary anti-COVID-19 measures.[227]

226 ADB COVID-19 Policy Database. Tajikistan. https://covid19policy.adb.org/policy-measures/TAJ.

227 IMF. Policy Responses to COVID-19 - Tajikistan. https://www.imf.org/en/Topics/imf-and-covid19/Policy-Responses-to-COVID-19#T.

The central bank eased monetary and liquidity conditions and adopted an action plan to address the pandemic effects on banking. It allowed for a 17% exchange rate depreciation during 2020 to narrow the gap between the official and market rate. Banks were provided with liquidity in foreign currency.[228] The policy rate was cut by 100 basis points in April 2020 and 100 basis points in August 2020 to 10.75%. Under mounting pressure, it lowered reserve requirements, relaxed the enforcement of prudential requirements, and provided foreign exchange liquidity. It also promoted the use of electronic payments for remote transactions.[229]

Prices of staple goods pushed headline inflation outside of the central bank's target range in April–May 2020, slowing to 9.4% by December 2020. A presidential decree mandated price controls for key consumer goods and medical supplies.

In April 2020, the central bank recommended banks review loan terms to support borrowers facing temporary difficulties. It also recommended banks to waive penalties for businesses and individuals that faced difficulties in repaying their loan obligations between May and October 2020. The central bank temporarily (until September 2020) waived supervisory sanctions against banks providing adequate loan loss provisions and as a result failed to meet capital adequacy and liquidity ratios. Banks have restructured over 46,000 loans which are being tracked separately. Despite the temporary waiving of penalties, credit institutions must ensure that established prudential requirements are met. The central bank recommended that credit institutions not pay dividends or bonuses to shareholders but use these profits to boost capital. Credit institutions are exempt from paying fees for the settlement system and have been asked to avoid non-essential expenditures. To reduce dollarization, the income tax rate for interest income on domestic currency deposits was lowered by 5% until end-December 2020.

In April 2020, reserve ratios were lowered from 3% to 1% for local currency and from 9% to 5% for foreign exchange deposits until 31 December 2020. The government disbursed preferential loans to food and medical supply companies through the Fund for State Support to Entrepreneurship. Interest rates on bank deposits were lowered from 12% to 6% from 1 July to 31 December 2020. The central bank also recommended banks to consider restructuring difficult loans (for example, extending maturities).

The government allocated TJS40.8 million to increase salaries of health and social protection workers for 3 months to provide hospitals with food, and the Ministry of Health and Social Protection to improve the operations of hospitals, polyclinics, sanatoriums, medical institutions, and to supply them with medicines and modern equipment. In addition, on 17 July 2020, the government decree allowed a one-time payment to vulnerable groups in the amount of the minimum monthly wage.[230]

The COVID-19 response also included financial support for SMEs as subsidies to business. Grain, seeds, and fuel were provided to farmers to improve food security and assist targeted industries and small businesses.

International assistance for the COVID-19 Active Response and Expenditure Support Program reached $716.8 million in loans and grants, of which $82.2 million or 11.5% was from ADB with the rest from other international finance institutions.

Response to Russian Invasion of Ukraine

With the COVID-19 pandemic recovery spreading across the global economy, another external shock battered growth forecasts. The Russian invasion of Ukraine and the ensuing unprecedented economic sanctions affected

[228] https://www.imf.org/en/Topics/imf-and-covid19/Policy-Responses-to-COVID-19#T
[229] https://covid19policy.adb.org/policy-measures/TAJ;
[230] https://covid19policy.adb.org/policy-measures/TAJ

countries near and far. The impact on Tajikistan has been significant. Landlocked Tajikistan is heavily dependent on the Russian Federation for exports, trade routes and logistics, its labor market and remittances, and many infrastructure projects.

The government adopted an anti-crisis program in March 2022, creating an Interdepartmental Headquarters to develop an action plan to identify and reduce risks to the national economy. The plan's goal was to ensure food security, financial and exchange rate stability, and improve the investment climate. Also in March, a decree imposed a moratorium on monitoring entrepreneurs from April 2022 until January 2023. To stabilize the domestic market, the government exempted the Agency for State Material Reserves from paying customs duties, taxes and excise taxes on 100,000 tons of wheat, 40,000 tons of sugar, 20,000 tons of flour, 5,000 tons of vegetable oil, 5,000 tons of meat, and other goods.

More than half of Tajikistan enterprises have faced rising production costs, given that many source products and raw materials from the Russian Federation. Imports from the Russian Federation and Ukraine stopped. Together, businesses have been forced to raise product prices as they face declining profitability.

Those selling their products to exporters or multinational corporations from the Russian Federation or Ukraine report a decrease in sales by an average of 5% (with significant variations—from an increase in sales of about 3% to a decrease of about 13%). Those not selling products to the Russian Federation or Ukraine had sales increase by an average of 5%. Financial difficulties have increased from reduced profitability and difficulties accessing new loan financing, forcing them to adjust loan obligations to reduce their debt burden.

There is also the significant problem of paying bills of partner clients in US dollars, even as 70% of contracts of Tajik suppliers of goods and products from the Russian Federation were already transferred to the *ruble*. Banks generally use correspondent accounts with Russian banks. About 95% of remittances from the Russian Federation to Tajikistan were received in *rubles*, which led to a decrease in demand for US dollars and, accordingly, an appreciating exchange rate of from TJS11.30/$1 to TJS10.26/$1. One of the Action Plan points was the transition from the *US dollar* to the *ruble* and *yuan* when importing goods and products from the Russian Federation and the PRC.

Data Tables

Table 7.1: SME Definitions

A. Definition after 2017

Item	Small	Medium	Large
Annual gross income	TJS1,000,000	Between TJS1,000,000 and TJS25,000,000	Above TJS25,000,000
Average number of employees	No more than 30 people and for agricultural producers 50 people	From 30 to 100 people and for agricultural producers from 50 to 200 people	Over 100 people and for agricultural producers over 200 people

The law restricts the following activities of small enterprises: (i) excisable manufacturing, e.g., production of pharmaceuticals, spirits, and perfume; (ii) supply of primary aluminum; (iii) banking and insurance; (iv) management of investment funds; and (v) stock market activities.

Source: ADB Asia SME Monitor 2022 database. Data from Ministry of Economic Development and Trade of the Republic of Tajikistan and Agency on Statistics under President of the Republic of Tajikistan; amendment of the Law No.1107 of 2014 on the Government Protection and Support of Entrepreneurship dated 2 January 2020.

B. Definition after 18 March 2015

Item	Small	Medium	Large
Annual gross income	TJS500,000	Between TJS500,000 and TJS15,000,000	Above TJS15,000,000
Average number of employees	No more than 30 people and for agricultural producers 50 people	From 30 to 100 people and for agricultural producers from 50 to 200 people	Over 100 people and for agricultural producers over 200 people

The law restricts the following activities of small enterprises: (i) excisable manufacturing, e.g., production of pharmaceuticals, spirits, and perfume; (ii) supply of primary aluminum; (iii) banking and insurance; (iv) management of investment funds; and (v) stock market activities.

Source: ADB Asia SME Monitor 2022 database. Data from Ministry of Economic Development and Trade of the Republic of Tajikistan and Agency on Statistics under President of the Republic of Tajikistan.

C. Definition before 17 March 2015

Item	Small	Medium	Large
Annual turnover	TJS500,000	Between TJS500,000 and TJS15,000,000	Above TJS15,000,000
Average number of employees	No more than 30 people and for agricultural producers 50 people	From 30 to 100 people and for agricultural producers from 50 to 200 people	Over 100 people and for agricultural producers over 200 people

The law restricts the following activities of small enterprises: (i) excisable manufacturing, e.g., production of pharmaceuticals, spirits, and perfume; (ii) supply of primary aluminum; (iii) banking and insurance; (iv) management of investment funds; and (v) stock market activities.

Sources: ADB Asia SME Monitor 2022 database. Data from Ministry of Economic Development and Trade of the Republic of Tajikistan and Agency on Statistics under President of the Republic of Tajikistan.

SME = small and medium-sized enterprise.

Note: There is no microenterprise category in Tajikistan.

Table 7.2: SME Landscape

End-of-period data

Item	2004	2005	2006	2007	2008	2009*	2010	2011	2012	2013	2014	2015*	2016	2017	2018	2019	2020	2021
NUMBER OF ENTERPRISES																		
Number of enterprises, total[1]	...	...	...	...	57,172	57,172	25,083	28,594	31,875	38,323	39,401	39,401	38,299	25,923	26,854	27,069	28,056	29,967
Number of SMEs	...	...	...	...	55,750	55,750	24,459	27,964	31,144	37,832	38,907	38,907	37,804	25,451	26,453	26,691	27,650	29,555
Small	...	...	...	...	48,682	48,682	21,358	23,670	25,882	32,206	33,256	33,256	32,237	20,324	21,438	21,734	22,508	24,350
Medium	...	...	...	...	7,068	7,068	3,101	4,294	5,262	5,626	5,651	5,651	5,567	5,127	5,015	4,957	5,142	5,205
Number of large enterprises	...	...	...	...	1,422	1,422	624	630	731	491	494	494	495	472	401	378	406	412
SME to total (%)	...	...	...	...	97.5	97.5	97.5	97.8	97.7	98.7	98.7	98.7	98.7	98.2	98.5	98.6	98.6	98.6
SME growth (%)	...	...	...	...	...	...	...	14.3	11.4	21.5	2.8	...	(2.8)	(32.7)	3.9	0.9	3.6	6.9
SMEs by sector (% share)																		
Agriculture, forestry, and fisheries	...	...	...	...	60.7	60.7	24.7	26.0	27.9	24.5	24.9	22.1	21.4	16.5	16.6	15.5	14.4	15.2
Manufacturing	...	...	...	...	3.5	3.5	6.1	6.0	5.4	6.1	6.7	6.7	6.9	7.6	7.6	7.7	7.7	7.9
Transportation and communication	...	...	...	...	1.3	1.3	2.8	2.9	2.9	2.7	2.8	2.8	3.0	3.3	3.4	3.6	2.1	4.3
Construction	...	...	...	...	3.5	3.5	6.5	6.3	6.1	5.9	6.5	6.5	7.0	6.2	6.3	6.7	6.8	6.9
Wholesale and retail trade	...	...	...	...	3.5	3.5	10.8	10.9	11.3	17.2	16.3	17.2	19.1	13.9	14.0	14.7	13.4	13.3
Other services[2]	...	...	...	...	27.6	27.6	49.2	47.9	46.4	43.7	42.7	44.6	42.6	52.5	52.0	51.9	55.5	52.4
SMEs by region (% share)																		
Capital city (Dushanbe)	...	...	...	...	14.3	14.3	25.9	23.6	25.3	23.5	24.3	24.3	25.3	21.1	21.4	21.4	21.3	21.9
Others	...	...	...	...	85.7	85.7	74.1	76.4	74.7	76.5	75.7	75.7	74.7	78.9	78.6	78.6	78.7	78.1
EMPLOYMENT																		
Number of employment, total (thousand)	2,090	2,112	2,137	2,150	2,168	2,219	2,233	2,249	2,292	2,307	2,325	2,380	2,384	2,407	1,167	1,198	1,214	1,239
Number of employment by SMEs (thousand)	16.5	17.2	18.1	18.9	19.4	20.9	19.9	18.7	19.6	27.5	30.2	28.4	21.4	...	248.5	250.8	251.3	252.7
Small	16.5	17.2	18.1	18.9	19.4	20.9	19.9	18.7	19.6	27.5	30.2	28.4	21.4	...	154.7	157.5	157.4	158.9
Medium	...	...	...	...	...	...	...	...	...	...	...	...	...	...	93.9	93.3	93.9	93.9
Number of employment by large enterprises	2,074	2,095	2,119	2,131	2,149	2,198	2,213	2,231	2,272	2,280	2,295	2,351	2,363	...	918	947	963	986
SME employees to total (%)	0.8	0.8	0.9	0.9	0.9	0.9	0.9	0.8	0.9	1.2	1.3	1.2	0.9	...	21.3	20.9	20.7	20.4
SME employees growth (%)	...													...	....	0.9	0.2	0.6
Share of female employees to total employees (%)	...	...	...	...	...	...	...	...	...	...	...	...	...	...	...	...	...	...
Employment by SME by sector (% share)																		
Agriculture, forestry, and fisheries	...	...	...	...	...	...	...	...	...	...	...	...	...	...	11.9	12.5	13.0	13.6
Manufacturing	...	...	...	...	...	...	...	...	...	...	...	...	...	...	6.6	6.8	7.0	7.2
Transportation and communication	...	...	...	...	...	...	...	...	...	...	...	...	...	...	2.3	2.3	2.2	2.2
Construction	...	...	...	...	...	...	...	...	...	...	...	...	...	...	5.1	5.1	5.0	4.9
Wholesale and retail trade	...	...	...	...	...	...	...	...	...	...	...	...	...	...	6.4	6.2	6.1	6.0
Other services	...	...	...	...	...	...	...	...	...	...	...	...	...	...	67.7	67.2	66.7	66.1
Employment by SMEs by region (% share)																		
Capital city (Dushanbe)	...	...	...	...	...	...	...	...	...	...	...	...	...	...	...	...	...	...
Others	...	...	...	...	...	...	...	...	...	...	...	...	...	...	...	...	...	...
CONTRIBUTION TO GDP																		
GDP of SMEs (TJS million)[3]	...	...	...	...	8,287	9,799	11,934	14,885	18,841	22,005	28,322	32,881	36,381	42,849	41,356	47,070	49,032	58,753
SME contribution to GDP (% share)	...	...	...	...	46.8	47.5	48.3	49.5	52.1	54.3	62.1	64.5	66.4	66.5	58.2	59.5	58.4	59.4
SME GDP growth (%)	...	...	...	...	...	18.2	21.8	24.7	26.6	16.8	28.7	16.1	10.6	17.8	(3.5)	13.8	4.2	19.8
SME labor productivity (TJS million)[4]	...	...	...	...	0.2	0.2	0.3	0.4	0.5	0.4	0.4	0.5	0.8	...	...	...	...	...

continued on next page

Table 7.2 *continued*

Item	2004	2005	2006	2007	2008	2009*	2010	2011	2012	2013	2014	2015*	2016	2017	2018	2019	2020	2021
SME GDP by sector (% share)																		
Agriculture, forestry, and fisheries	...	...	...	...	...	...	...	...	...	...	...	...	...	...	...	...	...	...
Manufacturing	...	...	...	...	...	...	...	...	...	...	...	...	...	...	...	...	...	...
Transportation and communication	...	...	...	...	...	...	...	...	...	...	...	...	...	...	...	...	...	...
Construction	...	...	...	...	...	...	...	...	...	...	...	...	...	...	...	...	...	...
Wholesale and retail trade	...	...	...	...	...	...	...	...	...	...	...	...	...	...	...	...	...	...
Other services	...	...	...	...	...	...	...	...	...	...	...	...	...	...	...	...	...	...
SME GDP by region (% share)																		
Capital city (Dushanbe)	...	...	...	...	...	...	...	...	...	...	...	...	...	...	...	...	...	...
Others	...	...	...	...	...	...	...	...	...	...	...	...	...	...	...	...	...	...
EXPORTS																		
Total export value (TJS million)	2,779	2,907	4,794	5,087	4,863	4,416	5,260	5,983	6,478	4,504	5,187	6,225	7,078	10,565	10,121	11,377	15,898	24,290
Total export growth (%)	...	4.6	64.9	6.1	(4.4)	(9.2)	19.1	13.7	8.3	(30.5)	15.2	20.0	13.7	49.3	(4.2)	12.4	39.7	52.8
SME export value (TJS million)	...	...	...	...	...	...	...	...	...	...	...	...	...	...	...	...	...	...
SME export to total export value (%)	...	...	...	...	...	...	...	...	...	...	...	...	...	...	...	...	...	...
SME export growth (%)	...	...	...	...	...	...	...	...	...	...	...	...	...	...	...	...	...	...
IMPORTS																		
Total import value (TJS million)	3,618	4,255	5,912	8,826	11,297	11,232	11,699	15,256	18,002	19,313	22,810	24,016	23,874	24,472	29,713	32,445	35,605	47,567
Total import growth (%)	...	17.6	38.9	49.3	28.0	(0.6)	4.2	30.4	18.0	7.3	18.1	5.3	(0.6)	2.5	21.4	9.2	9.7	33.6
SME import value (TJS million)	...	...	...	...	...	...	...	...	...	...	...	...	...	...	...	...	...	...
SME import to total import value (%)	...	...	...	...	...	...	...	...	...	...	...	...	...	...	...	...	...	...
SME import growth (%)	...	...	...	...	...	...	...	...	...	...	...	...	...	...	...	...	...	...

GDP = gross domestic product, SME = small and medium-sized enterprise.

Notes: There is no official category of microenterprises in Tajikistan. Aggregate SME figures not include *dekhkan* farms.

* The same number of SMEs is reported between 2008-2009 and between 2014-2015 according to the national statistics.

** The data for 2004-2017 are based on the old definition, and the data for 2018-2021 are based on the new definition and electronically based.

[1] In 2009, a single window was created for business registration with the legislation change not counting dekkan farms in the list of enterprises. Due to this, the statistical number of enterprises sharply decreased in 2010.

[2] "Other services" includes health and social services, education, public administration and defense, real estate, financial intermediation, recreation and entertainment, culture and sports, as well as other community, social, and personal services.

[3] Data for GDP of private sector businesses, which is regarded as SMEs' GDP.

[4] Calculated based on SMEs' outputs (using wage data) divided by the number of SME employees.

Source: ADB Asia SME Monitor 2022 database. Data from Agency on Statistics under President of the Republic of Tajikistan.

Table 7.3: Bank Credit

End-of-period data

Item	2004	2005	2006	2007	2008	2009	2010	2011	2012	2013	2014	2015	2016	2017	2018	2019	2020	2021
OPERATING BANKS																		
Number of operating banks, total	12	12	10	11	12	13	14	15	16	16	17	17	18	17	17	17	19	14
State-owned commercial banks	1	1	1	1	1	1	1	1	1	1	1	1	1	1	1	1	2	2
State-owned development financial institutions	...	...	...	...	...	...	...	...	...	...	...	...	...	...	...	...	...	...
Private commercial banks	8	8	6	7	7	8	8	8	8	8	9	9	10	9	9	10	10	7
Foreign commercial banks	3	3	3	3	4	4	5	6	7	7	7	7	7	7	7	6	7	5
Credit																		
Loans outstanding, total (TJS million)	941	1,138	2,174	3,631	4,401	4,955	3,087	3,967	4,356	6,021	7,767	9,236	8,122	6,812	6,607	7,578	8,809	9,437
Loans outstanding in domestic currency (TJS million)	333	405	401	681	1,818	3,355	1,301	1,400	1,310	2,019	2,773	2,814	2,443	2,058	2,052	3,061	4,392	5,627
Loans outstanding in foreign currency (TJS million)	608	733	1,773	2,950	2,583	1,601	1,786	2,567	3,046	4,002	4,994	6,422	5,679	4,754	4,554	4,517	4,417	3,810
Loan growth (%)[1]	...	20.9	91.1	67.0	21.2	12.6	(37.7)	28.5	9.8	38.2	29.0	18.9	(12.1)	(16.1)	(3.0)	14.7	16.2	7.1
Total bank loans to GDP (%)	12.8	14.2	16.6	26.0	17.7	7.9	9.4	9.4	7.1	7.8	10.0	12.6	8.5	9.0	7.0	8.0	9.0	10.3
Lending rate (%, annual average)	22.9	20.8	21.9	21.6	22.2	23.7	22.1	22.1	22.8	23.7	23.3	22.9	22.5	23.3	22.6	20.5	18.9	20.6
Gross nonperforming loans (NPLs) (TJS million)	...	...	...	...	...	...	231	286	414	963	1,949	2,766	4,389	2,894	2,521	2,489	2,444	1,526
Gross NPLs to total loans (%)	...	...	...	...	...	...	7.5	7.2	9.5	16.0	25.1	29.9	54.0	42.5	38.2	32.8	27.7	16.2
Deposits																		
Deposits, total (TJS million)	...	...	...	...	1,914	2,614	3,222	4,354	4,817	5,296	6,446	8,167	8,849	8,720	9,041	8,975	10,501	8,982
Deposits in domestic currency (TJS million)	...	...	...	...	696	946	1,356	1,604	1,567	1,686	2,244	2,503	3,296	3,788	4,335	4,613	5,716	4,735
Deposits in foreign currency (TJS million)	...	...	...	...	1,218	1,668	1,866	2,750	3,250	3,610	4,202	5,664	5,553	4,932	4,706	4,362	4,785	4,247
Deposit rate (%, annual average)	0.7	0.7	0.7	0.9	1.0	1.4	1.3	1.2	1.0	0.9	0.9	0.7	0.7	0.5	0.5	0.3	0.4	0.4
SME LOANS																		
SME loans outstanding, total (TJS million)	...	...	...	...	...	...	...	1,029	1,219	1,570	988	1,820	844	1,270	1,304	1,284	1,147	1,510
SME loans to total loans outstanding (%)	...	...	...	...	...	...	...	25.9	28.0	26.1	12.7	19.7	10.4	18.6	19.7	16.9	13.0	16.0
SME loans to GDP (%)[2]	...	...	...	...	...	...	...	4.0	3.8	4.6	5.3	3.8	2.0	1.7	1.9	1.8	2.0	2.5
SME loan growth (%)	...	...	...	...	...	...	...	...	18.5	28.8	(37.1)	84.2	(53.6)	50.4	2.7	(1.6)	(10.7)	31.7
SME lending rate (%, annual average)	...	...	...	...	...	...	...	...	...	...	...	...	...	...	...	...	...	...
Nonperforming SME loans (NPLs) (TJS million)	...	...	...	...	...	...	...	93	122	113	231	361	677	548	470	318	78	70
SME NPLs to total SME loans (%)	...	...	...	...	...	...	...	9.0	10.0	7.2	23.4	19.8	80.2	43.2	36.1	24.8	6.8	4.6
Number of SME loan borrowers	...	...	...	...	...	...	...	...	...	...	...	...	...	...	...	...	...	...
SME loan borrowers to total bank borrowers (%)	...	...	...	...	...	...	...	...	...	...	...	...	...	...	...	...	...	...
SME loan rejection rate (% of total applications)	...	...	...	...	...	...	...	...	...	...	...	...	...	...	...	...	...	...
Number of SME savings account in banks	...	...	...	...	...	...	...	...	...	...	...	...	...	...	...	...	...	...
Guaranteed SME loans (TJS million)	...	...	...	...	...	...	...	...	...	...	...	...	...	...	...	...	...	...
Non-collateral SME loans (TJS million)	...	...	...	...	...	...	...	...	...	...	...	...	...	...	...	...	...	...
SME loans outstanding by sector (% share)																		
Agriculture, forestry, and fisheries	...	...	...	...	...	30.4	24.5	23.7	20.2	23.8	23.5	23.7	22.8	23.5	21.2	27.4	32.1	31.1
Manufacturing	...	...	...	...	...	15.7	13.2	11.8	8.3	10.5	11.7	12.1	11.2	10.8	6.3	4.7	3.5	3.0
Construction	...	...	...	...	...	10.1	9.7	11.2	7.8	10.0	13.0	13.4	12.9	11.0	12.3	10.6	8.1	6.2
Transport	...	...	...	...	...	1.8	1.8	1.6	0.8	1.6	2.3	1.6	1.4	0.9	1.5	1.1	1.4	1.5
Catering	...	...	...	...	...	2.3	2.1	2.0	2.7	1.1	1.0	1.0	1.0	1.0	1.1	0.9	0.5	0.4
Services	...	...	...	...	...	2.7	3.6	4.2	6.7	9.7	10.5	10.2	9.8	10.8	11.4	12.2	12.9	14.9
International trade	...	...	...	...	...	26.7	38.1	37.9	38.6	35.1	34.0	34.3	37.3	38.5	44.1	39.0	35.0	34.9
Others	...	...	...	...	...	10.2	7.0	7.6	14.9	8.3	4.0	3.8	3.6	3.5	2.2	4.1	6.5	7.9
SME loans outstanding by region (% share)																		
Capital city (Dushanbe)	...	...	...	...	...	...	...	...	...	...	...	...	...	...	...	...	...	...
Other	...	...	...	...	...	...	...	...	...	...	...	...	...	...	...	...	...	...
SME loans outstanding by type of use (% share)																		
For working capital	...	...	...	...	...	...	...	...	...	...	...	...	...	...	...	...	...	...
For capital investment	...	...	...	...	...	...	...	...	...	...	...	...	...	...	...	...	...	...
SME loans outstanding by tenor (% share)																		
Less than 1 year	...	...	...	...	...	...	...	...	...	...	...	...	...	...	...	...	...	...
1-5 years	...	...	...	...	...	...	...	...	...	...	...	...	...	...	...	...	...	...
More than 5 years	...	...	...	...	...	...	...	...	...	...	...	...	...	...	...	...	...	...

GDP = gross domestic product, SME = small and medium-sized enterprise.

Note: Data for SME loans. There is no category of "microenterprise" in the banking sector.

[1] Loan growth in 2010 and 2016-2018 was negative due to the 2008-2009 global financial crisis and the sanctions of crisis in the Russian Federation.

[2] SME loans to GDP (%) after 2015 decreased as two large banks (Agroinvestbank and Tajiksodirotbank) were excluded in the central bank statistics due to the deterioration of their financial condition and the consequences of declaring bankrupt.

Source: ADB Asia SME Monitor 2022 database. Data from National Bank of Tajikistan.

Table 7.4: Public Financing and Guarantees

End-of-period data

Item	2013	2014	2015	2016	2017	2018	2019	2020	2021
SUBSIDIZED LOANS TO SMEs									
Number of funds	1	1	1	1	2	2	2	2	2
Number of subsidized loans (new approval)	12	63	36	23	28	15	32	15	205
Outstanding of subsidized loans to SMEs (TJS million)	17.3	53.5	74.1	81.1	122.7	127.1	157.1	147.4	217.2
Growth (%)	...	208.4	38.6	9.5	51.2	3.6	23.6	(6.2)	47.4
Subsidized loans disbursed to SMEs (TJS million)	19.3	37.2	37.6	21.7	63.2	40.8	50.6	33.7	128.3
Number of SMEs that accepted subsidized loans	12	74	102	106	115	110	119	101	263
SME access to subsidized loans (% of total SMEs)			...	...	...	...	...	...	...

Source: ADB Asia SME Monitor 2022 database. Data from SUE Sanoatsodirotbank.

End-of-period data

Item	2013	2014	2015	2016	2017	2018	2019	2020	2021
CREDIT GUARANTEES									
Number of guarantee schemes	...	...	1	1	1	1	1	1	1
Guaranteed loans outstanding to SMEs (TJS million)	...	...	14.8	66.0	106.5	114.7	277.1	204.3	176.4
Growth (%)	...	...	...	345.5	61.3	7.7	141.6	(26.3)	(13.6)
Guaranteed loans approved to SMEs (TJS million)	...	...	15.5	85.0	130.7	108.2	313.7	140.6	171.6
Guaranteed loans disbursed to SMEs (TJS million)	...	...	15.5	85.0	130.7	108.2	313.7	140.6	171.6
Number of SMEs guaranteed	...	...	53	293	456	296	999	497	707
SME access to credit guarantees (% of total SMEs)	...	...	...	...	...	17.0	28.3	15.8	18.3
Guaranteed SME loans to total SME loans (%)	...	...	...	...	...	4.2	8.1	2.1	1.5
Nonperforming guaranteed SME loans to total guaranteed SME loans (NPL ratio; %)	...	...	...	...	...	0.03	0.01	0.01	0.03

SME = small and medium-sized enterprise.

Source: ADB Asia SME Monitor 2022 database. Data from Credit Guarantee Fund Tajikistan.

Table 7.4a: Refinancing Schemes for SMEs

Name of the Fund	Year of the Launch	Fund Size (TJS million)	Taget Beneficiaries	Amount of Refinance (TJS million)*	Number of SMEs benefited*	Status (ongoing/closed)
Entrepreneurship Support Fund	2013	5.0	SMEs	212.6 (national budget)	202	transformed**
SUE Sanoatsodirotbank	2020	200.0	SMEs	180.0 (national budget)	80	ongoing
Microcredit Fund "Refinancing Fund"	2017	298.4	SMEs through MFIs	123.7	1,237	ongoing
Grant Total (TJS million)		503.4		516.3	1,519	

SME = small and medium-sized enterprise.

* Data as of end-2021 includes SUE Sanoatsodirotbank and the Microcredit Fund (MCF) "Refinancing Fund".

** In 2020, the Entrepreneurship Support Fund under the Government of the Republic of Tajikistan (2013) was transformed to SUE "Sanoatsodirotbank" and the Microcredit Fund (MCF) "Refinancing Fund" that has been supported by the Government of Tajikistan, ADB, and the German Development Bank/KfW (Kreditanstalt für Wiederaufbau) since 2017. The major goal of the MCF "Refinancing Fund" is to promote entrepreneurship and expand the financial access to economically active population through credit institutions regulated by the National Bank of Tajikistan.

Source: ADB Asia SME Monitor 2022 database. Data from Credit Guarantee Fund Tajikistan.

Table 7.5: Nonbank Finance

End-of-period data

Item	2004	2005	2006	2007	2008	2009	2010	2011	2012	2013	2014	2015	2016	2017	2018	2019	2020	2021
NUMBER OF NONBANK FINANCE INSTITUTIONS																		
Nonbank Finance Institutions, total	12	35	65	78	100	123	124	124	159	149	149	106	86	67	62	58	50	67
Microfinance institutions[1]		21	55	70	92	116	121	122	125	120	120	106	86	67	62	58	50	49
Nonbank credit institutions[2]	12	14	10	8	8	7	3	2	1	1	...	...	...	...	...	...	...	...
Leasing companies	...	...	...	...	...	...	...	...	7	12	12	...	...	...	...	...	...	...
Insurance companies	...	...	...	...	...	...	...	...	26	16	17	...	...	...	...	...	...	18
MICROFINANCE INSTITUTIONS																		
Loans outstanding, total (TJS million)	...	21	59	156	273	317	421	622	934	1,376	1,894	1,993	1,701	1,695	2,041	2,125	2,058	2,496
Growth (%)	...	....	179.8	162.7	75.6	15.9	32.9	47.8	50.1	47.3	37.6	5.2	(14.6)	(0.4)	20.4	4.1	(3.2)	21.3
Total financing to GDP (%)	...	0.3	0.6	1.2	1.5	1.5	1.7	2.1	2.6	3.4	4.2	4.1	3.1	2.8	3.0	2.7	2.5	2.1
Annual lending rate (%, on average)	...	...	...	...	...	...	...	...	...	...	...	...	...	...	...	...	...	...
Gross nonperforming loans (NPLs) (TJS million)	...	0.3	0.5	2.5	4.7	17.8	21.4	21.7	27.4	27.1	55.1	139.9	209.8	152.3	110.6	70.4	102.1	80.6
Gross NPLs to total loans (%)	...	0.05	0.1	0.1	0.2	0.8	4.9	3.4	2.9	2.0	2.9	7.0	12.3	9.0	5.4	3.3	5.0	3.2
Savings (TJS million)	...	...	1	3	9	27	48	69	110	226	245	441	395	563	683	767	914	1,177
Number of customers financed, total	...	...	...	...	...	141,671	148,389	188,112	232,656	280,676	318,934	307,877	267,115	291,200	333,404	475,844	280,790	329,220
Financing outstanding by sector/purpose (% share)																		
Agriculture, forestry, and fisheries	...	...	...	...	...	35.1	29.8	29.6	29.9	27.4	29.3	30.3	27.5	25.3	25.2	26.0	29.9	31.1
Manufacturing	...	...	...	...	...	30.9	32.2	24.8	20.6	18.4	19.5	15.0	15.1	13.8	12.1	10.8	11.8	11.8
Construction	...	...	...	...	...	2.6	3.6	3.2	3.3	3.2	4.2	4.3	3.7	3.6	3.6	3.0	3.2	3.0
Transport	...	...	...	...	...	0.3	0.7	0.5	0.6	0.7	0.9	0.7	0.6	0.4	0.4	0.3	0.4	0.3
Catering	...	...	...	...	...	1.7	1.2	0.1	0.4	0.7	0.6	0.8	0.6	0.6	0.7	0.6	0.8	0.7
Services	...	...	...	...	...	5.4	6.7	7.6	8.3	12.9	11.5	13.8	12.4	12.2	13.6	13.9	15.7	16.0
International trade	...	...	...	...	...	7.4	8.2	11.2	9.6	9.7	6.9	6.3	6.1	5.5	4.9	4.6	3.5	3.4
Financial intermediation	...	...	...	...	...	...	...	0.00	0.00	0.01	0.00	0.06	0.01	0.03	0.01	(0.00)	0.00	0.01
Consumption	...	...	...	...	...	14.7	14.8	15.4	21.0	23.6	22.1	23.0	27.5	32.2	34.7	36.5	30.9	31.3
others	...	...	...	...	...	1.9	2.8	7.5	6.4	3.4	4.9	5.7	6.6	6.3	5.0	4.3	3.9	2.3
Financing outstanding by region (% share)																		
Capital city (Dushanbe)	...	...	...	11.4	12.2	18.8	19.5	17.8	16.8	17.2	16.8	18.0	19.0	19.3	18.3	19.1	16.6	15.1
Others	...	...	...	88.6	87.8	81.2	80.5	82.2	83.2	82.8	83.2	82.0	81.0	80.7	81.7	80.9	83.4	84.9
NONBANK CREDIT INSTITUIONS																		
Financing outstanding, total (TJS million)[3]	654.0	622.9	668.6	1,948.4	1,990.6	1,776.4	15.4	9.8	1.3	....	....	....	....	....	....	....	....	....
Growth (%)	...	(4.8)	7.3	191.4	2.2	(10.8)	(99.1)	(36.4)	(86.9)	....	....	....	....	....	....	....	....	....
Total financing to GDP (%)	10.6	8.6	7.2	15.2	11.2	8.6	0.1	0.03	0.004	....	....	....	....	....	....	....	....	....
Annual lending rate (%, on average)	...	...	...	...	...	...	...	...	...	...	...	...	...	...	...	...	...	...
Gross nonperforming loans (NPLs) (TJS million)	...	...	...	...	...	...	...	...	...	...	...	...	...	...	...	...	...	...
Gross NPLs to total loans (%)	...	...	...	...	...	...	...	...	...	...	...	...	...	...	...	...	...	...
Number of customers financed, total	...	...	...	...	...	...	...	...	...	...	...	...	...	...	...	...	...	...

GDP = gross domestic product, SME = small and medium-sized enterprise.

[1] Microfinance institutions include microcredit deposit organization, microcredit organization, and microcredit fund.

[2] Nonbank credit institutions are credit institutions entitled to implement certain banking operations. The list of banking operations for nonbank credit institutions shall be determined by the central bank.

[3] Due to the closure of the Nonbanking Financial Organization CJSC Credit Invest in 2009, the nonbank credit institutions' total financing outstanding sharply decreased from TJS1,776.4 million in 2009 to TJS15.4 million in 2010.

Source: ADB Asia SME Monitor 2022 database. Data from National Bank of Tajikistan.

Table 7.6: Capital Markets

A. Central Asian Stock Exchange Markets

End-of-period data

Item	2019	2020	2021
Main Board			
Market capitalization (TJS million)	1,511	1,836	2,646
Growth (%)	...	21.5	44.1
Trading value (TJS million)	...	833	529.5
Trading volume (million shares)	2	18	5
Number of listed companies	40	38	38
Specialized Board that SMEs can tap			
Market capitalization (TJS million)	40.1	40.0	40.1
Growth (%)	...	0.1	0.2
Trading value (TJS million)	...	0.02	0.10
Trading volume (million shares)	0.046	0.000	0.001
Number of listed companies	1	2	3

SME = small and medium-sized enterprise.

Note: Data represents the Central Asian Stock Exchange (CASE) market as the organized security market. CASE markets include both the main board and the specialized board for SMEs.

Source: ADB Asia SME Monitor 2022 database. Data from Central Asian Stock Exchange.

B. Markets Supervised by the Agency for the Development of Securities and Specialized Registration

End-of-period data

Item	2008	2009	2010*	2011	2012	2013	2014	2015*	2016	2017	2018	2019	2020	2021**
Market capitalization (TJS million)	1,488	570	7,248	305	865	310	376	8,306	4,901	6,319	3,737	4,581	6,734	11,493
Growth (%)	...	(61.7)	1,171.3	(95.8)	183.7	(64.1)	21.0	2,110.5	(41.0)	28.9	(40.9)	22.6	47.0	70.7
Trading value (TJS million)	...	...	...	...	...	...	...	...	...	...	...	...	...	...
Trading volume (million shares)	...	...	...	...	...	...	...	...	...	...	...	...	...	...
Number of listed companies	49	58	51	29	34	34	36	39	34	27	40	80	64	95
Number of IPOs	18	29	31	12	15	16	21	25	23	13	26	26	20	54
Number of delisted companies	...	...	...	...	...	...	...	...	...	...	...	...	...	...

IPO = initial public offering.

Note: Data represents the unorganized securities market in the form of accounting for the issue of securities of companies.

* Sharp increase was triggered by additional shares issued for construction of Rogun dam.

** Sharp increase was triggered by additional shares issued for construction of Rogun dam and industrial enterprises.

Source: ADB Asia SME Monitor 2022 database. Data from the Agency for the Development of Securities and Specialized Registration of the Ministry of Finance of the Republic of Tajikistan.

Table 7.6a-1: Listing Requirements—Central Asian Stock Exchange

Criteria	Stock	
	Main Board	Specialized Board
Share capital	From TJS5.0 million to TJS100 million.	Not less than TJS100,000.
Financial reporting	Audited financial statements for the last 3 years of activity.	Having a business plan.
Volume of placement on the Stock Exchange	Without restrictions.	No more than 20% of shares.

Note: There is one stock exchange operating in Tajikistan, "Central Asian Stock Exchange (CASE)".

Table 7.6a-1: Listing Requirements–Agency for the Development of Securities and Specialized Registration

Criteria	Stock
	Main Board
1. Status of the firm	The issuer must be a legal entity of the Republic of Tajikistan, or have documents properly legalized or apostilled for their use in the Republic of Tajikistan, confirming its registration as a legal entity of another state.
2. Financial statements	The issuer must prepare its financial statements in accordance with the standards of the Republic of Tajikistan and international financial reporting standards, including on a quarterly basis.
3. Registration	The register of holders of the Issuer's securities must be maintained by an independent Registrar.
4. Debt condition	The issuer must not have debts to fulfill obligations on securities issued by him, except for current and unclaimed debts on payment of income on these securities.
5. Requirements	Articles of Association and other documents of the issuer shall not impose restrictions on the free disposal of securities issued by it for their owners and other restrictions on other rights under securities.
6. Audit	The Issuer's annual financial statements must be confirmed by an opinion of an independent auditor recognized by the Exchange.
7. Due diligence	The issuer must undergo due diligence.
8. Investment memorandum	The issuer must sign an investment memorandum with a professional participant in the securities market serving it.
9. Volume of issued securities	The volume of issued securities, which are included or declared for inclusion in the Official List of the Exchange, must be at least 10,000 shares.
10. Disclosure	An issuer, whose securities are included in the Official List, must disclose to the Exchange, in a timely manner and to the extent required, the information provided for by the Listing Rules for the purpose of maintaining the listing.

Source: ADB Asia SME Monitor 2022 database. Data from the Ministry of Finance Agency for the Development of Securities and Specialized Registration and CASE.

Table 7.7: Policies and Regulations

Regulations

Name	Outline
Law No.1107 on the Government Protection and Support of Entrepreneurship (2014)	SME definition, regulation of civil affairs concerned with the government protection, and support and development of entrepreneurship.
Tax Code No.549 (2021)	Simplifying tax administration and reducing the tax burden on SMEs (corporate income tax reduction).
Law No.816 on Microfinance Organisations (2012)	Regulation of microfinance activities.
Law No.524 on Banking Activities (2009)	Regulation of banking activities.

Regulators and Policymakers

Name	Responsibility
National Bank of Tajikistan (NBT)	The central bank regulates and supervises commercial banks and nonbank finance institutions.
State Committee on Investment and Property Management of Tajikistan (SCISPM)	Develop policies related to the private sector development.
Entrepreneurship Support Fund of Tajikistan/SUE Sanoatsodirotbank	Financial support for SMEs.
Ministry of Finance (MOF)	SME financial support and development.
Ministry of Economic Development and Trade (MEDT)	Responsible for developing, implementing, and monitoring the state socioeconomic policies in Tajikistan.
Ministry of Industrial and New Technologies	Assistance for accelerating industrialization.
Agency for the Development of Securities and Specialized Registration, MOF	Regulate capital markets.

Policies

Name	Responsible Entity	Outline
Program for Government Support of Entrepreneurship in Tajikistan up to 2020 (2012)	SCISPM	The program, as a long-term strategy, identifies the set of measures that are to be undertaken and supported by the government: (i) reforming the legislation governing entrepreneurial activity; (ii) modernization of production and technological processes; (iii) attracting foreign and local investments; (iv) strengthening the Institute of public- private partnerships; (v) enhancing access to finance for SMEs; and (vi) providing SMEs with government subsidies and guarantees.
National Development Strategy of the Republic of Tajikistan for 2030 (2016)	MEDT, SCISPM	The strategy has been developed, considering the changes that have taken place in the country and in the world, and in particular, the impact of the global financial and economic crisis of 2007–2009 on the national economy, including priorities for the development of SMEs and serves as a directive action plan for all bodies of state administration and an indicative action plan for the private sector and civil society. Three basic principles of the national development strategy are: (i) Prevention or reduction of vulnerability of future development. (ii) Industrialization or increasing the efficiency of the use of national resources. (iii) Innovation based development in all spheres of social and economic life of the country.
Creation of the Entrepreneurship Support Fund of Tajikistan (2013)	MOF	(i) Provide loans to SMEs at a subsidized interest rate fixed at 12% and (ii) target startup projects and those from the areas where entrepreneurship is least developed.
Transformation of Entrepreneurship Support Fund of Tajikistan to State Unitary Enterprise Industrial and Export Bank of Tajikistan "Sanoatsodirotbonk"	MOF	SUE Sanoatsodirotbank was established on the basis of the State Fund for the Support of Entrepreneurship to finance projects of entrepreneurs to provide concessional (preferential) loans to SMEs. The bank passed state registration with the Tax Committee under the government and received a license from the NBT. Concessional lending to entrepreneurs in the amount of TJS180 million under the ADB Project TA-9894 TAJ Preparation of the Financial sector and Fiscal Management Improvement Program has received funds from the Ministry of Finance of the Republic of Tajikistan in 2020.
National Strategy for Financial Inclusion (NSFI) for 2022-2026 (Government Decision No.314 dated 1 July 2022)	NBT	The NSFI includes four key areas: (i) delivery channels and digital financial services, (ii) variety of financial products, (iii) protection of the rights of consumers of financial services, and (iv) financial literacy. It aims to ensure the stability of banking system, improve the financial literacy of population in the direction of using modern banking services, and thereby contribute to the development of national economy and financial inclusion of population.

SME = small and medium-sized enterprise.
( ) refers to the year when the program/initiative was launched.
Source: ADB Asia SME Monitor 2022. Data from National Bank of Tajikistan; State Committee on Investment and State Property Management of Tajikistan.

Table 7.7a: COVID-19 Emergency Measures

Name	Fund Size (TJS million)	Outline
1. Support program State Unitary Enterprise Industrial and Export Bank "Sanoatsodirotbank" (Entrepreneurship Support Fund) for SMEs	180	Provision of concessional loans to SMEs, of which 24% owned by women affected by the pandemic.
2. Enhanced support for business entities and measures to safeguard employment	n/a	1) Adopt the Law of the Republic of Tajikistan "On Amendments to the Law on the State Budget of the Republic of Tajikistan for 2020," which provides for a number of temporary incentives and benefits for vulnerable sectors of the economy. 2) Provide tax benefits to at least 40,000 eligible SMEs, of which 24% owned by women.
3. Monetary easing	271	1) The National Bank of Tajikistan reduced the policy interest rate from 12.75% to 11.75% in May 2020 and further to 10.75% in July 2020 to support the economy. 2) In April 2020, it slashed reserve requirements from 9% to 5% on US dollar accounts and from 3% to 1% on somoni accounts to the end of 2020, which increased liquidity by about 6.5%.
Grand Total	451	

SME = small, and medium-sized enterprise.

Source: ADB Asia SME Monitor 2022. Data from the Ministry of Finance and the National Bank of Tajikistan.

Country Review

Uzbekistan

Overview

Uzbekistan is the second most-developed country in Central Asia. It is one of two double-landlocked countries in the world, with a population of 34.2 million people. Uzbekistan shares its borders with all five Central Asian countries: Kazakhstan to the north; Tajikistan to the southeast; the Kyrgyz Republic to the northeast; Turkmenistan to the southwest; and a short border with Afghanistan to the south. Uzbekistan is rich in natural resources—including oil, gas, gold, and is the world's fifth-largest exporter and sixth-largest producer of cotton. Uzbekistan holds 74% of all condensed gas in Central Asia, 31% of its oil, 40% of natural gas, and 55% of coal deposits. Gross domestic product (GDP) grew by 7.4% in 2021. The inflation rate is below 10%. Export value increased by almost $1.3 billion compared to 2020, reaching $16.5 billion in 2021.

As of end-2021, 99.3% of existing businesses were micro and small enterprises (MSEs)—there is no category of medium-sized enterprises in Uzbekistan. The number of MSEs has grown by double digits since 2018 (12.6% growth in 2021). MSE development has accelerated since 2016, when the Acting President of the Republic of Uzbekistan, Shavkat Mirziyoyev, signed a decree on 5 October 2016 which said, "On additional measures to ensure the accelerated development of entrepreneurial activity, the comprehensive protection of private property and the qualitative improvement of the business climate." The document said the transition to a qualitatively new level of state policy would aim to strengthen legal protection of private property, create favorable conditions and all-round support for small businesses and private entrepreneurship, as well as increase the investment attractiveness of Uzbekistan.

MSEs generate about 10.0 million jobs, or 74.4% of all employees in 2021. Legally registered microenterprises and small enterprises accounted for just 15% of MSEs, with the remaining 85% informal private entrepreneurs. By sector, MSEs in agriculture, forestry, and fisheries provided the largest number of jobs (34.3% in 2021).

MSEs contributed 54.9% of GDP in 2021 (SUM374.4 trillion). The MSE contribution to GDP has changed significantly from 2004 to 2021. In 2004, the MSE share of GDP was 35.6%, increasing to 60.8% in 2010 and reached a maximum 66.8% in 2016. Since 2017, however, the MSE contribution to GDP has declined. Nearly half (47.3%) of MSE GDP came from agriculture in 2021, followed by manufacturing (11.5%), and trade, accommodation, and food services (10.6%).

Foreign trade grew by 16% and exceeded $42 billion in 2021. Exports amounted to $16.7 billion (up 10.3%) with imports of $25.5 billion (20.6%). Uzbekistan has trade relations with 182 countries, yet just small fraction of MSEs cater to foreign markets, with the majority operating in small, stable domestic markets.

The MSE credit market remains small. It accounts for 18.2% of bank loans and 8.1% of GDP. Interest subsidies are available to promote MSE access. Nonbank financial institutions (NBFIs), represented by microfinance institutions (MFIs), remain underdeveloped; unable to effectively compete with banks. Some small firms have issued bonds through the capital market.

The coronavirus disease (COVID-19) pandemic had a significant but short-lived dampening effect on the economy. Lockdowns had a severe impact on businesses and were a severe test of MSE resilience. Decisive and timely measures taken by the government mitigated much of the economic damage as the economy—and MSEs—shifted to the recovery stage. It allowed Uzbekistan to suffer much less than most economies around the world.

The Russian invasion of Ukraine seriously affected the economy and businesses in Uzbekistan. Deliveries of goods from the Russian Federation and Ukraine were reduced. There were difficulties moving goods in and out of the European Union (EU), with transportation costs several times higher than before. As the Russian Federation plays a key role in trade logistics, the impact on MSE operations is significant.

1. Impact of the Global Economy on MSEs

COVID-19 Impact

A few days after the World Health Organization labeled the COVID-19 outbreak a pandemic on 11 March 2020, Uzbekistan detected its first infection—a citizen returning from France tested positive. The government reacted quickly. International road and air transport were closed from 16 March, and rail connections from 19 March. On 27 March, Uzbekistan recorded its first death from COVID-19.

From 24 March, the government temporarily closed markets in Tashkent covering nonfood products, construction, automotive, household appliances, and shopping complexes, regardless of ownership. Only groceries, stores selling essential goods, and pharmacies retained their work permits. Catering outlets could only operate for takeout or delivery. Delivery services were upgraded. From 1 April, self-isolation was introduced in Tashkent, Nukus, and regional centers. And from 6 April, self-isolation became mandatory for all citizens; people could only leave home to go to work, shop at a nearby store or pharmacy, or visit a doctor. If caught outside without good reason, an administrative protocol was drawn up with a fine of up to SUM6.7 million (about $700) was levied (up to SUM11.1 million (about $1,167) for officials.

The pandemic caused significant but short-lived damage to the economy. Lockdowns had a severe impact on businesses, with MSEs most affected. The economic impact was mitigated due to decisive and timely measures taken by the government. Uzbekistan fared much better than most other countries. Economic growth remained positive. Although GDP growth decreased from 5.7% in 2019 to 1.9% in 2020, by 2021, it had recovered to 7.4%.

Among business sectors, tourism, trade, and food catering were most affected. They had to suspend activities, switch to a new work format, improve delivery services, and find new ways to maintain international relations. Also, many employees were either put on leave (mostly unpaid), or fired. There were wage cuts and additional payments for remaining state employees. MSEs worked or serviced most of these areas.

Tourism was one of the sectors hardest hit by the pandemic. Despite state support, it suffered heavy losses. An analysis of foreign visitors at the time shows dramatic changes over the past 2 years. There were 2.5 million tourists in 2017, rising to 5.3 million in 2018 and 6.7 million in 2019, before crashing to 1.5 million in 2020. By 2021, it had slightly recovered to 1.9 million. In terms of revenue, tourism brought in $1.0 billion in 2018 and $1.3 billion in 2019 before dropping to $261 million in 2020. Many travel companies restructured their operations in 2021 to adapt to the new reality.

Another sector of the economy struck by the pandemic was catering. On 19 March 2020, a resolution was adopted to temporarily suspend all catering activities in the country. During the pandemic, catering faced a collapse in revenue and radically reduced income, which threatened closure. Some catering establishments closed, but most changed formats to concentrate on delivery and takeout. Nonetheless, these were mostly survival tactics.

Trade has also suffered due to lockdowns and other restrictions. As incomes fell during the early stages of the pandemic, so did demand—for fruits and vegetables, clothing, and building materials, among others. Border closures had a huge impact on trade, particularly with major trading partners like the People's Republic of China (PRC) and the Russian Federation.

Least affected was agriculture. Here, production and wages remained relatively stable or increased (wages). Demand for agricultural products continued to support revenue earnings.

The major beneficiary during the pandemic was the information technology (IT) industry. Due to quarantine measures, cafés and restaurants switched to online e-commerce. Messenger bots were created to simplify home food delivery. Shops and bazaars also moved online. E-commerce, fintech, and the IT industry in general all benefited. And there was a sharp increase in demand for IT specialists. Other positive effects included the development of an electronic currency exchange, cashless payments, internet banking, and online shopping.

According to the State Statistics Committee, in January-June 2020, exports of fruits and vegetables reached 720,400 tons (down 3.9% from January-June 2019), worth $416.6 million (down 39.8%). This reflects lower prices in importing countries.

The Ministry of Employment and Labor Relations reported that most public agencies continued to work and thus saved jobs during the pandemic. At the same time, however, 55% of small businesses and 60% of microenterprises closed operations. The pandemic also affected the informal sector, which accounted for more than 7.8 million people, or about 57.9% of the labor force, as of February 2020. Informal work provides income for a large part of the population and is very vulnerable to economic shocks. In the first quarter of 2020, the unemployment rate was 9.5%, rising to 13.2% amid quarantine restrictions.

In April 2020, industrial production declined 28% compared with April 2019—services fell 39% and exports 23%. As of 20 April 2020, about half of all enterprise were not operating at full capacity—189,239 out of 380,211 firms.

Impact of the Russian Invasion of Ukraine

According to the State Committee on Statistics, in 2021 the Russian Federation replaced the PRC as Uzbekistan's top trading partner for the first time since 2016. Bilateral trade amounted to $7.51 billion: with Russian Federation imports worth $5.45 billion (up 31%) and exports $2.05 billion (up 39%). Food, oil products, timber, and other goods are imported, while the Russian Federation is the main buyer of Uzbekistan textiles.

In 2021, Ukraine ranked ninth of Uzbekistan's top 10 trading partners. Bilateral trade amounted to $704 million—with $231.6 million in exports (up 87%) and $472.4 million in import (up 49.6%). Ukraine exports medicines, semi-finished metal products, vegetable oil, confectioneries, sugar, and other goods, while it exports fruits and vegetables.

The Russian Federation is the leading foreign investor, accounting for more than $10 billion in investments. As of end-2021, Uzbekistan and the Russian Federation had more than 150 joint ventures, valued at about $14 billion. The number of enterprises using Russian capital increased by 2.5 times from 2017 to 2021 to more than 2,000.

The Russian Federation is also the main destination for Uzbekistan's migrant workers (more than 3 million). According to a World Bank report *Recovery COVID-19 Crisis Through Migration Lens, November 2021,* labor migrants were projected to remit $7.6 billion, or 11.6% of the country's GDP—highest among CIS countries.

The invasion and ensuing sanctions against the Russian Federation also posed problems with trade logistics in the EU, leading to huge increases in transportation costs (by a factor of 5). The Russian Federation plays a key role in EU export-import cargo logistics. Of Uzbekistan's total cargo turnover (66.9 billion tons-kilometer in 2020), some 70% travels through the Russian Federation territory. At the same time, Uzbekistan has been working for several years to increase use of southern routes for the supply of goods, as they offer faster and cheaper access to available seaports—Poti in Georgia and Bandar Abbas in Iran.

Since the beginning of 2022, over 3,000 foreign IT specialists have moved to Uzbekistan, according to the Technological Park of Software Products and Information Technologies in Tashkent. Starting 1 April 2022, special 3-year IT visas were made available for foreign IT specialists and their families.

Tourists from the the Russian Federation and Belarus have increased rapidly. The ban on Russian airlines and credit card use have seriously limited the number of Russian tourists traveling to the EU and other countries. Uzbekistan can still host tourists and open a bank card to those from the Russian Federation and Belarus. The Russian Federal Tourism Agency predicts an increase in the number of Russian tourists to Uzbekistan in 2022 to reach 700,000, 30% more than before the pandemic. Over the next 3-5 years, tourist flows could grow by a factor of four—up to 2 million people a year.

Given the sanctions against the Russian Federation and its need to open new markets, foreign trade between Uzbekistan and the Russian Federation is estimated to grow by 10%-12% by the end of 2022, to $8.3 billion-$8.5 billion.[231] Uzbekistan is also looking for new markets for its fruits and vegetables, building materials, and consumer goods. On 5 March 2022, for example, the Russian Federation canceled previously imposed restrictions and resumed imports of vegetable products from nine countries (including Uzbekistan).

There is no specific assessment of the impact of the Russian invasion of Ukraine on MSEs. But in general, a prolonged invasion will be mixed for Uzbekistan's MSEs—tourism and IT may benefit even as trade with the Russian Federation slows.

2. MSE Development

- As of end-2021, 99.3% of all enterprises were MSEs, or 462,834 firms. One-third operated in trade—with many of them women-led MSEs. Most were located in the heavily populated capital of Tashkent and the nearby Tashkent region.
- MSEs generated jobs for 10 million people, or 74.4% of the labor force in 2021. Agricultural MSEs held the largest share (34.3%).
- MSEs contributed SUM374.4 trillion to GDP in 2021, or 54.9% of country's total. Its share has declined gradually as the rest of the economy has grown faster. Nearly half (47.3%) was generated through agriculture.
- MSE exports reached $3.3 billion in 2021 (20.0% of total exports), up 7.6% from 2020. MSEs rely on imported goods and services for production and business operations, much of that from the Russian Federation. MSE imports in 2021 amounted to $11.5 billion (45.2% of total imports), up 5.4% from 2020.
- The government promotes digitalization—2020 was labeled the "digital economy development year"—with MSE exports expanding by increased use of digital trading platforms.
- There are several active business associations and various bodies supporting small businesses—such as the Chamber of Commerce and Industry, and the Business Women's Association. The government also supports MSE development and entrepreneurships through its special Fund.

[231] https://anhor.uz/economy/economy-uz/?ysclid=l8xevtcp9n778312515

Scale of MSEs

Businesses are classified based on the Decree of the Cabinet of Ministers of the Republic of Uzbekistan No.275 dated 24 August 2016. MSEs are classified by number of employees and by sector (Table 8.1). Microenterprises are defined as firms with up to 5 employees (annual average) for wholesale and retail trade, up to 10 employees for services (arts, entertainment, and recreation; transportation and storage; and accommodation and food services), and up to 20 for other services and industries (financial and insurance activities; education; agriculture; power supply; water supply; real estate; professional, scientific, and technical activities; support services; repair of motor vehicles and motorcycles; information and communications; health and social services; mining and quarrying; manufacturing; and construction).

Small enterprises are defined as those with (i) not more than 25 average annual employees for wholesale and retail trade and services (arts, entertainment, and recreation; financial and insurance activities; and education); (ii) not more than 50 employees for agriculture, infrastructure (power supply and water supply), and services (real estate; professional, scientific, and technical activities; and support services); (iii) not more than 100 employees for other services (transportation and storage; accommodation and food services; repair of motor vehicles and motorcycles; information and communications; and health and social services); and (iv) not more than 200 employees for industries (mining and quarrying; manufacturing, and construction).

There is no legally defined medium-sized enterprise category. Besides MSEs, there is a category for individual entrepreneurs, legally defined as "an individual who carries out entrepreneurial activities without forming a legal entity (individual entrepreneur). Individual entrepreneurship is carried out by an individual entrepreneur independently, without the right to hire employees, on the basis of property belonging to him on the basis of ownership, as well as by virtue of another real right that allows possession and (or) use of property."

As of end-2021, there were 462,834 active MSEs, or 99.3% of all firms excluding *dekhkan* (a family farm) and other farming enterprises (Figure 8.1A and Table 8.2).[232] MSEs have seen double-digit growth since 2018 (12.6% in 2021). By firm size, microenterprises account for 94.0% of all enterprises (437,844 firms), while small enterprises held a 5.4% share (24,990 firms). There were 98,886 newly registered MSEs as of end-2021. The largest number were in wholesale and retail trade (38,459 MSEs, or 38.9% of those registered), followed by industry (19,285 MSEs or 19.5%). The number in retail trade is growing, largely due to simplified procedures for opening a trading business.

The sector classification of MSEs has changed since 2013 (10 sectors until 2013 and nine sectors from 2014: Table 8.2). The largest number of MSEs in 2021 were in trade (33.8% or 156,539 MSEs), followed by industry (manufacturing) (19.5% or 90,313), agriculture (9.9% or 45,897), construction (9.4% or 43,410), accommodation and food services (7.1% or 32,948), transportation and storage (3.9% or 18,045), information and communications (2.2% or 10,247), health and social services (1.9% or 8,814), and others (12.2% or 56,621) (Figure 8.1B). The largest number of women-led MSEs were in trade (14,147 firms), followed by other services (10,057) and industry (5,543). Just 6.4% of MSEs in 2021 were women-led (29,747).

The capital Tashkent and nearby region accounted for 30% of MSEs in 2021, with 20.4% in the capital and 9.5% in the Tashkent region (Figure 8.1C). Other regions with MSEs include Samarkand (8.8%), Fergana (8.7%), and Andijan (7.6%). The Tashkent region had a population of 2.7 million as of 2021, the highest among all regions. Tashkent attracts most MSEs because of its market, infrastructure, and foreigner visitors. In 2021, Tashkent had the largest number of operating women-led MSEs (9,764 firms, or 11.3% of the region's total MSEs), followed by Tashkent region (4,760), Samarkand (2,974), and Navoi (2,544).

[232] A *dekhkan* farm is a small-scale family-owned farm that produces and sells agricultural products produced by family members. The land was provided to the head of the household and is inheritable.

A significant increase in MSE development began in 2016, when Acting President Shavkat Mirziyoyev signed a decree on 5 October 2016 "On additional measures to ensure the accelerated development of entrepreneurial activity, the comprehensive protection of private property and the qualitative improvement of the business climate." This began a transition to a qualitatively new state policy aimed at strengthening the legal protection of private property, creating favorable conditions and all-around support for small businesses and private entrepreneurs, as well as bolstering the investment climate. This was also specified in an Action Strategy for five priority areas covering 2017–2021.

Figure 8.1: Number of MSEs

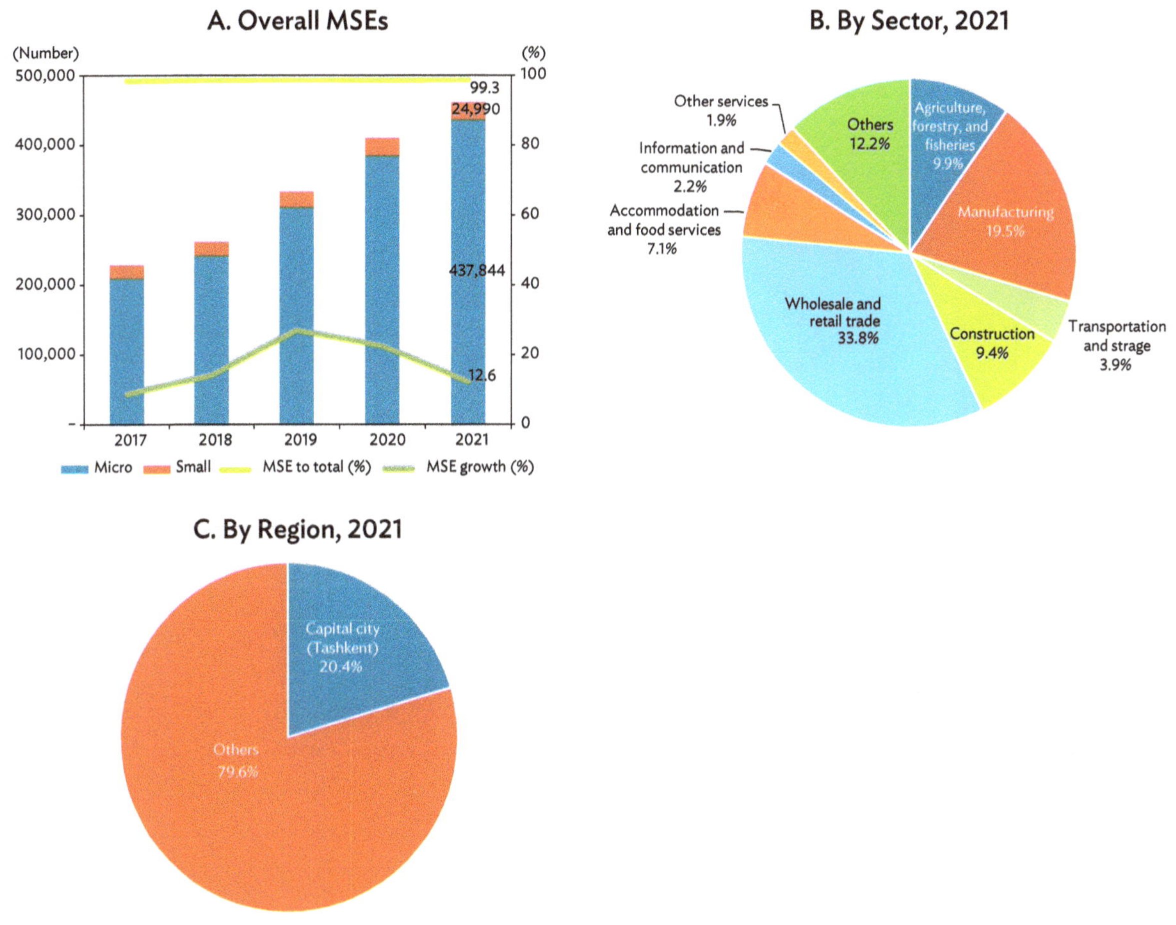

MSE = micro and small enterprise.

Source: ADB Asia SME Monitor 2022 database. Data from the State Committee on Statistics.

Employment

In 2004, MSEs generated jobs for about 6 million people, or 60.3% of the total workforce. It rose to 8.6 million people (74.3%) in 2010, and 10.0 million (74.4%) in 2021, 2.1% more than 2019 despite the pandemic impact (Figure 8.2A and Table 8.2). The overall labor force (MSME employees to total) increased 14.1% from 2004 to 2021, with MSE workers adding 4.1 million people. Legally registered MSEs were just 15% of the total with the remaining 85% unregistered private entrepreneurs (without creating a legal entity).

Agriculture absorbed the largest number of MSE jobs (34.3% of MSE workers in 2021), followed by wholesale and retail trade (14.6%), manufacturing (13.1%), construction (12.0%), other services (8.0%), transportation and communication (5.2%), and other sectors (12.8%) (Figure 8.2B). Female employees accounted for 41.4% of the total as of end-2020, down from 48.1% in 2004.

The government set a priority to increase quality jobs through the April 2021 Decree of the President of Uzbekistan No.PP-5094 "On the state program for creating new jobs and promoting employment of the population for 2021."

The program targets the creation of 457,127 new jobs and employment for 513,575 citizens by end-2021. The government provided financial assistance in 2021 through SUM92.3 billion in subsidies; an unemployed allowance of SUM65.1 billion; SUM40.6 billion for vocational training; and SUM125 billion for commercial bank microcredits for small job-creating projects.

Figure 8.2: Employment by MSEs

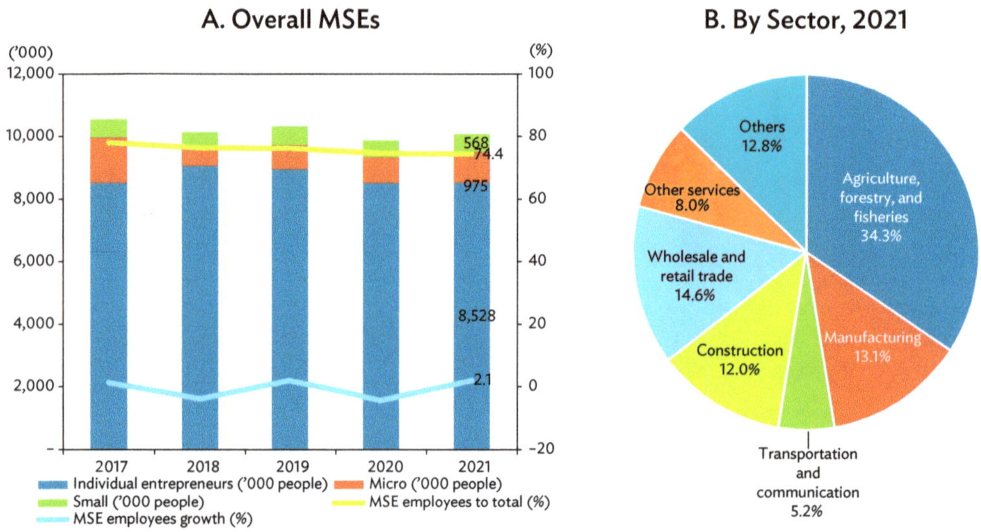

MSE = micro and small enterprise.

Source: ADB Asia SME Monitor 2022 database. Data from the State Committee on Statistics.

Business Productivity

MSEs added SUM374.4 trillion to GDP, contributing 54.9% of the total in 2021 (Figure 8.3A and Table 8.2). The MSE share of GDP changed significantly during 2004–2021. In 2004, its share of GDP was 35.6%, increasing to 60.8% in 2010, peaking at 66.8% in 2016. Since 2017, the share has dropped.

In 2021, nearly half (47.3%) of the MSE share was generated by agriculture, followed by manufacturing (11.5%); trade, accommodation, and food services (10.6%); construction (9.2%); transportation and storage, information and communications (6.7%); and other services (14.6%) (Figure 8.3B).

By region, the largest GDP share was in Jizzakh (81.2% of GDP in the region in 2021), followed by Surkhandarya (77.3%), and Bukhara (75.4%). The smallest MSE share of GDP was in Navoi (27.1%) and Tashkent (46.8%) regions, along with Tashkent city (48.1%). Once primarily an agricultural and raw material producer, the Jizzakh region has successfully become an industrial center with several firms operating in the automotive, textile, food, construction, leather and footwear, and chemical industries. The "Jizzakh" free economic zone offers special tax and customs benefits. For example, enterprises are exempt from all taxes and customs duties on imported equipment, raw materials, and components for production.

Less than 30% of MSEs (138,105) were profitable in 2021. Most were in trade (60,566 firms), followed services (32,408), manufacturing (24,043), and construction (17,324). Male-led small enterprises (121,746) earned net profits totaling SUM27,966 billion, while 16,359 women-led small enterprises earned SUM2,313 billion. Male-led small firms averaged SUM229.7 million in profits, while women-led small firms averaged just SUM141.4 million.

A government rural housing program (2016) helped small enterprises steadily grow as the volume of construction work increased. Aside from residential construction, small enterprises also built social infrastructure facilities, rural medical centers, educational institutions, and related services.

Figure 8.3: MSE Contribution to GDP

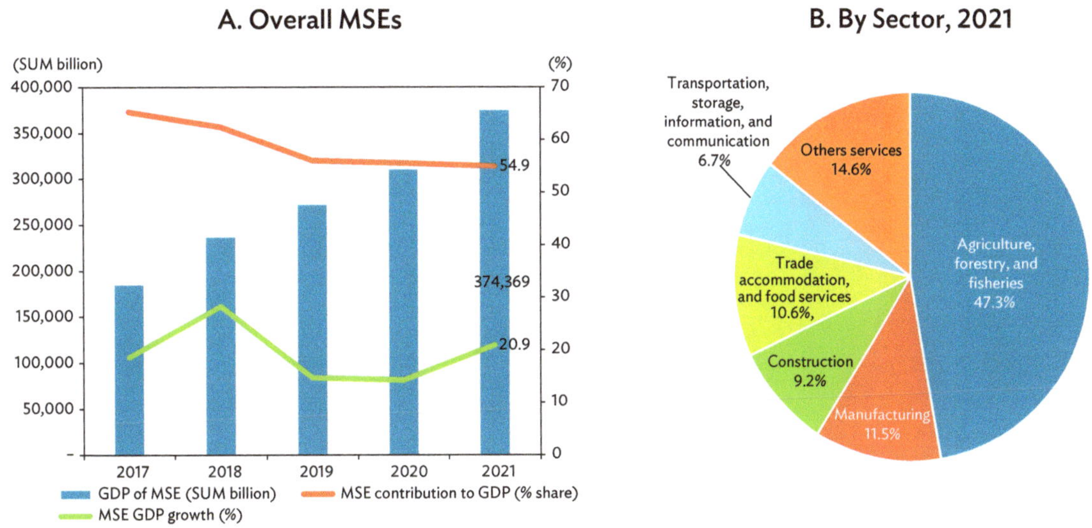

MSE = micro and small enterprise, GDP = gross domestic product.

Source: ADB Asia SME Monitor 2022 database. Data from the State Committee on Statistics.

Market Access

In 2021, Uzbekistan saw a V-shape recovery in international trade from the 2020 pandemic effects. Foreign trade turnover grew by 16% to over $42 billion. Exports were valued at $16,663 million (up 10.3%) with imports rising to $25,508 million (up 20.6%). Uzbekistan has trade relations with 182 countries worldwide. Only a few MSEs cater to foreign markets, with the majority catering to small, relatively stable domestic markets.

According to the State Committee on Statistics, MSE exports in 2021 amounted to $3.3 billion (20.0% of total exports), 7.6% above 2020 ($3.1 billion) (Figure 8.4A and Table 8.2). During pandemic-affected 2020, MSE exports were hit harder than non-MSE exporters, contracting 34.2% from 2019 as opposed to a 13.5% drop overall (Figure 8.4B). MSE exports recovered in 2021, but remain small. In 2004, MSE exports accounted for only 7.3% of exports. In 2011, its share jumped to 18.8%, a 58.5% increase from 2010, backed by government assistance under the State Program that declared 2011 the Year of Small Business and Private Entrepreneurship. The share of MSE exports peaked in 2018 at 27.2%, afterward it gradually decreased. Although details are unavailable, in 2021, the main overall export items were manufactured goods (26.1% of total exports), gold (24.7%), services (15.3%), and food products (8.3%).

MSEs largely rely on imported goods and services for production and business. MSE imports amounted to $11.5 billion in 2021, or 45.2% of all imports, up 5.4% from 2020 ($10.9 billion), when imports fell by 26.9% from 2019 due to the pandemic (Figure 8.4A). The share of MSE imports was 32.7% in 2004, growing steadily until 2019 (61.6%). MSE imports grew fastest in 2018 (45.3% higher than 2017). After the COVID-19 outbreak in 2020, however, the share of MSE imports has decreased. The main overall import items in 2021 were machinery and equipment (32.4% of all imports, but down 5.2% from 2020), manufactured goods (18.5%), chemical products (14.3%), food products (9.9%), and services (6.8%).

The Russian Federation displaced the PRC as top trading partner in 2021 with a 17.9% share of total trade, followed by the PRC (17.7%). The switch also occurred with MSE foreign trade.

Figure 8.4: MSE Exports and Imports

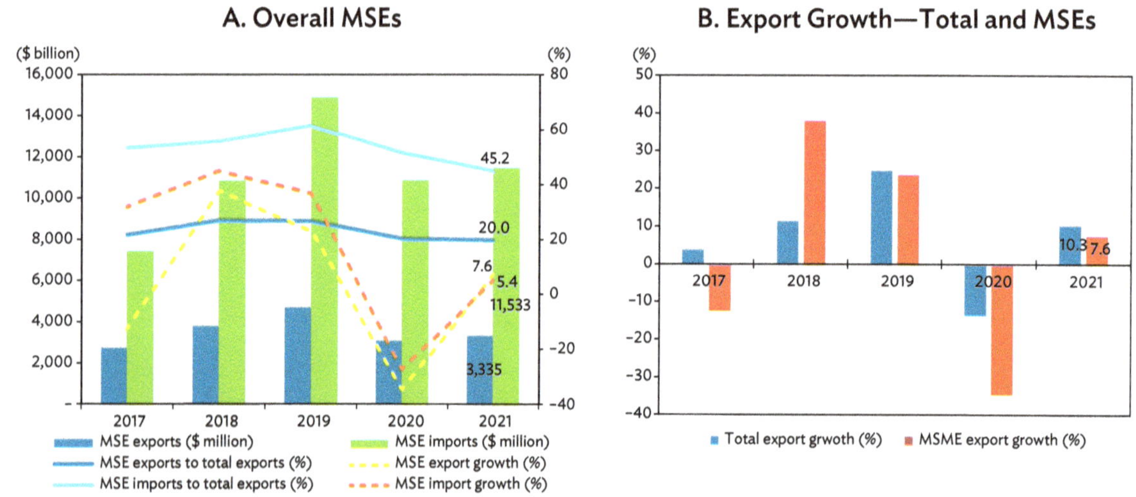

MSE = micro and small enterprise.

Source: ADB Asia SME Monitor 2022 database. Data from the State Committee on Statistics.

Technology and Innovation

Advances in technology drive economic growth, create new employment opportunities overall—especially for youth, women, and the socially vulnerable—and enable MSEs to expand market access, both domestic and global. The information and technology (IT) sector continues to grow rapidly, especially as demand accelerated during the pandemic. For the first time in Uzbekistan, virtual offices appeared as the ability to work remotely deepened, attracting young IT specialists from abroad.

More digital infrastructure and digital skills are needed. For example, digital trade is developing at a relatively slow pace, with 60% of new job openings requiring skills that only 20% of the population possess. Many businesses remain unprepared to digitize operations. To stimulate progress, a presidential decree was adopted under which IT companies are granted tax exemptions. While active support for IT firms began in 2017, a formal IT Park was established in Tashkent in 2019 to register and monitor IT companies along with offering facilities and consulting services.

A Cybernetics Innovation IT Park was added in 2021. Under the Ministry of Innovative Development, there are three Youth technoparks (Okhangaran, Andijan, and Samarkand), an Innovative Training and Production Technopark in Tashkent (a 1.94 hectare campus), and a Yashnabad Innovation technopark. These offer production sites, 3D modeling labs, office space, co-working centers, and conference rooms for events. The production sites are equipped with modern machine tools and prototyping equipment, such as laser cutting machines, 3D printers, rover equipment, welding equipment, hydraulic sheet presses, lathes, universal drilling machines, and universal milling machines.

MSEs are also digitizing, using international trading platforms to export products to countries both near and far, targeting CIS countries, the Middle East, Europe, and the United States (US). Improving connectivity and expanding internet use allow MSEs to partner with e-commerce firms and accelerate their use of technology. For example, the mobile operator Ucell in 2021 launched a pilot 5G communications system in central Tashkent.

The development of online payment systems is also gaining momentum. A 2018 presidential decree "On measures to evolve the national payment system" led to a National Interbank Processing Center and *Humo* payment system, which began operations in 2019. Payment systems such as PayMe, Click Evolution, and Apelsin were created later so people could easily pay their utility bills, internet subscriptions, mobile communications, and much more. The pandemic also accelerated the use of bots for ordering food, clothes and much more, the creation of a variety of applications—such as Express 24, Le Bazaar and others—that help the gradual shift to online payment formats.

Box 8.1: Startup Projects in Nanotechnology

Brothers Amir and Sultan Abidov from Tashkent created a unique startup related to nanotechnology. Their projects have already attracted interest in Israel; the Republic of Korea; Taipei,China; the Russian Federation, and other economies. It all started in their father's garage, where Sultan began experimenting while at university. Amir had studied at a university in the Republic of Korea and was preparing a dissertation on nanoparticles. He was interested in superhydrophobic (waterproof) coatings that protect metal from corrosion, and other materials from pollution, ice and moisture. His brother and then his friend Azamat Norkhozhaev joined in, and the three began using the garage for their first small discoveries, which led to three inventions, with patents pending.

Germ Killer CleanBox: CleanBox is something like a wooden box with special nanofilters installed inside. Fans drive air through the box, bursting bacteria and killing 99.99% of the germs. The device operates at room temperature. The young scientists won first place for their invention at the international exhibition Start Haifa 2018 in Israel. The plan is to install the filters in air conditioners to purify the air before circulation—as people get sick not because they sit under the air conditioner, but because of bacteria that multiply in a cold environment. Built-in nanofilters will solve this problem.

Lotus Tower Air Purifier: Another of their inventions is the Lotus Tower, an air purification tower. It could be either small or large. A small one is used to filter local places, for example, near a garbage dump. A large one can filter air on a city scale. The installation is designed so that it does not need any engines. Everything follows the laws of physics: cold and hot air flows into the tower from outside, rising through nanofilters and cleaned of many bacteria, including E.coli, and exit as purified air.

continued on next page

Box 8.1 continued

Nanopowder made in Uzbekistan: The third invention relates to how nanopowder is manufactured. The principle behind the powder's action—the premise the scientists used—is borrowed from nature and called the lotus effect. Thus the team named their project Lotus Engineering. The lotus grows in swamps, where there are many putrefactive bacteria. And its flower—so beautiful on the outside— is considered a symbol of beauty and purity. The surface of the flower, as seen under a microscope, is covered with tiny hairs, which are sufficiently strong and elastic to repel anything foreign that tries to interfere. Water just beads up and rolls off the petals without getting inside. This method formed the basis of their work of the "trinity"—they mimicked the coating. Their nanopowder is coated with the same materials used for camping tents. In medicine, they are used on bandages. Air, entering through the bandage, is cleared of bacteria, allowing the wound to heal faster. It is also possible to purify water from any oil spilled on it. Thus, the range of applications of the invention is very wide. The benefits for the economy are also considerable—it is possible to export the nanopowder itself and the materials or objects it processes. These technologies and products—Clean Box, Lotus Tower and others—are thus far unique worldwide.

Grants and Achievements: The Ministry of Innovative Development of the Republic of Uzbekistan allocated a grant of SUM850 million to the Lotus Engineering team for the development and promotion of their projects. Startup CleanBox, according to Skolkovo experts, is considered the most commercially attractive.

Source: https://uznews.uz/posts/15812.

Networking and Support

There are several active business associations and other groups supporting small businesses. One of the largest is the Chamber of Commerce and Industry of the Republic of Uzbekistan. Large enterprises and companies—including commercial banks and joint ventures—are members of the chamber. As of 1 June 2021, there were 25,481 business members including MSEs. The chamber's main goals are to create favorable conditions to develop entrepreneurship, improve the business climate, represent and protect the rights and legitimate interests of its members, and promote relationships between entrepreneurs and foreign partners. In 2018–2020, the chamber assisted 948 entrepreneurs in exporting products worth $356 million and 988 joint ventures with a total authorized capital of $791 million.

The chamber (i) helps entrepreneurs expand business contacts and relations with foreign partners, along with promoting exports; (ii) offers a wide range of services for entrepreneurs, including information support and consulting, organizing and publishing business catalogs, including information about domestic manufacturers; (iii) represents and protects the rights and legitimate interests of entrepreneurs, including relations with the government and other economic authorities; and (iv) supports education and skills development though training activities.

On 28 January 2020, the Chamber of Commerce and Industry and the Korea International Cooperation Agency signed an agreement in Tashkent on "Promoting the business incubation system in Uzbekistan." The $5.5 million project will help entrepreneurs implement their business projects based on the experience in the Republic of Korea. As part of the project, a business incubator will be created in Tashkent, where entrepreneurs can receive assistance from qualified specialists on implementing new business ideas.

With support from the World Bank, the chamber is implementing a project to create "Development of rural entrepreneurship in the Ferghana Valley" (2020). The $3 million project will create nine business incubators in nine districts of the Fergana, Andijan, and Namangan regions to expand economic opportunities and jobs by developing rural enterprises and entrepreneurship.

The Business Women's Association, established in 1991, expands and protects the economic and social rights of women, supports their entrepreneurial and social initiatives, and helps ensure their use of financial and information resources. The association has trained more than 50,000 women since 1991 in professional skills and 43,000 in business skills, 75% of whom have their own business.

Aside from private sector initiatives on business networking and support, several government institutions assist MSEs and entrepreneurs—such as the State Fund for Entrepreneurial Development Support. The fund provides financial support to small businesses in local and foreign currencies through commercial banks. It offers two types of financial assistance—guarantee and partial compensation of interest expenses. The fund aims to strengthen legal mechanisms for protecting and guaranteeing the activities of private entrepreneurships, introduce new tools for state support, expand access to credit, create new jobs, and further improve the financial and banking system. As of 1 July 2021, the fund provided financial support amounting to SUM12.4 trillion on loans totaling SUM58.8 billion for 38,161 projects.

Box 8.2: Entrepreneurs from Kashkadarya, Samarkand, and Jizzakh Receive Equipment for Production and Employment

To counter some of the economic damage caused by the pandemic, an Integrated Business Support program was launched in 2021—a joint project of the United Nations Development Programme and the Ministry of Employment and Labor Relations, in cooperation with the Chamber of Commerce and Industry. The project helps small enterprises improve competitiveness, efficiency and growth through technical assistance in business skills training and advisory support, along with equipment.

The program included 4 weeks of training and consulting services organized for entrepreneurs selected from a competition. It included personal coaching from Uzbekistan experts to solve individual business problems in strategic planning, marketing, and operational and financial management, among others. Program participants received equipment free of charge for implementing their projects.

From 13 to 15 June 2022, ceremonies were held in Karshi, Samarkand, and Jizzakh to hand over a second consignment of equipment. One of the beneficiaries from the Kashkadarya region, Mamayunus Allayerov, explained: "Having heard about the Integrated Business Support Program of UNDP and the Chamber, we applied for participation on behalf of the Karshi Training and Production Complex of the Society of the Blind of Uzbekistan. They successfully passed the selection, thanks to which they were able to take part in training, as well as receive free equipment for edging mattresses. With the receipt of the new equipment, we were able to employ an additional 10 people. We thank the organizers of the program for their support."

Entrepreneurs from these regions received 221 pieces of free equipment worth SUM2.2 billion. The initiatives in Kashkadarya, Samarkand, and Jizzakh are expected to create an additional 205 jobs—of which 131 are for women—with 278 youth learning modern professions and entrepreneurial skills—186 are for women. Additional grant funds for the initiative were provided by the Government of Japan.

Grants of SUM4.1 billion were provided to cover 478 pieces of equipment to 43 entrepreneurs from five regions (Samarkand 12 entrepreneurs, Jizzakh 7, Namangan 9, Fergana 9, and Kashkadarya 6) for agriculture, bakery products, garments, construction, waste processing, and information technology, among others. As a result, 398 new jobs were created, of which 267 are for women. About 715 young people (526 women) will learn modern professions and develop entrepreneurial skills.

Source: Chamber of Commerce and Industry of the Republic of Uzbekistan.

3. Access to Finance

- Due to the COVID-19 pandemic, MSE loans outstanding dropped by 12.7% in 2020. They recovered strongly in 2021 backed by government assistance, to SUM59.6 trillion, a 23.1% increase over 2020. Still, MSE bank credit remains small—18.2% of bank lending in 2021 and 8.1% of GDP.
- The government and central bank offer several incentives to assist MSEs borrow through soft loan programs and the State Entrepreneurship Support Fund, which offers a 50% partial guarantee and interest rate subsidy for MSE bank credit.
- The nonbank finance industry remains in its infancy, mostly through microfinance institutions and pawnshops. They partly support working capital for small firms, with high lending rates and nonperforming financing.
- Remote banking has expanded as digital payment infrastructure (*Humo*) grows and digital banks operate—more than 900,000 entities and individual enterprises use internet banking.
- The capital market remains at an early stage of development. There is no dedicated equity board for MSEs, but some small businesses raise funds by issuing bonds. Private venture funds have begun to finance startups.
- There are two credit bureaus: the Credit Information Analytical Center (KIAC) and CRIF Kredit-Axborot Xizmatlari (CRIF KAX). The information database holds consumer and corporate records, and acts as a collateral registry for loans. It remains weak, however, and needs to collect more information.

Bank Credit

Uzbekistan has a two-tier banking system; consisting of the (i) central bank and (ii) commercial banks. The Central Bank of Uzbekistan is a legal entity owned exclusively by the state. The law mandates the central bank's political and economic independence. Its primary task is to ensure macroeconomic stability and a sound banking system. The central bank creates the conditions for people and businesses to access loans, and use monetary policy instruments to ensure banks have adequate liquidity.

The second tier covers the 33 commercial banks operating in Uzbekistan (as of end-2021), of which 12 are state-owned, 16 privately owned, and 5 foreign-owned (Table 3). Their main task is to lend to industry, agriculture, housing construction, trade, and provide insurance and mortgages for business. Bank resources include initial capital, deposits and issued funds. Own funds—including equity and reserve capital and profits—covers about 10% of bank resources.

The state's share is highly concentrated, with 84% of all bank assets held by state-owned banks—64% are held by the National Bank, Asaka Bank, Promstroy Bank, Ipoteka Bank, and Agrobank. Despite their larger number, private banks hold just 16% of the market.

In 2011, Uzbekistan began to rapidly develop and prioritize entrepreneurship. It was declared the year of "Small Business and Entrepreneurship," emphasizing the provision of soft loans.

The bank credit market remained robust even during the pandemic. Loans outstanding increased 30.9% from SUM211.6 trillion in 2019 to SUM277.0 trillion in 2020, supported by government and central bank assistance. It expanded further in 2021, reaching SUM326.4 trillion, up 17.8% from 2020. There remains plenty of room to expand, however. Its share of GDP was 44.4% as of end-2021. Nonperforming loans (NPLs) have increased since 2017, sharply rising in 2021 with a gross NPL ratio of 5.2%

MSE loans outstanding dropped by 12.7% from SUM55.4 trillion in 2019 to SUM48.4 trillion in 2020. However, it recovered in 2021 backed by government subsidized loans, increasing by 23.1% to SUM59.6 trillion (Figure 8.5 and Table 8.3). MSE loans outstanding was highest in 2021, but the share of MSE loans to total loans was 18.2%, lower than the pre-pandemic period (26.2% in 2019). The MSE bank credit market in 2021 remained small at 8.1% of GDP.

Uzbekistan's national currency, the *sum*, has been freely convertible since 5 September 2017.[233] Legal entities and individuals can freely buy and sell foreign currency at market rates. Freeing up the market played a key role in economic reforms, helping create a better business climate for entrepreneurship, investment, export development, and increasing competitiveness.

Figure 8.5: MSE Loans

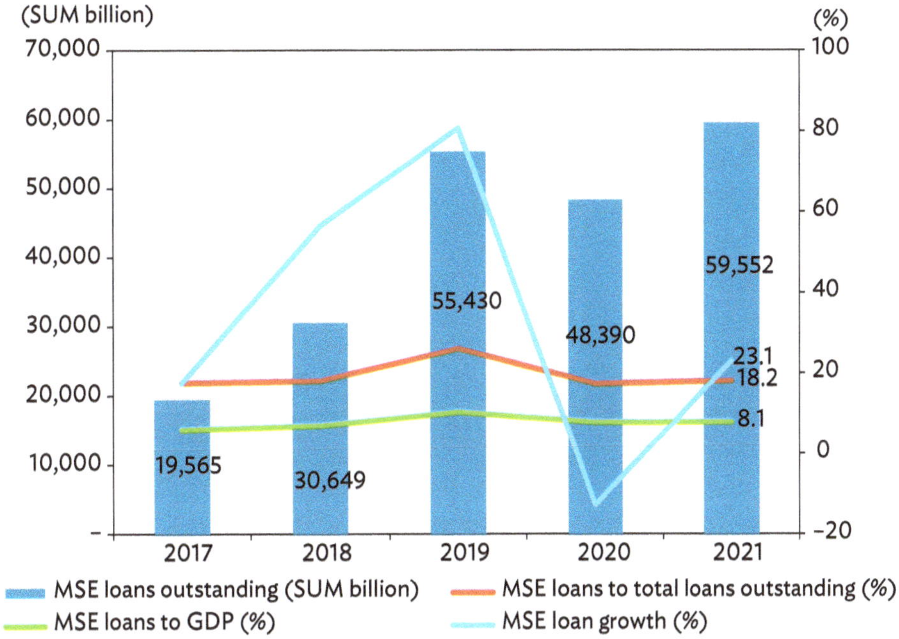

MSE = micro and small enterprise.

Source: ADB Asia SME Monitor 2022 database. Data from Central Bank of Uzbekistan.

Public Financing and Guarantees

a. Soft loan programs

The government and central bank offer several incentives to encourage lending to specific sectors or groups that have difficulty accessing credit. The government provides several loan schemes with interest subsidies. They vary considerably in terms of loan size, interest concessions, collateral requirements, tenure, credit guarantees, documentation requirements, and target groups.

One of the most popular is "Every family is an entrepreneur," a state program that supports initiatives for those wishing to engage in entrepreneurship (loans, practical assistance, onsite training, financial support for micro

233 Decree of the President of the Republic of Uzbekistan No.UP-5177 "On priority measures for the liberalization of foreign exchange policy" dated 2 September 2017.

enterprises, creating micro-clusters, developing family entrepreneurships, and company restoration, among many others). The interest rate on preferential loans was 15% until 1 January 2020 (central bank refinancing rate). Setting interest rates shifted to the discretion of banks starting 1 January 2021.

For loans issued at rates set independently by commercial banks—based on market principles—a compensatory mechanism is used for interest expenses. As of end-2021, only three banks provided preferential lending—Agrobank (SUM400 billion), Xalq Bank (SUM300 billion), and Microcreditbank (SUM300 billion). Loan amounts are set (i) up to SUM33 million for individuals opening a business based on the recommendation of the local mayor's assistant; (ii) up to SUM225 million for small businesses properly registered, based on the recommendation of the mayor's assistant, and guarantees from third parties and insurance policies; and (iii) over SUM225 million, following the recommendation of the mayor's assistant for lending to business investments based on the types of security required by law.

Under family business development programs during 2021, SUM3.6 trillion was allocated for concessional loans covering more than 148,000 projects. Of this, SUM648 billion (18%) went to legal entities and individual entrepreneurs, with SUM2.9 trillion (82%) allocated to self-employed individuals. The main criteria are to provide additional income sources for the population and the creation of new jobs. The "Every family is an entrepreneur" program accounts for 84% (SUM3.0 trillion), with the remaining 16% (SUM576.2 billion) for other programs. SUM1.6 trillion of these funds went to develop women entrepreneurship, and SUM1.6 trillion for developing young entrepreneurs.

In April 2022, the government launched a large-scale concessional lending program for small businesses by providing commercial banks a credit line of $300 million, allocated out of the Fund for Reconstruction and Development. Commercial banks would provide loans to implement projects for the production and provision of services up to SUM5 billion for up to 5 years, including a grace period of up to 2 years, at a rate of 14% per annum. Loans would be allocated to businesses:

- up to 6 months in amounts up to SUM1 billion,
- from 6 months to 1 year up to SUM2 billion,
- from 1 to 2 years up to SUM3 billion,
- from 2 to 3 years up to SUM4 billion, and
- more than years up to SUM5 billion.

b. Special funds

There are several public funds that support small businesses. The State Fund for Entrepreneurship Support, for example, provides financial support to small businesses in national and foreign currency through commercial banks. The fund offers two types of financial assistance—guarantees and partial compensation of interest expenses. It strengthens the legal mechanisms for protecting and guaranteeing activities of private entrepreneurship, introduces new tools for state support, expands access of businesses to credit resources, creates new jobs, and further develops the financial and banking system. As of 1 July 2021, the Fund provided loans to enterprises amounting to SUM12.4 trillion for 38,161 projects.

The State Fund for Entrepreneurship Support compensates small businesses for part of the interest on loans and leasing agreements, as well as loan guarantees. Loan guarantees from commercial banks cover up to 50% of the loan amount but (i) not more than 100 times the base amount for implementing the initiative supporting vulnerable segments of the population, and (ii) not more than SUM8 billion.

c. State MSE finance programs through commercial banks

As part of state programs, several banks directly support MSEs—such as Agrobank, Halkbank, and Mikrokreditbank. These commercial banks offer 45% of total MSE financing. Mikrokreditbank is one of the leading financial institutions for small business development. It allocates loans at reduced interest rates, and can be tapped online through the "oila kredit.uz" platform. Loans are mainly allocated to low-income families, the unemployed, or people from regions to support entrepreneurs expand their business. The interest rate is 14% for a 3-year maturity, sometimes amended to 7 years. The maximum loan amount for individuals is SUM33 million and SUM224 million for legal entities. Mikrokreditbank covers all sectors, industry, agriculture, and trade, but most are in agriculture and industry. Industry includes sewing workshops, food production, and small textile enterprises. It has more than 70 branches and 60 central banking offices.

By 2021, there were nine state funds fully allocated, with 7,278 newly approved subsidized loans. A total of 7,250 MSEs (71.8%) received subsidized loans amounting to SUM667 billion. Outstanding subsidized loans to MSEs amounted to SUM625 billion as of end-2021 (Figure 8.6 and Table 8.4).

Figure 8.6: Public Financing—Subsidized Loans

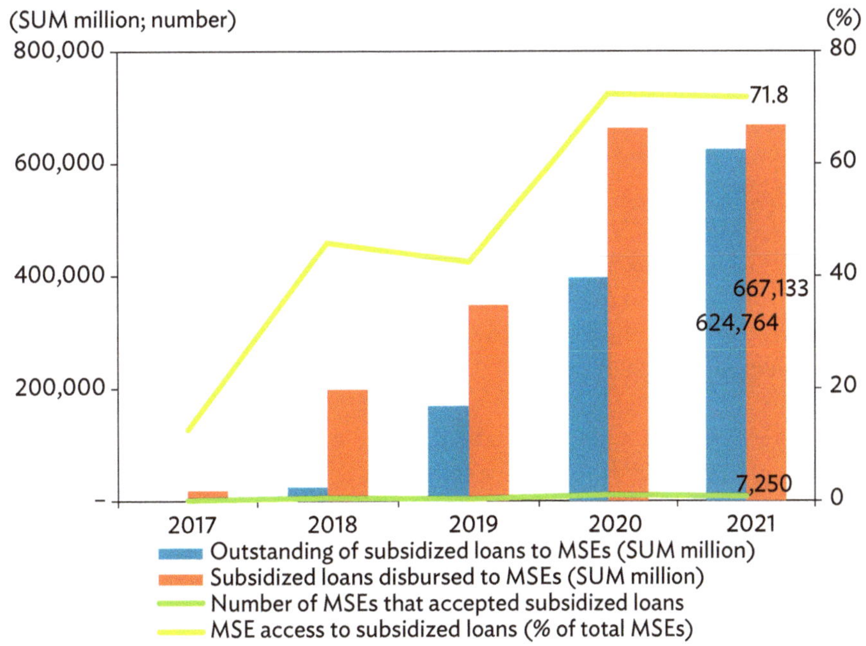

MSE = micro and small enterprise.

Source: ADB Asia SME Monitor 2022 database. Data from Central Bank of Uzbekistan.

Nonbank Financing

Nonbank finance institutions (NBFIs) include (i) microfinance institutions (MFIs) with minimum authorized capital of SUM2 billion; (ii) pawnshops engaged in issuing short-term microloans to individuals using movable property as collateral, with minimum authorized capital of SUM500 million; and (iii) mortgage refinancing entities that raise funds for refinancing mortgages, with minimum authorized capital of SUM25 billion.[234]

234 Law of the Republic of Uzbekistan, No.ZRU-765 "On non-bank credit organizations and microfinance activities" dated 20 April 2022.

NBFIs are regulated and supervised by the central bank. As of end-2021, 69 microfinance institutions and 73 pawnshops serviced 112,382 and 69,483 borrowers, respectively (Figure 8.7A and Table 8.5). Demand is high with borrowers constantly increasing: it expanded 6.2 times from 2014 (17,973) for MFIs and 1.6 times from 2014 (43,474) for pawnshops. As of June 2022, registered NBFIs totaled 150 institutions—72 MFIs, 77 pawnshops, and 1 mortgage refinancing organization.

The central bank licenses NBFIs. Their resources include their own funds, bank loans, grants, and borrowed funds from heir shareholders. MFIs and mortgage refinancing organizations derive resources from

- funds from corporate bond placements;
- funds from the state budget and state funds;
- loans from international financial institutions, foreign government financial organizations, and nongovernment nonprofit organizations (can be foreign);
- loans from legal entities, including foreign;
- funds from the placement of securities corresponding to Islamic finance (for MFIs); and
- funds from the placement of mortgage-backed securities (for mortgage refinancing organizations).

MFIs can provide microcredits or microloans; loans and guarantees, render Islamic finance services to individuals in an amount not exceeding the amount of a microloan; purvey leasing and guarantees, factoring services and Islamic financing services to businesses in an amount not exceeding the amount of a microcredit; and provide of other types of microfinance services, including consumer loans. The maximum amount is SUM50 million for a microloan, SUM300 million for microcredit, and SUM600 million for micro leasing. The interest rate on microcredits varies from 40% to 60% per annum. Almost all microcredits require collateral, most often jewelry and vehicles.

Most MFIs are in Tashkent (27) and the Fergana region (18) as of June 2022. Their total assets amounted to SUM1.6 trillion, with capital of SUM798 billion (up 41.2% compared with June 2021) and SUM404 billion in authorized capital. Liabilities amounted to SUM771.3 billion, of which 89% were loans and leasing payables. The ratio of liabilities to equity was 0.97, indicating a low debt burden.

As of end-2021, MFI loans outstanding reached SUM1.2 trillion, a 43.3% increase from 2020 (Figure 8.7B). Over 2014–2021, the amount of loans issued increased significantly: up 25 times in 2021 from SUM46 billion in 2014. The MFI lending market remains small; its loans outstanding accounted for just 0.2% of GDP. The annual lending rate was quite high—over 65% as of end-2021. NPLs increased sharply in 2020 due to the pandemic, with an NPL ratio of 17.8%—it fell dramatically to 4.6% in 2021, but still above the pre-pandemic period (2.7% in 2019). MFI clients grew to reach 112,382 as of end-2021. As of June 2022, the total portfolio of loans and micro leasing issued by the 72 MFIs increased to SUM1.4 trillion, an increase of 64.1% compared to June 2021. There remains significant unmet demand for microfinance services among the public and businesses including MSEs.

Pawnshop financing is a small fraction of the NBFI total, though it helps small businesses obtain working capital. As of June 2022, most pawnshops were in Tashkent city (41), the Tashkent region (10), and Bukhara region (7). Total assets amounted to SUM237 billion, with total capital of SUM213 billion (39.4% more than June 2021), including authorized capital of SUM72 billion. Liabilities amounted to SUM24 billion, of which SUM15 billion or 63.2% came from loans and leasing payables.

In 2021, pawnshop financing outstanding amounted to SUM176 billion, a 39.7% increase from 2020 (Figure 8.7C). It expanded more than 7 times from 2014 (SUM23.9 billion). Nonperforming financing was high (and rising) at 33.9% of the total as of end-2021. As of June 2022, the total financing portfolio of 77 pawnshops was SUM198 billion, up 30.3% compared to June 2021. This also shows a growing demand for pawnshop financing.

Figure 8.7: Nonbank Finance

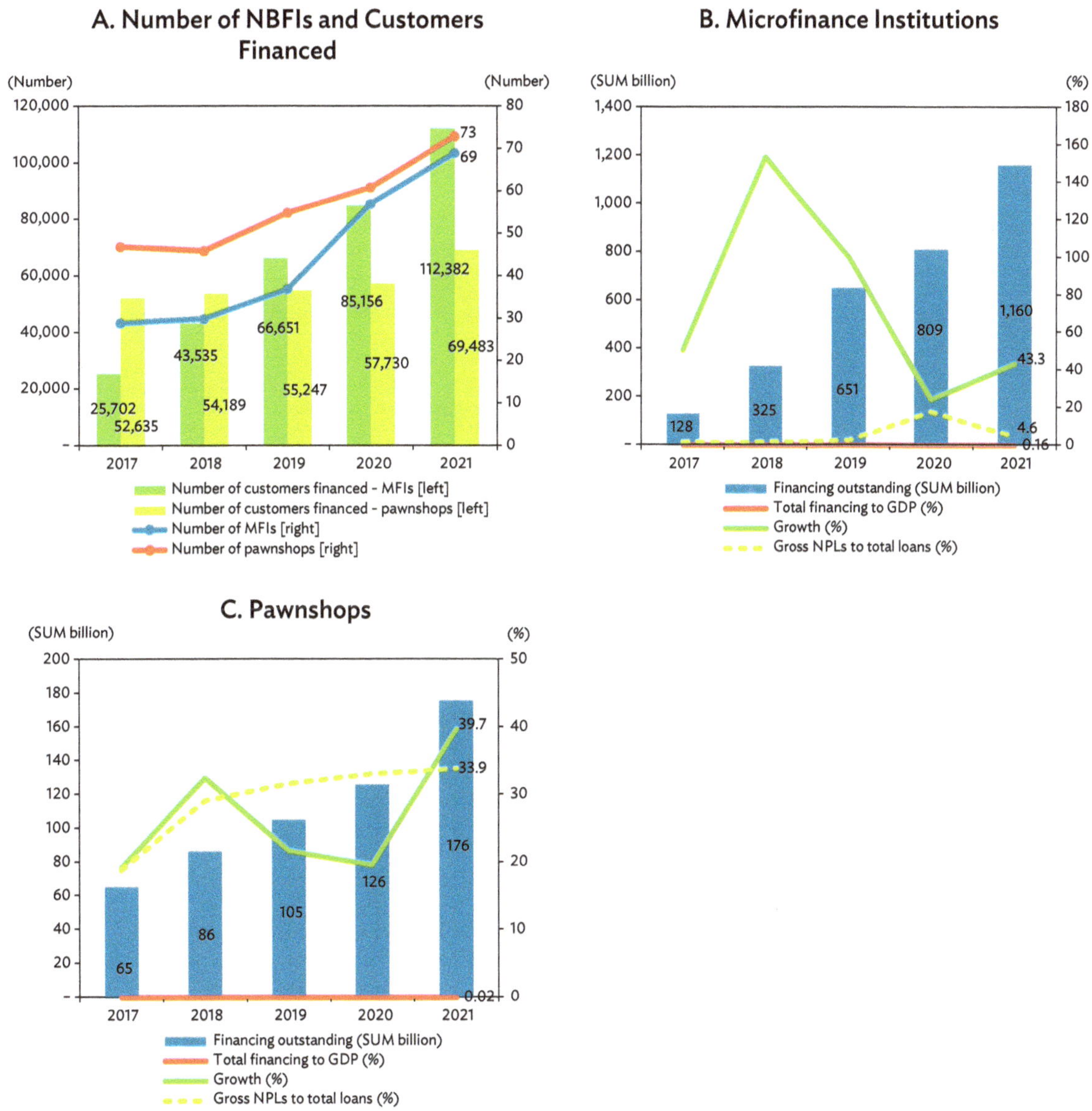

GDP = gross domestic product, NBFI = nonbank finance institution, MFI = microfinance institution, NPL = nonperforming loan.

Source: ADB Asia SME Monitor 2022 database. Data from Central Bank of Uzbekistan.

Digital Financial Services

Uzbekistan is taking comprehensive measures to embrace a more digital economy, including the widespread introduction of modern information and communication technology (ICT) in public administration, education, healthcare, and agriculture. There are currently over 220 priority projects underway to improve e-government, further develop the domestic market for software products and ICT, to set up IT parks in all regions of the country, and to attract or train qualified personnel.[235]

According to the central bank, as of January 2022, there were more than 20 million users of remote banking services, of which more than 19 million were individuals, with more than 900,000 businesses or individual enterprises (Figure 8.8). Since 2018, effective steps have been taken to radically improve interactions between commercial banks, businesses, and the general public by introducing remote banking services via the internet and mobile banking.

The Law of the Republic of Uzbekistan "On payments and payment systems" dated 1 November 2019 promotes infrastructure for e-payment service operators. There were 28 payment firms specializing providing digital financial services registered as of March 2021. For contactless payments, the *Humo* retail payment system was created, fully complying with international standards, which has created a competitive environment for bank card transactions.

Figure 8.8: Internet Banking

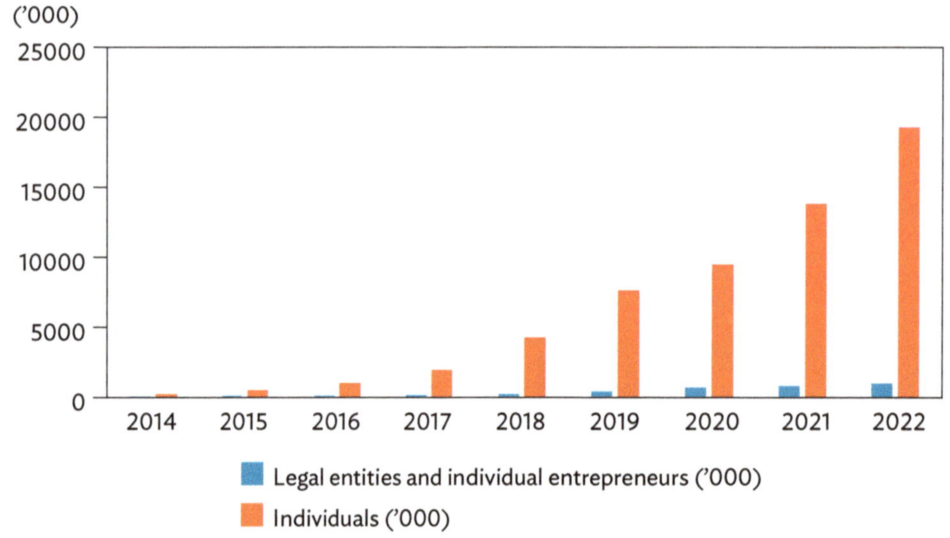

Source: ADB Asia SME Monitor 2022 database. Data from Central Bank of Uzbekistan

In 2020, the central bank launched a quick response (QR)-online instant payment information system that allows customers to make payments for goods and services using funds on a bank card without directly using the card or a payment terminal. People can apply to a commercial bank to receive a QR code generated based on existing bank details, while buyers get the opportunity to pay for goods and services by scanning the code using their mobile applications. As of July 2021, there were 74,117 registered QR-online customers making transactions worth more than SUM3 billion.

235 Decree of the President of the Republic of Uzbekistan, No.UP-6079 "On approval of the Digital Uzbekistan-2030 strategy and measures for its effective implementation," dated 5 October 2020.

Many banks have developed their own mobile applications, which people use to carry out real-time person-to-person (P2P) transfers from card to card, make budgetary and utility payments, receive and repay microloans, make online deposits, open remote deposit and loan accounts, access an international bank card account, and perform online conversion operations.

Enterprises and organizations can manage their bank account funds in real time, make payments, apply electronically to purchase (convert) foreign currency from a servicing bank, provide the bank an electronic statement for transferring monthly wages or equivalent payments, and use other services. For the first half of 2021, customers—using mobile banking applications—managed their online deposit transactions (worth SUM6.7 trillion), online currency conversions (SUM3.6 trillion), obtained online microloans (SUM1.5 trillion), repaid loans (SUM400 billion), and made other payments for utilities, communications, and others (SUM400 billion).

Uzbekistan is developing the infrastructure for *Uzcard* and *Humo* retail payment systems that service bank cards, as well as services provided within payment systems. As of July 2021, there were 23.7 million bank cards in circulation. ATMs and info kiosks installed in public places increased by 1,194 compared to the same period in 2020, totaling 12,298, while the number of payment terminals used by businesses increased by 8,375 to 438,000. For the first half of 2021, SUM95.5 trillion were transferred to bank cards, 20% more than the same period in 2020. Transactions carried out using payment terminals increased by 15% to SUM49.8 trillion, with the amount transacted through ATMs rising to SUM29.3 trillion.

In 2020, Anorbank (domestic) and TBC Bank (foreign) were registered as digital banks. A new digital bank, Bank Apelsin, was registered in Tashkent in November 2021. Anorbank, TBC Bank, and Apelsin Bank offer a full range of digital services through mobile applications or personal computers. Clients‘ mobile applications allow high flexibility in banking operations using high-tech IT infrastructure.

On 16 June 2020, the Humans international group of companies opened the first version of its mobile application in Uzbekistan. The fintech platform combines the services of a virtual mobile operator, a financial service, a showcase for goods and services, and a cashback system from each purchase. The application allows the customer to control money quickly and conveniently in one click. The customer controls expenses on both the Humans card and on other cards. The application allows customers to pay for any service or product, restaurant bill, mobile phone, and groceries. When paying for Humans partner services, it offers the user with a cashback (return of part of the cost of services to the account).

The Finextra Group has become a bridge to the global financial product ecosystem. Fenestra, an international productivity management platform, has an office in the IT PARK and partners with some of the world's fintech leaders such as Finestra and Neoflex. Finextra provides modern software solutions following central bank requirements. With an extensive global network and local knowledge, Finextra offers solutions for banks of all types and any size, in trade finance, risk management, treasury products, and Islamic finance.

The development of digital financial services has had a significant impact on the business operations of MSEs. Entrepreneurs can take advantage of digital financial services when conducting various transactions such as contract payments, loan repayments, currency conversion, and other transactions without visiting the bank. This was especially useful for entrepreneurs operating in remote areas where there are no bank branches.

In September 2020, the Instant Payment System offered a way to transfer budget and tax payments to the Treasury of the Ministry of Finance, as well as making payments from loan accounts 24/7. As a result, for the first half of 2021, 5.4 million transactions worth SUM127 trillion were carried out through the Instant Payment System, of which more than 724,000 payments were made to the state budget in the amount of SUM4.3 trillion.

Capital Markets

Uzbekistan's capital market remains at an early stage of the development. The Capital Market Development Agency, established in April 2019, was responsible for the regulation, control, and development of the capital market. However, in 2021, a Presidential Decree No.PP-5073 "On measures to further improve the capital market regulation system" dated 13 April 2021 directed that all tasks, functions, and powers of the agency were transferred to the Ministry of Finance. A Department for the Development of the Capital Market was established, responsible for capital market operations.

The Republican Stock Exchange "Tashkent" (Tashkent Stock Exchange) is the major securities trading platform and only corporate securities exchange in Uzbekistan. It was established in April 1994, founded by the government as an open joint stock company, located in Tashkent (Decree of the President of the Republic of Uzbekistan No.745 "On measures to further deepen economic reforms, ensure the protection of private property and evolve entrepreneurship" dated 21 January 1994).

There is no dedicated equity board under the stock exchange, but SMEs can tap the bond market, traded on the stock exchange. At the end of 2021, the trading value and number of transactions doubled compared with 2020—value increased from SUM 578 billion in 2020 to SUM1.3 trillion in 2021, while volume grew from 35,000 to about 73,000. Also, funds raised through bond issuance also increased in 2021—to SUM113.4 billion from SUM64.3 billion in 2020.

The Tashkent Stock Exchange had 139 companies listed on its main board as of end-2021, with a market capitalization of SUM59.2 trillion (Figure8. 9A and Table 8.6). The largest number of transactions were in banking stocks (51% of all listed companies) and construction (25%) (Figure 8.9B). As of June 2022, there were just over 600 registered joint-stock companies, with about 100 listed on the exchange. About 170 financial instruments (equities, bonds) are traded on the stock exchange (about 20 are actively traded), with more than 40 brokers registered as members of the exchange.

About 80% of share capital is state-owned. Thus, privatization is part of the 2021 capital market development strategy. As this happens, trading volumes are expected to rise, as new higher-tech listing and trading methods are adopted. Once in place, qualified MSEs should be able to tap these markets as a much-needed alternative source of growth finance. Many SMEs operate on Islamic principles, meaning they cannot avail of interest-bearing financing using banks or bonds. With Islam the main religion in Uzbekistan, some MSEs would prefer a more developed Islamic finance system.

A UzVC National Venture Fund was established as a limited liability company—with initial authorized capital of SUM15 billion—to support innovative ideas and startups.[236] For example, a National Venture Fund, together with the British company Sturgeon Capital, financed the TASS Vision startup for $100,000 in June 2022.

[236] Resolution of the Cabinet of Ministers No.684 "On measures to organize the activities of the National Venture Fund "UzVC" dated 3 November 2020.

There are two private venture funds—Semurg Ventures and Uzcard Ventures:

- Semurg Ventures—SUM6 billion in authorized capital—combines a venture fund that focuses on the CIS market and Venture Builder, which creates and helps grow technology startups. For example, in September 2021 Semurg Ventures invested $120,000 in Micros24, a young startup company that is creating a multibank module to replace internet banking.
- UZCARD Ventures—$1 million in authorized capital—invests in technological startups and growth firms in science and technology. In May 2022, the fund invested $550,000 in eight Startup Bridge program firms.

Capital market development is hampered by the low level of financial literacy, a complex legal frameworfk, lack of institutional investors, the large share of state joint-stock companies, as well as an insufficient number of tools to protect shareholder interests.

Figure 8.9: Equity Market

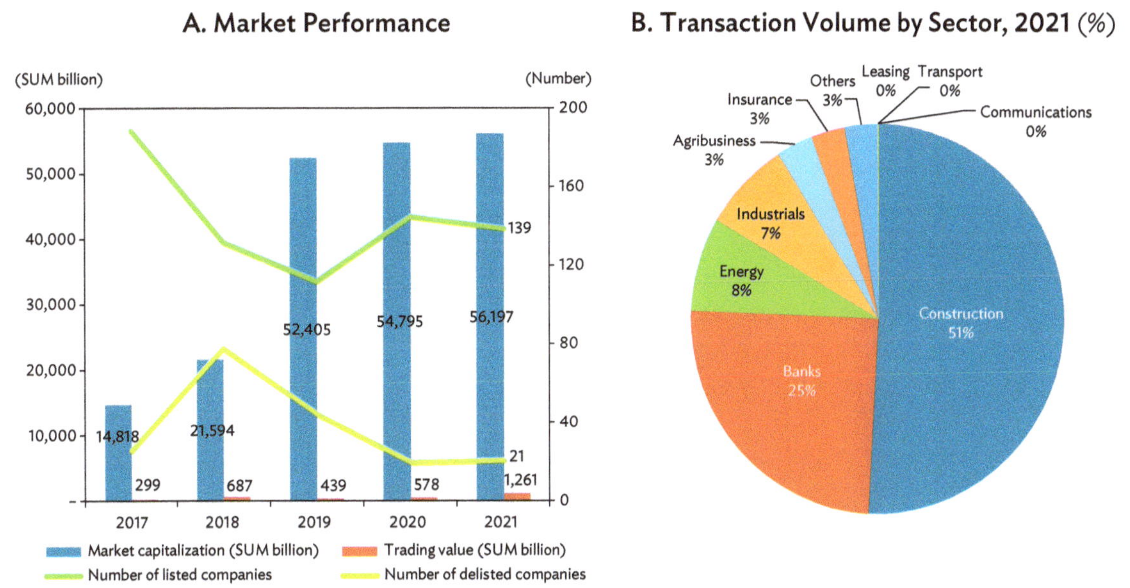

Source: ADB Asia SME Monitor 2022 database. Data from Stock Exchange Tashkent.

Financial Infrastructure

The Law of the Republic of Uzbekistan No.301 "On the exchange of credit information" dated 4 October 2011 defines a credit bureau in a way to ensure data security and bank secrecy. To do this, IT is used to protect against unauthorized use by third parties. But this has been difficult as the credit system relies only on wages and information from tax services, limiting its ability to properly create a credit scoring system. The two credit bureaus in Uzbekistan are KIAC and CRIF KAX.

Another decree adopted a proposal of the central bank, Association of Banks of Uzbekistan, and commercial banks to establish, a society based on the Interbank Credit Bureau called the "Credit Information Analytical Center."[237]

In 2016, within the framework of the central bank's Action Plan, the Association of Banks of Uzbekistan (ABU), and the World Bank Group's International Finance Corporation (IFC), an international competition was held to choose a foreign partner to join the local credit bureau. The Italian global credit company CRIF bought 35% of the Credit Information Analytical Center in May 2018.[238] As of January 2019, the credit bureau database contained credit information on more than 9,135 individuals and 685,006 businesses.

Uzbekistan also joined the IFC's Azerbaijan and Central Asia Financial Infrastructure Project (ACAFI)—in cooperation with the Government of Switzerland—to improve access to finance for individuals, MSEs, and medium-sized enterprises developing an efficient, reliable credit reporting and secured transactions system.

CRIF KAX was founded in May 2020 in Tashkent with six local commercial banks joining CRIF as shareholders—Uzbek Industrial and Construction Bank, Asia Alliance Bank, Invest Finance Bank, Ipak Yuli Bank, Ipoteka-Bank, and Hamkorbank. CRIF KAX supports banks, financial institutions, and lenders work with clients on acquisitions, portfolio management, and collections. Its platform allows lenders to share customer credit information uploaded to the system, providing information on a client's credit history as collected from lenders. Any data lacking can be requested from the tax committee.

As of May 2022, CRIF KAX had a database of 2 million businesses and individuals. It remains at an early stage of information gathering, as IT companies and specialists continue to upgrade database software for commercial banks and MFIs. Most creditors (MFIs, commercial banks, and pawnshops) remain unable to efficiently upload needed information on the data exchange.

The pledge registry is an information database containing records of the rights of creditors to debtor collateral and disposal.[239] An agreement is made with each legal entity or individual applicant—and for using it in real time—providing them with consulting services on how the registry works. Each entry has its own taxpayer-debtor identification number or unique registration number.

In 2021, a scoring system was set up with banks through Wings Partners—one of Asia's largest scoring companies—in cooperation with Asakabank, TBC Bank, Tenge Bank, and Anorbank. The scoring system helps banks significantly reduce the risk of loan defaults. The scoring system independently connects all the required information sources on a borrower's credit history, and income to quickly and accurately assess creditworthiness. Banks using the system have already been able to reduce the time for loan approvals from several days to several minutes.

237 Decree of the Cabinet of Ministers of the Republic of Uzbekistan No.74 "On measures to implement the Law of the Republic of Uzbekistan on the exchange of credit information" dated 17 March 2012.

238 CRIF is a global company specializing in credit and business information systems, analytics, outsourcing and processing services, as well as advanced digital solutions for business development and open banking.

239 Law of the Republic of Uzbekistan No.ZRU-356 "On Pledge Registry" dated 23 October 2013.

4. Policies and Regulations

- Several government initiatives support MSE development. The strategy for five priority areas of development for 2017–2021 includes development of MSEs and private entrepreneurship, including women-led rural MSEs.
- Barriers to MSE development include government intervention, taxation, limited access to finance, and the need for a better investment climate.
- Banking reforms are ongoing through 2025, including privatizing state-owned shares in banks and increasing the quality of financial services for small businesses.
- The National Financial Inclusion Strategy for 2021–2023 targets expanded banking services through agent banks, more developed digital financial services and alternative financing, strengthened consumer protection, and increased financial literacy.
- The government launched several emergency assistance programs to individuals and businesses affected by the COVID-19 pandemic—such as an Anti-Crisis Fund including tax relief and debt deferrals.
- Since February 2022, the government has begun implementing several measures to rescue businesses affected by the Russian invasion of Ukraine, such as diversifying export markets and supply chains, and offering financial support through concessional loans.

MSME Development

Several government initiatives support MSE development (Table 8.7).[240] They set medium-term priority areas for government policies, with one of its main goals boosting small business and private entrepreneurship. So far, about 2,000 laws, decrees, and resolutions have been adopted to support small business development. Particular attention was paid to ensuring legal protection, eliminating numerous administrative barriers for business, and limiting government agencies' interference in business activities. The government cancelled 114 licenses and permits, and a notification procedure was introduced for 33 types of activities. Procedures for obtaining permits were simplified, in many cases reducing approval times by half. Other transactions were also simplified, with restrictions associated with the circulation of cash, currency, and raw materials lifted. The reforms appear to be working. For example, in the World Bank's former Doing Business survey, Uzbekistan rose from 138th to 69th place in the rankings. The measures taken were aimed at improving the legal framework and regulatory procedures in doing business, creating a favorable business climate and create a more positive international image of the country.

A presidential decree dated 8 April 2022 "On the next reforms to create conditions for stable economic growth by improving the business environment and developing the private sector," aims to improve the investment climate and accelerate privatization by making it easier to buy state-owned assets. In general, it promotes private sector development across all economic sectors.

On 28 January 2022, President of Uzbekistan signed a decree "On the Development Strategy of New Uzbekistan for 2022–2026." The strategy targets a reduction in tax revenues to 25% of GDP; $120 billion in new investments; advance a general resettlement scheme; replace dilapidated housing with "modern" housing estates through renovation and the resettlement of 275,000 families; and reduce inflation to 5% by 2023. About 200 companies will be selected through open competition to become the country's primary exporters. Free trade zones would be built in border areas. The private sector's share of GDP is targeted to increase to 80%. About 200 new industrial zones will be built in rural regions. Business incubators will be promoted along with factoring services.

[240] The President of Uzbekistan signed a decree on the "Strategy of actions in five priority areas of development of the country in 2017–2021" dated 7 February 2017, and a decree "On the State Program for the Implementation of the Action Strategy in five priority areas of development of the Republic of Uzbekistan in 2017–2021 in the Year of Support for Active Entrepreneurship, Innovative Ideas and Technologies" dated 22 January 2018.

With a larger rural population than urban population, developing women entrepreneurship in the countryside is of particular importance, increasing welfare as employment and incomes rise among the rural population with more women involved in production. Rural women general work in MSEs as ateliers, in pharmacies, small wholesale stores, and producing souvenirs, aside from working at home. The majority of women entrepreneurs are involved in small-scale wholesale production of consumer goods, trade, health care, and educational and other professional services.

According to the State Statistics Committee, as of January 2022 there were 36,472 MSEs managed by women, earning a net income of SUM22.6 trillion. Compared to 2021, the net profit of small enterprises and micro enterprises managed by women has grown to about SUM7 trillion.

The barriers to MSE development include excessive government control and intervention, taxes, limited access to finance, and an unattractive investment climate. Entrepreneurs continue to face procedural delays by certain authorized state bodies when issuing licenses, permits, and providing public services. Also, many entrepreneurs point to the high lending rates and commissions on bank operations—for example, a fee is charged for the credit commission to consider submitted documents.

Other obstacles include inefficiencies in promoting MSE products on regional and world markets, poor marketing and logistics services, a need for consulting centers, and poor personnel training. The current tax system does not promote MSE growth given sharp differences in the relative tax burden between registered MSEs and large enterprises.

Data show that over 30,000 state-owned enterprises and facilities have been privatized in the 30 years since 1991 However, laws have not kept up with changes in managing state property and privatization (including auctions). A system better harmonized with international standards is needed.

The government is moving to resolve these challenges in several ways: (i) the time limit for registering a small business is 30 minutes, reducing to just one document required to register an individual entrepreneur, and two documents to register a small enterprise; and (ii) financial support for MSEs, including preferential bank loans with subsidized rates, a guarantee from the State Fund for Supporting the Development of Entrepreneurial Activities to businesses up to 50% of the loan amount along with compensation for interest expenses on commercial bank loans.

Financial Inclusion

Various incentives and subsidies support MSE access to finance—which in turn supports financial inclusion.

A revised November 2019 Law No.582 “On the Central Bank” said the bank should take measures to ensure the protection of the rights and legitimate interests of consumers of services of banks and nonbank credit organizations, increase the availability of financial services and the level of financial literacy of the population and businesses. Also, the central bank is responsible for price stability and the development of banking and payment systems.

On 12 May 2020, another Decree of the President of the Republic of Uzbekistan No.UP-5992 “On the strategy for reforming the banking system of the Republic of Uzbekistan for 2020-2025” was adopted. it included a banking reform strategy for 2020–2025, developed by the central bank and Ministry of Finance in cooperation with the World Bank.

The strategy cited the low level of financial inclusion due to banks' concentration on servicing corporate clients—individuals account for 19% of all loans, while the corporate share is 81%. It also cited underdeveloped NBFIs and innovation and information systems.

Under the decree, priorities for bank reform included (i) improving the efficiency of the banking system; (ii) ensuring its financial stability; (iii) reducing the state share in banking; (iv) increasing the availability and quality of financial services by targeting underserved and vulnerable segments, introducing remote services for MSEs and individuals, developing a network of low-cost service outlets, and; (v) developing nonbank credit organizations as part of a more unified financial system.

In 2021, a National Strategy for Increasing Financial Inclusion for 2021–2023 was approved by the central bank covering five specific reforms:

- increasing basic financial coverage by expanding service outlets, introducing alternative ways of accessing bank services and creating a network of agent banks;
- developing digital financial services by attracting fintech companies, introducing a remote identification system, and modernizing the national payment system;
- expanding small business financing by developing financial instruments aimed at entrepreneurial projects, and developing nonbank credit organizations;
- strengthening consumer rights and protection by ensuring transparency of information on financial products and services, and introducing mechanisms for resolving disputes; and
- spreading financial literacy throughout the population (and MSEs) by raising awareness through the media, introducing a financial literacy curriculum in schools, and developing financial literacy training programs.

The central bank, together with the European Bank for Reconstruction and Development (EBRD), developed a 2021–2023 Action Plan for gender inclusiveness in finance and entrepreneurship. The paper outlined nine initiatives aligned with the Agency for Financial Inclusion's Denarau Action Plan to increase women's access to financial services. The Action Plan (i) develops networks of women entrepreneurs, (ii) carries out short-term business and financial education programs for women starting their own business, (iii) promotes gender diversity within the central bank itself through leadership and diversity education.

For example, the European Bank for Reconstruction and Development, together with Davr Bank and consulting companies—in particular the German Sparkassenstiftung for International Cooperation's Internationale Projekt Consult—launched a "Women in Business" program in May 2022. It provides a package of services for women including Davr Bank financial products and nonfinancial services for business development. It makes it possible to finance and evolve business projects through Zamona Credit for experienced women entrepreneurs and Zamona Start for those aspiring to open a business.

From 1 January 2020, commercial bank interest rates on loans issued in *sum* had to be set at a level not lower than the central bank refinancing rate. From 1 January 2021, commercial banks were allowed to independently determine their own interest rates. The World Bank estimates a decline in inflation allowed the central bank to lower its main rate from 16% to 14%.

The Ministry of Innovative Development allocates grants (from the national budget) to startups through competitions. Of thyen more than 600 projects submitted during 2019–2021, 138 (23%) startups were approved for funding. Thirteen projects made it to the growth phase, eight projects failed, while the others are continuing operations.

Currently, venture capitalists, business angels, and crowdfunding remain undeveloped. Over the long term, the government should move away from providing grant money to foster a more competitive environment that attracts venture capitalists, business angels, and crowdfunding.

Response to COVID-19

From March to June 2020, 14 decrees and resolutions were adopted to mitigate the economic effects of the pandemic. The state provided SUM82 trillion, including an Anti-Crisis Fund of SUM16 trillion allocated from the budget. Over 500,000 state-owned enterprises and businesses, as well as nearly 8 million individuals received tax benefits, deferrals on SUM66 trillion in loans as of end-2020. As part of the "Kindness and Support movement" program, over 800,000 needy families received over SUM1 trillion in material support. These timely government support measures reduced the economic damage caused by the pandemic.

For example, on 19 March 2020, a presidential decree was signed to ensure macroeconomic stability, uninterrupted operation of industries and other economic sectors, stimulate foreign economic activity, provide social support for the population and prevent a sharp decline in individual incomes.

The Anti-Crisis Fund attracted external borrowed funds, and increased the State Fund for Entrepreneurship Support SUM500 billion. The fund was used for measures combating the spread of infection; support entrepreneurship and employment; expand social support; and ensure the economy could continue to operate.

The decree provided a wide range of stimulus for entrepreneurs:

- from April to October 2020, the minimum amount of social tax was reduced to 50% of the base calculated amount per month for individual entrepreneurs; deductions from wholesalers of alcoholic products were reduced from 5% to 3%; the fees to carry out retail trade in alcoholic products for restaurants and others was reduced by 25%;
- from April to July 2020, tourist (hotel) fees were suspended; tax rates on water for agricultural irrigation was reduced by 50% for 2020;
- exporters of goods did not need guarantees for those with existing overdue receivables not exceeding 10% of the total export value for the reporting year; during 2020, one-time transactions for importing technological equipment and raw materials could be exchanged for repaying overdue receivables from foreign trade operations; and
- other measures to support entrepreneurs on exports, taxes, and other fees.

In April 2020, assistance to entrepreneurs from the State Fund for Entrepreneurship Support was expanded. From April to October 2020, the procedure for State Fund coverage of interest expenses on loans from commercial banks applied to existing business loan as well. The fund covered 8% of entrepreneur's loan expenses with interest rates not exceeding 24%. It also offered to cover 12% of the cost of loans with an interest rate up to 28%. More than SUM400 billion was allocated from the fund to entrepreneurs to cover interest on loans totaling SUM3 trillion. The restriction on providing guarantees for just one project per entrepreneur was canceled.

For entrepreneurs with a positive credit history, the fund provided guarantees of up to 75% of the loan amount (previously 50%). The upper limit of the guaranteed amount was increased from SUM8 billion to SUM10 billion. For people, individual entrepreneurs and enterprises with cash flow problems, deadlines for fulfilling loan obligations were extended (loans worth SUM12 trillion). Small businesses with revenues down 50% from the previous month, payments were deferred for taxes on turnover, land, property, social, and water resources until 1 October 2020. Through end-2020, customs duties and excise taxes were waived on the import of basic consumer goods like flour, vegetable oil, meat and dairy products, sugar, and hygiene products.

In May 2020, a decree on next measures exempted small businesses from paying property and land taxes from 1 June to 1 September 2020. The social tax rate was also reduced from 12% to 1%. For individual entrepreneurs forced to suspend operations during quarantine, the accrued personal income tax and social tax was suspended.

Response to the Russian Invasion of Ukraine

The invasion of Ukraine and sanctions imposed against the Russian Federation affected Uzbekistan's economy, as it did most countries worldwide. In general, businesses in Uzbekistan faced reduced productivity and competitiveness, business closures, job losses and reduced economic growth. Since February 2022, 65% of businesses in Uzbekistan, the Kyrgyz Republic, and Tajikistan have been hit with rising production costs.

In addition, some enterprises in Uzbekistan have had increased financial difficulties, possibly due to reduced profitability and difficulties accessing new loan financing. Thus, many businesses had to adjust their loans and reduce their debt burden. In response, businesses, including MSEs, had to deal with several challenges:

- trade flows affected by sanctions against the Russian Federation had to be redirected or alternative markets identified for purchases and exports;
- transport and logistics problems had to be resolved, including trade-related payments—including those related to sanctioned correspondent banks;
- financial and nonfinancial support for businesses required adjustments so the support only those enterprises that really needed it, and to avoid unnecessary budgetary expenses;
- ensuring deadlines and transparency procedures against insolvent debtors and protection from creditors followed bankruptcy laws.

On 31 March 2022, the President announced several measures to ensure macroeconomic stability and provide additional business support. It offers business assistance in several areas:

- banks would provide entrepreneurs an additional SUM10 trillion in "revolving" loans for purchasing raw materials and working capital, directed primarily to exporters and manufacturers of food and consumer goods;
- the amounts and preferential rates on loans provided under state programs would remain for horticulture (SUM2 trillion in 2022), family businesses (SUM10 trillion), mortgages (SUM13 trillion), and education (SUM1 trillion);
- until end-2022, companies operating in the Russian Federation, Ukraine, and Belarus would not pay fines for receivables—their debt on bank loans would be extended, with fines and penalties waived;
- wholesale trade zones will be created in Navoi, Samarkand, Tashkent, Bukhara, and Surkhandarya regions to supply products to the markets of Uzbekistan's neighbors; and
- an additional 100,000 jobs would be created to absorb returning migrant workers.

In September 2022, the President held a meeting on measures to ensure price stability for basic food products, with several benefits for farmers announced. The impact of the Russian invasion made production and delivery of food products more difficult. In Uzbekistan, 25 types of food products remain dependent on imports. The Ministry of Agriculture, together with regional administrative authorities, was instructed to prepare projects to boost domestic production.

It was decided to allocate about 20,000 hectares of land for new production. By 2023, 100,000 hectares of sown land should be distributed to the population on a competitive basis. Areas for growing food crops would increase to 300,000 hectares. In addition, from 15 September 2022:

- unsecured loans would be provided up to SUM150 million for seeds, fertilizers, fuels and lubricants, plant protection products and working capital for growing vegetables, legumes and oilseeds;
- half of the funds can be issued in cash, with the Horticulture Agency receiving an additional SUM300 billion; and
- for clusters and *dehkans* growing potatoes, vegetables, and oilseeds, 50% of the cost of crop insurance will be covered by the state, with the insurance acting as collateral for loans directed at growing food products.

Data Tables

Table 8.1: MSE Definition

Item	Micro	Small
Number of employees:		
Wholesale and retail trade	1–5	6–25
Arts, entertainment, and recreation	1–10	11–25
Transportation and storage Accommodation and food services	1–10	11–100
Financial and insurance activities Education	1–20	21–25
Agriculture, forestry, fisheries Power supply, gas, steam and air-conditioning Water supply; sewerage, waste collection and disposal Operations with real estate Professional, scientific, and technical activities Activities for the management and provision of support services Provision of other types of services	1–20	21–50
Repair of motor vehicles and motorcycles Information and communications Health and social service delivery	1–20	21–100
Mining and quarrying Manufacturing Construction	1–20	21–200

MSE = micro and small enterprise.
Source: ADB Asia SME Monitor 2022 database. Data from Resolution of the Cabinet of Ministers of the Republic of Uzbekistan No.275 dated on 24 August 2016.

Table 8.2: MSE Landscape

End-of-period data

Item	2004	2005	2006	2007	2008	2009	2010	2011	2012	2013	2014	2015	2016	2017	2018	2019	2020	2021
NUMBER OF ENTERPRISES																		
Number of enterprises, total	106,301	106,272	116,544	132,940	139,098	155,794	167,274	180,950	180,471	192,718	198,734	209,621	213,111	231,989	265,016	337,096	414,182	465,889
Number of MSEs	99,780	100,751	112,260	129,211	135,561	152,246	164,052	177,876	177,551	189,867	196,014	207,104	210,594	229,666	262,930	334,767	411,203	462,834
Micro	86,214	87,361	97,595	111,956	117,269	131,124	143,397	157,436	154,497	167,291	174,094	184,887	192,962	210,744	242,585	312,609	386,105	437,844
Small	13,566	13,390	14,665	17,255	18,292	21,122	20,655	20,440	23,054	22,576	21,920	22,217	17,632	18,922	20,345	22,158	25,098	24,990
Number of large enterprises	6,521	5,521	4,284	3,729	3,537	3,548	3,222	3,074	2,920	2,851	2,720	2,517	2,517	2,323	2,086	2,329	2,979	3,055
MSE to total (%)	93.9	94.8	96.3	97.2	97.5	97.7	98.1	98.3	98.4	98.5	98.6	98.8	98.8	99.0	99.2	99.3	99.3	99.3
MSE growth (%)	...	1.0	11.4	15.1	4.9	12.3	7.8	8.4	(0.2)	6.9	3.2	5.7	1.7	9.1	14.5	27.3	22.8	12.6
MSEs by sector (% share)																		
Industry (manufacturing)	20.1	19.3	18.5	16.9	16.3	16.9	17.8	18.9	19.7	19.0	19.9	19.8	20.3	21.1	21.4	20.9	20.1	19.5
Construction	11.0	11.6	11.5	11.5	11.3	11.4	10.9	10.3	10.2	9.7	10.0	10.1	10.3	10.4	11.0	10.8	9.9	9.4
Agriculture (until 2012)/ Agriculture, forestry, and fisheries (after 2013)*	8.5	8.9	9.4	8.9	8.9	8.6	8.5	9.3	9.5	8.8	8.5	8.4	8.5	8.9	9.1	8.6	9.9	9.9
Transportation and communication (until 2012)/ Transportation and storage (after 2013)*	2.3	2.7	3.4	3.5	4.1	4.5	4.7	4.8	4.7	4.1	4.3	4.6	5.0	5.1	5.0	4.5	4.1	3.9
Other manufacturing industries	6.5	7.1	7.5	7.7	8.1	8.6	8.8	10.1	10.5	...	...	...	...	...	...	...	...	...
Trade and public catering (until 2012)/ Trade (after 2013)*	42.0	40.7	39.6	40.1	39.7	38.7	38.0	36.2	35.2	30.2	29.4	28.5	29.1	27.3	26.8	30.0	32.0	33.8
Non-productive types of consumer services	1.7	1.8	1.8	1.9	2.0	2.1	2.0	1.9	1.9	...	...	...	...	...	...	...	...	...
Health care, physical education, sports and social welfare (until 2012)/ Healthcare and provision social services (after 2013)*	3.5	3.6	4.1	4.9	4.8	4.5	4.3	4.1	3.9	3.0	2.9	2.8	1.8	1.9	2.0	1.9	1.8	1.9
Education, culture, science and scientific service	2.4	2.4	2.3	2.3	2.3	3.0	3.6	3.0	2.9	...	...	...	...	...	...	...	...	...
Other non-manufacturing industries	2.0	1.9	2.0	2.3	2.4	1.7	1.4	1.5	1.5	...	...	...	...	...	...	...	...	...
Accommodation and food services*	...	...	...	...	...	...	...	...	...	6.3	6.6	6.9	7.3	7.4	7.5	7.6	7.3	7.1
Information and communication*	...	...	...	...	...	...	...	...	...	3.4	3.3	3.1	2.9	2.7	2.6	2.3	2.2	2.2
Other types*	...	...	...	...	...	...	...	...	...	15.5	15.0	16.0	14.7	15.1	14.6	13.4	12.6	12.2
MSEs by region (% share)																		
Capital city (Tashkent)	17.9	18.9	19.2	20.1	21.5	20.9	20.3	19.3	19.6	19.9	19.9	21.0	22.0	22.8	22.8	22.1	20.8	20.4
Others	82.1	81.1	80.8	79.9	78.5	79.1	79.7	80.7	80.4	80.1	80.1	79.0	78.0	77.2	77.2	77.9	79.2	79.6
Republic of Karakalpakstan	5.1	5.6	4.8	4.6	4.5	4.7	4.5	4.7	4.7	4.4	4.8	4.7	4.6	4.6	4.6	4.4	4.4	4.3
Andijan Region	11.6	8.6	9.3	9.1	9.0	9.4	9.8	10.0	10.5	10.5	10.6	10.6	10.3	8.9	8.6	7.7	7.7	7.6
Bukhara Region	6.7	6.5	6.4	6.4	6.7	6.4	6.3	5.8	5.5	4.6	4.8	5.4	5.5	5.5	5.6	6.0	6.0	6.0
Jizzakh Region	2.7	3.4	3.7	3.6	3.7	3.3	3.5	3.9	3.8	3.8	3.8	3.8	3.8	4.1	4.3	4.2	4.3	4.2
Kashkadarya Region	8.8	8.5	7.9	7.8	7.4	7.9	8.8	9.4	9.4	8.5	8.1	7.2	6.5	6.2	6.2	6.1	6.2	6.7
Navoi Region	3.2	3.2	3.1	3.1	3.3	3.5	3.3	3.4	3.4	3.3	3.2	3.2	3.2	3.3	3.5	4.4	4.4	4.4
Namangan Region	5.3	5.9	5.9	6.1	5.9	6.5	6.5	6.1	6.4	6.5	6.7	6.8	7.0	6.9	6.5	6.4	6.5	6.3
Samarkand Region	10.3	9.6	9.3	9.0	7.6	7.0	6.5	7.0	6.3	6.7	6.6	6.7	6.6	7.0	7.5	7.7	8.1	8.8
Surkhandarya Region	6.3	6.7	7.2	7.1	7.1	5.9	5.3	5.1	4.6	5.6	4.6	4.4	4.5	4.5	4.4	4.6	5.2	5.3
Syrdarya Region	3.3	3.0	2.9	2.7	2.8	3.2	3.4	3.3	3.2	3.2	3.3	3.1	3.3	3.2	3.2	3.3	3.2	3.0
Tashkent Region**	7.7	7.9	7.6	7.8	7.7	8.1	8.5	8.7	9.3	9.4	9.7	9.4	9.2	9.4	9.7	9.7	9.8	9.5
Fergana Region	7.4	8.3	8.5	8.2	8.2	7.9	8.1	7.9	8.0	8.5	8.6	8.7	8.5	8.8	8.9	8.8	8.8	8.7
Khorezm Region	3.7	3.8	4.0	4.6	4.7	5.3	5.1	5.3	5.4	5.2	5.3	5.0	4.9	4.7	4.5	4.6	4.6	4.7
EMPLOYMENT																		
Number of employment, total ('000)	9,911	10,196	10,467	10,735	11,035	11,328	11,628	11,919	12,224	12,523	12,818	13,058	13,298	13,520	13,273	13,541	13,236	13,539
Number of employment by MSEs	5,975	6,603	7,234	7,743	8,071	8,370	8,644	8,951	9,240	9,604	9,951	10,170	10,398	10,542	10,129	10,319	9,866	10,071
Individual entrepreneurs, dekhan farms, and self-employed	4,756	6,127	5,469	5,649	5,963	6,435	6,434	6,637	7,002	7,340	7,722	7,993	8,230	8,517	9,056	8,946	8,517	8,528
Micro	962	185	1,406	1,586	1,563	1,334	1,456	1,527	1,393	1,411	1,403	1,419	1,394	1,451	592	781	812	975
Small	257	291	359	509	545	601	753	788	845	853	826	758	774	575	481	592	537	568
Number of employment by large enterprises	3,550	3,156	2,798	2,552	2,522	2,516	2,537	2,521	2,536	2,472	2,420	2,440	2,453	2,531	2,697	2,774	2,923	3,020
Unclassified	386	438	435	440	442	442	448	448	448	448	448	448	448	448	448	448	448	448
MSE employees to total (%)	60.3	64.8	69.1	72.1	73.1	73.9	74.3	75.1	75.6	76.7	77.6	77.9	78.2	78.0	76.3	76.2	74.5	74.4
MSE employees growth (%)	9.9	10.5	9.6	7.0	4.2	3.7	3.3	3.5	3.2	3.9	3.6	2.2	2.2	1.4	(3.9)	1.9	(4.4)	2.1
Share of female employees to total employees (%)	48.1	47.8	47.8	46.7	45.8	45.9	45.5	45.4	45.4	45.7	45.6	45.7	45.7	45.8	41.6	41.4	41.4	...

continued on next page

Table 8.2 *continued*

Item	2004	2005	2006	2007	2008	2009	2010	2011	2012	2013	2014	2015	2016	2017	2018	2019	2020	2021
Employment by MSEs by sector (% share)																		
Agriculture, forestry, and fisheries	...	...	...	...	...	33.2	34.5	34.5	33.5	34.2	34.7	34.8	34.5	34.3	34.3	33.8	34.9	34.3
Manufacturing	...	...	...	...	...	13.1	12.8	12.7	12.6	12.5	12.4	12.5	12.5	12.7	13.2	13.2	12.9	13.1
Transportation and communication	...	...	...	...	...	4.2	4.2	4.3	4.4	4.4	4.7	4.8	5.0	5.1	5.2	5.0	4.9	5.2
Construction	...	...	...	...	...	11.1	11.2	11.2	11.3	11.3	11.2	11.3	11.5	11.6	11.4	12.3	12.5	12.0
Wholesale and retail trade	...	...	...	...	...	13.8	13.8	13.6	13.6	13.4	13.3	13.4	13.4	13.5	13.2	13.3	13.6	14.6
Other services	...	...	...	...	...	10.2	10.4	10.6	10.3	10.4	10.2	9.9	9.6	9.1	7.8	7.4	6.6	8.0
Others	...	...	...	...	...	14.3	13.2	13.1	14.3	13.8	13.5	13.4	13.4	13.8	14.9	14.8	14.6	12.8
Employment by MSEs by region (% share)																		
Capital city (Tashkent)	...	...	...	...	...	...	...	...	...	...	...	...	...	...	...	...	...	...
Other regions	...	...	...	...	...	...	...	...	...	...	...	...	...	...	...	...	...	...
CONTRIBUTION TO GDP																		
GDP of MSEs (SUM million)	3,750,841	5,437,089	7,993,216	11,576,245	16,925,513	22,350,327	42,255,869	56,687,970	68,859,120	83,634,480	104,189,696	129,890,228	155,653,215	184,519,023	236,571,151	271,316,838	309,735,627	374,368,780
MSE contribution to GDP (% share)	35.6	38.2	42.1	45.7	48.2	50.1	60.8	61.9	60.8	60.9	61.9	64.6	66.8	65.3	62.4	56.0	55.5	54.9
MSE GDP growth (%)	...	45.0	47.0	44.8	46.2	32.1	89.1	34.2	21.5	21.5	24.6	24.7	19.8	18.5	28.2	14.7	14.2	20.9
MSE labor productivity (SUM million)	...	...	...	...	...	...	...	...	...	...	...	...	...	...	...	...	...	...
MSE GDP by sector (% share)																		
Agriculture, forestry, and fisheries	...	...	...	...	...	...	...	...	...	...	...	49.3	47.0	48.3	47.2	47.0	47.2	47.3
Industry (manufacturing)	...	...	...	...	...	...	...	...	...	...	...	12.2	12.5	12.7	14.0	11.3	11.8	11.5
Construction	...	...	...	...	...	...	...	...	...	...	...	5.4	6.0	5.7	7.2	8.9	9.1	9.2
Trade, accommodation, and food services	...	...	...	...	...	...	...	...	...	...	...	8.9	10.7	10.3	10.0	10.5	10.5	10.6
Transportation, storage, information, and communication	...	...	...	...	...	...	...	...	...	...	...	7.9	7.6	7.0	6.3	6.4	6.3	6.7
Others services	...	...	...	...	...	...	...	...	...	...	...	16.4	16.3	16.0	15.4	15.8	15.0	14.6
MSE GDP to total GDP of the region (% share)																		
Capital city (Tashkent)	...	...	...	...	...	...	...	...	...	...	...	66.7	68.1	63.0	64.8	53.1	51.2	48.1
Republic of Karakalpakstan	...	...	...	...	...	...	...	...	...	...	...	69.7	63.6	58.5	57.0	56.3	58.1	56.4
Andijan Region	...	...	...	...	...	...	...	...	...	...	...	78.5	83.6	80.2	73.1	69.6	69.9	71.8
Bukhara Region	...	...	...	...	...	...	...	...	...	...	...	77.4	79.3	79.9	80.9	74.3	75.6	75.4
Jizzakh Region	...	...	...	...	...	...	...	...	...	...	...	83.0	84.2	85.6	86.2	83.1	83.0	81.2
Kashkadarya Region	...	...	...	...	...	...	...	...	...	...	...	63.2	66.7	73.6	72.7	70.8	71.5	69.0
Navoi Region	...	...	...	...	...	...	...	...	...	...	...	51.0	50.4	49.4	42.3	30.7	25.4	27.1
Namangan Region	...	...	...	...	...	...	...	...	...	...	...	78.7	79.8	80.8	80.5	75.9	74.6	73.5
Samarkand Region	...	...	...	...	...	...	...	...	...	...	...	80.2	81.2	82.6	80.8	75.2	74.2	73.4
Surkhandarya Region	...	...	...	...	...	...	...	...	...	...	...	77.4	79.1	79.5	81.2	78.8	77.1	77.3
Syrdarya Region	...	...	...	...	...	...	...	...	...	...	...	75.1	75.9	77.9	77.8	69.8	70.5	69.2
Tashkent Region**	...	...	...	...	...	...	...	...	...	...	...	66.5	67.9	65.0	58.9	51.3	49.2	46.8
Ferghana Region	...	...	...	...	...	...	...	...	...	...	...	69.7	73.9	71.7	71.3	69.3	70.5	69.9
Khorezm Region	...	...	...	...	...	...	...	...	...	...	...	77.1	79.4	79.1	79.1	76.4	76.1	73.9
EXPORTS																		
Total export value ($ million)	4,853	5,409	6,390	8,992	11,493	11,771	13,023	15,021	13,600	14,323	13,546	12,508	12,095	12,554	13,991	17,459	15,102	16,663
Total export growth (%)	30.3	11.5	18.1	40.7	27.8	2.4	10.6	15.3	(9.5)	5.3	(5.4)	(7.7)	(3.3)	3.8	11.4	24.8	(13.5)	10.3
MSE export value ($ million)	354	326	715	1,334	1,420	1,724	1,783	2,826	1,911	3,752	3,658	3,378	3,139	2,759	3,811	4,715	3,101	3,335
MSE export to total export value (%)	7.3	6.0	11.2	14.8	12.4	14.6	13.7	18.8	14.0	26.2	27.0	27.0	26.0	22.0	27.2	27.0	20.5	20.0
MSE export growth (%)	30.3	(8.1)	119.4	86.6	6.5	21.4	3.4	58.5	(32.4)	96.4	(2.5)	(7.7)	(7.1)	(12.1)	38.1	23.7	(34.2)	7.6
IMPORTS																		
Total import value ($ million)	3,816	4,091	4,782	6,728	9,704	9,438	9,176	11,345	12,817	13,947	13,984	12,417	12,138	14,012	19,439	24,292	21,154	25,508
Total import growth (%)	28.7	7.2	16.9	40.7	44.2	(2.7)	(2.8)	23.6	13.0	8.8	0.3	(11.2)	(2.2)	15.4	38.7	25.0	(12.9)	20.6
MSE import value ($ million)	1,249	1,380	1,634	2,155	3,460	4,011	3,288	3,896	4,946	5,909	6,353	5,523	5,677	7,512	10,916	14,972	10,943	11,533
MSE import to total import value (%)	32.7	33.7	34.2	32.0	35.7	42.5	35.8	34.3	38.6	42.4	45.4	44.5	46.8	53.6	56.2	61.6	51.7	45.2
MSE import growth (%)	25.2	10.5	18.4	31.9	60.6	15.9	(18.0)	18.5	27.0	19.5	7.5	(13.1)	2.8	32.3	45.3	37.2	(26.9)	5.4

GDP = gross domestic product, MSE = micro and small enterprise.

Note: There is no category of medium-sized enterprises in Uzbekistan.

* Classification of MSEs by sector changed in 2013.

*** Tashkent Region is excluded from Tashkent City.

Source: ADB Asia SME Monitor 2022 database. Data from State Committee on Statistics of Uzbekistan.

Table 8.3: Bank Credit

End-of-period data

Item	2004	2005	2006	2007	2008	2009	2010	2011	2012	2013	2014	2015	2016	2017	2018	2019	2020	2021
OPERATING BANKS																		
Number of operating banks, total	31	29	28	28	30	30	31	30	29	28	26	26	27	28	28	30	32	33
State-owned commercial banks	11	10	10	10	10	10	10	10	10	10	10	10	10	11	12	13	13	12
State-owned development financial institutions	...	...	...	...	...	...	...	...	...	...	...	...	...	...	...	...	...	...
Private commercial banks	16	15	14	14	16	16	17	16	15	15	13	13	14	14	13	13	14	16
Foreign commercial banks	4	4	4	4	4	4	4	4	4	3	3	3	3	3	3	4	5	5
Credit																		
Loans outstanding, total (SUM million)	...	...	...	...	...	...	...	...	...	...	32,160,906	39,718,335	52,610,507	110,572,058	167,390,630	211,580,509	276,974,809	326,385,581
Loans outstanding in domestic currency (SUM million)	...	...	...	...	...	...	...	...	...	...	19,605,948	23,591,531	30,104,371	41,733,904	73,863,622	110,633,178	138,868,458	163,722,894
Loans outstanding in foreign currency (SUM million)	...	...	...	...	...	...	...	...	...	...	12,554,958	16,126,804	22,506,136	68,838,154	93,527,008	100,947,331	138,106,351	162,662,686
Loan growth (%)	...	...	...	...	...	...	...	...	...	...	28.2	23.5	32.5	110.2	51.4	26.4	30.9	17.8
Total bank loans to GDP (%)	...	...	...	...	...	...	...	...	...	...	17.2	17.9	20.6	34.8	39.4	40.0	46.0	44.4
Lending rate (%, annual average)	...	...	...	...	...	...	...	...	...	...	...	...	...	...	...	...	...	...
Gross nonperforming loans (NPLs) (SUM million)	...	...	...	...	...	...	...	...	...	...	674,372	580,847	391,468	1,324,440	2,140,452	3,169,081	5,784,828	16,974,028
Gross NPLs to total loans (%)	...	...	...	...	...	...	...	...	...	...	2.1	1.5	0.7	1.2	1.3	1.5	2.1	5.2
Deposits																		
Deposits, total (SUM million)	...	...	...	...	...	...	...	...	...	...	23,670,695	30,057,531	37,183,157	59,578,667	70,001,437	91,009,009	114,746,891	156,189,834
Deposits in domestic currency (SUM million)	...	...	...	...	...	...	...	...	...	...	17,327,538	22,905,286	27,176,409	30,753,388	43,323,504	51,040,035	65,318,346	95,578,157
Deposits in foreign currency (SUM million)	...	...	...	...	...	...	...	...	...	...	6,343,157	7,152,245	10,006,749	28,825,279	26,677,933	39,968,974	49,428,545	60,611,677
Deposit rate (%, annual average)	...	...	...	...	...	...	...	...	...	...	...	...	...	...	...	...	...	...
MSE LOANS																		
MSE loans outstanding, total (SUM million)	...	...	...	...	...	...	...	...	...	...	...	12,459,134.0	16,630,818.3	19,564,668.5	30,648,846.0	55,430,002.9	48,389,693.3	59,552,127.3
MSE loans to total loans outstanding (%)	...	...	...	...	...	...	...	...	...	...	...	31.4	31.6	17.7	18.3	26.2	17.5	18.2
MSE loans to GDP (%)	...	...	...	...	...	...	...	...	...	...	...	5.6	6.5	6.2	7.2	10.5	8.0	8.1
MSE loan growth (%)	...	...	...	...	...	...	...	...	...	...	...	...	33.5	17.6	56.7	80.9	-12.7	23.1
MSE lending rate (%, annual average)	...	...	...	...	...	...	...	...	...	...	...	...	...	...	...	...	...	...
Nonperforming MSE loans (NPLs) (SUM million)	...	...	...	...	...	...	...	...	...	...	...	...	...	...	...	...	...	...
MSE NPLs to total MSE loans (%)	...	...	...	...	...	...	...	...	...	...	...	...	...	...	...	...	...	...
Number of MSE loan borrowers	...	...	...	...	...	...	...	...	...	...	...	...	...	...	...	...	...	...
MSE loan borrowers to total bank borrowers (%)	...	...	...	...	...	...	...	...	...	...	...	...	...	...	...	...	...	...
MSE loan rejection rate (% of total applications)	...	...	...	...	...	...	...	...	...	...	...	...	...	...	...	...	...	...
Number of MSE savings account in banks	...	...	...	...	...	...	...	...	...	...	...	...	...	...	...	...	...	...
Guaranteed MSE loans (SUM million)	...	...	...	...	...	...	...	...	...	...	...	...	...	...	...	...	...	...
Non-collateral MSE loans (SUM million)	...	...	...	...	...	...	...	...	...	...	...	...	...	...	...	...	...	...
MSE loans outstanding by sector (% share)																		
Agriculture, forestry, and fisheries	...	...	...	...	...	...	...	...	...	...	...	...	...	...	...	...	...	...
Manufacturing	...	...	...	...	...	...	...	...	...	...	...	...	...	...	...	...	...	...
Transportation and communication	...	...	...	...	...	...	...	...	...	...	...	...	...	...	...	...	...	...
Construction	...	...	...	...	...	...	...	...	...	...	...	...	...	...	...	...	...	...
Wholesale and retail trade	...	...	...	...	...	...	...	...	...	...	...	...	...	...	...	...	...	...
Other services	...	...	...	...	...	...	...	...	...	...	...	...	...	...	...	...	...	...
Others	...	...	...	...	...	...	...	...	...	...	...	...	...	...	...	...	...	...
MSE loans outstanding by region (% share)																		
Capital city (Tashkent)	...	...	...	...	...	...	...	...	...	...	...	...	...	...	...	...	...	...
Other	...	...	...	...	...	...	...	...	...	...	...	...	...	...	...	...	...	...
MSE loans outstanding by type of use (% share)																		
For working capital	...	...	...	...	...	...	...	...	...	...	...	...	...	...	...	...	...	...
For capital investment	...	...	...	...	...	...	...	...	...	...	...	...	...	...	...	...	...	...
MSE loans outstanding by tenor (% share)																		
Less than 1 year	...	...	...	...	...	...	...	...	...	...	...	...	...	...	...	...	...	...
1-5 years	...	...	...	...	...	...	...	...	...	...	...	...	...	...	...	...	...	...
More than 5 years	...	...	...	...	...	...	...	...	...	...	...	...	...	...	...	...	...	...

GDP = gross domestic product, MSE = micro and small enterprise.

Source: ADB Asia SME Monitor 2022. Data from Central Bank of Uzbekistan.

Table 8.4: Public Financing

End-of-period data

Item	2017	2018	2019	2020	2021
SUBSIDIZED LOANS TO MSEs					
Number of funds	1	6	7	7	9
Number of subsidized loans (new approvals)	622	4,958	2,941	9,760	7,278
Outstanding of subsidized loans to MSEs (SUM million)	...	23,853	167,306	396,051	624,764
Subsidized loans disbursed to MSEs (SUM million)	17,336	197,135	347,108	661,860	667,133
Number of MSEs that accepted subsidized loans	622	4,932	2,932	9,742	7,250
MSE access to subsidized loans (% of total MSEs)	12.6	45.8	42.4	72.3	71.8

MSE = micro and small enterprise.

Source: ADB Asia SME Monitor 2022 database. Data from Microcredit Bank of Uzbekistan.

Table 8.4a: Public Funds and Financing Programs for MSEs

Name of the Fund	Year of the launch	Fund Size (SUM million)	Taget Beneficiaries	Amount of Refinance (SUM million)*	Number of MSEs benefitted*	Status (ongoing/ closed)	Responsible Ministry/ Agency	Outline
1. State Fund for Entrepreneurship Support	2018	341,000	Firms in agriculture, industry, and services.	89,000	980	Ongoing	Central Bank of Uzbekistan, Ministry of Finance	Forms of financial assistance provided: 1. Guarantees for loans from commercial banks for implementing entrepreneurial initiative for vulnerable groups. 2. Guaranteed loans from commercial banks. 3. Compensation of interest expenses on loans from commercial banks.
2. Craft Development Program	2017	n/a	Business entities engage in their activities in handicraft	344,627	11,451	Ongoing	Ministry of Finance, Central Bank of Uzbekistan, Ministry of Employment and Labor Relations	Further development of national handicrafts, folk arts and crafts; implementing targeted and comprehensive measures to broadly support handicrafts and encourage citizens involved in handicrafts in every possible way; ensure employment of the population on this basis, especially young people, women, and low-income families.
3. Program "Every Family is an Entrepreneur"	2018	n/a	Firms in agriculture, industry, and services.	1,014,225	10,961	Ongoing	Family Business Support Center	Ensure the provision of full support for entrepreneurial initiatives of the population wishing to engage in entrepreneurship.
4. Fund for Support of Farmers, Dekhkan Farms and Landowners	2018	n/a	Business entities operating in agriculture	49,821	109	Ongoing	Farmers Council	The main objective of the fund is to provide financial support to farmers, *dekhkan* farms, and owners of homestead lands.
5. Funds of local governments	2018	n/a	Firms in agriculture, industry, and services.	41,655	176	Ongoing	Regional municipalities	Support and development of entrepreneurship in the regions.
6. Employment Promotion Fund	2018	n/a	Firms in agriculture, industry, and services.	24,138	366	Ongoing	Ministry of Labor and Social Protection	The funds are used to open credit lines on the terms of public-private partnership of enterprises, providing for the creation of new jobs mainly for socially vulnerable segments of the population, with the condition of further sale of the share of regional funds in established enterprises to private partners.
7. Women's Support Fund	2018	n/a	Firms in agriculture, industry, and services.	24,832	457	Ongoing	Heads of the sectors of municipalities, State Committee for Family and Women Affairs	Financing social and economic assistance to needy women from the "Women's Notebook."
8. Program Foundation "Youth is our future"	2019	n/a	Firms in agriculture, industry, and services.	260,490	841	Closed	Cabinet of Ministers, Central Bank of Uzbekitan	The program aims to (i) provide youth employment by facilitating and supporting implementation of youth business initiatives, startups, ideas, and projects; (ii) teach unemployed youth in high-demand specialties and business skills; (iii) increase their socio economic activity in general.
9. Youth Entrepreneurship Support Program (YOUE) (PQ-4862)	2021	n/a	Firms in agriculture, industry, and services.	99,630	1,164	Ongoing	Cabinet of Ministers, Central Bank of Uzbekitan	Broad involvement of the population, especially youth and women in entrepreneurships, improvement of the microfinance system, and state support for entrepreneurship.
10. Lead Entrepreneur (PQ-5214)	2021	n/a	Business entities classified as leader entrepreneurs	31,155	34	Ongoing	Cabinet of Ministers, Central Bank of Uzbekitan	To further support entrepreneurship in *mahallas* (difficult conditions) that are lagging in socio economic development and with a high level of unemployment and expanding economic cooperation between business entities and households based on the *mahallabai* work system.
Grand Total (SUM million and number)				1,979,573	26,539			

* Data as of end-2021.

MSE = micro and small enterprise, NPL = nonperforming loan.

Source: ADB Asia SME Monitor 2022 database. Data from Microcredit Bank of Uzbekistan.

Table 8.5: Nonbank Finance

End-of-period data

Item	2004	2005	2006	2007	2008	2009	2010	2011	2012	2013	2014	2015	2016	2017	2018	2019	2020	2021
NUMBER OF NONBANK FINANCE INSTITUTIONS																		
Nonbank Finance Institutions, total	15	26	31	50	92	138	183	209	84	76	72	71	70	76	76	92	118	142
Microfinance institutions	...	...	...	...	13	26	32	35	34	30	28	25	27	29	30	37	57	69
Credit unions/cooperatives	14	20	24	36	55	78	103	116	...	...	...	...	...	...	...	...	...	...
Pawnshops	1	6	7	14	24	34	48	58	50	46	44	46	43	47	46	55	61	73
MICROFINANCE INSTITUTIONS																		
Financing outstanding, total (SUM million)	...	...	...	...	...	...	...	...	...	...	46,019	61,593	85,019	128,140	325,145	650,685	809,109	1,159,636
Growth (%)	...	...	...	...	...	...	...	...	...	...	...	33.8	38.0	50.7	153.7	100.1	24.3	43.3
Total financing to GDP (%)	...	...	...	...	...	...	...	...	...	...	0.02	0.03	0.03	0.04	0.08	0.12	0.13	0.16
Annual lending rate (%, on average)	...	...	...	...	...	...	...	...	...	...	65.1	63.6	62.2	62.0	60.3	61.8	61.5	65.5
Gross nonperforming loans (NPLs) (SUM million)	...	...	...	...	...	...	...	...	...	...	950	982	1,750	2,126	5,697	17,801	143,659	53,815
Gross NPLs to total loans (%)	...	...	...	...	...	...	...	...	...	...	2.1	1.6	2.1	1.7	1.8	2.7	17.8	4.6
Savings (SUM million)	...	...	...	...	...	...	...	...	...	...	...	...	...	...	...	...	...	...
Number of customers financed, total	...	...	...	...	...	...	...	...	...	...	17,973	18,705	21,047	25,702	43,535	66,651	85,156	112,382
PAWNSHOPS																		
Financing outstanding, total (SUM million)	...	...	...	...	...	...	...	...	...	...	23,925	52,477	54,610	65,125	86,288	105,014	125,642	175,536
Growth (%)	...	...	...	...	...	...	...	...	...	...	...	119.3	4.1	19.3	32.5	21.7	19.6	39.7
Total financing to GDP (%)	...	...	...	...	...	...	...	...	...	...	0.01	0.02	0.02	0.02	0.02	0.02	0.02	0.02
Annual financing rate (%, on average)	...	...	...	...	...	...	...	...	...	...	165.0	153.6	149.1	151.6	145.9	140.5	106.1	104.0
Gross nonperforming financing (NPFs) (SUM million)	...	...	...	...	...	...	...	...	...	...	2,143	4,215	7,277	12,347	25,223	33,340	41,713	59,448
Gross NPFs to total financing (%)	...	...	...	...	...	...	...	...	...	...	9.0	8.0	13.3	19.0	29.2	31.7	33.2	33.9
Number of customers financed, total	...	...	...	...	...	...	...	...	...	...	43,474	46,291	51,350	52,635	54,189	55,247	57,730	69,483

GDP = gross domestic product.

Note: There is no financing data available for credit unions and cooperatives.

Source: ADB Asia SME Monitor 2022. Data from Central Bank of Uzbekistan.

Table 8.6: Capital Markets

End-of-period data

Item	2010	2011	2012	2013	2014	2015	2016	2017	2018	2019	2020	2021
EQUITY MARKET												
Main Board												
Index	...	1,000.0	1,000.1	1,000.0	1,000.0	1,000.0	1,000.9	1,001.7	854.8	642.0	641.4	1,099.2
Market capitalization (SUM million)	4,746,600	5,255,500	5,448,900	6,320,000	7,018,800	8,436,300	7,963,460	14,817,700	21,594,400	52,405,271	54,794,500	56,197,495
Growth (%)	...	10.7	3.7	16.0	11.1	20.2	(5.6)	86.1	45.7	142.7	4.6	2.6
Trading value (SUM million)	64,378	213,100	170,700	93,200	97,600	161,049	38,440	298,550	687,300	438,820	578,150	1,260,510
Trading volume (million shares)	179	109	228	122	178	357	469	1,552	10,063	8,111	99,077	1,416
Number of listed companies	101	108	110	135	133	259	192	189	132	112	145	139
Number of IPOs	...	...	...	...	...	...	...	...	1	...	1	...
Number of delisted companies	1	1	...	37	32	2	156	26	78	45	20	21

Note: There is no market board dedicated for small and medium-sized enterprises in Uzbekistan.

IPO = initial public offering.

Source: ADB Asia SME Monitor 2022 database. Data from Republican Stock Exchange "Toshkent."

Table 8.7: Policies and regulations

Regulations	
Name	**Outline**
Decree of the President of the Republic of Uzbekistan of 8 April 2022 N UP-101 "On the next reforms to create conditions for stable economic growth by improving the business environment and developing the private sector"	(i) Implement the Development Strategy of New Uzbekistan for 2022–2026, (ii) reduce poverty by half by achieving inclusive and stable economic growth, (iii) ensure competition in the economy, (iv) create equal conditions for business entities, (v) accelerate a full transition to market relations, (vi) increase the competitiveness of the national economy, and (vii) increase in private investment and strengthening the confidence of the business community.
Decree of the President of the Republic of Uzbekistan dated 15 September 2021 N UP-6314 "On measures to further reduce the administrative and tax burden for business entities, improve the system for protecting the legitimate interests of business"	(i) Accelerate the development of the activities of business entities, (ii) reduce the administrative and tax burden by improving state control and the "Taxman-Assistant" system, and (iii) ensure the fulfillment of the tasks identified in the framework of the open dialogue of the President of the Republic of Uzbekistan with entrepreneurs, held on 20 August 2021 to directly study the problems and proposals of entrepreneurs and determine the main directions for the development of entrepreneurship.
Decree of the President of the Republic of Uzbekistan of 23 August 2021 N PP-5228 "On additional measures to create a favorable investment climate, encourage small businesses and family entrepreneurship in the Surkhandarya region"	(i) Encourage small businesses and family businesses, production and support for the export of competitive products and (ii) improve the efficiency of the *mahallabai* system of work to ensure employment and increase the income of the population in the Surkhandarya region.
Decree of the President of the Republic of Uzbekistan dated 5 August 2021 N PP-5214 "On additional measures to further support entrepreneurship and develop cooperation between business entities and the population in mahallas"	(i) Support entrepreneurship in *mahallas* that are lagging behind in socio-economic development and with a high level of unemployment (hereinafter referred to as *mahalla* with difficult conditions) and (ii) expanding economic cooperation between business entities and households based on the mahallabay system of work.
Decree of the President of the Republic of Uzbekistan dated 21 April 2021 N PP-5084 "On measures to further support entrepreneurship and develop engineering and communication networks in the Namangan region"	(i) Support entrepreneurship, (ii) ensure employment, and (iii) allocate financial resources for the development of engineering and communications networks in the Namangan region.
Decree of the President of the Republic of Uzbekistan dated 21 April 2021 N PP-5087 "On additional measures to improve the business support system, further improve the business climate"	(i) Improve the conditions for doing business, (ii) consistently continue reforms to develop entrepreneurship, (iii) expand mechanisms to support entrepreneurs, and (iv) provide them with the necessary financial and infrastructure resources.
Decree of the President of the Republic of Uzbekistan dated 20 April 2021 N UP-6208 "On additional measures to support entrepreneurial activity, promote employment, social protection and meaningful organization of free time for young people"	(i) Improve the youth support system, (ii) promote employment, (iii) stimulate business ideas and initiatives, (iv) create additional conditions for young people to receive a decent income, and (v) raise the work carried out in this direction to a new level.
Decree of the President of the Republic of Uzbekistan of 8 June 2020 N PP-4742 "On measures to simplify state regulation of entrepreneurial activity and self-employment"	(i) Broadly involve the population in entrepreneurial activities and (ii) create additional conditions for the implementation of legal labor activities.
Decree of the President of the Republic of Uzbekistan dated 20 May 2020 N PP-4720 "On additional measures to finance the program: Every family is an entrepreneur"	Provide financial resources for projects implemented within the framework of the program "Every Family is an Entrepreneur," the development of family entrepreneurship, and increasing employment.
Decree of the President of the Republic of Uzbekistan of 20 November 2019 N PP-4525 "On measures to further improve the business environment and improve the business support system in the country"	(i) Improve the business environment, (ii) continue reforms initiated in the country to provide even greater freedom to entrepreneurship, and (iii) ensure the correct application of the adopted legislative acts on the ground.
Decree of the Cabinet of Ministers of the Republic of Uzbekistan dated 1 August 2019 N 643 "On measures to support the development of entrepreneurship and the expansion of industrial production in the Jizzakh region"	(i) Comprehensively develop the Jizzakh region by organizing additional capacities for higher quality processing of raw materials, (ii) attract more direct investment in the production of high-tech and export-oriented products, and (iii) create new jobs and improving the welfare of the population of the region.
Resolution of the Cabinet of Ministers of the Republic of Uzbekistan of 14 July 2019 N 584 "On measures for the effective organization of the activities of the Commissioner under the President of the Republic of Uzbekistan to protect the rights and legitimate interests of business entities"	Effectively organize the activities of the Commissioner under the President of the Republic of Uzbekistan for the protection of rights and legitimate interests business entities (hereinafter referred to as the Commissioner for the Protection of the Rights of Entrepreneurs) and its office.
Decree of the President of the Republic of Uzbekistan dated 14 May 2019 N UP-5718 "On measures to radically improve the system of support and protection of entrepreneurial activity"	(i) Improve the quality and efficiency of organizing work with requests from entrepreneurs including foreign investors, (ii) ensure an open and direct dialogue with them, (iii) effectively and efficiently implement their legal requirements and resolve problematic issues, (iv) increase a real contribution to the socio-economic development of regions, and (v) increase employment population and the growth of its material well-being.

continued on next page

Table 8.7 *continued*

Decree of the President of the Republic of Uzbekistan dated 15 March 2019 N UP-5690 "On measures to radically improve the system for protecting business activities and optimizing the activities of the prosecutor's office"	(i) Strengthen legal mechanisms for protecting the rights and interests of business entities, (ii) ensure legality guarantees of their activities, (iii) improve the investment climate and business environment in the country, and (iv) optimize the activities of the prosecution authorities by eliminating tasks and functions outside their purview.
Resolution of the Cabinet of Ministers of the Republic of Uzbekistan, dated 22 May 2020 No. 313 "On measures to establish youth technology parks in the country"	(i) Attract young people to scientific activities more widely, (ii) prepare young talents, and (iii) develop the main directions of science and scientific activity.
Resolution of the President of the Republic of Uzbekistan, dated 14 July 2018 No. PP-3855 "On additional measures to increase the effectiveness of commercialization of scientific developments and scientific-technical activities"	(i) Ensure the rapid implementation of local scientific-practical and innovative projects, (ii) increase the contribution of science to the competitiveness of the country's economy, and (iii) create effective ways to promote the promising local scientific developments and scientific-technical activities.
Resolution of the Cabinet of Ministers of the Republic of Uzbekistan, dated 5 July 2017 No. 468 "On measures to organize the activities of the innovation technology park in Yashnabad district of Tashkent"	Create a state unitary enterprise "Directorate of the Innovative Technopark "Yashnabad"" (hereinafter referred to as the Directorate of the Technopark "Yashnabad"), the founder of which is the *khokimiyat* of the city of Tashkent.
Resolution of the Cabinet of Ministers of the Republic of Uzbekistan, 9 March 2020, No. 133 "On measures to further improve the normative and legal basis for the development of research and innovative activity"	Improve the regulatory and legal framework for the formation and implementation of the state order for scientific research works.
Decree of the Cabinet of Ministers of the Republic of Uzbekistan № 222 on 19 April 2021 "On measures to support talented young people in scientific and innovative activities"	Under this Resolution, the Regulations on the procedure for conducting the startup competition "Future Scientist" was developed to support talented young people and young scientists engaged in scientific and innovative activities.
Decree of the President of the Republic of Uzbekistan, dated 21 October 2020 No. UP-6091 "On measures to further expand financial support for export activities"	Ensure macroeconomic stability at the present stage of socio economic development of the republic by increasing the volume of exports, additional financial and organizational incentives for suppliers of finished products.
Decree of the President of the Republic of Uzbekistan, dated 21 January 2022 No. UP-53 "On measures to stimulate deep processing, production and export of finished products with high added value by textile and sewing and knitting enterprises"	Introduce mechanisms for further stimulating high-quality processing, production, and export of finished products with high added value by textile and sewing and knitting enterprises with effective use of the available raw materials base in the republic.
Decree of the President of the Republic of Uzbekistan of 7 June 2018 N PP-3777 "On the implementation of the program "Every family is an entrepreneur"	Create conditions for doing business and acquire a stable source of income in every family.
Regulators and Policymakers	
Name	**Outline**
Cabinet of Ministers	The Cabinet of Ministers is the executive branch of the Republic of Uzbekistan. It provides for effective work of economy, social and spiritual spheres, execution of laws, and other resolutions by Oliy Majlis, decrees, resolutions, and orders issues by the President of Uzbekistan. It also issues resolutions and orders, binding for execution on the entire territory of the country by all bodies, enterprises, institutions, organizations, authorities, and citizens.
Ministry of Economic Development and Poverty Reduction (MEDPR)	Its main tasks include (i) systematic monitoring and analysis of the processes of market reforms and economic liberalization, (ii) developing and monitoring the main macroeconomic indicators, (iii) developing measures to ensure macroeconomic stability and economic growth in the interconnection of the main macroeconomic indicators with monetary aggregates, (iv) developing proposals based on a critical analysis to expand the introduction of market methods and mechanisms of economic management, and (v) reduce and optimize state regulation of the economy.
Ministry of Finance (MOF)	The main tasks are (i) the implementation of the unified state fiscal policy, (ii) concentration of financial resources on the most priority areas of economic development and acceleration of the development of the social sphere, (iii) consistent improvement of the tax system by reducing the tax burden on the economy and the populatio, and (iv) formation of the basic principles and methods of monetary and financial policy.

continued on next page

Table 8.7 *continued*

State Tax Committee		The committee is a republican body of state administration for control in the field of ensuring compliance with tax legislation and protecting the economic interests of the state. It is guided in its activities by the Constitution and laws of the Republic of Uzbekistan; resolutions of the Chambers of the Oliy Majlis of the Republic of Uzbekistan; decrees, resolutions and orders of the President of the Republic of Uzbekistan; and resolutions and orders of the Cabinet of Ministers of the Republic of Uzbekistan.
Ministry of Investments and Foreign Trade (MIFT)		The ministry is an authorized state body responsible for the implementation of a unified state investment policy, coordination of attracting foreign investment, primarily direct investment, cooperation with international financial institutions (manager's offices) and foreign government financial organizations, as well as the formation and coordination of a unified state policy in the field of foreign trade and international economic cooperation.
Ministry of Agriculture (MOA)		The ministry is a government body that implements a unified state policy in the field of agriculture and food security, promoting the creation of the value chain of agricultural and food products, creation of conditions for mutually beneficial relations between enterprises growing (producing) fruits and vegetables, meat, dairy and other agricultural food products, and enterprises engaged in processing, procurement and sale of these products.
Ministry of Labor (MOL)		Its mission is to promote the growth of living standards and welfare of the population through the implementation of state policy in the field of employment, regulation of labor relations and migration, employment and vocational training of the unemployed, youth, women, persons with disabilities and other socially vulnerable groups of the population, improving mechanisms stimulation of labor, ensuring its protection and guarantees.
Ministry of Justice (MOJ)		The main tasks are (i) elaboration of proposals for the consistent improvement of the legislative base of democratic, socio-economic, socio-political reforms ensuring effective control over the observance of human rights and freedoms in the activities of public administration bodies, law enforcement and regulatory structures in the center and on the ground; and (ii) ensuring the rule of law, improving the organizational and legal foundations of the functioning of nongovernment, nonprofit organizations.
Central Bank of Uzbekistan (CBU)		In accordance with Article 4 of the Law of the Republic of Uzbekistan "On Banks and Banking Activities", the central bank is a state body that regulates the field of banking activities and exercises powers of licensing, regulations, and prudential supervision.
Policies		
Name	**Responsible Entity**	**Outline**
Development Strategy of New Uzbekistan for 2022-2026	Cabinet of Ministers	(i) Reducing poverty in half by achieving inclusive and stable economic growth, (ii) ensuring competition in the economy, (iii) creating a level playing field for businesses, (iv) accelerating the full transition to a market economy, (v) increasing the competitiveness of the national economy, (vi) a sharp increase in private investment, and (vii) further strengthening the confidence of the business community.
Program "Every family is an entrepreneur"	Cabinet of Ministers, MOF	Ensuring a fundamental improvement in material conditions, significant positive changes in the quality, and level of the lifestyle of the population.
"Roadmap" to improve the position of the Republic of Uzbekistan in the annual report of the World Bank and the International Finance Corporation "Doing Business"	MOF and interested ministries	(i) Further improvement of the business environment, (ii) continuation of the reforms initiated in the country to provide even greater freedom of entrepreneurship, and (iii) ensuring the correct application of the adopted legislative acts on the ground.
Action strategy for five priority areas of development of the Republic of Uzbekistan in 2017-2021 in the "Year of Youth Support and Public Health Promotion"	Agency for Youth Affairs, MOL, MOF	Continued institutional and structural reforms aimed at reducing the presence of the state in the economy, further strengthening the protection of the rights and the priority role of private property, and stimulating the development of small businesses and private entrepreneurship.
		Improvement of the state youth policy: employment and involvement in the sphere of private entrepreneurship of graduates of secondary specialized, professional, and higher educational institutions.

continued on next page

Table 8.7 *continued*

"Roadmap" to facilitate doing business and improve the system for protecting the legitimate interests of business	Business Ombudsman, concerned departments	(1) Development of a procedure for coordinating and conducting inspections carried out in the activities of business entities, implementing preventive measures, electronic registration of inspections, and maintaining the book of registration of inspections.
		(2) Development of a procedure for determining the index of freedom of entrepreneurial activities.
		(3) Approval, in agreement with the Commissioner for the Protection of the Rights and Legitimate Interests of Business Entities, by each regulatory body of questionnaires to verify the activities of business entities.
	Business Ombudsman, Anti-Corruption Agency, MOJ, other regulatory authorities	(4) Establishing a procedure for notifying a business entity of the start of an inspection by the regulatory authority at least 10 working days in advance.
		(5) Development of a draft regulatory legal act that provides for the formation and maintenance of electronic registers of state control functions, mandatory requirements, and officials entitled to check the activities of business entities. The form of control and the object of control are indicated in the register of state control functions and the controlling body. The list of mandatory requirements by types of entrepreneurial activity and questionnaires with reference to the relevant regulatory legal acts are indicated in the register of mandatory requirements.
	Business Ombudsman, MEDPR, MOJ, Chamber of Commerce and Industry	(6) Revision of state control functions and the list of types of inspections at least once every 3 years, taking into account the level of security in the relevant areas and the current state of socio-economic and technological development.
"Roadmap" for attracting grants and concessional long-term financing for measures to counter the negative consequences of the global coronavirus pandemic"	National Bank, Asaka Bank, Uzpromstroybank, Ipoteka Bank	(1) Attraction of credit lines and trade finance from the European Bank for Reconstruction and Development (EBRD) in the amount of $220 million. National Bank ($70 million), Asakabank ($60 million), Uzpromstroybank ($60 million) and Ipotekabank ($30 million) without a state guarantee.
	Cabinet of Ministers, National Bank, MIFT	(2) Attracting a credit line from the Asian Infrastructure Investment Bank (AIIB) in the amount of up to $200 million to finance exporters and small and medium-sized businesses.
	Cabinet of Ministers, MIFT, MOF, MOA	(3) Attracting an additional credit line from JICA in the amount of up to $200.0 million to finance enterprises in the horticulture sector (subject to the approval of the Japanese government).
	MIFT, MEDPR, MOF, Microcreditbank, Uzpromstroybank, Hamkorbank, Qishloq Qurilish Bank	(4) Attracting funds from the European Investment Bank in the amount of $80 million for credit lines to commercial banks to finance exporters and small and medium-sized businesses through the project "Improving the energy efficiency of industrial enterprises."
Innovative Development Strategy for 2019–2021 (Decree of the President of the Republic of Uzbekistan, dated 21 July 2018, No.UP-5544)	Cabinet of Ministers	The main goal of the Strategy is the development of human capital as the main factor determining the level of a country's competitiveness on the world stage and its innovative progress.
Banking Reform Strategy for 2020–2025	CBU	Reform priorities: (i) improving the efficiency of the banking system; (ii) ensuring its financial stability; (iii) reducing the state share in banking; (iv) increasing the availability and quality of financial services by targeting underserved and vulnerable segments, introducing remote services for MSEs and individuals, developing a network of low-cost service outlets; and (v) developing nonbank credit organizations as part of a more unified financial system.
National Strategy for Increasing Financial Inclusion for 2021–2023	CBU	Five reforms: (i) increasing basic financial coverage by expanding service outlets, introducing alternative ways of accessing bank services and creating a network of agent banks; (ii) developing digital financial services by attracting fintech companies, introducing a remote identification system, and modernizing the national payment system; (iii) expanding small business financing by developing financial instruments aimed at entrepreneurial projects, and developing nonbank credit organizations; (iv) strengthening consumer rights and protection by ensuring transparency of information on financial products and services, and introducing mechanisms for resolving disputes; and (v) spreading financial literacy throughout the population (and MSEs) by raising awareness through the media, introducing a financial literacy curriculum in schools, and developing financial literacy training programs.

MSE = micro and small enterprise.

Source: ADB Asia SME Monitor 2022 database. Data from the national database of legislation of the Republic of Uzbekistan (https://lex.uz/en/).

Table 8.7a: COVID-19 Emergency Measures

Name	Fund Size (SUM and $)	Outline
Decree of the President of the Republic of Uzbekistan, dated 3 April 2020 No. UP-5978 "On additional measures to support the population, economic sectors and business entities during the coronavirus pandemic"	SUM2 trillion	Reduce the mandatory requirements for prepayments by legal entities for gas and electricity to 30% from 1 April 2020; in cases where a legal entity or individual has been forced to suspend its activities due to restrictive measures introduced to counter the spread of coronavirus disease (COVID-19) infection, the procedure for applying increased rates of property tax and land tax in respect of unused production areas, nonresidential buildings, including those identified before 1 April 2020, as well as the accrual of penalties and the adoption of measures for the enforcement of debts resulting from the application of increased rates for these taxes.
Decree of the President of the Republic of Uzbekistan dated 19 March 2020 No. UP-5969 "On priority measures to mitigate the negative impact on the economy of the coronavirus pandemic and global crisis phenomena"	SUM10 trillion	(i) Ensure macroeconomic stability, uninterrupted operation of industries and sectors of the economy; (ii) stimulate foreign economic activities; (iii) make effective social support for the population during the period of countering the spread of coronavirus infection and other global risks; (iv) prevent a sharp decline in the income of the country's population; and (v) create an Anti-Crisis Fund under the Ministry of Finance of the Republic of Uzbekistan (hereinafter - Anti-Crisis Fund) without forming a legal entity.
Decree of the President of the Republic of Uzbekistan dated 18 May 2020 No. UP-5996 "On regular measures to support the population and business entities during the coronavirus pandemic"	n/a.,	(i) Stimulate economic growth and investment activities, (ii) restore production rates, (iii) increase employment, (iv) increase household incomes, and (v) support businesses during the coronavirus pandemic.
Decree of the President of the Republic of Uzbekistan dated 22 April 2020 N PP-4691 "On measures to attract external assistance funds to support the population, budget, basic infrastructure and business entities during the coronavirus pandemic"	$3 billion	(i) Increase the efficiency and expand the capabilities of the healthcare system and the sanitary and epidemiological service for the timely detection and medical care of patients infected with coronavirus infection and (ii) provide additional budget support to enterprises in the agricultural, utilities, and energy sectors.
Decree of the President of the Republic of Uzbekistan dated 3 April 2020 N UP-5978 "On additional measures to support the population, economic sectors and business entities during the coronavirus pandemic"	n/a.,	(i) Strengthen the social protection of the population and ensure the stability of the functioning of economic sectors and (ii) provide support to individual business entities during the period of countering the spread of coronavirus infection.
Measures to implement the "Program to Combat the Coronavirus Pandemic" with the participation of the Asian Development Bank	$500 million	Ensure the implementation of the Decree of the President of the Republic of Uzbekistan No. PQ-4691 dated April 22, 2020 "On measures to attract foreign aid to support the population, budget, basic infrastructure and business entities during the coronavirus pandemic."
Decree of the President of the Republic of Uzbekistan dated 28 May 2020 No. UP-6002 "On urgent measures to support the tourism sector to reduce the negative impact of the coronavirus pandemic"	SUM1.5 billion	(i) Support the tourism and related industries most severely affected and continue to be adversely affected by the coronavirus pandemic, (ii) save hundreds of thousands of jobs and qualified professionals, (iii) maintain their incomes, and (iv) accelerate the recovery of tourism as the sanitary and epidemiological situation in the country improves.
Measures to implement the project "Emergency support for businesses affected by the global coronavirus pandemic in Uzbekistan" with the participation of the European Investment Bank	$100 million	Ensure the implementation of the Decree of the President of the Republic of Uzbekistan No. PQ-4691 dated April 22, 2020 "On measures to attract foreign aid to support the population, budget, basic infrastructure and business entities during the coronavirus pandemic" and to further expand cooperation with the European Investment Bank, to further support business entities.
Decree of the President of the Republic of Uzbekistan dated 20 July 2020 No. UP-6029 "On additional measures to support the population, businesses, catering, trade and services to reduce the negative impact of the coronavirus pandemic"	n/a.,	(i) Additionally support the population and business entities, especially in the field of catering, trade and services, during the coronavirus pandemic; (ii) maintain their incomes, their accelerated recovery as the sanitary and epidemiological situation improves; and (iii) save jobs.
Measures to attract and use the credit line of the Asian Infrastructure Investment Bank to support businesses during the coronavirus pandemic	$200 million	Combat the negative consequences of the global coronavirus pandemic following measures that the Cabinet of Ministers decides.
Ground Total	SUM13 trillion	
	$3.8 billion ($800 million as loans)	

Source: ADB Asia SME Monitor 2022 database. Data from the national database of legislation of the Republic of Uzbekistan (https://lex.uz/en/).

Appendixes

Appendix 1: Rationale and Methodology

Background

In response to heightened demand for high-quality multicountry analytical data on micro, small, and medium-sized enterprises (MSMEs) and regional best practices that support their development, the Asian Development Bank (ADB) has published the *Asia Small and Medium-Sized Enterprise Monitor* (ASM) since 2020. The ASM is a knowledge-sharing product developed as a key resource for MSME development policies in Asia and the Pacific. The ASM, as an annual periodical, reviews financial and nonfinancial conditions of MSMEs at the country and regional level. The ASM has several main objectives: (i) provide in-depth analyses on MSMEs, finance, and policy interventions; (ii) exchange country best practices and experiences on MSME development; and (iii) present timely comparative financial and nonfinancial data on MSMEs. Its target clientele are ADB's developing member country (DMC) government authorities responsible for MSME development and access to finance to support their promotion of evidence-based policy design—but it also serves additional audiences. The ASM expects that analyzed data on MSME development and access to finance will contribute to increasing analytical output on MSMEs from academia; thus, it will promote global and regional dialogue on MSME policies and financial inclusion.

The ASM was developed through two testing phases. The Phase 1 project (September 2012–May 2014) designed a feasible framework for a MSME data platform for Asia and the Pacific. As a pilot product, the inaugural ASM 2013 was published in April 2014 with 14 countries from five ADB regions.[1] The Phase 2 project (July 2014–September 2015) improved the ASM platform based on feedback from DMC partner institutions. It expanded country coverage and designed a pilot online ASM database (for internal use only). With the success of the inaugural volume of ASM 2013, ASM 2014 (second edition) was published in September 2015 covering 20 DMCs from five ADB regions.[2] After Phase 2, ADB conducted evaluation surveys for both DMCs and ADB operations. It received positive feedback from both external and internal clients asking to regularize the ASM. In July 2019, after a 4-year interval, the ASM project became a multi-year project, strengthening its global reach and data comparability, and developing a user-friendly online data portal. The ASM 2013 and 2014 focused specifically on MSME access to finance, but ASM 2020 and following editions upgraded prior ASM products by extending its analytical coverage to nonfinancial issues on MSME development.

1 The five regions and countries were (i) Kazakhstan in Central Asia; (ii) the People's Republic of China (PRC) and the Republic of Korea (ROK) in East Asia; (iii) Bangladesh, India, and Sri Lanka in South Asia; (iv) Cambodia, Indonesia, Malaysia, the Philippines, Thailand, and Viet Nam in Southeast Asia; and (v) Papua New Guinea and Solomon Islands in the Pacific.

2 The five regions and countries were (i) Kazakhstan, the Kyrgyz Republic, and Tajikistan in Central Asia; (ii) the PRC, the ROK, and Mongolia in East Asia; (iii) Bangladesh, India, and Sri Lanka in South Asia; (iv) Cambodia, Indonesia, the Lao People's Democratic Republic (Lao PDR), Malaysia, Myanmar, the Philippines, Thailand, and Viet Nam in Southeast Asia; and (v) Fiji, Papua New Guinea, and Solomon Islands in the Pacific.

Components

In October 2020, ADB released the four-volume ASM 2020, focusing on 10 Southeast Asian countries.[3] The 2021 edition extended country coverage to five South Asian countries—Bangladesh, India, Nepal, Pakistan, and Sri Lanka—together with data updates from Southeast Asia. The 2022 edition further extends country coverage to seven Central and West Asian countries—Armenia, Azerbaijan, Georgia, Kazakhstan, the Kyrgyz Republic, Tajikistan, and Uzbekistan; for a total of 22 countries covered in the ASM.

The ASM normally comprises three key components: (i) country and regional reviews, (ii) thematic analysis, and (iii) technical assessments. Because of the coronavirus disease (COVID-19) pandemic that started in 2020, ADB prepared two special chapters to assess its impact on MSMEs in ASM 2020 and ASM 2021.

The Country and Regional Review Volume (main ASM report) offers in-depth analyses on financial and nonfinancial issues of a country's MSME development. Each has three review dimensions with 15 sub-dimensions (16 for 2022) for analysis: (i) MSME development (scale of MSMEs, employment, business productivity, market access, technology and innovation, and networking and support); (ii) access to finance (bank credit, public financing and guarantees, nonbank financing, digital financial services, capital markets, and financial infrastructure); and (iii) policies and regulations (MSME development, financial inclusion, and response to COVID-19 [with the response to the Russian invasion of Ukraine added for 2022]). This volume analyzes these dimensions based on data collected from DMC partner institutions by using a standardized ASM data request form. This report is Volume I of the ASM 2022.

The Thematic Chapter explores each country's best practices related to MSME development by using an impact evaluation approach—an approach that assesses how an intervention affects particular conditions compared with non-intervention. This is a useful analytical tool to evaluate the impact of policy interventions on national MSME development. The analysis will also be used as a pilot project exercise for MSME development in DMCs. Thematic chapters focused on fintech loans to tricycle drivers in the Philippines for ASM 2020, digitalizing microfinance in Bangladesh (findings from baseline surveys) for ASM 2021, and the Russian invasion of Ukraine and its impact on small firms in Central and West Asia for ASM 2022.

Separately, given the heightened needs of DMC governments, ADB published two special chapters that analyzed the impact of the COVID-19 pandemic on MSMEs in Indonesia, the Lao PDR, the Philippines, and Thailand. The special study was based on the findings from year-long MSME surveys conducted in March 2020–April 2021 in the four countries.

The Technical Chapter is a new feature. It aims to design and test a new composite index called the Small and Medium-Sized Enterprise Development Index (SME-DI) to measure two dimensions affecting MSME development, finance and nonfinance, by using multivariate analysis based on country data received during the ASM project. Technical chapters were published in the ASM 2020 and ASM 2021 as pilot exercises. The SME-DI was applied for the regional analysis in Volume I of ASM 2022.

[3] ADB. Asia Small and Medium-Sized Enterprise Monitor. https://www.adb.org/publications/series/asia-small-medium-sized-enterprise-monitor

Data Processing

To collect reliable and accurate data with periodic updates, ADB first built strategic partnerships with key institutions that hold MSME data—including SME agencies, relevant line ministries, statistics offices, central banks, financial authorities, SME banks, and chambers of commerce. To systematically compile the data, ADB prepared a Standardized Data Request Form for collecting MSME data from partner institutions, comprising two separate forms on finance and nonfinance. Missing data and information from the data forms were supplemented by surveys, field research, and virtual interviews. For ASM 2022, virtual missions were conducted in February–May 2022 in Armenia, Azerbaijan, Georgia, Kazakhstan, the Kyrgyz Republic, Tajikistan, and Uzbekistan. A total of 84 virtual meetings and interviews were conducted with key stakeholders including central banks, financial authorities, SME agencies, line ministries, and private sector institutions across the seven Central and West Asian countries—which became the basis for Country Chapter analysis. All data collected were interactively reviewed and finalized by an ADB team and DMC partner institutions. Volume I country and regional data are downloadable from the ADB Asia SME Monitor database (online data portal). The ASM also has a feedback mechanism for participating DMCs through training and dissemination programs. An example was a Serendipity Knowledge Program on Strengthening MSME Dynamics for Resilient Economic Growth in Sri Lanka held on 24 August 2022.

Reading Note

In Central and West Asia, MSME definitions vary by country. They use different criteria and categories—such as micro and small enterprises (MSEs) for Uzbekistan; small and medium-sized enterprises (SMEs) for Georgia and Tajikistan; and micro, small, and medium-sized enterprises (MSMEs) for Armenia, Azerbaijan, Kazakhstan, and the Kyrgyz Republic. The ASM relies on country MSME definitions for comparative analysis as they are a benchmark for MSME policies, and collectively uses "MSME" throughout, unless otherwise stated.

Moving Forward

The ASM uses a regionally focused approach for analysis. It provides deep analysis of a designated region and countries, with data updates of past analyses of regions and countries each year. Following this approach, ASM 2020 focused on 10 Southeast Asian countries with ASM 2021 covering five countries in South Asia, with data updates of Southeast Asian countries. ASM 2022 expanded country coverage further to Central and West Asia.

We faced extremely difficult working conditions when preparing ASM 2020 and 2021 due to the COVID-19 pandemic and a series of outbreaks of coronavirus variants through 2021. Planned fieldwork was restricted, with counterpart government offices long closed due to the lockdowns and strict mobility restrictions. Against this backdrop, however, we published the ASM series in 2020 and 2021 as planned. It was made possible due to the strong commitment to emergency analytical needs and constant networking (through virtual communications) among the team and counterpart DMC institutions.

In largely post-pandemic 2022, we could more systematically prepare the ASM in close collaboration between ADB's knowledge and operations departments. For preparation of ASM 2023, virtual work arrangements will shift to hybrid netwoking and more fieldwork.

Appendix 2: Regional Data Tables

A. MSME Landscape

A1. Number of MSMEs

Country	2003	2004	2005	2006	2007	2008	2009	2010	2011	2012	2013	2014	2015	2016	2017	2018	2019	2020	2021
Southeast Asia																			
Brunei Darussalam	...	...	...	...	...	...	...	5,566	...	...	...	...	5,434	5,896	6,047	6,085	6,169	...	...
Cambodia	...	...	...	...	...	...	376,069	...	462,582	...	...	512,870	...	...	...	...	...	...	...
Indonesia	...	...	...	...	...	...	...	52,764,750	54,114,821	55,206,444	56,534,592	57,895,721	59,262,772	61,651,177	62,922,617	64,194,057	65,465,497	...	...
Lao People's Democratic Republic	...	...	...	126,717	...	...	...	...	...	...	124,510	...	...	...	...	124,567	...	133,721	...
Malaysia	548,267	...	...	...	...	...	...	638,790	...	...	...	...	907,065	1,086,157	1,154,809	1,149,629	1,181,631	1,151,339	1,226,494
Myanmar*	...	...	...	39,949	40,811	40,529	40,396	39,272	38,978	38,590	38,654	39,062	39,162	59,694	61,949	71,290	75,116	...	...
Philippines	...	...	...	780,469	781,201	758,436	777,357	774,664	816,759	940,886	937,327	942,925	896,839	911,768	920,677	998,342	995,745	952,969	1,076,279
Singapore	...	...	...	...	...	...	...	...	...	...	...	242,800	246,200	247,800	254,100	262,400	271,800	279,700	290,300
Thailand	...	...	...	...	2,366,227	2,827,633	2,896,106	2,913,167	2,646,549	2,730,591	2,763,997	2,736,744	2,765,986	3,004,679	3,046,790	3,077,822	3,105,096	3,134,442	2,621,725
Viet Nam	...	...	...	...	143,622	186,379	230,365	272,283	316,941	338,916	365,181	393,915	433,453	495,010	544,212	593,865	651,138	...	...
South Asia																			
Bangladesh	...	...	...	...	...	...	...	...	...	...	7,813,315	...	...	...	...	...	...	...	...
India*	...	...	...	...	...	36,176,000	37,736,000	39,370,000	41,080,000	42,873,000	44,764,000	46,754,000	48,846,000	51,057,000	51,299,000	63,387,673	...	...	...
Nepal*	...	...	...	...	...	...	...	156,343	171,004	189,026	204,582	226,711	244,365	268,682	300,721	337,864	390,493	...	...
Pakistan	...	...	3,210,000	...	...	...	...	...	...	...	...	...	...	...	...	...	...	5,200,000	...
Sri Lanka	...	...	...	...	...	...	...	...	...	...	1,017,267	...	...	...	...	...	...	...	...
Central and West Asia																			
Armenia	...	93,825	99,820	79,595	81,953	129,985	132,923	59,267	68,682	73,295	77,999	76,589	69,360	76,763	59,467	68,654	75,045	83,032	...
Azerbaijan	...	161,434	178,540	184,281	196,972	204,960	205,028	207,120	135,353	141,422	165,277	186,898	187,375	191,695	169,603	244,883	271,304	316,370	...
Georgia	...	27,217	34,783	33,374	33,072	32,961	37,990	42,365	57,325	54,418	58,761	70,491	90,092	97,627	124,614	126,770	128,204	129,268	...
Kazakhstan	...	...	507,365	572,738	643,376	707,821	663,374	661,598	846,111	809,750	888,233	926,844	1,242,579	1,106,353	1,145,994	1,241,328	1,330,244	1,357,311	1,431,647
Kyrgyz Republic	...	8,485	8,471	9,267	9,852	11,988	12,221	12,161	12,211	11,931	12,549	13,505	14,027	14,368	14,653	15,289	16,978	17,019	17,050
Tajikistan	...	...	...	...	...	55,750	55,750	24,459	27,964	31,144	37,832	38,907	38,907	37,804	25,451	26,453	26,691	27,650	29,555
Uzbekistan	...	99,780	100,751	112,260	129,211	135,561	152,246	164,052	177,876	177,551	189,867	196,014	207,104	210,594	229,666	262,930	334,767	411,203	462,834

MSME = micro, small, and medium-sized enterprise.

Notes: End-of-year data except * fiscal year data (ended 31 March in India and Myanmar, and 15 July in Nepal). For Kazakhstan, data for operating MSMEs.

Source: ADB Asia SME Monitor 2022 database.

A2. MSMEs to Total (%)

Country	2003	2004	2005	2006	2007	2008	2009	2010	2011	2012	2013	2014	2015	2016	2017	2018	2019	2020	2021
Southeast Asia																			
Brunei Darussalam	...	...	...	...	...	...	...	97.5	...	...	...	...	96.6	97.0	97.2	97.3	97.3	...	...
Cambodia	...	...	...	...	...	...	99.8	...	99.8	...	...	99.8	...	...	...	...	...	...	...
Indonesia	...	...	...	...	...	...	...	100.0	100.0	100.0	100.0	100.0	100.0	100.0	100.0	100.0	100.0	...	...
Lao People's Democratic Republic	...	...	...	99.8	...	...	...	...	...	...	99.8	...	...	...	...	99.8	...	99.8	...
Malaysia	99.2	...	...	...	...	...	...	98.5	...	...	...	...	98.5	97.9	97.6	97.4	97.3	97.2	97.4
Myanmar*	...	...	...	92.0	92.0	91.8	91.6	90.3	89.1	88.4	87.9	87.4	87.1	90.2	89.6	90.1	89.9	...	...
Philippines	...	...	...	99.7	99.7	99.6	99.6	99.6	99.6	99.6	99.6	99.6	99.5	99.6	99.6	99.5	99.5	99.5	99.6
Singapore	...	...	...	...	...	...	...	...	...	...	...	99.5	99.4	99.5	99.5	99.5	99.5	99.5	99.6
Thailand	...	...	...	...	99.6	99.7	99.8	99.6	99.8	97.2	97.2	99.7	99.7	99.7	99.8	99.8	99.5	99.5	99.8
Viet Nam	...	...	...	...	96.3	97.0	97.4	97.5	97.6	97.7	97.8	97.9	98.0	98.0	97.1	97.2	97.4	...	...
South Asia																			
Bangladesh	...	...	...	...	...	...	...	...	...	...	100.0	...	...	...	...	...	...	...	...
India	...	...	...	...	...	...	...	...	...	...	...	...	...	99.9	...	...	...	...	...
Nepal	...	...	...	...	...	...	...	...	...	...	...	...	...	...	...	...	...	...	...
Pakistan	...	...	99.1	...	...	...	...	...	...	...	...	...	...	...	...	...	...	98.6	...
Sri Lanka	...	...	...	...	...	...	...	...	...	...	99.8	...	...	...	...	...	...	...	...
Central and West Asia																			
Armenia	...	97.8	97.7	97.7	97.8	97.7	97.7	98.0	98.0	98.0	99.0	99.0	99.0	99.0	99.8	99.8	99.8	99.8	...
Azerbaijan	...	...	...	...	...	...	...	...	...	...	...	...	...	...	...	...	99.6	99.7	...
Georgia	...	99.6	99.6	99.6	99.5	99.5	99.5	99.6	99.6	99.5	99.5	99.6	99.7	99.7	99.7	99.7	99.7	99.7	...
Kazakhstan	...		99.6	99.7	99.7	99.7	99.7	99.7	99.7	99.7	99.7	99.7	99.8	99.8	99.8	99.8	99.8	99.8	99.8
Kyrgyz Republic	...	95.7	95.7	96.0	96.4	96.9	97.3	97.6	97.6	97.6	97.7	97.9	98.0	98.0	97.9	98.0	98.2	98.3	98.2
Tajikistan	...	...	...	...	...	97.5	97.5	97.5	97.8	97.7	98.7	98.7	98.7	98.7	98.2	98.5	98.6	98.6	98.6
Uzbekistan	...	93.9	94.8	96.3	97.2	97.5	97.7	98.1	98.3	98.4	98.5	98.6	98.8	98.8	99.0	99.2	99.3	99.3	99.3

MSME = micro, small, and medium-sized enterprise.

Note: End-of-year data except * fiscal year data (ended 31 March in Myanmar).

Source: ADB Asia SME Monitor 2022 database.

A3. MSMEs by Sector (% share, latest available year)

Item / Southeast Asia	Brunei Darussalam	Cambodia	Indonesia	Lao People's Democratic Republic	Malaysia	Myanmar	Philippines	Singapore	Thailand	Viet Nam
Agriculture	2.9	...	...	1.4	1.9	...	0.9	...		1.1
Manufacturing	10.8	13.9	16.7	14.7	5.8	...	11.6	...	17.2	15.7
Transportation and communication	5.5	...	7.3	3.0	...	...	...	...	0.5	7.9
Construction	9.8	...	0.9	1.7	8.0	...	...	...	2.5	13.7
Wholesale and retail trade	34.5	59.6	63.5	61.2	83.8*	...	46.4	...	46.4	37.5
Other services	35.3	26.5	10.7	3.2	...	...	40.4	...	33.3	22.8
Others	1.2	...	0.9	14.8	0.4	...	0.7	...	0.2	1.2
Year	2019	2014	2016	2020	2021		2020		2021	2019

Item / South Asia	Bangladesh	India*	Nepal*	Pakistan	Sri Lanka
Agriculture	...	...	16.3	1.0	...
Manufacturing	11.1	31.0	33.2	20.0	23.6
Transportation and communication	16.9	...	...	2.0	4.2
Construction	0.1	...	3.0	0.1	0.8
Wholesale and retail trade	45.9	36.3	...	53.0	41.1
Other services	25.7	32.6	46.7	22.0	29.2
Others	0.3	0.01	0.7	1.9	1.2
Year	2013	FY 2018	FY 2019	2005	2013

Item / Central and West Asia	Armenia	Azerbaijan	Georgia	Kazakhstan	Kyrgyz Republic	Tajikistan	Uzbekistan
Agriculture	...	1.0	1.2	18.2	3.3	15.2	9.9
Manufacturing	12.7	3.9	8.9	4.5	14.6	7.9	19.5
Transportation and communication	4.0	23.1	8.6	5.4	5.3	4.3	6.1
Construction	2.6	3.7	6.6	5.7	12.2	6.9	9.4
Wholesale and retail trade	58.1	32.8	39.5	31.9	28.0	13.3	33.8
Other services	22.3	35.0	20.4	20.0	36.6	52.4	9.0
Others	0.3	0.5	14.8	14.3	...	...	12.2
Year	2020	2020	2020	2021	2021	2021	2021

MSME = micro, small, and medium-sized enterprise.

Notes: End-of-year data except * fiscal year (FY) data (ended 31 March in India and 15 July in Nepal). For Malaysia, "wholesale and retail trade" includes transportation and storage, telecommunication, and real estate. For Nepal, "others" include energy-based, mining and minerals; other services include information and technology, and tourism. For Armenia, "other services" include electricity, gas, steam and air-conditioning supply; water supply, sewerage, waste management and remediation activities; information and communication; real estate activities; professional, scientific and technical activities; administrative and support service activities; repair of computers and personal and household goods; accommodation and food service activities, while "others" include mining and quarrying. For Tajikistan, "other services" include health and social services, education, public administration and defense, real estate, financial intermediation, recreation and entertainment, culture and sports, as well as other community, social and personal services.

Source: ADB Asia SME Monitor 2022 database.

A4. MSMEs by Region (% share, latest available year)

Item / Southeast Asia	Brunei Darussalam	Cambodia	Indonesia	Lao People's Democratic Republic	Malaysia	Myanmar*	Philippines	Singapore	Thailand	Viet Nam
Capital city	...	18.8	...	22.3	14.7	15.3	20.3	...	11.3	...
Other areas	...	81.2	...	77.7	85.3	84.7	79.7	...	88.7	...
Year		2014		2020	2015	FY2019	2020		2021	

Item / South Asia	Bangladesh	India*	Nepal*	Pakistan	Sri Lanka
Capital city	28.5	48.8	19.5	0.6	13.3
Other areas	71.5	51.3	80.5	99.4	86.7
Year	2013	FY 2018	FY 2019	2005	2013

Item / Central and West Asia	Armenia	Azerbaijan	Georgia	Kazakhstan	Kyrgyz Republic	Tajikistan	Uzbekistan
Capital city	51.5	47.5	45.2	11.4	62.5	21.9	20.4
Other areas	48.5	52.5	54.8	88.6	37.5	78.1	79.6
Year	2020	2020	2020	2021	2021	2021	2021

MSME = micro, small, and medium-sized enterprise.

Notes: End-of-year data except * fiscal year (FY) data (ended 31 March in India and Myanmar, and 15 July in Nepal). Capital city: Yerevan in Armenia; Baku in Azerbaijan; Phnom Penh in Cambodia; Tbilisi in Georgia; Astana in Kazakhstan; Bishkek in the Kyrgyz Republic; Vientiane in the Lao PDR; Kuala Lumpur in Malaysia; Yangon in Myanmar; National Capital Region in the Philippines; Bangkok in Thailand; Kathmandu in Nepal; Islamabad in Pakistan; Colombo in Sri Lanka. For Bangladesh and India, Urban/Rural.

Source: ADB Asia SME Monitor 2022 database.

A5. Number of Employees by MSMEs

Country	2003	2004	2005	2006	2007	2008	2009	2010	2011	2012	2013	2014	2015	2016	2017	2018	2019	2020	2021
Southeast Asia																			
Brunei Darussalam	...	...	...	...	...	...	...	59,179	...	...	...	...	64,722	65,486	66,123	64,384	64,487	...	...
Cambodia	...	...	...	...	...	...	1,099,647	...	1,158,871	...	...	1,345,100	...	...	...	...	...	...	...
Indonesia	...	...	...	...	...	...	...	96,193,623	98,238,913	101,722,458	107,657,509	114,144,082	123,229,386	112,828,610	116,431,224	116,978,631	119,562,843	...	...
Lao People's Democratic Republic	...	...	...	238,703	...	...	...	...	...	...	472,231	...	...	...	...	472,529	...	...	...
Malaysia	...	...	5,707,000	5,846,000	6,133,000	6,283,000	6,476,000	6,798,000	7,074,000	7,339,000	7,785,000	8,836,000	9,069,000	6,663,000	6,889,000	7,106,000	7,318,000	7,253,000	...
Myanmar	...	...	...	...	...	...	...	...	...	...	...	...	...	...	...	...	...	...	...
Philippines	...	...	...	3,327,855	3,355,742	3,395,505	3,595,641	3,532,935	3,872,406	4,930,851	4,770,445	4,891,836	4,784,870	4,879,179	4,922,251	5,714,262	5,510,760	5,380,815	5,461,731
Singapore	...	...	...	...	...	...	...	...	...	...	...	2,450,000	2,470,000	2,480,000	2,470,000	2,480,000	2,500,000	2,360,000	2,410,000
Thailand	...	...	...	...	8,900,567	...	9,701,354	10,507,507	10,995,977	11,783,143	11,414,702	10,501,166	10,749,735	11,747,093	13,088,802	13,950,241	12,060,369	12,714,916	9,964,249
Viet Nam	...	...	...	...	2,834,950	3,347,883	3,872,711	4,394,037	5,060,430	5,107,958	5,179,702	5,321,882	5,682,980	6,205,320	5,538,134	5,627,952	5,681,518	...	...
South Asia																			
Bangladesh	...	...	...	...	...	...	...	...	...	...	21,033,994	...	...	...	...	...	...	...	...
India*	...	...	...	...	...	80,523,000	84,200,000	88,084,000	92,179,000	96,515,000	101,169,000	106,140,000	111,429,000	117,132,000	111,228,000	110,989,000.0	...	...	...
Nepal*	...	...	...	...	...	1,761,863	1,843,908	1,914,469	1,987,387	2,062,497	2,140,706	2,157,744	2,263,363	2,337,373	2,466,992	2,606,086	2,808,052	...	...
Pakistan*	...	...	...	...	...	...	...	...	...	...	...	...	24,066,900	...	...	27,324,000	...	...	...
Sri Lanka	...	...	...	...	...	...	...	...	...	...	2,255,182	...	...	...	...	...	...	...	...
Central and West Asia																			
Armenia	...	365,486	375,802	383,432	448,311	471,394	465,761	258,619	280,927	290,388	...	370,269	365,262	238,311	168,185	212,963	248,069	232,955	...
Azerbaijan	...	68,565	73,447	87,524	92,108	103,246	105,902	93,205	90,182	95,503	108,976	115,035	284,066	281,099	290,132	283,432	332,255	348,723	...
Georgia	...	205,685	253,481	246,516	244,953	226,064	257,776	265,939	349,993	364,953	372,463	405,637	428,153	448,990	474,576	490,897	491,668	442,164	...
Kazakhstan**	...	...	1,875.5	1,951.9	2,121.2	2,153.0	2,296.6	2,630.6	2,427.1	2,383.3	2,576.9	2,811.0	3,183.8	3,166.8	3,190.1	3,312.5	3,448.7	3,472.6	3,463.0
Kyrgyz Republic**	...	87.0	84.2	87.9	90.8	96.8	92.9	88.6	86.0	87.4	88.0	88.5	88.3	87.4	89.4	91.0	107.8	100.8	92.9
Tajikistan**	...	16.5	17.2	18.1	18.9	19.4	20.9	19.9	18.7	19.6	27.5	30.2	28.4	21.4	...	248.5	250.8	251.3	252.7
Uzbekistan**	...	5,974.9	6,602.5	7,234.1	7,743.1	8,071.1	8,370.1	8,643.9	8,950.7	9,239.7	9,604.0	9,950.8	10,170.4	10,397.5	10,541.5	10,128.8	10,318.9	9,865.7	10,070.7

MSME = micro, small, and medium-sized enterprise.

Notes: End-of-year data except * fiscal year data (ended 31 March in India, 15 July in Nepal, and 30 June in Pakistan). ** thousand people.

Source: ADB Asia SME Monitor 2022 database.

A6. MSME Employees to Total (%)

Country	2003	2004	2005	2006	2007	2008	2009	2010	2011	2012	2013	2014	2015	2016	2017	2018	2019	2020	2021
Southeast Asia																			
Brunei Darussalam	...	...	...	...	...	...	...	59.4	...	...	...	...	55.1	56.5	57.3	57.4	55.7	...	...
Cambodia	...	...	...	...	...	...	74.8	...	72.0	...	...	71.8	...	...	...	...	...	...	...
Indonesia	...	...	...	...	...	...	...	97.3	97.3	97.2	97.2	97.0	96.7	97.0	96.8	97.0	96.9	...	...
Lao People's Democratic Republic	...	...	...	87.4	...	...	...	...	...	...	82.9	...	...	...	...	82.4	...	...	...
Malaysia	56.4	56.6	56.8	56.9	58.2	58.9	58.0	55.5	57.3	57.2	57.5	63.8	46.6	47.0	47.6	48.0	48.4	48.0	...
Myanmar	...	...	...	...	...	...	...	...	...	...	...	...	...	...	...	...	...	...	...
Philippines	...	...	...	66.8	64.7	61.2	63.2	62.3	61.0	64.9	63.7	62.8	61.6	63.3	62.8	63.2	62.4	62.7	64.7
Singapore	...	...	...	...	...	...	...	...	...	...	...	72.1	72.2	72.3	72.2	71.7	71.4	70.4	70.9
Thailand	...	...	...	...	76.0	...	78.2	77.9	83.9	81.0	81.0	80.3	80.4	78.5	82.2	85.5	69.5	71.7	76.9
Viet Nam	...	...	...	...	39.2	42.1	44.4	45.1	46.8	46.4	45.2	44.2	44.2	44.3	38.1	38.0	37.5	...	...
South Asia																			
Bangladesh	...	...	...	...	...	...	...	...	...	...	85.9	...	...	...	...	...	...	...	...
India*	...	...	...	...	...	...	...	...	...	...	...	...	...	...	...	...	...	...	...
Nepal*	...	...	...	...	...	...	...	...	...	...	...	...	...	...	...	...	...	73.5	...
Pakistan*	...	...	...	...	...	...	...	...	...	...	...	...	72.6	...	...	72.0	...	...	...
Sri Lanka	...	...	...	...	...	...	...	...	...	...	75.1	...	...	...	...	...	...	...	...
Central and West Asia																			
Armenia	...	68.2	68.2	68.2	68.2	68.2	68.2	68.2	68.2	68.2	...	68.2	68.2	64.3	66.2	68.3	69.8	68.7	...
Azerbaijan	...	5.4	5.6	6.5	6.7	7.3	7.6	6.7	6.5	6.4	7.9	7.6	6.3	20.4	20.8	42.9	43.7	42.1	...
Georgia	...	63.7	65.2	68.3	67.8	64.7	66.5	66.9	69.5	68.3	67.6	68.5	68.3	67.3	67.0	66.9	65.0	62.8	...
Kazakhstan	...	...	25.8	26.4	27.8	27.4	29.1	32.4	29.2	28.0	30.1	33.0	37.8	37.0	37.2	38.1	39.3	39.8	39.3
Kyrgyz Republic	...	44.1	43.4	43.6	44.2	45.6	47.2	48.2	47.2	48.3	48.5	48.5	48.8	48.2	48.7	48.9	53.0	52.6	49.3
Tajikistan	...	0.79	0.81	0.85	0.88	0.89	0.94	0.89	0.83	0.86	1.19	1.30	1.19	0.90	...	21.3	20.9	20.7	20.4
Uzbekistan	...	60.3	64.8	69.1	72.1	73.1	73.9	74.3	75.1	75.6	76.7	77.6	77.9	78.2	78.0	76.3	76.2	74.5	74.4

MSME = micro, small, and medium-sized enterprise.

Notes: End-of-year data except * fiscal year data (ended 31 March in India, 15 July in Nepal, and 30 June in Pakistan). For Malaysia, data in 2015–2019 was revised based on a methodology change. Revised data include the government, informal sector excluding agriculture, unregistered businesses in agriculture, and outsourcing activities in computing the overall employment which signified as denominator. For Nepal, data were extracted from the Industrial Statistics 2019–2020, and small and medium-sized enterprises only.

Source: ADB Asia SME Monitor 2022 database.

A7. MSME Employees by Sector (% share, latest available year)

Item / Southeast Asia	Brunei Darussalam	Cambodia	Indonesia	Lao People's Democratic Republic	Malaysia	Myanmar	Philippines	Singapore	Thailand	Viet Nam
Agriculture	1.6	...	...	2.1	10.7	...	1.9	...	...	1.5
Manufacturing	10.2	15.2	20.5	22.5	16.4	...	13.5	...	29.9	25.4
Transportation and communication	5.9	...	4.7	3.1	...	...	...	...	1.3	8.3
Construction	14.8	...	...	2.8	9.3	...	...	...	5.2	17.3
Wholesale and retail trade	31.2	46.7	54.4	46.6	63.3	...	36.1	...	38.3	24.2
Other services	34.0	38.1	19.5	1.8	...	...	45.4	...	24.7	21.6
Others	2.3	...	0.9	21.1	0.3	...	3.0	...	0.5	1.7
Year	2019	2014	2016	2020	2020		2020		2021	2019

Item / South Asia	Bangladesh	India*	Nepal	Pakistan*	Sri Lanka
Agriculture	...	...	...	...	...
Manufacturing	20.3	32.5	...	22.8	28.1
Transportation and communication	9.4	...	...	11.5	3.4
Construction	0.2	...	...	16.2	2.1
Wholesale and retail trade	39.9	34.9	...	32.5	30.8
Other services	29.9	32.6	...	16.0	33.2
Others	0.4	0.01	...	1.0	2.4
Year	2013	FY 2018		FY 2018	2013

Item / Central and West Asia	Armenia	Azerbaijan	Georgia	Kazakhstan	Kyrgyz Republic	Tajikistan	Uzbekistan
Agriculture	...	5.2	2.0	13.0	4.2	13.6	34.3
Manufacturing	22.2	13.6	12.7	10.0	32.4	7.2	13.1
Transportation and communication	3.9	11.0	8.8	5.5	3.9	2.2	5.2
Construction	8.9	16.8	11.6	8.6	12.7	4.9	12.0
Wholesale and retail trade	31.6	15.9	29.8	28.5	17.7	6.0	14.6
Other services	32.3	28.0	33.7	26.3	29.1	66.1	8.0
Others	1.0	9.5	1.5	8.0	...	...	12.8
Year	2020	2020	2020	2021	2021	2021	2021

MSME = micro, small, and medium-sized enterprise.

Notes: End-of-year data except * fiscal year (FY) data (ended 31 March in India and 30 June in Pakistan). For Malaysia, "wholesale and retail trade" includes transportation and storage, telecommunication, and real estate. For Armenia, "other services" include electricity, gas, steam and air-conditioning supply; water supply, sewerage, waste management and remediation activities; information and communication; real estate activities; professional, scientific and technical activities; administrative and support service activities; repair of computers and personal and household goods; accommodation and food service activities, while "others" include mining and quarrying.

Source: ADB Asia SME Monitor 2022 database.

A8. MSME Employees by Region (% share, latest available year)

Item / Southeast Asia	Brunei Darussalam	Cambodia	Indonesia	Lao People's Democratic Republic	Malaysia	Myanmar	Philippines	Singapore	Thailand	Viet Nam
Capital city	...	20.0	...	...	15.7	...	27.9	...	15.8	...
Other areas	...	80.0	...	...	84.3	...	72.1	...	84.2	...
Year		2014			2015		2020		2021	

Item / South Asia	Bangladesh	India*	Nepal	Pakistan	Sri Lanka
Capital city	34.4	44.9	...	...	18.5
Other areas	65.6	55.2	...	...	81.5
Year	2013	FY 2018			2013

Item / Central and West Asia	Armenia	Azerbaijan	Georgia	Kazakhstan	Kyrgyz Republic	Tajikistan	Uzbekistan
Capital city	65.0	62.6	52.9	12.0	49.9	...	...
Other areas	35.0	37.4	47.1	88.0	50.1	...	...
Year	2020	2020	2020	2021	2021		

MSME = micro, small, and medium-sized enterprise.

Notes: End-of-year data except * fiscal year (FY) data (ended 31 March in India). Capital city: Yerevan in Armenia; Baku in Azerbaijan; Phnom Penh in Cambodia; Tbilisi in Georgia; Astana in Kazakhstan; Bishkek in the Kyrgyz republic; Kuala Lumpur in Malaysia, National Capital Region in the Philippines, Bangkok in Thailand, Colombo in Sri Lanka. For Bangladesh and India, Urban/Rural.

Source: ADB Asia SME Monitor 2022 database.

A9-1. GDP of MSMEs (local currency)

Country	2003	2004	2005	2006	2007	2008	2009	2010	2011	2012	2013	2014	2015	2016	2017	2018	2019	2020	2021
Southeast Asia																			
Brunei Darussalam	...	...	...	...	...	...	...	3,233	3,472	3,808	3,984	...	3,612	5,399	5,323	5,126	4,898	...	...
Cambodia	...	...	...	...	...	...	...	...	...	...	...	...	...	...	...	...	...	...	...
Indonesia	...	...	...	...	...	...	...	2,969,346	3,411,575	4,321,830	4,869,568	5,440,008	6,228,285	7,009,283	7,820,283	8,573,895	9,580,763	...	...
Lao People's Democratic Republic	...	...	...	...	...	...	...	...	...	...	...	...	...	...	...	...	...	...	...
Malaysia	190,199	205,999	220,213	234,359	257,883	274,766	275,324	298,180	319,832	339,121	360,916	409,776	435,072	458,686	491,568	522,415	553,458	512,798	...
Myanmar	...	...	...	...	...	...	...	...	...	...	...	...	...	...	...	...	...	...	...
Philippines	...	...	...	751,943	...	...	...	...	...	...	...	...	...	...	...	...	...	...	...
Singapore	...	...	...	...	...	...	...	...	...	...	...	180	181	191	201	204	207	183	213
Thailand	...	...	...	...	3,758,130	3,863,743	3,858,146	4,258,542	4,445,932	4,831,990	5,044,252	5,261,090	5,631,426	6,099,185	6,557,750	7,013,971	5,963,156	5,376,066	...
Viet Nam	...	...	...	...	...	...	...	...	...	...	...	...	...	...	...	...	...	...	...
South Asia																			
Bangladesh*	...	...	...	...	...	...	...	...	...	225,691	245,579	261,131	283,426	309,094	339,458	370,864	411,480	443,476	...
India*	...	...	...	...	...	24,366	25,621	27,582	30,457	25,833	27,584	29,169	30,888	33,517	36,001	39,196	42,322	...	...
Nepal	...	...	...	...	...	...	...	...	...	...	...	...	...	...	...	...	...	...	...
Pakistan	...	...	...	...	101,162	122,473	145,946	167,383	208,611	241,951	283,107	327,030	373,595	406,648	457,088	506,839	571,951	621,977	...
Sri Lanka	...	...	...	...	...	...	...	...	...	...	...	...	...	...	...	...	...	...	...
Central and West Asia																			
Armenia	...	736,467	892,667	1,070,445	1,291,206	1,487,951	1,335,202	1,487,887	1,643,407	1,698,993	1,559,516	1,564,691	1,616,739	1,681,700	1,371,222	1,417,780	1,708,535	1,625,388	...
Azerbaijan	...	143	203	365	449	719	845	1,120	1,692	2,081	2,453	2,363	3,735	3,587	3,808	9,837	11,072	10,941	...
Georgia	...	...	...	1,608	2,228	2,342	2,857	3,379	5,140	6,203	6,794	7,357	8,578	9,795	11,722	12,534	13,805	13,528	...
Kazakhstan	...	...	797,576	1,003,032	1,370,578	2,673,017	3,002,660	4,498,009	4,890,986	5,303,593	6,027,426	10,294,709	10,196,652	12,584,004	14,257,284	17,569,900	22,029,151	23,189,145	28,115,260
Kyrgyz Republic	...	40,825	44,397	51,505	60,433	85,319	85,635	90,763	113,131	124,072	138,043	161,264	173,292	186,602	218,608	242,499	265,441	244,373	309,513
Tajikistan	...	...	...	...	...	8,287	9,799	11,934	14,885	18,841	22,005	28,322	32,881	36,381	42,849	41,356	47,070	49,032	58,753
Uzbekistan	...	3,750,841	5,437,089	7,993,216	11,576,245	16,925,513	22,350,327	42,255,869	56,687,970	68,859,120	83,634,480	104,189,696	129,890,228	155,653,215	184,519,023	236,571,151	271,316,838	309,735,627	374,368,780

GDP = gross domestic product; MSME = micro, small, and medium-sized enterprise.

Notes: End-of-year data except * fiscal year data (ended 30 June in Bangladesh and 31 March in India). For Malaysia, real GDP data. For Singapore, nominal value added of SMEs. For Bangladesh, manufacturing gross value added of cottage and small enterprises. For Pakistan, GDP of small manufacturing only. Armenia: AMD million; Azerbaijan: AZN million; Brunei Darussalam: B$ million; Georgia: GEL million; India: Rs billion; Indonesia: Rp billion; Kazakhstan: KZT million; Kyrgyz Republic: KGS million; Malaysia: RM million; Pakistan: PRs million; Philippines: P million; Singapore: S$ billion; Tajikistan: TJS million; Thailand: B million; Bangladesh: Tk million; Uzbekistan: SUM million.

Source: ADB Asia SME Monitor 2022 database.

A9-2. GDP of MSMEs ($ million)

Country	2003	2004	2005	2006	2007	2008	2009	2010	2011	2012	2013	2014	2015	2016	2017	2018	2019	2020	2021
Southeast Asia																			
Brunei Darussalam	...	...	...	...	...	...	...	2,506	2,671	3,122	3,137	...	2,562	3,723	3,972	3,742	3,628	...	...
Cambodia	...	...	...	...	...	...	...	...	...	...	...	...	...	...	...	...	...	...	...
Indonesia	...	...	...	...	...	...	...	330,258	376,221	446,932	399,505	437,300	451,489	521,679	577,228	592,079	689,214	...	...
Lao People's Democratic Republic	...	...	...	...	...	...	...	...	...	...	...	...	...	...	...	...	...	...	...
Malaysia	50,052	54,210	58,257	66,391	77,910	79,412	80,504	96,812	100,576	110,824	110,035	117,079	101,415	102,157	121,076	126,187	135,320	127,880	...
Myanmar	...	...	...	...	...	...	...	...	...	...	...	...	...	...	...	...	...	...	...
Philippines	...	...	...	15,305	...	...	...	...	...	...	...	...	...	...	...	...	...	...	...
Singapore	...	...	...	...	...	...	...	...	...	...	...	138,462	129,286	136,429	154,615	145,714	159,231	140,769	...
Thailand	...	...	...	...	111,451	110,709	115,791	141,245	140,294	157,754	153,741	159,620	156,038	170,226	200,666	216,147	197,783	178,964	...
Viet Nam	...	...	...	...	...	...	...	...	...	...	...	...	...	...	...	...	...	...	...
South Asia																			
Bangladesh*	...	...	...	...	...	...	...	...	...	2,826	3,159	3,350	3,611	3,927	4,105	4,420	4,847	5,230	...
India*	...	...	...	...	...	502,799	548,873	615,535	571,859	471,583	445,618	460,585	465,675	493,264	563,139	561,629	593,823	...	...
Nepal	...	...	...	...	...	...	...	...	...	...	...	...	...	...	...	...	...	...	...
Pakistan	...	...	...	...	1,652	1,548	1,732	1,953	2,319	2,491	2,679	3,255	3,562	3,880	4,139	3,652	3,693	3,897	...
Sri Lanka	...	...	...	...	...	...	...	...	...	...	...	...	...	...	...	...	...	...	...
Central and West Asia																			
Armenia	...	1,516	1,983	2,945	4,245	4,851	3,533	4,094	4,260	4,210	3,845	3,294	3,342	3,475	2,833	2,931	3,562	3,110	...
Azerbaijan	...	145	221	419	531	897	1,052	1,404	2,151	2,651	3,127	3,012	2,395	2,026	2,240	5,786	6,513	6,436	...
Georgia	...	...	...	938	1,400	1,405	1,695	1,906	3,077	3,744	3,913	3,948	3,582	3,701	4,522	4,683	4,814	4,129	...
Kazakhstan	...	...	5,953	7,898	11,393	22,129	20,225	30,495	32,958	35,184	39,124	56,456	29,989	37,757	42,901	45,731	57,579	55,093	65,112
Kyrgyz Republic	...	981	1,075	1,351	1,702	2,164	1,942	1,927	2,434	2,617	2,803	2,739	2,283	2,695	3,176	3,472	3,811	2,957	3,652
Tajikistan	...	...	...	...	...	2,401	2,242	2,710	3,128	3,955	4,609	5,336	4,704	4,619	4,859	4,386	4,859	4,339	5,199
Uzbekistan	...	3,545	4,608	6,446	8,974	12,150	14,792	25,766	31,581	34,707	37,978	43,011	46,225	48,168	22,724	28,367	28,537	29,564	34,543

GDP = gross domestic product; MSME = micro, small, and medium-sized enterprise.

Notes: End-of-year data except * fiscal year data (ended 30 June in Bangladesh and 31 March in India). Exchange rates of local currency to US dollar refer to end-of-year currency rates from the International Monetary Fund (IMF) International Financial Statistics in designated years.

Source: ADB Asia SME Monitor 2022 database.

A10. MSME Contribution to GDP (%)

Country	2003	2004	2005	2006	2007	2008	2009	2010	2011	2012	2013	2014	2015	2016	2017	2018	2019	2020	2021
Southeast Asia																			
Brunei Darussalam	...	...	...	...	...	...	...	17.3	14.9	16.0	17.6	...	20.3	34.3	31.8	28.0	26.7	...	...
Cambodia	...	...	...	...	...	...	...	...	...	...	...	...	...	...	...	...	...	...	...
Indonesia	...	...	...	...	...	...	...	56.2	56.2	58.0	59.1	60.3	61.4	59.8	60.9	61.1	60.5	...	...
Lao People's Democratic Republic	...	...	...	...	...	...	...	...	...	...	...	...	...	...	...	...	...	...	...
Malaysia	29.3	29.7	30.2	30.4	31.5	32.0	32.6	32.8	33.4	33.6	34.2	36.6	37.0	37.3	37.8	38.3	38.9	38.2	...
Myanmar	...	...	...	...	...	...	...	...	...	...	...	...	...	...	...	...	...	...	...
Philippines	...	...	...	35.7	...	...	...	...	...	...	...	...	...	...	...	...	...	...	...
Singapore	...	...	...	...	...	...	...	...	...	...	...	50.1	47.5	47.7	46.9	44.4	44.7	42.8	43.9
Thailand	...	...	...	...	41.4	39.8	39.9	39.4	39.3	39.1	39.1	39.8	41.0	41.9	42.4	43.0	35.3	34.2	...
Viet Nam	...	...	...	...	...	...	...	...	...	...	...	...	...	...	...	...	...	...	...
South Asia																			
Bangladesh*	...	...	...	...	...	...	...	...	...	18.7	18.5	18.1	17.8	17.3	17.2	16.5	16.1	16.4	...
India*	...	...	...	...	...	35.4	36.1	36.1	36.7	29.6	29.9	29.8	29.3	29.5	29.3	29.8	30.3	...	...
Nepal	...	...	...	...	...	...	...	...	...	...	...	...	...	...	...	...	22.0	...	...
Pakistan	...	...	...	...	1.2	1.2	1.3	1.4	1.5	1.5	1.6	1.7	1.7	1.8	1.8	1.9	2.0	2.0	...
Sri Lanka	...	...	...	...	...	...	...	...	...	...	...	...	...	...	...	...	...	...	...
Central and West Asia																			
Armenia	...	38.6	39.8	40.3	41.0	41.7	42.5	43.0	43.5	42.5	34.2	32.4	32.0	33.1	24.6	23.6	26.0	26.3	...
Azerbaijan	...	1.8	1.6	1.9	1.6	1.8	2.6	2.8	3.5	4.1	4.5	4.3	7.5	6.4	5.9	13.4	14.9	16.7	...
Georgia	...	...	...	46.2	49.1	45.4	52.3	50.4	55.5	55.4	56.0	57.3	56.1	58.4	61.6	60.5	59.3	60.8	...
Kazakhstan	...	...	10.5	9.8	10.7	16.7	17.7	20.6	17.3	17.1	16.7	25.9	24.9	26.8	26.8	28.4	31.7	32.8	33.5
Kyrgyz Republic	...	43.3	44.0	45.2	42.6	45.5	42.6	41.2	39.5	39.9	38.9	40.3	40.3	39.1	41.2	42.5	42.8	40.6	42.8
Tajikistan	...	...	...	...	...	46.5	45.0	48.0	48.0	51.8	54.6	58.6	56.9	66.1	64.5	56.5	58.5	53.0	59.4
Uzbekistan	...	35.6	38.2	42.1	45.7	48.2	50.1	60.8	61.9	60.8	60.9	61.9	64.6	66.8	65.3	62.4	56.0	55.5	54.9

GDP = gross domestic product; MSME = micro, small, and medium-sized enterprise.

Notes: End-of-year data except * fiscal year data (ended 30 June in Bangladesh and 31 March in India). For Malaysia, real GDP data. For Singapore, nominal value added of SMEs. For Bangladesh, contribution of cottage and small enterprises to manufacturing gross value added. For Nepal, data cited from the 2019 Nepal Rastra Bank Report. For Pakistan, small manufacturing contribution to GDP.

Source: ADB Asia SME Monitor 2022 database.

A11. MSME GDP by Sector (% share, latest available year)

Item / Southeast Asia	Brunei Darussalam	Cambodia	Indonesia	Lao People's Democratic Republic	Malaysia	Myanmar	Philippines	Singapore	Thailand	Viet Nam
Agriculture	...	...	...	...	10.5	...	1.0	...	0.3	...
Manufacturing	...	...	26.8	...	20.7	...	19.3	...	32.0	...
Transportation and communication	...	...	4.8	...	...	...	...	...	...	...
Construction	...	...	...	...	5.1	...	...	...	4.0	...
Wholesale and retail trade	...	...	47.8	...	62.1	...	18.4	...	21.6	...
Other services	...	...	20.6	...	...	...	41.9	...	40.5	...
Others	...	...	...	...	1.7	...	19.3	...	1.6	...
Year			2016		2020		2006		2020	

Item / South Asia	Bangladesh	India	Nepal	Pakistan	Sri Lanka
Agriculture	...	...	...	...	...
Manufacturing	...	...	...	12.5	...
Transportation and communication	...	...	...	...	...
Construction	...	...	...	...	...
Wholesale and retail trade	...	...	...	...	...
Other services	...	...	...	...	...
Others	...	...	...	...	...
Year				2020	

Item / Central and West Asia	Armenia	Azerbaijan	Georgia	Kazakhstan	Kyrgyz Republic	Tajikistan	Uzbekistan
Agriculture	...	3.7	1.7	...	20.8	...	47.3
Manufacturing	24.1	13.5	12.3	...	14.7	...	11.5
Transportation and communication	5.8	11.4	10.5	...	4.9	...	6.7
Construction	12.8	14.5	20.9	...	10.3	...	9.2
Wholesale and retail trade	34.2	29.4	26.5	...	39.3	...	10.6
Other services	22.3	27.5	24.4	...	3.0	...	14.6
Others	0.8	...	3.8	...	7.0	...	...
Year	2020	2020	2020		2021		2021

GDP = gross domestic product; MSME = micro, small, and medium-sized enterprise.

Notes: End-of-year data. For Malaysia, real GDP data, and "wholesale and retail trade" includes transportation and storage, telecommunication, and real estate. For Pakistan, GDP of small manufacturing only. For Uzbekistan, "wholesale and retail trade" includes accommodation and food services.

Source: ADB Asia SME Monitor 2022 database.

A12. MSME GDP by Region (% share, latest available year)

Item / Southeast Asia	Brunei Darussalam	Cambodia	Indonesia	Lao People's Democratic Republic	Malaysia	Myanmar	Philippines	Singapore	Thailand	Viet Nam
Capital city	...	...	...	...	23.0	...	...	...	...	...
Other areas	...	...	...	...	77.0	...	...	...	...	...
Year					2015					

Item / South Asia	Bangladesh	India	Nepal	Pakistan	Sri Lanka
Capital city	...	...	...	...	...
Other areas	...	...	...	...	...
Year					2015

Item / Central and West Asia	Armenia	Azerbaijan	Georgia	Kazakhstan	Kyrgyz Republic	Tajikistan	Uzbekistan
Capital city	65.0	...	62.9	...	...	15.3	
Other areas	35.0	...	37.1	...	...	84.7	
Year	2012		2020			FY2019	

GDP = gross domestic product; MSME = micro, small, and medium-sized enterprise.

Notes: End-of-year data. For Malaysia, real GDP data. Capital city: Yerevan in Armenia; Tbilisi in Georgia; Dushanbe in Tajikistan; Kuala Lumpur in Malaysia.

Source: ADB Asia SME Monitor 2022 database.

A13-1. MSME Export Value (local currency)

Country	2003	2004	2005	2006	2007	2008	2009	2010	2011	2012	2013	2014	2015	2016	2017	2018	2019	2020	2021
Southeast Asia																			
Brunei Darussalam	...	...	...	...	...	...	...	...	...	...	...	...	...	...	...	...	...	...	...
Cambodia	...	...	...	...	...	...	...	...	...	...	...	...	...	...	...	...	...	...	...
Indonesia	...	...	...	...	...	...	...	162,255	175,895	187,442	166,627	182,113	185,975	255,126	301,630	293,841	339,191	...	...
Lao People's Democratic Republic	...	...	...	...	...	...	...	...	...	...	...	1,238	...	...	...	...	...	...	...
Malaysia	...	...	...	...	...	...	...	116,800	131,000	134,700	136,900	145,200	145,000	155,100	166,200	171,800	176,300	117,800	...
Myanmar	...	...	...	...	...	...	...	...	...	...	...	...	...	...	...	...	...	...	...
Philippines	...	...	...	...	...	...	...	...	...	...	...	...	...	...	...	...	...	...	...
Singapore	...	...	...	...	...	...	...	...	...	...	...	...	...	...	...	...	...	...	...
Thailand	...	...	...	...	1,576,000	1,691,000	1,564,000	1,669,000	1,971,000	2,065,460	1,761,800	1,922,500	1,978,300	2,190,500	1,990,420	2,325,852	1,023,713	839,750	...
Viet Nam	...	...	...	...	...	...	...	...	...	...	...	...	...	...	...	...	...	...	...
South Asia																			
Bangladesh	...	...	...	...	...	...	...	...	...	...	...	...	...	...	...	...	...	...	...
India*	...	...	...	...	...	...	...	...	...	...	7,922,321	8,442,912	9,212,416	8,886,300	8,762,387	10,286,693	11,345,380	11,308,805	...
Nepal	...	...	...	...	...	...	...	...	...	...	...	...	...	...	...	...	...	...	...
Pakistan	...	...	...	...	...	...	...	404,365	...	...	...	...	...	...	...	...	...	...	...
Sri Lanka	...	...	...	...	...	...	...	...	...	...	...	...	...	...	...	...	...	...	...
Central and West Asia																			
Armenia	...	60,153	73,059	69,252	68,730	57,895	45,747	...	...	...	...	...	...	...	...	...	...	...	...
Azerbaijan	...	...	...	...	...	...	...	...	...	...	...	...	...	...	...	...	...	...	...
Georgia	...	...	...	...	...	...	...	...	...	...	...	...	1,355	1,352	1,601	1,806	1,982	1,864	2,372
Kazakhstan	...	...	...	...	...	...	...	...	...	...	...	...	...	...	...	...	...	...	...
Kyrgyz Republic	...	9,275	8,992	13,758	13,719	30,474	18,948	21,383	29,099	32,026	28,474	27,406	41,031	39,317	42,183	50,485	48,939	40,663	63,738
Tajikistan	...	...	...	...	...	...	...	...	...	...	...	...	...	...	...	...	...	...	...
Uzbekistan	...	374,974	384,427	886,149	1,720,226	1,977,827	2,604,359	2,923,762	5,072,967	3,790,440	8,263,408	8,860,554	9,491,276	10,144,141	22,406,111	31,780,519	44,825,836	32,488,398	36,145,582

MSME = micro, small, and medium-sized enterprise.

Notes: End-of-year data except * fiscal year data (ended 31 March in India). For Pakistan, data from Pakistan Economic Survey 2009-2010. Armenia: AMD million; Georgia: GEL million; Indonesia: Rp billion; Kyrgyz Republic: KGS million; Lao PDR: KN million; Malaysia: RM million; Thailand: B million; India: Rs million; Pakistan: PRs million; Uzbekistan: SUM million.

Source: ADB Asia SME Monitor 2022 database.

A13-2. MSME Export Value ($ million)

Country	2003	2004	2005	2006	2007	2008	2009	2010	2011	2012	2013	2014	2015	2016	2017	2018	2019	2020	2021
Southeast Asia																			
Brunei Darussalam	...	...	...	...	...	...	...	...	...	...	...	...	...	...	...	...	...	...	...
Cambodia	...	...	...	...	...	...	...	...	...	...	...	...	...	...	...	...	...	...	...
Indonesia	...	...	...	...	...	...	...	18,046	19,397	19,384	13,670	14,639	13,481	18,988	22,264	20,291	24,400	...	...
Lao People's Democratic Republic	...	...	...	...	...	...	...	...	...	...	...	0	...	...	...	...	...	...	...
Malaysia	...	...	...	...	...	...	...	37,922	41,195	44,020	41,738	41,486	33,800	34,543	40,936	41,498	43,105	29,377	...
Myanmar	...	...	...	...	...	...	...	...	...	...	...	...	...	...	...	...	...	...	...
Philippines	...	...	...	...	...	...	...	...	...	...	...	...	...	...	...	...	...	...	...
Singapore	...	...	...	...	...	...	...	...	...	...	...	...	...	...	...	...	...	...	...
Thailand	...	...	...	...	46,738	48,453	46,939	55,357	62,196	67,433	53,697	58,328	54,816	61,136	60,906	71,675	33,954	27,954	...
Viet Nam	...	...	...	...	...	...	...	...	...	...	...	...	...	...	...	...	...	...	...
South Asia																			
Bangladesh	...	...	...	...	...	...	...	...	...	...	...	...	...	...	...	...	...	...	...
India*	...	...	...	...	...	...	...	...	...	...	127,986	133,316	138,888	130,777	137,062	147,395	159,189	154,809	...
Nepal	...	...	...	...	...	...	...	...	...	...	...	...	...	...	...	...	...	...	
Pakistan	...	...	...	...	...	...	...	4,718	...	...	...	...	...	...	...	...	...	...	...
Sri Lanka	...	...	...	...	...	...	...	...	...	...	...	...	...	...	...	...	...	...	...
Central and West Asia																			
Armenia	...	124	162	191	226	189	121	...	...	...	...	...	...	...	...	...	...	...	...
Azerbaijan	...	...	...	...	...	...	...	...	...	...	...	...	...	...	...	...	...	...	...
Georgia	...	...	...	...	...	...	...	...	...	...	...	...	566	511	617	675	691	569	766
Kazakhstan	...	...	...	...	...	...	...	...	...	...	...	...	...	...	...	...	...	...	...
Kyrgyz Republic	...	223	218	361	386	773	430	454	626	676	578	465	541	568	613	723	703	492	752
Tajikistan	...	...	...	...	...	...	...	...	...	...	...	...	...	...	...	...	...	...	...
Uzbekistan	...	354	326	715	1,334	1,420	1,724	1,783	2,826	1,911	3,752	3,658	3,378	3,139	2,759	3,811	4,715	3,101	3,335

MSME = micro, small, and medium-sized enterprise.

Notes: End-of-year data except * fiscal year data (ended 31 March in India). For Pakistan, data from Pakistan Economic Survey 2009-2010. Exchange rates of local currency to US dollar refer to end-of-year currency rates from the International Monetary Fund (IMF) International Financial Statistics in designated years.

Source: ADB Asia SME Monitor 2022 database.

A14. MSME Exports to Total (%)

Country	2003	2004	2005	2006	2007	2008	2009	2010	2011	2012	2013	2014	2015	2016	2017	2018	2019	2020	2021
Southeast Asia																			
Brunei Darussalam	...	...	...	...	...	...	...	...	...	...	...	...	...	...	...	...	...	...	...
Cambodia	...	...	...	...	...	...	...	...	...	...	...	...	...	...	...	...	...	...	...
Indonesia	...	...	...	...	...	...	...	17.0	15.8	16.4	14.1	15.7	15.7	14.4	14.5	14.4	15.7	...	...
Lao People's Democratic Republic	...	...	...	...	...	...	...	...	...	...	...	...	...	...	...	...	...	...	...
Malaysia	...	...	...	...	...	...	...	16.4	16.9	17.5	17.8	17.8	17.7	18.6	17.3	17.3	17.9	13.5	
Myanmar	...	...	...	...	...	...	...	...	...	...	...	...	...	...	...	...	...	...	...
Philippines	...	...	...	...	...	...	...	...	...	...	...	...	...	...	...	...	...	...	...
Singapore	...	...	...	...	...	...	...	...	...	...	...	...	...	...	...	...	...	...	...
Thailand	...	...	...	...	30.1	28.9	30.1	27.3	29.4	29.9	25.5	27.9	28.2	29.0	28.9	28.7	13.4	11.7	
Viet Nam	...	...	...	...	...	...	...	...	...	...	...	...	...	...	...	...	...	...	...
South Asia																			
Bangladesh	...	...	...	...	...	...	...	...	...	...	...	...	...	...	...	...	...	...	...
India*	...	...	...	...	...	...	...	...	...	...	42.6	42.4	44.8	49.9	49.7	48.6	48.1	49.8	...
Nepal	...	...	...	...	...	...	...	...	...	...	...	...	...	...	...	...	...	...	...
Pakistan	...	...	...	...	...	...	...	25.0	...	...	...	...	...	...	...	...	...	...	...
Sri Lanka	...	...	...	...	...	...	...	...	...	...	...	...	...	...	...	...	...	...	...
Central and West Asia																			
Armenia	...	15.7	16.4	16.9	17.4	17.9	17.7	...	...	...	...	...	...	...	...	...	...	...	...
Azerbaijan	...	...	...	...	...	...	...	...	...	...	...	...	...	...	...	...	...	...	...
Georgia	...	...	...	...	...	...	...	...	...	...	...	...	61.5	63.8	58.3	53.4	52.2	55.8	55.9
Kazakhstan	...	...	...	...	...	...	...	...	...	...	...	...	...	...	...	...	...	...	...
Kyrgyz Republic	...	30.9	32.3	40.5	29.3	41.7	25.7	25.9	27.9	35.0	28.8	24.7	36.5	36.1	34.7	39.3	35.4	24.9	27.3
Tajikistan	...	...	...	...	...	...	...	...	...	...	...	...	...	...	...	...	...	...	...
Uzbekistan	...	7.3	6.0	11.2	14.8	12.4	14.6	13.7	18.8	14.0	26.2	27.0	27.0	26.0	22.0	27.2	27.0	20.5	20.0

MSME = micro, small, and medium-sized enterprise.

Notes: End-of-year data except * fiscal year data (ended 31 March in India). For Pakistan, data from Pakistan Economic Survey 2009-2010.

Source: ADB Asia SME Monitor 2022 database.

B. MSME Access to Finance (Banking)

B1-1. MSME Bank Loans Outstanding (local currency)

Country	2003	2004	2005	2006	2007	2008	2009	2010	2011	2012	2013	2014	2015	2016	2017	2018	2019	2020	2021
Southeast Asia																			
Brunei Darussalam	...	...	...	...	...	...	...	...	...	...	...	...	...	...	...	3,304,913	8,996,023	11,367,828	12,219,363
Cambodia	...	...	...	...	...	...	...	...	...	...	...	...	...	...	...	...	...	...	...
Indonesia	...	...	...	...	...	...	...	...	458,164	526,397	608,823	763,307	790,467	856,997	942,388	1,032,643	1,111,340	1,091,232	1,223,433
Lao People's Democratic Republic	...	...	...	...	...	...	...	...	...	...	...	...	14,919	13,997	15,939	14,241	14,104	15,731	12,848
Malaysia	...	...	...	...	127,984	138,859	141,608	141,159	165,316	187,039	211,038	243,708	274,412	299,733	315,660	297,615	278,355	305,064	319,952
Myanmar*	...	...	...	...	...	...	...	...	...	...	...	...	...	...	733,235	896,840	1,131,665	...	...
Philippines	...	...	...	...	...	270,526	257,894	311,452	351,693	384,082	395,031	425,155	461,650	496,863	532,198	577,719	588,837	488,013	470,078
Singapore	...	...	...	...	...	...	...	46,424	56,869	60,497	66,752	74,190	76,018	77,983	80,667	78,204	86,242	90,429	92,501
Thailand	...	...	...	...	2,688	2,768	2,585	3,594	4,272	4,627	5,123	5,460	5,974	6,096	6,288	6,560	6,581	4,916	5,179
Viet Nam	...	...	...	...	...	...	...	...	...	...	...	...	...	...	...	...	...	1,818,233	...
South Asia																			
Bangladesh	...	...	...	...	...	...	...	671	785	977	1,123	1,318	1,433	1,655	1,926	1,785	2,092	2,273	2,408
India	...	...	...	...	...	...	...	...	...	...	...	...	12,368,744	12,377,008	13,924,802	16,208,160	17,419,130	17,496,199	19,011,873
Nepal	...	...	...	...	...	...	...	...	...	...	...	...	...	...	...	...	...	...	...
Pakistan	...	...	...	...	411,675	383,698	348,199	336,553	294,306	266,144	272,528	287,881	305,090	401,480	450,384	513,459	477,232	481,780	...
Sri Lanka	...	...	...	...	...	...	...	...	...	...	...	...	...	...	...	...	...	743,024	...
Central and West Asia																			
Armenia	...	...	...	...	...	...	...	...	...	...	...	...	...	...	...	...	...	1,180,675	1,169,815
Azerbaijan	...	...	...	...	...	...	...	...	...	...	...	...	...	...	...	2,877	3,725	3,441	4,451
Georgia	...	...	...	...	...	...	...	...	...	...	...	...	3,612	4,451	5,266	6,006	7,062	7,788	8,516
Kazakhstan	...	288,367	470,168	861,045	1,505,487	1,570,734	1,708,189	1,384,956	1,341,578	1,412,005	1,283,441	1,788,059	2,060,455	3,002,974	2,788,589	2,363,861	2,108,945	2,515,308	3,772,244
Kyrgyz Republic	...	5,056	6,550	8,814	16,194	19,894	20,099	21,647	25,483	32,466	43,563	63,778	75,922	75,471	87,188	101,863	113,900	127,914	139,642
Tajikistan	...	...	...	...	...	...	...	...	1,029	1,219	1,570	988	1,820	844	1,270	1,304	1,284	1,147	1,510
Uzbekistan	...	...	...	...	...	...	...	...	...	...	...	...	12,459,134	16,630,818	19,564,668	30,648,846	55,430,003	48,389,693	59,552,127

MSME = micro, small, and medium-sized enterprise.

Notes: End-of-year data except * fiscal year data (ended 31 March in Myanmar). For India, urban cooperative banks only for 2007-2014; urban cooperative banks plus commercial banks for 2015-2020. Armenia: AMD million; Azerbaijan: AZN million; Bangladesh: Tk billion; Brunei Darussalam: B$; Georgia: GEL million; India: Rs million; Indonesia: Rp billion; Kazakhstan: KZT million; Kyrgyz Republic: KGS million; Lao PDR: KN billion; Malaysia: RM million; Myanmar: MK million; Pakistan: PRNotes: End-of-year data except * fiscal year data (ended 31 March in Myanmar). For India, urban cooperative banks only for 2007-2014; urban cooperative banks plus commercial banks for 2015-2020. Armenia: AMD million; Azerbaijan: AZN million; Bangladesh: Tk billion; Brunei Darussalam: B$; Georgia: GEL million; India: Rs million; Indonesia: Rp billion; Kazakhstan: KZT million; Kyrgyz Republic: KGS million; Lao PDR: KN billion; Malaysia: RM million; Myanmar: MK million; Pakistan: PRs million; Philippines: P million; Singapore: S$ million; Sri Lanka: SLRs million; Tajikistan: TJS million; Thailand: B billion; Uzbekistan: SUM million; Viet Nam: D billion.

Source: ADB Asia SME Monitor 2022 database.

B1-2. MSME Bank Loans Outstanding ($ million)

Country	2003	2004	2005	2006	2007	2008	2009	2010	2011	2012	2013	2014	2015	2016	2017	2018	2019	2020	2021
Southeast Asia																			
Brunei Darussalam	...	...	...	...	...	...	...	...	...	...	...	...	...	...	...	2.4	6.7	8.5	9.0
Cambodia	...	...	...	...	...	...	...	...	...	...	...	...	...	...	...	...	...	...	...
Indonesia	...	...	...	...	...	...	...	...	50,525	54,436	49,949	61,359	57,301	63,784	69,559	71,310	79,947	77,365	85,741
Lao People's Democratic Republic	...	...	...	...	...	...	...	...	...	...	...	...	1,831	1,710	1,922	1,669	1,592	1,696	1,164
Malaysia	...	...	...	...	38,666	40,133	41,406	45,831	51,986	61,124	64,341	69,631	63,965	66,756	77,749	71,888	68,057	76,076	76,544
Myanmar*	...	...	...	...	...	...	...	...	...	...	...	...	...	...	538	579	772	...	...
Philippines	...	...	...	...	...	5,696	5,563	7,096	8,006	9,325	8,895	9,528	9,787	9,975	10,661	10,958	11,605	10,158	9,259
Singapore	...	...	...	...	...	...	...	35,987	43,745	49,588	52,561	56,205	53,913	53,781	60,199	57,503	63,883	68,507	68,519
Thailand	...	...	...	...	79,710	79,313	77,586	119,206	134,807	151,048	156,154	165,641	165,544	170,126	192,421	202,154	218,289	163,648	154,967
Viet Nam	...	...	...	...	...	...	...	...	...	...	...	...	...	...	...	...	...	78,606	...
South Asia																			
Bangladesh	...	...	...	...	...	...	...	9,478	9,594	12,237	14,445	16,904	18,260	21,024	23,295	21,273	24,638	26,803	28,066
India	...	...	...	...	...	...	...	...	...	...	...	...	186,473	182,149	217,813	232,242	244,410	239,510	255,880
Nepal	...	...	...	...	...	...	...	...	...	...	...	...	...	...	...	...	...	...	...
Pakistan	...	...	...	...	6,725	4,851	4,132	3,927	3,271	2,740	2,579	2,866	2,909	3,831	4,078	3,700	3,082	3,019	...
Sri Lanka	...	...	...	...	...	...	...	...	...	...	...	...	...	...	...	...	...	3,986	...
Central and West Asia																			
Armenia	...	...	...	...	...	...	...	...	...	...	...	...	...	...	...	...	...	2,259	2,436
Azerbaijan	...	...	...	...	...	...	...	...	...	...	...	...	...	...	...	1,693	2,191	2,024	2,619
Georgia	...	...	...	...	...	...	...	...	...	...	...	...	1,508	1,682	2,032	2,244	2,463	2,377	2,749
Kazakhstan	...	2,218	3,509	6,780	12,514	13,003	11,503	9,390	9,040	9,370	8,329	9,803	6,060	9,010	8,392	6,153	5,512	5,976	8,736
Kyrgyz Republic	...	121	159	231	456	505	456	460	548	685	885	1,083	1,000	1,090	1,267	1,458	1,635	1,548	1,648
Tajikistan	...	...	...	...	...	...	...	...	216	256	329	186	260	107	144	138	133	101	134
Uzbekistan	...	...	...	...	...	...	...	...	...	...	...	...	4,434	5,147	2,409	3,675	5,830	4,619	5,495

MSME = micro, small, and medium-sized enterprise.

Notes: End-of-year data except * fiscal year data (ended 31 March in Myanmar). Exchange rates of local currency to US dollar refer to end-of-year currency rates from the International Monetary Fund (IMF) International Financial Statistics in designated years.

Source: ADB Asia SME Monitor 2022 database.

B2. MSME Bank Loans to Total (%)

Country	2003	2004	2005	2006	2007	2008	2009	2010	2011	2012	2013	2014	2015	2016	2017	2018	2019	2020	2021
Southeast Asia																			
Brunei Darussalam	...	...	...	...	...	...	...	...	...	...	...	...	...	...	...	0.1	0.2	0.2	0.2
Cambodia	...	...	...	...	...	...	...	...	...	...	...	...	...	...	...	...	...	...	...
Indonesia	...	...	...	...	...	...	...	...	20.8	19.4	18.5	20.4	19.3	19.4	19.7	19.3	19.6	19.7	21.0
Lao People's Democratic Republic	...	...	...	...	...	...	...	...	...	...	...	...	30.9	23.4	23.8	20.6	19.8	17.1	11.5
Malaysia	...	...	...	...	18.2	17.4	16.3	14.4	15.0	15.3	15.7	16.6	17.4	18.0	18.3	16.1	14.5	15.4	15.4
Myanmar*	...	...	...	...	...	...	...	...	...	...	...	...	...	...	4.5	4.6	4.8	...	...
Philippines	...	...	...	...	...	11.6	10.6	11.7	11.0	10.6	9.3	8.3	7.9	7.2	6.6	6.2	6.1	4.9	4.5
Singapore	...	...	...	...	...	...	...	7.2	7.1	6.9	6.3	6.5	6.6	6.7	6.5	6.0	6.3	6.7	7.0
Thailand	...	...	...	...	33.6	29.1	25.4	30.9	32.3	30.9	31.3	32.1	33.5	32.9	31.5	31.8	30.9	21.6	21.5
Viet Nam	...	...	...	...	...	...	...	...	...	...	...	...	...	...	...	...	...	21.5	...
South Asia																			
Bangladesh	...	...	...	...	...	...	...	...	...	...	...	...	23.7	23.7	23.4	19.0	20.1	20.2	19.7
India	...	...	...	...	...	...	...	...	...	...	...	...	17.1	16.5	16.8	17.2	17.3	15.6	16.2
Nepal*	...	...	...	...	...	...	...	...	...	...	...	...	11.2	11.7	11.5	...	...	...	...
Pakistan	...	...	...	...	16.2	12.0	10.1	9.6	8.3	6.8	6.5	8.0	6.1	9.2	8.7	8.5	7.6	7.3	...
Sri Lanka	...	...	...	...	...	...	...	...	...	...	...	...	...	...	...	...	...	11.1	...
Central and West Asia																			
Armenia	...	...	...	...	...	...	...	...	...	...	...	...	...	...	...	...	...	30.2	31.6
Azerbaijan	...	...	...	...	...	...	...	...	...	...	...	...	...	...	...	22.8	25.0	24.3	26.7
Georgia	...	...	...	...	...	...	...	...	...	...	...	...	22.6	23.5	23.6	22.6	22.1	20.4	19.8
Kazakhstan	...	19.0	18.0	18.0	21.0	21.0	22.0	18.0	15.0	14.0	11.0	15.0	16.0	24.0	22.0	18.0	15.0	17.0	20.0
Kyrgyz Republic	...	87.1	84.9	77.7	77.7	77.7	79.7	82.1	81.6	81.0	80.7	81.0	80.8	80.7	80.5	79.7	77.8	78.7	76.8
Tajikistan	...	...	...	...	...	...	...	...	25.9	28.0	26.1	12.7	19.7	10.4	18.6	19.7	16.9	13.0	16.0
Uzbekistan	...	...	...	...	...	...	...	...	...	...	...	...	31.4	31.6	17.7	18.3	26.2	17.5	18.2

MSME = micro, small, and medium-sized enterprise.

Notes: End-of-year data except * fiscal year data (ended 31 March in Myanmar and 15 July in Nepal). For Bangladesh, commercial banks' MSME loans outstanding divided by total loans outstanding of all operating banks; actual percentage share of MSME loans to total loans outstanding in commercial banks would be higher. For India, commercial banks only. For Nepal, data from Nepal Rastra Bank Report, SME Financing in Nepal 2019. For Pakistan, SME loans to total domestic private loans outstanding. For Sri Lanka, MSME loans to total outstanding loans to the private sector.

Source: ADB Asia SME Monitor 2022 database.

B3. MSME Bank Loans to GDP (%)

Country	2003	2004	2005	2006	2007	2008	2009	2010	2011	2012	2013	2014	2015	2016	2017	2018	2019	2020	2021
Southeast Asia																			
Brunei Darussalam	...	...	...	...	...	...	...	...	...	...	...	...	...	...	...	0.0	0.1	0.0	0.0
Cambodia	...	...	...	...	...	...	...	...	...	...	...	...	...	...	...	...	...	...	...
Indonesia	...	...	...	...	...	...	...	...	6.2	6.4	6.7	7.2	6.9	6.9	6.9	7.0	7.0	7.1	7.2
Lao People's Democratic Republic	...	...	...	...	...	...	...	...	...	...	...	...	12.7	10.8	11.3	9.3	8.5	9.1	7.0
Malaysia	...	...	...	...	19.3	18.0	19.9	17.2	18.1	19.3	20.7	22.0	23.3	24.0	23.0	20.6	18.4	21.5	20.7
Myanmar*	...	...	...	...	...	...	...	...	...	...	...	...	...	...	0.9	1.0	...	...	...
Philippines	...	...	...	...	...	3.5	3.2	3.5	3.6	3.6	3.4	3.4	3.5	3.4	3.4	3.3	3.2	2.7	2.4
Singapore	...	...	...	...	...	...	...	14.2	15.8	14.7	16.8	17.6	17.2	16.2	15.9	15.1	...	...	...
Thailand	...	...	...	...	29.6	28.5	26.8	25.9	28.6	29.0	31.8	33.2	33.7	32.3	32.3	31.6	30.3	31.3	32.0
Viet Nam	...	...	...	...	...	...	...	...	...	...	...	...	...	...	...	...	...	28.9	...
South Asia																			
Bangladesh	...	...	...	...	...	...	...	8.4	8.6	9.3	9.4	9.8	9.5	9.5	9.8	7.9	8.2	8.1	...
India	...	...	...	...	...	...	...	...	...	...	...	...	9.0	8.0	8.1	8.6	8.6	8.9	...
Nepal	...	...	...	...	...	...	...	...	...	...	...	...	...	...	...	...	...	...	...
Pakistan	...	...	...	...	4.5	3.6	2.6	2.3	1.6	1.3	1.2	1.1	1.1	1.4	1.4	1.5	1.3	1.2	...
Sri Lanka	...	...	...	...	...	...	...	...	...	...	...	...	...	...	...	...	...	5.0	...
Central and West Asia																			
Armenia	...	...	...	...	...	...	...	...	...	...	...	...	...	...	...	...	...	19.1	16.8
Azerbaijan	...	...	...	...	...	...	...	...	...	...	...	...	...	...	...	3.6	4.5	4.6	4.8
Georgia	...	...	...	...	...	...	...	...	...	...	...	...	10.6	12.4	12.9	13.5	14.3	15.8	14.1
Kazakhstan	...	4.9	6.2	8.4	11.7	9.8	10.0	6.3	4.8	4.6	3.6	4.5	5.0	6.4	5.1	3.8	3.0	3.6	4.6
Kyrgyz Republic	...	5.4	6.5	7.7	11.4	10.6	10.0	9.8	8.9	10.5	12.3	15.9	17.6	15.8	16.4	17.9	18.4	21.3	19.3
Tajikistan	...	...	...	...	...	...	...	...	4.0	3.8	4.6	5.3	3.8	2.0	1.7	1.9	1.8	2.0	2.5
Uzbekistan	...	...	...	...	...	...	...	...	...	...	...	...	5.6	6.5	6.2	7.2	10.5	8.0	8.1

GDP = gross domestic product; MSME = micro, small, and medium-sized enterprise.

Notes: End-of-year data except * fiscal year data (ended 31 March in Myanmar). For India, data for commercial banks only.

Source: ADB Asia SME Monitor 2022 database.

B4. MSME Bank Loans by Sector (% share, latest available year)

Item	Brunei Darussalam	Cambodia	Indonesia	Lao People's Democratic Republic	Malaysia	Myanmar*	Philippines	Singapore	Thailand	Viet Nam
Agriculture	8.5	...	11.9	3.8	4.7	1.0	...	0.4	2.0	3.2
Manufacturing	16.9	...	10.3	7.9	15.5	18.9	...	7.4	20.3	...
Transportation and communication	30.5	...	3.9	1.1	...	3.4	...	8.0	2.9	...
Construction	1.3	...	5.4	20.7	12.8	1.5	...	40.2	4.8	40.0
Wholesale and retail trade	12.4	...	48.6	37.0	66.1	45.6	...	23.9	33.0	56.8
Other services	28.2	...	17.5	18.6	...	11.4	...	13.6	32.5	...
Others	2.2	...	2.3	11.0	0.4	18.3	...	6.6	4.6	...
Year	2021		2020	2019	2020	FY2019		2020	2020	2020

Item	Bangladesh	India	Nepal	Pakistan	Sri Lanka
Agriculture	...	...	...	0.5	11.9
Manufacturing	38.5	...	...	45.7	50.5
Transportation and communication	...	...	...	6.2	...
Construction	...	...	...	2.9	...
Wholesale and retail trade	41.1	...	...	30.0	...
Other services	20.4	...	...	5.2	37.6
Others	...	...	...	9.4	...
Year	2021			2020	2020

Item	Armenia	Azerbaijan	Georgia	Kazakhstan	Kyrgyz Republic	Tajikistan	Uzbekistan
Agriculture	6.6	...	4.6	24.1	23.8	31.1	...
Manufacturing	14.3	...	8.8	4.0	11.6	3.0	...
Transportation and communication	3.8	...	2.5	8.6	3.1	1.5	...
Construction	15.2	...	7.2	5.5	9.7	6.2	...
Wholesale and retail trade	28.4	...	18.8	1.8	36.7	34.9	...
Other services	11.9	...	14.0	23.9	4.8	15.3	...
Others	19.9	...	44.2	32.1	10.4	7.9	...
Year	2021		2021	2021	2021	2021	

MSME = micro, small, and medium-sized enterprise.

Notes: End-of-year data except * fiscal year (FY) data (ended 31 March in Myanmar). For Malaysia, "wholesale and retail trade" includes transportation and storage, telecommunication, and real estate. For Viet Nam, "wholesale and retail trade" refers to commercial services. Data for Brunei Darussalam refers to SME Bank data only. For Tajikistan, "wholesale and retail trade" refers to international trade, and "other services" include catering.

Source: ADB Asia SME Monitor 2022 database.

B5. MSME Bank Loans by Region (% share, latest available year)

Item	Brunei Darussalam	Cambodia	Indonesia	Lao People's Democratic Republic	Malaysia	Myanmar	Philippines	Singapore	Thailand	Viet Nam
Capital city	92.2	...	...	...	...	...	...	...	...	26.9
Other areas	7.8	...	...	...	...	...	...	...	...	73.1
Year	2021									2020

Item	Bangladesh	India	Nepal	Pakistan	Sri Lanka
Capital city	84.2	...	...	...	...
Other areas	15.8	...	...	...	...
Year	2020				

Item	Armenia	Azerbaijan	Georgia	Kazakhstan	Kyrgyz Republic	Tajikistan	Uzbekistan
Capital city	75.9	73.7	50.9	16.2	55.0	...	...
Other areas	24.1	26.3	49.1	83.8	45.0	...	...
Year	2021	2021	2021	2021	2021		

MSME = micro, small, and medium-sized enterprise.

Notes: End-of-year data. Data for Brunei Darussalam refers to SME Bank data only. Capital city: Yerevan in Armenia; Baku in Azerbaijan; Bandar Seri Begawan in Brunei Darussalam; Tbilisi in Georgia; Astana in Kazakhstan; Bishkek in the Kyrgyz Republic; Viet Nam: Ha Noi. For Bangladesh, Urban/Rural.

Source: ADB Asia SME Monitor 2022 database.

B6-1. Nonperforming MSME Bank Loans (local currency)

Country	2003	2004	2005	2006	2007	2008	2009	2010	2011	2012	2013	2014	2015	2016	2017	2018	2019	2020	2021
Southeast Asia																			
Brunei Darussalam	...	...	...	...	...	...	...	...	...	...	...	...	...	...	...	...	...	26,741	83,829
Cambodia	...	...	...	...	...	...	...	...	...	...	...	...	...	...	...	...	...	...	...
Indonesia	...	...	...	...	...	...	...	...	15,674	17,011	19,515	31,560	33,208	35,597	38,520	35,504	40,089	43,110	46,757
Lao People's Democratic Republic	...	...	...	...	...	...	...	...	...	...	...	...	...	...	...	...	...	...	...
Malaysia	...	...	...	...	12,083	9,882	8,895	10,590	9,552	8,574	8,216	8,553	8,880	8,874	10,065	10,203	10,313	9,798	10,060
Myanmar	...	...	...	...	...	...	...	...	...	...	...	...	...	...	...	...	...	...	...
Philippines	...	...	...	...	...	...	...	23,656	26,078	25,347	25,512	25,097	25,209	26,217	25,989	30,030	32,306	48,072	52,636
Singapore	...	...	...	...	...	...	...	696	783	612	561	627	1,458	2,330	4,758	4,919	3,874	4,134	4,044
Thailand	...	...	...	...	...	...	184	153	130	125	136	137	164	205	220	230	231	247	254
Viet Nam	...	...	...	...	...	...	...	...	...	...	...	...	...	...	...	...	...	205,909	...
South Asia																			
Bangladesh	...	...	...	...	...	...	...	...	...	...	...	...	...	...	...	...	...	...	342,770
India	...	...	...	...	...	...	...	...	...	...	...	...	1,156,321	1,246,214	1,482,100	1,637,547	1,545,805	1,623,223	1,821,214
Nepal	...	...	...	...	...	...	...	...	...	...	...	...	...	...	...	...	...	...	...
Pakistan	...	...	...	...	35,003	60,692	79,141	97,091	95,472	95,440	86,615	87,055	77,170	66,601	69,368	75,440	80,001	81,429	...
Sri Lanka	...	...	...	...	...	...	...	...	...	...	...	...	...	...	...	...	...	...	...
Central and West Asia																			
Armenia	...	...	...	...	...	...	...	...	...	...	...	...	...	...	...	...	...	62,943	25,069
Azerbaijan	...	...	...	...	...	...	...	...	...	...	...	...	...	...	...	960	800	412	301
Georgia	...	...	...	...	...	...	...	145	134	111	102	101	161	206	221	407	400	974	748
Kazakhstan	...	...	...	...	...	...	...	...	...	...	...	...	...	...	...	...	...	...	...
Kyrgyz Republic	...	...	...	...	...	...	...	...	...	...	...	...	...	...	...	...	...	...	...
Tajikistan	...	...	...	...	...	...	...	...	93	122	113	231	361	677	548	470	318	78	70
Uzbekistan	...	...	...	...	...	...	...	...	...	...	...	...	...	...	...	...	...	...	...

MSME = micro, small, and medium-sized enterprise.

Notes: End-of-year data. For India, data for commercial banks only. Armenia: AMD million; Azerbaijan: AZN million; Georgia: GEL million; India: Rs million; Indonesia: Rp billion; Malaysia: RM million; Pakistan: PRs million; Philippines: P million; Singapore: S$ million; Tajikistan: TJS million; Thailand: B billion.

Source: ADB Asia SME Monitor 2022 database.

B6-2. Nonperforming MSME Bank Loans ($ million)

Country	2003	2004	2005	2006	2007	2008	2009	2010	2011	2012	2013	2014	2015	2016	2017	2018	2019	2020	2021
Southeast Asia																			
Brunei Darussalam	...	...	...	...	...	...	...	...	...	...	...	...	...	...	...	...	...	0.0	0.1
Cambodia	...	...	...	...	...	...	...	...	...	...	...	...	...	...	...	...	...	...	...
Indonesia	...	...	...	...	...	...	...	...	1,728	1,759	1,601	2,537	2,407	2,649	2,843	2,452	2,884	3,056	3,277
Lao People's Democratic Republic	...	...	...	...	...	...	...	...	...	...	...	...	...	...	...	...	...	...	...
Malaysia	...	...	...	...	3,650	2,856	2,601	3,438	3,004	2,802	2,505	2,444	2,070	1,976	2,479	2,465	2,521	2,443	2,407
Myanmar	...	...	...	...	...	...	...	...	...	...	...	...	...	...	...	...	...	...	...
Philippines	...	...	...	...	...	...	...	539	594	615	574	562	534	526	521	570	637	1,001	1,037
Singapore	...	...	...	...	...	...	...	540	602	502	441	475	1,034	1,607	3,551	3,617	2,870	3,132	2,996
Thailand	...	...	...	...	...	...	5,530	5,060	4,091	4,079	4,150	4,164	4,535	5,727	6,722	7,076	7,668	8,222	7,600
Viet Nam	...	...	...	...	...	...	...	...	...	...	...	...	...	...	...	...	...	8,902	...
South Asia																			
Bangladesh	...	...	...	...	...	...	...	...	...	...	...	...	...	...	...	...	...	...	3,995
India	...	...	...	...	...	...	...	...	...	...	...	...	17,433	18,340	23,183	23,464	21,689	22,221	24,512
Nepal	...	...	...	...	...	...	...	...	...	...	...	...	...	...	...	...	...	...	...
Pakistan	...	...	...	...	572	767	939	1,133	1,061	982	820	867	736	635	628	544	517	510	...
Sri Lanka	...	...	...	...	...	...	...	...	...	...	...	...	...	...	...	...	...	...	...
Central and West Asia																			
Armenia	...	...	...	...	...	...	...	...	...	...	...	...	...	...	...	...	...	120.4	52.2
Azerbaijan	...	...	...	...	...	...	...	...	...	...	...	...	...	...	...	564.7	470.6	242.1	176.9
Georgia	...	...	...	...	...	...	...	81.5	80.4	67.2	58.7	54.0	67.3	77.7	85.2	152.1	139.6	297.2	241.6
Kazakhstan	...	...	...	...	...	...	...	...	...	...	...	...	...	...	...	...	...	...	...
Kyrgyz Republic	...	...	...	...	...	...	...	...	...	...	...	...	...	...	...	...	...	...	...
Tajikistan	...	...	...	...	...	...	...	...	19.4	25.4	23.6	43.6	51.5	85.7	62.3	50.0	32.8	6.9	6.2
Uzbekistan	...	...	...	...	...	...	...	...	...	...	...	...	...	...	...	...	...	...	...

MSME = micro, small, and medium-sized enterprise.

Notes: End-of-year data. Exchange rates of local currency to US dollar refer to end-of-year currency rates from the International Monetary Fund (IMF) International Financial Statistics in designated years.

Source: ADB Asia SME Monitor 2022 database.

B7. MSME NPL to Total MSME Bank Loans (%)

Country	2003	2004	2005	2006	2007	2008	2009	2010	2011	2012	2013	2014	2015	2016	2017	2018	2019	2020	2021
Southeast Asia																			
Brunei Darussalam	...	...	...	...	...	...	...	...	...	...	...	...	...	...	...	...	...	0.2	0.7
Cambodia	...	...	...	...	...	...	...	...	...	...	...	...	...	...	...	...	...	...	...
Indonesia	...	...	...	...	...	...	...	...	3.4	3.2	3.2	4.1	4.2	4.2	4.1	3.4	3.6	4.0	3.8
Lao People's Democratic Republic	...	...	...	...	...	...	...	...	...	...	...	...	...	...	...	...	...	...	...
Malaysia	...	...	...	...	9.4	7.1	6.3	7.5	5.8	4.6	3.9	3.5	3.2	3.0	3.2	3.4	3.7	3.2	3.1
Myanmar	...	...	...	...	...	...	...	...	...	...	...	...	...	...	...	...	...	...	...
Philippines	...	...	...	...	...	...	...	7.6	7.4	6.6	6.5	5.9	5.5	5.3	4.9	5.2	5.5	9.9	11.2
Singapore	...	...	...	...	...	...	...	1.5	1.4	1.0	0.8	0.8	1.9	3.0	5.9	6.3	4.5	4.6	4.4
Thailand	...	...	...	...	...	...	7.1	5.4	4.0	3.5	3.3	3.1	3.5	4.4	4.5	4.6	4.7	7.7	7.5
Viet Nam	...	...	...	...	...	...	...	...	...	...	...	...	...	...	...	...	...	11.3	...
South Asia																			
Bangladesh	...	...	...	...	...	...	...	3.6	3.6	6.4	7.9	11.8	...	...	...	...	...	...	14.2
India	...	...	...	...	...	...	...	...	...	...	...	...	9.6	10.3	10.9	10.4	9.1	9.6	9.9
Nepal	...	...	...	...	...	...	...	...	...	...	...	...	...	...	...	...	...	...	...
Pakistan	...	...	...	...	8.5	15.8	22.7	28.8	32.4	35.9	31.8	30.2	25.3	16.6	15.4	14.7	16.8	16.9	...
Sri Lanka	...	...	...	...	...	...	...	...	...	...	...	...	...	...	...	...	...	...	...
Central and West Asia																			
Armenia	...	...	...	...	...	...	...	...	...	...	...	...	...	...	...	...	...	5.3	2.1
Azerbaijan	...	...	...	...	...	...	...	...	...	...	...	...	...	...	...	33.4	21.5	12.0	6.8
Georgia	...	...	...	...	...	...	...	10.3	8.7	6.4	5.0	4.2	4.4	5.2	4.3	6.1	4.9	9.8	6.5
Kazakhstan	...	...	...	...	...	...	...	...	...	...	...	...	...	...	...	...	...	...	...
Kyrgyz Republic	...	...	...	...	...	...	...	...	...	...	...	...	...	...	...	...	...	...	...
Tajikistan	...	...	...	...	...	...	...	...	9.0	10.0	7.2	23.4	19.8	80.2	43.2	36.1	24.8	6.8	4.6
Uzbekistan	...	...	...	...	...	...	...	...	...	...	...	...	...	...	...	...	...	...	...

MSME = micro, small, and medium-sized enterprise; NPL = nonperforming loan.

Notes: End-of-year data. For India, data for commercial banks only.

Source: ADB Asia SME Monitor 2022 database.

B8-1. Outstanding Guaranteed Loans (local currency)

Country	2003	2004	2005	2006	2007	2008	2009	2010	2011	2012	2013	2014	2015	2016	2017	2018	2019	2020	2021
Southeast Asia																			
Brunei Darussalam	...	...	...	...	...	...	...	...	...	...	...	...	...	...	...	...	...	...	...
Cambodia	...	...	...	...	...	...	...	...	...	...	...	...	...	...	...	...	...	...	...
Indonesia	...	...	...	...	...	...	8,154	5,010	30,486	40,760	47,422	49,546	22,757	70,669	75,004	125,912	163,722	178,067	192,590
Lao People's Democratic Republic	...	...	...	...	...	...	...	...	...	...	...	...	...	...	...	...	...	...	...
Malaysia	...	...	...	...	39	42	45	47	50	51	53	56	60	64	67	71	75	81	87
Myanmar	...	...	...	...	...	...	...	...	...	...	...	...	...	...	...	...	...	...	...
Philippines	...	...	...	215	131	108	58	67	26	126	80	175	230	123	595	185	78	349	992
Singapore	...	...	...	...	...	...	...	...	...	...	...	...	...	...	...	...	...	...	...
Thailand	...	...	...	...	22	22	40	73	113	180	244	270	309	331	354	374	389	451	626
Viet Nam	...	...	...	...	...	...	...	...	...	...	...	...	...	...	...	...	...	...	...
South Asia																			
Bangladesh	...	...	...	...	...	...	...	...	...	...	...	...	...	...	...	...	...	...	...
India*	...	...	...	...	...	10,560	21,990	68,750	125,890	137,840	160,620	181,880	212,750	199,490	199,310	190,660	301,680	458,510	368,990
Nepal*	...	...	...	...	...	...	...	...	...	...	...	...	350	523	578	810	...	...	...
Pakistan	...	...	...	...	...	...	...	...	...	...	...	...	...	...	...	...	...	...	...
Sri Lanka	...	...	...	...	...	...	...	...	...	...	...	...	...	...	...	...	...	...	...
Central and West Asia																			
Armenia	...	47	366	628	748	429	598	181	122	578	1,104	1,091	860	84	710	370	351	128	...
Azerbaijan	...	...	...	...	...	...	...	...	...	...	...	...	...	...	...	...	...	...	...
Georgia	...	...	...	...	...	...	...	...	...	...	...	...	...	...	...	...	...	101	205
Kazakhstan	...	...	...	...	...	...	...	677	4,238	10,991	7,090	15,448	26,964	27,474	42,846	65,348	102,748	275,466	365,286
Kyrgyz Republic	...	...	...	...	...	...	...	...	5	16	43	75	55	41	790	1,752	2,967	5,015	5,759
Tajikistan	...	...	...	...	...	...	...	...	...	...	...	...	15	66	106	115	277	204	176
Uzbekistan	...	...	...	...	...	...	...	...	...	...	...	...	...	...	...	...	...	...	...

Notes: End-of-year data except * fiscal year data (ended 31 March in India and 15 July in Nepal). For Malaysia, data from Credit Guarantee Corporation. For the Philippines, approved guaranteed loans data from the Small Business Corporation until August 2019; outstanding guaranteed loan from PhilGuarantee for 2020. For India, guaranteed loans approved to MSMEs (CGTMSE). For Nepal, data from Deposit and Credit Guarantee Fund (DCGF). Armenia: AMD million; Georgia: GEL million; India: Rs million; Indonesia: Rp billion; Kazakhstan: KZT million; Kyrgyz Republic: KGS million; Malaysia: RM million; Nepal: NRs million; Philippines: P million; Tajikistan: TJS million; Thailand: B billion.

Source: ADB Asia SME Monitor 2022 database.

B8-2. Outstanding Guaranteed Loans ($ million)

Country	2003	2004	2005	2006	2007	2008	2009	2010	2011	2012	2013	2014	2015	2016	2017	2018	2019	2020	2021
Southeast Asia																			
Brunei Darussalam	...	...	...	...	...	...	...	...	...	...	...	...	...	...	...	...	...	...	...
Cambodia	...	...	...	...	...	...	...	...	...	...	...	...	...	...	...	...	...	...	...
Indonesia	...	...	...	...	...	...	867	557	3,362	4,215	3,891	3,983	1,650	5,260	5,536	8,695	11,778	12,624	13,497
Lao People's Democratic Republic	...	...	...	...	...	...	...	...	...	...	...	...	...	...	...	...	...	...	...
Malaysia	...	...	...	...	11,722	12,081	13,129	15,388	15,804	16,797	16,128	16,029	13,869	14,187	16,522	17,092	18,289	20,125	20,766
Myanmar	...	...	...	...	...	...	...	...	...	...	...	...	...	...	...	...	...	...	...
Philippines	...	...	...	4.4	3.2	2.3	1.3	1.5	0.6	3.1	1.8	3.9	4.9	2.5	11.9	3.5	1.5	7.3	19.5
Singapore	...	...	...	...	...	...	...	...	...	...	...	...	...	...	...	...	...	...	...
Thailand	...	...	...	...	660	626	1,197	2,418	3,567	5,892	7,425	8,178	8,560	9,239	10,828	11,520	12,892	15,027	18,737
Viet Nam	...	...	...	...	...	...	...	...	...	...	...	...	...	...	...	...	...	...	...
South Asia																			
Bangladesh	...	...	...	...	...	...	...	...	...	...	...	...	...	...	...	...	...	...	...
India*	...	...	...	...	...	218	471	1,534	2,364	2,516	2,595	2,872	3,207	2,936	3,118	2,732	4,233	6,277	4,966
Nepal*	...	...	...	...	...	...	...	...	...	...	...	...	3.3	4.8	5.6	7.0	...	...	...
Pakistan	...	...	...	...	...	...	...	...	...	...	...	...	...	...	...	...	...	...	...
Sri Lanka	...	...	...	...	...	...	...	...	...	...	...	...	...	...	...	...	...	...	...
Central and West Asia																			
Armenia	...	0.1	0.8	1.7	2.5	1.4	1.6	0.5	0.3	1.4	2.7	2.3	1.8	0.2	1.5	0.8	0.7	0.2	...
Azerbaijan	...	...	...	...	...	...	...	...	...	...	...	...	...	...	...	...	...	...	...
Georgia	...	...	...	...	...	...	...	...	...	...	...	...	...	...	...	...	...	30.6	66.0
Kazakhstan	...	...	...	...	...	...	...	4.6	28.6	72.9	46.0	84.7	79.3	82.4	128.9	170.1	268.6	654.5	846.0
Kyrgyz Republic	...	...	...	...	...	...	...	...	0.1	0.3	0.9	1.3	0.7	0.6	11.5	25.1	42.6	60.7	67.9
Tajikistan	...	...	...	...	...	...	...	...	...	...	...	...	2.1	8.4	12.1	12.2	28.6	18.1	15.6
Uzbekistan	...	...	...	...	...	...	...	...	...	...	...	...	...	...	...	...	...	...	...

Notes: End-of-year data except * fiscal year data (ended 31 March in India and 15 July in Nepal). Exchange rates of local currency to US dollar refer to end-of-year currency rates from the International Monetary Fund (IMF) International Financial Statistics in designated years.

Source: ADB Asia SME Monitor 2022 database.

B8-3. Number of MSMEs Guaranteed

Country	2003	2004	2005	2006	2007	2008	2009	2010	2011	2012	2013	2014	2015	2016	2017	2018	2019	2020	2021
Southeast Asia																			
Brunei Darussalam	...	...	...	...	...	...	...	...	...	...	...	...	...	...	...	...	...	...	...
Cambodia	...	...	...	...	...	...	...	...	...	...	...	...	...	...	...	...	...	...	...
Indonesia	...	...	...	...	3,623	1,652,965	718,320	1,437,650	1,909,912	1,962,121	2,347,429	2,443,907	722,621	4,362,599	4,086,971	4,440,028	4,728,330	6,112,058	1,765,991
Lao People's Democratic Republic	...	...	...	...	...	...	...	...	...	...	...	...	...	...	...	...	...	...	...
Malaysia	...	...	...	...	13,004	10,368	14,073	7,670	7,504	2,152	2,368	6,839	8,225	7,568	8,637	8,999	10,827	13,472	21,736
Myanmar	...	...	...	...	...	...	...	...	...	...	...	...	...	...	...	...	...	...	...
Philippines	...	...	...	64	43	36	17	10	9	44	22	91	142	181	14,799	327	80	2,923	...
Singapore	...	...	...	...	...	...	...	...	...	...	...	...	...	...	...	...	...	...	...
Thailand	...	...	...	...	2,206	1,335	5,507	12,259	15,992	21,950	25,256	23,117	75,799	53,842	109,087	77,858	88,215	166,418	226,308
Viet Nam	...	...	...	...	...	...	...	...	...	...	...	...	...	...	...	...	...	...	...
South Asia																			
Bangladesh	...	...	...	...	...	...	...	...	...	...	...	...	...	...	...	...	...	...	...
India	...	...	...	...	...	...	...	...	...	...	...	...	...	...	...	...	...	...	...
Nepal*	...	...	...	...	...	...	...	...	...	...	...	...	505	851	867	530	...	...	...
Pakistan	...	...	...	...	...	...	...	...	...	...	...	...	...	...	...	...	...	...	...
Sri Lanka	...	...	...	...	...	...	...	...	...	...	...	...	...	...	...	...	...	...	...
Central and West Asia																			
Armenia	...	7	56	87	129	97	122	53	28	150	243	235	176	18	81	64	82	30	...
Azerbaijan	...	...	...	...	...	...	...	...	...	...	...	...	...	...	...	...	...	...	...
Georgia	...	...	...	...	...	...	...	...	...	...	...	...	...	...	...	...	...	133	318
Kazakhstan	...	...	...	...	...	...	...	3	24	87	143	443	941	979	1,317	1,944	2,673	7,347	17,219
Kyrgyz Republic	...	...	...	...	...	...	...	...	16	36	106	159	98	64	291	469	515	732	977
Tajikistan	...	...	...	...	...	...	...	...	...	...	...	...	53	293	456	296	999	497	707
Uzbekistan	...	...	...	...	...	...	...	...	...	...	...	...	...	...	...	...	...	...	...

MSME = micro, small, and medium-sized enterprise.

Note: End-of-year data except * fiscal year data (ended 15 July in Nepal).

Source: ADB Asia SME Monitor 2022 database.

C. MSME Access to Finance (Nonbanking)

C1-1. NBFI Financing, Total (local currency)

Country	2003	2004	2005	2006	2007	2008	2009	2010	2011	2012	2013	2014	2015	2016	2017	2018	2019	2020	2021
Southeast Asia																			
Brunei Darussalam	...	...	...	...	...	...	...	1,415	1,562	1,716	1,815	2,023	1,881	1,677	1,570	1,552	1,537	1,576	1,583
Cambodia	...	...	...	...	617,271	1,130,585	1,244,970	1,724,841	2,591,263	3,538,889	5,261,752	7,299,407	12,589,330	13,146,529	17,761,787	22,527,051	30,527,095	28,877,763	33,315,455
Indonesia	...	...	...	...	...	...	...	...	...	...	...	...	...	423,126	452,048	477,590	503,199	427,983	417,487
Lao People's Democratic Republic	...	...	...	...	...	...	...	49,209	93,042	103,110	459,065	430,988	835,488	1,461,276	2,196,508	4,808,287	6,075,379	5,405,244	6,480,546
Malaysia	...	...	...	...	2,479	2,277	2,097	553	953	1,130	1,364	1,487	1,392	1,641	1,245	1,386	1,503	1,312	1,063
Myanmar*	...	...	...	...	...	...	...	...	...	49,194	67,245	110,069	169,293	260,948	426,016	793,197	1,800,232	...	...
Philippines	...	...	...	...	...	...	6,544	5,947	7,711	8,876	8,538	130,201	310,467	382,749	403,599	527,932	610,164	624,152	...
Singapore	...	...	...	...	...	...	...	8,058	9,460	11,312	11,654	12,385	13,252	12,547	12,849	13,254	14,712	14,080	13,930
Thailand	...	...	...	...	...	...	...	...	...	...	...	...	...	...	...	...	...	...	...
Viet Nam	...	...	...	...	...	...	...	23,708,082	29,076,880	36,450,034	45,557,772	53,221,190	61,880,958	71,700,966	84,896,048	96,140,373	75,707,125	92,405,581	...
South Asia																			
Bangladesh	...	...	...	...	...	...	...	...	...	268,628	344,538	407,375	448,478	530,724	615,962	662,449	671,768	669,232	673,542
India	...	...	...	...	...	...	...	...	...	...	...	...	574,766	755,150	1,108,210	1,282,338	1,257,732	1,503,208	1,644,339
Nepal*	...	...	...	...	...	...	...	...	...	...	...	...	...	...	106,515	145,952	234,153	262,732	...
Pakistan	...	...	...	...	38,141	39,641	37,121	36,249	32,989	37,062	42,694	52,088	63,097	80,283	90,590	113,193	118,694	109,491	...
Sri Lanka	...	...	...	...	106,211	128,378	213,397	265,456	388,416	471,698	553,085	641,349	837,672	1,006,306	1,108,691	1,205,002	1,200,314	1,164,440	1,266,666
Central and West Asia																			
Armenia	...	2,393	4,848	16,390	38,230	57,382	55,443	69,584	93,742	128,347	149,826	174,209	186,502	173,611	199,721	236,217	347,603	311,137	309,792
Azerbaijan	...	...	...	...	...	...	...	...	...	343	453	539	578	399	318	252	284	276	347
Georgia	...	1	2	4	56	114	131	232	352	523	626	858	1,204	1,450	1,143	1,103	1,545	1,597	2,308
Kazakhstan	...	4,400	9,200	12,500	18,000	22,000	22,600	19,100	17,900	25,300	36,500	50,400	127,460	176,944	1,001,497	1,331,466	1,875,350	2,099,765	2,515,111
Kyrgyz Republic	...	1,244	2,128	2,804	4,921	7,191	9,061	11,011	15,261	14,960	18,643	21,019	13,628	9,682	10,563	14,536	18,349	18,416	20,514
Tajikistan	...	654	644	728	2,104	2,264	2,093	436	632	935	1,377	1,894	1,993	1,701	1,695	2,041	2,125	2,058	2,496
Uzbekistan	...	...	...	...	...	...	...	...	...	...	...	69,943	114,069	139,629	193,265	411,433	755,698	934,752	1,335,172

MSME = micro, small, and medium-sized enterprise; NBFI = nonbank finance institution.

Notes: End-of-year data except * fiscal year data (ended 15 July in Nepal and 31 March in Myanmar). Armenia: AMD millions (microfinance institutions and pawnshops); Azerbaijan: AZN million (microfinance institutions and credit unions/cooperatives); Bangladesh: Tk million (nonbank finance institutions regulated by Bangladesh Bank); Brunei Darussalam: B$ million (finance companies and pawnbrokers); Cambodia: KR million (microfinance institutions and leasing companies); Georgia: GEL million (microfinance institutions, credit unions/cooperatives, and pawnshops); India: Rs million (nonbank finance institutions regulated by Reserve Bank of India; MSME financing only); Indonesia: Rp billion (finance companies, microfinance institutions, and government pawnshops); Kazakhstan: KZT million (microfinance institutions, credit unions/cooperatives, finance companies, and pawnshops); Kyrgyz Republic: KGS million (microfinance institutions, credit unions/cooperatives, finance companies, pawnshops, and leasing companies); Lao PDR: KN million (microfinance institutions, pawnshops, and leasing companies); Malaysia: RM million (private equity, venture capital, factoring, and leasing companies); Myanmar: MK million (microfinance institutions); Nepal: NRs million (microfinance institutions); Pakistan: PRs million (microfinance institutions and leasing companies); Philippines: P million (credit unions and cooperatives [2015-2018], pawnshops [2009-2018], and nonstock savings and loans associations [NSSLAs; 2014-2020]); Singapore: S$ million (finance companies); Sri Lanka: SLRs million (nonbank finance institutions regulated by Central Bank of Sri Lanka); Tajikistan: TJS million (microfinance institutions and nonbank credit institutions); Uzbekistan: SUM million (microfinance institutions and pawnshops); Viet Nam: D million (People's Credit Funds and microfinance institutions).

Source: ADB Asia SME Monitor 2022 database.

C1-2. NBFI Financing, Total ($ million)

Country	2003	2004	2005	2006	2007	2008	2009	2010	2011	2012	2013	2014	2015	2016	2017	2018	2019	2020	2021
Southeast Asia																			
Brunei Darussalam	...	...	...	...	...	...	...	1,097	1,201	1,406	1,429	1,533	1,334	1,156	1,171	1,133	1,139	1,176	1,164
Cambodia	...	...	...	...	154	277	299	426	642	886	1,317	1,791	3,107	3,250	4,395	5,586	7,475	7,084	8,099
Indonesia	...	...	...	...	...	...	...	...	...	...	...	...	...	31,492	33,366	32,980	36,199	30,343	29,258
Lao People's Democratic Republic	...	...	...	...	...	...	...	6	12	13	57	53	103	179	265	564	686	583	587
Malaysia	...	...	...	...	749	658	613	180	300	369	416	425	325	366	307	335	368	327	254
Myanmar*	...	...	...	...	...	...	...	...	...	58	68	107	130	192	313	512	1,228	...	...
Philippines	...	...	...	...	...	...	141	135	176	215	192	2,918	6,582	7,684	8,085	10,014	12,025	12,992	...
Singapore	...	...	...	...	...	...	...	6,247	7,277	9,272	9,176	9,383	9,398	8,653	9,589	9,746	10,898	10,667	10,319
Thailand	...	...	...	...	...	...	...	...	...	...	...	...	...	...	...	...	...	...	...
Viet Nam	...	...	...	...	...	...	...	1,252	1,396	1,750	2,166	2,505	2,827	3,236	3,786	4,212	3,270	3,995	...
South Asia																			
Bangladesh	...	...	...	...	...	...	...	...	...	3,364	4,431	5,226	5,713	6,744	7,448	7,896	7,912	7,892	7,850
India	...	...	...	...	...	...	...	...	...	...	...	...	8,665	11,113	17,335	18,374	17,647	20,578	22,131
Nepal*	...	...	...	...	...	...	...	...	...	...	...	...	...	...	1,035	1,269	2,067	2,230	...
Pakistan	...	...	...	...	623	501	441	423	367	382	404	518	602	766	820	816	766	686	...
Sri Lanka	...	...	...	...	977	1,135	1,866	2,393	3,410	3,709	4,230	4,894	5,815	6,718	7,253	6,611	6,609	6,247	6,320
Central and West Asia																			
Armenia	...	5	11	45	126	187	147	191	243	318	369	367	385	359	413	488	725	595	645
Azerbaijan	...	...	...	...	...	...	...	...	...	437	578	687	371	225	187	148	167	163	204
Georgia	...	0.8	0.9	2.1	35	68	78	131	211	316	360	460	503	548	441	412	539	487	745
Kazakhstan	...	34	69	98	150	182	152	129	121	168	237	276	375	531	3,014	3,466	4,902	4,989	5,825
Kyrgyz Republic	...	30	52	74	139	183	205	234	328	316	379	357	180	140	154	208	264	223	242
Tajikistan	...	218	201	214	601	647	476	99	132	195	287	357	285	215	193	217	219	182	221
Uzbekistan	...	...	...	...	...	...	...	...	...	...	...	29	41	43	24	49	79	89	123

NBFI = nonbank finance institution.

Notes: End-of-year data except * fiscal year data (ended 15 July in Nepal and 31 March in Myanmar). Exchange rates of local currency to US dollar refer to end-of-year currency rates from the International Monetary Fund (IMF) International Financial Statistics in designated years.

Source: ADB Asia SME Monitor 2022 database.

C2. NBFI Financing to Bank Loans (%)

Country	2003	2004	2005	2006	2007	2008	2009	2010	2011	2012	2013	2014	2015	2016	2017	2018	2019	2020	2021
Southeast Asia																			
Brunei Darussalam	...	...	...	...	...	...	...	27.3	30.7	33.0	32.3	35.4	30.8	31.0	30.6	28.4	26.1	27.1	26.0
Cambodia	...	...	...	...	9.7	11.5	11.9	13.1	14.8	15.2	17.9	19.2	27.0	23.5	27.1	27.7	29.8	23.0	21.2
Indonesia	...	...	...	...	...	...	...	...	...	...	...	...	...	9.2	9.0	9.5	11.3	7.7	7.2
Lao People's Democratic Republic	...	...	...	...	...	...	...	0.4	0.5	0.4	1.3	1.1	1.7	2.4	3.3	7.0	8.5	6.9	...
Malaysia	...	...	...	...	0.38	0.31	0.27	0.06	0.09	0.10	0.11	0.11	0.10	0.11	0.08	0.08	0.10	0.10	0.10
Myanmar*	...	...	...	...	...	...	...	...	...	1.7	1.6	1.7	1.9	2.1	2.6	4.1	7.7	...	...
Philippines	...	...	...	...	...	...	...	...	...	0.2	0.2	2.5	5.3	5.6	5.0	5.7	6.3	6.3	...
Singapore	...	...	...	...	...	...	...	1.3	1.2	1.3	1.1	1.1	1.2	1.1	1.0	1.0	1.1	1.0	1.1
Thailand	...	...	...	...	...	...	...	...	...	...	...	...	...	...	...	...	...	...	...
Viet Nam	...	...	...	...	...	...	...	...	...	1.2	1.3	1.3	1.3	1.3	1.3	1.3	0.9	1.0	...
South Asia																			
Bangladesh	...	...	...	...	...	...	...	...	...	...	...	...	7.4	7.6	7.5	7.1	6.5	5.9	5.2
India	...	...	...	...	...	...	...	...	...	...	...	...	0.8	1.0	1.3	1.4	1.2	1.3	1.4
Nepal*	...	...	...	...	...	...	...	...	...	...	...	...	...	...	5.3	6.0	8.0	8.0	...
Pakistan	...	...	...	...	1.4	1.2	1.1	1.0	0.9	0.9	1.0	1.1	1.2	1.4	1.3	1.4	1.4	1.2	...
Sri Lanka	...	...	...	...	6.9	7.9	13.6	13.5	14.9	15.0	16.1	16.5	17.8	18.2	17.2	15.7	14.8	12.8	12.1
Central and West Asia																			
Armenia	...	1.8	2.6	7.1	9.4	9.3	7.9	7.8	7.7	8.4	8.8	8.4	9.3	7.5	7.9	8.1	10.2	8.0	8.4
Azerbaijan	...	...	...	...	...	...	...	...	...	3.0	3.0	3.0	2.8	2.5	2.8	2.0	1.9	2.0	2.1
Georgia	...	0.2	0.1	0.1	1.2	2.0	2.6	3.8	4.7	6.2	6.1	6.7	7.5	7.7	5.1	4.1	4.8	4.2	5.4
Kazakhstan	...	0.3	0.4	0.3	0.2	0.3	0.3	0.3	0.2	0.3	0.3	0.4	1.0	1.4	7.9	10.2	13.5	14.4	13.6
Kyrgyz Republic	...	21.4	27.6	24.7	23.6	28.1	35.9	41.7	48.9	37.3	34.5	26.7	14.5	10.4	9.8	11.4	12.5	11.3	11.3
Tajikistan	...	69.5	56.6	33.5	58.0	51.4	42.2	14.1	15.9	21.5	22.9	24.4	21.6	20.9	24.9	30.9	28.0	23.4	26.4
Uzbekistan	...	...	...	...	...	...	...	...	...	...	...	0.2	0.3	0.3	0.2	0.2	0.4	0.3	0.4

NBFI = nonbank finance institution.

Note: End-of-year data except * fiscal year data (ended 15 July in Nepal and 31 March in Myanmar).

Source: ADB Asia SME Monitor 2022 database.

C3. NBFI Financing to GDP (%)

Country	2003	2004	2005	2006	2007	2008	2009	2010	2011	2012	2013	2014	2015	2016	2017	2018	2019	2020	2021
Southeast Asia																			
Brunei Darussalam	...	...	...	...	...	...	...	7.6	6.7	7.2	8.0	9.3	10.6	10.6	9.4	8.5	8.4	9.5	8.4
Cambodia	...	...	...	...	1.8	2.7	2.9	3.7	5.0	6.2	8.6	10.8	17.1	16.2	19.8	22.6	27.7	27.9	30.1
Indonesia	...	...	...	...	...	...	...	...	...	...	...	...	...	3.4	3.3	3.2	3.2	2.8	2.5
Lao People's Democratic Republic	...	...	...	...	...	...	...	0.1	0.1	0.1	0.5	0.4	0.7	1.1	1.6	3.2	3.7	3.1	3.5
Malaysia	...	...	...	...	0.4	0.3	0.3	0.1	0.1	0.1	0.1	0.1	0.1	0.1	0.1	0.1	0.1	0.9	0.7
Myanmar*	...	...	...	...	...	...	...	...	...	0.1	0.1	0.2	0.2	0.3	0.5	2.4	...	...	...
Philippines	...	...	...	...	...	...	0.1	0.1	0.1	0.1	0.1	1.0	2.2	2.5	2.4	2.9	3.1	3.5	...
Singapore	...	...	...	...	...	...	...	2.5	2.7	3.1	3.0	3.1	3.1	2.9	2.7	2.6	2.9	3.0	2.6
Thailand	...	...	...	...	...	...	...	...	...	...	...	...	...	...	...	...	...	...	...
Viet Nam	...	...	...	...	...	...	...	0.0	0.0	0.0	0.0	0.0	0.0	0.0	0.0	0.0	0.0	0.0	...
South Asia																			
Bangladesh	...	...	...	...	...	...	...	...	...	2.5	2.9	3.0	3.0	3.1	3.1	2.9	2.6	2.4	1.9
India	...	...	...	...	...	...	...	...	...	...	...	...	0.4	0.5	0.6	0.7	0.6	0.8	...
Nepal*	...	...	...	...	...	...	...	...	...	...	...	...	...	...	3.5	4.2	6.1	6.7	...
Pakistan	...	...	...	...	0.4	0.4	0.3	0.2	0.2	0.2	0.2	0.2	0.2	0.3	0.3	0.3	0.3	0.3	...
Sri Lanka	...	...	...	...	3.0	2.9	4.4	4.1	5.4	5.4	5.8	6.2	7.6	8.4	8.3	8.4	8.0	7.8	7.5
Central and West Asia																			
Armenia	...	0.1	0.2	0.6	1.2	1.6	1.8	2.0	2.5	3.0	3.3	3.6	3.7	3.4	3.6	3.9	5.3	5.0	4.4
Azerbaijan	...	...	...	...	...	...	...	...	...	0.6	0.8	0.9	1.1	0.7	0.5	0.3	0.3	0.4	0.4
Georgia	...	0.0	0.0	0.0	0.3	0.6	0.7	1.1	1.4	1.9	2.2	2.8	3.5	4.0	2.8	2.5	3.1	3.2	3.8
Kazakhstan	...	0.1	0.2	0.2	0.2	0.2	0.1	0.1	0.1	0.1	0.1	0.1	0.3	0.4	2.1	2.4	3.0	3.0	3.6
Kyrgyz Republic	...	1.3	2.1	2.5	3.5	3.8	4.5	5.0	5.3	4.8	5.2	5.2	3.2	2.0	2.0	2.6	3.0	3.1	2.8
Tajikistan	...	13.7	10.4	10.1	22.5	17.7	11.8	2.1	2.6	3.1	3.8	4.7	4.4	3.3	3.1	3.2	3.0	2.6	3.0
Uzbekistan	...	...	...	...	...	...	...	...	...	...	...	0.0	0.1	0.1	0.1	0.1	0.2	0.2	0.2

GDP = gross domestic product, NBFI = nonbank finance institution.

Note: End-of-year data except * fiscal year data (ended 15 July in Nepal and 31 March in Myanmar).

Source: ADB Asia SME Monitor 2022 database.

C4-1. Nonperforming NBFI Financing (local currency)

Country	2003	2004	2005	2006	2007	2008	2009	2010	2011	2012	2013	2014	2015	2016	2017	2018	2019	2020	2021
Southeast Asia																			
Brunei Darussalam	...	...	...	...	...	...	...	12.9	13.2	18.9	20.3	23.5	20.4	19.1	20.1	15.1	17.2	25.3	15.6
Cambodia	...	...	...	...	1,171	4,719	34,847	20,361	5,753	10,284	30,880	52,119	94,788	210,885	298,210	335,399	262,692	563,564	845,912
Indonesia	...	...	...	...	...	...	...	...	...	...	...	...	...	12,644	12,260	11,810	10,853	14,829	12,861
Lao People's Democratic Republic	...	...	...	...	...	...	...	...	...	...	...	...	...	...	...	...	74,235	225,592	149,387
Malaysia	...	...	...	...	...	...	...	...	...	...	...	...	...	...	...	...	...	...	...
Myanmar*	...	...	...	...	...	...	...	...	...	42.1	40.6	68.0	258	1,645	2,769	9,085	14,376	...	...
Philippines	...	...	...	...	...	...	...	...	...	...	...	...	20,356	32,840	24,868	29,302	38,268	42,612	...
Singapore	...	...	...	...	...	...	...	...	...	...	...	...	...	...	...	15	20	...	...
Thailand	...	...	...	...	...	...	...	...	...	...	...	...	...	...	...	...	...	...	...
Viet Nam	...	...	...	...	...	...	...	...	83.8	912.1	140.2	86.6	115	554	16,319	18,669	644,466	705,880	...
South Asia																			
Bangladesh	...	...	...	...	...	...	...	...	...	13,871	18,064	20,223	40,012	38,693	45,232	54,394	63,988	100,536	130,166
India	...	...	...	...	...	...	...	...	...	...	...	...	467,032	606,742	867,226	1,530,874	1,540,101	1,265,910	2,079,118
Nepal	...	...	...	...	...	...	...	...	...	...	...	...	...	...	...	...	...	...	...
Pakistan	...	...	...	...	1,589	2,031	2,862	3,390	2,961	3,312	3,014	1,620	2,174	2,288	1,970	2,109	2,176	6,589	...
Sri Lanka	...	...	...	...	...	...	6,053	20,911	19,904	23,627	37,024	44,095	47,429	52,973	65,895	93,010	127,626	161,602	139,318
Central and West Asia																			
Armenia	...	...	...	...	...	...	...	...	...	...	...	...	...	...	...	...	...	...	...
Azerbaijan	...	...	...	...	...	...	...	...	...	...	...	...	...	...	...	96.0	66.0	81.0	70.0
Georgia	...	...	...	...	...	...	...	...	...	...	...	...	...	...	...	93.7	89.4	79.7	...
Kazakhstan	...	...	...	...	...	...	...	...	...	...	...	...	...	...	83,275	79,915	88,553	121,246	134,640
Kyrgyz Republic	...	...	...	...	...	...	...	...	...	...	...	...	...	...	...	...	...	...	...
Tajikistan	...	0.3	0.5	2.5	4.7	17.8	21.4	21.7	27.4	27.1	55.1	139.9	209.8	152.3	110.6	70.4	102.1	80.6	80.6
Uzbekistan	...	...	...	...	...	...	...	...	...	...	3,093	5,197	9,027	14,473	30,920	51,142	185,372	113,263	113,263

NBFI = nonbank finance institution.

Notes: End-of-year data except * fiscal year data (ended 31 March in Myanmar). Azerbaijan: AZN million (microfinance institutions); Bangladesh Tk million (nonbank finance institutions regulated by Bangladesh Bank); Brunei Darussalam: B$ million (finance companies only for 2010–2011; finance companies and pawnbrokers for 2012–2020); Cambodia: KR million (microfinance institutions and leasing companies); Georgia: GEL million (microfinance institutions); India: Rs million (nonbank finance institutions regulated by Reserve Bank of India); Indonesia: Rp billion (data from 2016 to 2019 based on New Business Activities [POJK 35/POJK.05/2018] and New Economy Sector [SEOJK 3/SEOJK.05/2016]; data from 2007 to 2015 based on the old classification; excludes microfinance institutions and government pawnshops because of no nonperforming financing data); Kazakhstan: KZT million (microfinance institutions [2017–2021], finance companies [2017–2021], and pawnshops [2020–2021]); Myanmar: MK million (microfinance institutions); Pakistan: PRs million (microfinance institutions and leasing companies); Philippines: P million (credit unions and cooperatives only); Sri Lanka: SLRs million (nonbank finance institutions regulated by Central Bank of Sri Lanka); Tajikistan: TJS million (microfinance institutions); Uzbekistan: SUM million (microfinance institutions and pawnshops); Viet Nam: D million (microfinance institutions only for 2011–2018; microfinance institutions and People's Credit Funds for 2019–2020).

Source: ADB Asia SME Monitor 2022 database.

C4-2. Nonperforming NBFI Financing ($ million)

Country	2003	2004	2005	2006	2007	2008	2009	2010	2011	2012	2013	2014	2015	2016	2017	2018	2019	2020	2021
Southeast Asia																			
Brunei Darussalam	...	...	...	...	...	...	...	10.0	10.2	15.5	16.0	17.8	14.5	13.2	15.0	11.0	12.8	18.9	11.4
Cambodia	...	...	...	...	0.3	1.2	8.4	5.0	1.4	2.6	7.7	12.8	23.4	52.1	73.8	83.2	64.3	138.2	205.6
Indonesia	...	...	...	...	...	...	...	...	...	...	...	...	...	941.0	904.9	815.6	780.7	1,051.3	901.3
Lao People's Democratic Republic	...	...	...	...	...	...	...	...	...	...	...	...	...	...	...	...	8.4	24.3	13.5
Malaysia	...	...	...	...	...	...	...	...	...	...	...	...	...	...	...	...	...	...	...
Myanmar*	...	...	...	...	...	...	...	...	...	0.05	0.04	0.07	0.20	1.21	2.03	5.86	9.81	...	...
Philippines	...	...	...	...	...	...	...	...	...	...	...	...	431.5	659.3	498.2	555.8	754.2	887.0	...
Singapore	...	...	...	...	...	...	...	...	...	...	...	...	...	...	...	10.9	14.6	...	...
Thailand	...	...	...	...	...	...	...	...	...	...	...	...	...	...	...	...	...	...	...
Viet Nam	...	...	...	...	...	...	...	...	0.004	0.044	0.007	0.004	0.005	0.025	0.728	0.8	27.8	30.5	...
South Asia																			
Bangladesh	...	...	...	...	...	...	...	...	...	173.7	232.3	259.4	509.7	491.6	546.9	648.3	753.7	1,185.5	1,517.1
India	...	...	...	...	...	...	...	...	...	...	...	...	7,041.0	8,929.2	13,565.2	21,935.4	21,609.4	17,329.4	27,982.7
Nepal	...	...	...	...	...	...	...	...	...	...	...	...	...	...	...	...	...	...	...
Pakistan	...	...	...	...	26.0	25.7	34.0	39.6	32.9	34.1	28.5	16.1	20.7	21.8	17.8	15.2	14.1	41.3	...
Sri Lanka	...	...	...	...	...	...	52.9	188.5	174.8	185.8	283.2	336.5	329.2	353.6	431.1	510.3	702.7	866.9	695.1
Central and West Asia																			
Armenia	...	...	...	...	...	...	...	...	...	...	...	...	...	...	...	...	...	...	...
Azerbaijan	...	...	...	...	...	...	...	...	...	...	...	...	...	...	...	56.5	38.8	47.6	41.2
Georgia	...	...	...	...	...	...	...	...	...	...	...	...	...	...	...	...	32.7	27.3	25.7
Kazakhstan	...	...	...	...	...	...	...	...	...	...	...	...	...	...	250.6	208.0	231.5	288.1	311.8
Kyrgyz Republic	...	...	...	...	...	...	...	...	...	...	...	...	...	...	...	...	...	...	-
Tajikistan	...	...	0.1	0.1	0.7	1.4	4.0	4.9	4.5	5.7	5.6	10.4	20.0	26.6	17.3	11.8	7.3	9.0	7.1
Uzbekistan	...	...	...	...	...	...	...	...	...	...	...	1.3	1.8	2.8	1.8	3.7	5.4	17.7	10.5

NBFI = nonbank finance institution.

Notes: End-of-year data except * fiscal year data (ended 31 March in Myanmar). Exchange rates of local currency to US dollar refer to end-of-year currency rates from the International Monetary Fund (IMF) International Financial Statistics in designated years.

Source: ADB Asia SME Monitor 2022 database.

C5. NBFI NPF to Total Financing (%)

Country	2003	2004	2005	2006	2007	2008	2009	2010	2011	2012	2013	2014	2015	2016	2017	2018	2019	2020	2021
Southeast Asia																			
Brunei Darussalam	...	...	...	...	...	...	...	0.9	0.8	1.1	1.1	1.2	1.1	1.1	1.3	1.0	1.1	1.6	1.0
Cambodia	...	...	...	...	0.2	0.4	2.8	1.2	0.2	0.3	0.6	0.7	0.8	1.6	1.7	1.5	0.9	...	...
Indonesia	...	...	...	...	...	...	...	...	...	...	...	...	...	3.3	3.0	2.7	2.4	4.0	3.5
Lao People's Democratic Republic	...	...	...	...	...	...	...	...	...	...	...	...	...	...	...	...	1.2	4.2	2.3
Malaysia	...	...	...	...	...	...	...	...	...	...	...	...	...	...	...	...	...	...	...
Myanmar*	...	...	...	...	...	...	...	...	...	0.09	0.06	0.06	0.2	0.6	0.7	1.1	0.8	...	...
Philippines	...	...	...	...	...	...	...	...	...	...	...	...	0.3	0.5	0.3	0.3	0.4	0.4	...
Singapore	...	...	...	...	...	...	...	...	...	...	...	...	...	...	...	0.0	0.0	...	...
Thailand	...	...	...	...	...	...	...	...	...	...	...	...	...	...	...	...	...	...	...
Viet Nam	...	...	...	...	...	...	...	...	0.02	0.03	0.004	0.002	0.002	0.01	0.2	0.3	7.8	7.9	...
South Asia																			
Bangladesh	...	...	...	...	...	...	...	...	...	5.2	5.2	5.0	8.9	7.3	7.3	8.2	9.5	15.0	19.3
India	...	...	...	...	...	...	...	...	...	...	...	...	3.7	3.9	4.8	7.1	6.4	5.8	7.3
Nepal*	...	...	...	...	...	...	...	...	...	...	...	...	...	0.9	0.8	1.0	1.2	2.3	...
Pakistan	...	...	...	...	4.2	5.1	7.7	9.4	9.0	8.9	7.1	3.1	3.4	2.9	2.2	1.9	1.8	6.0	...
Sri Lanka	...	...	...	...	...	...	2.8	7.9	5.1	5.0	6.7	6.9	5.7	5.3	5.9	7.7	10.6	13.9	11.0
Central and West Asia																			
Armenia	...	...	...	...	...	...	...	...	...	...	...	...	...	...	...	...	...	...	...
Azerbaijan	...	...	...	...	...	...	...	...	...	...	...	...	...	...	...	42.1	24.5	30.8	21.0
Georgia**	...	...	...	...	...	...	...	...	...	...	...	...	...	...	...	...	8.3	7.5	5.9
Kazakhstan	...	...	...	...	...	...	...	...	...	...	...	...	...	...	8.3	6.0	4.7	5.8	5.4
Kyrgyz Republic	...	...	...	...	...	...	...	...	...	...	...	...	...	...	...	...	...	...	...
Tajikistan**	...	...	0.05	0.06	0.12	0.21	0.8	4.9	3.4	2.9	2.0	2.9	7.0	12.3	9.0	5.4	3.3	5.0	3.2
Uzbekistan	...	...	...	...	...	...	...	...	...	...	...	4.4	4.6	6.5	7.5	7.5	6.8	19.8	8.5

NBFI = nonbank finance institution, NPF = nonperforming financing.

Notes: End-of-year data except * fiscal year data (ended 15 July in Nepal and 31 March in Myanmar). ** Microfinance institutions only.

Source: ADB Asia SME Monitor 2022 database.

C6. NBFI Financing by Sector (% share, latest available year)

Item	Brunei Darussalam	Cambodia	Indonesia	Lao People's Democratic Republic	Malaysia	Myanmar	Philippines	Singapore	Thailand	Viet Nam
Agriculture	...	19.2	5.6	7.4	...	30.8	...	...	...	...
Manufacturing	...	1.0	10.4	0.4	...	10.5	...	...	...	...
Transportation and communication	97.7	5.9	6.7	0.1	...	...	...	...	...	...
Construction	...	3.8	3.3	3.0	...	...	...	...	...	...
Wholesale and retail trade	...	20.9	23.0	21.0	...	33.2	...	...	...	...
Other services	...	15.9	6.3	2.5	72.4	25.6	...	...	...	...
Others	2.3	33.3	44.6	65.7	27.6	...	...	...	...	...
Year	2021	2020	2021	2020	2020	September 2019				

Item	Bangladesh	India*	Nepal*	Pakistan	Sri Lanka
Agriculture	2.5	...	42.2	42.0	...
Manufacturing	43.9	36.7	...	8.0	...
Transportation and communication	3.9	...	...	...	...
Construction	14.3	...	...	...	...
Wholesale and retail trade	14.0	63.3	...	20.0	...
Other services	...	...	33.8	11.0	...
Others	21.4	...	24.1	19.0	...
Year	2021	FY2021	FY 2020	2020	

Item	Armenia	Azerbaijan	Georgia	Kazakhstan	Kyrgyz Republic	Tajikistan	Uzbekistan
Agriculture	22.8	13.0	6.6	...	...	31.1	...
Manufacturing	7.4	...	...	...	...	11.8	...
Transportation and communication	1.3	...	...	...	...	0.3	...
Construction	2.6	...	...	...	...	3.0	...
Wholesale and retail trade	6.9	8.0	13.0	...	...	3.4	...
Other services	36.3	10.0	...	...	...	48.0	...
Others	22.7	69.0	80.4	...	...	2.3	...
Year	2021	2021	2021			2021	

NBFI = nonbank finance institution.

Notes: End-of-year data except * fiscal year (FY) data (ended 31 March in India and 15 July in Nepal) and September 2019 data in Myanmar. For Brunei Darussalam, finance companies only. For Cambodia and the Lao PDR, microfinance institutions only. For Indonesia, NBFI financing based on new economic sector (SEOJK 3/SEOJK.05/2016). For Malaysia, "other services" include life sciences and information and communication technology. For Bangladesh, nonbank finance institutions regulated by Bangladesh Bank. For India, data for wholesale and retail trade refers to all services sectors. For Nepal, microfinance institutions only; "others" includes wholesale credit, and cottage and micro industries. For Pakistan, microfinance institutions only. For Armenia, microfinance institutions only. For Tajikistan, microfinance institutions only.

Source: ADB Asia SME Monitor 2022 database.

C7. NBFI Financing by Region (% share, latest available year)

Item	Brunei Darussalam	Cambodia	Indonesia	Lao People's Democratic Republic	Malaysia	Myanmar	Philippines	Singapore	Thailand	Viet Nam
Capital city	...	11.3	...	...	...	99.3	36.5	...	...	...
Other areas	...	88.8	...	...	...	0.7	63.5	...	...	...
Year		2020				September 2019	2019			

Item	Bangladesh	India	Nepal	Pakistan	Sri Lanka
Capital city	...	...	...	0.4	...
Other areas	...	...	...	99.6	...
Year				2020	

Item	Armenia	Azerbaijan	Georgia	Kazakhstan	Kyrgyz Republic	Tajikistan	Uzbekistan
Capital city	...	60.0	37.8	...	...	15.1	...
Other areas	...	40.0	62.2	...	...	84.9	...
Year		2021	2021			2021	

NBFI = nonbank finance institution.

Notes: For Cambodia, Myanmar, and Pakistan, microfinance institutions only. For the Philippines, credit unions and cooperatives only. Capital city: Baku in Azerbaijan; Phnom Penh in Cambodia; Tbilisi in Georgia; Yangon in Myanmar; Islamabad in Pakistan; National Capital Region in the Philippines; Dushanbe in Tajikistan.

Source: ADB Asia SME Monitor 2022 database.

C8-1. Market Capitalization (local currency)

Country	2003	2004	2005	2006	2007	2008	2009	2010	2011	2012	2013	2014	2015	2016	2017	2018	2019	2020	2021
Southeast Asia																			
BRU (no exchange market)	...	...	...	...	...	...	...	...	...	...	...	...	...	...	...	...	...	...	...
CAM - Main board	...	...	...	...	...	...	...	...	...	539,234	466,176	658,682	716,387	804,539	1,230,678	1,771,677	2,805,807	2,410,829	1,745,424
INO - Main board	...	...	...	...	1,988,326	1,076,491	2,019,375	3,247,097	3,537,294	4,126,995	4,219,020	5,228,043	4,872,702	5,753,613	7,052,389	7,023,497	7,265,016	6,970,010	8,255,624
INO - Acceleration Board	...	...	...	...	...	...	...	...	...	...	...	...	...	...	...	...	...	1,068	3,218
LAO - Main board	...	...	...	...	...	...	...	...	4,638,300	8,136,540	8,826,800	10,968,690	12,047,100	10,414,100	11,352,400	9,868,000	9,618,492	7,908,931	7,894,062
MAL - ACE	...	...	...	...	...	...	5,293	5,761	6,415	6,935	9,865	9,665	11,853	9,956	15,646	12,141	18,829	35,590	29,389
MAL - LEAP	...	...	...	...	...	...	...	...	...	...	...	...	...	...	213	920	2,435	3,146	4,685
MYA - Main board	...	...	...	...	...	...	...	...	...	...	...	...	...	583,957	578,721	554,599	627,449	...	...
PHI - SME board	...	263	290	322	4,509	2,226	335	549	713	586	871	34,470	28,513	17,029	20,657	11,308	11,587	58,431	29,956
SIN - Catalist	...	...	...	...	...	3,562	5,325	6,462	5,347	6,782	9,326	10,791	9,521	9,233	12,819	10,534	9,809	10,975	11,706
THA - mai	...	...	...	...	38	22	39	55	77	133	177	383	323	425	339	241	215	235	472
VIE - UPCoM	...	...	...	...	...	...	4,259,814	16,237,680	22,663,598	28,868,424	25,745,000	37,169,559	61,033,252	303,359,258	677,705,000	893,777,000	911,940,645	1,000,696,230	1,418,465,448
South Asia																			
BAN - CSE*	...	...	...	...	399,268	777,743	974,948	1,538,393	2,237,585	1,878,171	1,919,891	2,286,679	2,370,421	2,496,849	3,113,243	3,123,522	3,293,303	2,447,567	4,384,258
BAN - DSE*	...	...	...	...	475,855	931,025	1,241,339	2,700,745	2,853,892	2,491,613	2,530,246	2,943,202	3,247,306	3,185,749	3,801,001	3,847,348	3,998,164	3,119,670	5,142,821
IND - BSE SME Exchange	...	...	...	...	...	...	...	...	...	2,871	30,124	90,699	89,577	188,444	215,740	186,110	183,489	212,795	475,666
IND - NSE Emerge	...	...	...	...	...	...	...	...	...	1,490	2,746	4,292	5,174	14,105	105,207	126,396	79,942	56,048	95,464
NEP - NPSE*	...	...	...	...	...	366,248	514,940	376,870	323,484	368,262	514,430	1,057,166	989,404	1,890,130	1,856,829	1,435,138	1,567,499	1,792,763	...
PAK - PSX	...	...	...	...	4,329,910	1,858,699	2,705,880	3,268,949	2,945,785	4,242,278	6,051,696	7,380,532	6,947,358	9,628,514	8,570,926	7,692,787	7,811,812	8,035,363	...
SRI - Colombo Stock Exchange	...	...	...	...	820,652	488,813	1,092,138	2,210,452	2,213,873	2,167,581	2,459,897	3,104,864	2,937,998	2,745,406	2,899,291	2,839,446	2,851,313	2,960,648	5,489,168
Central and West Asia																			
ARM - AMX	...	8,796	18,877	21,872	32,090	53,991	53,097	52,621	53,847	53,333	61,698	73,001	103,771	134,305	143,799	145,740	148,926	134,949	173,900
AZE - BSE	...	...	...	...	...	...	...	...	...	...	...	...	...	2,681	3,234	3,554	3,688	3,958	4,367
GEO - GSX	...	...	...	...	...	...	...	...	...	1,462	2,074	2,152	1,324	1,729	3,327	1,963	1,963	2,366	2,368
KAZ - KASE	...	512,287	1,407,419	7,189,648	6,475,829	3,853,313	8,506,238	8,959,446	6,425,940	5,363,455	4,351,085	4,542,276	12,382,405	14,271,471	16,565,407	14,852,007	16,368,545	18,585,732	28,233,280
KAZ - Alternative Board for SMEs	...	...	...	...	...	...	...	...	...	...	...	...	...	...	576,252	635,411	852,494	464,369	528,080
KGZ - KSE	...	4,000	3,750	4,705	4,865	3,697	3,168	3,740	7,671	7,820	9,052	9,037	11,953	17,422	19,199	26,435	26,285	33,223	51,090
TAJ - CASE	...	...	...	...	...	...	...	...	...	...	...	...	...	...	...	...	1,511	1,836	2,646
UZB - TSE	...	...	...	...	...	...	...	4,746,600	5,255,500	5,448,900	6,320,000	7,018,800	8,436,300	7,963,460	14,817,700	21,594,400	52,405,271	54,794,500	56,197,495

AMX = Armenian Securities Exchange; ARM = Armenia; AZE = Azerbaijan; BAN = Bangladesh; BRU = Brunei Darussalam; BSE = Baku Stock Exchange/Bombay Stock Exchange; CAM = Cambodia; CASE = Central Asian Stock Exchange; CSE = Chittagong Stock Exchange; DSE = Dhaka Stock Exchange; GEO = Georgia; GSX = Georgian Stock Exchange; INO = Indonesia; LAO = Lao People's Democratic Republic; KAZ = Kazakhstan; KASA = Kazakhstan Stock Exchange; KGZ = the Kyrgyz Republic; KSE = Kyrgyz Stock Exchange; MAL = Malaysia; MYA = Myanmar; NEP = Nepal; NPSE = Nepal Stock Exchange; NSE = National Stock Exchange; PAK = Pakistan; PHI = Philippines; PSX = Pakistan Stock Exchange; SIN = Singapore; SME = small and medium-sized enterprise; SRI = Sri Lanka; TAJ = Tajikistan; THA = Thailand; TSE = Republic Stock Exchange "Toshkent"; UZB = Uzbekistan; VIE = Viet Nam.

Notes: End-of-year data except * fiscal year data (ended 30 June in Bangladesh and 15 July in Nepal). Armenia: AMD million; Azerbaijan AZN million; Bangladesh: Tk million; Cambodia: KR million; Georgia: GEL million; India: Rs million; Indonesia: Rp billion; Kazakhstan: KZT million; Kyrgyz Republic: KGS million; Lao PDR: KN million; Malaysia: RM million; Myanmar: MK million; Nepal: NRs million; Pakistan: PRs million; Philippines: P million; Singapore: S$ million; Sri Lanka: SLRs million; Tajikistan: TJS million; Thailand: B billion; Uzbekistan: SUM million; Viet Nam: D million.

Source: ADB Asia SME Monitor 2022 database.

C8-2. Market Capitalization ($ million)

Country	2003	2004	2005	2006	2007	2008	2009	2010	2011	2012	2013	2014	2015	2016	2017	2018	2019	2020	2021
Southeast Asia																			
BRU (no exchange market)	...	...	...	...	...	...	...	...	...	...	...	...	...	...	...	...	...	...	...
CAM - Main board	...	...	...	...	...	...	...	...	...	135	117	162	177	199	305	439	687	591	424
INO - Main board	...	...	...	...	211,097	98,310	214,827	361,150	390,085	426,783	346,133	420,261	353,222	428,224	520,548	485,015	522,625	494,151	578,570
INO - Acceleration Board	...	...	...	...	...	...	...	...	...	...	...	...	...	...	...	...	...	76	226
LAO - Main board	...	...	...	...	...	...	...	...	578	1,019	1,100	1,357	1,479	1,272	1,369	1,157	1,085	853	715
MAL - ACE	...	...	...	...	...	...	1,548	1,870	2,017	2,266	3,008	2,762	2,763	2,217	3,854	2,933	4,604	8,875	7,031
MAL - LEAP	...	...	...	...	...	...	...	...	...	...	...	...	...	...	52	222	595	785	1,121
MYA - Main board	...	...	...	...	...	...	...	...	...	...	...	...	...	430	425	358	428	...	...
PHI - SME board	...	4.7	5.5	6.5	108.9	46.9	7.2	12.5	16.2	14.2	19.6	773	604	342	414	214	228	1,216	590
SIN - Catalist	...	...	...	...	...	2,474	3,804	5,010	4,113	5,559	7,343	8,175	6,753	6,368	9,567	7,746	7,266	8,314	8,671
THA - mai	...	...	...	...	1,135	635	1,174	1,828	2,440	4,343	5,406	11,622	8,963	11,872	10,368	7,421	7,136	7,823	14,123
VIE - UPCoM	...	...	...	...	...	...	237	858	1,088	1,386	1,224	1,749	2,788	13,690	30,221	39,158	39,384	43,262	61,286
South Asia																			
BAN - CSE*	...	...	...	...	5,822	11,285	14,075	21,744	27,338	23,521	24,693	29,335	30,196	31,726	37,645	37,229	38,790	28,863	51,099
BAN - DSE*	...	...	...	...	6,939	13,509	17,920	38,173	34,867	31,204	32,543	37,758	41,367	40,480	45,961	45,856	47,093	36,789	59,940
IND - BSE SME Exchange	...	...	...	...	...	...	...	...	...	52	487	1,432	1,350	2,773	3,375	2,667	2,575	2,913	6,402
IND - NSE Emerge	...	...	...	...	...	...	...	...	...	27	44	68	78	208	1,646	1,811	1,122	767	1,285
NEP - NPSE*	...	...	...	...	...	4,717	6,918	5,260	3,783	4,237	5,175	10,607	9,221	17,501	18,036	12,475	13,835	15,215	...
PAK - PSX	...	...	...	...	70,727	23,498	32,113	38,140	32,742	43,672	57,264	73,467	66,247	91,866	77,614	55,428	50,441	50,350	...
SRI - Colombo Stock Exchange	...	...	...	...	7,548	4,320	9,548	19,923	19,437	17,046	18,814	23,692	20,394	18,327	18,968	15,577	15,698	15,882	27,386
Central and West Asia																			
ARM - AMX	...	18	42	60	105	176	141	145	140	132	152	154	215	278	297	301	310	258	362
AZR - BSE	...	...	...	...	...	...	...	...	...	...	...	...	...	1,514	1,902	2,090	2,169	2,328	2,569
GEO - GSX	...	...	...	...	...	...	...	...	...	882	1,195	1,155	553	653	1,283	733	685	722	764
KAZ - KASE	...	3,941	10,505	56,611	53,831	31,901	57,296	60,742	43,301	35,581	28,243	24,910	36,418	42,820	49,846	38,657	42,784	44,156	65,385
KAZ - Alternative Board for SMEs	...	...	...	...	...	...	...	...	...	...	...	...	...	...	1,734	1,654	2,228	1,103	1,223
KGZ - KSE	...	96	91	123	137	94	72	79	165	165	184	153	157	252	279	378	377	402	603
TAJ - CASE	...	...	...	...	...	...	...	...	...	...	...	...	...	...	...	...	156	162	234
UZB - TSE	...	...	...	...	...	...	...	2,894	2,928	2,746	2,870	2,897	3,002.26	2,464	1,825	2,589	5,512	5,230	5,185

AMX = Armenian Securities Exchange; ARM = Armenia; AZE = Azerbaijan; BAN = Bangladesh; BRU = Brunei Darussalam; BSE = Baku Stock Exchange/Bombay Stock Exchange; CAM = Cambodia; CASE = Central Asian Stock Exchange; CSE = Chittagong Stock Exchange; DSE = Dhaka Stock Exchange; GEO = Georgia; GSX = Georgian Stock Exchange; INO = Indonesia; LAO = Lao People's Democratic Republic; KAZ = Kazakhstan; KASA = Kazakhstan Stock Exchange; KGZ = the Kyrgyz Republic; KSE = Kyrgyz Stock Exchange; MAL = Malaysia; MYA = Myanmar; NEP = Nepal; NPSE = Nepal Stock Exchange; NSE = National Stock Exchange; PAK = Pakistan; PHI = Philippines; PSX = Pakistan Stock Exchange; SIN = Singapore; SME = small and medium-sized enterprise; SRI = Sri Lanka; TAJ = Tajikistan; THA = Thailand; TSE = Republic Stock Exchange "Toshkent"; UZB = Uzbekistan; VIE = Viet Nam.

Notes: End-of-year data except * fiscal year data (ended 30 June in Bangladesh and 15 July in Nepal). Exchange rates of local currency to US dollar refer to end-of-year currency rates from the International Monetary Fund (IMF) International Financial Statistics in designated years.

Source: ADB Asia SME Monitor 2022 database.

C8-3. Market Capitalization to GDP (%)

Country	2003	2004	2005	2006	2007	2008	2009	2010	2011	2012	2013	2014	2015	2016	2017	2018	2019	2020	2021
Southeast Asia																			
BRU (no exchange market)	...	...	...	...	...	...	...	...	...	...	...	...	...	...	...	...	...	...	...
CAM - Main board	...	...	...	...	...	...	...	...	...	1.0	0.8	1.0	1.0	1.0	1.4	1.8	2.6	9.5	6.5
INO - Main board	...	...	...	...	50.3	21.8	36.0	47.3	45.2	47.9	44.2	49.5	42.3	46.4	51.9	47.3	45.9	45.2	48.6
INO - Acceleration Board	...	...	...	...	...	...	...	...	...	...	...	...	...	...	...	...	...	0.01	0.00
LAO - Main board	...	...	...	...	...	...	...	...	7.2	10.0	9.4	10.3	10.3	8.1	8.1	6.5	5.9	4.6	4.3
MAL - ACE	...	...	...	...	...	...	0.7	0.7	0.7	0.7	1.0	0.9	1.0	0.8	1.1	0.8	1.2	2.5	1.9
MAL - LEAP	...	...	...	...	...	...	...	...	...	...	...	...	...	...	0.0	0.1	0.2	0.2	0.3
MYA - Main board	...	...	...	...	...	...	...	...	...	...	...	...	...	0.7	0.6	1.7	...	...	...
PHI - SME board	...	0.005	0.005	0.005	0.065	0.029	0.004	0.006	0.007	0.005	0.007	0.261	0.204	0.113	0.125	0.062	0.059	0.003	0.002
SIN - Catalist	...	...	...	...	...	...	...	2.0	1.5	1.8	2.4	2.7	2.2	2.1	2.7	2.1	1.9	2.3	2.2
THA - mai	...	...	...	...	0.4	0.2	0.4	0.5	0.7	1.1	1.4	2.9	2.4	2.9	2.2	1.5	1.3	1.5	2.9
VIE - UPCoM	...	...	...	...	...	...	...	0.2	0.6	0.7	0.8	0.7	0.9	1.4	6.1	12.2	14.8	15.9	16.9
South Asia																			
BAN - CSE*	...	...	...	...	7.3	12.4	13.8	19.3	24.4	17.8	16.0	17.0	15.6	14.4	15.8	13.9	13.0	8.8	...
BAN - DSE*	...	...	...	...	8.7	14.8	17.6	33.9	31.2	23.6	21.1	21.9	21.4	18.4	19.2	17.1	15.7	11.2	...
IND - BSE SME Exchange	...	...	...	...	...	...	...	...	...	0.003	0.027	0.073	0.065	0.122	0.126	0.099	0.090	0.108	...
IND - NSE Emerge	...	...	...	...	...	...	...	...	...	0.001	0.002	0.003	0.004	0.009	0.062	0.067	0.039	0.028	...
NEP - NPSE*	...	...	...	...	...	44.9	52.1	31.6	20.7	20.9	26.4	47.4	40.8	72.5	60.3	41.5	40.6	45.8	...
PAK - PSX	...	...	...	...	46.9	17.5	20.5	22.0	16.1	21.2	27.0	29.3	25.3	33.1	26.8	22.2	20.5	19.3	...
SRI - Colombo Stock Exchange	...	...	...	...	22.9	11.1	22.6	34.5	30.7	24.8	25.6	30.0	26.8	22.9	21.8	19.9	19.0	19.8	...
Central and West Asia																			
ARM - AMX	...	0.5	0.8	0.8	1.0	1.5	1.7	1.5	1.4	1.3	1.4	1.5	2.1	2.7	2.6	2.4	2.3	2.2	2.5
AZR - BSE	...	...	...	...	...	...	...	...	...	...	...	...	...	4.4	4.6	4.4	4.5	5.5	4.7
GEO - GSX	...	...	...	...	...	...	...	...	...	5.4	7.3	6.9	3.9	4.8	8.2	4.4	4.0	4.8	3.9
KAZ - KASE	...	8.7	18.5	70.4	50.4	24.0	50.0	41.1	22.8	17.3	12.1	11.4	30.3	30.4	30.5	24.0	23.5	26.3	34.3
KAZ - Alternative Board for SMEs	...	...	...	...	...	...	...	...	...	...	...	...	...	...	1.1	1.0	1.2	0.7	0.6
KGZ - KSE	...	4.2	3.7	4.1	3.4	2.0	1.6	1.7	2.7	2.5	2.5	2.3	2.8	3.7	3.6	4.6	4.2	5.5	7.1
TAJ - CASE	...	...	...	...	...	...	...	...	...	...	...	...	...	...	...	...	1.9	2.2	2.7
UZB - TSE	...	...	...	...	...	...	...	6.0	5.1	4.3	4.1	3.8	3.8	3.1	4.7	5.1	9.9	9.1	7.7

AMX = Armenian Securities Exchange; ARM = Armenia; AZE = Azerbaijan; BAN = Bangladesh; BRU = Brunei Darussalam; BSE = Baku Stock Exchange/Bombay Stock Exchange; CAM = Cambodia; CASE = Central Asian Stock Exchange; CSE = Chittagong Stock Exchange; DSE = Dhaka Stock Exchange; GEO = Georgia; GSX = Georgian Stock Exchange; INO = Indonesia; LAO = Lao People's Democratic Republic; KAZ = Kazakhstan; KASA = Kazakhstan Stock Exchange; KGZ = the Kyrgyz Republic; KSE = Kyrgyz Stock Exchange; MAL = Malaysia; MYA = Myanmar; NEP = Nepal; NPSE = Nepal Stock Exchange; NSE = National Stock Exchange; PAK = Pakistan; PHI = Philippines; PSX = Pakistan Stock Exchange; SIN = Singapore; SME = small and medium-sized enterprise; SRI = Sri Lanka; TAJ = Tajikistan; THA = Thailand; TSE = Republic Stock Exchange "Toshkent"; UZB = Uzbekistan; VIE = Viet Nam.

Note: End-of-year data except * fiscal year data (ended 30 June in Bangladesh and 15 July in Nepal).

Source: ADB Asia SME Monitor 2022 database.

C8-4. Number of Listed Companies

Country	2003	2004	2005	2006	2007	2008	2009	2010	2011	2012	2013	2014	2015	2016	2017	2018	2019	2020	2021
Southeast Asia																			
BRU (no exchange market)	...	...	...	...	...	...	...	...	...	...	...	...	...	...	...	...	...	...	...
CAM - Main board	...	...	...	...	...	...	...	...	...	1	1	2	3	4	5	5	5	7	8
INO - Main board	...	...	...	...	383	396	398	420	440	459	483	506	521	537	566	619	668	713	766
INO - Acceleration Board	...	...	...	...	...	...	...	...	...	...	...	...	...	...	...	...	...	5	15
LAO - Main board	...	...	...	...	...	...	...	...	2	2	3	4	5	5	6	9	11	11	11
MAL - ACE	...	...	...	...	...	...	116	113	119	112	109	107	109	113	115	119	129	135	141
MAL - LEAP	...	...	...	...	...	...	...	...	...	...	...	...	...	...	2	13	28	34	44
MYA - Main board	...	...	...	...	...	...	...	...	...	...	...	...	...	3	4	5	5	...	...
PHI - SME board	...	3	3	3	2	2	2	2	2	2	2	4	4	4	4	4	5	7	7
SIN - Catalist	...	...	...	...	...	133	134	133	136	139	139	155	172	185	200	214	216	217	217
THA - mai	...	...	...	...	48	49	60	66	73	81	95	111	122	134	150	159	169	175	183
VIE - UPCoM	...	...	...	...	...	...	34	109	131	132	142	169	256	417	690	810	872	910	892
South Asia																			
BAN - CSE*	...	...	...	...	204	...	228	204	200	207	220	232	252	261	266	274	288	293	310
BAN - DSE*	...	...	...	...	259	...	282	243	232	238	251	263	283	292	297	305	317	321	341
IND - BSE SME Exchange	...	...	...	...	...	...	...	...	...	11	43	82	119	162	216	281	314	331	358
IND - NSE Emerge	...	...	...	...	...	...	...	...	...	2	4	6	11	33	111	192	206	214	236
NEP - NPSE*	...	...	...	...	...	142	159	176	207	216	228	235	232	230	208	196	215	212	...
PAK - PSX	...	...	...	...	654	653	651	644	638	573	560	557	554	558	559	546	534	531	...
SRI - Colombo Stock Exchange	...	...	...	...	235	235	231	241	272	287	289	294	294	295	296	297	289	283	296
Central and West Asia																			
ARM - AMX	...	...	197	35	33	10	11	11	11	11	11	11	10	11	10	10	10	11	10
AZR - BSE	...	...	...	...	...	...	...	...	...	...	...	...	...	5	4	6	11	28	28
GEO - GSX	...	276	250	242	161	157	145	138	135	133	129	129	124	124	124	22	19	10	8
KAZ - KASE	...	54	62	68	69	74	72	65	67	78	81	76	85	98	61	59	74	77	58
KAZ - Alternative Board for SMEs	...	...	...	...	...	...	...	...	...	...	...	...	...	...	43	51	48	44	89
KGZ - KSE	...	...	...	10	10	9	9	11	13	18	20	21	23	26	29	29	26	26	26
TAJ - CASE	...	...	...	...	...	...	...	...	...	...	...	...	...	...	...	...	1	2	3
UZB - TSE	...	...	...	...	...	...	...	101	108	110	135	133	259	192	189	132	112	145	139

AMX = Armenian Securities Exchange; ARM = Armenia; AZE = Azerbaijan; BAN = Bangladesh; BRU = Brunei Darussalam; BSE = Baku Stock Exchange/Bombay Stock Exchange; CAM = Cambodia; CASE = Central Asian Stock Exchange; CSE = Chittagong Stock Exchange; DSE = Dhaka Stock Exchange; GEO = Georgia; GSX = Georgian Stock Exchange; INO = Indonesia; LAO = Lao People's Democratic Republic; KAZ = Kazakhstan; KASA = Kazakhstan Stock Exchange; KGZ = the Kyrgyz Republic; KSE = Kyrgyz Stock Exchange; MAL = Malaysia; MYA = Myanmar; NEP = Nepal; NPSE = Nepal Stock Exchange; NSE = National Stock Exchange; PAK = Pakistan; PHI = Philippines; PSX = Pakistan Stock Exchange; SIN = Singapore; SME = small and medium-sized enterprise; SRI = Sri Lanka; TAJ = Tajikistan; THA = Thailand; TSE = Republic Stock Exchange "Toshkent"; UZB = Uzbekistan; VIE = Viet Nam.

Note: End-of-year data except * fiscal year data (ended 30 June in Bangladesh and 15 July in Nepal).

Source: ADB Asia SME Monitor 2022 database.

www.ingramcontent.com/pod-product-compliance
Lightning Source LLC
Chambersburg PA
CBHW041801220926
51847CB00015B/165
* 9 7 8 9 2 9 2 6 9 8 7 2 0 *